Out of Many

A History of the American People

Volume 2: Since 1865

John Mack Faragher
Yale University

Mari Jo Buhle
Emerita, *Brown University*

Daniel Czitrom
Mount Holyoke College

Susan H. Armitage
Emerita, *Washington State University*

 Pearson

Executive Portfolio Manager: Ed Parsons
Content Producer: Rob DeGeorge
Content Developer: John Reisbord
Portfolio Manager Assistant: Andy Maldonado
Product Marketer: Nicholas Bolt
Field Marketer: Alexa Macri
Content Producer Manager: Ken Volcjak
Content Development Manager: Darcy Betts
Art/Designer: Pearson CSC
Digital Studio Course Producer: Heather Pagano
Full-Service Project Manager: Julie Kidd, Pearson CSC

Compositor: Pearson CSC
Printer/Binder: LSC Communications, Inc.
Cover Printer: LSC Communications, Inc.
Cover Design: Dutton & Sherman Design
Cover Credit: Combined: Artimages/Alamy Stock Photo Volume 1: Courtesy, Winterthur Museum, Painting: Audience given by the Trustees of Georgia to a Delegation of Creek Indians by William Verelst, 1734-1735, London, England, Oil paint on canvas, Gift of Henry Francis du Pont, 1956.567 Volume 2: Niday Picture Library/Alamy Stock Photo

Acknowledgements of third party content appear on page C-1, which constitutes an extension of this copyright

Brief Contents

Contents

The Source Collection at the end of each chapter is available only in the Revel version of *Out of Many*, Ninth Edition.

27 America at Mid-Century 1952–1963 660

28 The Civil Rights Movement 1945–1966 688

Communities *in* Conflict

SEEING History

Maps

Figures & Tables

Documents

The Source Collection documents listed here are available only in the Revel version of *Out of Many*, Ninth Edition.

Videos

The videos listed here are available only in the Revel version of *Out of Many*, Ninth Edition.

Preface

*O*ut of Many: A History of the American People, ninth edition, offers a distinctive and timely approach to American history, highlighting the experiences of diverse communities of Americans in the unfolding story of our country. The stories of these communities offer a way of examining the complex historical forces shaping people's lives at various moments in our past. The debates and conflicts surrounding the most momentous issues in our national life—independence, emerging democracy, slavery, westward settlement, imperial expansion, economic depression, war, technological change—were largely worked out in the context of local communities. Through communities we focus on the persistent tensions between everyday life and those larger decisions and events that continually reshape the circumstances of local life. Each chapter opens with a description of a representative community. Some of these portraits feature American communities struggling with one another: African slaves and English masters on the rice plantations of colonial Georgia, or *Tejanos* and Americans during the Texas war of independence. Other chapters feature portraits of communities facing social change: the feminists of Seneca Falls, New York, in 1848, or the African Americans of Montgomery, Alabama, in 1955. As the story unfolds we find communities growing to include ever larger groups of Americans: the soldiers from every colony who forged the Continental Army into a patriotic national force at Valley Forge during the American Revolution, or the moviegoers who aspired to a collective dream of material prosperity and upward mobility during the 1920s.

Out of Many is also the only American history text with a truly continental perspective. With community vignettes from New England to the South, the Midwest to the far West, we encourage students to appreciate the great expanse of our nation. For example, a vignette of seventeenth-century Santa Fé, New Mexico, illustrates the founding of the first European settlements in the New World. We present territorial expansion into the American West from the viewpoint of the Mandan villagers of the upper Missouri River of North Dakota. We introduce the policies of the Reconstruction era through the experience of African Americans in Hale County, Alabama. A continental perspective drives home to students that American history has never been the preserve of any particular region.

Out of Many includes extensive coverage of our diverse heritage. Our country is appropriately known as "a nation of immigrants," and the history of immigration to America, from the seventeenth to the twenty-first centuries, is fully integrated into the text. There is sustained and close attention to our place in the world, with special emphasis on our relations with the nations of the Western Hemisphere, especially our near neighbors, Canada and Mexico. The statistical data in the final chapter has been completely updated with the results of the 2010 census.

In these ways *Out of Many* breaks new ground, but without compromising its coverage of the traditional turning points that we believe are critically important to an understanding of the American past. Among these watershed events are the Revolution and the struggle over the Constitution, the Civil War and Reconstruction, and the Great Depression and World War II. In *Out of Many*, however, we seek to integrate the narrative of national history with the story of the nation's many diverse communities. The Revolutionary and Constitutional period tested the ability of local communities to forge a new unity, and success depended on their ability to build a nation without compromising local identity. The Civil War and Reconstruction formed a second great test of the balance between the national ideas of the Revolution and the power of local and sectional communities. The Depression and the New Deal demonstrated the importance of local communities and the growing power of national institutions during the greatest economic challenge in our history. *Out of Many* also looks back in a new and comprehensive way—from the vantage point of the beginning of a new century and the end of the Cold War—at the salient events of the last 65 years and their impact on American communities. The community focus of *Out of Many* weaves the stories of the people and the nation into a single compelling narrative.

Out of Many, ninth edition, is completely updated with the most recent scholarship on the history of America and the United States. All the chapters have been extensively reviewed, revised, and rewritten. The chapters covering the period from 1974 to the present have been rewritten and reorganized to emphasize the profound impact of social and economic inequality on contemporary American life. Throughout the book the text and graphics are presented in a stunning new design.

Content Highlights

Special Features

Out of Many offers a wealth of special features and pedagogical aids that reinforce our narrative and help students grasp key topics and concepts.

Community and Diversity. This special introductory essay begins students' journey into the narrative history that unfolds in *Out of Many*. The essay acquaints students with the major themes of the book and provides them with a framework for understanding American history. (pp. xlv–xlvii)

American Communities. Each chapter opens with a story that highlights the experiences of diverse communities of Americans as a way of examining the complex historical forces shaping people's lives at various moments in our past.

Communities in Conflict. This special feature highlights two primary sources that offer opposing voices on a controversial historical issue. With introductory source notes and critical thinking questions, "Communities in Conflict" offers students and instructors the opportunity to discuss how Americans have struggled to resolve their differences at every point in our past.

SEEING History. This feature helps students use visual culture to make sense of the past. These carefully chosen images, with critical thinking questions for interpretation, include a broad array of fine art, drawings, political cartoons, advertisements, and photographs. Encouraged to look at the image with an analytical eye, students will think critically about how visual sources can illuminate their understanding of American history and the important role visuals play in our knowledge of the past.

Tables. Tables provide students with a summary of complex issues.

Photos and Illustrations. The abundant illustrations in *Out of Many* include extensive captions that treat the images as visual primary source documents from the American past, describing their source and explaining their significance.

Time Lines and Key Terms. A time line at the end of each chapter helps students build a framework of key events. Key Terms bolded within chapters help students review, reinforce, and retain the material in each chapter.

Revel for the Ninth Edition

The eighth edition of *Out of Many* was the first to be available in the powerful and innovative Revel platform. The ninth edition features a revised Revel program that takes even greater advantage of all that Revel has to offer. This program was designed with the specific content of *Out of Many* 9e in mind. For example, at the same time that the chapters covering the period 1974 to the present were revised to emphasize issues of social and economic inequality, new interactive elements and videos were created to amplify and enhance the new content.

Videos. Every chapter features selections from an exciting new series of videos. Created in partnership with the Smithsonian Institution, these videos focus on a wide range of unique artifacts from the Smithsonian collection, using these artifacts as starting points for explaining and illuminating the American historical experience. *Out of Many* uses more than 90 videos from the series.

The ninth edition also features more than 20 "History 360" experiences. "History 360" experiences allow students to learn through the exploration of historical sites. Each immersive experience combines 360-degree photographs and videos with sound, images, and text to help bring the past to life.

Primary Source Documents. Each chapter features its own primary document source collection. These excerpts include explanatory introductions to help provide students with necessary context, as well as questions for reflection. With the addition of more than 90 new primary source documents and videos, students and instructors now have access to over 250 primary source resources to explore U.S. history.

Interactive Maps and Figures. *Out of Many* provides a rich and engaging map program with over 120 maps. Many offer interactive elements, such as toggles to illustrate movement over time, as well as clickable map keys and pan/zoom capability.

In addition, the ninth edition features Social Explorer maps and figures in every chapter. Social Explorer maps and figures allow students to dig deeper by merging graphics and data in an interactive format.

Integrated Writing Opportunities. To help students connect chapter content with personal meaning, each chapter offers three varieties of writing prompts: the Journal prompt, eliciting free-form topic-specific responses addressing subjects at the module level; the Shared Writing prompt, which encourages students to share and respond to each other's brief response to high-interest topics in the chapter; and Chapter Essays drawn from primary source documents.

For more information about all of the tools and resources in Revel and access to your own Revel account for *Out of Many* 9e go to www.pearsonhighered .com/Revel.

Supplements for Instructors

Pearson is pleased to offer the following resources to qualified adopters of *Out of Many*. These supplements are available to instantly download on the Instructor Resource Center (IRC); please visit the IRC at www.pearsonhighered.com/irc to register for access.

Instructor's Resource Manual. The Instructor's Resource Manual provides a Detailed Chapter Review, Learning Objectives, Discussion Suggestions and Possible Answers, Lecture Outline, Resources (Web and Film/Video, which will include a list of Revel videos), and Critical Thinking Exercises for each chapter.

Test Bank. Thoroughly reviewed, revised, and updated, the Ninth Edition Test Bank file contains more than 1,700 multiple-choice and essay test questions.

PowerPoint Presentations. PowerPoints contain chapter outlines and full-color images of maps and art. All PowerPoints are accessible.

MyTest. MyTest is a powerful assessment-generation program that helps instructors easily create and print quizzes and exams. Questions and tests can be authored online, allowing instructors ultimate flexibility and the ability to efficiently manage assessments anytime, anywhere! Instructors can easily access existing questions and edit, create, and store using simple drag-and-drop and Word-like controls.

Revel Combo Card. The Revel Combo Card provides an all-in-one access code and loose-leaf print reference (delivered by mail).

Acknowledgments

In the years it has taken to bring *Out of Many* from idea to reality and to improve it in successive editions, we have often been reminded that although writing history sometimes feels like isolated work, it actually involves a collective effort. We want to thank the dozens of people whose efforts have made the publication of this book possible.

We wish to thank our many friends at Pearson, Ohlinger Studios, and SPi Global for their efforts in creating the ninth edition of *Out of Many*: Ed Parsons, Executive Portfolio Editor; Darcy Betts, Managing Editor; John Reisbord, Development Editor; Emsal Hasan, Program Manager (Ohlinger Studios); Julie Kidd, Project Manager (SPi Global); Natalee Sperry, Project Manager; Brooks Hill-Whilton, Rights and Permissions; Caitlin Bonaventure, Digital Media Manager; Alexa Macri, Field Marketer; and Nick Bolt, Product Marketer.

Although we share joint responsibility for the entire book, the chapters were individually authored: John Mack Faragher wrote Chapters 1–8; Susan Armitage wrote Chapters 9–16; Mari Jo Buhle wrote Chapters 18–20, 25–26 and 29; and Daniel Czitrom wrote Chapters 17, 21–24 and 27–28. For this edition Buhle and Czitrom co-authored Chapters 30–31.

Each of us depended on a great deal of support and assistance with the research and writing that went into this book. We want to thank: Kathryn Abbott, Nan Boyd, Krista Comer, Jennifer Cote, Crista DeLuzio, Keith Edgerton, Carol Frost, Jesse Hoffnung Garskof, Pailin Gaither, Jane Gerhard, Todd Gernes, Mark Krasovic, Daniel Lanpher, Melani McAlister, Rebecca McKenna, Cristiane Mitchell, J. C. Mutchler, Keith Peterson, Alan Pinkham, Tricia Rose, Gina Rourke, Jessica Shubow, Gordon P. Utz Jr., Maura Young, Teresa Bill, Gill Frank, and Naoko Shibusawa. Our families and close friends have been supportive and ever so patient over the many years we have devoted to this project. But we want especially to thank Paul Buhle, Meryl Fingrutd, Bob Greene, and Michele Hoffnung.

About the Authors

John Mack Faragher

John Mack Faragher is the Howard R. Lamar Professor of History and director of the Howard R. Lamar Center for the Study of Frontiers and Borders at Yale University. Born in Arizona and raised in southern California, he received his B.A. at the University of California, Riverside, and his Ph.D. at Yale University. He is the author of *Women and Men on the Overland Trail* (1979), *Sugar Creek: Life on the Illinois Prairie* (1986), *Daniel Boone: The Life and Legend of an American Pioneer* (1992), *The American West: A New Interpretive History* (2000), *A Great and Noble Scheme: The Tragic Story of the Expulsion of the French Acadians from Their American Homeland* (2005), and *Eternity Street: Violence and Justice in Frontier Los Angeles* (2016).

Mari Jo Buhle

Mari Jo Buhle is William R. Kenan, Jr. University Professor *Emerita* of American Civilization and History at Brown University, specializing in American women's history. She received her B.A. from the University of Illinois, Urbana-Champaign, and her Ph.D. from the University of Wisconsin, Madison. She is the author of *Women and American Socialism, 1870–1920* (1981) and *Feminism and Its Discontents: A Century of Struggle with Psychoanalysis* (1998). She is also coeditor of the *Encyclopedia of the American Left* (second edition, 1998). Professor Buhle held a fellowship (1991–1996) from the John D. and Catherine T. MacArthur Foundation. She is currently an Honorary Fellow of the History Department at the University of Wisconsin, Madison.

Daniel Czitrom

Daniel Czitrom is Professor of History at Mount Holyoke College. Born and raised in New York City, he received his B.A. from the State University of New York at Binghamton and his M.A. and Ph.D. from the University of Wisconsin, Madison. He is the author of *New York Exposed: The Gilded Age Police Scandal That Launched the Progressive Era* (2016), *Media and the American Mind: From Morse to McLuhan* (1982), and co-author of *Rediscovering Jacob Riis: Exposure Journalism and Photography in Turn of the Century New York* (2008). He served as the historical adviser for the BBC America dramatic series *Copper* (2011–13), and he has appeared as featured on-camera commentator in numerous documentary film projects, including the PBS productions *New York: A Documentary Film; The Rise and Fall of Penn Station; American Photography: A Century of Images;* and the forthcoming *Joseph Pulitzer: Voice of the People.*

Susan H. Armitage is Professor of History and Women's Studies, *Emerita*, at Washington State University, where she was a Claudius O. and Mary R. Johnson Distinguished Professor. She earned her Ph.D. from the London School of Economics and Political Science. Among her many publications on western women's history are three co-edited books, *The Women's West* (1987), *So Much To Be Done: Women on the Mining and Ranching Frontier* (1991), and *Writing the Range: Race, Class, and Culture in the Women's West* (1997). She served as editor of the feminist journal *Frontiers* from 1996 to 2002. Her most recent publications are *Speaking History: Oral Histories of the American Past, 1865–Present* (2009) and *Shaping the Public Good: Women Making History in the Pacific Northwest* (2015).

Susan H. Armitage

Community & Diversity

One of the most characteristic features of our country is its astounding variety. The American people include the descendants of native Indians; colonial Europeans of British, French, and Spanish background; Africans; and migrants from virtually every country and continent. Indeed, at the beginning of the new century the United States is absorbing a flood of immigrants from Latin America and Asia that rivals the great tide of people from eastern and southern Europe 100 years before. What's more, our country is one of the world's most spacious, sprawling across than 3.6 million square miles of territory. The struggle to meld a single nation out of our many far-flung communities is what much of American history is all about. That is the story told in this book.

Every human society is made up of communities. A community is a set of relationships linking men, women, and their families to a coherent social whole that is more than the sum of its parts. In a community people develop the capacity for unified action. In a community people learn, often through trial and error, how to transform and adapt to their environment.

The sentiment that binds the members of a community together is the mother of group consciousness and ethnic identity. In the making of history, communities are far more important than even the greatest of leaders, for the community is the institution most capable of passing a distinctive historical tradition to future generations.

Communities bind people together in multiple ways. They can be as small as local neighborhoods, in which people maintain face-to-face relations, or as large as the nation itself. This book examines American history from the perspective of community life—an ever-widening frame that has included larger and larger groups of Americans.

Networks of kinship and friendship, and connections across generations and among families, establish the bonds essential to community life. Shared feelings about values and history establish the basis for common identity. In communities, people find the power to act collectively in their own interest. But American communities frequently took shape as a result of serious conflicts among groups, and within communities there was often significant fighting among competing groups or classes. Thus the term *community*, as we use it here, includes conflict and discord as well as harmony and agreement.

For decades Americans have complained about the "loss of community." But community has not disappeared—it has been continuously reinvented. Until the late eighteenth century, community was defined primarily by space and local geography. But in the nineteenth century communities were reshaped by new and powerful historical forces such as the marketplace, industrialization, the corporation, mass immigration, mass media, and the growth of the nation-state. In the twentieth century, Americans struggled to balance commitments to multiple communities. These were defined not simply by local spatial arrangements, but by categories as varied as race and ethnicity, occupation, political affiliation, and consumer preference.

The "American Communities" vignettes that open each chapter reflect these transformations. Most of the vignettes in the pre–Civil War chapters focus on geographically defined communities, such as the ancient Indian city at Cahokia, or the experiment in industrial urban planning in early nineteenth-century Lowell, Massachusetts. Post–Civil War chapters explore different and more modern kinds of communities. In the 1920s, movies and radio offered communities of identification with dreams of freedom, material success, upward mobility, youth, and beauty. In the

1950s, rock 'n' roll music helped germinate a new national community of teenagers, with profound effects on the culture of the entire country in the second half of the twentieth century. In the late 1970s, fear of nuclear accidents like the one at Three Mile Island brought concerned citizens together in communities around the country and encouraged a national movement opposing nuclear power.

The title for our book was suggested by the Latin phrase selected by John Adams, Benjamin Franklin, and Thomas Jefferson for the Great Seal of the United States: *E Pluribus Unum*—"Out of Many, One." These men understood that unity could not be imposed by a powerful central authority but had to develop out of mutual respect among Americans of different backgrounds. The Revolutionary leadership expressed the hope that such respect could grow on the basis of a remarkable proposition: "We hold these truths to be self-evident, that all men are created equal; that they are endowed by their Creator with certain unalienable rights; that among these are life, liberty, and the pursuit of happiness." The national government of the United States would preserve local and state authority but would guarantee individual rights. The nation would be strengthened by guarantees of difference.

"Out of Many" comes strength. That is the promise of America and the premise of this book. The underlying dialectic of American history, we believe, is that as a people we must locate our national unity in the celebration of the differences that exist among us; these differences can be our strength, as long as we affirm the promise of the Declaration of Independence. Protecting the "right to be different," in other words, is absolutely fundamental to the continued existence of democracy, and that right is best protected by the existence of strong and vital communities. We are bound together as a nation by the ideal of local and cultural differences protected by our common commitment to the values of the American Revolution.

Today those values are endangered by those who use the tactics of mass terror. In the wake of the September 11, 2001 attack on the United States, and with the continuing threat of biological, chemical, or even nuclear assaults, Americans cannot afford to lose faith in our historic vision. The thousands of victims buried in the smoking ruins of the World Trade Center included people from dozens of different ethnic and national groups. The United States is a multicultural and transnational society. We must rededicate ourselves to the protection and defense of the promise of diversity and unity.

Our history demonstrates that the promise has always been problematic. Centrifugal forces have been powerful in the American past, and at times the country seemed about to fracture into its component parts. Our transformation from a collection of groups and regions into a nation was marked by painful and often violent struggles. Our past is filled with conflicts between Indians and colonists, masters and slaves, Patriots and Loyalists, Northerners and Southerners, Easterners and Westerners, capitalists and workers, and sometimes the government and the people. War can bring out our best, but it can also bring out our worst. During World War II thousands of Japanese American citizens were deprived of their rights and locked up in isolated detention centers because of their ethnic background. Americans often appear to be little more than a contentious collection of peoples with conflicting interests, divided by region and background, race and class.

Our most influential leaders have also sometimes suffered a crisis of faith in the American project of "liberty and justice for all." Thomas Jefferson not only believed in the inferiority of African Americans but feared that immigrants from outside the Anglo-American tradition might "warp and bias" the development of the nation "and render it a heterogeneous, incoherent, distracted mass." We have not always lived up to the American promise and there is a dark side to our history. It took the bloodiest war in American history to secure the human rights of African Americans, and the struggle for full equality for all our citizens has yet to be won. During the great influx of immigrants in the early twentieth century, fears much like Jefferson's led to movements to Americanize the foreign-born by forcing them, in the words of one leader, "to give up the languages, customs, and methods of life which they have brought with them across the ocean, and adopt instead the language, habits, and customs of this country, and the general standards and ways of American living." Similar thinking motivated Congress at various times to bar the immigration of Africans, Asians, and other people of color into the country, and to force assimilation on American Indians by denying them the freedom to practice their religion or even to speak their own language. Such calls for restrictive unity resound in our own day.

But other Americans have argued for a more fulsome version of Americanization. "What is the American, this new man?" asked the French immigrant Michel Crévecoeur in 1782. "A strange mixture of blood which you will find in no other country." In America, he wrote, "individuals of all nations are melted into a new race of men." A century later Crévecoeur was echoed by historian Frederick Jackson Turner, who believed that "in the crucible of the frontier, the immigrants were Americanized, liberated, and fused into a mixed race, English in neither nationality nor characteristics. The process has gone on from the early days to our own."

The process by which diverse communities have come to share a set of common American values is one of the most fundamental aspects of our history. It did not occur, however, because of compulsory Americanization programs, but because of free public education, popular participation in democratic politics, and the impact of popular culture. Contemporary America does have a common culture: we share a commitment to freedom of thought and expression, we join in the aspirations to own our own homes and send our children to college, we laugh at the same television programs or video clips on YouTube.

To a degree that too few Americans appreciate, this common culture resulted from a complicated process of mutual discovery that took place when different ethnic and regional groups encountered one another. Consider just one small and unique aspect of our culture: the barbecue. Americans have been barbecuing since before the beginning of written history. Early settlers adopted this technique of cooking from the Indians— the word itself comes from a native term for a framework of sticks over a fire on which meat was slowly cooked. Colonists typically barbecued pork, fed on Indian corn. African slaves lent their own touch by introducing the use of spicy sauces. The ritual that is a part of nearly every American family's Fourth of July silently celebrates the heritage of diversity that went into making our common culture.

The American educator John Dewey recognized this diversity early in the last century. "The genuine American, the typical American, is himself a hyphenated character," he declared, "international and interracial in his make-up." It was up to all Americans, Dewey argued, "to see to it that the hyphen connects instead of separates." We, the authors of *Out of Many*, endorse Dewey's perspective. "Creation comes from the impact of diversity," the American philosopher Horace Kallen wrote about the same time. We also endorse Kallen's vision of the American promise: "A democracy of nationalities, cooperating voluntarily and autonomously through common institutions . . . a multiplicity in a unity, an orchestration of mankind." And now, let the music begin.

Chapter 17
Reconstruction 1863–1877

ON TO LIBERTY In this 1867 painting by Theodor Kaufmann, runaway slaves escape through the woods.

The Metropolitan Museum of Art/Art Resource, NY.

 ## Contents and Focus Questions

American Communities

Hale County, Alabama: From Slavery to Freedom in a Black Belt Community

On a bright Saturday morning in May 1867, 4,000 former slaves streamed into the town of Greensboro, bustling seat of Hale County in west-central Alabama. They came to hear speeches from two delegates to a recent freedmen's convention in Mobile and to find out about the political status of black people under the Reconstruction Act just passed by Congress. Tensions mounted in the days following this unprecedented gathering, as military authorities began supervising voter registration for elections to the upcoming constitutional convention that would rewrite the laws of Alabama. On June 13, John Orrick, a local white, confronted Alex Webb, a politically active freedman, on the streets of

Greensboro. Webb had recently been appointed a voter registrar for the district. Orrick swore he would never be registered by a black man and shot Webb dead. Hundreds of armed and angry freedmen formed a posse to search for Orrick but failed to find him. Galvanized by Webb's murder, 500 local freedmen formed a chapter of the Union League, the Republican Party's organizational arm in the South. The chapter functioned as both a militia company and a forum to agitate for political rights.

Violent political encounters between black people and white people were common in southern communities in the wake of the Civil War. Communities throughout the South struggled over the meaning of freedom in ways that reflected their particular circumstances. The 4 million freed people constituted roughly one-third of the total southern population, but the black/white ratio in individual communities varied enormously. In some places, the Union army had been a strong presence during the war, hastening the collapse of the slave system and encouraging experiments in free labor. Other areas had remained relatively untouched by the fighting. In some areas, small farms prevailed; in others, including Hale County, large plantations dominated economic and political life.

West-central Alabama had emerged as a fertile center of cotton production just two decades before the Civil War. There, African Americans, as throughout the South's black belt, constituted more than three-quarters of the population. With the arrival of federal troops in the spring of 1865, African Americans in Hale County, like their counterparts elsewhere, began to challenge the traditional organization of plantation labor.

One owner, Henry Watson, found that his entire workforce had deserted him at the end of 1865. "I am in the midst of a large and fertile cotton growing country," Watson wrote to a partner. "Many plantations are entirely without labor, many plantations have insufficient labor, and upon none are the laborers doing their former accustomed work." Black women refused to work in the fields, preferring to stay home with their children and tend garden plots. Nor would male field hands do any work, such as caring for hogs, that did not directly increase their share of the cotton crop.

Above all, freed people wanted more autonomy. Overseers and owners grudgingly allowed them to work the land "in families," letting them choose their own supervisors and find their own provisions. The result was a shift from the gang labor characteristic of the antebellum period, in which large groups of slaves worked under the harsh and constant supervision of white overseers, to the sharecropping system, in which African American families worked small plots of land in exchange for a small share of the crop.

Only a small fraction—perhaps 15 percent—of African American families were fortunate enough to be able to buy land. The majority settled for some version of sharecropping, while others managed to rent land from owners, becoming tenant farmers. Still, planters throughout Hale County had to change the old routines of plantation labor. Local African Americans also organized politically. In 1866, Congress had passed the Civil Rights Act and sent the Fourteenth Amendment to the Constitution to the states for ratification; both promised full citizenship rights to former slaves. Hale County freedmen joined the Republican Party and local Union League chapters. They used their new political power to press for better labor contracts, demand greater autonomy for the black workforce, and agitate for the more radical goal of land confiscation and redistribution. "The colored people are very anxious to get land of their own to live upon independently; and they want money to buy stock to make crops," reported one black Union League organizer. "The only way to get these necessaries is to give our votes to the [Republican] party." Two Hale County former slaves, Brister Reese and James K. Green, won election to the Alabama state legislature in 1869.

It was not long before these economic and political gains prompted a white counterattack. In the spring of 1868, the Ku Klux Klan—a secret organization devoted to terrorizing and intimidating African Americans and their white Republican allies—came to Hale County. Disguised in white sheets, armed with guns and whips, and making nighttime raids on horseback, Klansmen flogged, beat, and murdered freed people. They intimidated voters and silenced political activists. Planters used Klan terror to dissuade former slaves from leaving plantations or organizing for higher wages. With the passage of the Ku Klux Klan Act in 1871, the federal government cracked down on the Klan, breaking its power temporarily in parts of the former Confederacy. But no serious effort was made to stop Klan terror in the west Alabama black belt, and planters there succeeded in reestablishing much of their social and political control.

The events in Hale County illustrate the struggles that beset communities throughout the South during the Reconstruction era after the Civil War. The destruction of slavery and of the Confederacy forced African Americans and white people to renegotiate their old roles. These community battles both shaped and were shaped by the victorious and newly expansive federal government in Washington. But the new arrangements of both political power sharing and the organization of labor had to be worked out within local communities. In the end, Reconstruction was only partially successful. Not until the "Second Reconstruction" of the twentieth-century civil rights movement would the descendants of Hale County's African Americans begin to enjoy the full fruits of freedom—and even then not without challenge.

Greensboro

17.1 The Politics of Reconstruction

*What were the competing political plans
for reconstructing the defeated Confederacy?*

When General Robert E. Lee's men stacked their guns at Appomattox, the bloodiest war in American history ended. At least 600,000 soldiers—and perhaps as many as 800,000—had died during the four years of fighting, 360,000 Union and 260,000 Confederate. Another 275,000 Union and 190,000 Confederate troops had been wounded. Although President Abraham Lincoln insisted early on that the purpose of the war was to preserve the Union, by 1863 it had evolved as well into a struggle for African American liberation. Indeed, the political, economic, and moral issues posed by slavery were the root cause of the Civil War, and the war ultimately destroyed slavery—although not racism—once and for all.

The Civil War also settled the constitutional crisis provoked by the secession of the Confederacy and its justification in appeals to states' rights. The old notion of the United States as a voluntary union of sovereign states gave way to the new reality of a single nation, in which the federal government took precedence over the individual states. The key historical developments of the Reconstruction era revolved around precisely how the newly strengthened national government would define its relationship with the defeated Confederate states and the 4 million newly freed slaves.

17.1.1 The Defeated South

The white South paid an extremely high price for secession, war, and defeat. In addition to the battlefield casualties, the Confederate states sustained deep material and psychological wounds. Much of the best agricultural land was laid to waste, including the rich fields of northern Virginia; the Shenandoah Valley; and large sections of Tennessee, Mississippi, Georgia, and South Carolina. Many towns and cities—including Richmond, Atlanta, and Columbia, South Carolina—were in ruins. By 1865, the South's most precious commodities, cotton and African American slaves, no longer were measures of wealth and prestige. Retreating Confederates destroyed most of the South's cotton to prevent its capture by federal troops. What remained was confiscated by Union agents as contraband of war. The former slaves, many of whom had fled to Union lines during the latter stages of the war, were determined to chart their own course in the reconstructed South as free men and women.

Emancipation proved the bitterest pill for white Southerners to swallow, especially the planter elite. Conquered and degraded, and in their view robbed of their slave property, white people responded by regarding African Americans, more than ever, as inferior to themselves. In the antebellum South, white skin gave even the poorest white a badge of superiority over even the most skilled slave or prosperous free African American. The specter of political power and social equality for African Americans made racial order the consuming passion of most white Southerners during the Reconstruction years. In fact, racism can be seen as one of the major forces driving Reconstruction and, ultimately, undermining it.

17.1.2 Abraham Lincoln's Plan

By late 1863, Union military victories had convinced President Lincoln of the need to fashion a plan for the reconstruction of the South. (See Chapter 16.) Lincoln based his reconstruction program on bringing the seceded states back into the Union as quickly as possible. His Proclamation of Amnesty and Reconstruction of December 1863 offered "full pardon" and the restoration of property, not including slaves, to white Southerners willing to swear an oath of allegiance to the United States and its laws, including the Emancipation Proclamation. Prominent Confederate military and civil leaders were excluded from Lincoln's offer, though he indicated that he would freely pardon them.

The president also proposed that when the number of any Confederate state's voters who took the oath of allegiance reached 10 percent of the number who had voted in the election of 1860, this group could establish a state government that Lincoln would recognize as legitimate. Fundamental to this Ten Percent Plan was that the reconstructed governments accept the abolition of slavery. Lincoln's plan was designed less as a blueprint for reconstruction than as a way to shorten the war and gain white people's support for emancipation.

Lincoln's amnesty proclamation angered those Republicans—known as **Radical Republicans**—who advocated not only equal rights for the freedmen but also a tougher stance toward the white South. In July 1864, Senator Benjamin F. Wade of Ohio and Congressman Henry W. Davis of Maryland, both Radicals, proposed a harsher alternative to the Ten Percent Plan. The Wade-Davis bill required 50 percent of a seceding state's white male citizens to take a loyalty oath before elections could be held for a convention to rewrite the state's constitution. The Radical Republicans saw reconstruction as a chance to effect a fundamental transformation of southern society. They thus

"DECORATING THE GRAVES OF REBEL SOLDIERS" After the Civil War, both Southerners and Northerners created public mourning ceremonies honoring fallen soldiers. Women led the memorial movement in the South that, by establishing cemeteries and erecting monuments, offered the first cultural expression of the Confederate tradition. This engraving depicts citizens of Richmond, Virginia, decorating thousands of Confederate graves with flowers at the Hollywood Memorial Cemetery on the James River. A local women's group raised enough funds to transfer more than 16,000 Confederate dead from northern cemeteries for reburial in Richmond.

wanted to delay the process until war's end and to limit participation to a small number of southern Unionists. Lincoln viewed Reconstruction as part of the larger effort to win the war and abolish slavery. He wanted to weaken the Confederacy by creating new state governments that could win broad support from southern white people. The Wade-Davis bill threatened his efforts to build political consensus within the southern states. Lincoln, therefore, pocket-vetoed the bill by refusing to sign it within ten days of the adjournment of Congress.

As Union armies occupied parts of the South, commanders improvised a variety of arrangements involving confiscated plantations and the African American labor force. For example, in 1862 General Benjamin F. Butler began a policy of transforming slaves on Louisiana sugar plantations into wage laborers under the close supervision of occupying federal troops. Butler's policy required

slaves to remain on the estates of loyal planters, where they would receive wages according to a fixed schedule, as well as food and medical care for the aged and sick. Abandoned plantations would be leased to northern investors.

In January 1865, General William T. Sherman issued **Special Field Order 15**, setting aside the Sea Islands off the Georgia coast and a portion of the South Carolina Lowcountry rice fields for the exclusive settlement of freed people. Each family would receive 40 acres of land and the loan of mules from the army—the origin, perhaps, of the famous call for "40 acres and a mule" that would soon capture the imagination of African Americans throughout the South. Sherman's intent was not to revolutionize southern society but to relieve the demands placed on his army by the thousands of impoverished African Americans who followed his march to the sea. By the summer of 1865 some 40,000 freed people, eager to take advantage of the general's order, had been settled on 400,000 acres of "Sherman land."

Conflicts within the Republican Party prevented the development of a systematic land distribution program. Still, Lincoln and the Republican Congress supported other measures to aid the emancipated slaves. In March 1865 Congress established the Freedmen's Bureau. Along with providing food, clothing, and fuel to destitute former slaves, the bureau was charged with supervising and managing "all the abandoned lands in the South and the control of all subjects relating to refugees and freedmen." The act that established the bureau also stated that 40 acres of abandoned or confiscated land could be leased to freed slaves or white Unionists, who would have an option to purchase after three years and "such title thereto as the United States can convey."

On the evening of April 14, 1865, while attending the theater in Washington, President Lincoln was shot by John Wilkes Booth; he died of his wounds several hours later. At the time of his assassination, Lincoln's reconstruction policy remained unsettled and incomplete. In their broad outlines, the president's plans had seemed to favor a speedy restoration of the southern states to the Union and a minimum of federal intervention in their affairs. But with his death, the specifics of postwar Reconstruction had to be hammered out by a new president: Andrew Johnson of Tennessee, a man whose personality, political background, and racist leanings put him at odds with the Republican-controlled Congress.

AFRICAN AMERICAN FAMILY Photography pioneer Timothy O'Sullivan took this portrait of a multigenerational African American family on the J. J. Smith plantation in Beaufort, South Carolina, in 1862. Many white plantation owners in the area had fled, allowing slaves like these to begin an early transition to freedom before the end of the Civil War.

17.1.3 Andrew Johnson and Presidential Reconstruction

Andrew Johnson, a Democrat and former slaveholder, was a most unlikely successor to the martyred Lincoln. Throughout his career, Johnson had championed yeoman farmers and viewed the South's plantation aristocrats with contempt. He was the only southern member of the U.S. Senate to remain loyal to the Union, and he held the planter elite responsible for secession and defeat. In 1862, Lincoln appointed Johnson to the difficult post of military governor of Tennessee. There he successfully began wartime Reconstruction and cultivated Unionist support in the mountainous eastern districts of that state.

In 1864, the Republicans, in an appeal to northern and border state **War Democrats**, nominated Johnson for vice president. In the immediate aftermath of Lincoln's murder, however, Johnson appeared to side with those Radical Republicans who sought to treat the South as a conquered territory. Any support for Johnson quickly faded as the new president's policies unfolded. Johnson defined Reconstruction as the province of the executive, not the legislative, branch, and he planned to restore the Union as quickly as possible. He blamed individual Southerners—the planter elite—rather than entire states for leading the South down the disastrous road to secession. In line with this philosophy, Johnson outlined mild terms for reentry to the Union.

In the spring of 1865, Johnson granted amnesty and pardon, including restoration of property rights except slaves, to all Confederates who pledged loyalty to the Union and support for emancipation. Fourteen classes of Southerners, mostly major Confederate officials and wealthy landowners, were excluded. But these men could apply individually for presidential pardons. (During his tenure Johnson pardoned roughly 90 percent of those who applied.) Significantly, Johnson instituted this plan while Congress was not in session.

By the autumn of 1865, ten of the eleven Confederate states claimed to have met Johnson's requirements to reenter the Union. On December 6, 1865, in his first annual message to Congress, the president declared the "restoration" of the Union virtually complete. But a serious division within the federal government was taking shape, for the Congress was not about to allow the president free rein in determining the conditions of southern readmission.

Andrew Johnson used the term "restoration" rather than "reconstruction." A lifelong Democrat with ambitions to be elected president on his own in 1868, Johnson hoped to build a new political coalition composed of northern Democrats, conservative Republicans, and southern Unionists. Firmly committed to white supremacy, he opposed political rights for the freedmen. Johnson's open sympathy for his fellow white Southerners, his antiblack bias, and his determination to control the course of Reconstruction placed him on a collision course with the powerful Radical wing of the Republican Party.

17.1.4 Free Labor and the Radical Republican Vision

Most Radicals were men whose careers had been shaped by the slavery controversy. One of the most effective rhetorical weapons used against slavery and its spread had been the ideal of a society based upon free labor. The model of free individuals, competing equally in the labor market and enjoying equal political rights, formed the core of this worldview.

Radicals now looked to reconstruct southern society along these same lines, backed by the power of the national government. They argued that once free labor, universal education, and equal rights were implanted in the South, that region would be able to share in the North's material wealth, progress, and social mobility. Representative George W. Julian of Indiana typified the Radical vision for the South. He called for elimination of the region's large plantations, arguing that the South needed to develop "small farms, thrifty tillage, free schools, social independence, flourishing manufactures and the arts, respect for honest labor, and equality of political rights." In the most far-reaching proposal, Representative Thaddeus Stevens of Pennsylvania called for the confiscation of 400 million acres belonging to the wealthiest 10 percent of Southerners to be redistributed to black and white yeomen and northern land buyers. "The whole fabric of Southern society must be changed," Stevens told Pennsylvania Republicans in September 1865, "and never can it be done if this opportunity is lost. How can republican institutions, free schools, free churches, free social intercourse exist in a mingled community of nabobs and serfs?"

Northern Republicans were especially outraged by the stringent **black codes** passed by South Carolina, Mississippi, Louisiana, and other states. These were designed to restrict the freedom of the black labor force and keep freed people as close to slave status as possible. Laborers who left their jobs before contracts expired would forfeit wages already earned and be subject to arrest by any white citizen. Vagrancy, very broadly defined, was punishable by fines and involuntary plantation labor. Apprenticeship clauses obliged black children to work without pay for employers. Some states attempted to bar African Americans from land ownership. Other laws specifically denied African Americans equality with white people in civil rights, excluding them from juries and prohibiting interracial marriages. The black codes underscored the unwillingness of white Southerners to accept freedom for African Americans.

The Radicals, although not a majority of their party, were joined by moderate Republicans as growing numbers of Northerners grew suspicious of white southern intransigence and the denial of political rights to freedmen. When the Thirty-Ninth Congress convened in December 1865, the large Republican majority prevented the seating of the white Southerners elected to Congress under President Johnson's provisional state governments. Republicans also established the Joint Committee on Reconstruction. After hearing extensive testimony from a broad range of witnesses, it concluded that not only were old Confederates back in power in the South but also that black codes and racial violence required increased protection for African Americans.

In the spring of 1866, Congress passed two important bills designed to aid African Americans. The landmark **Civil Rights bill**, which bestowed full citizenship on African Americans, overturned the 1857 *Dred Scott* decision and the black codes. Under this bill, African Americans acquired "full and equal benefit of all laws and proceedings for the security of person and property as is enjoyed by white citizens."

Congress also voted to enlarge the scope of the **Freedmen's Bureau**, empowering it to build schools and pay teachers, and also to establish courts to prosecute those charged with depriving African Americans of their civil rights. The bureau achieved important, if limited,

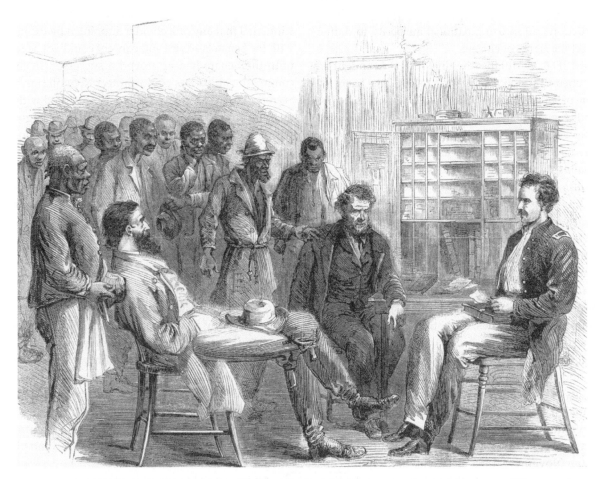

"OFFICE OF THE FREEDMEN'S BUREAU, MEMPHIS, TENNESSEE" Established by Congress in 1865, the Freedmen's Bureau provided economic, educational, and legal assistance to former slaves in the post-Civil War years. Bureau agents were often called on to settle disputes between black and white Southerners over wages, labor contracts, political rights, and violence. Although most southern whites only grudgingly acknowledged the Bureau's legitimacy, freed people gained important legal and psychological support through testimony at public hearings like this one.

success in aiding African Americans. Bureau-run schools helped lay the foundation for southern public education. The Bureau's network of courts allowed freed people to bring suits against white people in disputes involving violence, nonpayment of wages, or unfair division of crops. The very existence of courts hearing public testimony by African Americans provided an important psychological challenge to traditional notions of white racial domination.

But an angry President Johnson vetoed both of these bills. In opposing the Civil Rights bill, Johnson denounced the assertion of national power to protect African American civil rights, claiming it was a "stride toward centralization, and the concentration of all legislative powers in the national Government." But Johnson's intemperate attacks on the Radicals—he damned them as traitors unwilling to restore the Union—united moderate and Radical Republicans, and they succeeded in overriding the vetoes. Congressional Republicans, led by the Radical faction, were now unified in challenging the president's power to direct Reconstruction and in using national authority to define and protect the rights of citizens.

In June 1866, fearful that the Civil Rights Act might be declared unconstitutional, and eager to settle the basis for the seating of southern representatives, Congress passed the Fourteenth Amendment. The amendment defined national citizenship to include former slaves ("all persons born or naturalized in the United States") and prohibited the states from violating the privileges of citizens without due process of law. It also empowered Congress to reduce the representation of any state that denied suffrage to males over 21. Republicans adopted the Fourteenth Amendment as their platform for the 1866 congressional elections and suggested that southern states would have to ratify it as a condition of readmission. President Johnson, meanwhile, took to the stump in August to support conservative Democratic and Republican candidates. His unrestrained speeches often degenerated into harangues, alienating many voters and aiding the Republican cause.

For their part, the Republicans skillfully portrayed Johnson and northern Democrats as disloyal and white Southerners as unregenerate. Republicans began an effective campaign tradition known as "waving the bloody shirt"—reminding northern voters of the hundreds of thousands of Yankee soldiers left dead or maimed by the war. In the November 1866 elections, the Republicans increased their majority in both the House and the Senate and gained control of all the northern states. The stage was now set for a battle between the president and Congress. Was it to be Johnson's "restoration" or Congressional Reconstruction?

17.1.5 Congressional Reconstruction and the Impeachment Crisis

United against Johnson, moderate and Radical Republicans took control of Reconstruction early in 1867. In March, Congress passed the **First Reconstruction Act** over Johnson's veto. This act divided the South into five military districts subject to martial law. To achieve restoration, southern states were first required to call new constitutional conventions, elected by universal manhood suffrage. Once these states had drafted new constitutions, guaranteed African American voting rights, and ratified the Fourteenth Amendment, they were eligible for readmission to the Union. Supplementary legislation, also passed over the president's veto, invalidated the provisional governments established by Johnson, empowered the military to administer voter registration, and required an oath of loyalty to the United States. (See Map 17.1.)

Congress also passed several laws aimed at limiting Johnson's power. One of these, the **Tenure of Office Act**, stipulated that any officeholder appointed by the president with the Senate's advice and consent could not be removed until the Senate had approved a successor. In this way, congressional leaders could protect Republicans, such as Secretary of War Edwin M. Stanton, entrusted with implementing **Congressional Reconstruction**. In August 1867, with Congress adjourned, Johnson suspended Stanton and appointed General Ulysses S. Grant interim Secretary of War. In January 1868, when the Senate overruled Stanton's suspension, Grant broke openly with Johnson and vacated the office. Stanton resumed his position and barricaded himself in his office when Johnson attempted to remove him once again.

Outraged by Johnson's relentless obstructionism, and seizing upon his violation of the Tenure of Office Act as a pretext, moderate and Radical Republicans in the House of Representatives again joined forces and voted to impeach the president by a vote of 126 to 47 on February 24, 1868, charging him with 11 counts of high crimes and misdemeanors. To ensure the support of moderate Republicans, the articles of impeachment focused on violations of the Tenure of Office Act. The case against Johnson would have to be made on the basis of willful violation of the law. Left unstated were the Republicans' real reasons for wanting the president removed: Johnson's political views and his opposition to the Reconstruction Acts.

An influential group of moderate Senate Republicans feared the damage a conviction might do to the constitutional separation of powers. They also worried about the political and economic policies that might be pursued by Benjamin Wade, the president pro tem of the Senate and

Map 17.1 RECONSTRUCTION OF THE SOUTH, 1866–1877

Dates for the readmission of former Confederate states to the Union and the return of Democrats to power varied according to the specific political situations in those states.

a leader of the Radical Republicans, who—because there was no vice president—would succeed to the presidency if Johnson were removed from office. Behind the scenes during his Senate trial, Johnson agreed to abide by the Reconstruction Acts. In May, the Senate voted 35 for conviction, 19 for acquittal—1 vote shy of the two-thirds necessary for removal from office. Johnson's narrow acquittal established the precedent that only criminal actions by a president—not political disagreements—warranted removal from office.

17.1.6 The Election of 1868

By the summer of 1868, seven former Confederate states (Alabama, Arkansas, Florida, Louisiana, North Carolina, South Carolina, and Tennessee) had ratified the revised constitutions, elected Republican governments, and ratified the Fourteenth Amendment. They had thereby earned readmission to the Union. In 1868 Republicans nominated Grant, the North's foremost military hero, for president. Grant enjoyed tremendous popularity after the war, especially when he broke with Johnson. Totally lacking in political experience, Grant admitted, after receiving the nomination, that he had been forced into it in spite of himself.

Significantly, at the very moment that the South was being forced to enfranchise former slaves as a prerequisite for readmission to the Union, the Republicans rejected a campaign plank endorsing black suffrage in the North. Supporting black suffrage in the South did not translate into supporting African American voting rights in the North. State referendums calling for black suffrage failed in eight northern states between 1865 and 1868, succeeding only in Iowa and Minnesota. The Democrats, determined to reverse Congressional Reconstruction, nominated Horatio Seymour, former governor of New York and a longtime foe of emancipation and supporter of states' rights.

The **Ku Klux Klan** emerged as a potent instrument of terror. (See the opening of this chapter.) In Louisiana, Arkansas, Georgia, and South Carolina, the Klan threatened, whipped, and murdered black and white Republicans to prevent them from voting. This terrorism enabled the Democrats to carry Georgia and Louisiana, but it ultimately cost them votes in the North. In the final tally, Grant carried 26 of the 34 states for an Electoral College victory of 214 to 80. Significantly, more than 500,000 African American voters cast their ballots for Grant, demonstrating their overwhelming support for the Republican

THE FIFTEENTH AMENDMENT The Fifteenth Amendment, ratified in 1870, stipulated that the right to vote could not be denied "on account of race, color, or previous condition of servitude." This illustration expressed the optimism and hopes of African Americans generated by this constitutional landmark aimed at protecting black political rights. Note the various political figures (Abraham Lincoln, John Brown, Frederick Douglass) and movements (abolitionism and black education) invoked here, providing a sense of how the amendment ended a long historical struggle.

Library of Congress (Photoduplication).

Party. The Republicans also retained large majorities in both houses of Congress.

In February 1869, Congress passed the **Fifteenth Amendment**, providing that "the right of citizens of the United States to vote shall not be denied or abridged on account of race, color, or previous condition of servitude." To enhance the chances of ratification, Congress required the four remaining unreconstructed states—Mississippi, Georgia, Texas, and Virginia—to ratify both the Fourteenth and Fifteenth Amendments before readmission. They did so and rejoined the Union in early 1870. The Fifteenth Amendment was ratified in February 1870. In the narrow sense of simply readmitting the former Confederate states to the Union, Reconstruction was complete. (See Table 17.1.)

17.1.7 Woman Suffrage and Reconstruction

Many women's rights advocates had long been active in the abolitionist movement. The Fourteenth and Fifteenth Amendments, which granted citizenship and the vote to freedmen, both inspired and frustrated these activists. Insisting that the causes of the African American vote and the women's vote were linked, Elizabeth Cady Stanton, Susan B. Anthony, and Lucy Stone founded the American Equal Rights Association in 1866. The group launched a series of lobbying and petition campaigns to remove racial and sexual restrictions on voting from state constitutions. Throughout the nation, the old abolitionist

Table 17.1 RECONSTRUCTION AMENDMENTS TO THE CONSTITUTION, 1865–1870

Amendment and Date Passed by Congress	Main Provisions	Ratification Process (3/4 of all States Including Ex-Confederate States Required)
13 (January 1865)	• Prohibited slavery in the United States	December 1865 (27 states, including 8 southern states)
14 (June 1866)	• Conferred national citizenship on all persons born or naturalized in the United States	July 1868 (after Congress made ratification a prerequisite for readmission of ex-Confederate states to the Union)
	• Reduced state representation in Congress proportionally for any state disfranchising male citizens	
	• Denied former Confederates the right to hold state or national office	
	• Repudiated Confederate debt	
15 (February 1869)	• Prohibited denial of suffrage because of race, color, or previous condition of servitude	March 1870 (ratification required for readmission of Virginia, Texas, Mississippi, and Georgia)

NATIONAL WOMAN SUFFRAGE ASSOCIATION This engraving depicts a meeting of the National Woman Suffrage Association in Chicago, ca. 1870. The suffrage campaign attracted many middle-class women into political activism for the first time.

organizations and the Republican Party emphasized passage of the Fourteenth and Fifteenth Amendments and withdrew funds and support from the cause of woman suffrage. Disagreements over these amendments divided suffragists for decades.

The radical wing, led by Stanton and Anthony, opposed the Fifteenth Amendment, arguing that ratification would establish an "aristocracy of sex," enfranchising all men while leaving women without political privileges. They argued for a Sixteenth Amendment that would secure the vote for women. Other women's rights activists, including Lucy Stone and Frederick Douglass, asserted that "this hour belongs to the Negro." They feared a debate over woman suffrage at the national level would jeopardize passage of the two amendments.

By 1869 woman suffragists had split into two competing organizations: the moderate American Woman Suffrage Association (AWSA), which sought the support of men, and the more radical all-female National Woman Suffrage Association (NWSA). For the NWSA, the vote represented only one part of a broad spectrum of goals inherited from the Declaration of Sentiments manifesto adopted at the first women's rights convention held in 1848 at Seneca Falls, New York. (See Chapter 13.)

Although women did not win the vote in this period, they did establish an independent suffrage movement that eventually drew millions of women into political life. The NWSA in particular demonstrated that self-government and democratic participation in the public sphere were crucial for women's emancipation. The failure of woman suffrage after the Civil War was less a result of factional fighting than of the larger defeat of Radical Reconstruction and the ideal of expanded citizenship.

17.2 The Meaning of Freedom

What were the most important changes in the lives of African Americans in the years immediately following the war?

For nearly 4 million slaves, freedom arrived in various ways in different parts of the South. In many areas, slavery had collapsed long before Lee's surrender at Appomattox. In regions far removed from the presence of federal troops, African Americans did not learn of slavery's end until the spring of 1865. There were thousands of sharply contrasting stories, many of which revealed the need for freed slaves to confront their owners. One Virginia slave, hired out to another family during the war, had been working in the fields when a friend told her she was now free. "Is dat

so?" she exclaimed. Dropping her hoe, she ran the seven miles to her old place, confronted her former mistress, and shouted, "I'se free! Yes, I'se free! Ain't got to work fo' you no mo'." But regardless of specific regional circumstances, the meaning of "freedom" would be contested for years to come. The deep desire for independence from white control formed the underlying aspiration of newly freed slaves. For their part, most southern white people sought to restrict the boundaries of that independence. As individuals and as members of communities transformed by emancipation, former slaves struggled to establish economic, political, and cultural autonomy. They built on the twin pillars of slave culture—the family and the church—to consolidate and expand African American institutions, and thereby laid the foundation for the modern African American community.

17.2.1 Moving About

The first impulse of many emancipated slaves was to test their freedom. The simplest, most obvious way to do this involved leaving home. Throughout the summer and fall of 1865, observers in the South noted enormous numbers of freed people on the move. One former slave squatting in an abandoned tent outside Selma, Alabama, explained his feeling to a northern journalist: "I's want to be free man, come when I please, and nobody say nuffin to me, nor order me roun'." When urged to stay on with the South Carolina family she had served for years as a cook, a slave woman replied firmly: "No, Miss, I must go. If I stay here I'll never know I am free."

Yet many who left their old neighborhoods returned soon afterward to seek work in the general vicinity or even on the plantation they had left. Many wanted to separate themselves from former owners, but not from familial ties and friendships. Others moved away altogether, seeking jobs in nearby towns and cities. Many former slaves left predominantly white counties, where they felt more vulnerable and isolated, for new lives in the relative comfort of predominantly black communities. In most southern states, there was a significant population shift toward black belt plantation counties and towns after the war. Many African Americans, attracted by schools, churches, and fraternal societies as well as the army, preferred the city. Between 1865 and 1870, the African American population of the South's ten largest cities doubled, while the white population increased by only 10 percent.

Disgruntled planters had difficulty accepting African American independence. During slavery, they had expected obedience, submission, and loyalty from African Americans. Now many could not understand why so many former slaves wanted to leave, despite urgent pleas to continue working at the old place. The deference and humility white people expected from African Americans could no longer be taken for granted. Indeed, many freed people went out of their way to reject the old subservience. Moving about freely was one way of doing this, as were refusing to tip one's hat to white people, ignoring former masters or mistresses in the streets, and refusing to step aside on sidewalks.

When freed people staged parades, dances, and picnics to celebrate their new freedom—as they did, for example, when commemorating the Emancipation Proclamation—white people invariably condemned them angrily for "insolence," "outrageous spectacles," or "putting on airs."

17.2.2 African American Families, Churches, and Schools

Emancipation allowed freed people to strengthen family ties. For many former slaves, freedom meant the opportunity to find long-lost family members. To track down these relatives, freed people trekked to faraway places, put ads in newspapers, sought the help of Freedmen's Bureau agents, and questioned anyone who might have information about loved ones. Many thousands of family reunions, each with its own story, took place after the war. Thousands of African American couples who had lived together under slavery streamed to military and civilian authorities and demanded to be legally married. By 1870, the two-parent household was the norm for a large majority of African Americans.

For many freed people, the attempt to find lost relatives dragged on for years. Searches often proved frustrating, exhausting, and ultimately disappointing. Some "reunions" ended painfully with the discovery that spouses had found new partners and started new families.

Emancipation brought changes to gender roles within the African American family as well. By serving in the Union army, African American men played a more direct role than women in the fight for freedom. In the political sphere, black men could now serve on juries, vote, and hold office; black women, like their white counterparts, could not. Freedmen's Bureau agents designated the husband as household head and established lower wage scales for women laborers. African American editors, preachers, and politicians regularly quoted the biblical injunction that wives submit to their husbands.

African American men asserted their male authority, denied under slavery, by insisting their wives work at home instead of in the fields. African American women generally wanted to devote more time than they had under slavery to caring for their children and to performing such domestic chores as cooking, sewing, gardening, and laundering. Yet African American women continued to work outside the home, engaging in seasonal field labor for wages or working a family's rented plot. Most rural black families barely eked out a living and, thus, the labor of every family member was essential to survival. The key difference from slave times was that African American families themselves, not white masters and overseers, decided when and where women and children worked.

The creation of separate African American churches proved the most lasting and important element of the energetic institution building that went on in postemancipation years. Before the Civil War, southern Protestant churches had relegated slaves and free African Americans to second-class membership. Even in larger cities, where all-black congregations sometimes built their own churches, the law required white pastors.

In communities around the South, African Americans now pooled their resources to buy land and build their own churches. Before these structures were completed, African Americans might hold services in a railroad boxcar, where Atlanta's First Baptist Church began, or in an outdoor arbor, the original site of the First Baptist Church of Memphis. Churches became the center not only for religious life but also for many other activities that defined the African American community: schools, picnics, festivals, and political meetings. The church became the first social institution fully controlled by African Americans. In nearly every community, ministers, respected for their speaking and organizational skills, were among the most influential leaders. Black Baptist churches, with their decentralized and democratic structure and more emotional services, attracted the greatest number of freed people. By the end of Reconstruction, the vast majority of African American Christians belonged to black Baptist or Methodist churches.

The rapid spread of schools reflected African Americans' thirst for self-improvement. Southern states had prohibited education for slaves. But many free black people managed to attend school, and a few slaves had been able to educate themselves. Still, over 90 percent of the South's adult African American population was illiterate in 1860. Access to education thus became a central part of the meaning of freedom. Freedmen's Bureau agents repeatedly expressed amazement at the number of makeshift classrooms organized by African Americans in rural areas. A Bureau officer described these "wayside schools": "A negro riding on a loaded wagon, or sitting on a hack waiting for a train, or by the cabin door, is often seen, book in hand, delving after the rudiments of knowledge. A group on the platform of a depot, after carefully conning an old spelling book, resolves itself into a class."

African American communities received important educational aid from outside organizations. By 1869, the

FIRST AFRICAN BAPTIST CHURCH An overflow congregation crowds into Richmond's First African Baptist Church in 1874. Despite their poverty, freed people struggled to save money, buy land, and erect new buildings as they organized hundreds of new black churches during Reconstruction. As the most important African American institution outside the family, the black church—in addition to tending to spiritual needs—played a key role in the educational and political life of the community.

Getty Images.

Freedmen's Bureau was supervising nearly 3,000 schools serving more than 150,000 students throughout the South. Over half of the roughly 3,300 teachers in these schools were African Americans, many of whom had been free before the Civil War. Other teachers included dedicated northern white women, volunteers sponsored by the American Missionary Association (AMA). The Bureau and the AMA also assisted in the founding of several black colleges, including Tougaloo, Hampton, and Fisk, designed to train black teachers. Black self-help proved crucial to the education effort. Throughout the South in 1865 and 1866, African Americans raised money to build schoolhouses, buy supplies, and pay teachers. Black artisans donated labor for construction, and black families offered room and board to teachers.

17.2.3 Land and Labor after Slavery

Most newly emancipated African Americans aspired to quit the plantations and to make new lives for themselves. Some freed people did find jobs in railroad building, mining, ranching, or construction work. Others raised subsistence crops and tended vegetable gardens as squatters. White planters, however, tried to retain African Americans as permanent agricultural laborers. Restricting the employment of former slaves was an important goal of the black codes.

The majority of African Americans hoped to become self-sufficient farmers. Many former slaves believed they were entitled to the land they had worked throughout their lives. General Oliver O. Howard, chief commissioner of the Freedmen's Bureau, observed that many "supposed that the Government [would] divide among them the lands of the conquered owners, and furnish them with all that might be necessary to begin life as an independent farmer." This perception was not merely a wishful fantasy. Frequent reference in the Congress and the press to the question of land distribution made the idea of "40 acres and a mule" not just a pipe dream but a matter of serious public debate. But by 1866, the federal government had already pulled back from the various wartime experiments involving the breaking up of large plantations and the leasing of small plots to individual families. President Johnson directed General Howard of the Freedmen's Bureau to evict tens of thousands of freed people settled on confiscated and abandoned land in southeastern Virginia, southern Louisiana, and the Georgia and South Carolina Lowcountry.

In communities throughout the South, freed people and their former masters negotiated new arrangements for organizing agricultural labor. In Hale County, Alabama, for example, local black farmhands contracted to work on Henry Watson's plantation in 1866 deserted him when they angrily discovered that their small share of the crop left them in debt. Local Union League activists encouraged newly freed slaves to remain independent of white farmers, and political agitation for freedmen's rights encouraged them to push for better working conditions as well. Yet few owners would sell or even rent land to blacks. Watson, desperate for field hands, finally agreed to subdivide his plantation and rent it to freedmen, who would work under their own supervision without overseers. Black families left the old slave quarters and began building cabins scattered around the plantation. By 1868, Watson was convinced that black farmers made good tenants; like many other landowners, he grudgingly accepted greater independence for black families in exchange for a more stable labor force. By 1869, as one Hale County correspondent reported, "Many planters have turned their stock, teams, and every facility to farming, over to the negroes, and only require an amount of toll for the use of the land." (See Map 17.2.)

By the late 1860s, **sharecropping** and tenant farming had emerged as the dominant forms of working the land. Sharecropping represented a compromise between planters and former slaves. Under sharecropping arrangements that were usually very detailed, individual families contracted with landowners to be responsible for a specific plot. Large plantations were thus broken into family-sized farms. Generally, sharecropper families received one-third of the year's crop if the owner furnished implements, seed, and draft animals, or one-half if they provided their own supplies. African Americans preferred sharecropping to gang labor, as it allowed families to set their own hours and tasks, and offered freedom from white supervision and control. Although black sharecroppers clearly enjoyed more autonomy than in the past, the vast majority never achieved economic independence or land ownership. For planters, the system stabilized the workforce by requiring sharecroppers to remain until the harvest and to employ all family members. It also offered a way around the chronic shortage of cash and credit that plagued the postwar South. Freed people did not aspire to sharecropping. They remained a largely subordinate agricultural labor force.

17.2.4 The Origins of African American Politics

Hundreds of African American delegates, selected by local meetings or churches, attended statewide political conventions held throughout the South in 1865 and 1866. Convention debates sometimes reflected the tensions within African American communities, such as friction between poorer former slaves and better-off free black people, or between lighter- and darker-skinned African Americans. But most of these state gatherings concentrated on passing resolutions on issues that united all African Americans. The central concerns were suffrage and equality before the law. (See SEEING History.)

The passage of the First Reconstruction Act in 1867 encouraged even more political activity among African Americans. The military started registering the South's electorate, ultimately enrolling approximately 735,000 black and 635,000 white voters in the ten unreconstructed states. Five states—Alabama, Florida, Louisiana, Mississippi, and South Carolina—had black electoral majorities. Fewer than half the registered white voters participated in the elections for state constitutional conventions in 1867 and 1868. In contrast, four-fifths of the registered black voters cast ballots in these elections. Much of this new African American political activism was channeled through local Union League chapters throughout the South. However, as the fate of Alex Webb in Hale County, Alabama, again makes clear, few whites welcomed this activism.

Begun during the war as a northern, largely white middle-class patriotic club, the **Union League** now became the political voice of the former slaves. Union League chapters brought together local African Americans, soldiers, and Freedmen's Bureau agents to demand the vote and

Map 17.2 **THE BARROW PLANTATION, OGLETHORPE COUNTY, GEORGIA, 1860 AND 1881 (APPROX. 2,000 ACRES)**

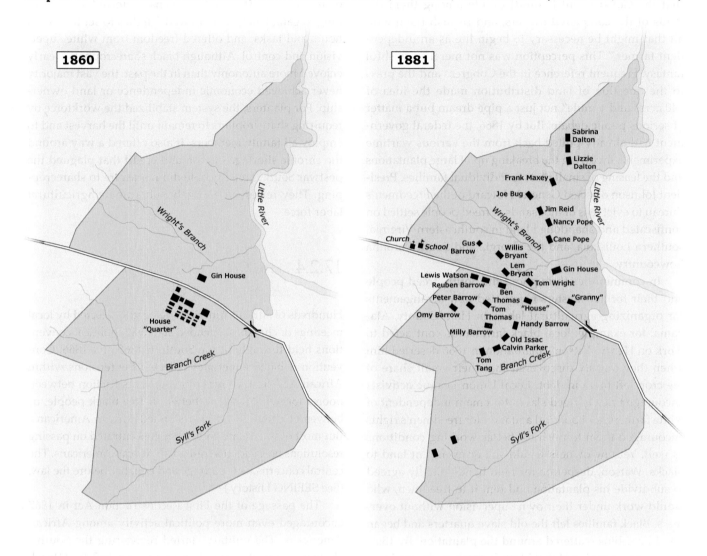

These two maps, based on drawings from *Scribner's Monthly*, April 1881, show some of the changes brought by emancipation. In 1860, the plantation's entire black population lived in the communal slave quarters, right next to the white master's house. In 1881, black sharecropper and tenant families lived on individual plots, spread out across the land. The former slaves had also built their own school and church.

an end to legal discrimination against African Americans. It brought out African American voters, instructed freedmen in the rights and duties of citizenship, and promoted Republican candidates. Not surprisingly, newly enfranchised freedmen voted Republican and formed the core of the Republican Party in the South. For most ordinary African Americans, politics was inseparable from economic issues, especially the land question. Grassroots political organizations frequently intervened in local disputes with planters over the terms of labor contracts. African American political groups closely followed the congressional debates over Reconstruction policy and agitated for land confiscation and distribution.

17.3 Southern Politics and Society

How successful were southern Republicans in reshaping southern society and government?

By the summer of 1868, when the South had returned to the Union, the majority of Republicans believed the task of Reconstruction to be finished. Most Republican congressmen were moderates, conceiving Reconstruction in limited terms. They rejected radical calls for confiscation and redistribution of land, as well as permanent military rule of the South. The Reconstruction Acts of 1867 and 1868 laid out

"THE FIRST VOTE" This *Harper's Weekly* illustration from November 16, 1867, reflected the optimism felt by much of the northern public as former slaves began to vote for the first time. The caption noted that freedmen went to the ballot box "not with expressions of exultation or of defiance of their old masters and present opponents depicted on their countenances, but looking serious and solemn and determined."

the requirements for the readmission of southern states, along with the procedures for forming and electing new governments.

Yet over the next decade, the political structure created in the southern states proved too restricted and fragile to sustain itself. To most southern whites, the active participation of African Americans in politics seemed extremely dangerous. Federal troops were needed to protect Republican governments and their supporters from violent opposition. Congressional action to monitor southern elections and protect black voting rights became routine. Despite initial successes, southern Republicanism proved an unstable coalition of often conflicting elements, unable to sustain effective power for very long. By 1877, Democrats had regained political control of all the former Confederate states.

17.3.1 Southern Republicans

Three major groups composed the fledgling Republican coalition in the postwar South. African American voters made up a large majority of southern Republicans throughout the Reconstruction era. Yet African Americans outnumbered whites in only three southern states; Republicans would have to attract white support to win elections and sustain power.

A second group consisted of white Northerners, derisively called **carpetbaggers** by native white Southerners. Most were veterans of the Union army who stayed in the South after the war. Others included Freedmen's Bureau agents and businessmen who had invested capital in cotton plantations and other enterprises. Albert Morgan, for example, was an army veteran from Ohio who settled in

SEEING History

Changing Images of Reconstruction

After the Civil War, northern journalists and illustrators went south to describe Reconstruction in action. They took a keen interest in how the newly freed slaves were reshaping local and national politics. A drawing by *Harper's Weekly* illustrator William L. Sheppard titled "Electioneering in the South" clearly approved of the freedmen's exercise of their new citizenship rights. "Does any man seriously doubt," the caption asked, "whether it is better for this vast population to be sinking deeper and deeper in ignorance and servility, or rising into general intelligence and self-respect? They can not be pariahs; they can not be peons; they must be slaves or citizens."

Thomas Nast was the nation's best-known political cartoonist during the 1860s and 1870s. During the Civil War, he strongly supported the Union cause and the aspirations of the newly freed slaves. But by 1876, like many Northerners originally sympathetic to guaranteeing blacks full political

and civil rights, Nast had turned away from the early ideals of Reconstruction. Nast used grotesque racial caricature to depict southern African Americans and northern Irish immigrants as undeserving of the right to vote. The aftermath of the disputed 1876 presidential election included charges of widespread vote fraud from both Republicans and Democrats. Nast's view—published in *Harper's Weekly* in December 1876, while the election's outcome was still in doubt—reflected concerns among many middle-class Northerners that the nation's political system was tainted by the manipulation of "ignorant" voters in both the South and the North.

- **How does the portrayal of the larger African American community in "Electioneering in the South" reflect the political point being made?**

- **What do the caricatures in "The Ignorant Vote" suggest about Reconstruction-era ideas about the meaning of "whiteness"?**

"ELECTIONEERING IN THE SOUTH"

Everett Collection Historical/Alamy Stock Photo.

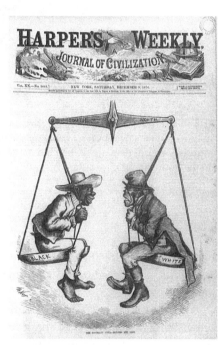

"THE IGNORANT VOTE"

Library of Congress (Photoduplication).

Mississippi after the war. When he and his brother failed at running a cotton plantation and sawmill, Morgan became active in Republican politics as a way to earn a living. He won election to the state constitutional convention, became a power in the state legislature, and risked his life to keep the Republican organization alive in the Mississippi Delta region. Although they made up a tiny percentage of the population, carpetbaggers played a disproportionately large role in southern politics. They won a large share of Reconstruction offices, particularly in Florida, South Carolina, and Louisiana, and in areas with large African American constituencies.

The third major group of southern Republicans was the native whites pejoratively termed **scalawags**. They had even more diverse backgrounds and motives than the northern-born Republicans. Some were prominent prewar Whigs who saw the Republican Party as their best chance to regain political influence. Others viewed the party as an agent of modernization and economic expansion. "Yankees and Yankee notions are just what we want in this country," argued Thomas Settle of North Carolina. "We want their capital to build factories and workshops. We want their intelligence, their energy and enterprise." Loyalists during the war and traditional enemies of the planter elite (most were small farmers), these white Southerners looked to the Republican Party for help in settling old scores and for relief from debt and wartime devastation.

Southern Republicanism also reflected prewar political divisions, the influence of which was greatest in those regions that had long resisted the political and economic power of the plantation elite. Thus, southern Republicans could dominate the mountainous areas of western North Carolina, eastern Tennessee, northern Georgia, and southwestern Virginia as much as Democrats controlled other areas. Yet few white Southerners identified with the political and economic aspirations of African Americans. Moderate elements more concerned with maintaining white control of the party, and encouraging economic investment in the region, outnumbered and defeated "confiscation radicals" who focused on obtaining land for African Americans.

17.3.2 Reconstructing the States: A Mixed Record

With the old Confederate leaders barred from political participation, and with carpetbaggers and newly enfranchised African Americans representing many of the plantation districts, Republicans managed to dominate the 10 southern constitutional conventions from 1867 to 1869. Most of these conventions produced constitutions that expanded democracy and the public role of the state. In 1868, only three years after the end of the war, Republicans came to power in most of the southern states. By 1869, new constitutions had been ratified in all the old Confederate states.

Republican governments in the South faced a continual crisis of legitimacy that limited their ability to legislate change. They had to balance reform against the need to gain acceptance, especially by white Southerners. Their achievements were thus mixed. In the realm of race relations there was a clear thrust toward equal rights and against discrimination. Republican legislatures followed up the federal Civil Rights Act of 1866 with various antidiscrimination clauses in new constitutions and laws prescribing harsh penalties for civil rights violations.

Segregation, though, became the norm in public school systems. African American leaders often accepted segregation because they feared that insistence on integrated education would jeopardize funding for the new school systems. Segregation in railroad cars and other public places was more objectionable. By the early 1870s, as black influence and assertiveness grew, laws guaranteeing equal access to transportation and public accommodation were passed in many states. By and large, though, such civil rights laws were difficult to enforce in local communities.

In economic matters, Republican governments failed to fulfill African Americans' hopes of obtaining land. Most former slaves did not possess the cash to buy land in the open market, and they looked to the state for help. Republicans tried to weaken the plantation system and promote black ownership by raising taxes on land. Yet even when state governments seized land for nonpayment of taxes, the property was never used to help create black homesteads.

Republican leaders envisioned promoting northern-style capitalist development—factories, large towns, and diversified agriculture—through state aid. Much Republican state lawmaking was devoted to encouraging railroad construction. But in spite of all the new laws, it proved impossible to attract significant amounts of northern and European investment capital. The obsession with railroads withdrew resources from education and other programs. As in the North, it also opened the door to widespread corruption and bribery of public officials. Railroad failures eroded public confidence in the Republicans' ability to govern.

17.3.3 White Resistance and "Redemption"

The emergence of a Republican Party in the reconstructed South brought two parties, but not a two-party system, to the region. The opponents of Reconstruction, the Democrats, refused to acknowledge Republicans' right to participate in southern political life. Republicans were split between those who urged conciliation in an effort to gain white acceptance and those who emphasized consolidating the party under the protection of the military.

From its founding in 1868 through the early 1870s, the Ku Klux Klan waged an ongoing terrorist campaign against Reconstruction governments and local leaders. Just as the institution of slavery had depended on violence and the threat of violence, the Klan acted as a kind of guerrilla military force in the service of the Democratic Party, the planter class, and all those who sought the restoration of white supremacy. It employed a wide array of terror tactics: destroying ballot boxes, issuing death threats, and beating and murdering politically active blacks and their white allies. Freedmen and their allies sometimes resisted the Klan. In Hale County, Alabama, Union Leaguers set up a warning system using buglers to signal the activities of Klan raiders. But violence and intimidation decimated Union League leadership in the countryside by 1869. (See Communities *in* Conflict.)

In October 1870, after Republicans carried Laurens County in South Carolina, bands of white people drove 150 African Americans from their homes and murdered 13 white and black Republican activists. In March 1871, 3 African Americans were arrested in Meridian, Mississippi, for giving "incendiary" speeches. At their court hearing, Klansmen killed 2 of the defendants and the Republican judge, and 30 more African Americans were murdered in a day of rioting. The single bloodiest episode of Reconstruction-era violence took place in Colfax, Louisiana, on Easter Sunday 1873. Nearly 100 African Americans were murdered after they failed to hold a besieged courthouse during a contested election.

Southern Republicans looked to Washington for help. In 1870 and 1871, Congress passed three Enforcement Acts designed to counter racial terrorism. The most sweeping measure was the Ku Klux Klan Act of April 1871, which made the violent infringement of civil and political rights a federal crime punishable by the national government. By the election of 1872, the federal government's intervention had helped break the Klan and restore a semblance of law and order.

The Civil Rights Act of 1875 outlawed racial discrimination in theaters, hotels, railroads, and other public places. But the law proved more an assertion of principle than a direct federal intervention in southern affairs. Enforcement required African Americans to take their cases to the federal courts, a costly and time-consuming procedure.

In many southern communities, persistent organized violence aimed at restoring white supremacy overwhelmed limited federal efforts to protect freedpeople. As wartime idealism faded, northern Republicans became less inclined toward direct intervention in southern affairs. They had enough trouble retaining political control in the North. In 1874, the Democrats gained a majority in the House of Representatives for the first time since 1856. Key northern states also began to fall to the Democrats. Northern Republicans slowly abandoned the freedmen and their white allies in the South. Southern Democrats were also able to exploit a deepening fiscal crisis by blaming Republicans for excessive extension of public credit and the sharp increase in tax rates.

Gradually, conservative Democrats "redeemed" one state after another. Virginia and Tennessee led the way in 1869, and North Carolina followed in 1870, Georgia in 1871, Texas in 1873, and Alabama and Arkansas in 1874. In Mississippi, white conservatives employed violence and intimidation to wrest control in 1875 and "redeemed" the state the following year. Republican infighting in Louisiana in 1873 and 1874 led to a series of contested election results, including bloody clashes between black militia and armed whites, and finally to "redemption" by the Democrats in 1877.

Several Supreme Court rulings involving the Fourteenth and Fifteenth amendments effectively constrained federal protection of African American civil rights. In the so-called **Slaughterhouse cases** of 1873, the Court issued its first ruling on the Fourteenth Amendment. The cases involved a Louisiana charter that gave a New Orleans meatpacking company a monopoly over the city's butchering business on the grounds of protecting public health. A rival group of butchers had sued, claiming the law violated the Fourteenth Amendment, which prohibited states from depriving any person of life, liberty, or property without due process of law. The Court held that the Fourteenth Amendment protected only the former slaves, not butchers, and that it protected only national citizenship rights, not the regulatory powers of states. The Court separated national citizenship from state citizenship and declared that most of the rights that Americans enjoyed on a daily basis—freedom of speech, fair trials, the right to sit on juries, protection from unreasonable searches, and the right to vote—were under the control of state law. The ruling in effect denied the original intent of the Fourteenth Amendment—to protect against state infringement of national citizenship rights as spelled out in the Bill of Rights.

Three other decisions curtailed federal protection of black civil rights. In *United States v. Reese* (1876) and *United*

Communities *in* Conflict

The Ku Klux Klan in Alabama

*Ku Klux Klan: Sincere protectors
or vicious terrorists?*

During Reconstruction the Ku Klux Klan (KKK) claimed as many as 12,000 members in Alabama, or about one in every nine white male voters. The KKK enjoyed deep and widespread support from many whites, including women and children, who viewed the Klan as the protector of white supremacy and a weapon against the Republican Party. Democratic newspapers routinely printed favorable accounts of Klan activities, as well as pro-Klan advertisements, songs, and jokes—and threats directed at intended Klan victims. The following excerpt from a sympathetic newspaper report of Klan activities in the central Alabama town of Florence was published in the *Shelby County Guide* on December 3, 1868.

African Americans and their Republican allies, however, experienced the Klan as a terrorist organization responsible for murder, beatings, arson, and violent intimidation aimed at preventing African American political organizing and economic advancement. This view is vividly presented in a first-person account of Klan terror given by George Houston, an ex-slave and tailor, who had been elected to represent Sumter County in the Alabama state legislature. Houston had helped organize a Union League chapter and actively registered black voters. After local Klansmen wounded his son and broke down the door to his house, Houston grabbed his gun and shot back. In this testimony to a congressional committee investigating the KKK's terrorist campaign, he describes the immediate scene and the campaign to intimidate him.

- **How do the documents reveal profoundly different understandings of the consequences of freedom for African Americans?**

- **What do the sources tell us about the connections between political dominance and economic power in the Reconstruction-era South?**

Movements of the Mystic Klan, from the *Shelby County Guide,* December 3, 1868

About a week ago Saturday night the Ku Klux came into town to regulate matters. They were here from eleven P.M. to three o'clock A.M.—five hundred in all. They shot one very bad Negro, putting six balls through his head. Many heard the noise, but did not know what was going on. They also hung three or four Negroes nearly dead, and whipped others severely in order to make them tell them about their nightly meetings, and what their object was in holding the same; also, as to who their leaders were. They made a clean breast of the whole matter, telling everything. The strongest thing about these Ku Klux was that they did not hesitate to unmask themselves when asked to do so; and out of the whole party none were identified.—Every one who saw them says their horses were more beautiful than, and far superior to, any in the country round about. They spoke but little but always to a purpose. They went to several stores and knocked; the doors were opened at once. They then called for rope, and at each place a coil was rolled out to them. They cut it in suitable length to hang a man with. No one asked for money and they offered none. They did not disturb any one else, nor did they take any thing except some few Enfield rifles which were found in possession of some very bad Negroes.—They called on the revenue officer and passed a few remarks with him. What transpired is not known, but it has made a great improvement in his conversation. The visitants advent has been productive of much good and benefit to the community, though all regret such steps should have to be resorted to, every one says "give us peace," and really I believe them to be truly sincere.

Source: Alabama Department of Archives and History, Montgomery, Alabama.

George Houston's Testimony, Montgomery, October 17, 1871

Q: How many were there in the crowd that attacked your house?

A. I can't tell. It looked like a great many men. It was starlight and before day. There was a good deal of cursing after they got shot and broke down my door. The reason they were afraid to come in was, I think, because that shot was fired. They didn't come back.

Q: Did you notice whether they were disguised?

A. Only the one that I shot at. He looked like he was wrapped up in some white cloth; it looked so by starlight. That is all I could see.

Q: Had you any trouble with your neighbors?

A. Nothing more than some talk that I didn't like from some wealthy men of the county. One of them had come to me, and told me if I turned against them they would turn against me. They looked upon me as being the prominent Negro of the county. I know the men that told me that thing very well. It was in a dry goods store in that town.

Q: What did they want you to do?

A. They wanted me to deny what was called the Union League. They had understood I belonged to it. The reason they took a great fancy to me was, I was a tailor in that place. My master had learned me this trade on account of my health and crippleness when I was a slave. I had run a shop for sixteen years there. They came to me, and said I made my living off of them and not off of the damned niggers, and if I turned against them they would turn against me. I said my belonging to the Union League didn't do them any harm. They said, 'Yes, it does.' I said, 'It's only to teach our ignorant colored men.' This was our talk privately, and this was only a few months before I was shot. That is all I could assign for the cause of it, and taking the fact that the other colored men were shot down just before, and I was a representative of that county. There was a public meeting; we had made some public speeches, some white and some black men, and I told them I was opposed to this.

Q: Opposed to what?

A. Opposed to colored men being shot down like dogs, when I knew that the officers of the county could stop it. I told the sheriff that to his face. If they took exceptions to me on that account, that is all I can tell, for I was raised there, and they never could put a scratch of a pen against me before, and nothing else could they have taken from it except that I tried to hold up the men that had been shot down by violence; some at night, some by daylight; some were found in the stock pools with their guts cut out. All this came to my ears and the other men's ears.

Q: How many colored men were assassinated in that county?

A. I think eight or nine, before I was shot, were killed dead, according to the accounts of the white men and black men I got through the county. I stop at eight or nine, but I really think there were a few more.

Q: Is the bullet there now in the leg?

A. Yes sir; and it will stay there until God Almighty takes it out. I had a doctor fifteen minutes probing to get that out. The ball went through my child's flesh, too. My child had to go fifteen miles to his grandfather and I had to suffer and go off. I had to sacrifice my property. And yet I am a Republican, and I will die one. I say the Republican Party freed me, and I will die on top of it. I don't care who is pleased. I vote every time. I was register of my county, and my master sent in and lent me his pistols to carry around my waist when I was register, to protect myself against my enemies. I am a Republican today, and if the Republican Party can't do me any good, I will never turn against it. I can work in the cotton patch and work at my trade, and get along without any benefit from my party, and so I will stick to the Republican Party and die in it.

Source: "Affairs in Insurrectionary States: Report and Minority Reviews, Alabama, vol. 2," *Senate Reports*, 42nd Congress, 2nd Session, vol. 2, pt. 9, no. 41.

THE KU KLUX KLAN The Ku Klux Klan emerged as a potent political and social force during Reconstruction, terrorizing freed people and their white allies.

States v. Cruikshank (1876), the Court restricted congressional power to enforce the Ku Klux Klan Act. Future prosecution would depend on the states rather than on federal authorities. In these rulings, the Court held that the Fourteenth Amendment extended the federal power to protect civil rights only in cases involving discrimination by states; discrimination by individuals or groups was not covered. The Court also ruled that the Fifteenth Amendment did not guarantee a citizen's right to vote; it only barred certain specific grounds for denying suffrage—"race, color, or previous condition of servitude." This interpretation opened the door for southern states to disenfranchise African Americans for allegedly nonracial reasons.

Finally, in the 1883 *Civil Rights Cases* decision, the Court declared the Civil Rights Act of 1875 unconstitutional, holding that the Fourteenth Amendment gave Congress the power to outlaw discrimination by states but not by private individuals. The majority opinion held that black people must no longer "be the special favorite of the laws." Together, these Supreme Court decisions marked the end of federal attempts to protect African American rights until well into the next century.

17.3.4 King Cotton: Sharecroppers, Tenants, and the Southern Environment

The Republicans' vision of a "New South" remade along the lines of the northern economy failed to materialize. Instead, the South declined into the country's poorest agricultural region. In the post-Civil War years, "King Cotton" expanded its realm, as greater numbers of small white farmers found themselves forced to switch from subsistence crops to growing cotton for the market. (See Map 17.3.)

A chronic shortage of capital and banking institutions made local merchants and planters the sole source of credit. They advanced loans and supplies to small owners, tenant farmers, and sharecroppers in exchange for a lien, or claim, on the year's cotton crop. They often charged extremely high interest rates on advances, while marking up the prices of the goods sold in their stores. At the end of the year, sharecroppers and tenants found themselves deep in debt to stores for seed, supplies, and clothing. Despite hard work and even bountiful harvests, few small farmers could escape from heavy debt. The spread of the "crop lien" system as the South's main form of agricultural credit forced more and more farmers into cotton growing.

As the "crop lien" system spread, and as more and more farmers turned to cotton growing as the only way to obtain credit, expanding production depressed prices. Competition from new cotton centers in the world market, such as Egypt and India, accelerated the downward spiral. As cotton prices declined alarmingly, from roughly 11 cents per pound in 1875 to 5 cents by the early 1890s, per capita wealth in the South fell steadily, equaling only one-third that of the East, Midwest, or West by the 1890s. Small farmers caught up in a vicious cycle of low cotton prices, debt, and dwindling food crops found their old ideal of independence sacrificed to the cruel logic of the cotton market.

To obtain precious credit, most southern farmers, both black and white, found themselves forced to produce cotton for market and thus became enmeshed in the debt-ridden crop lien system. In traditional cotton-producing areas, especially the black belt, landless farmers growing cotton had replaced slaves growing cotton. In the Upcountry and newer areas of cultivation, cotton-dominated commercial agriculture, with landless tenants and sharecroppers as the main workforce, had replaced the more diversified subsistence economy of the antebellum era. These patterns hardened throughout the late nineteenth century. By 1900, roughly half of the South's 2,620,000 farms were operated by tenants, who rented land, or sharecroppers, who pledged a portion of the crop to owners in exchange for some combination of work animals, seed, and tools. Over one-third of the white farmers and nearly three-quarters of the African American farmers in the cotton states were tenants or sharecroppers. Large parts of the southern landscape would remain defined by this system well into the twentieth century: small farms operated by families who did not own their land, mired in desperate poverty and debt.

17.4 Reconstructing the North

How did the northern political landscape change in the decades after the Civil War?

Abraham Lincoln liked to cite his own rise as proof of the superiority of the northern system of "free labor" over slavery. "There is no permanent class of hired laborers amongst us," Lincoln asserted. "Twenty-five years ago, I was a hired laborer. The hired laborer of yesterday, labors on his own account today; and will hire others to labor for him

Map 17.3 SOUTHERN SHARECROPPING AND THE COTTON BELT, 1880

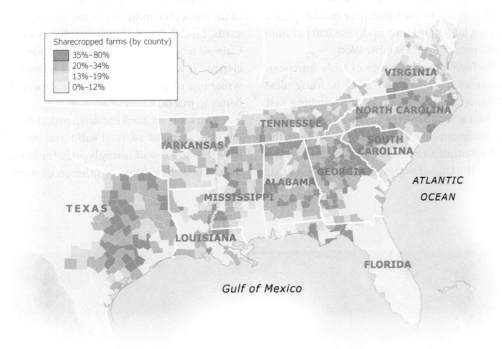

Sharecropped farms (by county)
- 35%–80%
- 20%–34%
- 13%–19%
- 0%–12%

The economic depression of the 1870s forced increasing numbers of southern farmers, both white and black, into sharecropping arrangements. Sharecropping was most pervasive in the cotton belt regions of South Carolina, Georgia, Alabama, Mississippi, and eastern Texas.

tomorrow. Advancement—improvement in condition—is the order of things in a society of equals." But the triumph of the North brought with it fundamental changes in the economy, labor relations, and politics that brought Lincoln's ideal vision into question. The spread of the factory system, the growth of large and powerful corporations, and the rapid expansion of capitalist enterprise all hastened the development of a large unskilled and routinized workforce. Rather than becoming independent producers, more and more workers found themselves consigned permanently to wage labor.

The old Republican ideal of a society bound by a harmony of interests had become overshadowed by a grimmer reality of class conflict. A violent national Great Railroad Strike in 1877 was broken only with the direct intervention of federal troops. That conflict struck many Americans as a turning point. Northern society, like the society of the South, appeared more hierarchical than equal.

17.4.1 The Age of Capital

In the decade following Appomattox, the North's economy continued the industrial boom begun during the Civil War. By 1873, America's industrial production had grown 75 percent over the 1865 level. By that time, too, the number of nonagricultural workers in the North had surpassed the number of farmers. Between 1860 and 1880, the number of wage earners in manufacturing and construction more than doubled, from 2 million to more than 4 million. Only Great Britain boasted a larger manufacturing economy than the United States. During the same period, nearly 3 million immigrants arrived in America, almost all of whom settled in the North and West.

The railroad business both symbolized and advanced the new industrial order. Shortly before the Civil War, enthusiasm mounted for a transcontinental line. Private companies took on the huge and expensive job of construction, but the federal government funded the project, providing the largest subsidy in American history. The Pacific Railway Act of 1862 granted the Union Pacific and the Central Pacific rights to a broad swath of land extending from Omaha, Nebraska, to Sacramento, California. An 1864 act bestowed a subsidy of $15,000 per mile of track laid over smooth plains country and varying larger amounts up to $48,000 per mile in the foothills and mountains of the Far West.

The Union Pacific employed gangs of Irish American and African American workers to lay track heading west from Omaha. Meanwhile the Central Pacific, pushing east from California, had a tougher time finding workers, and began recruiting thousands of men from China. In 1868, the Senate ratified the Burlingame Treaty, giving Chinese the right to emigrate to the United States, while specifying that "nothing contained herein shall be held to confer naturalization." The right to work in America, in other words, did not bestow any right to citizenship. Some 12,000 Chinese laborers (about 90 percent of the workforce) bore the brunt of the difficult conditions in the Sierra Nevada, where blizzards, landslides, and steep rock faces took an awful toll. Chinese workers earned a reputation for toughness and efficiency. "If we found we were in a hurry for a job of work," wrote one of the Central Pacific's superintendents, "it was better to put on Chinese at once."

Working in baskets suspended by ropes, Chinese laborers chipped away at solid granite walls and became expert in the use of nitroglycerin for blasting through the mountains. But after completion of the transcontinental

CHINESE RAILROAD WORKERS Chinese immigrants, like these section gang workers, provided labor and skills critical to the successful completion of the first transcontinental railroad.

line threw thousands of Chinese railroad workers onto the California labor market, the open-door immigration pledge in the Burlingame Treaty would soon be eclipsed by a virulent tide of anti-Chinese agitation among western politicians and labor unions. In 1882, Congress passed the Chinese Exclusion Act, suspending any further Chinese immigration.

On May 10, 1869, Leland Stanford, the former governor of California and president of the Central Pacific Railroad, traveled to Promontory Point in Utah Territory to hammer a ceremonial golden spike, marking the finish of the first transcontinental line. Other railroads went up with less fanfare. The Southern Pacific, chartered by the state of California, stretched from San Francisco to Los Angeles, and on through Arizona and New Mexico to connections with New Orleans. The Atchison, Topeka, and Santa Fe reached the Pacific in 1887 by way of a southerly route across the Rocky Mountains. The Great Northern, one of the few lines financed by private capital, extended west from St. Paul, Minnesota, to Washington's Puget Sound.

Railroad corporations became America's first big businesses. Railroads required huge outlays of investment capital, and their growth increased the economic power of banks and investment houses centered in Wall Street. Bankers often gained seats on the boards of directors of railroad companies, and their access to capital sometimes gave them the real control of the corporations. By the early 1870s the Pennsylvania Railroad was the nation's largest single company, with more than 20,000 employees. A small group of railroad executives, including Cornelius Vanderbilt, Jay Gould, Collis P. Huntington, and James J. Hill, amassed unheard-of fortunes. When he died in 1877, Vanderbilt left his son $100 million. By comparison, a decent annual wage for working a 6-day week was around $350.

Some of the nation's most prominent politicians routinely accepted railroad largesse. Republican Senator William M. Stewart of Nevada, a member of the Committee on Pacific Railroads, received a gift of 50,000 acres of land from the Central Pacific for his services. The worst scandal of the Grant administration grew out of corruption involving railroad promotion. As a way of diverting federal funds for the building of the Union Pacific Railroad, an inner circle of Union Pacific stockholders created the dummy Crédit Mobilier construction company. In return for political favors, a group of prominent Republicans received stock in the company. When the scandal broke in 1872, it politically ruined Vice President Schuyler Colfax and led to the censure of two congressmen.

Other industries also boomed in this period, especially those engaged in extracting minerals and processing natural resources. Railroad growth stimulated expansion in the production of coal, iron, stone, and lumber, and these industries also received significant government aid. For example, under the National Mineral Act of 1866, mining companies received millions of acres of free public land. Oil refining enjoyed a huge expansion in the 1860s and 1870s. As with railroads, an early period of fierce competition soon gave way to concentration. By the late 1870s, John D. Rockefeller's Standard Oil Company controlled almost 90 percent of the nation's oil-refining capacity.

17.4.2 Liberal Republicans and the Election of 1872

With the rapid growth of large-scale, capital-intensive enterprises, Republicans increasingly identified with the interests of business rather than the rights of freedmen or the antebellum ideology of "free labor." State Republican parties now organized themselves around the spoils of federal patronage rather than grand causes such as preserving the Union or ending slavery. Republicans had no monopoly on political scandal. In 1871 New York City newspapers reported the shocking story of how Democratic Party boss William M. Tweed and his friends had systematically stolen tens of millions from the city treasury. But to many the scandal represented only the most extreme case of the routine corruption that now plagued American political life.

By the end of President Grant's first term, a large number of disaffected Republicans sought an alternative. The **Liberal Republicans**, as they called themselves, emphasized the doctrines of classical economics. They called for a return to limited government, arguing that bribery, scandal, and high taxes all flowed from excessive state interference in the economy.

Liberal Republicans were also suspicious of expanding democracy. They believed that politics ought to be the province of "the best men"—educated and well-to-do men like themselves, devoted to the "science of government." They proposed civil service reform as the best way to break the hold of party machines on patronage.

Although most Liberal Republicans had enthusiastically supported abolition, the Union cause, and equal rights for freedmen, they now opposed continued federal intervention in the South. The national government had done all it could for the former slaves; they must now take care of themselves. In the spring of 1872, a diverse collection of Liberal Republicans nominated Horace Greeley to run for president. A longtime foe of the Democratic Party, Greeley nonetheless won that party's presidential nomination as well. All Americans, Greeley urged, must put the Civil War behind them and "clasp hands across the bloody chasm."

Grant easily defeated Greeley, carrying every state in the North and winning 56 percent of the popular vote. But the 1872 election accelerated the trend toward federal abandonment of African American citizenship rights. The Liberal Republicans quickly faded as an organized political force. But their ideas helped define a growing conservative consciousness among the northern public. Their agenda included retreat from the ideal of racial justice, hostility toward trade unions, suspicion of immigrant and working-class political power, celebration of competitive individualism, and opposition to government intervention in economic affairs.

17.4.3 The Depression of 1873

In the fall of 1873, the postwar boom came to an abrupt halt as a severe financial panic triggered a deep economic depression. The collapse resulted from commercial overexpansion, especially speculative investing in the nation's railroad system. By 1876, half the nation's railroads had defaulted on their bonds. Over the next 2 years more than 100 banks folded and 18,000 businesses shut their doors. The depression that began in 1873 lasted 65 months—the longest economic contraction in the nation's history until then.

The human toll was enormous. As factories began to close across the nation, the unemployment rate soared to about 15 percent. In many cities the jobless rate was much higher; roughly one-quarter of New York City workers were unemployed in 1874. Many thousands of men took to the road in search of work, and the "tramp" emerged as a new and menacing figure on the social landscape. Farmers were also hard hit by the depression. Agricultural output continued to grow, but prices and land values fell sharply. As prices for their crops fell, farmers had a more difficult time repaying their fixed loan obligations; many sank deeper into debt.

Mass meetings of workers in New York and other cities issued calls to government officials to create jobs through public works. But these appeals were rejected. Indeed, many business leaders and political figures denounced even meager efforts at charity. They saw the depression as a natural, if painful, part of the business cycle, one that would allow only the strongest enterprises (and workers) to survive. The depression of the 1870s prompted workers and farmers to question the old free-labor ideology that celebrated a harmony of interests in northern society. More people voiced anger at and distrust of large corporations that exercised great economic power from outside their local communities.

17.4.4 The Electoral Crisis of 1876

With the economy mired in depression, Democrats looked forward to capturing the White House in 1876. New scandals plaguing the Grant administration also weakened the Republican Party. In 1875, a conspiracy surfaced between distillers and U.S. revenue agents to cheat the government out of millions in tax revenues. The government secured indictments against more than 200 members of this "Whiskey Ring," including Orville E. Babcock, Grant's private secretary. Though acquitted, thanks to Grant's intervention, Babcock resigned in disgrace. In 1876, Secretary of War William W. Belknap was impeached for receiving bribes for the sale of trading posts in Indian Territory, and he resigned to avoid conviction.

Democrats nominated Governor Samuel J. Tilden of New York, who brought impeccable reform credentials to his candidacy. In 1871 he had helped expose and prosecute the "Tweed Ring" in New York City. As governor he had toppled the "Canal Ring," a graft-ridden scheme involving inflated contracts for repairs on the Erie Canal. In their platform, the Democrats linked the issue of corruption to an attack on Reconstruction policies. They blamed the Republicans for instituting "a corrupt centralism."

Republican nominee Rutherford B. Hayes, governor of Ohio, also sought the high ground. As a lawyer in Cincinnati he had defended runaway slaves. Later he had distinguished himself as a general in the Union army. Hayes promised, if elected, to support an efficient civil service system, to vigorously prosecute officials who betrayed the public trust, and to introduce a system of free universal education.

On an election day marred by widespread vote fraud and violent intimidation, Tilden received 250,000 more popular votes than Hayes. But Republicans refused to concede victory, challenging the vote totals in the electoral college. Tilden garnered 184 uncontested electoral votes, one shy of the majority required to win, while Hayes received 165. (See Map 17.4.)

The problem centered on 20 disputed electoral votes from Florida, Louisiana, South Carolina, and Oregon. In each of the three southern states the vote was extremely close, and both parties claimed to have earned the electoral vote. In Oregon, which Hayes had unquestionably carried, the Democratic governor nevertheless replaced a disputed Republican elector with a Democrat.

The crisis was unprecedented. In January 1877, Congress moved to settle the deadlock, establishing an Electoral Commission composed of five senators, five representatives, and five Supreme Court justices; eight were Republicans and seven were Democrats. The commission voted along strict partisan lines to award all the contested electoral votes

Map 17.4 THE ELECTION OF 1876

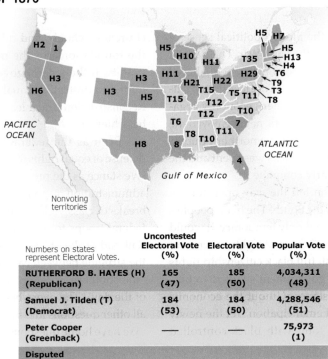

Numbers on states represent Electoral Votes.	Uncontested Electoral Vote (%)	Electoral Vote (%)	Popular Vote (%)
RUTHERFORD B. HAYES (H) (Republican)	165 (47)	185 (50)	4,034,311 (48)
Samuel J. Tilden (T) (Democrat)	184 (53)	184 (50)	4,288,546 (51)
Peter Cooper (Greenback)	—	—	75,973 (1)
Disputed			

The presidential election of 1876 left the nation without a clear-cut winner.

to Hayes. Outraged by this decision, Democratic congressmen threatened a filibuster to block Hayes's inauguration. Violence and stalemate were avoided when Democrats and Republicans struck a compromise in February. In return for Hayes's ascendance to the presidency, the Republicans promised to appropriate more money for southern internal improvements, to appoint a Southerner to Hayes's cabinet, and to pursue a policy of noninterference ("home rule") in southern affairs.

Shortly after assuming office, Hayes ordered removal of the remaining federal troops in Louisiana and South Carolina. Without this military presence to sustain them, the Republican governors of those two states quickly lost power to Democrats. "Home rule" meant Republican abandonment of freed people, Radicals, carpetbaggers, and scalawags. It also effectively nullified the Fourteenth and Fifteenth amendments and the Civil Rights Act of 1866. The **Compromise of 1877** completed repudiation of the idea, born during the Civil War and pursued during Congressional Reconstruction, of a powerful federal government protecting the rights of all American citizens.

Conclusion

Reconstruction succeeded in the limited political sense of reuniting a nation torn apart by the Civil War. The Radical Republican vision, emphasizing racial justice, equal civil and political rights guaranteed by the Fourteenth and Fifteenth Amendments, and a new southern economy organized around independent small farmers, never enjoyed the support of the majority of its party or the northern public. By 1877, the political force of these ideals was spent and the national retreat from them nearly complete.

The end of Reconstruction left the way open for the return of white domination in the South. The freed people's political and civil equality proved only temporary. It would take a "Second Reconstruction," the civil rights movement of the next century, to establish full black citizenship rights once and for all. The federal government's failure to pursue land reform left former slaves without the economic independence needed for full emancipation. Yet the newly autonomous black family, along with black-controlled churches, schools, and other social institutions, provided the foundations for the modern African American community. If the federal government was not yet fully committed to protecting equal rights in local communities, the Reconstruction Era at least pointed to how that goal might be achieved.

Even as the federal government retreated from the defense of equal rights for black people, it took a more aggressive stance as the protector of business interests. The Hayes administration responded decisively to one of the worst outbreaks of class violence in American history by dispatching federal troops to several northern cities to break the Great Railroad Strike of 1877. In the aftermath of Reconstruction, the struggle between capital and labor had clearly replaced "the southern question" as the number one political issue of the day. "The overwhelming labor question has dwarfed all other questions into nothing," wrote an Ohio Republican. "We have home questions enough to occupy attention now."

Key Terms

Radical Republicans A shifting group of Republican congressmen, usually a substantial minority, who favored the abolition of slavery from the beginning of the Civil War and later advocated harsh treatment of the defeated South. p. 371

Special Field Order 15 Order by General William T. Sherman in January 1865 to set aside abandoned land along the southern Atlantic coast for 40-acre grants to freedmen; rescinded by President Andrew Johnson later that year. p. 372

War Democrats Those from the North and the border states who broke with the Democratic Party and supported Abraham Lincoln's military policies during the Civil War. p. 374

black codes Laws passed by states and municipalities denying many rights of citizenship to free black people. p. 374

Civil Rights bill The 1866 act that gave full citizenship to African Americans. p. 375

Freedmen's Bureau Agency established by Congress in March 1865 to provide social, educational, and economic services, advice, and protection to former slaves and destitute whites; lasted seven years. p. 375

First Reconstruction Act 1877 act that divided the South into five military districts subject to martial law. p. 376

Tenure of Office Act Act stipulating that any officeholder appointed by the president with the Senate's advice and consent could not be removed until the Senate had approved a successor. p. 376

Congressional Reconstruction Name given to the period of 1867–1870, when the Republican-dominated Congress controlled Reconstruction-era policy. p. 376

Ku Klux Klan Perhaps the most prominent of the vigilante groups that terrorized black people in the South during the Reconstruction era, founded by Confederate veterans in 1866. p. 377

Fifteenth Amendment Passed by Congress in 1869; guaranteed the right of American men to vote, regardless of race. p. 378

sharecropping Labor system that evolved during and after Reconstruction whereby landowners furnished laborers with a house, farm animals, and tools and advanced credit in exchange for a share of the laborers' crop. p. 383

Union League Republican party organizations in northern cities that became an important organizing device among freedmen in southern cities after 1865. p. 383

carpetbaggers Northern transplants to the South, many of whom were Union soldiers who stayed in the South after the war. p. 385

scalawags Southern whites, mainly small landowning farmers and well-off merchants and planters, who supported the southern Republican Party during Reconstruction. p. 387

Slaughterhouse cases Group of cases resulting in one sweeping decision by the U.S. Supreme Court in 1873 that contradicted the intent of the Fourteenth Amendment by decreeing that most citizenship rights remained under state, not federal, control. p. 388

Liberal Republicans Disaffected Republicans who emphasized the doctrines of classical economics. p. 395

Compromise of 1877 The congressional settling of the 1876 election which installed Republican Rutherford B. Hayes in the White House and ultimately gave Democrats control of all state governments in the South. p. 397

CHRONOLOGY

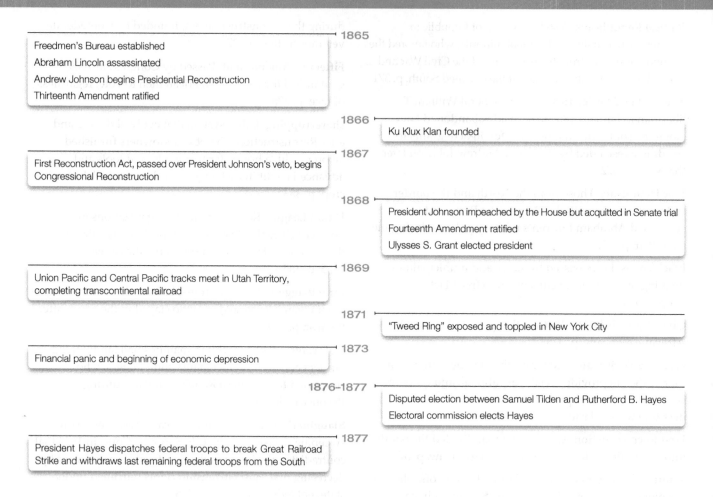

1865

Freedmen's Bureau established

Abraham Lincoln assassinated

Andrew Johnson begins Presidential Reconstruction

Thirteenth Amendment ratified

1866

Ku Klux Klan founded

1867

First Reconstruction Act, passed over President Johnson's veto, begins Congressional Reconstruction

1868

President Johnson impeached by the House but acquitted in Senate trial

Fourteenth Amendment ratified

Ulysses S. Grant elected president

1869

Union Pacific and Central Pacific tracks meet in Utah Territory, completing transcontinental railroad

1871

"Tweed Ring" exposed and toppled in New York City

1873

Financial panic and beginning of economic depression

1876–1877

Disputed election between Samuel Tilden and Rutherford B. Hayes

Electoral commission elects Hayes

1877

President Hayes dispatches federal troops to break Great Railroad Strike and withdraws last remaining federal troops from the South

Chapter 18
The Trans-Mississippi West 1860–1900

FORT LARAMIE TREATY General William T. Sherman and the Peace Commission negotiate the 1868 Fort Laramie Treaty during the Great Sioux War.

MPI/Getty Images.

Contents and Focus Questions

American Communities

The Oklahoma Land Rush

Decades after the event, cowboy Evan G. Barnard vividly recalled the preparations settlers made when Oklahoma territorial officials announced the biggest "land rush" in American history. "Thousands of people gathered along the border. . . . As the day for the race drew near, the settlers practiced running their horses and driving carts." Finally, the morning of April 22, 1889, arrived. "At ten o'clock people lined up . . . ready for the great race of their lives." Like many others, Barnard displayed his guns prominently on his hips, determined to discourage competitors from claiming the 160 acres of prime land that he intended to grab for himself.

Evan Barnard's story was one strand in the larger tale of the destruction and creation of communities in the trans-Mississippi West. In the 1830s, the federal government designated what was to become the state of Oklahoma as Indian Territory, reserved for the Five Civilized Tribes (Cherokees, Chickasaws, Choctaws, Creeks, and Seminoles) who had been forcibly removed from their eastern lands. All five tribes had reestablished themselves as sovereign republics in Indian Territory. The Cherokees and Choctaws became prosperous cotton growers. The Creeks managed large herds of hogs and cattle, and the Chickasaws grazed not only cattle but also sheep and goats on their open fields. The Five Tribes also ran sawmills, gristmills, and cotton gins. Indian merchants were soon dealing with other tribespeople as well as licensed white traders, and even contracting with the federal government.

The Civil War, however, took a heavy toll on their success. Some tribes, slaveholders themselves, sided with the Confederacy; others with the Union. When the war ended, more than 10,000 people—nearly one fifth of the population of Indian Territory—had died. To make matters worse, new treaties required the Five Civilized Tribes to cede the entire western half of the territory, including the former northern Indian territory of Nebraska and Kansas, for the resettlement of tribes from other regions.

Western Oklahoma thereby became home to thousands of newly displaced peoples, including the Pawnees, Peorias, Ottawas, Wyandots, and Miamis. Many small tribes readily took to farming and rebuilt their communities. But the nomadic, buffalo-hunting Kiowas, Cheyennes, Comanches, and Arapahoes did not settle so peacefully. They continued to traverse the plains until the U.S. Army finally forced them onto reservations. Eventually, more than 80,000 tribespeople were living on 21 separate reservations in western Oklahoma, all governed by agents appointed by the federal government.

The opening of the unassigned far western district of Oklahoma, however, signaled the impending end of Indian sovereignty. Many non-Indians saw this almost 2-million-acre strip as a Promised Land, perfect for dividing into thousands of small farms. African Americans, many of whom were former slaves of Indian planters, appealed to the federal government for the right to stake claims there. Another group of would-be homesteaders, known as "Boomers," quickly tired of

petitioning and invaded the district in 1880, only to be booted out by the Tenth Cavalry. Meanwhile, the railroads, seeing the potential for lucrative commerce, put constant pressure on the federal government to open No Man's Land for settlement. In 1889, the U.S. Congress finally gave in.

Cowboy Barnard was just one of thousands to pour into No Man's Land on April 22, 1889. Many homesteaders simply crossed the border from Kansas. Southerners, dispossessed by warfare and economic ruin in their own region, were also well represented. Market-minded settlers claimed the land nearest the railroads, and by nightfall of April 22, they had set up tent cities along the tracks. In a little over two months, after 6,000 homestead claims had been filed, the first sod houses appeared, sheltering growing communities of non-Indian farmers, ranchers, and other entrepreneurs. Some Indian leaders petitioned the federal government for the right to resettle on new land distant from white settlers, but nothing came from their efforts.

Dramatic as it was, the land rush of 1889 was only one in a series of events that soon dispossessed Oklahoma's Indians of their remaining lands. First, the federal government broke up the estates held collectively by various tribes in western Oklahoma, assigning to individuals the standard 160-acre allotment and allowing non-Indian homesteaders to claim the rest. Then, in 1898, Congress passed the Curtis Act, which abolished tribal jurisdiction over all Indian Territory. Members of the former Indian nations were directed to dismantle their governments and abandon their estates. (See Map 18.1.). Before a decade had passed,

Map 18.1 OKLAHOMA TERRITORY

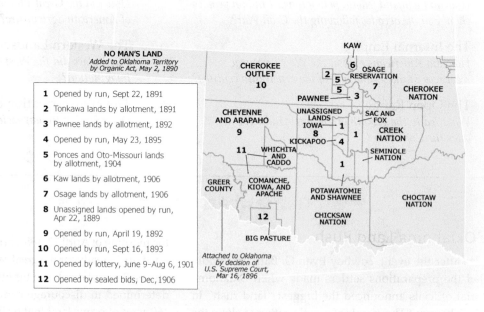

1 Opened by run, Sept 22, 1891
2 Tonkawa lands by allotment, 1891
3 Pawnee lands by allotment, 1892
4 Opened by run, May 23, 1895
5 Ponces and Oto-Missouri lands by allotment, 1904
6 Kaw lands by allotment, 1906
7 Osage lands by allotment, 1906
8 Unassigned lands opened by run, Apr 22, 1889
9 Opened by run, April 19, 1892
10 Opened by run, Sept 16, 1893
11 Opened by lottery, June 9–Aug 6, 1901
12 Opened by sealed bids, Dec, 1906

Land openings to settlers came at different times, making new land available through various means.

tribespeople in Oklahoma were outnumbered by 10 to 1. In 1907, at the festivities marking statehood, a huge crowd witnessed a mock wedding ceremony uniting a white man representing Oklahoma Territory and a demure part-Cherokee bride representing Indian Territory.

By this time, nearly one-quarter of the entire population of the United States lived west of the Mississippi River. Hundreds of new communities, supported primarily by cattle ranching, agriculture,

Indian Territory
(Oklahoma)

mining, or other industries, had not only grown with the emerging national economy but also helped to shape it in the process. The newcomers had displaced communities that had formed centuries earlier. They also drastically transformed the physical landscape. Through their activities and the support of Easterners, the United States realized an ambition that John L. O'Sullivan had described in 1845 as the nation's "manifest destiny to overspread the continent" and remake it in a new image.

18.1 Indian Peoples Under Siege

How and why did federal policy toward Indian peoples change in the decades following the Civil War?

The Indians living west of the Mississippi River keenly felt the pressure of the gradual incorporation of the West into the American nation. California became a state in 1850, Oregon in 1859. In the next decades, Congress granted territorial status to Utah, New Mexico, Washington, Dakota, Colorado, Nevada, Arizona, Idaho, Montana, and Wyoming. The purchase of Alaska in 1867 added an area twice the size of Texas. The federal government made itself the custodian of these thinly settled regions, with appointed white governors supervising the transition from territorial status to statehood.

A series of events brought large numbers of white settlers into these new states and territories: the discovery of gold in California in 1848, the opening of western lands to homesteaders in 1862, and the completion of the transcontinental railroad in 1869. With competition for the land and its resources escalating into violent skirmishes and small wars, federal officials became determined to end tribal rule and bring Indians into the American mainstream.

18.1.1 Indian Territory and Reservation Policy

Before the European colonists reached the New World, hundreds of tribes, totaling perhaps a million members, had occupied western lands for more than 20,000 years. Invasion by the English, the Spanish, and other Europeans brought disease, religious conversion, and new patterns of commerce. But geographic isolation still gave many tribes a margin of survival unknown in the East. At the close of the Civil War, approximately 360,000 Indian peoples still lived in the trans-Mississippi West, the majority of them in the Great Plains.

The surviving tribes adapted to changing conditions. The Plains Indians learned to ride the horses and shoot the guns introduced by Spanish and British traders and became formidable warriors. The Pawnees migrated farther westward to evade encroaching non-Indian settlers, while the Sioux and the Comanches fought neighboring tribes to gain control of large stretches of the Great Plains. The southwestern Hopis and Zunis, conquered earlier by the Spanish, continued to trade with the Mexicans who lived near them. Some tribes took dramatic steps toward accommodation with white ways. Even before they were uprooted and moved across the Mississippi River, the Cherokees had learned English, converted to Christianity, established a constitutional republic, and become a nation of farmers.

Legally, the federal government had long regarded Indian tribes as autonomous nations residing within American boundaries and had negotiated numerous treaties with them over land rights and commerce. But pressured by land-hungry whites, several states had violated these federal treaties so often that in 1830, Congress passed the Indian Removal Act (see Chapter 10), which provided funds to relocate all eastern tribes by force, if necessary. The Cherokees challenged this legislation, and the Supreme Court ruled in their favor. But ignoring the Court's decision, President Andrew Jackson forced many tribes to cede their land and remove to Indian Territory. There, it was believed, they might live undisturbed by whites and gradually adjust to "civilized" ways. But soon, the onslaught of white settlers, railroad entrepreneurs, and gold rush prospectors pressured tribes to cede millions of their acres to the United States. As demand for resources and land accelerated, the entire plan for a permanent Indian Territory fell apart.

United States officials had outlined a plan to subdue the intensifying rivalry over natural resources and land. Under the terms of their proposal, individual tribes would agree to live within smaller, clearly defined zones—reservations. In return, the Bureau of Indian Affairs would provide essential services, while U.S. military forces ensured protection. By the end of the 1850s, eight western reservations had been established.

But tribes confined to reservations often found provisions inadequate to their needs. The Medicine Lodge Treaty of 1867 assigned reservations in existing Indian Territory to Comanches, Plains (Kiowa) Apaches, Kiowas, Cheyennes, and Arapahoes, bringing these tribes together with Sioux, Shoshones, and Bannocks. All told, more than 100,000 people found themselves competing intensely for survival. Corrupt officials of the Bureau of Indian Affairs routinely diverted funds for their own use and reduced food supplies, a policy promoting malnutrition, demoralization, and desperation.

Bureau of Indian Affairs agents tried to rein in the tribes of the Great Plains who routinely left their reservation to hunt bison, or buffalo, which were central to their economy and culture. Often seizing hunting territory from their rivals, the Pawnees and the Crows, the Lakotas (Western Sioux), had learned to follow the herds on horseback. Buffalo meat and hides fed, clothed, and sheltered the tribe. The Western Sioux used buffalo horns to make cups and spoons, and twisted bison hair to stuff dolls. But, as Luther Standing Bear of the Lakota tribe remarked, "The Indian was frugal in the midst of plenty. When the buffalo roamed the plains in multitudes, he slaughtered only what he could eat and these he used to the hair and bones."

By the early 1870s, as gunpowder and the railroad moved west, the buffalo herds that once darkened the western skies fell rapidly. Non-Indian traders avidly sought fur for coats, hide for leather, bones for fertilizer, and heads for trophies. Army commanders encouraged the slaughter, accurately predicting that starvation would break tribal resistance to the reservation system. With their food sources practically destroyed, and diseases such as smallpox and cholera (brought by fur traders) sweeping through their villages, many Great Plains tribes, including several Sioux, concluded that they could only fight or die.

18.1.2 The Indian Wars

In 1864, large-scale war erupted after Colorado territorial governor John Evans decided to open up the Cheyenne and Arapaho buffalo hunting grounds for white settlements. Hoping to force the defiant tribes onto reservations, he called up a volunteer militia to stage raids through the Cheyenne and Arapaho campgrounds. Seeking peace and protection, Chief Black Kettle brought a band of 800 followers to U.S. Fort Lyon and received orders to set up camp at Sand Creek. Feeling secure in this arrangement, Black Kettle sent out most of his young warriors to hunt. Several weeks later, on November 29, 1864, the Colorado Volunteers and soldiers attacked. While Black Kettle held up a U.S. flag and a white truce banner, a disorderly group of nearly 700 men, many of them drunk, slaughtered as many as 200 Cheyennes and Arapahos, the majority elderly men, women, and children. They mutilated the corpses and took scalps back to Denver to exhibit as trophies. Months after the **Sand Creek Massacre**, bands of Cheyennes, Sioux, and Arapahoes were still retaliating, burning civilian outposts and sometimes killing whole families.

The Sioux played the most dramatic roles in the avenging wars that raged for the next quarter-century. Earlier, in 1851, believing the U.S. government would recognize their own rights of conquest over other Indian tribes, the Sioux had relinquished large tracts of land as a demonstration of good faith. But within a decade, a mass invasion of miners and the construction of military forts along the Bozeman Trail in Wyoming, the Sioux's principal buffalo range, threw the tribe's future into doubt. During the **Great Sioux War** of 1865–1867, the Oglala Sioux warrior Red Cloud fought the U.S. Army to a stalemate. The Treaty of Fort Laramie, signed in 1868, brought peace to the region, but only temporarily.

The **Treaty of Fort Laramie** granted the Sioux the right to occupy the Black Hills, or Paha Sapa—their sacred land—"as long as the grass shall grow," but the discovery of gold soon undermined this guarantee. Directed to map a site for a new fort while quietly looking for gold, Lieutenant Colonel George Armstrong Custer led an expedition to the Black Hills during the summer of 1874. Contrary to the plan, the Civil War hero broadcast his discovery of the precious ore. White prospectors soon overran the territory. Determined to fight for the right to this land, thousands of Sioux, Cheyenne, and Arapaho warriors moved into war camps during the summer of 1876 and prepared for battle. (See Map 18.2.)

After several months of skirmishes between the U.S. Army and Indian warriors, Custer decided to rush ahead to a site in Montana known to white soldiers as Little Bighorn and to Lakotas as Greasy Grass. This foolhardy move offered the allied Cheyenne and Sioux warriors a perfect opportunity to cut off Custer's logistical and military support. On June 25, 1876, one of the largest Indian contingents ever assembled, an estimated 2,000–4,000 warriors, wiped out Custer and his ill-trained troops.

"Custer's Last Stand" gave Indian-haters the emotional ammunition to whip up public sentiment against the Indians. After Custer's defeat, Sitting Bull reportedly said, "Now they will never let us rest." The U.S. Army tracked down the disbanded Indian contingents one by one and forced them to surrender or flee to Canada. In February 1877, Sioux leadership in the Indian Wars ended.

Map 18.2 MAJOR INDIAN BATTLES AND INDIAN RESERVATIONS, 1860–1900

As commercial routes and white populations passed through and occupied Indian lands, warfare inevitably erupted. The displacement of Indians to reservations opened access by farmers, ranchers, and investors to natural resources and to markets.

BATTLE OF SAND CREEK This painting depicts the Battle of Sand Creek, fought in November 1864. Colorado militia volunteers, under Colonel John Chivington, led the deadly attack on the Cheyennes and their allies in southeastern Colorado Territory.

State Historical Society of Colorado, Denver, USA/De Agostini Picture Library/Bridgeman Images.

Among the last to strike out against the reservation system were the Apaches in the Southwest. Unable to tolerate the harsh conditions on the reservation, and angered by the encroachment of whites, some of the Apache bands returned to their old ways of seizing territory and stealing cattle. Pursued by the U.S. Army, the Apaches earned a reputation as intrepid warriors. Brilliant strategists like Geronimo and skilled horse-riding braves became legendary for lightning-swift raids against the white outposts in the rugged Arizona terrain.

In 1874–1875, the Kiowas and the Comanches, both powerful tribes, joined the Apaches in one of the bloodiest conflicts of the era, the Red River War. The U.S. Army ultimately prevailed, although less by military strategy than by new technologies of warfare and by denying Indians access to food. Small-scale warfare sputtered on until September 1886, when Geronimo, his band reduced to only 10 people, finally surrendered, thereby ending the Indian Wars.

18.1.3 The Nez Perces

For generations, the Nez Perces (Nimiipuu) had regarded themselves as good friends to white traders and settlers. Living in the plateau where Idaho, Washington, and Oregon now meet, they had saved the Lewis and Clark expedition from starvation in 1806. The Nez Perces had occasionally assisted American armies against hostile tribes, and many of them converted to Christianity. But the discovery of gold on Nez Perce land in 1860 changed their relations with whites for the worse and also challenged their tribal identity. Pressed by prospectors and mining companies, U.S. government officials demanded, in the Treaty of 1863, that the Nez Perces cede about nine-tenths of their holdings, at less than 10 cents per acre. Some of the Nez Perce leaders agreed to the terms of the treaty, which had been fraudulently signed on behalf of the entire tribe, but others refused. Joseph, who became chief of the Wallowa band in 1871, held out. He kept his faith in the teachings of his ancestors and refused to join other Nez Perces in their conversion to Christianity. Only to avoid warfare did he agree to move his band to the small Lapwai Reservation in Idaho.

In 1877, Chief Joseph's band reluctantly set out from the Wallowa. Along the way, some young members of another Indian band traveling with them rode away from camp to avenge the death of one of their own by killing several white settlers. Hoping to explain the situation, a Nez Perce truce team approached U.S. troops. The troops opened fire, and the Indian riders fired back, killing one-third of the soldiers. Brilliantly outmaneuvering vengeful U.S. troops sent to intercept them, the 750 Nez Perce retreated for some 1,400 miles into Montana and Wyoming. Over the three-and-a-half months of their journey, Nez Perce braves fought 2,000 regular U.S. troops and 18 Indian auxiliary detachments in 18 separate engagements and 2 major battles. U.S. troops finally trapped the Nez Perces in the Bear Paw Mountains of northern Montana, just 30 miles from the Canadian border. Suffering from hunger and cold, they surrendered.

The Nez Perces were sent to disease-ridden bottomland near Fort Leavenworth in Kansas and then to Oklahoma. Arguing for the right of his people to return to their ancestral land, Joseph spoke eloquently, through an interpreter: "Treat all men alike. Give them all the same law. Give them all an even chance to live and grow. All men were made by the same Great Spirit Chief." The last remnants of Joseph's band were eventually deported to a non-Nez Perce reservation in Washington, where Chief Joseph died in 1904 of a broken heart, according to a reservation doctor, and where his descendants continue to live in exile to this day.

18.2 The Internal Empire

How did Americans exploit the West's natural resources in the second half of the nineteenth century?

In the nineteenth century, numerous adventurers traveled west, determined to make their fortunes from the abundant natural resources, be it from copper in Arizona, timber in Washington, wheat in Montana, or oranges in California. As a group, they carried out the largest migration and greatest commercial expansion in American history.

But the settlers themselves were subject to the operations of a huge "internal empire" whose financial, political, and industrial centers of power remained in the East. Only a small number of settlers actually struck it rich in the great extractive industries—mining, lumbering, ranching, and farming—that ruled the western economy and supported industrial development in the East. Meanwhile, older populations—Indian peoples, Hispanic peoples, and more recently settled communities like the Mormons—struggled to create places for themselves in this new expansionist order.

18.2.1 Mining Towns

The discovery of gold in California in 1848 attracted fortune seekers from across the United States, from Europe, and from as far away as Chile, Australia, and China. Prospecting parties soon overran the territories, setting a pattern for intermittent rushes for gold, silver, and copper that extended from the Colorado mountains to the Arizona deserts, from California to Washington, and from Alaska to the Black Hills of South Dakota. Mining camps and boomtowns soon dotted what had once been thinly settled regions and speeded the urban development of the West. The population of California alone jumped from 14,000 in 1848 to 223,856 just four years later. Mining soon brought the West into a vast global market for capital, commodities, and labor. (See Map 18.3.)

Map 18.3 RAILROAD ROUTES, CATTLE TRAILS, GOLD AND SILVER RUSHES, 1860–1900

By the end of the nineteenth century, the vast region of the West was crosscut by hundreds of lines of transportation and communication. The trade in precious metals and in cattle helped build a population almost constantly on the move, following the rushes for gold or the herds of cattle.

The mining industry quickly grew from its treasure-hunt origins into a grand corporate enterprise. The most successful mine owners bought out the smaller claims and built an entire industry around their stakes. They found investors to finance their expansion and used the borrowed capital to purchase the latest in extractive technology. They gained access to timber to fortify their underground structures and water to feed the hydraulic pumps that washed down mountains. They built smelters to refine the crude ore into ingots and often financed railroads to transport the product to distant markets. The Anaconda Copper Mining Company, which had mining interests throughout the West, soon became one of the most powerful corporations in the nation.

The mining corporations laid the basis for a new economy, as well as an interim government, and established many of the region's first white settlements. Before the advent of railroads, ore had to be brought out of, and supplies brought into, mining areas by boats, wagons, and mules traveling hundreds of miles over rough territory. The railroad made transportation of supplies and products easier and faster. The shipping trade meanwhile grew into an important industry of its own, employing thousands of merchants, peddlers, and sailors.

The many boomtowns, known as "Helldorados," flourished, if only temporarily. Men outnumbered women by as much as 10 to 1, and very few stayed very long. They often bunked with male kin and worked alongside friends or acquaintances from their hometown or with fellow immigrants. The town center was usually the saloon, where, as one observer complained, men "without the restraint of law, indifferent to public opinion, and unburdened by families, drink whenever they feel like it, whenever they have the money to pay for it, and whenever there is nothing else to do." And for a time, some miners lived unusually well, enjoying fresh fruits and vegetables provided by Chinese merchants and feasting on oysters trucked in at great expense. The western labor movement began in these camps, partly as a response to dangerous working conditions. In the hardrock mines of the 1870s, 1 of every 30 workers was disabled, and 1 of every 80 killed. Miners began to organize in the 1860s, demanding good pay for dangerous and life-shortening work.

By the end of the century, miners had established the strongest unions in the West. They helped to secure legislation mandating a maximum eight-hour day for certain jobs and compensation for injuries. Such laws were enacted in Idaho, Arizona, and New Mexico by the 1910s, long before similar laws in most eastern states.

The unions fought hard, but they did so exclusively for the benefit of white workers. The native-born and the Irish and Cornish immigrants (these last from Cornwall, England) far outnumbered other groups before the turn of the century, when Italians, Slavs, and Greeks began to replace them. Labor unions eventually admitted these new immigrants but drove away Chinese, Mexican, Indian, and African American workers.

When prices and ore production fell sharply, not even unions could stop the owners from shutting down the mines and leaving ghost towns in their wake. Often they also left behind an environmental disaster. Hydraulic mining, which used water cannons to blast hillsides and expose gold deposits, drove tons of rock and earth into the rivers and canyons. By the late 1860s, California's rivers were clogged, producing floods that wiped out towns and farms. In 1893, Congress finally passed the Caminetti Act, giving states the power to regulate the mines. Underground mining continued unregulated, using up whole forests for timbers and filling the air with dangerous, sulfurous smoke.

18.2.2 Mormon Settlements

Led by their new prophet, Brigham Young, a group of persecuted Mormons, or Latter-day Saints, fled the Midwest and migrated to the Great Salt Lake Basin in 1847 in order to live and worship according to their religious doctrine, which included the sanctity of plural marriage, or polygamy. By 1870, more than 87,000 Mormons lived in Utah Territory, creating relatively sizable communities

GOLD RUSH IN THE BLACK HILLS
Thousands of prospectors rushed to the Black Hills of South Dakota after George Armstrong Custer reported discovering large deposits of gold in 1874. Although the Treaty of Fort Laramie guaranteed the land to the Lakota people, the federal government allowed the white fortune-hunters to set up camp and to claim parcels in mineral-rich locations. Repeated violations of the treaty led to the Great Sioux War of 1876–1877.

National Park Service.

complemented by satellite villages joined to communal farmlands and a common pasture. Relying on agricultural techniques learned from local Indian tribes, they built dams for irrigation and harvested a variety of crops from desert soil. Eventually, nearly 500 Mormon communities spread from Oregon to Idaho to northern Mexico. (See Map 18.4.)

As territorial rule tightened, the Mormons saw their unique and tightly organized way of life threatened. The newspapers and the courts repeatedly assailed the Mormons, often condemning them as heathens and savages. Preceded by prohibitory federal laws enacted in 1862 and 1874, the Supreme Court finally ruled against the practice of polygamy in 1879. In 1882, Congress passed the **Edmunds Act**, which disfranchised those who believed in or practiced polygamy and threatened them with fines and imprisonment. More devastating was the **Edmunds–Tucker Act**, passed five years later, which disincorporated the Latter-day Saints church, seizing assets over $50,000 and establishing a federal commission to oversee all elections in the territory. By the early 1890s, Mormon leaders officially renounced the practice of plural marriage.

Forced to abandon the practice, they gave up many other aspects of their distinctive communal life, including the common ownership of land. By the time Utah became a state in 1896, Mormon communities resembled in some ways the society that the original settlers had sought to escape. Nevertheless, they combined their religious cohesion with leadership in the expanding regional economy to become a major political force in the West.

18.2.3 Mexican Borderland Communities

The Treaty of Guadalupe Hidalgo, which ended the Mexican-American War in 1848, allowed the Hispanic people north of the Rio Grande to choose between immigrating to Mexico or staying in what was now the United States. But the new Mexican-American border did not sever communities that had been connected for centuries. What gradually emerged was an economically and socially interdependent zone, the Anglo-Hispanic borderlands linking the United States and Mexico.

For a time, the borderlands held out hope for a mutually beneficial interaction between Mexicanos and Anglos (as Mexicans called white Americans). A prosperous class of Hispanic landowners, with long-standing ties to Anglos through marriage, had established itself in cities like Albuquerque and Tucson, old Spanish towns that had been founded in the seventeenth and eighteenth centuries. Estevan Ochoa—merchant, philanthropist, and the first Mexican to serve as mayor of Tucson, following the Gadsden Purchase in 1853–54—managed to build one of the largest business empires in the West. In Las Cruces, New Mexico, the wealthy family of Martin Amador and Refugio Ruiz de Amador could shop Bloomingdale's by mail, travel to the World's Fair in Chicago, and send their children to English-language Catholic schools. Even the small and struggling Mexicano middle class could afford such modern conveniences as kitchen stoves and sewing machines. These Mexican elites, well-integrated into the emerging national economy, continued to wield political power as ranchers, landlords, and real estate developers until the end of the century. They secured passage of bills for education in their regions and often served as officers on local school boards. Several prominent merchants became territorial delegates to Congress.

Map 18.4 MORMON CULTURAL DIFFUSION, CA. 1883

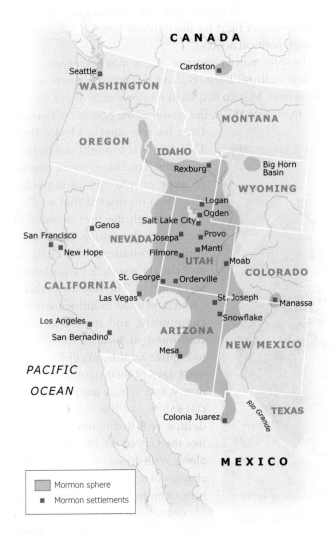

Mormon settlements permeated many sparsely populated sections of Idaho, Nevada, Arizona, Wyoming, Colorado, and New Mexico. Built with church backing and the strong commitment of community members, they survived and even prospered in adverse climates.

The majority of Mexicans, who had lived in the mountains and deserts of the Southwest for more than two centuries, were less prepared for these changes. Most had worked outside the commercial economy, farming and herding sheep for their own subsistence. With the Anglos came land closures as well as commercial expansion, prompted by the railroad, mining, and timber industries. Many poor families found themselves crowded onto plots of land too small for subsistence farming. Many men turned to seasonal labor on the new Anglo-owned commercial farms. Others took jobs on the railroad or in the mines. Meanwhile, their wives and daughters moved to the new towns and cities in such numbers that by the end of the century Mexicanos had become a predominantly urban population, dependent on wages for survival.

Women were quickly drawn into the expanding network of market relations. They tried to make ends meet by selling produce from their backyard gardens; more often they worked as seamstresses or laundresses. Formerly at the center of a communal society, Mexicanas found themselves with fewer options in the cash economy. What wages they could earn fell below even the low sums paid to their husbands, and women lost status within both the family and the community.

Commercial expansion occasionally strained relations between Mexicanos and Anglos to the breaking point.

Although the Treaty of Guadalupe Hidalgo formally guaranteed Mexicanos U.S. citizenship, with rights to the "free enjoyment of their liberty and property," local Anglos often violated these provisions and, through fraud or coercion, took control of the land. The Santa Fe Ring, a powerful and ruthless group of lawyers, politicians, and land speculators, stole millions of acres from the public domain and grabbed over 80 percent of the Mexicano landholdings in New Mexico alone.

Mexicanos organized to reverse these trends, or at least to limit the damage done to their communities. In the late 1880s, Las Gorras Blancas, a band of agrarian rebels in northern New Mexico, destroyed railroad ties and farm machinery, and posted demands for justice on new fences enclosing Anglo farms and ranches that shut off grazing land. In 1890, Las Gorras turned from social banditry to political organization, forming *El Partido del Pueblo Unido* (The People's Party). Organized along similar lines, *El Alianzo Hispano-Americano* (The **Hispanic-American Alliance**) was formed "to protect and fight for the rights of Spanish Americans" through political action.

Despite many pressures, Mexicanos preserved much of their cultural heritage, and the influx of new immigrants from Mexico helped to reinforce older ways. Beginning in the late 1870s, the modernizing policies of Porfirio Díaz, the president of Mexico from 1876 to 1911, brought deteriorating living conditions to the masses of poor people and prompted a migration northward that accelerated through the first decades of the twentieth century. These newcomers revitalized old customs and rituals associated with family and religion. The Roman Catholic Church retained its influence in the community, and most Mexicans continued to turn to the church to baptize infants, to celebrate the feast days of their patron saints, to marry, and to bury their dead. Special saints like the Virgin of Guadalupe and distinctive holy days like the Day of the Dead survived, along with fiestas celebrating the change of seasons. Many communities continued to commemorate Mexican national holidays, such as *Cinco de Mayo* (Fifth of May), marking the Mexican victory over French invaders in the battle of Puebla in 1862. Spanish language and Spanish place names continued to distinguish the Southwest.

AMADOR FAMILY The Amador family prospered by running several businesses in Las Cruces, New Mexico, a railroad town and major crossroad. Martin Amador inherited a mercantile store from his mother, who had moved there from Juarez, Mexico, in 1850. He then built a successful freight-hauling business. The family also ran the Amador Hotel, which included a theater, jail, and post office. The wealthy Amadors could shop by mail from Bloomingdale's, travel to the Chicago World's Fair, and send their children to English-language Catholic schools.

18.3 The Open Range

What led to the growth of the cattle industry after the Civil War?

The borderlands, especially the Mexican territory that became Texas in 1836, gave birth to the enormously profitable cattle industry. Texas longhorns, introduced by the Spanish in the late fifteenth century, numbered more than 5 million at the close of the Civil War and represented a potentially plentiful supply of beef for eastern consumers. Entrepreneurs such as Joseph G. McCoy began to build a spectacular cattle market in the eastern part of Kansas, where the Kansas Pacific Railroad provided crucial transportation links to slaughtering and packinghouses and commercial distributors in Kansas City, St. Louis, and Chicago. By 1880, nearly 2 million cattle were being slaughtered each year in Chicago alone. "Beef barons" Philip Armour and Gustavus Swift made fortunes shipping the meat to distant markets in refrigerated rail cars. By the 1880s a new era of regional food production and national distribution had taken hold.

18.3.1 The Long Drives

The great cattle drives depended on the cowboy, a seasonal or migrant worker. After the Civil War, cowboys rounded up herds of Texas cattle and drove them as much as 1,500 miles north to grazing ranches or to the stockyards, where they were readied for shipping by rail to eastern markets. The boss supplied the horses, the cowboy his own bedroll, saddle, and spurs. The workday lasted from sunup to sundown, with short night shifts for guarding the cattle. Scurvy, a widespread ailment, could be traced to the basic chuckwagon menu of sowbelly, beans, and coffee, a diet bereft of fruits and vegetables. The cowboy worked without protection from rain or hail, and severe dust storms could cause temporary blindness.

In return for his labor, the cowboy received at the best of times about $30 per month. Wages were usually paid in one lump sum at the end of a drive, a policy that encouraged cowboys to spend their money quickly and recklessly in the booming cattle towns. In the 1880s, when wages began to fall along with the price of beef, cowboys fought back by stealing cattle or by forming unions. In 1883, many Texas cowboys struck for higher wages; nearly all Wyoming cowboys struck in 1886. Aided by the legendary camaraderie fostered in the otherwise desolate conditions of the long drive, cowboys, along with miners, were among the first western workers to organize against employers.

Like other parts of the West, the cattle range was ethnically diverse. Mexican cowboys, or *vaqueros*, had worked the great herds before Texas became a state in 1845, and they passed on their skills to Americans. During the peak of the cattle drives, between one-fifth and one-third of all workers were Indian, Mexican, or African American. Indian cowboys worked mainly on the northern plains and in Indian Territory; the *vaqueros* continued to work in the borderlands. African American cowboys worked primarily in Texas. (See SEEING History.) The majority of cowboys were white, and often former soldiers hoping to avoid the indoor work that prevailed in the cities.

Like the *vaqueros*, African American cowboys were highly skilled managers of cattle. Unlike Mexicans, they earned wages comparable to those paid to Anglos and, especially during the early years, worked in integrated drover parties. By the 1880s, as the center of the cattle industry shifted to the more settled regions around the northern ranches, African Americans were forced out, and they turned to other kinds of work.

Very few women participated in the long drives. Sally Redus, wife of an early Texas cattleman, once accompanied her husband on the trip from Texas to Kansas. Carrying her baby on her lap, she most likely rode the enormous distance sidesaddle, with both legs on one side of the horse. Most women stayed back at the ranch. Occasionally, a husband and wife worked as partners, sharing even the labor of wrangling cattle, and following her husband's death, a woman might take over altogether. Elizabeth Collins, for example, turned her husband's large ranch into an extraordinarily prosperous business, earning for herself the title "Cattle Queen of Montana." The majority of wives attended to domestic chores, caring for children and maintaining the household. Their daughters, however, often tagged along after their fathers and learned to love outdoor work. They were soon riding astride, clothespin style, roping calves, branding cattle or cutting their ears to mark them, and castrating bulls. But not until 1901 did a woman dare to enter an official rodeo contest.

18.3.2 The Sporting Life

In cattle towns as well as mining camps, saloons, gambling establishments, and dance halls were regular features. The hurdy-gurdy, a form of hand organ, supplied raucous music for cowboys eager to spend their money and blow off steam after the long drive. Here they found dancing partners, often called hurdy-girls or hurdies. If they wanted to do more than dance, the cowboy and his partner could retreat to one of the small rooms for rent, which were often located at the rear of the building.

During the first cattle drive to Abilene, in 1867, only a few women worked as prostitutes; but by the following spring, Joseph G. McCoy's assistant recalled, "they came in swarms, & as the weather was warm 4 or 5 girls could huddle together in a tent very comfortably." Although some women worked in trailside "hoghouses," the best-paid prostitutes congregated in the brothel districts. Most cattle towns boasted at least one bawdy house. Dodge City

SEEING History

The Legendary Cowboy: Nat Love, Deadwood Dick

Nat Love was born a slave in 1854 and spent his childhood on a plantation in Tennessee. In 1907, he published a short autobiography, *The Life and Adventures of Nat Love, Better Known in the Cattle Country as "Deadwood Dick,"* recounting his "unusually adventurous" life during the decades after emancipation. He worked as a cowboy, a ranch hand, an Indian fighter, and a rodeo performer. His most famous episode occurred in the boomtown of Deadwood, South Dakota, where in 1876 he won a cowboy tournament. It began with a roping contest, in which Love roped, saddled, and mounted a mustang in just nine minutes, winning the almost unbelievably large prize of $200. In the second part of this competition, a shooting contest, Love once again came out on top, hitting the bull's-eye in 10 out of 12 shots. He boasted that the miners and gamblers who had gathered for the tournament were so awed that they called him "Deadwood Dick," a name he proudly claimed until his death in 1921.

That name became familiar to the many readers of Edward Wheeler's *Deadwood Dick* dime novels, and at least five of Love's contemporaries claimed to be that character. Wheeler published the first installment in this popular series in 1877 as *Deadwood Dick, the Prince of the Road, or, The Black Rider of the Black Hills*. It is said that Love's autobiography reads like a dime novel, packed with adventures that no historian has yet been able to authenticate.

The photograph illustrating Love's popular autobiography captures the standard image of the cowboy of the legendary Wild West—the chaps, firearm, and ammunition in the cartridge belt circling his waist, the tack on the floor (saddle, harness, and rope), and the assertive body language. But in Love's case, the cowboy is a black man.

- **How does Nat Love fit into the legendary Wild West? How readily would you expect nineteenth-century readers of the *Deadwood Dick* dime novels to accept the hero's identity as a black man?**

DEADWOOD DICK

Nat Love.

- **How does Nat Love's identity as an African American line up with the image of the heroic cowboy in modern American popular culture?**

---

had two: one with white prostitutes for white patrons, another with black prostitutes for both white and black men. Although prostitution was illegal in most towns, the laws were rarely enforced until the end of the century, when reformers led campaigns to shut down the red-light districts. Until then, prostitution supplied these women with the largest source of employment outside the home.

Like the cowboys who bought their services, most prostitutes were unmarried and in their teens or twenties. Often fed up with underpaid jobs in dressmaking or domestic service, they found few alternatives to prostitution in the cattle towns, where the cost of food and lodging was notoriously high. Still, earnings in prostitution were slim, except during the cattle-shipping season, when young men outnumbered women by as much as three to one. Injury or even death from violent clients, addiction to narcotics such as cocaine or morphine, and venereal disease were workaday dangers.

18.3.3 Frontier Violence and Range Wars

The combination of prostitution, gambling, and drinking discouraged the formation of stable communities. Acts of personal violence were notoriously commonplace on the streets and in the barrooms of cattle towns and mining camps populated mainly by young, single men. Many western towns, such as Wichita, outlawed the carrying of handguns, but enforcement usually lagged. Local specialty shops and mail-order catalogs continued to sell weapons with little regulation. But contrary to popular belief, gunfights were relatively rare. Homicides in Dodge City, Kansas, averaged only 1.5 a year during its 10-year run as a major center of the cattle trade. Local marshals, such as William Barclay "Bat" Masterson, Wyatt Earp, and James Butler "Wild Bill" Hickok, worked mainly to break up fights among drunken cowboys.

After the Civil War, violent crime, assault, and robbery rose sharply throughout the United States. In the West, the most prevalent crimes were horse theft and cattle rustling, which peaked during the height of the open range period and then fell back by the 1890s. Death by legal hanging or illegal lynching—"necktie parties," in which the victims were "jerked to Jesus"—was the usual sentence. On occasion, attacks were racially motivated. In 1885 in Wyoming, a mob of 150 white miners—many of them members of the Knights of Labor—brutally attacked the Chinese immigrants who were brought by the Union Pacific company to mine coal at lower wages. The Rock Springs massacre claimed at least 28 lives.

Conflicts over land and water erupted into the brutal "range wars" of the 1880s. By this time, farmers and sheepherders were encroaching on the fields where cattle had once grazed freely and erecting fences to protect their crops and livestock and to control their water supply. The powerful cattle barons, demanding "open range" to graze their herds, fought back by cutting the new barbed wire fences.

The cattle barons helped to bring about their own demise, but they did not go down quietly. Eager for greater profits, and often backed by foreign capital, they overstocked their herds, and eventually the cattle began to deplete the limited supply of grass. Finally, during 1885–1887, a combination of summer drought and winter blizzards killed 90 percent of the cattle in the northern Plains. Many ranchers went bankrupt. Along the way, they often took out their grievances against the former cowboys who had gathered small herds for themselves. They charged these small ranchers with cattle rustling, taking them to court or, in some cases, rounding up lynching parties. As one historian has written, violence was "not a mere sideshow" but "an intrinsic part of western society."

18.4 Farming Communities

How did the Great Plains become a center of American agriculture?

The first explorers who traveled through the Great Plains called the region "The Great American Desert." Few trees blocked the blazing sun of summer or promised a supply of lumber for homes and fences. The occasional river or stream flowed with "muddy gruel" rather than pure, sweet water. Economically, the entire region appeared as hopelessly barren as it was vast. It took massive improvements in both transportation and farm technology—as well as unrelenting advertising and promotional campaigns—to open the Great Plains to widescale agriculture.

By the end of the nineteenth century, prosperity lay farther west, with the commercial farmers who employed the most advanced methods of agricultural production in the world. They brought huge numbers of acres under cultivation and used new technologies to achieve unprecedented levels of efficiency in the planting and harvesting of crops. As a result, bonanza farming became increasingly tied to international trade, and modern capitalism soon ruled western agriculture, as it did the mining and cattle industries.

COSMOPOLITAN SALOON IN TELLURIDE, COLORADO As early as 1879, the local newspaper described Leadville, Colorado, as a mining town that never slept: "The dancing houses and liquoring shops are never shut. . . . The streets are full of drunken carousers taking the town." This photograph, dating to the turn of the twentieth century, captures the elegance and masculine exclusivity of the Cosmopolitan Saloon in Telluride, Colorado. Founded in 1878, Telluride prospered from the mining of lead, zinc, silver, and gold, and boomed after the railroad arrived in 1890.

Library of Congress.

18.4.1 Populating the Plains

The **Homestead Act of 1862** offered the first meaningful incentive to prospective farmers. This act granted a quarter section (160 acres) of the public domain free to any household head who lived on the land for at least five years and improved it, or who could buy the land for $1.25 per acre after only six months' residence. Unmarried women filed between 5 percent and 15 percent of the claims.

Homesteaders achieved their greatest success in the central and upper Midwest, where the soil was rich and weather relatively moderate. But those settlers lured to the Great Plains by advertisements depicting land "carpeted with soft grass—a sylvan paradise" found themselves locked in a fierce struggle with the harsh climate and arid soil.

The dream of a homestead nevertheless died hard. Five years after the passage of the Homestead Act, *New York Tribune* editor Horace Greeley still advised his readers to strike off "into the broad, free West" and "make yourself a farm from Uncle Sam's generous domain, you will crowd nobody, starve nobody, and . . . neither you nor your children need evermore beg for Something to Do." He was wrong. The Homestead Act did not provide the solution to urban poverty and unemployment, as Greeley predicted, because few Easterners had either the resources or the experience with farming to strike out for themselves. Only 10 percent of all farmers got their start under the terms of the Homestead Act, and nearly half of all homesteaders lost their claims.

Rather than filing a homestead claim with the federal government, most settlers acquired their land outright. State governments and land companies usually held the most valuable land near transportation and markets, and the majority of farmers were willing to pay a hefty price for those benefits. The big-time land speculators did even better, plucking choice locations at bargain prices and selling high. And the railroads, which received land grants from the federal government, did best, selling off the holdings near their routes at top dollar.

Although the Homestead Act offered prospective farmers free land, it was the railroad that promoted settlement, brought people to their new homes, and carried crops and cattle to eastern markets. Unlike the railroads built before the Civil War, which followed the paths of villages and towns, the western lines preceded settlement. Bringing

CHRISMAN SISTERS In 1887, Lizzie Chrisman filed the first homestead claim on Lieban Creek in Custer County, Nebraska. Joined by her three sisters, she is shown here standing in front of her sod cabin. "Soddies," as these small houses were called, were constructed of stacked layers of cut prairie turf, which were eventually fortified by a thick network of roots. The roofs, often supported by timber, were usually covered with more sod, straw, and small branches.

Library of Congress.

people west became their top priority, and the railroad companies conducted aggressive promotional and marketing campaigns. Agents enticed Easterners and Europeans alike with long-term loans and free transportation by rail to distant points in the West. The railroads also sponsored land companies to sell parcels of their own huge allotments from the federal government.

More than 2 million Europeans, many recruited by professional promoters hired by the railroads, settled the Great Plains between 1870 and 1900. Some districts in Minnesota seemed to be virtual colonies of Sweden; others housed the largest number of Finns in the New World. Nebraska, whose population was 25 percent foreign-born in 1870, concentrated Germans, Swedes, Danes, and Czechs. But Germans outnumbered all other immigrants by far. A smaller portion of European immigrants reached Kansas, and still fewer reached the territories to the south, where Indian and Hispanic peoples and African Americans remained the major ethnic groups.

Traveling the huge distance with kin or members of their Old World villages meant immigrants formed tight-knit communities with their fellow travelers on the Great Plains. Most married only within their own group. Like many Mexicanos in the Southwest, several immigrant groups retained their languages well into the twentieth century, usually by sponsoring parochial school systems and publishing their own newspapers. A few groups closed their communities to outsiders.

Among the native-born settlers of the Great Plains, the largest number had migrated from states bordering the

Mississippi River. Settling as individual families rather than as whole communities, they faced an exceptionally solitary life on the Great Plains. To stave off isolation, homesteaders sometimes built their homes on the adjoining corners of their homestead plots. Still, the prospect of improving their lives, which brought most homesteaders to the Great Plains in the first place, caused many families to keep seeking greener pastures. Mobility was so high that between one-third and one half of all households pulled up stakes within a decade.

Communities eventually flourished in prosperous towns like Grand Island, Nebraska; Coffeyville, Kansas; and Fargo, North Dakota, that served the larger agricultural region. Built alongside the railroad, they grew into commercial centers, home to banking, medical, legal, and retail services. Town life fostered a special intimacy; even in the county graveyard, it was said, a town resident remained among neighbors. Closeness did not necessarily promote social equality or even friendship. A social hierarchy based on education (for the handful of doctors and lawyers) and, more important, investment property (held mainly by railroad agents and bankers) governed relationships between individuals and families. Reinforced by family ties and religious and ethnic differences, this hierarchy often persisted across generations.

18.4.2 Work, Dawn to Dusk

By the 1870s, the Great Plains, once the home of buffalo and Indian hunters, was becoming a vast farming region populated mainly by immigrants from Europe and white Americans from east of the Mississippi. In place of the first one-room shanties, sod houses, and log cabins stood substantial frame farmhouses, along with a variety of other buildings like barns, smokehouses, and stables. The built environment took nothing away from the predominating vista—the expansive fields of grain. "You have no idea, Beulah," wrote a Dakota farmer to his wife, "of what [the wheat farms] are like until you see them. For mile after mile there is not a sign of a tree or stone and just as level as the floor of your house. . . . Wheat never looked better and it is nothing but wheat, wheat, wheat."

Most farm families survived, and prospered if they could, through hard work, often from dawn to dusk. Men's activities in the fields tended to be seasonal, with heavy work during planting and harvest. At other times, their labor centered on construction or repair of buildings and on taking care of livestock. Women's activities were usually far more routine, week in and week out: cooking and canning of seasonal fruit and vegetables, washing, ironing, churning cream for butter, and keeping chickens for their eggs. Women tended to the young children, and they might occasionally take in boarders, usually young men working temporarily in railroad construction. Many women complained about the ceaseless drudgery, especially when they

watched their husbands invest in farm equipment rather than in domestic appliances. Others relished the challenge.

Milking the cows, hauling water, and running errands to neighboring farms could be done by the children, once they had reached the age of nine or so. The "one-room school," where all grades learned together, taught the basics of literacy and arithmetic that a future farmer or commercial employee would require.

The harsh climate and unyielding soil forced all but the most reclusive families to seek out friends and neighbors. Many hands were needed to clear the land for cultivation or for roadbeds, to raise houses and barns, or to bring in a harvest before a threatening storm. Neighbors might agree to work together haying, harvesting, and threshing grain. A well-to-do farmer might "rent" his threshing machine in exchange for a small cash fee and, for instance, three days' labor. His wife might barter her garden produce for her neighbor's bread and milk or for help during childbirth or illness. Women often combined work and leisure in quilting bees and sewing circles. Whole communities turned out for special events, such as the seasonal husking bees, which were organized mainly by women.

For many farmers, the soil simply would not yield a livelihood, and they often owed more money than they took in. Start-up costs, including the purchase of land and equipment, put many farmers deep in debt. Some lost their land altogether. By the turn of the century, more than one-third of all farmers in the United States were tenants on someone else's land.

No matter how hard the average farm family worked, again and again foreclosures wiped out the small landowner through dips in commodity prices, bad decisions, natural disasters, or illness. The swift growth of rural population soon ended. Although writers and orators alike continued to celebrate the family farm as the source of virtue and economic well-being, the hard reality of big money and political power told a far different story.

18.4.3 New Production Technologies

Agricultural productivity depended as much on new technology as on the farmers' hard labor. In 1837, John Deere designed his famous "singing plow," which easily turned prairie grasses under and turned up even highly compacted soils. Around the same time, Cyrus McCormick's reaper began to be used for cutting grain. The harvester, invented in the 1870s, drew the cut stalks upward to a platform where two men could bind them into sheaves; by the 1880s, an automatic knotter tied them together. By drastically reducing the number of people required for this work, the harvester increased the pace many times over. The introduction of mechanized corn planters and mowing or raking machines for hay all but completed the technological arsenal. (See Table 18.1.) The improvements in the last half

Table 18.1 MACHINE LABOR ON THE FARM, CA. 1880

Crop	Time Worked		Labor Cost	
	Hand	Machine	Hand	Machine
Wheat	61 hours	3 hours	$3.55	$0.66
Corn	39 hours	15 hours	3.62	1.51
Oats	66 hours	7 hours	3.73	1.07
Loose Hay	21 hours	4 hours	1.75	0.42
Baled Hay	35 hours	12 hours	3.06	1.29

of the century allowed an average farmer to produce up to 10 times more than was possible with the old implements.

Scientific study of soil, grain, and climate conditions was another factor in the record output. Beginning in the mid-nineteenth century, federal and state governments added inducements to the growing body of expertise, scientific information, and hands-on advice. Through the **Morrill Act of 1862**, "land-grant" colleges acquired space for campuses in return for promising to institute agricultural programs. The Department of Agriculture, which attained cabinet-level status in 1889, and the Weather Bureau (transferred from the War Department in 1891) also made considerable contributions to farmers' knowledge. The federal Hatch Act of 1887, which created a series of state experimental stations, provided for basic agricultural research, especially in the areas of soil minerals and plant growth. Many states added their own agricultural stations, usually connected with state colleges and universities.

The technologies of production did not necessarily guarantee success. Land, draft animals, and equipment remained very expensive, and start-up costs could keep a family in debt for decades. A year of good returns often preceded a year of financial disaster. Nature often seemed to take revenge against these early successes. West of the 98th meridian—a north-south line extending through western Oklahoma, central Kansas and Nebraska, and eastern Dakota—perennial dryness due to an annual rainfall of less than 20 inches constantly threatened to turn soil into dust and to break plows on the hardened ground. Summer heat burned out crops and ignited grass fires. Mountains of winter snows turned rivers into spring torrents that flooded fields; heavy fall rains washed crops away. Even good weather invited worms and flying insects to infest the crops. During the 1870s, grasshoppers in clouds a mile long ate everything organic, including tree bark and clothes.

18.4.4 Bonanza Farming in California

The new technology and scientific expertise favored the large, well-capitalized farmer over the small one. The majority of farmers continued to plant vegetable gardens and usually kept fowl or livestock for the family's consumption, but they understood that a major success depended on raising crops for a market that stretched across the world. To keep pace, farmers in the seven leading grain-growing states increased their individual holdings from approximately 64 acres on average in 1880 to more than 100 acres in 1900.

The trend toward large-scale or bonanza farming reached an apex in California, where farming as a business surpassed farming as a way of life. Bankers, railroad magnates, and other Anglos made rich by the gold rush took possession of the best farming land in the state. They introduced the latest technologies, built dams and canals, and invested huge amounts of capital, setting the pattern for the state's prosperous agribusiness. Farms of nearly 500 acres dominated the California landscape in 1870; by the turn of the century, two-thirds of the state's arable land was in 1,000-acre farms.

This scale of production made California the national leader in wheat production by the mid-1880s. But the state also produced tons of fruits and vegetables. Large- and medium-sized growers, shrewdly combined in cooperative marketing associations during the 1870s and 1880s, used the new refrigerator cars to ship produce in large quantities to the East and to Europe. By 1890, cherries, apricots, and oranges, packed in mountains of ice, were making their way into homes across the United States.

MECHANICAL HARVESTER This "thirty-three horse team harvester" was photographed at the turn of the century in Walla Walla, Washington. Binding the grain into sheaves before it could hit the ground, the "harvester" cut, threshed, and stacked wheat in one single motion.

California growers learned quickly that they could satisfy consumer appetites and even create new ones. Orange producers packed their products individually in tissue paper, a technique designed to convince eastern consumers that they were about to eat a luxury fruit. By the turn of the century, advertisers for the California Citrus Growers' Association described oranges as a necessity for good health, inventing the "Sunkist" trademark, which they stamped on each orange. Meanwhile grape growing grew into a big business. Long considered inferior to French wines, California wines found a ready market at lower prices. Other grape growers made their fortunes in raisins. One company trademarked its raisins as "Sun Maid" and packaged them in small boxes for schoolchildren.

By 1900, California had become the model for large-scale agriculture—not the home of self-sufficient homesteaders, but the showcase of heavily capitalized farm factories that employed a huge tenant and migrant workforce, including many Chinese. After the mines gave out and work on the transcontinental railroad ended, thousands of Chinese helped to bring new lands under cultivation. Chinese tenant farmers specialized in labor-intensive crops, such as vegetables and fruits, and peddled their crops door-to-door or sold them in roadside stands. Others worked in packing and preserving in all the major agricultural regions of the state. However, the Chinese, like the majority of field hands, rarely rose to the ranks of agricultural entrepreneurs. By the turn of the century, amid intense legislative battles over land and irrigation rights, it was clear that the rich and powerful dominated California agriculture.

18.4.5 The Toll on the Environment

Viewing the land as a resource to command, the new inhabitants often looked past the existing flora and fauna toward a landscape remade strictly for commercial purposes. The changes they produced in some areas were nearly as cataclysmic as those that occurred during the Ice Age.

Farmers "improved" the land by introducing exotic plants and animals—that is, biological colonies indigenous to other regions and continents. Farmers also unintentionally introduced new varieties of weeds, insect pests, and rats. Surviving portions of older grasslands and meadows eventually could be found only alongside railroad tracks, in graveyards, or inside national parks. Numerous species disappeared altogether or suffered drastic reduction. The grizzly bear, for example, an animal exclusive to the West, once could be found in large numbers from the Great Plains to California and throughout much of Alaska; by the early decades of the twentieth century, one nature writer estimated that only 800 survived, mostly in Yellowstone National Park. At the same time, the number of wolves declined from perhaps as many as 2 million to just 200,000. By the mid-1880s, no more than 5,000 buffalo survived in the entire United States, and little remained of the once vast herds except great heaps of bones sold for $7.50 per ton.

The slaughter of the buffalo had a dramatic impact, not only on the fate of the species, but also on the grasslands of the Great Plains. Overall, the biological diversity of the region had been drastically reduced. Having killed off the giant herds, ranchers and farmers quickly shifted to cattle and sheep production. Unlike the roaming buffalo, these livestock did not range widely and soon devoured the native grasses down to their roots. With the ground cover destroyed, the soil eroded and became barren. By the end of the century, huge dust storms swept across the plains.

Large-scale commercial agriculture also took a heavy toll on inland waters. Before white settlement, rainfall had drained naturally into lakes and underground aquifers, and watering spots were abundant throughout the Great Plains. Farmers mechanically rerouted and dammed water to irrigate their crops, causing many bodies of water to disappear and the water table to drop significantly. In the 1870s, successful ranchers in California pressed for ever-greater supplies of water and contracted Chinese work gangs to build the largest irrigation canal in the West. In 1887, the state of

IRRIGATING AT STRAWBERRY FARM This painting by the British-born artist Thomas Hill (1829–1908) depicts workers tending strawberry fields in the great agricultural valley of northern California. Chinese field hands, such as the two men shown here, supplied not only cheap labor but also invaluable knowledge of specialized fruit and vegetable crops.

California formed irrigation districts, securing bond issues for the construction of canals, and other western states followed. But by the 1890s, irrigation had seemed to reach its limit without federal support. The Newlands Reclamation Act, or **National Reclamation Act**, of 1902 added 1 million acres of irrigated land, and state irrigation districts added more than 10 million acres. Expensive to taxpayers, and ultimately benefiting corporate farmers rather than small landowners, these projects further diverted water and totally transformed the landscape.

Although western state politicians and federal officials debated water rights for decades, they rarely considered the impact of water policies on the environment. Lake Tulare in California's Central Valley, for example, had occupied up to 760 square miles. After farmers began to irrigate their land by tapping the rivers that fed Tulare, the lake shrank dramatically, covering a mere 36 square miles by the early twentieth century. Finally the lake disappeared entirely. The land left behind, now wholly dependent on irrigation, grew so alkaline in spots that it could no longer be used for agricultural purposes.

The need to maintain the water supply indirectly led to the creation of the first national forests. Western farmers supported the **Forest Reserve Act of 1891**, which gave the president the power to establish forest reserves to protect watersheds against the threats posed by lumbering, overgrazing, and forest fires. In the years that followed, President Benjamin Harrison established 16 forest reserves exceeding 20 million acres, and President Grover Cleveland added another 20 million acres. In 1897 the secretary of the interior gained the authority to regulate the use of these reserves.

These policies set the federal government on the path of large-scale regulatory activities to conserve the nation's natural resources. At the same time, these measures enhanced the role of the federal government in the economic development of the West.

18.5 The Western Landscape

What place did the West hold in the national imagination?

Throughout the nineteenth century, many Americans viewed western expansion as the nation's "manifest destiny," and just as many marveled at the region's natural and cultural wonders. The public east of the Mississippi craved stories about the West. Beginning in the 1860s, magazines such as *Harper's Weekly*, *Atlantic Monthly*, and *Scribner's* published frontier tales and expedition reports, often illustrated with striking visual images. The region and its peoples came to represent what was both unique and magnificent about the American landscape.

18.5.1 Nature's Majesty

Artists, writers, and scientists soon built their reputations on what they saw and imagined. Scores of writers described spectacular, breathtaking natural sites like the Grand Tetons and High Sierra. Geologists, botanists, historians, and anthropologists toured the trans-Mississippi West in pursuit of new information. Landscape painters, particularly the group that became known as the Rocky Mountain

***HETCH HETCHY CAÑON, CALIFORNIA* (1890)** Albert Bierstadt became one of the first artists to capture on enormous canvases the legendary vastness and rugged terrain of western mountains and wilderness. Many other artists joined Bierstadt to form the Rocky Mountain School. In time, the camera largely replaced the paintbrush, and most Americans formed an image of these majestic peaks from postcards and magazine illustrations.

SuperStock/Alamy Stock Photo.

School, also piqued the public's interest in the scenery of the unsettled West. In 1859, German-born Albert Bierstadt, equipped with his sketchbook, traveled the territories of Colorado and Wyoming. After he returned to his studio, Bierstadt painted mountains so wondrous that they seemed nearly surreal, projecting a divine aura behind the majesty of nature. His "earthscapes"—huge canvases with exacting details of animals and plants—thrilled viewers and sold for tens of thousands of dollars.

Moved by the depictions of the West's natural beauty, the federal government set aside huge tracts of wilderness. In 1864, Congress passed the Yosemite Act, which placed the spectacular cliffs and giant sequoias under the management of the State of California. In 1872, Congress named Yellowstone the first national park. Yosemite and Sequoia in California, Crater Lake in Oregon, Mount Rainier in Washington, and Glacier in Montana all became national parks between 1890 and 1910. (See Map 18.5.) The railroad companies, with their eyes on passenger revenue, lobbied vigorously for the creation of these parks. By the 1880s, the Northern Pacific Railroad was advertising the splendors of Yellowstone National Park and transporting an ever-increasing number of eastern tourists to the western wilderness.

18.5.2 The Legendary Wild West

The West as a land of promise and opportunity and, above all, of excitement and adventure found an expanding market in popular entertainments. The first "westerns," the "dime novels" that sold in the 1860s in editions of 50,000 or more, competed against tales about pirates, wars, crime, and sea adventures, and soon outsold all other genres. Edward Zane Carroll Judson's *Buffalo Bill, the King of the Border Men*, first published in 1869, spawned hundreds of other novels and even an entire magazine devoted to Buffalo Bill. In these sensational stories, Buffalo Bill, "a revolver in each hand" and a Bowie knife in his pocket, braves countless dangers to

Map 18.5 **THE ESTABLISHMENT OF NATIONAL PARKS AND FORESTS**

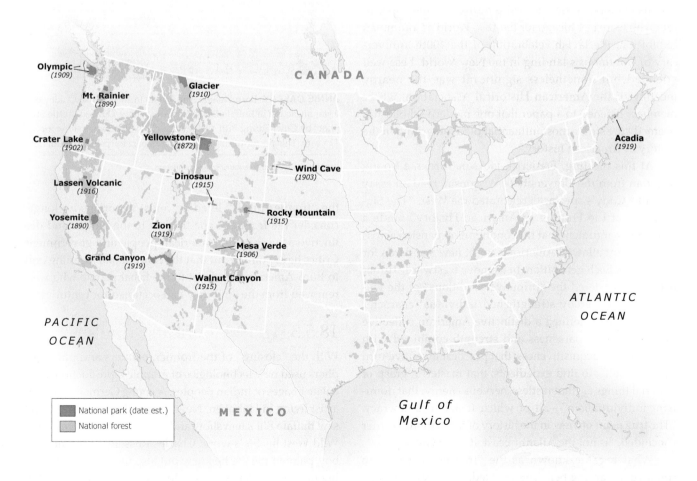

The setting aside of land for national parks saved large districts of the West from early commercial development and industrial degradation, setting a precedent for the later establishment of additional parks in economically marginal, but scenic, territory. The West, home to the vast majority of park space, became a principal site of tourism by the end of the nineteenth century.

maintain a moral order repeatedly jeopardized by outlaws or Indian warriors.

Many cowboys played up this role, dressing and talking to match the stories told about them. The first professional photographers who made their living touring the West set up studios where cowboys and prostitutes posed in elaborate costumes. Railroad promoters and herd owners also promoted this heroic imagery. Cowman Joseph G. McCoy staged Wild West shows in St. Louis and Chicago, where Texas cowboys entertained prospective buyers by roping calves and breaking horses. In 1883, the famed buffalo hunter William F. Cody, the inspiration for Judson's stories, created a spectacular entertainment that made the Wild West a staple of American popular culture. He headlined sharpshooter Annie Oakley. Entrancing crowds with her stunning accuracy with pistol or rifle, Oakley shot dimes in midair and cigarettes from her husband's mouth. "Little Sure Shot" soon became the main attraction of the touring company. Cody also hired Chief Sitting Bull and other Sioux Indians and hundreds of cowboys to perform in mock stagecoach robberies and battles, including the popular reenactment of "Custer's Last Stand."

Buffalo Bill's Wild West toured Europe eight times and also opened in time to entice nearly 3 million spectators who were in Chicago for the 1893 World's Columbian Exhibition, the lavish celebration of the 400th anniversary of Columbus's landing in the New World. Less well attended but nonetheless significant was the nearby meeting of the American Historical Association, where members listened to a paper that one modern scholar has deemed "the single most influential piece of writing in the history of American history."

At this meeting, Frederick Jackson Turner, a young historian from the University of Wisconsin, read an essay that, like Cody's spectacle, celebrated the West. "The Significance of the Frontier in American History" made a compelling argument that the continuous expansion across the continent allowed Americans to set new standards for democracy. Each generation, in its move westward, Turner reasoned, mastered the "primitive conditions" of the wilderness and thereby strengthened individual character and, ultimately, defined a distinctive American collective identity—"that coarseness and strength combined with acuteness and acquisitiveness; that practical inventive turn of mind, quick to find expedients; that masterful grasp of material things . . . that restless, nervous energy; that dominant individualism"—all of which fostered democracy. "The true point of view in the history of this nation," Turner concluded, "is not the Atlantic coast, it is the Great West."

What became known as the "frontier thesis" also sounded a warning bell. The 1890 federal census revealed that the "free land" had been depleted, prompting Turner to conclude that the "closing" of the frontier marked the end of the formative period of American history. Although

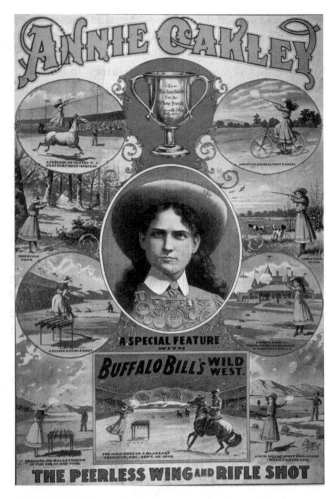

ANNIE OAKLEY Born Phoebe Ann Moses in 1860, Annie Oakley was a star attraction in Buffalo Bill's Wild West show. Dubbed "Little Sure Shot" by Chief Sitting Bull, Oakley traveled with Cody's show for 17 years. This poster from 1901 advertises her sharpshooting talents.

Peter Newark Western Americana/Bridgeman Images.

the "frontier thesis" lived on, most historians no longer consider the frontier to be the key to the unique and distinctive aspects of the American people and government. Critics have pointed out that the concept had meaning only to Euro-Americans and not to the tribal people who were removed from the land they had occupied for centuries.

18.5.3 The "American Primitive"

With the "closing" of the frontier, painters and photographers used new technologies of graphic reproduction to circulate images of Indian peoples. A young German American artist living in Hoboken, New Jersey, Charles Schreyvogel, saw Buffalo Bill's tent show and decided to make the mythic Wild West his life's work. Charles Russell, a genuine cowboy, painted the life he knew but also indulged in fashioning imaginary scenes of buffalo hunts and first encounters between Indian peoples and white explorers. Frederic Remington, the most famous of all the western artists, left Yale Art School to visit Montana in 1881. Painstakingly accurate in physical details, especially of horses, his paintings and popular magazine illustrations celebrated the "winning of the West" from the Indian peoples.

Photographers often produced highly nuanced portraits of Indian peoples. Dozens of early photographers from the Bureau of American Ethnology captured the gaze of noble tribespeople or showed them hard at work digging clams or grinding corn. President Theodore Roosevelt praised Edward Sheriff Curtis for vividly conveying tribal virtue. Generations later, in the 1960s and 1970s, Curtis's photographs again captured the imagination of western enthusiasts, who were unaware or unconcerned that he often posed his subjects or retouched his photos to blur out any artifacts of white society.

Painters and photographers led the way for scholarly research on the various Indian societies. The early ethnographer and pioneer of fieldwork in anthropology Lewis Henry Morgan devoted his life to the study of Indian family or kinship patterns, mostly of eastern tribes such as the Iroquois, who adopted him into their Hawk Clan. In 1851, he published *League of the Ho-de-no-sau-nee, or Iroquois*, considered the first scientific account of an Indian tribe. A decade later, Morgan ventured into Cheyenne country to examine the naming patterns of that tribe. His major work, *Ancient Society*, published in 1877, outlines a universal process of social evolution leading from savagery to barbarism to civilization.

One of the most influential interpreters of the cultures of living tribespeople was the pioneering ethnographer Alice Cunningham Fletcher. In 1879, Fletcher met Susette (Bright Eyes) La Flesche of the Omaha tribe, who was on a speaking tour to gain support for her people, primarily to prevent their removal from tribal lands. Fletcher, then 42 years old, accompanied La Flesche to Nebraska, telling the Omahas that she had come "to learn, if you will let me, something about your tribal organization, social customs, tribal rites, traditions and songs. Also to see if I can help you in any way." After transcribing hundreds of songs, Fletcher

became well known as an expert on Omaha music. She also promoted assimilation through the allotment of individual claims to 160-acre homesteads, eked out of tribal lands, and helped to draft the model legislation that was enacted by Congress as the **Omaha Act of 1882**. As a founder of the American Anthropological Society and president of the American Folklore Society, she encouraged further study of Indian societies.

While white settlers and the federal government threatened the survival of tribal life, Indian lore became a major pursuit of scholars and amateurs alike. Adults and children delighted in discovering arrowheads. Fraternal organizations such as the Elks and Eagles borrowed tribal terminology. The Boy Scouts and Girl Scouts, the nation's premier youth organizations, used tribal lore to instill strength of character. The U.S. Treasury stamped images of tribal chiefs and buffalo on the nation's most frequently used coins.

18.6 The Transformation of Indian Societies

What kind of Indian society did reformers envision?

In 1871, under the terms of the Indian Appropriations Act, the U.S. government formally ended the treaty system and no longer recognized any group of Indians as an independent nation. Still, the tribes persisted. Using a mixture of survival strategies from farming and trade to the leasing of reservation lands, they both adapted to changing conditions and maintained old traditions.

18.6.1 Reform Policy and Politics

By 1881, many Indian tribes had been forcibly resettled on reservations, although few had adapted to white ways. The majority lived in poverty, deprived of their traditional

---

Table 18.2 **MAJOR INDIAN TREATIES AND LEGISLATION OF THE LATE NINETEENTH CENTURY**

1863	**Nez Perce Treaty**	Signed illegally on behalf of the entire tribe, the treaty in which the Nez Perces abandoned 6 million acres of land in return for a small reservation in northeastern Oregon. Led to the Nez Perce wars, which ended in 1877 with the surrender of Chief Joseph.
1867	**Medicine Lodge Treaty**	Assigned reservations in existing Indian Territory to Comanches, Plains (Kiowa), Apaches, Kiowas, Cheyennes, and Arapahoes, bringing these tribes together with Sioux, Shoshones, Bannocks, and Navajos.
1868	**Treaty of Fort Laramie**	Successfully ended Red Cloud's war by evacuating federal troops from Sioux Territory along the Bozeman Trail; additionally granted Sioux ownership of the western half of South Dakota and rights to use Powder River country in Wyoming and Montana.
1871	**Indian Appropriations Act**	Congress declares end to treaty system. The U.S. government no longer recognizes the sovereignty of Indian nations.
1887	**Dawes Severalty Act**	Divided communal tribal land, granting the right to petition for citizenship to those Indians who accepted the individual land allotment of 160 acres. Designed to encourage assimilation by encouraging Indian peoples to adopt American farming practices.
1889	**Springer Amendment, Indian Appropriations Act**	Opened unassigned lands to white homesteaders, prompting the Oklahoma Land Rush.

means of survival and, more often than not, subjected to fraud by corrupt government agents and private suppliers. Conceding the failure of the reservation system, sympathetic reformers nevertheless remained unshaken in their belief that tribespeople must be raised out of the darkness of ignorance into the light of civilization.

One of the most influential reformers was Helen Hunt Jackson, a noted poet and author of children's stories. In 1879, Jackson heard a chief of the Ponca tribe describe the sufferings of his people after they had been forced from their Dakota homeland. Heart-struck, she began to lobby for Indians' rights and to write against government policy. Her book-length exposé, *A Century of Dishonor*, was published in 1881.

Jackson threw herself into the Indian Rights Association, an offshoot of the Women's National Indian Association (WNIA), which had formed in 1874 to rally public support for a program of assimilation. According to the reformers' plans, men would now farm as well as hunt, while women would leave the fields to take care of home and children. Likewise, all communal practices would be abandoned in favor of individually owned homesteads, where families could develop in the "American" manner. Children, hair trimmed short, would be placed in boarding schools where, removed from their parents' influence, they would shed traditional values and cultural practices. By 1882, the WNIA had gathered 100,000 signatures on petitions urging Congress to phase out the reservation system, to establish universal education for Indian children, and to award title to 160 acres to any Indian individual willing to work the land.

The **Dawes Severalty Act**, passed by Congress in 1887, incorporated many of these measures and established federal Indian policy for decades to come. The act allowed the president to distribute land not to tribes, but to individuals legally "severed" from their tribes. The commissioner of Indian Affairs rendered the popular interpretation that "tribal relations should be broken up, socialism destroyed and the family and autonomy of the individual substituted. The allotment of land in severalty, the establishment of local courts and police, the development of a personal sense of independence and the universal adoption of the English language are means to this end." Those individuals who accepted the land allotment of 160 acres and agreed to allow the government to sell the remaining tribal lands (with some funds set aside for education) could petition to become citizens of the United States. A little over a decade after its enactment, many reformers believed that the Dawes Act had resolved the "Indian problem." Hollow Horn Bear, a Sioux chief, offered a different opinion, judging the Dawes Act to be "only another trick of the whites."

The Dawes Act successfully undermined tribal sovereignty but offered little compensation. Indian religions and sacred ceremonies were banned, the telling of legends and myths forbidden, and shamans and medicine men imprisoned or exiled for continuing their traditional practices. "Indian schools" forbade Indian languages, clothing styles, and even hair fashions. (See Communities *in* Conflict.)

These and other measures did little to integrate Indians into white society. Government agencies did little to help Indians succeed as farmers and instead allotted them inferior land, inadequate tools, and little training for agricultural self-sufficiency. Seeing scant advantage in assimilating, only a minority of adults dropped their tribal religion for Christianity or their communal ways for the accumulation of private property. Within the next 40 years, the Indian peoples lost 60 percent of the reservation land remaining in 1887 and 66 percent of the land allotted to them as homesteaders. The tenets of the Dawes Act were not reversed until 1934. In that year, Congress passed the Indian Reorganization Act, which affirmed the integrity of Indian cultural institutions and returned some land to tribal ownership. (See Chapter 24.)

18.6.2 The Ghost Dance

After the passage of the Dawes Severalty Act, one more cycle of rebellion remained for the Sioux. In 1889, the Northern Paiute Wovoka had a vision during a total eclipse of the sun. In Wokova's vision, the Creator told him that if the Indian peoples learned to love each other, they would be granted a special place in the afterlife. The Creator also gave him the Ghost Dance, which he taught to his followers. The Sioux, among others, elaborated Wovoka's prophecy into a religion of resistance. They came to believe that when the day of judgment arrived, all Indian peoples who had ever lived would return to their lost world and white peoples would vanish from the earth. They chanted:

The whole world is coming.

A nation is coming, a nation is coming.

The eagle has brought the message to the tribe.

The father says so, the father says so.

Over the whole earth they are coming.

The buffalo are coming, the buffalo are coming.

The crow has brought the message to the tribe,

The father says so, the father says so.

Many white settlers and federal officials feared the Ghost Dancers, even though belief in a sudden divine judgment was common among Christians and Jews. Before the Civil War, Protestant groups such as the Millerites, who had renounced personal property and prepared themselves for the millennium, were tolerated by other Americans. After decades of Indian warfare, however, white Americans took the Ghost Dance as a warning of tribal retribution

Communities *in* Conflict

The Carlisle Indian Industrial School

. . . thrust into an alien world . . . the "civilizing" process began.

Richard Henry Pratt (1840–1924) founded the Indian school in Carlisle, Pennsylvania, in 1879 with the approval of the Department of the Interior and the War Department. He had served in a volunteer regiment during the Civil War and then continued his military assignment in the Indian Territory, where he began to develop ideas of "civilizing" Native Americans. Before his first encounter he had anticipated meeting "atrocious aborigines," but he soon came to believe that, if given sufficient opportunities and guidance, Indian peoples could thrive and become equal citizens of the United States.

Pratt headed the Carlisle Indian School for 25 years, until he retired from military service in 1904. Together with his wife, Anna Mason Pratt, he supervised every aspect of the Indian children's life, including language, dress, and deportment. Sharing with many well-intentioned white reformers the conviction that Christianity provided the best moral guidance, the Pratts forbade the children to practice their native religion. Pratt's motto, "Kill the Indian, but save the man," aptly expressed his belief that the salvation of the Indians depended on the sacrifice of their culture.

Luther Standing Bear (1868–1939), the son of the Oglala Sioux chief Standing Bear, was born on the Sioux Pine Ridge reservation in South Dakota and educated at the Carlisle Indian School. He was a member of the first class to graduate. In 1898, he joined Buffalo Bill's Wild West Show as an interpreter and chaperon for Indian performers and also performed, along with his wife. In 1912, he moved on to the motion picture industry in California, where he became an actor and consultant on movies about Indians. He wrote several books about his experiences; an excerpt from one of them appears here.

- **Why did Richard Henry Pratt choose haircuts and new clothing as important measures in training Indian children for citizenship?**

- **How did Luther Standing Bear interpret this act?**

Richard Henry Pratt Explains How He Made Indian Children "White"

Just before starting for the Indian Territory party, I employed a couple of barbers to cut the hair of the boys. This work was scarcely begun when I had to leave and the barbers were to finish the work under Mrs. Pratt's oversight. Upon my return Mrs. Pratt gave me this experience: The interpreter came to her saying all the boys had their hair cut except two of the older ones who refused to part with their long braids. She went at once to the room where the hair cutting was being done and asked these big boys why they refused to carry out the Captain's order. "Well," said one, "we were told we would have new clothes like the white men. We have none so we keep our long hair." "All right," said Mrs. Pratt, "the clothes will come later, and if you do not want to have your hair cut now, I must send away these barbers and then you must wait until the Captain returns." The spokesman relented and said that if she would stand by, he would let the man cut his hair, which she willingly did. The other, however, stubbornly held to his decision. Later that night she was aroused by a very discordant wailing, which grew in volume. Mrs. Pratt sent a boy for the interpreter. When the interpreter came, he gave the explanation that the young man who had refused to have his hair cut afterwards relented and did the job himself with a knife. He then said his people always wailed after cutting their hair, as it was an evidence of mourning, and he had come onto the parade ground to show his grief. His voice had awakened the girls, who joined with their shrill voices, then other boys joined and hence the commotion. . . .

There was a very considerable delay in the arrival of clothing, and when it finally came it was delivered under a Bureau contract with one of our great American merchants. It was the shoddiest of shoddy clothing. As the price was insignificant, the worth was the same, but it illustrated the ill-considered system of buying the cheapest materials. Agent Miles stopped off on his way to Washington. I made a bundle of a cloth cap, through which I could push my finger, a coat out at the elbows and ripped, and trousers torn and worn out at the knees and seat, all in use less than a month. . . .

We were scarcely underway when I received a letter from the Commissioner of Indian Affairs, enclosing a printed table of the per capita allowance of food for Indian schools. Experience in army service showed that children living on that ration would be hungry all the time. . . .

The next time I visited Washington, the Commissioner, Mr. Hayt, laughingly told me that he wanted me to see how that table came to be adopted by the Bureau and sent for the chief of the division in the Indian Office having the matter in charge. When he came in, the Commissioner said, "I want you to tell Captain Pratt how you came to make up that school food supply table." The man said: "We had a rational allowance considerably more liberal than that for several years, and as nobody complained about it I thought there could be a reduction.

"I accordingly made up that table and have been waiting for complaints." I said, "You did that, without investigating allowances at boarding schools for young people or making inquiries of people who know about such things, and pushed it on the Indians as the conclusion of this Bureau?" "Well," he said, "I knew no other way. No one complained and I thought it right to economize."

Source: Excerpt from Pratt and Utley, *Battlefield and Classroom: Four Decades with the American Indian*, pp. 232–234. Copyright © 2003 University of Oklahoma Press. Reprinted by permission.

Luther Standing Bear Remembers Being Made "White"

At the age of eleven years, ancestral life for me and my people was most abruptly ended without regard for our wishes, comforts, or rights in the matter. At once I was thrust into an alien world, into an environment as different from the one into which I had been born as it is possible to imagine, to remake myself, if I could, into the likeness of the invader.

By 1879, my people were no longer free, but were subjects confined on reservations under the rule of agents. One day there came to the agency a party of white people from the East. Their presence aroused considerable excitement when it became known that these people were school teachers who wanted some Indian boys and girls to take away with them to train as were white boys and girls. . . .

I could think of no reason why white people wanted Indian boys and girls except to kill them, and not having the remotest idea of what a school was, I thought we were going East to die. . . . In my decision to go, I gave up many things dear to the heart of a little Indian boy, and one of the things over which my child mind grieved was the thought of saying good-bye to my pony. I rode him as far as I could on the journey, which was to the Missouri River, where we took the boat. There we parted from our parents, and it was a heart-breaking scene, women and children weeping. Some of the children changed their minds and were unable to go on the boat, but for many who did go it was a final parting. . . .

At last at Carlisle the transforming, the "civilizing" process began. It began with clothes. Never, no matter what our philosophy or spiritual quality, could we be civilized while wearing the moccasin and blanket. The task before us was not only that of accepting new ideas and adopting new manners, but actual physical changes and discomfort had to be borne uncomplainingly until the body adjusted itself to new tastes and habits. Our accustomed dress was taken and replaced with clothing that felt cumbersome and awkward. Against trousers and handkerchiefs we had a distinct feeling—they were unsanitary and the trousers kept us from breathing well. High collars, stiff-bosomed shirts, and suspenders fully three inches in width were uncomfortable, while leather boots caused actual suffering. We longed to go barefoot, but were told that dew on the grass would give us colds. That was a new warning for us, for our mothers had never told us to beware of colds, and I remember as a child coming into the tipi with moccasins full of snow. . . . My niece once asked me what it was that I disliked the most during those first bewildering days, and I said, "red flannel." Not knowing what I meant, she laughed, but I still remember those horrid, sticky garments which we had to wear next to the skin, and I still squirm and itch when I think of them.

Source: Reproduced from Luther Standing Bear, *Land of the Spotted Eagle*, by permission of the University of Nebraska Press. Copyright © 1933 by Luther Standing Bear. Copyright renewed 1960 by May Jones.

rather than as a religious ceremony. As thousands of Sioux danced to exhaustion, local whites demanded the practice be stopped. The U.S. Seventh Cavalry, led in part by survivors of the Battle of Little Bighorn, rushed to the Pine Ridge Reservation, and a group of Sioux led by Big Foot, fearing mass murder, moved into hiding in the Badlands of South Dakota. Falsely targeted as an instigator, the great Sioux chief Sitting Bull was killed by Lieutenant Bull Head, a Sioux who had allied with U.S. troops. The Ghost Dancers concluded that the U.S. government planned to exterminate them.

The Seventh Cavalry pursued the Sioux Ghost Dancers and 300 undernourished Sioux, freezing and without horses, to Wounded Knee Creek on the Pine Ridge Reservation. There, on December 29, 1890, while the peace-seeking Big Foot—who had personally raised a white flag of surrender—lay dying of pneumonia, the Sioux were surrounded by soldiers armed with Hotchkiss guns and rifles. The U.S. troops expected the Sioux to surrender their few remaining weapons, but an accidental gun shot from one

deaf brave who misunderstood the command caused panic on both sides.

Within minutes, at least 150 Sioux had been cut down and 25 soldiers mortally wounded, mostly by their own crossfire. For two hours soldiers continued to shoot at anything that moved—mostly women and children running for cover. Many of the injured froze to death in the snow; others were transported in open wagons and finally laid out on beds of hay under Christmas decorations at the Pine Ridge Episcopal Church. The massacre, which took place almost exactly 400 years after Columbus "discovered" the New World for Christian civilization, seemed to mark the final conquest of the continent's indigenous peoples.

18.6.3 Endurance and Rejuvenation

The most tenacious tribes were those occupying land rejected by white settlers and those distant from their new communities. Still, not even an insular, peaceful agricultural existence on semiarid, treeless terrain necessarily provided protection. Nor did a total willingness to peacefully accept white offers prevent attack.

The Pimas of Arizona, for instance, had a well-developed agricultural system adapted to a scarce supply of water, and they rarely warred with other tribes. After the arrival of white settlers, they integrated Christian symbolism into their religion, learned to speak English, and even fought with the U.S. cavalry against the Apaches. Still, the Pimas saw their lands stolen, their precious waterways diverted, and their families impoverished.

The similarly peaceful Yana tribes of California, hunters and gatherers rather than farmers, were even less fortunate. Suffering enslavement, prostitution, and multiple new diseases from white settlers, they faced near extinction within a generation. One Yana tribe, the Yahi, chose simply to disappear. For more than a decade, they lived in caves and avoided all contact with white settlers.

Many tribes found it difficult to survive in proximity to white settlers. The Flatheads, for example, seemed to Indian commissioners in the Bitterroot region of Montana to be destined for quick assimilation. They had refused to join the Ghost Dance and had agreed to sell their rich tribal land and move to a new reservation. While waiting to be moved, however, the dispossessed Flatheads nearly starved. When they finally reached the new reservation in October 1891, the remaining 250 Flatheads put on their finest war paint and whooped and galloped their horses, firing guns in the air in celebration. Disappointment and tragedy lay ahead. The federal government drastically reduced the size of the reservation, using a large part of it to provide a national reserve for buffalo. Only handfuls of Flatheads, mostly elderly, continued to live together, in pockets of rural poverty.

A majority of tribes, especially smaller ones, sooner or later reached numbers too low to maintain their collective existence. Intermarriage, although widely condemned by the white community, drew many young people outside their Indian communities. Some tribal leaders also deliberately chose a path toward assimilation. The Quapaws, for example, formally disbanded in the aftermath of the Dawes Severalty Act. The minority that managed to prosper in white society as tradespeople or farmers abandoned their language, religious customs, and traditional ways of life. Later generations petitioned the federal government and regained tribal status, established ceremonial grounds and cultural centers (or Bingo halls), and built up one of the most durable powwows in the state. Even so, much of the tribal lore that had underpinned their distinct identity had simply vanished.

For those tribes who remained on reservations, the aggressively assimilationist policies of the Office of Indian Affairs (OIA) challenged their traditional ways. The Southern Ute, for example, at one time hunted, fished, and gathered throughout a huge region spanning the Rocky Mountains and the Great Basin. In 1848, they began to sign a series of treaties in accord with the reservation policy of the U.S. government. Twenty years later, their territory had been reduced to approximately one-quarter of Colorado Territory, and in 1873, they had further relinquished about one-quarter of this land. After the passage of the Dawes Act, the U.S. government, pressured by white settlers, gave the tribe two choices: They could break up their communal land holdings and accept the 160 acres granted to each of the male heads of families, or they could maintain their tribal status and move to a reservation in Utah. The Utes were divided over the issue, but a considerable number chose to live on reservations under the administration of the OIA.

Under the terms of the Dawes Act, Southern Ute men and women endured continuous challenges to their egalitarian practices. The OIA assumed, for example, that Ute men would represent the tribe in all official matters, a policy that forced Ute women to petition the U.S. government to recognize their rights and concerns. Similarly, Ute women struggled to hold on to their roles as producers within the subsistence family economy against the efforts of the OIA agents to train them for homemaking alone. In the 1880s, the OIA established a matrons program to teach Ute women to create a "civilizing" home, which included new lessons about sanitation, home furnishings, and health care. But even 50 years later, some Ute preferred to live at least part of the year in a teepee in a multigenerational family, rather than in a private residence designed for a single married couple and their children.

A small minority of tribes, grown skillful in adapting to dramatically changing circumstances, managed to persist and even grow. Never numbering more than a few thousand people, during the late eighteenth century the Cheyennes found themselves caught geographically between aggressive tribes in the Great Lakes region and migrated into the Missouri area, where they split into small village-sized communities. By the mid-nineteenth century, they had become expert horse traders on the Great Plains, well prepared to meet the massive influx of white settlers by shifting their location frequently. They avoided the worst of the pestilence that spread from the diseases white people carried and likewise survived widespread intermarriage with the Sioux in the 1860s and 1870s. Instructed to settle, many Cheyennes took up elements of the Christian religion and became farmers, also without losing their tribal identity. Punished by revenge-hungry soldiers after the battle of Little Bighorn, their lands repeatedly taken away, they still held on. The Cheyennes were survivors.

The Navajos experienced an extraordinary renewal, largely because they built a life in territory considered worthless by whites. Having migrated to the Southwest from the northwestern part of the continent perhaps 700 years earlier, the Diné ("the People"), as they called themselves, had already survived earlier invasions by the Spanish. In 1863,

JOHN WESELY POWELL AND TAU-GUE The explorer John Wesley Powell led
an expedition of 10 men in 1869 to map the Colorado River, its tributaries, and its
canyons. He became fascinated with the culture of the tribespeople he encountered,
and learned to speak the Ute language. In 1871–1872 Powell, accompanied by a
photographer, remade the trip to the Grand Canyon, which he named. In this image,
Powell appears alongside Tau-gue, Chief of the Paiutes, overlooking the Virgin River.

Time Life Pictures/Getty Images.

alone as a food reserve during years of bad
crops. With their wool rugs and blankets
much in demand in the East, the Navajos
increasingly turned to crafts, eventually
including silver jewelry as well as weaving,
to survive. Although living on the economic
margin, they persevered to become the largest
Indian nation in the United States.

The nearby Hopis, like the Navajos,
survived by stubbornly clinging to lands
unwanted by white settlers, and by adapting
to drastically changing conditions. A famous
tribe of "desert people," the Hopis had lived
for centuries in their cliff cities. Their highly
developed theological beliefs, peaceful social
system, sand paintings, and kachina dolls
interested many educated and influential
whites. The resulting publicity helped them
gather the public supporters and financial
resources needed to fend off further threats to
their reservations.

Fortunate northwestern tribes remained
relatively isolated from white settlers until
the early twentieth century, although they had
begun trading with white visitors centuries
earlier. Northwestern peoples relied largely
on salmon and other resources of the region's
rivers and bays. In potlatch ceremonies, leaders redistributed tribal wealth and maintained
their personal status and the status of their
tribe by giving lavish gifts to invited guests.
Northwestern peoples also made intricate
wood carvings, including commemorative
"totem" poles that recorded their history and
identified their regional status. Northwestern
peoples maintained their cultural integrity in
part through connections with kin in Canada,
as did southern tribes with kin in Mexico. In
Canada and Mexico, native populations suffered less pressure from new populations and retained more tribal authority than in the United States.

Indian nations approached their nadir as the nineteenth
century came to a close. The descendants of the great pre-
Columbian civilizations had been conquered by foreigners,
their population reduced below 250,000. Under the pressure
of assimilation, the remaining tribespeople became known
to non-Indians as "the vanishing Americans." It would take
several generations before Indian sovereignty experienced
a resurgence.

they had been conquered again through the cooperation of
hostile tribes led by the famous Colonel Kit Carson. Their
crops burned, their fruit trees destroyed, 8,000 Navajos were
forced in the 300-mile "Long Walk" to the desolate Bosque
Redondo reservation, where they nearly starved. Four years
later, the Indian Bureau allowed the severely reduced tribe
to return to a fraction of its former lands.

By 1880, the Navajos' population had returned to
nearly what it had been before their conquest by white
Americans. Quickly depleting the deer and antelope on
their hemmed-in reservation, they had to rely on sheep

Conclusion

Amid the land rush of April 22, 1889, the town of Guthrie, Oklahoma, was built, contemporaries liked to brag, not in a day but in a single afternoon, its population leaping from a dozen or so to 10,000 by sundown. Throughout the territory, new communities formed almost as rapidly and often displaced old ones. Farms and ranches owned by white settlers soon spread out across the vast countryside that earlier had been Indian Territory. This spectacular development of Oklahoma was, however, but one chapter in the history of the trans-Mississippi West as an internal empire.

The West, rich in natural resources, soon served the nation in supplying ore and timber for its expanding industries and agricultural products for the growing urban populations. Envisioning the West as a cornucopia whose boundless treasures would offer themselves to the willing pioneer, most of the new residents failed to calculate the odds against their making a prosperous livelihood as miners, farmers, or petty merchants. Nor could they appreciate the long-term consequences of the violence they brought with them from the battlefields of the Civil War to the far reaches of the West.

The new settlers adapted their political and legal systems, as well as many of their economic and cultural institutions, to western circumstances. Ironically though, even after statehood, they would still be only distant representatives of an empire whose financial, political, and industrial centers remained in the Northeast. They were often frustrated by their isolation and enraged at the federal regulations that governed them, and at the eastern investors and lawyers who seemed poised on all sides to rob them of the fruits of their labor. Embittered Westerners, along with Southerners, would form the core of a nationwide discontent that would soon threaten to uproot the American political system.

Key Terms

Sand Creek Massacre The near annihilation in 1864 of Black Kettle's Cheyenne band by Colorado troops under Colonel John Chivington's orders to "kill and scalp all, big and little." p. 404

Great Sioux War From 1865 to 1867 the Oglala Sioux warrior Red Cloud waged war against the U.S. Army, forcing the United States to abandon its forts built on land relinquished to the government by the Sioux. p. 404

Treaty of Fort Laramie The treaty acknowledging U.S. defeat in the Great Sioux War in 1868 and supposedly guaranteeing the Sioux perpetual land and hunting rights in South Dakota, Wyoming, and Montana. p. 404

Edmunds Act 1882 act that effectively disenfranchised those who believed in or practiced polygamy and threatened them with fines and imprisonment. p. 409

Edmunds–Tucker Act 1887 act that destroyed the temporal power of the Mormon Church by confiscating all assets over $50,000 and establishing a federal commission to oversee all elections in the Utah territory. p. 409

Hispanic-American Alliance Organization formed to protect and fight for the rights of Spanish Americans. p. 410

Homestead Act of 1862 Granted a quarter section (160 acres) of the public domain free to any settler who lived on the land for at least five years and improved it. p. 414

Morrill Act of 1862 Act by which "land-grant" colleges acquired space for campuses in return for promising to institute agricultural programs. p. 416

National Reclamation Act 1902 act that added 1 million acres of irrigated land to the United States. p. 418

Forest Reserve Act of 1891 Act that allowed the President to set aside forest reserves from land in the public domain. p. 418

Omaha Act of 1882 Act that allowed the establishment of individual title to tribal lands. p. 421

Dawes Severalty Act An 1887 law terminating tribal ownership of land and allotting some parcels of land to individual Indians, with the remainder opened for white settlement. p. 422

CHRONOLOGY

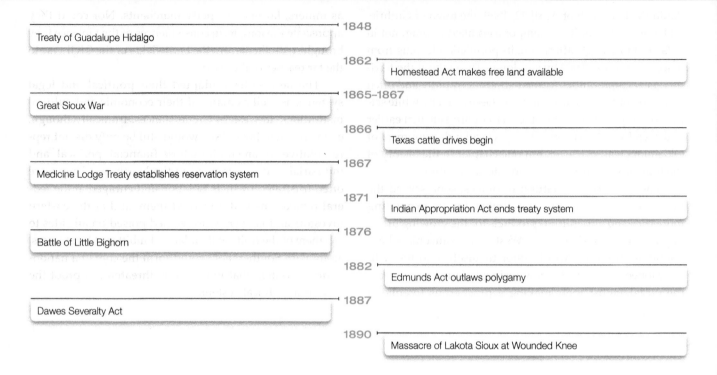

Treaty of Guadalupe Hidalgo	1848
	1862 — Homestead Act makes free land available
Great Sioux War	1865–1867
	1866 — Texas cattle drives begin
Medicine Lodge Treaty establishes reservation system	1867
	1871 — Indian Appropriation Act ends treaty system
Battle of Little Bighorn	1876
	1882 — Edmunds Act outlaws polygamy
Dawes Severalty Act	1887
	1890 — Massacre of Lakota Sioux at Wounded Knee

Chapter 19
Production and Consumption in the Gilded Age 1865–1900

BLOODSHED IN HAYMARKET SQUARE Swedish-born illustrator Thure de Thulstrup depicted the events in Haymarket Square in *The Anarchist Riot: A Dynamite Bomb Exploding among the Police.*

North Wind Picture Archives/Alamy Stock Photo.

 ## Contents and Focus Questions

American Communities

Haymarket Square, Chicago, May 4, 1886

As rain approached the city, approximately 1,500 people gathered for a mass meeting in Haymarket Square to protest the brutality of the previous day, when Chicago police killed four strikers at the fiercely antiunion McCormick Reaper Works. The crowd listened peacefully as several speakers denounced the violence. Around 10:00 P.M., when the winds picked up, most headed for home, including the city's longtime mayor, Democrat Carter Harrison. According to newspaper reports, the crowd quickly dwindled to only 600 people. The final speaker, stone hauler Samuel Fielden, jumped up on the hay wagon that served as a makeshift stage and concluded on an ominous note. He warned that, "war has been declared on us" and advised the crowd, "to get hold of anything that will help you to resist the onslaught of the enemy and the usurper."

Within minutes, a column of 176 police marched down the street, pushing what remained of the crowd onto the wooden sidewalks and commanding them to disperse. Then, according to the city's leading newspaper, the *Tribune*, "something like a miniature rocket suddenly rose out of the crowd on the east sidewalk." The bomb exploded "with terrific force, shaking buildings on the street and creating havoc among the police." One policeman died immediately, provoking others to open fire into the scattering crowd. At the end of just a few minutes of chaos, 7 policemen had received mortal wounds and as many as 60 more were injured, many in their own crossfire. Several civilians were killed, and dozens were injured.

Those who attended the rally were mainly disgruntled workers, recent immigrants from central and eastern Europe who had come to Chicago to take advantage of the city's growing industries. At this moment, though, they were primarily determined to establish unions and a workday shorter than the customary 10 or 12 hours.

Since early in the year, an eight-hour campaign had been sweeping the nation, with its center in Chicago. Workers and sympathetic consumers alike boycotted brands of beer, tobacco, bread, and other products made in longer-hour shops. They wanted *"Eight hours for work, eight hours for rest / Eight hours for what we will."* With more than wages at stake, workers were joining unions and striking so often that the era became known as the "Great Upheaval." Their leaders responded to this upsurge by calling for a general strike across all industries on May 1, 1886.

A community of radical workers who had emigrated from Germany and settled in Chicago's near North Side made up the most militant contingent of the movement. They called themselves "revolutionary socialists," and sought a government of working people in place of politicians and corporate power. Writing in the *Arbeiter-Zeitung (Workers' Newspaper)*, the local German-language newspaper, editor August Spies greeted May 1, hailed as "Emancipation Day," calling, "Workmen, let your watchword be: No compromise! Cowards to the Rear! Men to the front!"

On May Day, Spies renewed the cry of "Eight for ten!" and helped to lead the spectacular parade of 80,000 men, women, and children up Michigan Avenue, Chicago's main street. A Saturday, the day passed peacefully. However, when the workweek resumed on Monday, May 3, the deadly confrontation of strikers and police at the McCormick Reaper Works set the stage for virtual class warfare.

Feelings of animosity intensified on all sides. In the days following the tragedy at Haymarket Square, Chicago police arrested hundreds of working people, rounded up known leaders, and searched their homes and detained them without warrants. Meanwhile, newspapers denounced them as "enemy forces" and the "scum" of Europe. Sentiment swung sharply against immigrants.

Ultimately, eight men were charged with incitement to murder. In the most celebrated trial of the nineteenth century, a jury of middle-class men pronounced all eight guilty despite the lack of evidence linking the defendants to the bombing. Three of the eight had not even been at Haymarket Square on the evening of May 4. The judge sentenced them to death by hanging.

At the other end of the social scale, for middle- and upper-class Chicagoans the 1880s were a time of unprecedented prosperity. Incorporated in 1837, the city boasted a population of 200,000—second only to New York—and dozens of new mass industries and vibrant new classes of consumers. Many of the workers, especially immigrants, could barely make ends meet. But thousands of better-off Chicagoans rushed to Marshall Field & Company to survey the ever-expanding range of goods in one of the finest department stores in the nation and a major source of pride for the city. Others could turn to less expensive goods offered by Chicago-based Montgomery Ward, the nation's first large-scale mail-order business.

By the final decades of the nineteenth century, the nation's eyes were fixed on Chicago because the city was marking the steps being taken by the nation as a whole. If class differences sharpened and led to violence, the rise in living standards provided a different, more appealing focus. The city with the most technologically advanced industries in the world seemed to be leading the way—but to what?

Chicago

19.1 The Rise of Industry, the Triumph of Business

What explains the rise of big business in the late nineteenth century?

At the time of the Civil War, the typical American business firm was a small enterprise, owned and managed by a single family and producing goods for a local or regional market. By the turn of the century, businesses depending on large-scale investments had organized as corporations and grown to unforeseen size. These mammoth firms could afford to mass-produce goods for national and even international markets. At the helm stood unimaginably wealthy men, powerful representatives of a new national business community. With the help of government and friendly politicians, these business leaders and financiers sped the transformation of the United States from a rural to an urban industrial nation.

19.1.1 Mechanization Takes Command

The Centennial Exposition of 1876, held in Philadelphia, celebrated not so much the American Revolution 100 years earlier as the industrial and technological promise of the

THOMAS ALVA EDISON Thomas Alva Edison (1847–1931), shown here working on the phonograph, moved his laboratory from Menlo Park to West Orange, New Jersey. There, he invented the alkaline storage battery, the phonograph, and the kinetoscope, the first machine to allow one person at a time to view motion pictures.

Ian Dagnall/Alamy Stock Photo.

century to come. The visiting emperor of Brazil spoke into an unfamiliar device on display and gasped, "My God, it talks!" The telephone, patented that year by Alexander Graham Bell, signaled the rise of the United States to world leadership in industrial technology.

The year 1876 also marked the opening of Thomas Alva Edison's laboratory in Menlo Park, New Jersey, one of the first devoted to industrial research. Three years later, his team produced an incandescent lamp that burned for 13 hours. By 1882, the Edison Electric Light Company had launched its service in New York City's financial district. Electricity revolutionized both urban life and industry.

The second industrial revolution (1871–1914) proceeded at a pace that was not only unprecedented but also previously unimaginable. In 1865, the annual production of goods was valued at approximately $2 billion; by 1900, it stood at $13 billion, transforming the United States from fourth to first in the world in terms of productivity. Fostering major advances in manufacturing and technology, American industry had outstripped industry in its European rivals, Germany and Great Britain, and produced one-third of the world's goods.

Government at all levels, from municipal to federal, played important and multifaceted roles in this development. The U.S. Congress enacted steep tariffs to protect American manufacturers, and the federal government created new agencies to further technological development. In 1863 the National Academy of Sciences was founded as a consulting body, and in 1870 the U.S. patent office was reorganized to keep up with a rapidly growing number of applications.

A major force behind economic growth was the vast transcontinental railroad, completed in 1869. The addition of three more major rail lines (the Southern Pacific, the Northern Pacific, and the Atchison, Topeka, and Santa Fe) in the early 1880s, and of the Great Northern, a decade later, completed the most extensive transportation network in the world. As the nation's first big business and recipient of generous government subsidies, railroads linked cities in every state and served as nationwide distributors of goods. Freight trains carried the bountiful natural resources, such as iron, coal, and minerals, that supplied the raw materials for industry, as well as food and other commodities for the growing urban populations. (See Map 19.1.)

No factor was more important in promoting economic growth than the application of new technologies to increase the productivity of labor and the volume of goods. Machines, factory managers, and workers together created a system of continuous production by which more could be made—and faster—than

Map 19.1 PATTERNS OF INDUSTRY, 1900

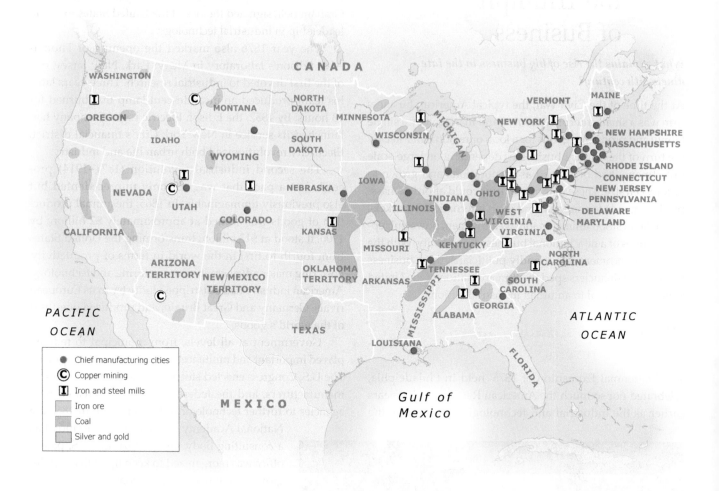

Industrial manufacturing concentrated in the Northeast and Midwest, whereas the raw materials for production came mostly from other parts of the nation.

anywhere else on earth. Higher productivity depended not only on machinery and technology but also on economies of scale and speed, reorganization of factory labor and business management, and the unparalleled growth of a market for goods of all kinds.

New systems of mass production replaced wasteful and often chaotic practices and speeded up the delivery of finished goods. In the 1860s, meatpackers set up one of the earliest production lines. Sometimes the invention of a single machine could instantly transform production, mechanizing every stage from processing the raw material to packaging the product. The cigarette-making machine, patented in 1881, could produce more than 7,000 cigarettes per hour, replacing the worker who at best made 3,000 per day. After a few more improvements, 15 machines could meet the total demand for American cigarettes. Within a generation, continuous production—the assembly line—became standard in most areas of manufacturing, thus revolutionizing the making of furniture, cloth, grain products, soap, and canned goods; the

refining, distilling, and processing of animal and vegetable fats; and eventually, the manufacture of automobiles.

19.1.2 Expanding the Market for Goods

To distribute the growing volume of goods and to create a dependable market, businesses demanded new techniques of merchandising on a national and, in some cases, an international scale. For generations, legions of sellers, or "drummers," had worked their routes, pushing goods, especially hardware and patent medicines, to individual buyers and local retail stores. After the Civil War, mail-order houses, which accompanied the consolidation of the railroad lines and the expansion of the postal system, helped to get new products to consumers.

Growing directly out of these services, the successful Chicago-based mail-orderhouses drew rural and urban consumers into a common marketplace. Sears, Roebuck and

Company and Montgomery Ward became huge businesses
by offering an enormous variety of goods, from shoes to
buggies to gasoline stoves and cream separators. By the end
of the century, Montgomery Ward's catalog had grown to
nearly 1,000 pages.

Chain stores achieved similar economies of scale. By
1900, a half-dozen grocery chains had sprung up. Frank and
Charles Woolworth, for example, offered inexpensive variety goods in five-and-ten-cent stores. Other chains selling
drugs, costume jewelry, shoes, cigars, and furniture soon
appeared, offering a greater selection of goods and lower
prices than the small, independent stores.

Opening shortly after the Civil War, department
stores began to take up much of the business formerly
enjoyed by specialty shops, offering a spectrum of services that included restaurants, restrooms, ticket agencies, nurseries, reading rooms, and post offices. Elegantly
appointed with imported carpets, sweeping marble
staircases, and crystal chandeliers, the department store
raised retailing to new heights. By the close of the century, the names of Marshall Field of Chicago, Filene's of
Boston, The Emporium of San Francisco, Wanamaker's of
Philadelphia, and Macy's of New York came to represent
the splendors of those great cities as well as the apex of
mass retailing.

Advertising lured customers to the department
stores, the chains, and the independent neighborhood
stores. The advertising revolution began in 1869, when
Francis Wayland Ayer founded the earliest advertising
agency. In Chicago, the mail-order firms hired scores
of copywriters and commercial artists to produce their
illustrated catalogs. With the help of this new sales tool,
gross revenues of retailers raced upward from $8 million
in 1860 to $102 million in 1900.

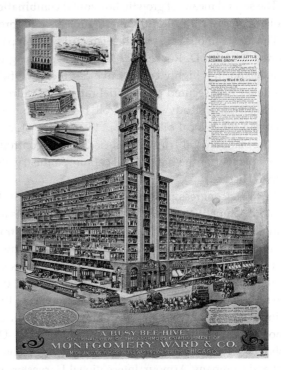

MONTGOMERY WARD BUILDING Montgomery Ward & Company
was founded in 1872 by Aaron Montgomery Ward as a dry-goods
mail order business with the commercial goal of getting thousands
of products to rural customers. By 1903, the company's catalog listed
more than 10,000 items for sale and delivery. To handle distribution,
a 1.25 million-square foot warehouse opened in Chicago in 1908.

19.1.3 Integration, Combination, and Merger

The business community sought to enlarge their commercial empires by gaining greater control over the economy.
From sourcing raw materials and managing workers to

influencing public opinion, business leaders acted forcefully. The shrewdest and most successful among them took advantage of economic cycles alternating between rapid growth and sharp decline by consolidating their enterprises. Major economic setbacks in 1873 and in 1893 wiped out weaker competitors, allowing the strongest firms to rebound swiftly and to expand their scale of operation during the recovery period.

Businesses grew in two distinct, if overlapping, ways. Through **vertical integration**, a firm gained control of production at every step of the way—from raw materials through processing to the transporting and merchandising of the finished items. In 1899, the United Fruit Company began to build a network of wholesale houses in the United States, and within two years it had opened distribution centers in 21 major cities. Eventually, it controlled an elaborate system of Central American plantations and temperature-controlled shipping and storage facilities for its highly perishable bananas.

The second means of growth, **horizontal combination**, entailed gaining control of the market for a single product. The most famous case was the Standard Oil Company, founded by John D. Rockefeller in 1870. Operating out of Cleveland in a highly competitive but lucrative field, Rockefeller first secured preferential rates from railroads eager to ensure a steady supply of oil. He then convinced or coerced other local oil operators to sell their stock to him. The Standard Oil Trust, established in 1882, controlled over 90 percent of the nation's oil-refining industry. (See SEEING History.)

In 1890, Congress passed the Sherman Antitrust Act to restore competition by encouraging small business and outlawing "every . . . combination . . . in restraint of trade or commerce." Ironically, the courts interpreted the law in ways that inhibited the organization of trade unions and actually helped the consolidation of business. More than 2,600 firms vanished between 1898 and 1902 alone. By 1910, the industrial giants that would dominate the American economy until the last half of the twentieth century—U.S. Rubber, Goodyear, General Electric, Westinghouse, Nabisco, Swift and Company, Armour, International Harvester, and Eastman Kodak—had already formed.

19.1.4 The Gospel of Wealth

Several leaders of industry promoted a philosophy that justified their unprecedented wealth and specified their duty to the growing number of Americans less fortunate then themselves. Ninety percent of them were Protestant, and the majority attended church services regularly. They attributed their personal success to hard work and perseverance, and made these the principal tenets of a new faith that imbued the pursuit of wealth with old-time religious zeal.

One version of this **gospel of wealth** justified the ruthless behavior of the entrepreneurs who accumulated wealth and power even through shady deals and conspiracies. Speculator Jay Gould, known in the popular press as the "Worst Man in the World," wrung his fortune, it was widely alleged, from the labor of others. Through a series of unsavory financial maneuvers, Gould rose quickly from his modest origins to become one of the richest men of the era.

Speculation in railroads proved to be Gould's forte. He took over the Erie Railroad, paying off New York legislators to get the state to finance its expansion, and he acquired the U.S. Express Company by pressuring and tricking its stockholders. When threatened with arrest, Gould sold off his shares for $9 million and moved on to the Union Pacific, where he cut wages, precipitated strikes, and manipulated elections in the western and Plains states. Tired of being caricatured in the press as a great swindler, he bought the leading newspapers and directed their editorial policy in his favor. At his death, one obituary described Jay Gould as "an incarnation of cupidity and sordidness."

Andrew Carnegie—the "Richest Man in the World"—offered a strikingly different model. A poor immigrant from Scotland, he set himself to learn about business by working in textile mills and then, during the Civil War, the railroad industry. By 1900, he had built an empire in steel, undercutting his competitors by using the latest technology and designing his own system of cost analysis. The most efficient in the world, Carnegie's steel mills accounted for one-third of the nation's total output of steel and operated as a model of vertical integration.

Carnegie was well known as a civic leader. From one point of view, he was a factory despot who underpaid his employees and ruthlessly managed their working conditions. But to the patrons of the public libraries, art museums, concert halls, colleges, and universities that he funded, Carnegie appeared to be the single greatest philanthropist of the age. Late in his life, he outlined his personal philosophy of altruism in a popular essay, *The Gospel of Wealth* (1889), explaining that, "there is no genuine, praiseworthy success in life if you are not honest, truthful, and fair-dealing." By the time he died, he had given away his massive personal fortune.

Whether following the rough road of Gould or the smooth path of Carnegie, the business community fashioned a new conservative ideology that became known as Social Darwinism. Grafted onto the biological theory of evolution propounded by the famed British naturalist Charles Darwin, social Darwinism raised the principle of the "survival of the fittest" as an ideal for modern society and as a rationale for free enterprise. In 1883, the Yale professor William Graham Sumner published an essay entitled *What Social Classes Owe to Each Other*, wherein he argued

SEEING History

The Standard Oil Company

John D. Rockefeller, who formed the Standard Oil Company in 1870, sought to control all aspects of the industry, from the transportation of crude oil to the marketing and distribution of the final products. By the end of the decade, after making shrewd deals with the railroads and underselling his rivals, he managed to control 90 percent of the oil-refining industry. To further consolidate his interests, in 1882 Rockefeller created the Standard Oil Trust, which, by integrating both vertically and horizontally, became a model for other corporations and an inspiration for critical commentary and antitrust legislation.

Rockefeller's best-known critic was Ida Tarbell. In 1904, she published *The History of the Standard Oil Company*, first in serial form in the popular *McClure's Magazine* and later as a book. Tarbell's muckraking exposé attracted a great deal of attention. Even more popular were political cartoons depicting Rockefeller's stranglehold on the entire oil industry. *Puck* magazine, which was founded in 1871 by Joseph Keppler, an immigrant from Austria, held up Rockefeller and his company to ridicule. This cartoon, published in *Puck* in 1904, shows Standard Oil as a sinister octopus, wrapping its arms around the White House and Congress as well as workers and even the denizens of Wall Street. In 1911, in response to an antitrust suit, the Supreme Court ordered the company to break up. The modern corporations Exxon, Mobil, and Chevron (some of which have merged) all descended from Rockefeller's Standard Oil.

- **What does this cartoon tell us about Rockefeller's reputation at the turn of the twentieth century?**

- **What does it suggest about Americans' feelings regarding the trusts?**

STANDARD OIL OCTOPUS

Library of Congress (Photoduplication).

that only a few individuals possessed the moral fiber and intelligence to drive the emerging industrial economy and, therefore, that they should be unrestrained in their pursuit of great fortunes. In contrast, the vast majority, too lazy or profligate to rise above poverty, deserved their own miserable fates. To tamper with this "natural" order by establishing welfare programs to help the poor or redistributing wealth in any way would be hazardous to society. Meanwhile, the popular writer Horatio Alger produced a more temperate version of this credo. Publishing more than 100 rags-to-riches novels, he created heroes who managed to rise out of poverty by both hard work and luck, and to ultimately acquire, if not vast wealth, middle-class respectability and comfort.

19.2 Labor in the Age of Big Business

How did American workers respond to the changing economic conditions of the late nineteenth century?

Like the gospel of wealth, the "gospel of work" affirmed the dignity of production and the importance of individual initiative. But unlike business leaders, the philosophers of American working people did not believe in riches as the proof of civic virtue or in the lust for power as the driving force of progress. On the contrary, they favored cooperation and contended that a hard day's work should be the badge of all respectable citizens.

Behind the "gospel of work" stood the reality of the second industrial revolution. Increasingly, Americans made their livelihoods by working not in small shops but in increasingly large and mechanized factories. Rather than learning the traditional methods of production, they saw their authority over the process slip away. In return for their labor, they earned wages. By the end of the nineteenth century, big business thus found its mirror image in a labor movement spawned by the consolidation of the wage system.

19.2.1 The Wage System

The accelerating growth of industry, especially the steady mechanization of production, dramatically changed employer/employee relations and created new categories of workers. Both in turn fostered competition among workers, particularly between native-born workers and the growing number from outside the United States. Moreover, where once working for wages served to prepare apprentices, journeymen, and even farm workers and domestic servants for owning and managing their own shops, farms, or households, now the desired path to independence often ended where it began. By 1870, nearly two-thirds of all productive Americans worked for wages and would continue to do so for their entire working lives.

For most craft workers, the new system destroyed longstanding practices and chipped away at their customary autonomy. Managers constantly supervised workers and set the pace of production and rate of payment. In addition, new, faster machinery made many skills obsolete. In the woodworking trades, highly skilled cabinetmakers, who for generations had brought their own tools to the factory, were largely replaced with "green hands"—immigrants, including many women—who with only minimal training and close supervision could operate new woodworking machines at cheaper rates of pay.

Not all trades conformed to this pattern. The garment industry, for example, grew at a very fast pace in New York, Boston, Chicago, Philadelphia, Cleveland, and St. Louis, but retained older systems of labor along with the new. The highly mechanized factories employed hundreds of thousands of young immigrant women, while the outwork system, established well before the Civil War, contracted ever-larger numbers of families to work in their homes on

WOMEN ASSEMBLY LINE WORKERS
John Henry Patterson formed National Cash Register Company in 1884 and became the leading manufacturer of mechanical cash registers, at more than 110,000 per year, by the end of the century. As an employer, he was known for his paternalistic programs for workers, many of whom were women. He provided chairs with backs to relieve stress, for example, as well as hot lunches, indoor toilets, and a ventilator system to clean the air.

Everett Collection Historical/Alamy Stock Photo.

sewing machines or by hand. Paid by the piece—a seam stitched, a collar turned, a button attached—workers in this "sweating" system labored faster and longer to forestall a dip in wages.

For women, industrial expansion offered new opportunities to work outside the home, and many young native-born women fled the family farm for cities where manufacturing thrived. African American and immigrant women found employment in trades least affected by technological advances, such as domestic service. In contrast, English-speaking white women moved into the better-paying clerical and retail positions in the rapidly expanding business sector. After the typewriter and telephone came into widespread use in the 1890s, the number of women employed in office work rose even faster. At the turn of the century, 8.6 million women worked outside their homes—nearly triple the number in 1870.

In contrast, African American men found themselves excluded from many fields. In Cleveland, for example, the number of black carpenters declined after 1870, just as the number of construction jobs grew. African American men were also systematically driven from restaurant service and barred from newer trades such as boilermaking, plumbing, electrical work, and paperhanging, which European immigrants secured for themselves.

Discriminatory or exclusionary practices fell hardest on workers recruited earlier from China. From the 1860s on, many Chinese established laundries and restaurants in West Coast cities, where they were viewed as potential competitors by both white workers and small business owners. A potent and racist anti-Chinese movement organized to protest "cheap" Chinese labor and to demand a halt to Chinese immigration. During the nationwide depression of the 1870s, white rioters razed Chinese neighborhoods and insistently called for deportation measures. The 1882 **Chinese Exclusion Act** created a 10-year moratorium on the immigration of Chinese laborers and for the first time denied entry to the United States based on race or ethnicity.

For even the best-placed wage earners, the new workplace could be unhealthy, even dangerous. Meatpacking produced its own hazards—the dampness of the pickling room, the sharp blade of the slaughtering knife, and the noxious odors of the fertilizer department. With few effective government regulations in place, factory owners often failed to mark high-voltage wires, locked fire doors, and allowed the emission of toxic fumes. Moreover, machines ran faster in American factories than anywhere else in the world, and workers who could not keep up or suffered serious injury found themselves without a job.

Even under less hazardous conditions, workers complained about the tedium of performing repetitive tasks

for many hours each day. Although federal employees had been granted the eight-hour day in 1868, most workers still toiled upward of 10 to 12 hours for six days a week. Nor could glamour be found in the work of saleswomen in the elegant department stores. Clerks could not sit down, despite workdays as long as 16 hours in the busy season, or hold "unnecessary conversations" with customers or other clerks. Despite these disadvantages, most women preferred sales and manufacturing jobs to domestic service, which required live-in servants to be on call seven days a week.

Moreover, steady employment was rare. Between 1866 and 1897, 14 years of prosperity stood against 17 years of hard times. The major depressions of 1873–1879 and 1893–1897 were the worst in the nation's history up to that time. Three "minor" recessions (1866–1867, 1883–1885, and 1890–1891) did not seem insignificant to the millions who lost their jobs.

THE DENVER RIOT The Denver Riot of 1880 was one of more than 150 anti-Chinese riots in the American West in the 1870s and 1880s. The mob depicted here, which numbered more than 3,000, attacked Chinese residents and destroyed their businesses and homes. The mob beat to death Sing Lee, who operated a laundry.

Library of Congress.

19.2.2 The Knights of Labor

The Noble and Holy Order of the **Knights of Labor**, founded by a group of Philadelphia garment cutters in 1869, grew to become the largest labor organization in the nineteenth century. Led by Grand Master Workman Terence V. Powderly, the order sought to bring together wage earners, regardless of skill. The Knights endorsed a variety of reform measures—the restriction of child labor, a graduated income tax, more land set aside for homesteading, the abolition of contract labor, and monetary reform—to offset the power of the industrialists. They believed that the "producing classes," once freed from the grip of corporate monopoly and the curses of ignorance and alcohol, would transform the United States into a genuinely democratic society. The Knights insisted that "labor creates all wealth" and all wealth "belongs to those who create it."

The Knights sought to overturn the wage system and, as an alternative to capitalist production, they promoted producers' cooperatives. In these factories, workers collectively made all decisions on prices charged for goods and shared all the profits. Local assemblies launched thousands of small coops, such as the Our Girls Co-operative Manufacturing Company, which a group of Chicago seamstresses established in the 1880s. Successful for a time, most cooperatives could not compete against the heavily capitalized enterprises and ultimately failed.

For women, the Knights of Labor created a special department within the organization "to investigate the abuses to which our sex is subjected by unscrupulous employers, to agitate the principles which our Order teaches of equal pay for equal work and the abolition of child labor." At the 1886 convention, delegates approved this plan, and Grand Master Powderly appointed knit-goods worker Leonora M. Barry general investigator. With perhaps 65,000 women members at its peak, the Knights ran daycare centers and occasionally even set up cooperative kitchens to reduce the drudgery of cooking.

The Knights reached their peak in 1886 during the great campaign for a shorter workday. The organization grew from a few thousand in 1880 to more than 700,000 six years later. The Knights welcomed workers usually excluded by other unions. Nearly 3,000 women formed their own "ladies assemblies" or joined mixed locals. The Knights also organized African American workers—20,000-30,000 nationally—mainly in separate assemblies within the organization. Chinese workers, however, were barred from membership.

The Haymarket affair in Chicago, where the Knights were headquartered, virtually crushed the organization. Local employers' associations successfully pooled funds to rid their factories of troublesome organizers. By 1890, membership had declined to below 100,000. The wage system had triumphed.

19.2.3 The American Federation of Labor

The events of 1886 also signaled the rise of a very different kind of organization, the **American Federation of Labor (AFL)**. Unlike the Knights, the AFL accepted the wage system. Following a strategy of "pure and simple unionism," the AFL sought recognition of its union status to bargain with employers for better working conditions, higher

WOMEN DELEGATES AT THE GENERAL ASSEMBLY OF THE KNIGHTS OF LABOR
At the 1886 General Assembly of the Knights of Labor, which met in Richmond, Virginia, 16 women attended as delegates. Elizabeth Rodgers, the first woman in Chicago to join the Knights and the first woman to serve as a master workman in a district assembly, attended with her two-week-old daughter. The convention established a Department of Women's Work and appointed Leonora M. Barry, a hosiery worker, as general investigator.

Bettmann/Getty Images.

Communities *in* Conflict

Regulating the Conditions and Limiting the Hours of Labor in the State of Illinois

"No child under fourteen years of age shall be employed in any manufacturing establishment."

In the late 1880s, labor unions continued the shorter-hours movement spearheaded by the Knights of Labor and campaigned for legislation to limit hours and regulate working conditions. Reformer Florence Kelley drafted legislation that focused on the women and children who worked in sweatshops throughout Chicago. The state legislature passed this bill over the strong opposition of employers and appointed Kelley the first factory inspector in the state of Illinois. However, in 1895 the Illinois Supreme Court declared the eight-hour provision of the law unconstitutional.

- **Why did the Illinois Supreme Court reject Kelley's argument for limiting the hours of work for women?**

Florence Kelley's Proposal for the Illinois Factory and Workshop Inspection Act, 1893

AN ACT to regulate the employment of women and children in manufacturing establishments, factories and workshops, and to provide for the appointment of inspectors to enforce the same.

SECTION 1. No minor under eighteen years of age, and no woman shall be employed in any factory or workshop more than eight hours in any one day or forty-eight hours in any one week.

SEC. 2. No process of making or finishing, altering or repairing for sale any coats, vests, trousers, overcoats, or any wearing apparel of any description whatsoever, intended for sale, shall be carried on in any dwelling by any woman or by any child under sixteen years of age.

SEC. 3. No child under fourteen years of age shall be employed in any manufacturing establishment, factory or workshop within this state. It shall be the duty of every person, firm, corporation, agent or manager of any corporation employing children to keep a register in which shall be recorded the name, birthplace, age and place of residence of every person employed by him, her or them, under the age of sixteen years; and it shall be unlawful for any person, firm or corporation to hire or employ in any manufacturing establishment, factory or workshop any child over the age of fourteen years and under the age of sixteen years, unless there is first provided and placed on file an affidavit made by the parent or guardian stating the age, date and place of birth of said child: if said child have no parent or guardian, then such affidavit shall be made by the child, which affidavit shall be kept on file by the employer and which said register and affidavit shall be produced for inspection on demand by the inspector, assistant inspector or any of the deputies appointed under this act. The factory inspector, assistant inspector and deputy inspectors shall have power to demand a certificate of physical fitness from some regular physician of good standing in the case of children who may appear to him or her physically unable to perform the labor at which they may be engaged, and shall have power to prohibit the employment of any minor that cannot obtain such a certificate.

SEC. 4. Every person, firm, or corporation, agent or manager of a corporation employing any woman or minor under the age of eighteen years in any manufacturing establishment, factory or workshop, shall post, and keep posted, in a conspicuous place in every room where such help is employed, a printed notice stating the hours for each day of the week between which work is required of such persons, and in every room where children under sixteen years of age are employed, a list of their names with their ages.

SEC. 5. No child, under the age of sixteen years and over fourteen years of age, shall be employed in any manufacturing establishment, factory or workshop, who cannot read or write simple sentences in the English language, except during the vacation of the public schools in the city where such minor lives. . . .

Source: *Report and Findings of the Joint Committee to Investigate the "Sweat Shop" System* (1893), pp. 139–140.

Factory Act Declared Unconstitutional: Opinion of Supreme Court of Illinois, March 18, 1895

It is not the nature of the things done, but the sex of the person doing them, which is made the basis of the claim that the act is a measure for the promotion of the public health. It is sought to sustain the act as an exercise of the police power upon the alleged ground that it is designed to protect woman on account of her sex and physique. It will not be denied that woman is entitled to the same rights, under the Constitution, to make contracts with reference to her labor as are secured thereby to men. The first section of the fourteenth amendment to the Constitution of the United States provides: "No State shall make or enforce any law which shall abridge the privileges or immunities of citizens of the United States, nor shall any State deprive *any person* of life, liberty or property without due process of law, nor deny to any person within its jurisdiction the equal protection of the law."

It has been held that a woman is both a "citizen" and a "person" within the meaning of this section. . . . The privileges and immunities here referred to are in general, Protection by the government, with the right to acquire and possess property of every kind, and to pursue and obtain happiness and safety, subject, nevertheless, to such restraints as the government may prescribe for the general good of the whole. . . ." As a citizen, woman has the right to acquire and possess property of every kind. As a "person" she has the right to claim the benefit of the constitutional provision that she shall not be deprived of life, liberty or property without due process of law. Involved in these rights thus guaranteed to her is the right to make and enforce contracts. The law accords to her, as to every other citizen, the right to gain a livelihood by intelligence, honesty and industry in the arts, the sciences, the professions, or other vocations. Before the law, her right to a choice of vocations cannot be said to be denied or abridged on account of sex. . . .

Source: *Third Annual Report of the Factory Inspectors of the State of Illinois for the Year Ending, December 15, 1895*, Appendix A. Springfield: State of Illinois, 1896.

wages, and shorter hours. In return, it offered compliant firms the benefit of amenable day-to-day relations with the most highly skilled wage earners. Only if companies refused to bargain in good faith would union members resort to strikes.

The new federation, with 12 national unions and 140,000 affiliated members in 1886, rapidly pushed ahead of the rival Knights by organizing craft workers. AFL president Samuel Gompers disregarded unskilled workers, racial minorities, and immigrants, believing they were impossible to organize and even unworthy of membership. He also believed in the "family wage," a wage paid to a male household head and sufficient to keep women and children at home and out of the factories. Women, Gompers insisted, did not belong in the workforce, where they served only to lower wages.

While Gompers advanced the interests of the "aristocrats of labor," the rank and file often pursued broader aims. Chicago's Central Labor Federation, for example, worked closely with urban reformers. Finding allies among women's clubs and church groups, within the state legislature, and even among some socially minded members of the business community, they cultivated an atmosphere of civic responsibility. The Illinois Factory Investigation Act of 1893 offered evidence of their hard work and patience: Under its terms, unionists secured funds from the state legislature to monitor working conditions and, particularly, to improve the terrible conditions under which women and children worked in sweatshops. (See Communities *in* Conflict.)

Although the AFL represented only a small minority of working Americans—about 10 percent at the end of the century—local unions often played important roles in their communities. They may not have been able to slow the steady advance of mass production, but AFL members managed to make their presence felt. Local politicians courted their votes, and Labor Day, first celebrated in the 1880s, became a national holiday in 1894.

19.3 The New South

Who benefited the most from economic developments in the post-Reconstruction South? Why?

Physically and financially devastated by the Civil War, the South remained economically stagnant, its per capita wealth only 27 percent of that of the northeastern states. While a few urban centers moved very slowly into the era of modern industry, the countryside receded into greater isolation and poverty. The southern economy in general was held back by dependence on northern finance capital, continued reliance on cotton production, and the legacy of slavery.

19.3.1 An Internal Colony

In the 1870s, a vocal and powerful new group of Southerners headed by Henry Woodfin Grady, editor of the *Atlanta Constitution*, insisted that the region enjoyed a great potential in its abundant natural resources of coal, iron, turpentine, tobacco, and lumber. Grady and his peers envisioned a "New South" where modern textile mills operated efficiently and profitably, close to the sources of raw goods, the expansive fields of cotton, and a plentiful and cheap supply of labor, unrestricted by unions or by legal limitations on the employment of children. Arguing against those planters who hoped to rejuvenate the agricultural economy by cultivating a few staple crops, this group forcefully promoted industrial development and welcomed northern investors.

Northern investors secured huge concessions from southern state legislatures, including land, forest, and mineral rights and large tax exemptions. Exploiting the incentives, railroad companies laid more than 22,000 miles of new track, connecting the region to national markets and creating new cities. By 1890, a score of large railroad companies, centered mainly in New York, owned more than half of all the track in the South.

Northerners also employed various means to protect their investments from southern competition. By the late

1870s, southern merchants, with help from foreign investors, had begun to run iron factories around Birmingham, Alabama. Southern iron production was soon encroaching on the northeastern market. To stave off this competition, Andrew Carnegie ordered the railroads to charge higher freight fees to Birmingham's iron producers. After the turn of the century, the U.S. Steel Corporation simply bought out the local merchants and took over much of Birmingham's production.

The production of cotton textiles followed a similar course. Powerful merchants and large landowners, realizing that they could make high profits by controlling the cotton crop from field to factory, promoted the vertical integration of the cotton industry. The number of mills in the South grew from 161 in 1880 to 400 in 1900. Southern investors supplied large amounts of the capital for the industrial expansion and technological improvements. The South boasted the first factory fully equipped with electricity. Recognizing the potential for great profit, many New England mill owners moved their operations to the South. By the 1920s, northern investors held much of the South's wealth, including the major textile mills, but returned through employment or social services only a small share of the profits to the region's people.

Beyond iron or steel and textiles, southern industry remained largely extractive and, like the South itself, rural. For the most part, southern enterprises mainly produced raw materials for consumption or use in the North, thereby perpetuating the economic imbalance between the sections.

The governing role of capital investments from outside the region buttressed long-standing relationships. Even rapid industrialization—in iron, railroads, and textiles—did not carry the same consequences engendered in the North. The rise of the New South reinforced, rather than diminished, the region's status as the nation's internal colony.

19.3.2 Southern Labor

The advance of southern industry did little to improve the working lives of most African Americans, who made up more than one-third of the region's population. Although the majority continued to work in agriculture, large numbers found jobs in industries such as the railroad. In booming cities like Atlanta, they even gained skilled positions as bricklayers, carpenters, and painters. For the most part, however, African Americans were limited to unskilled, low-paying jobs. Nearly all African American women and girls who earned wages did so as household workers.

Only at rare moments did southern workers unite across racial lines. In the 1880s, the Knights of Labor briefly organized both black and white workers. But when white politicians and local newspapers began to raise the specter of black domination, the Knights retreated. Across the region, their assemblies collapsed. Other unions remained the exclusive preserve of white workers. In 1897, in an Atlanta mill, 1,400 white women operatives went on strike when the company proposed to hire two black spinners.

Wages throughout the South were low for both black and white workers. Southern textile workers' wages were barely half those of New Englanders. Black men's earnings

TOBACCO PROCESSING (1899)

The processing of raw tobacco employed thousands of African American women, who sorted, stripped, stemmed, and hung tobacco leaves as part of the redrying process. After mechanization was introduced, white women took jobs as cigarette rollers, but black women kept the worst, most monotonous jobs in the tobacco factories. The women shown in this photograph, taken in 1899 at the R. B. Williams Tobacco Company in Richmond, Virginia, are sorting tobacco.

Library of Congress (Photoduplication).

were at or below the poverty line of $300 per year, while black women rarely earned more than $120 and white women about $220 annually. The most poorly paid workers were children, the mainstay of southern mill labor.

As industry expanded throughout the nation, so, too, did the number of children earning wages. This was especially so in the South. In 1896, only one in twenty Massachusetts mill workers was younger than 16, but one in four North Carolina cotton mill operatives was that age or younger. Traditions rooted in the agricultural economy reinforced the practice of using the labor of all family members, even the very young. Seasonal labor, such as picking crops or grinding sugarcane, put families on the move, making formal education all but impossible. Not until well into the twentieth century did compulsory school attendance laws effectively restrict child labor in the South.

A system of convict labor also thrived in the South. African Americans constituted up to 90 percent of the convict workforce. Transported and housed like animals—chained together by day and confined in portable cages at night—these workers suffered high mortality rates. White politicians expressed pride in what they called the "good roads movement"—the chief use of convict labor—as proof of regional progress.

19.3.3 The Transformation of Piedmont Communities

The impact of modern industry was nowhere greater than in the Piedmont, the region extending from southern Virginia and the central Carolinas into northern Alabama and Georgia. After 1870, long-established farms and plantations gave way to railroad tracks, textile factories, numerous mill villages, and a few sizable cities. Once the South's backcountry, the Piedmont surpassed New England in the production of yarn and cloth to stand first in the world.

Rural poverty, intensified by declining prices for cotton, and the appeal of a new life encouraged many farm families to strike out for a mill town. Those with the least access to land and credit—mainly widows and their children, and single women—were the first to go into the mills. Then families sent their children. Some families worked in the mills on a seasonal basis, between planting and harvesting. But more and more people abandoned the countryside entirely for what they called "public work."

A typical mill community was made up of rows of single-family houses, a small school, several churches, a company-owned store, and the home of the superintendent, who governed everyone's affairs. It was not unknown for a superintendent to prowl the neighborhood to see which families burned their lanterns past nine o'clock at night and, finding a violator, to knock on the door and tell the offenders to go to bed. Millworkers frequently complained that they had no private life at all. A federal report

published shortly after the turn of the century affirmed: "Practically speaking, the company owns everything and controls everything, and to a large extent controls everybody in the mill village."

Mill owners also relied on schoolteachers and clergy to set the tone of community life. They hired and paid the salaries of Baptist and Methodist ministers to preach a faith encouraging workers to be thrifty, orderly, temperate, and hardworking. The schools, similarly subsidized by the company, reinforced the lesson of moral and social discipline required of industrial life and encouraged students to follow their parents into the mill. It was mainly young children between six and eight years old who attended school. When more hands were needed in the mill, superintendents plucked out those youngsters and sent them to join their older brothers and sisters, who were already at work.

Piedmont mill villages like Greenville, South Carolina, and Burlington, Charlotte, and Franklinville, North Carolina, developed a cohesive character typical of isolated rural communities. The new residents maintained many aspects of their agricultural pasts, tilling small gardens and keeping chickens, pigs, and even cows in their yards. They strengthened community ties through marriage. Within a few generations, most of the village residents had, according to one study, "some connection to each other, however distant, by marriage," blood, or both.

19.4 The Industrial City

How did cities grow as industrial centers in late-nineteenth-century America?

Before the Civil War, manufacturing had centered in the countryside, in new factory towns such as Lowell, Massachusetts, and Troy, New York. By the end of the nineteenth century, 90 percent of all manufacturing took place in cities. The metropolis stood at the center of the growing industrial economy, a magnet drawing raw material, capital, and labor, and a key distribution point for manufactured goods throughout the nation and worldwide. The industrial city became the home of nearly 20 million immigrants, mainly the so-called "new immigrants" from southern and eastern Europe, who hoped to escape famine, political upheaval, or religious persecution in their homelands or simply to make a better life for themselves and their families.

19.4.1 Populating the City

The population of cities grew at double the rate of the nation's population as a whole. In 1860, only 16 cities had more than 50,000 residents. By 1890, one-third of all Americans were city dwellers. Eleven cities claimed more than 250,000 people. (See Table 19.1.)

Table 19.1 A GROWING URBAN POPULATION

	1870	1880	1890	1900
U.S. population	35,558,000	50,156,000	62,947,000	75,995,000
Urban population	9,902,000	14,130,000	22,106,000	30,160,000
Percent urban	25.7	28.2	35.1	39.7
Percent rural	74.3	71.8	64.9	60.3

Note that during each decade, the U.S. population as a whole grew between 20 percent and 30 percent. Figures in the table have been rounded to the nearest thousand.

Source: From *The Gilded Age* edited by Charles W. Calhoun. © 1996. Reprinted by permission of Rowman & Littlefield.

Many newcomers to the nation's largest cities had migrated from rural communities within the United States. Between 1870 and 1910, an average of nearly 7,000 African Americans moved north each year, hoping to escape the poverty and oppression in the South and to find better-paying jobs. By the end of the century, nearly 80 percent of African Americans in the North lived in urban areas.

The major source of urban growth in the late nineteenth century was immigrants and their children. Most of those in the first wave of immigration, before the Civil War, had settled in the countryside. In contrast, the so-called new immigrants, who came primarily from eastern and southern Europe, populated the industrial cities. By the turn of the century, Chicago had more Germans than all but a few German cities and more Poles than most Polish cities; New York had more Italians than a handful of the largest Italian cities, and Boston had nearly as many Irish as Dublin. In almost every group except the Irish, men outnumbered women. (See Map 19.2.)

Like rural migrants, immigrants headed for the American city to take advantage of the expanding opportunities for employment. While many hoped to build a new home in the land of plenty, many others intended to work hard, save money, and return to their families in the Old Country. In the 1880s, for example, nearly half of all Italian, Greek, and Serbian men in the United States returned to their native lands. Others could not return to their homelands or did not wish to. Jews, for instance, had emigrated to escape persecution in Russia and Russian-dominated Polish and Romanian lands.

Of all groups, Jews had the most experience with urban life. Forbidden to own land in most parts of Europe and boxed into *shtetls* (villages), Jews had also formed thriving urban communities in Vilna (in then-Russia), Berlin, London, and Vienna. Many had worked in garment manufacturing—in London's East End, for example—and followed a path to American cities like New York, Rochester, Philadelphia, and Chicago, where the needle trades flourished.

Other groups, the majority coming from rural parts of Europe, sought out their kinfolk in American cities, where they could most easily find housing and employment. Bohemians settled largely in Chicago, Pittsburgh, and Cleveland. French Canadians emigrated from Québec and settled almost exclusively in New England and upper New York State. Cubans, themselves often first- or second-generation immigrants from Spain, moved to Ybor City, a section of Tampa, Florida, to work in cigar factories. Still other groups tended toward cities dominated by fishing, shoemaking, or even glassblowing, a craft carried directly from the Old Country. Italians, the most numerous among the new immigrants, settled mainly in northeastern cities, laying railroad track, excavating subways, and erecting buildings.

Resettlement in an American city did not necessarily mark the end of the immigrants' travels. Newcomers, both native-born and immigrants, moved frequently from one neighborhood to another and from one city to another. As manufacturing advanced outward from the city center, working populations followed. American cities experienced a total population turnover three or four times during each decade of the last half of the century.

19.4.2 The Urban Landscape

Faced with a population explosion and an unprecedented building boom, the cities encouraged the creation of many beautiful and useful structures, including commercial offices, sumptuous homes, and efficient public services. At the same time, open space decreased as builders leveled hills, filled ponds, and pulled down any farms or houses in the way. Factories often occupied the best sites, typically near waterways, where goods could be easily transported and chemical wastes dumped. City officials usually lacked any master plan, save the idea of endless expansion. In Chicago, however, the great fire of 1871 wiped out several square miles at the center and allowed a planned rebuilding as a modern city of tall, fireproof commercial buildings made of brick and terra cotta instead of wood.

The majority of the population, in Chicago and elsewhere, worked in dingy factories and lived in crowded **tenements**. A typical tenement sat on a lot 25 feet by 100 feet and rose to five stories. There were four families on each floor, each with three rooms. By 1890, New York's Lower East Side packed more than 700 people per acre into back-to-back buildings, producing one of the highest population densities in the world. In Chicago, tenements were scattered, typically located near work sites throughout the city.

At the other end of the social scale, Chicago's Michigan Avenue, New York's Fifth Avenue, St. Paul's Summit Avenue, and San Francisco's Nob Hill fairly gleamed with

Map 19.2 POPULATION OF FOREIGN BIRTH BY REGION, 1880

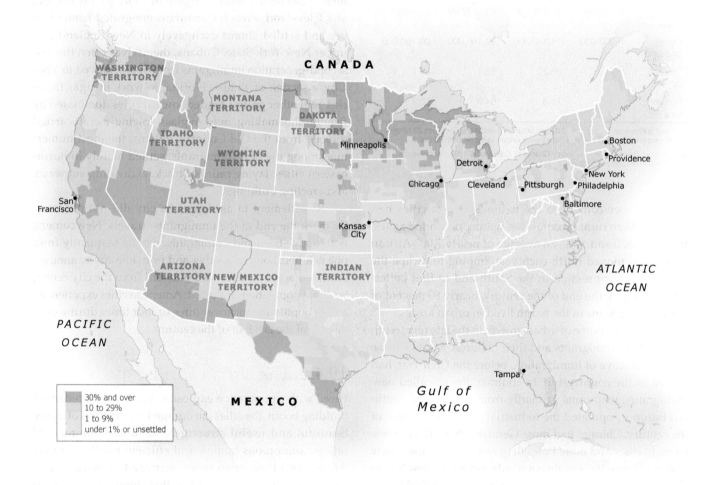

European immigrants after the Civil War settled primarily in the industrial districts of the northern Midwest and parts of the Northeast. French Canadians continued to settle in Maine, Cubans in Florida, and Mexicans in the Southwest, where earlier immigrants had established thriving communities.

new mansions and townhouses. Commonwealth Avenue marked Boston's fashionable Back Bay district, built on a filled-in 450-acre tidal flat. State engineers planned this community, with its magnificent boulevard, uniform five-story brownstones, and back alleys designed for deliveries. Like wealthy neighborhoods in other cities, Back Bay also provided space for the city's magnificent public architecture: its stately public library, fine arts and science museums, and orchestra hall. Back Bay opened onto the Fenway Park system designed by the nation's premier landscape architect, Frederick Law Olmsted.

The industrial city established a new style of commercial and civic architecture. The era's talented architects fashioned hundreds of buildings from steel, sometimes

decorating them with elaborate wrought-iron facades. The office building could rise 7, 10, even 20 stories high, and with the invention of the safety elevator, people and goods could easily be moved vertically.

Architects played a key role in the late-nineteenth-century City Beautiful movement. Influenced by American wealth and the country's enhanced role in the global economy, they turned to the monumental or imperial style common in European cities, laying grand concrete boulevards at enormous public cost. New sports amphitheaters spread pride in a city's accomplishments. New schools, courthouses, capitol buildings, hospitals, and huge art galleries, museums, and concert halls promoted urban excitement as well as cultural uplift.

LITTLE ITALY Mulberry Bend in Lower Manhattan was home to more than 10,000 Italians in 1910. The photographer Jacob Riis described the poverty-stricken neighborhood as "the foul core of New York's slums."

World History Archive/Alamy Stock Photo.

The city inspired other architectural marvels. Opened in 1883, the Brooklyn Bridge won wide acclaim as the most original American construction. Designed by John Roebling and his son Washington Roebling, the bridge was considered an aesthetic and practical wonder. In Chicago, civil engineers managed to reverse the flow of the Chicago River so that its heavily polluted water ran not into Lake Michigan, the source of the city's drinking water, but westward into the Mississippi watershed.

Like the railroad, but on a smaller scale, streetcars and elevated railroads changed business dramatically, because they moved traffic of many different kinds—information, people, and goods—faster and farther than before. In 1902, New York opened its subway system, which would grow to become the largest in the nation.

19.4.3 The City and the Environment

By making it possible for a great number of workers to live in communities distant from their place of employment, mass transportation allowed the metropolitan region to grow dramatically. Suburbs sprang up outside the major cities, offering many professional workers quiet residential retreats from the city's busy and increasingly polluted downtown.

Electric trolleys eliminated the tons of waste from horsecars that had for decades fouled city streets. The new rail systems also increased congestion and created new safety hazards for pedestrians. During the 1890s, 600 people were killed each year by Chicago's trains. Elevated trains, designed to avoid these problems, placed entire communities under the shadow of noisy and rickety wooden platforms.

Modern water and sewer systems constituted a hidden city of pipes and wires, mirroring the growth of the visible city aboveground. These advances, which brought indoor plumbing to most homes, did not, however, eradicate serious environmental or health problems. Most cities continued to unload sewage into nearby bodies of water. Rather than outlawing upriver dumping by factories, most municipal governments established separate clean-water systems through the use of reservoirs.

The unrestricted burning of coal to fuel the railroads and to heat factories and homes after 1880 greatly intensified urban air pollution. Noise levels continued to rise in the most compacted living and industrial areas. Overcrowded conditions and inadequate sanitary facilities bred tuberculosis, smallpox, and scarlet fever, among other contagious diseases. Only after the turn of the century, amid an intensive campaign against municipal corruption, did laws and administrative practices address the serious problems of public health.

Meanwhile, the distance between the city and the countryside narrowed. Naturalists had hoped for large open spaces—a buffer zone—to preserve farmland and wild areas, protect future water supplies, and diminish regional air pollution. But soon the industrial landscape invaded the countryside. Nearby rural lands not destined for private housing or commercial development became sites for water treatment and sewage plants, garbage dumps, and graveyards—services essential to the city's growing population.

THE BOWERY AT NIGHT In his watercolor *The Bowery at Night*, painted in 1895, W. Louis Sonntag, Jr., shows a New York City scene transformed by electric light. Electricity transformed the city in other ways as well, as seen in the electric streetcars and the elevated railroad.

The Museum of the City of New York/Art Resource, NY.

19.5 The Rise of Consumer Society

What accounts for the rise of a consumer society and how did various groups participate in its development?

The growth of industry and the spread of cities promoted—and depended on—the consumption of mass-produced goods. During the final third of the nineteenth century, the standard of living climbed, although unevenly and erratically. Real wages (pay in relation to the cost of living) rose, fostering improvements in nutrition, clothing, and housing. Meanwhile, prices dropped. More and cheaper products came into the reach of all but the very poor. Although many Americans continued to acknowledge the moral value of hard work, thrift, and self-sacrifice, the explosion of consumer goods and services promoted sweeping changes in behavior and beliefs, although in vastly and increasingly different ways.

19.5.1 "Conspicuous Consumption"

Labeled the **Gilded Age** by humorist and social critic Mark Twain, the era following the Civil War favored the growth of a new business class that pursued both money and leisure and formed national networks to consolidate its power. Business leaders built diverse stock portfolios and often served simultaneously on the boards of several corporations. Similarly, they intertwined their interests by joining the same religious, charitable, athletic, and professional societies. Their wives and children vacationed together in sumptuous new seashore and mountain resorts, while they themselves made deals in exclusive social clubs and on suburban golf links. Just as R.G. Dun and Company ranked the leading corporations, the Social Register identified the families that controlled most of the nation's wealth.

According to economist and social critic Thorstein Veblen, the rich had created a new style of **conspicuous consumption**, the public display of their wealth and status through luxury goods and services. The Chicago mansion of real estate tycoon Potter Palmer, for example, was constructed without exterior doorknobs. Not only could no one enter uninvited, but a visitor's calling card supposedly passed through the hands of 27 servants before admittance was allowed. A vice president of the Chicago & Northwestern Railroad, Perry J. Smith built his marble palace in the style of the Greek Renaissance. Its ebony staircase was trimmed in gold, its butler's pantry equipped with faucets not only for hot and cold water, but also for iced champagne. The women who oversaw these elaborate households served as measures of their husbands' status, according to Veblen, by adorning themselves in jewels, furs, and dresses of the latest Paris design.

Toward the end of the century, the wealthy added a dramatic dimension to the "high life." Families occasionally hosted dinner parties for their dogs or pet monkeys, dressing the animals in fancy outfits for the occasion. New York's Waldorf-Astoria hotel, which opened in 1893, incorporated the grandeur of European royalty but with an important difference. Because rich Americans wanted to be

LYNDHURST MANSION In 1838, the famed architect Alexander Jackson Davis designed this Gothic Revival mansion, which is situated along the banks of the Hudson River in Tarrytown, New York. In 1880, the wealthy railroad magnate Jay Gould purchased the property to be used as his summer home. Lyndhurst served as his country retreat until his death in 1892.

Philip Scalia/Alamy Stock Photo.

watched, the elegantly appointed corridors and restaurants were visible to the public through huge windows. The New York rich also established a unique custom to welcome the New Year: They opened wide the curtains of their Fifth Avenue mansions so that passersby could marvel at the elegant decor.

The wealthy became the leading patrons of the arts as well as the chief procurers of art treasures from Europe and Asia. They provided the bulk of funds for the new symphonies, operas, and ballet companies, which soon rivaled those of continental Europe.

19.5.2 Self-Improvement and the Middle Class

A new middle class, very different from its predecessor, formed during the last half of the century. The older middle class comprised the owners or superintendents of small businesses, doctors, lawyers, teachers, and ministers, and their families. The new middle class included these professionals but also the growing number of salaried employees—the managers, technicians, clerks, and engineers who worked in the complex web of corporations and government. They earned sufficient income to achieve a modest status in their communities and a home secure and comfortable for their families.

By the end of the century, many middle-class families were nestled in suburban retreats far from the noise, filth, and dangers of the city. This peaceful domestic setting, with its manicured lawns and well-placed shrubs, afforded both privacy and rejuvenation as well as the separation of business from leisure and of the breadwinner from his family for most of the day. Assisted by modern transportation systems,

men often traveled one to two hours each day, five or six days a week, to their city offices and back again. Women and children stayed behind.

Middle-class women devoted a large part of their day to care of the home. Improvements in the kitchen stove, such as the conversion from wood fuel to gas, saved a lot of time. Yet simultaneously, with the widespread circulation of cookbooks and recipes in newspapers and magazines, as well as the availability of new foods, the preparation of meals became more complex and time-consuming. New devices such as the eggbeater speeded up some familiar tasks, but the era's fancy culinary practices offset any gains in saving time. Similarly, the new carpet sweepers surpassed the broom in efficiency, but the fashionable high-napped carpeting demanded more care. Thus, rather than diminishing with technological innovation, household work expanded to fill the time available.

By the end of the century, middle-class women had added shopping to their list of household chores. They took charge of the household budget and purchased an ever-expanding range of machine-made goods, packaged foods, manufactured clothing, and personal luxuries. With the rise of department stores, which catered specifically to them, shopping combined work and pleasure and became a major pastime for women.

Almost exclusively white, Anglo-Saxon, and Protestant, the new middle class embraced "culture" not for purposes of conspicuous consumption but as a means of self-improvement. Whole families visited the new museums and art galleries. The middle class also provided the bulk of patrons for the new public libraries.

Middle-class families applied the same standards to their leisure activities. What one sporting-goods entrepreneur rightly called the "gospel of exercise" involved men and women engaged in calisthenics and outdoor activities, not so much for pleasure as for physical and mental discipline. Hiking was a favorite among both men and women. Soon men and women began camping out, with almost enough amenities to recreate a middle-class home in the woods. Roller-skating and ice-skating, which became crazes shortly after the Civil War, took place in specially designed rinks in almost every major town. By the 1890s, the "safety" bicycle had also been marketed. It replaced the large-wheel variety, which was difficult to keep upright. A good-quality "bike," like the piano, was a symbol of middle-class status. By 1895, Chicago's 33 cycle clubs boasted nearly 10,000 members.

Leisure became the special province of middle-class childhood. Removed from factories and shops and freed from many domestic chores, children enjoyed creative play and physical activity. The toy market boomed, and lower printing prices helped children's literature flourish. Uplifting classics such as *Little Women* and *Black Beauty* were popular.

19.5.3 Life in the Streets

Immigrants often weighed the material abundance they found in the United States against their memories of the Old Country. One could "live better" here, but only by working much harder. In letters home, immigrants described the riches of the new country but warned friends and relatives not to send weaklings, who would surely die of stress and strain amid the alien and intense commercialism of American society. Embittered German immigrants called their new land *Malhuerica*, "misfortune"; Jews called it *Ama Reka*, Hebrew for "without soul"; and Slavs referred to it as *Dollaryka*.

Many newcomers, having little choice about their place of residence, were concentrated in urban districts marked off by racial or ethnic lines. In the 1880s, Chinese San Franciscans, representing 10 percent of the city's population, crowded into a dozen blocks of restaurants, shops, and small factories known as Chinatown. In Los Angeles and San Antonio, Mexicans lived in distinctive barrios. In most cities, African American families were similarly compelled to remain in the dingiest, most crime-ridden, most dangerous sections of town.

The working-class home did not necessarily ensure privacy or offer protection from the dangers of the outside world. In the tenements, families often shared their rooms with other families or paying boarders. During the summer heat, adults, children, and boarders alike competed for a sleeping place on the fire escape or roof, and throughout the year, noise resounded through paper-thin walls.

Working-class women cared for their homes with their children's help but without the aid of new mechanical devices. In addition to cooking and cleaning, they often used their cramped domestic space for work that provided

NEW YORK SHOPGIRLS BUYING EASTER BONNETS Many women, including Christian shopgirls, celebrated the end of Lent and Easter by buying new outfits and fashionable broad-brimmed hats to wear to church services and the gala Easter Parade that followed. By 1890 dry-goods merchants and milliners advertised long lists of bonnets especially made for the occasion. From 1880 to 1950, the Easter Parade along Fifth Avenue in New York was a major event attracting thousands of participants and observers.

Science History Images/Alamy Stock Photo.

a small income. They gathered their children—and their husbands after a hard day's labor—to sew garments, wrap cigars, string beads, or paint vases for a contractor who paid them by the piece. And they cooked and cleaned for the boarders whose rent supplemented the family income.

Despite working people's slim resources, their combined buying power created new and important markets for consumer goods. Several leading clothing manufacturers specialized in inexpensive ready-to-wear items, usually copied from patterns designed for wealthier consumers but constructed hastily from flimsy materials. Patent medicines for ailments caused by working long periods in cramped conditions sold well in working-class communities, where money for doctors was scarce.

The close quarters of the urban neighborhood allowed immigrants to preserve many Old World customs. In immigrant communities such as Chicago's German North Side, Pittsburgh's Poletown, New York's Lower East Side, and San Francisco's Chinatown, people usually spoke their native language while visiting friends and relatives. The men might play cards while women and children gathered on the front stoop to trade stories. In good weather, they walked and talked, a pastime common in European cities. No organization was as important as the fraternal society, which sponsored social clubs and provided insurance benefits. Immigrants also recreated Old World religious institutions such as the temple, church, and synagogue, and secular institutions such as German family-style saloons and Russian Jewish tearooms. Chinese theaters, in inexpensive daily and nightly performances, presented dramas depicting historical events or explicating moral teachings, and thereby preserved much of Chinese native culture. Immigrants also replicated their native cuisine and married, baptized children, and buried their dead according to Old World customs.

In the cosmopolitan cities, immigrants, by being innovative entrepreneurs as well as the best customers, helped to shape the emerging popular culture. German immigrants, for example, created Tin Pan Alley, the center of the popular music industry. They also became the first promoters of ragtime, which found its way north from Storyville, the red-light district of New Orleans. Created by African American and Creole bands, ragtime captivated the teenage offspring of immigrants who rushed to the new dance halls.

Developers realized that "wholesome fun" for the masses could pay better than upper-class leisure or lower-class vice, and in 1895 they decided to transform Coney Island into a magnificent seaside park filled with ingenious amusements such as water slides, mechanized horse races, carousels, roller coasters, and fun houses. On the rides or at the nearby beach, young men and women could easily meet apart from their parents, cast off their inhibitions, and enjoy a hug or kiss. Or they could simply stroll through the grounds, looking at exotic performers, enjoying make-believe trips to the Far East and even the moon, entranced by fantastic towers, columns, minarets, and lagoons lit up at night to resemble dreams rather than reality. At Coney Island or at Riverview, Chicago's oldest amusement park, located on the city's North Side, millions of working-class people enjoyed cheap thrills that offset the hardships of their working lives.

19.6 Cultures in Conflict, Culture in Common

How did cultural developments in America's cities reflect larger social and economic tensions?

The new commercial entertainments gave Americans from various backgrounds more in common than they would otherwise have had. Even so, just as the changes in the conditions of labor fostered conflict, in the forms of strikes and workers' protests, so too did the concurrent transformation of the daily life of the community. Competing claims to the resources of the new urban, industrial society, such as public schools and parks, became more intense as the century moved to a close.

19.6.1 Education

Business and civic leaders understood that a democratic society demands an educated population, one possessing the skills and knowledge required to keep both industry and government running. Many also believed that, in light of the mass immigration since the Civil War, an expanded education system was necessary to prepare the vast numbers of newcomers for citizenship.

In the last three decades of the nineteenth century, individual cities and town directed an increasing portion of tax revenues toward education, and the idea of universal free schooling, if only for white children, took hold. Kindergartens in particular flourished. Public high schools, rare before the Civil War, also increased in number, from 160 in 1870 to 6,000 by the end of the century. Despite this spectacular growth, which was concentrated in urban industrial areas, as late as in 1890 only 4 percent of children between the ages of 14 and 17 were enrolled in school, the majority of them girls planning to become teachers or office workers. (See Figure 19.1.) Most high schools continued to serve mainly the middle class.

Higher education also expanded along several lines. Agricultural colleges formed earlier in the century developed into institutes of technology and took their places

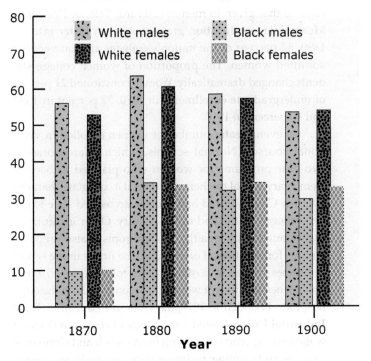

Figure 19.1 SCHOOL ENROLLMENT OF FIVE- TO NINETEEN-YEAR-OLDS, 1870–1900

In the final decades of the nineteenth century, elementary and high school enrollments grew across the board, but especially so for children of color and for girls.

U.S. Department of Commerce, Bureau of the Census, *Historical Statistics of the United States, Colonial Times to 1970.* U.S. Department of Education, Office of Educational Research and Improvement.

alongside the prestigious liberal arts colleges. To extend learning to the "industrial classes," Representative Justin Morrill (R., Vermont) sponsored the Morrill Federal Land Grant Act of 1862, which funded a system of state public colleges and universities for teaching agriculture and engineering "without excluding other scientific and classic studies."

Meanwhile, established private institutions like Harvard, Yale, Princeton, and Columbia grew with the help of huge endowments from business leaders. By 1900, 63 Catholic colleges were serving mainly the children of immigrants from Ireland and eastern and southern Europe. Still, while the overall number of colleges and universities grew from 563 in 1870 to nearly 1,000 by 1910, only 3 percent of the college-age population took advantage of these new opportunities. One of the most important developments occurred in the area of research and graduate studies, pioneered in this country in 1876 by Johns Hopkins University. By the end of the century, several American universities, including Stanford University and the University of Chicago, offered advanced degrees in the arts and sciences.

This expansion benefited women, who previously had little access to higher education. After the Civil War, a number of women's colleges were founded, beginning in 1865 with Vassar, which set the academic standard for the remainder of the century. Smith and Wellesley followed in 1875 and Bryn Mawr in 1885. By the end of the century, 125 women's colleges offered a first-rate education comparable to that given to men at Harvard, Yale, or Princeton. Meanwhile, coeducation grew at an even faster rate; by 1890, 47 percent of the nation's colleges and universities admitted women. The proportion of women college students changed dramatically. Women constituted 21 percent of undergraduate enrollments in 1870, 32 percent in 1880, and 40 percent in 1910.

An even greater number of women enrolled in vocational courses. Normal schools, which offered one- or two-year programs for women who planned to become elementary school teachers, developed a collegiate character after the Civil War and had become accredited state teachers' colleges by the end of the century. Other institutions, many founded by wealthy philanthropists, also prepared women for vocations. For example, the first training school for nurses opened in Boston in 1873, followed in 1879 by a diet kitchen that taught women to become cooks in the city's hospitals. Founded in 1877, the **Women's Educational and Industrial Union** offered a multitude of classes to Boston's wage-earning women, ranging from French and German to drawing and painting; to dressmaking and millinery, stenography and typing; as well as cabinet-making and carpentry. In the early 1890s, when the entering class at a large women's college like Vassar still averaged fewer than 100, the Boston Women's Educational and Industrial Union reported that its staff of 83 served an estimated 1,500 clients per day.

The leaders of the business community had also begun to promote manual training for working-class and immigrant boys. In 1884, the Chicago Manual Training School opened, teaching "shop work" along with a few academic subjects, and by 1895, all elementary and high schools in the city offered courses that trained boys for future jobs in industry and business.

The expansion of education did not benefit all Americans or benefit them all in the same way. Only in 1905, following a ruling of the U.S. Supreme Court, did California open public schools to Chinese children. Because African Americans were often excluded from colleges attended by white students, special colleges were founded shortly after the Civil War. All-black Atlanta and Fisk universities both soon offered rigorous curricula in the liberal arts. Other institutions, such as Hampton, founded in 1868, specialized in vocational training, mainly in manual trades.

Booker T. Washington, born into slavery, aspired to prepare African Americans for better, productive lives in the New South. He promoted practical knowledge above all and even encouraged African Americans to resist "the craze for Greek and Latin learning." Beginning in 1881, he headed the Tuskegee Institute in Alabama, and for the next 30 years he devoted himself to providing his students with both industrial education and moral uplift. By the turn of the century, Tuskegee enrolled 1,400 men and women in more than 30 different vocational courses, including special cooking classes for homemakers and domestic servants. Black colleges, including Tuskegee, trained so many teachers that by the century's end, the majority of black schools were staffed by African Americans.

The nation's educational system was becoming more inclusive and yet more differentiated. The majority of children attended school for several years or more. At the same time, students were tracked—by race, gender, and class—to fill particular roles in an industrial society.

19.6.2 Leisure and Public Space

Most large cities set aside open land for leisure-time use by residents. New York's Central Park, which opened for ice-skating in 1858, provided a model for urban park systems across the United States. In 1869, planners in Chicago secured funds to create a citywide system comprising six interconnected large parks, and within a few years, Lincoln Park, on the city's North Side, was attracting crowds of nearly 30,000 on Sundays. These parks were rolling expanses, cut across by streams and pathways and footbridges and set off by groves of trees, ornamental shrubs, and neat flower gardens. According to the designers' vision, the urban middle class might find here a respite from the stresses of modern life. To ensure this possibility, posted regulations forbade many activities, ranging from walking on the grass to gambling, picnicking, or ball playing without permission, to speeding in carriages.

Bettmann/Getty Images.

GEORGE WASHINGTON CARVER
George Washington Carver (1864–1943), who was born into slavery, had been invited by Booker T. Washington to direct agricultural research at the Tuskegee Institute in Alabama. A leader in development of agriculture in the New South, Carver promoted crop diversification to rejuvenate soil that was depleted by the continuous planting of cotton. He also encouraged the cultivation of alternative, high-protein crops such as peanuts and soybeans. He designed his programs in sustainable agriculture mainly for African American farmers and sharecroppers rather than for commercial purposes.

The working classes had their own ideas about the use of parks and open land in their communities. Trapped in overcrowded tenements or congested neighborhoods, they wanted space for sports, picnics, and lovers' trysts. Young people openly defied ordinances that prohibited play on the grassy knolls, while their elders routinely voted against municipal bonds that did not include funds for more recreational space.

Eventually, most park administrators set aside some sections for playgrounds and athletic fields and others for public gardens and band shells. Yet intermittent conflicts erupted. The Worcester, Massachusetts, park system, for example, allowed sports leagues to schedule events but prohibited pickup games. This policy gave city officials more control over the use of the park for outdoor recreation but at the same time forced many ball-playing boys into the streets. When working-class parents protested, city officials responded by instituting programs of supervised play, to the further dismay of the children.

Public drinking of alcoholic beverages, especially on Sunday, provoked similar disputes. Although civic leaders hoped to discourage Sunday drinking by sponsoring alternative events, such as free organ recitals and other concerts, many working people—especially beer-loving German immigrants—continued to treat Sunday as their one day of relaxation. In Chicago, when not riding the streetcars to the many beer gardens and taverns that thrived on the outskirts, Germans gathered in large numbers for picnics in the city's parks.

Toward the end of the century, many park administrators relaxed the rules and expanded the range of permitted activities. By that time, large numbers of the middle class had become sports enthusiasts and pressured municipal governments to turn meadowlands into tennis courts and golfing greens. In the 1890s, bicycling brought many women into the parks. Still, not all city residents enjoyed these facilities. Officials in St. Louis, for example, barred African Americans from the city's grand Forest Park and set aside the smaller Tandy Park for their use. After challenging this policy in court, African Americans won a few concessions, such as the rights to picnic at any time in Forest Park and to use the golf course on Monday mornings.

19.6.3 National Pastimes

Toward the end of the century, the younger members of the urban middle class had begun to find common ground in lower-class pastimes, especially ragtime music. Introduced to many Northerners by the African American composer Scott Joplin at the Chicago World's Fair of 1893, "rag" quickly became the staple of entertainment in the new cabarets and nightclubs. Middle-class urban dwellers began to seek out ragtime bands and congregated in nightclubs and even on the rooftops of posh hotels to listen and dance and even to drink.

Vaudeville, the most popular form of commercial entertainment since the 1880s, also bridged middle- and working-class tastes. Drawing on a variety-show tradition, "vaude" became a big business that made ethnic and racial stereotypes and the daily frustrations of city life into major topics of amusement. Vaudeville palaces attracted huge, "respectable" crowds that sampled between 20 and 30 dramatic, musical, and comedy acts averaging 15 minutes each.

Sports, however, outdistanced all other commercial entertainments in appealing to all kinds of fans and managing to create a sense of national community. Baseball clubs formed in many cities, and shortly after the Civil War, traveling teams with regular schedules made baseball a professional sport. The formation of the National League in 1876 encouraged other spectator sports, but for generations baseball remained the most popular.

Baseball, like many other sports, soon became incorporated into the larger business economy. In Chicago, local merchants such as Marshall Field supported teams, and by the end of the 1860s there were more than 50 company-sponsored teams playing in the local leagues. By 1870, a Chicago Board of Trade team emerged as the city's first professional club, the White Stockings. Capitalized as a joint stock company, the White Stockings soon succeeded in recruiting a star pitcher from the Boston Red Stockings, Albert Spalding, who eventually became manager and then president of the team. Spalding also came to see baseball as a source of multiple profits. He procured the exclusive rights to manufacture the official ball and the rule book, while producing large varieties of other sporting equipment. Meanwhile, he built impressive baseball parks in Chicago, with seating for 10,000 and special private boxes above the grandstands for the wealthy.

Spalding also succeeded in tightening the rules of participation in the sport. In 1879, he dictated the "reserve clause," which prevented players from negotiating a better deal and leaving the team that originally signed them. He encouraged his player-manager

BOSTON NATIONAL BLOOMER GIRL'S BASE BALL CLUB. L. J. GALBREATH, Originator and Owner.

BLOOMER GIRLS By the 1890s, Bloomer Girls baseball teams had organized in many parts of the country. To fill out a season, many of these clubs played against men's teams. To fill out a lineup, many of these women's clubs included male players, who at first wore wigs and women's clothing. By the early twentieth century, when this photograph was taken, men played openly in regulation uniforms. The last Bloomer Girl club disbanded in the 1930s. This photograph shows the Boston club with owner L. J. Galbreath.

Library of Congress (Photoduplication).

"Cap" Anson to forbid the White Stockings from playing against any team with an African American member. The firing of Moses "Fleet" Walker, an African American, from the Cincinnati Red Stockings in 1884 marked the first time the color line had been drawn in a major professional sport. Effectively excluded, African Americans organized their own traveling teams. In the 1920s, they formed the Negro Leagues, which produced some of the nation's finest ball players.

As attendance continued to grow, the enthusiasm for baseball straddled major social divisions, bringing together Americans of many backgrounds, if only on a limited basis. By the end of the century, no section of the daily newspaper drew more readers than the sports pages. Although it interested relatively few women, sports news riveted the attention of men from all social classes. Loyalty to the "home team" helped to create an urban identity, while individual players became national heroes.

Conclusion

By the end of the nineteenth century, industry and the growing cities had opened a new world for Americans. Fresh from Europe or from the native countryside, ordinary urban dwellers struggled to form communities of fellow newcomers through both work and leisure, in the factory, the neighborhood, the ballpark, and the public school. Meanwhile, their "betters," the wealthy and the new middle class, made and executed the decisions of industry and marketing, established the era's grand civic institutions, and set the tone for high fashion and art. Rich and poor alike shared many aspects of the new order. Yet inequality not only persisted but also increased and prompted new antagonisms.

The Haymarket tragedy highlighted the often-strained relationships between Chicago's immigrant working population and civic leaders, precipitating violence, which included the public hanging of four of the eight men brought to trial, August Spies among them. Although the new governor of Illinois, Peter Altgeld, pardoned the three who had their sentences commuted to life in prison, his attempt at amelioration did not signal a shift in the political climate. In the 1890s, hopes for a peaceful reconciliation of these tensions had worn thin, and the lure of an overseas empire appeared as one of the few goals that held together a suffering and divided nation.

Key Terms

vertical integration The consolidation of numerous production functions, from the extraction of the raw materials to the distribution and marketing of the finished products, under the direction of one firm. p. 434

horizontal combination The merger of competitors in the same industry. p. 434

gospel of wealth Thesis that hard work and perseverance lead to wealth, implying that poverty is a character flaw. p. 434

Chinese Exclusion Act Act that suspended Chinese immigration, limited the civil rights of resident Chinese, and forbade their naturalization. p. 437

Knights of Labor Labor union founded in 1869 that included skilled and unskilled workers irrespective of race or gender. p. 438

American Federation of Labor (AFL) Union formed in 1886 that organized skilled workers along craft lines and emphasized a few workplace issues rather than a broad social program. p. 438

tenements Four- to six-story residential dwellings, once common in New York, built on tiny lots without regard to providing ventilation or light. p. 443

Gilded Age Term applied to late-nineteenth-century America that refers to the shallow display and worship of wealth characteristic of that period. p. 446

conspicuous consumption Highly visible displays of wealth and consumption. p. 446

Women's Educational and Industrial Union Boston organization offering classes to wage-earning women. p. 450

CHRONOLOGY

Morrill Act authorizes "land-grant" colleges	1862	
	1869	Knights of Labor founded
Financial panic brings severe depression	1873	
	1876	Baseball National League founded
		Alexander Graham Bell patents telephone
Tuskegee Institute founded	1881	
	1882	Peak of immigration to the United States (1.2 million) in the nineteenth century
		Chinese Exclusion Act passed
Campaigns for eight-hour workday peak	1886	
American Federation of Labor founded		
	1890	Sherman Antitrust Act passed

Chapter 20
Democracy and Empire 1870–1900

DESTRUCTION OF THE *MAINE* This lithograph, produced by the Chicago firm Kurz and Allison to evoke patriotism rather than to convey accuracy, depicts the destruction of the U.S. battleship *Maine* in Havana Harbor, 1898.

Everett Collection Historical/Alamy Stock Photo.

 ## Contents and Focus Questions

American Communities

The Annexation of Hawai'i

On January 17, 1891, Lili'uokalani succeeded her brother, King Kalakaua, to become the queen of Hawai'i. Raised a Christian and fluent in English, the 52-year-old monarch was nevertheless intensely loyal to the Hawaiian people and to their language and customs. This allegiance—and

455

her strong opposition to a movement to annex Hawai'i to the United States—brought about her downfall. On January 17, 1893, the queen was deposed in a plot carried out by an American diplomat and his coconspirators.

This event followed more than a half century of intense economic and diplomatic maneuvering by the United States and other nations. Both American and British missionaries, who had arrived in the 1820s to convert Hawaiians to Christianity, had bought up huge parcels of land and had grown into a large and powerful community of planters. The missionaries in turn encouraged American businesses to buy into the sugar plantations, and by 1875, U.S. corporations dominated the sugar trade. Hawai'i was beginning to appear, in the opinion of Secretary of State James G. Blaine, to be "an outlying district of the state of California," and he pushed for formal annexation.

In 1888, American planters forced on the weak King Kalakaua a new constitution that severely limited his power and established wealth and property qualifications for voting. This so-called Bayonet Constitution, because it implied the use of U.S. arms to implement it, allowed noncitizens, Europeans as well as Americans, to vote, but denied the right of suffrage to poor native Hawaiians and the Chinese and Japanese who had come to work in the sugar fields.

The white planters had secured a constitutional government that was closely allied to their economic interests—until King Kalakaua died in 1891. After ascending to the throne, Queen Lili'uokalani struck back. She decided she must empower native Hawaiians and limit the political influence of the planter elite and noncitizens.

The U.S.-led annexation forces first denounced the queen for attempting to abrogate the Bayonet Constitution and then welcomed Blaine's decision to send in U.S. troops to protect American lives and property. Lili'uokalani was deposed and a new provisional government installed. Sanford B. Dole stepped in as the president of the new provisional government of Hawai'i, now a protectorate of the United States.

Lili'uokalani called on President Cleveland to recognize her authority as "the constitutional sovereign of the Hawaiian Islands" and to reinstate her as queen. After investigating the situation, Cleveland agreed and ordered Lili'uokalani's reinstatement. Ironically, Dole, who had been a major force for annexation, countered by refusing to recognize the right of the U.S. president "to interfere in our domestic affairs." On July 3, 1894, he proclaimed

Oahu

Hawai'i an independent republic, with himself retaining the office of president.

After Lili'uokalani's supporters attempted an unsuccessful military uprising in 1895, the deposed queen was arrested, tried by a military tribunal, and convicted of misprision of treason (having knowledge of treason but not informing the authorities). She was fined and sentenced to a five-year term in prison at hard labor, although Dole allowed her to serve a shorter sentence under "house arrest."

President Cleveland later declared privately that he was "ashamed of the whole affair" and stubbornly refused to listen to arguments for annexation. But he was powerless to stop the process before William McKinley succeeded him as president in 1896. Although more than a hundred members of Congress voted against annexation, an improper joint resolution passed to annex Hawai'i. In 1900, at McKinley's urging, Hawai'i became a territory. The people of Hawai'i were never consulted about this momentous change in their national identity.

Many Americans had long viewed Hawai'i as a stepping-stone to vast Asian markets, and by the 1890s they were determined to acquire the island nation to extend the reach of the United States beyond the continent. Domestic unrest increased pressures for overseas expansion. "American factories are making more than the American people can use; American soil is producing more than they can consume," declared Senator Albert J. Beveridge, Republican from Indiana. "[T]he trade of the world must and shall be ours." Others had different reasons for expanding the national boundaries, and a sizable number of Americans strongly opposed all such ventures. Nevertheless, the century closed on the heels of a war with Spain that won for the United States a swatch of new possessions that extended halfway around the world, from Puerto Rico to the Philippines.

The path to empire was paved with major changes in government. As the 1890s culminated in the acquisition of new territories, the United States also witnessed a decisive realignment of the party system. Voters not only changed affiliations that had been in place since the Civil War, but also waged significant challenges to the two-party system at the local, regional, and national levels. While Queen Lili'uokalani was trying to regain control of her government, a mass political movement was forming in the United States to revive the nation's own democratic impulse.

20.1 Toward a National Governing Class

What factors contributed to the growth of government in the late nineteenth century?

The basic structure of government changed dramatically in the last quarter of the nineteenth century. Mirroring the fast-growing economy, public administration expanded at all levels—municipal, county, state, and federal—and took on greater responsibility for regulating society, especially market and property relations. Growing numbers of citizens for the first time looked to the government to provide public education, military veterans' pensions, and social services covering public health and safety. The leaders of the business community looked to government just as eagerly, and with far more influence, for the protection of their property. Moreover, the expansion of government, particularly its increasing oversight of commerce, laid the foundation for economic and territorial expansion abroad.

Some notable politicians and business leaders acted to benefit directly, often competing with one another for control of the new mechanisms of power. Meanwhile, groups of citizens mobilized to rein in corruption and to promote both efficiency and professionalism in the multiplying structures of government. A lot was at stake.

20.1.1 The Growth of Government

Before the Civil War, local governments attended mainly to the promotion and regulation of trade and relied on private enterprise to supply vital services such as fire protection and public access to water. Cities gradually introduced professional police and firefighting forces and began to finance expanding school systems, public libraries, roads, and parks, an expansion requiring huge increases in local taxation. State governments grew in tandem, consolidating oversight of banking, transportation systems such as the railroads, and major enterprises such as the construction of dams and canals.

At the national level, mobilization for the Civil War and Reconstruction had demanded an unprecedented degree of resources and their coordination, as both revenues and administrative bureaucracy grew quickly. During the Civil War, for example, the federal government established a national currency and a system of taxation. After the war, the federal government as a whole continued to expand under the weight of new tasks and responsibilities. The federal bureaucracy soon doubled, from about 50,000 employees in 1871 to 100,000 only a decade later.

The modern apparatus of departments, bureaus, and cabinets took shape amid this upswing. The Department of the Interior, created in 1849, grew into the largest and most important federal office other than the Post Office.

It comprised some 20 agencies, including the Bureau of Indian Affairs and the U.S. Geological Survey. Through its authority, the federal government was the chief landowner in the West. The Department of the Treasury, responsible for collecting federal taxes and customs as well as printing money and stamps, quadrupled in size from 1873 to 1900. The Department of Justice was created in 1870, the Post Office in 1872. The Bureau of Pensions, pressured by a powerful Civil War veterans' lobby, accounted for nearly a third of all federal employees.

After the Civil War, Congress created several independent regulatory commissions. Foremost was the **Interstate Commerce Commission (ICC)**. Congress created the ICC in 1887 to bring order to the growing patchwork of state laws concerning railroads. The five-member commission appointed by the president approved freight and passenger rates set by the railroads. The ICC remained weak during that period, its rate-setting policies usually voided by the Supreme Court. But the activities of the ICC set a precedent for future regulation of trade as well as for positive government, making rules for business while superseding state laws with federal power—that is, for the intervention of the federal government into the affairs of private enterprise.

20.1.2 The Machinery of Politics

Only gradually did the nation's major political parties adapt to the demands of government expansion. The Republican Party continued to run on its Civil War record, pointing to its achievements in reuniting the nation and in passing new reform legislation. Democrats ridiculed Republicans for "waving the bloody shirt"—that is, making emotional appeals to voters. By contrast, Democrats promised to reduce the influence of the federal government, slash expenditures, repeal legislation, and protect states' rights. While Republicans held on to their longtime constituencies, Democrats gathered support from southern white voters and immigrants newly naturalized in the North.

Presidents in the last quarter of the century—Rutherford B. Hayes (1877–1881), James A. Garfield (1881), Chester A. Arthur (1881–1885), Grover Cleveland (1885–1889), Benjamin Harrison (1889–1893), and Cleveland again (1893–1897)—lacked luster. These so-called "forgotten presidents" lacked influence, and the members of Congress were often mired in corruption. Democrats usually held a majority in the House and Republicans a majority in the Senate, which was known as the "rich man's club." With neither party sufficiently engaged to govern effectively, Congress passed little legislation before 1890.

One major political issue that separated the two parties was the tariff. Manufacturing regions, especially the Northeast, favored a protective policy, while the southern and western agricultural regions opposed high tariffs as unfair to farmers and ranchers who had to pay the steep fees on imported necessities. Democrats, with a stronghold among southern voters, argued for sharp reductions in the tariff as a way to save the rural economy and to give a boost to workers. Republicans, who represented mainly business interests, raised tariffs to new levels on a wide array of goods during the Civil War and retained high tariffs as long as they held power. The so-called McKinley Tariff of 1890, introduced by Representative William McKinley (R-Ohio), further increased the tax rate on imported goods.

Despite differences over the tariff, the Democratic and Republican parties both operated mainly as regional organizations, and by the 1870s, partisan politics at the local level had become a full-time occupation. "We work through one campaign," quipped one candidate, "take a bath and start in on the next." Election paraphernalia—leaflets or pamphlets, banners, hats, flags, buttons, inscribed playing cards, and clay pipes featuring a likeness of a candidate's face or the party symbol—became a major expense for both parties. And voters did turn out. During the last quarter of the century, participation in presidential elections peaked at nearly 80 percent of those eligible to vote. At the state and municipal levels, voters went to the polls every two years.

The rising costs of maintaining local organizations and orchestrating mammoth campaigns drove party leaders to seek ever-larger sources of revenue. Winners

THE ELECTION OF 1888 In 1888, Grover Cleveland, with his running mate, Allen G. Thurman, led a spirited campaign for reelection to the presidency. Although he played up his strong record on civil service reform and tariff reduction, Cleveland, an incumbent, lost the election to his Republican challenger, Benjamin Harrison. In this lithograph campaign poster, the Democratic ticket highlighted the issue of tariff reform.

Chronicle/Alamy Stock Photo.

often seized and added to the "spoils" of office through an elaborate system of payoffs and patronage. Legislators who supported government subsidies for railroad corporations, for instance, commonly received stock and sometimes cash bribes in return. At the time, few politicians and business leaders regarded these practices as unethical.

At the local level, where a combination of ethnicity, race, and religion determined partisan loyalty, powerful bosses and political machines dominated both parties. Democrats William Marcy Tweed—of New York's powerful political organization, Tammany Hall—and Michael "Hinky Dink" Kenna, of Chicago, specialized in giving municipal jobs to loyal voters and holiday food baskets to their families. Elsewhere, hundreds of smaller political machines ruled city halls and county courthouses through a combination of "boodle" (bribe money) and personal favors. An advocate of "honest graft," Tammany Hall politician George Plunkitt once remarked, "Men ain't in politics for nothin'. They want to get somethin' out of it."

At the federal level, meanwhile, a large number of jobs changed hands each time the presidency passed from one party to another. More than 50 percent of all federal jobs—nearly 56,000 in 1881—were patronage positions, jobs that could be awarded to loyal supporters. In the aftermath of the 1828 presidential election, New York Senator William L. Marcy coined a phrase that took on ever-greater weight in the last decade of the century; "To the victor belongs the spoils."

Upon taking office, President James Garfield encountered loyal Republicans "lying in wait" for him "like vultures for a wounded bison." His colleagues in Congress were no less besieged. Observers estimated that decisions about patronage filled one-third of their time. Garfield himself served as president for only four months before being mortally wounded by a disturbed job-seeker, an event that prompted his successor, Chester A. Arthur, to encourage reform of the civil service system.

20.1.3 The Spoils System and Civil Service Reform

In January 1883, a bipartisan congressional majority passed the **Pendleton Civil Service Reform Act**. This measure, sponsored by Ohio Democratic Senator George H. Pendleton, allowed the president to create, with Senate approval, a three-person commission to draw up a set of guidelines for executive and legislative appointments. The bipartisan commission established a system of standards for various federal jobs and instituted "open, competitive examinations for testing the fitness of applicants for public service." The Pendleton Act also barred political candidates from funding their campaigns by assessing a "tax" on the salaries of party-sponsored government employees.

Although patronage did not disappear entirely, many departments of the federal government took on a professional character. At the same time, the federal judiciary began to act more aggressively to establish the parameters of government. With the Judiciary Act of 1891, Congress created nine new courts of appeal, thereby reducing the caseload of the U.S. Supreme Court and allowing the high court the right to review certain cases at will. Despite these reforms, many observers still viewed government as a sinkhole of self-interest and corruption. At the state level, the spoils system in many places persisted without restraint well into the twentieth century.

20.2 Farmers and Workers Organize Their Communities

What role did farmers' and workers' organizations play in the politics of the 1880s and 1890s?

Farmers and workers began to build regional as well as national organizations to oppose, as a Nebraska newspaper put it, "the wealthy and powerful classes who want the control of government to plunder the people." By the 1890s, many of these organizations came together to form a mass movement that presented the most significant challenge to the two-party system since the Civil War—**Populism**—and pledged themselves to restore the reins of government to "the hands of the people."

20.2.1 The Grange

In 1867, white farmers in the Midwest formed the Patrons of Husbandry for their own "social, intellectual, and moral improvement." Led by Oliver H. Kelley, this fraternal society resembled the secretive Masonic order but recruited women to its ranks. Whole families staffed a complex array of offices and engaged in mysterious rituals involving passwords, flags, songs, and costumes. In many farming communities, the headquarters of the local chapter, known as the **Grange** (a word for "farm"), became the main social center, the site of summer dinners and winter dances.

The Granger movement spread rapidly, especially in areas where farmers were experiencing their greatest hardships. Great Plains farmers barely survived the blizzards, grasshopper infestations, and droughts of the early 1870s. Meanwhile, farmers throughout the trans-Mississippi West and the South watched the prices for grains and cotton fall year by year in the face of growing competition from producers outside the United States. (See Figure 20.1.) Membership soon swelled to more than 775,000 in a network of 20,000 local chapters.

Figure 20.1 FALLING PRICE OF WHEAT FLOUR, 1865–1900

The falling price of wheat was often offset by increased productivity, giving farmers a steady, if not higher, income. Nevertheless, in the short term, farmers often carried more debt and faced greater risk, both of which were factors in sparking the Populists' protest by the end of the century.

Grangers blamed hard times on a band of "thieves in the night"—especially railroads and banks—that charged exorbitant and highly discriminatory fees for service. They mounted their greatest assault on the railroad corporations that commonly charged farmers more to ship their crops short distances than for long hauls.

Well in advance of the establishment of the ICC, in the late 1860s and mid-1870s, farmers began to petition their state legislatures to regulate rates. Several midwestern states responded to this pressure and passed a series of so-called **Granger laws** establishing maximum shipping rates. Grangers also complained to their lawmakers about the price-fixing policies of grain wholesalers and operators of grain elevators. In 1873, the Illinois legislature passed a Warehouse Act establishing maximum rates for storing grains. Chicago businesses challenged this measure, but in *Munn v. Illinois* (1877), the Supreme Court upheld the law, ruling that states had the power to regulate privately owned businesses like the railroads in the public interest.

Like the Knights of Labor, and aiming to escape the stranglehold by big corporations, Grangers embraced the principles of cooperation. Determined to buy less and produce more, they created a vast array of enterprises for both

GRANGE POSTER The symbols chosen by Grange artists represented their faith that all social value could be traced to honest labor and most of all to the work of the entire farm family. The hardworking American required only the enlightenment offered by the Grange to build a better community.

Library of Congress (Photoduplication).

20.2.2 The Farmers' Alliance

Agrarian unrest did not end with the downward turn of the Grange, but instead moved south. The falling price of cotton underscored the need for action, and farmers organized in communities where both poverty and the crop-lien system prevailed. In the 1880s, the **Southern Farmers' Alliance**, with more than 500 chapters in Texas alone, established cooperative stores complemented by the cooperative merchandising of crops, becoming a viable alternative to the capitalist marketplace—if only temporarily.

The Northern Farmers' Alliance took shape in the Great Plains states, drawing on larger organizations in Minnesota, Nebraska, Iowa, Kansas, and the Dakota Territory. During 1886 and 1887, summer drought followed winter blizzards and ice storms, reducing wheat harvests by one-third on the plains. Locusts and chinch bugs ate much of the rest. As if this were not enough, prices for wheat on the world market fell sharply for what little remained.

In 1889, the regional organizations joined forces to create the National Farmers' Alliance and Industrial Union. Within a year, the combined movement claimed 3 million white members. Excluded from the all-white chapters, the Colored Farmers' Alliance and Cooperative Union organized separately, established its own cooperative enterprises and fraternal orders, and quickly spread across the South. From its beginning in Texas in 1886, the Colored Farmers Alliance grew to claim more than one million members by 1890.

the purchase of supplies and the marketing of crops. They established local grain elevators, set up retail stores, and even manufactured some of their own farm machinery. Grangers ran banks as well as fraternal life and fire insurance companies and dreamed of a day when they might operate their own railroad.

The deepening depression of the late 1870s wiped out most of these cooperative programs, and Grange membership soon fell. In the mid-1880s, the Supreme Court overturned most of the key legislation regulating railroads. Despite these setbacks, the Patrons of Husbandry had nonetheless effectively promoted the idea of an activist government with primary responsibility to its producer-citizens. This idea would remain at the heart of farmer-worker protest movements until the end of the century.

The Grangers had pushed legislation that would limit the salaries of public officials, provide public school students with books at little or no cost, establish a program of teacher certification, and widen the admissions policies of the new state colleges. Only rarely, however, did they put up candidates for office. In comparison, the Northern and Southern Farmers' Alliances had few reservations about entering electoral races. At the end of the 1880s, regional alliances put up candidates on platforms demanding state ownership of the railroads, a graduated income tax, lower tariffs, restriction of land ownership to citizens, and easier access to money through "the free and unlimited coinage of silver." By 1890, the alliances had won several local and state elections, had gained control of the Nebraska legislature, and held the balance of power in Minnesota and South Dakota.

20.2.3 Workers Search for Power

The railroad became the locus of protest for workers as well as for farmers. The Great Uprising of 1877, the first nationwide strike, began in Martinsburg, West Virginia, where workers protested a 10 percent wage cut by uncoupling all engines. Within a few days, the strike spread along the railroad routes to New York, Buffalo, Pittsburgh, Chicago, Kansas City, and San Francisco. In all these cities, angry crowds defied armed militias ordered to disperse them by any means. The crowds halted train traffic, sometimes pulling up entire rails and seizing carloads of food for hungry families. Fearing a "national insurrection," President Hayes set a precedent by calling in the U.S. Army to put down the strikes. By the time the strike finally ended, more than 100 people were dead.

Before the end of the century, more than 6 million workers would strike in settings ranging from New England textile mills to southern tobacco factories to western mines. Although most of these strikes ended in failure, they showed that workers, like farmers, were ready to spell out their grievances in a direct and dramatic manner. They also revealed how strongly many townspeople, including merchants who depended on workers' wages, would support local strikes and turn them into community uprisings. (See Map 20.1.)

While the Farmers' Alliance put up candidates in the South and Plains states, workers launched labor parties in dozens of industrial towns and cities. In New York City, popular land reformer and economist Henry George, with the ardent support of the city's Central Labor Council and the Knights of Labor, put himself forward in 1886 as candidate for mayor on the United Labor Party ticket. In his best-selling book *Progress and Poverty* (1879), he advocated a sweeping "single tax" on all property and also called for the end of corruption in city politics. Tammany Hall delivered many thousands of the ballots cast for George straight into the Hudson River. Nevertheless, George managed to finish a respectable second with 31 percent of the vote. Although his campaign ended in defeat, his impressive showing encouraged trade unionists in other cities to form their own parties and put up candidates for local elections.

In the late 1880s, labor parties won seats on many city councils and state legislatures. The Milwaukee People's

Map 20.1 STRIKES BY STATE, 1880

Most strikes after the Great Uprising of 1877 could be traced to organized trades, concentrated in the manufacturing districts of the Northeast and Midwest.

From *Geographical Inquiry and American Historical Problems*, edited by Earl Carville. (Stanford, CA: Stanford University Press, 1992). Originally published in the *Third Annual Report of the Commissioner of Labor*, 1887.

Party elected the mayor, a state senator, six assemblymen, and one member of the United States Congress. In smaller industrial towns where workers outnumbered the middle classes, labor parties did especially well.

The victories of local labor parties caught the attention of farmers, who began to weigh their prospects for a political alliance with discontented urban workers. For the 1888 presidential election, they formed a coalition to sponsor the Union Labor Party, which ran on a plank of government ownership of the railroads. The new party made no headway against the two-party system, polling little more than 1 percent of the vote. Still, the successes in local communities nurtured hopes for a viable political alliance of the "producing classes," rural as well as urban.

20.2.4 Women Build Alliances

Women activists helped build both the labor and agrarian protest movements while campaigning for their own rights as citizens. The Grangers issued a charter to a local chapter only when women were well represented on its rolls, and in the 1870s, delegates to its conventions routinely gave speeches endorsing woman suffrage. In both the Northern and Southern Farmers' Alliances, women made up perhaps one-quarter of the membership, and several advanced through the ranks to become leading speakers and organizers. A Kansas newspaper editor claimed that orator Mary E. Lease "could recite the multiplication table and set a crowd hooting and harrahing at her will." Lease achieved lasting fame for purportedly advising farmers to raise less corn and more hell.

Women in both the Knights of Labor and the Farmers' Alliances found their greatest leader in Frances E. Willard, the most famous woman in the nineteenth century and a shrewd politician in her own right. Willard argued that women, who guarded their families' physical and spiritual welfare, should play a similar role outside their homes. From 1878 until her death in 1897, she presided over the **Woman's Christian Temperance Union (WCTU)**. Most numerous in the Midwest, WCTU members preached total abstinence from the consumption of alcohol, but ultimately endorsed Willard's "do everything" agenda. By the 1880s, the most militant branches were campaigning for an activist government and demanding an overhaul of the prison system, the eradication of prostitution, changes in the age of consent,

and even the elimination of the wage system. Willard went so far as to draw up plans for a new system of government whereby all offices, right up to the presidency, would be shared jointly by men and women. By 1890, Willard had mobilized nearly 200,000 paid members into the largest organization of women in the world, which pledged, in her words, to "make the whole world HOMELIKE."

Willard understood that for women to participate in politics they needed the right to vote. Under her leadership, the WCTU grew into the major force for woman suffrage and pushed the heart of the suffrage campaign into the Great Plains states and the West. In Iowa, Nebraska, Colorado, and especially Kansas, agitation for the right to vote provided a political bridge among women in the WCTU, Farmers' Alliance, Knights of Labor, and various local suffrage societies. The most active members were affiliated with several organizations or, in some cases, with all.

20.2.5 Populism and the People's Party

The leaders of all these organizations aimed to rein in the corruption and injustices that they associated with the entrenched two-party system by creating a new national third party. In December 1890, the Farmers' Alliance called a meeting in Ocala, Florida, for this purpose.

"FOR GOD AND HOME AND NATIVE LAND" Founded in Cleveland, Ohio, in 1874, the Woman's Christian Temperance Union grew quickly into a national organization. Its members crusaded against the dangers of alcohol and promoted a ban on the sale of liquor. "Agitate, Educate, Legislate" were its watchwords. By 1900, the National WCTU had become the largest women's organization in the United States and, in addition to temperance, endorsed a wide range of issues, including woman suffrage, labor reform, and broad educational programs.

The New York Historical Society/Getty Images.

This was a risky proposition, because the Southern Alliance hoped to capture control of the Democratic Party, whereas many farmers in the Plains states and African Americans nearly everywhere voted Republican. In some areas, however, labor unions and farmer organizations had established independent third parties, put up full slates of candidates for local elections, won majorities in state legislatures, and even sent representatives to Congress. Reviewing these successes, delegates in Ocala decided to push ahead and lay the groundwork for a national party.

On July 4, 1892, representatives met in Omaha, Nebraska, and drew up the platform for the People's Party, better known as the Populist party. The planks included government ownership of railroads, banks, and telegraph lines; the elimination of private banks; prohibition of large landholding companies; a graduated income tax; an eight-hour workday; and restriction of immigration. The most ambitious plan called for the national government to build local warehouses—"subtreasuries"—where farmers could store their crops until prices reached acceptable levels.

Despite their Jeffersonian motto, "Equal Rights to All, Special Privileges to None," the new Populist party did not cross the color line. As few as four African American men attended the Omaha meeting. The new national organization also bowed further to southern delegates by refusing to endorse universal suffrage, as advocated by Frances Willard and championed by several state branches.

The Populists, as supporters of the People's Party styled themselves, quickly became a major factor in American politics. Although Democrat Grover Cleveland regained the presidency in 1892 (he had previously served from 1885 to 1889), Populists scored a string of local victories. They elected three governors, ten representatives to Congress, and five U.S. senators. In Idaho, Nevada, Colorado, Kansas, and North Dakota, they won 50 percent or more of the vote. The national ticket headed by James Baird Weaver of Iowa received more than 1 million votes, nearly 9 percent of the total, and 22 electoral college votes—the first time since the Civil War that a third party had received any electoral votes. Despite poor showings among urban workers east of the Mississippi, Populists looked forward to the next round of state elections in 1894. But the great test would come with the presidential election in 1896.

20.3 The Crisis of the 1890s

How did the depression that began in 1893 threaten the existing political system?

The novelist and reformer Ignatius Donnelly, who drafted the preamble to the Omaha platform of the People's Party, observed that industrial society appeared to be a "wretched failure" for "the great mass of mankind." Americans, he added, were dividing into two hostile camps, the rich and the poor, and waiting only for "the drum beat and the trumpet to summon them to armed conflict." In the 1890s, a series of events shook the confidence of many citizens in the reigning political system. But nothing was more unsettling than the severe economic depression that consumed the nation and lasted for five years. Many feared—while others hoped—that the entire political system would topple.

20.3.1 Financial Collapse and Depression

By the spring of 1893, the nation was drawn into a depression that had been plaguing European nations since the late 1880s. The European market for imported goods, including those manufactured in the United States, sharply contracted. Financial panic in England spread across the Atlantic, as British investors began to sell off their American stocks to obtain funds. Other factors—tight credit, falling agricultural prices, a weak banking system, and overexpansion, especially in railroad construction—all helped to bring about the

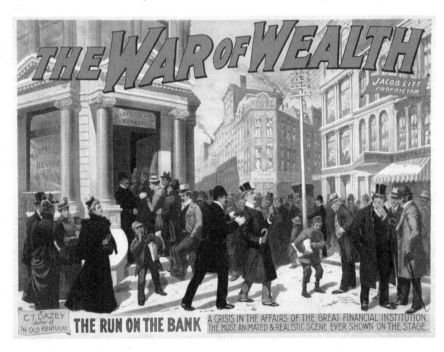

THE WAR OF WEALTH Charles Turner Dazey, a Kentucky-born poet and playwright, wrote *The War of Wealth*. The melodrama written in the aftermath of the Panic of 1893 sympathetically depicts a family threatened with financial ruin by a boisterous run on a bank. This poster advertises the play, which opened on Broadway in 1895 to great acclaim.

Everett Collection Inc/Alamy Stock Photo.

collapse of the U.S. economy. The business boom of nearly two decades ended, and the entire economy ground to a halt. The new century arrived before prosperity returned.

In many cities, unemployment rates reached 25 percent. Tens of thousands "rode the rails" or went "on the tramp" to look for work, hoping that their luck might change in a new city or town. Some panhandled for the nickel that could buy a mug of beer and a free lunch at a saloon. By night they slept in parks or sought temporary refuge in a city jail. Vagrancy laws (enacted during the 1870s) forced many without homes into prison. Inadequate diets prompted a rise in communicable diseases, such as tuberculosis and pellagra. Unable to buy food, clothes, or household items, many families learned to survive with the barest minimum.

As the depression deepened, so did demands on the federal government for positive action. Populist Jacob Sechler Coxey proposed that Congress fund a public works program to give jobs to the unemployed. To make his point, he decided to gather the masses of unemployed into a huge army and then to march to Washington, D.C. On Easter Sunday, 1894, Coxey left Massillon, Ohio, with several hundred followers. Meanwhile, brigades from across the country joined his "petition in boots." Only 600 men and women managed to reach the nation's capital, where the police first clubbed and then arrested the leaders for trespassing on the grass. **Coxey's Army** quickly disbanded, but not before voicing the public's expectation of federal responsibility for the welfare of its citizens, especially in times of crisis.

20.3.2 Strikes: Coeur d'Alene, Homestead, and Pullman

Even before the onset of the depression, the conflict between labor and capital had escalated to the brink of civil war. In the 1890s, three major strikes provided dramatic examples. In each case, state or federal authorities, at the behest of corporate owners, deployed troops to crush the labor uprising, providing a vivid lesson on the expanding power of government in this era.

Wage cuts in the silver and lead mines of northern Idaho led to one of the bitterest conflicts of the decade. To put a brake on organized labor, mine owners had formed a **protective association**, and in March 1892, they announced a wage cut throughout the Coeur d'Alene district. After the miners' union refused to accept the cut, the owners locked out all union members and brought in strikebreakers ("scab" laborers) by the trainload. Unionists tried peaceful methods of protest. But after three months of stalemate, they loaded a railcar with explosives and blew up a mine. The mineowners appealed to the governor, who proclaimed martial law and dispatched a combined state/federal force of about 1,500 troops to break the strike. In November, the mineowners declared victory, but the union survived. Many members became active in the Populist Party, which at the

next session of the Idaho legislature allied with Democrats to cut back all appropriations to the state militia.

At Homestead, Pennsylvania, the combined power of the corporation and government tested one of the strongest unions of the AFL. Members of the Amalgamated Iron, Steel and Tin Workers had carved out an admirable position for themselves in the Carnegie Steel Company. Well paid and proud of their skills, the unionists customarily directed their unskilled helpers without undue influence of company supervisors. Determined to gain control over every stage of production, however, Carnegie and his partner, Henry C. Frick, decided not only to lower wages but also to break the union.

In 1892, when Amalgamated's contract expired, Frick announced a drastic wage cut. He also ordered a wooden stockade built around the factory, with grooves for rifles and barbed wire on top. When Homestead's city government—the mayor and police chief were both union members—refused to assign police to disperse the strikers, Frick dispatched a barge carrying a private army. Gunfire broke out and continued throughout the day. Finally, the governor stepped in and sent the Pennsylvania state militia, 8,000 strong and armed with rifles and Gatling guns, to restore order, and Carnegie's factory reopened with strikebreakers doing the work.

After four months, the union was forced to concede a crushing defeat, not only for itself but, in effect, for all steelworkers. The Carnegie Company reduced its workforce by 25 percent, lengthened the workday, and cut wages 25 percent for those who remained on the job. Within a decade, every major steel company operated without union interference.

Pullman, Illinois, just south of Chicago, had been constructed as a model industrial community. Its creator and proprietor, George M. Pullman, had manufactured luxurious "sleeping cars" for railroads since 1881. He built his company as a self-contained community, with the factory at the center, surrounded by modern cottages, a library, churches, parks, an independent water supply, and even its own cemetery, but no saloons. The Pullman Palace Car Company deducted rent, library fees, and grocery bills from each worker's weekly wages. In good times, workers enjoyed a decent livelihood, although many resented Pullman's autocratic control of their daily affairs.

When times grew hard, the company cut wages by as much as one-half, in some cases down to less than $1 a day. Charges for food and rent remained unchanged. Furthermore, factory supervisors sought to make up for declining profits by driving workers to produce more. In May 1894, workers voted to strike.

Pullman workers found their champion in Eugene V. Debs, who had recently formed the American Railway Union (ARU) to bring railroad workers across the vast continent into one organization. Debs advised caution, but delegates to an ARU convention voted to support a nationwide boycott of all Pullman cars. This action soon turned into a sympathy strike by railroad workers across the country.

PULLMAN STRIKE In 1894, workers struck against the Pullman Palace Car Company after a severe cut in wages, and the company responded by shutting down operations. The American Railway Union, headed by Eugene V. Debs, then called for its members—approximately 260,000 nationwide—to join the strike, an action that halted all passenger service by train. The federal government secured a court injunction to force workers back to work, and following their refusal, President Grover Cleveland sent troops enforce the court order. On July 4, 1894, a violent melee broke out in Chicago, where the company was headquartered. A railroad yard was burned, and 26 civilians were killed.

North Wind Picture Archives/Alamy Stock Photo.

The Pullman strike at first produced little violence. ARU officials urged strikers to ignore all provocations and hold their ground peacefully. But Richard C. Olney, a former railroad lawyer, used his current office as attorney general to issue a blanket injunction against the strike. On July 4, President Cleveland sent army units to Chicago, over the objections of pro-labor Illinois governor John Peter Altgeld. After a bitter confrontation that left 13 people dead and more than 50 wounded, the army dispersed the strikers. For the next week, railroad workers in 26 other states resisted federal troops, and a dozen more people were killed. On July 17, the strike finally ended when federal marshals arrested Debs and other leaders.

Debs concluded that the labor movement could not regain its dignity without seizing the reins of government. He came out of jail committed to the ideals of socialism, and in 1898 helped to form a political party dedicated to its principles.

20.3.3 The Social Gospel

"What is socialism?" Debs once asked. "Merely Christianity in action. It recognizes the equality in men." During the 1890s, especially as hard times spread across the nation, a growing number of Protestants and Catholics came close to sharing Debs's perspective.

Social gospel ministers called on government at all levels to be more responsible toward the most impoverished and unprotected citizens. Supporting labor's right to organize and, if necessary, to strike, they petitioned government officials to regulate corporations and place a limit on profits. Washington Gladden, a Congregationalist minister, warned that if churches continued to ignore pressing social problems, they would devolve into institutions whose sole purpose was to preserve obscure rituals and superstitions. He addressed his most important book, *Applied Christianity* (1886), to the nation's business leaders, imploring them to return to Christ's teachings. The very popular and sensationalist *If Christ Came to Chicago* (1894), by British investigative journalist William T. Stead, forced readers to confront the "ugly sight" of a city with 200 millionaires and 200,000 unemployed men and women. Even more famous, *In His Steps* (1896), by Methodist minister Charles M. Sheldon, asked readers to contemplate a simple question; "What would Jesus do?"

Catholic clergy, doctrinally more inclined than Protestants to accept poverty as a natural condition, joined the social gospel movement in smaller numbers. Many of their parishioners, however, especially Polish and Irish Americans, allied with the labor movement, finding solace in Pope Leo XIII's encyclical *Rerum Novarum* (1891), which endorsed the right of workers to form trade unions.

Women, underrepresented in the clergy, guided the social gospel movement in many northern communities. Since the early part of the nineteenth century, middle-class women had formed numerous voluntary associations to improve the conditions of the poor and destitute. They founded orphanages, hospitals, and shelters for the homeless. During the hard times of the 1890s, a new generation of activists revived this legacy. In nearly every sizable city, groups of white women affiliated with various evangelical Protestant sects raised money to establish inexpensive residential hotels for working women, whose low wages rarely covered the price of safe, comfortable shelter. At the forefront of this movement was the Young Women's Christian Association (YWCA), which by 1900 had more than 600 local chapters. The "Y" sponsored a range of services for needy Christian women, ranging from homes for the elderly and for unmarried mothers to elaborate programs of vocational instruction and physical fitness. Meanwhile, Catholic laywomen and nuns served the poor women of their faith, operating numerous schools, hospitals, and orphanages.

African American women, excluded from the enterprises run by white women, sponsored their own self-help and charitable programs. Affiliated principally with the Baptist Church, they additionally emphasized the importance of education to racial uplift. The black branch of the YWCA organized in Ohio in 1890 was the first of several chapters that ran boarding houses for women migrating to northern cities in search of work or schooling. African American activists also branched out to sponsor nurseries, orphanages, hospitals, and nursing homes.

20.4 Politics of Reform, Politics of Order

In what ways did the election of 1896 represent a turning point in U.S. political history?

The severe hardships of the 1890s, following a quarter century of popular unrest, pushed economic issues to the forefront of politics. Voters were more than ready for a change. As a consequence, the presidential election of 1896, considered a turning point in American politics, marked a dramatic realignment. The election also sanctioned the popular call for a stronger government and, ultimately, established a clear link between domestic problems and overseas markets.

20.4.1 The Battle of the Standards

For Populists, as well as for Democrats and Republicans, currency reform emerged as a focal point in the campaigns of the 1890s. For decades farmers had railed against the Coinage Act of 1873, which had effectively ended the bimetallic standard of gold and silver that had been in place since 1792. The so-called "Crime of '73" had, by eliminating silver from circulation, tightened the money supply, put a brake on inflation, and made it more difficult for farmers to pay their debts. Finally, in 1890, Congress responded to the combined pressure of disgruntled farmers and western silver mineowners to pass the **Sherman Silver Purchase Act**, which directed the Treasury to increase the amount of currency coined from silver and also permitted the printing of paper currency backed by silver.

President Cleveland, who took office just as the depression of 1893 set in, breathed new life into the currency issue. He concluded that the crisis was, "largely the result of financial policy . . . embodied in unwise laws," and insisted that only the gold standard could pull the nation out of the depression. By exerting intense pressure on fellow Democrats, and after several months of contentious debate in a special session of Congress, Cleveland succeeded in securing the repeal the Sherman Act—but not without ruining his chances for renomination.

Mainly as a repudiation of Cleveland's leadership, the midterm elections of 1894 brought the largest shift in congressional power ever in American history. The president's party, the Democrats, lost control of both the House and the Senate. Vowing revenge, the "Silver Democrats" began to look to the Populists, who also did well in the midterm elections, increasing their vote by 42 percent over their 1892 total. Meanwhile, Republicans confidently began to prepare for the presidential election of 1896, warming to what they called the "battle of the standards."

20.4.2 Populism's Last Campaigns

As Populists prepared for the 1896 presidential campaign, they found themselves at a crossroad: What were they to do with the growing popularity of William Jennings Bryan, who had surprisingly emerged at the Democratic presidential candidate? A Nebraska lawyer, Bryan had won a congressional seat in 1890 and served two terms. He failed, however, in a campaign for the Senate in 1894. He was, however, a spellbinding orator, and for the nest two years he wooed voters in a tour that took him to every state in the nation. Pouring new life into his divided party, Bryan won back many disaffected Democrats by championing **free silver**.

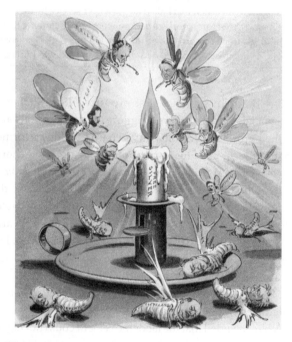

"FREE SILVER" Since the 1830s, political factions in the United States had complained that banks were too stingy in offering credit to otherwise eager borrowers. They believed more generous lending policies would bring greater prosperity to all. By the late 1880s, a demand for "bi-metalism"—silver alongside gold as the twin bases of the dollar's value— had become popular among many Democrats. In the run-up to the 1896 presidential election, Republicans ridiculed Democrat Williams Jennings Bryan, the first major-party candidate to build his platform on this principle. Anyone drawn to the flame of silver, Republicans warned, would perished. And Bryan did perish, losing the presidential election to Republican William McKinley.

Niday Picture Library/Alamy Stock Photo.

At the 1896 Democratic Party convention, the 36-year-old Bryan thrilled delegates with his evocation of agrarian ideals. "Burn down your cities and leave our farms," Bryan preached, "and your cities will spring up again as if by magic; but destroy our farms and the grass will grow in the streets of every city in the country." What became one of the most famous speeches in American political history closed on a yet more dramatic note. Spreading his arms to suggest the crucified Christ figure, he pledged to resist all demands for a gold standard by saying, "You shall not press down upon the brow of labor this crown of thorns, you shall not crucify mankind upon a cross of gold." The next day, Bryan carried the Democratic presidential nomination.

The Populists realized that by nominating Bryan, the Democrats had stolen their thunder. They also feared that the growing emphasis on currency would overshadow their more important planks calling for government ownership of the nation's railroads and communications systems. As the date of their own convention approached, delegates divided over strategy: They could "fuse" with the Democrats and endorse Bryan, or they could run an independent campaign and risk splitting the silver vote.

In the end, Populists nominated Bryan for president and one of their own, Georgian Tom Watson, for vice president. Most of the state Democratic Party organizations, however, refused to put this "fusion" ticket on the ballot and stuck to Bryan and his Democratic running mate, Arthur Sewall.

20.4.3 The Republican Triumph

Republicans had anticipated an easy victory in 1896, but Bryan's nomination, as party stalwart Mark Hanna warned, "changed everything." Luckily, they had their own handsome, knowledgeable, courteous, and ruthless candidate, Civil War veteran and former Ohio governor William McKinley.

The Republican campaign, in terms of sheer expense and skill of coordination, outdid all previous campaigns and established a precedent for future presidential elections. Hanna guided a strategy that outspent Bryan more than 10 to 1. Fearful that the silver issue would divide their own ranks, Republicans stepped around it while emphasizing the tariff. Delivering a hard-hitting, negative campaign, they consistently cast Bryan as a naysayer.

McKinley triumphed in the most important presidential election since Reconstruction. Bryan managed to win 46 percent of the popular vote, but failed to carry the Midwest, West Coast, or Upper South. (See Map 20.2.) Moreover, the free silver campaign rebuffed traditionally Democratic urban voters, who feared that soft money would bring higher prices. Many Catholics uncomfortable with Bryan's Protestant moral piety also deserted the Democrats. Finally, neither the reform-minded middle classes nor impoverished blue-collar workers were convinced that Bryan's grand reform vision really included them. The Populist following, already divided and now further disillusioned, dwindled away.

MCKINLEY CAMPAIGN POSTER This Republican campaign poster of 1896 depicts William McKinley standing on sound money and promising a revival of prosperity. The depression of the 1890s shifted the electorate into the Republican column.

Everett Collection Inc/Alamy Stock Photo.

Once in office, McKinley strengthened the executive branch and actively promoted a mixture of pro-business and expansionist measures. He supported the Dingley Tariff of 1897, which raised import duties to an all-time high. In 1897, McKinley also encouraged Congress to create the U.S. Industrial Commission, which would plan business regulation; in 1898, he promoted a bankruptcy act that eased the financial situation of small businesses, and he proposed the Erdman Act of the same year, which established a system of arbitration to avoid rail strikes. The Supreme Court ruled in concert with the president, finding 18 railways in violation of antitrust laws, and granting states the right to regulate hours of labor under certain circumstances. In 1900, McKinley settled the currency issue by overseeing the passage of the Gold Standard Act.

McKinley's triumphs ended the popular challenge to the nation's governing system. With the economy improving and nationalism rising swiftly, McKinley easily won reelection in the 1900 presidential campaign. With news of his second triumph, stock prices on Wall Street skyrocketed.

Map 20.2 ELECTION OF 1896

PACIFIC
OCEAN

ATLANTIC
OCEAN

Gulf of Mexico

Nonvoting
territories

Numbers on states represent Electoral Votes.	Electoral Vote (%)	Popular Vote (%)
WILLIAM McKINLEY (M) (Republican)	271 (61)	7,102,246 (51)
William J. Bryan (B) (Democrat)	176 (39)	6,492,559 (47)
Minor parties	—	315,398 (2)

Democratic candidate William Jennings Bryan carried most of rural America but could not overcome Republican William McKinley's stronghold in the populous industrial states.

20.4.4 Nativism and Jim Crow

Campaign rhetoric aside, McKinley and Bryan had differed only slightly on the major problems facing the nation in the 1890s. Neither Bryan, the reformer, nor McKinley, the prophet of business prosperity, addressed the escalation of racism and **nativism** (anti-immigrant feeling) throughout the nation.

Toward the end of the century, many political observers noted, patriotic fervor took on a strongly nationalistic and antiforeign tone. Striking workers and their employers alike tended to blame "foreigners" for the hard times. Semisecret organizations such as the American Protective Association sprang up to defend American institutions against the alleged threats posed by Catholics. Fireworks and parades continued to cheer up crowds celebrating Independence Day, but Fourth of July orators more typically than in the past boasted about the might and power of their nation.

African Americans became prime targets of this growing intolerance. In the post-Reconstruction South, local and state governments codified racist ideology by passing discriminatory and segregationist legislation, which became known as **Jim Crow laws**. The Jim Crow system covered services and facilities such as restaurants, public transportation, and libraries. Signs reading "White Only" and

"Colored" appeared over theaters, parks, rooming houses, toilets, and drinking fountains.

The U.S. Supreme Court upheld the Jim Crow system. Its decisions in the *Civil Rights Cases* (1883) overturned the Civil Rights Act of 1875 that had banned racial discrimination in public facilities; in *Plessy v. Ferguson* (1896), the Court upheld a Louisiana state law formally segregating railroad passenger cars. This landmark ruling established the legal rationale for **segregation**—"separate but equal"—in the North as well as the South, for the next 50 years. In *Cumming v. Richmond County Board of Education* (1899), the Court allowed separate schools for blacks and whites, even where facilities for African American children did not exist. This ruling reverberated in other parts of the country. For example, a year later, in 1900, the New Orleans school board decided to eliminate all schools for black children beyond the fifth grade, reasoning that African Americans needed only minimal education to fit them for menial jobs "to which they are best suited and seem ordained by the proper fitness of things."

Jim Crow struck hard at the voting rights of African American men. Southern states enacted new literacy tests and property qualifications for voting. Loopholes permitted poor whites to vote, except where they threatened the Democratic Party's rule. **Grandfather clauses**, invented in Louisiana, exempted from all restrictions those who had been entitled to vote on January 1, 1867, together with their sons and grandsons, a measure that effectively enfranchised whites while barring African Americans. In 1898, the Supreme Court ruled that poll taxes and literacy requirements enacted to prevent blacks (and some poor whites) from voting were a proper means of restricting the ballot to "qualified" voters. By this time, only 5 percent of the southern black electorate voted, and African Americans were barred from public office and jury service. (See Figure 20.2.)

Racial violence escalated. Race riots broke out in small towns like Rosewood, Florida, and Phoenix, South Carolina, and in large cities like New Orleans and Tulsa. In November 1898, in Wilmington, North Carolina, where a dozen African Americans had ridden out the last waves of the Populist insurgency to win appointments to minor political offices, a group of white opponents organized to root them out and ultimately staged a violent coup, restoring white rule and forcing black leaders to leave. As many as 100 African Americans were killed in what came to be known as the Wilmington massacre.

Not only murderous race riots, but also thousands of lynchings took place. Mobs often burned or dismembered victims to drag out their agony and entertain the crowd of onlookers. Announced in local newspapers, lynchings in the 1890s became public spectacles for entire white families, and railroads sometimes offered special excursion rates for travel to these events.

Figure 20.2 AFRICAN AMERICAN REPRESENTATION IN CONGRESS, 1867–1900

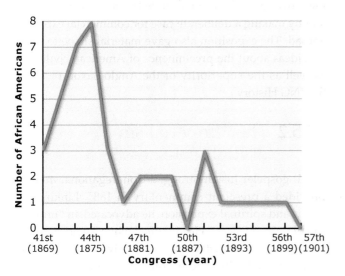

Black men served in the U.S. Congress from 1870 until 1900. All were Republicans.

Anti-lynching became the one-woman crusade of Ida B. Wells, the young editor of a black newspaper in Memphis. After three local black businessmen were lynched in 1892, Wells vigorously denounced the outrage, blaming the white business competitors of the victims. Local whites destroyed her press and forced Wells to leave the city. She then launched an international movement against lynching, lecturing across the country and in Europe, demanding an end to the silence about this barbaric crime. Her work inspired the growth of a black women's club movement. The National Association of Colored Women, founded in 1896, took up the anti-lynching cause and also fought to protect black women from sexual exploitation by white men.

Few white reformers rallied to defend African Americans. Even the National American Woman Suffrage Association, in an attempt to appease its southern members at its 1899 convention, voted down a resolution condemning racial segregation in public facilities. More than a few Americans had come to believe that their future welfare hinged on white supremacy, not only in their own country but across the globe as well.

20.5 The Path to Imperialism

How did the Spanish-American War change the place of the United States in world affairs?

Many Americans attributed the economic crisis of 1893–1897 not simply to the collapse of the railroads and banks but also to basic structural problems: an overbuilt economy and an insufficient market for goods. They witnessed the fabulous wealth of a new generation of businessmen and measured it against another, equally significant trend: The majority of Americans did not have enough money to buy a meaningful portion of what they produced. To solve problems brought on by low consumption, they looked for new markets overseas.

20.5.1 All the World's a Fair

On May Day 1893, less than two months after the nation's economy had collapsed, crowds began to flock to the World's Columbian Exposition. The fair, held in Chicago, commemorated the four hundredth anniversary of Columbus's landing by showcasing "the progress of civilization in the New World." The exhibits, staged in more than 400 newly constructed buildings, also heralded the future of American business in the emerging global economy.

"ALL NATIONS ARE WELCOME" This poster advertising the World's Columbian Exhibition, held in Chicago in 1893, features Uncle Sam and Lady Liberty welcoming representatives in native costume from around the world. Despite this portrayal of inclusion, African Americans were allotted no exhibitions or positions on the Board of Managers. The activist Ida B. Wells wrote and distributed a pamphlet protesting their exclusion and outlined the accomplishments of notable black Americans, such as Frederick Douglass, who should have been recognized at the fair. In response to Wells's publication and public demand, the fair administrators gave free admission to African Americans for one day, "Colored Day."

Science History Images/Alamy Stock Photo.

The section known as "The White City" highlighted international trade as a marker of American progress. Agriculture Hall illustrated the production of corn, wheat, and other crops for export and featured a gigantic globe encircled by samples of American-manufactured farm machinery. Another building housed a model of a canal cut across Nicaragua, suggesting the ease with which American traders might reach Asian markets if transport ships could travel directly from the Caribbean to the Pacific. One of the most popular exhibits featured a mock ocean liner built to scale where fairgoers could imagine themselves as "tourists" sailing in luxury to distant parts of the world.

In contrast to the White City was the Midway Plaisance, a wide strip nearly a mile long lined by amusements. The new, spectacular Ferris wheel, designed to rival the Eiffel Tower of Paris, was the largest attraction. But the Midway also offered entertainment in the form of "displays" of "uncivilized" people from foreign lands.

One enormous sideshow recreated Turkish bazaars and South Sea island huts. There were Javanese carpenters, Dahomean drummers, Egyptian swordsmen, and Hungarian Gypsies, as well as Eskimos, Syrians, Samoans, and Chinese. One favorite attraction was "Little Egypt," who performed at the Persian Palace of Eros; her *danse du ventre* became better known as the hootchy-kootchy. According to the guidebook, all these peoples had come "from the nightsome North and the splendid South, from the wasty West and the effete East, bringing their manners, customs, dress, religions, legends, amusements, that we might know them better."

By celebrating the brilliance of American industry and simultaneously presenting the "uncivilized" people of the world as a source of exotic entertainment, the planners of the fair delivered a powerful message. Former abolitionist Frederick Douglass, who attended the fair on "Colored People's Day," recognized it immediately. He noted that the physical layout of the fair, by carefully grouping exhibits, sharply divided the United States and Europe from the rest of the world—namely, from the nations of Africa, Asia, and the Middle East. Douglass objected to the stark contrast setting off Anglo-Saxons from people of color, an opposition between "civilization" and "savagery." He and Ida B. Wells also objected to the exclusion of African Americans from organizing an exhibit for the White City. Wells boycotted the special day set aside for African Americans, while Douglass attended, using the occasion to deliver a speech upbraiding white Americans for their racism.

Frederick Jackson Turner also spoke at the fair, delivering his famous essay on the disappearance of the frontier and its meaning for the fate of American democracy. With the closing of the frontier, the young historian warned, the nation is now "thrown back upon itself." His message seemed clear: If democracy were to survive, Americans required a new "frontier."

The Chicago World's Fair, which attracted 27 million visitors from all over the world, reassured Turner by marking the coming of age of the United States as a global power and by making a deliberate case for commercial expansion abroad. The exposition also gave material shape to prevalent ideas about the preeminence of American civilization as well as the superiority of the Anglo-Saxon race. (See SEEING History.)

20.5.2 The "Imperialism of Righteousness"

Social gospeler Josiah Strong, a Congregational minister, provided a prescient commentary in 1885. Linking economic and spiritual expansion, he advocated an "imperialism of righteousness." He identified white Americans as the best agents for "Christianizing" and "civilizing" the people of Africa, the Pacific, and beyond. It was the white American, Strong argued, who had been "divinely commissioned to be . . . his brother's keeper."

The push for overseas expansion coincided with a major wave of religious evangelism and foreign missions. Early in the nineteenth century, Protestant missionaries—hoping to fulfill what they believed to be a divine command to carry God's message to all peoples and to win converts for their church—had focused on North America. Many disciples, like Josiah Strong himself, headed west and stationed themselves on Indian reservations. Others, influenced by the Social Gospel, worked among the immigrant populations of the nation's growing cities. By the end of the nineteenth century, the major evangelical Protestant denominations were all sponsoring missions directed at foreign lands.

Protestant women rushed to join foreign missionary societies and raised large sums of money to fund overseas missions. By 1900, the various Protestant denominations had formed more than 40 women's missionary boards, representing no fewer than 3 million women. In total, the membership of women's missionary societies surpassed in size that of any other women's organization in the United States. The locations of missions ranged from China, India, and Africa to Syria, the Pacific Islands, and Latin America.

Outside the churches, the YMCA and YWCA—which had set up nondenominational programs for the working poor in many American cities—also embarked on a worldwide crusade to reach non-Christians. As foreign branches multiplied, a close observer ironically suggested that the United States had three great occupying forces: the army, the navy, and the "Y."

The missionaries did more than spread the gospel. They taught school, provided rudimentary medical care, offered vocational training programs, and sometimes encouraged young men and women to pursue a college education in

SEEING History

The White Man's Burden

In 1899, the British poet Rudyard Kipling published "The White Man's Burden" in the American magazine *McClure's* with the subtitle "The United States and the Philippine Islands." Some interpreted the poem as an endorsement of the U.S. imperialist ventures in the Pacific; others read it as a cautionary note warning against taking on colonies. Those who favored expansion embraced the notion of the "white man's burden" as means to justify their position as a noble enterprise—that is, "uplifting" those people of color who had not yet enjoyed the benefits of "civilization."

The concept even made its way into advertising for soap. In 1789, London soapmaster Andrew Pears began producing a distinctive oval bar of transparent amber glycerin and marketing it as a luxury item under the name Pears Soap. He found a talented promoter in Thomas J. Barratt, considered a pioneer of modern advertising, who built an international market for the product. By the end of the nineteenth century, Pears Soap had achieved brand-name status among middle- and upper-class Americans.

Barratt's advertising presented Pears Soap as safe and beneficial but suitable only for discerning consumers. Among its many other advantages, Pears Soap promised a smooth, white complexion, underscoring this message by associating dark skins with "uncivilized" people. The man pictured in this ad is probably a colonial official. The advertisement appeared first in 1899 in *McClure's*—the same magazine in which Kipling's poetic exhortation was published.

> *Take up the White Man's burden—*
> *Send forth the best ye breed—*
> *Go bind your sons to exile*
> *To serve your captives' need;*
> *To wait in heavy harness,*
> *On fluttered folk and wild—*
> *Your new-caught, sullen peoples,*
> *Half-devil and half-child.*
> *Take up the White Man's burden—*
> *In patience to abide,*
> *To veil the threat of terror*
> *. . . And check the show of pride . . .*

The first step towards lightening

The White Man's Burden

is through teaching the virtues of cleanliness.

Pears' Soap

is a potent factor in brightening the dark corners of the earth as civilization advances, while amongst the cultured of all nations it holds the highest place—it is the ideal toilet soap.

"THE WHITE MAN'S BURDEN"

North Wind Picture Archives/Alamy Stock Photo.

- **What did the readers of *McClure's* magazine understand as "the white man's burden"? How did this responsibility relate to the belief in a hierarchy of races and civilizations expressed in Kipling's poem?**

---

preparation for careers in their homelands. They also played important roles in generating public interest in foreign lands and in preparing the way for American economic expansion. As Strong aptly put it, "Commerce follows the missionary."

20.5.3 The Quest for Empire

Not only missionaries but also business and political leaders had set their sights on distant lands, which held out the prospect of new markets. During the Civil War, the Lincoln administration correctly predicted that foreign trade would play an increasingly important part in the American economy. Between 1870 and 1900, exports more than tripled, from about $400 million to over $1.5 billion, with textiles and agricultural products leading the way. But as European markets for American goods began to contract, business and political leaders, of necessity, looked more eagerly at lands closer by.

THE FOOCHOW MISSION Emily Susan Hartwell, far left, graduated from Wheaton College and, as a Congregational Christian missionary, traveled to Foochow, China, in 1884. She taught English at Foochow College for the next 20 years, and founded an orphanage, a kindergarten, a girls' school, and several other charitable institutions. She is pictured here with Bible students at the Foochow Mission in 1902. She remained in Foochow until 1937, when she was forced to evacuate at the beginning of the Sino-Japanese war.

Library of Congress.

The drive toward expansion rested on a cornerstone of U.S. foreign policy that had been outlined in 1823 by President James Monroe. The Monroe Doctrine called for the end of European colonization in the New World, arguing that the entire Western Hemisphere fell naturally within the U.S. territorial realm, destined for exploration and acquisition when the opportunity allowed. Secretary of State William Henry Seward, appointed by Lincoln in 1861, took one of the first major steps to implement this policy. In 1867, despite critics who dubbed his proposal "Seward's Folly" or "Seward's Icebox," he negotiated the purchase of Alaska from Russia for $7.2 million. Seward hoped, too, to see the American flag flying over Canada and Mexico. Meanwhile, others who shared his expansionist views discussed the Caribbean as an "American lake" and imagined all Latin America as a vast market for U.S. goods.

The Alaska Purchase raised the stakes for territorial expansion into Canada, especially for the railroad magnates who hoped to run a line linking the new region to the established western territories in the United States. The most ambitious Americans aspired to dislodge Britain from its rule of Canada. In 1867, when several Canadian colonies joined to become a self-governing confederation or dominion, American diplomats hoped Britain would back away and allow the United States to annex its northern neighbor. But Britain refused to give up Canada, and the majority of Canadians opposed annexation. Americans advocates of expansion hoped for better prospects in Central and South America. (See Map 20.3.)

Republican stalwart James G. Blaine, secretary of state under presidents Garfield and Harrison, emerged as an important architect of U.S. foreign policy in Latin America. "What we want," he explained, "are the markets

of these neighbors of ours that lie to the south of us." Bilateral treaties with Mexico, Colombia, the British West Indies, El Salvador, and the Dominican Republic allowed American businesses to dominate local economies,

QUEEN LILI'UOKALANI Brought to power with the assistance of American businessmen, Queen Lili'uokalani sought to limit outsider influence. American Marines, Christian missionaries, and sugar planters joined in 1893 to drive her from her throne. A century later, the U.S. government apologized to native Hawaiians for this illegal act.

Design Pics Inc/Alamy Stock Photo.

Map 20.3 THE AMERICAN DOMAIN, CA. 1900

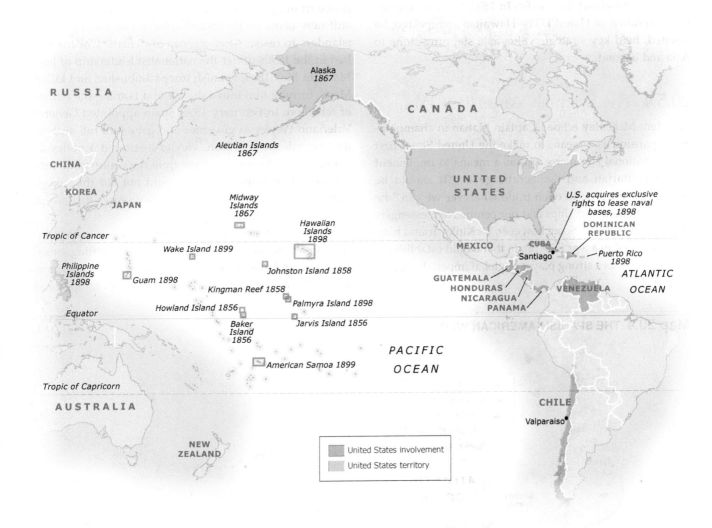

RUSSIA

CHINA

KOREA

JAPAN

Tropic of Cancer

Philippine
Islands
1898

Guam 1898

Equator

Tropic of Capricorn

AUSTRALIA

NEW
ZEALAND

Alaska
1867

Aleutian Islands
1867

Midway
Islands
1867

Wake Island 1899

Johnston Island 1858

Kingman Reef 1858

Howland Island 1856

Baker
Island
1856

Jarvis Island 1856

Palmyra Island 1898

American Samoa 1899

Hawaiian
Islands
1898

CANADA

UNITED
STATES

MEXICO

GUATEMALA
HONDURAS
NICARAGUA
PANAMA

CUBA
Santiago

U.S. acquires exclusive
rights to lease naval
bases, 1898

DOMINICAN
REPUBLIC

Puerto Rico
1898

VENEZUELA

ATLANTIC
OCEAN

PACIFIC
OCEAN

CHILE

Valparaiso

United States involvement

United States territory

The United States claimed numerous islands in the South Pacific and intervened repeatedly in Latin America to secure its own economic interests.

importing their raw materials at low prices and flooding their local markets with goods manufactured in the United States. Often, American investors simply took over the principal industries of these small nations, undercutting local business classes. Blaine, who had his eye on a future presidency for himself, hoped to provide stability to U.S. leadership by bringing together nations of North, Central, and South America in a Pan-American Conference, which convened for the first time in 1889. The success of this loose affiliation of nations depended, Blaine knew, on peace and order in the Latin American states, and during times of disruption, the United States stood ready to step in.

To promote stability and expand U.S. interests abroad, Congress appropriated funds to build up American sea power. Beginning with a fleet of outdated ships, over

one-third of them wooden, the navy began to grow in the 1880s to become a large, modern fleet of steel-hulled armored cruisers and battleships. By 1920 the U.S. Navy surpassed the British Royal Navy, which had until that time ruled the seas. In 1884 Congress established the Naval War College in Newport, Rhode Island, to train the growing officer corps.

Captain Alfred Thayer Mahan—one of the first lecturers at the Naval War College, and its president in the late 1880s—achieved international fame for outlining an imperialist strategy based on command of the seas. His major book, *The Influence of Sea Power upon History, 1660–1873* (1890), helped to define foreign policy not only for the United States but also for Great Britain, Japan, and Germany by identifying sea power as the key to world dominance. Viewing the U.S. Navy as the "handmaid of expansion," Mahan advocated the creation of bases beyond the Western Hemisphere, not only in the nearby Caribbean but also throughout the Pacific. In 1893, he came out for the annexation of Hawai'i. The Hawaiian archipelago, he insisted, held key strategic value as a stepping-stone to Asia and beyond.

20.5.4 The Spanish-American War

President McKinley echoed Captain Mahan in championing expansion as a means to make the United States first in international commerce and as a means to implement its humanitarian and democratic goals. "It should be our settled purpose to open trade wherever we can," he argued, "making our ships and our commerce messengers of peace and amity." Soon, however, McKinley found himself embroiled in a war with Spain that would establish the United States as a strong player in global imperialism. (See Map 20.4.)

The rationale for the war extended back to the mid-1860s, when Cuba launched a movement for independence from Spain. Its empire in ruins, Spain had levied stiff new taxes on its distant colony and provoked the islanders to resist. After a series of defeats, Cubans rallied in the 1890s under the nationalist leadership of José Martí. In May 1895, Spanish troops ambushed and killed Martí, turning him into a martyr and fanning the flames of rebellion. In February 1896, Spain appointed General Valeriano Weyler as governor and gave him full authority to crush the rebellion. Weyler instituted a policy of *reconcentrado*, forcing civilians from the countryside into concentration camps so they could not aid the rebels. Thousands starved or died from the diseases that swept these crowded, dirty camps.

In the United States, the popular press whipped up support for the movement for *Cuba Libre*, circulating sensationalistic and even false stories of atrocities. Newspapers ran stories on mass executions in the "death camps" and

Map 20.4 THE SPANISH-AMERICAN WAR

In two theaters of action, the United States used its naval power adeptly against a weak foe.

featured drawings of emaciated children. This so-called "yellow journalism," practiced brilliantly by publishers Joseph Pulitzer and William Randolph Hearst, boosted circulation and simultaneously aroused sympathy for the Cubans and abundant patriotic fervor.

Public sympathy, again whipped up by the press, turned into frenzy on February 15, 1898, when an explosion ripped through the battleship USS *Maine*, stationed in Havana harbor to protect American interests. The newspapers ran banner headlines charging a Spanish conspiracy, although there was no proof. The impatient public, meanwhile, demanded revenge for the death of 266 American sailors. Within days, a new slogan appeared; "Remember the Maine! To Hell with Spain!"

Finally, on April 11, President McKinley asked Congress for a declaration of war against Spain. Congress barely passed the war resolution on April 25, and only with the inclusion of an amendment by Senator Henry Teller (R-CO) that disclaimed, "any disposition or intention to exercise sovereignty, jurisdiction or control over said island, except for the pacification thereof." McKinley called for volunteers, and by the end of April, the fighting had begun.

Ten weeks later, the war was all but over. On land, Lieutenant Colonel Theodore Roosevelt led his Rough Riders to victory. On July 3, the main Spanish fleet near Santiago Bay was destroyed; two weeks later Santiago itself surrendered, and the war drew to a close. Although the Americans were poorly trained and lacking supplies, fewer than 400 died in battle. Disease and the inept treatment of the wounded created a medical disaster, however, spreading sickness and disease to more than 20,000 in the regiments. Nevertheless, Roosevelt agreed with McKinley's secretary of state, John Hay, that it had been a "splendid little war."

On August 12, at a small ceremony in McKinley's office marking Spain's surrender, the United States secured Cuba's independence from Spain, but not its own sovereignty. American businesses proceeded to tighten their hold on Cuban sugar plantations, while U.S. military forces oversaw the formation of a constitutional convention that made Cuba a protectorate of the United States. Under the Platt Amendment, sponsored by Republican senator Orville H. Platt of Connecticut in 1901, Cuba was required to provide land for American bases, including a navy base at Guantanamo Bay; to devote national revenues to pay back debts to the United States; to sign no treaty that would be detrimental to American interests; and to acknowledge the right of the United States to intervene at any time to protect its interests in Cuba.

McKinley and Roosevelt also viewed the Philippines, another of Spain's colonies, as an especially attractive prospect, its 7,000 islands a natural way station to the markets of mainland Asia. On May 4, shortly after Congress declared war on Spain, the president dispatched 5,000 troops to occupy the Philippines. During the first week of the conflict, the American Asiatic Squadron demolished the Spanish fleet in Manila Bay. Once the war ended, McKinley refused to sign the armistice unless Spain relinquished all claims to its Pacific islands. When Spain conceded, McKinley quickly drew up plans for colonial administration. He pledged "to educate the Filipinos, and to uplift and civilize and Christianize them." After centuries of Spanish rule, however, the majority of islanders were eager to create their own nation.

The Filipino rebels, like the Cubans, at first welcomed American troops and fought with them against Spain. But after the Spanish-American War ended and they perceived that American troops were not preparing to leave, the rebels, led by Emilio Aguinaldo, turned against their former allies and attacked the American base of operations in Manila in February 1899. Predicting a brief skirmish, American commanders seriously underestimated the population's capacity to endure great suffering for the sake of independence. Moreover, U.S. troops abused civilians, routinely insulting them and raping women, and whipped up resentment.

By the time the fighting slowed down in 1902, 4,300 American lives had been lost, and one of every five Filipinos had died in battle or from starvation or disease. Beginning in 1901, President McKinley appointed federal judge William Howard Taft to serve as the civilian governor of the Philippines; after 1905 Theodore Roosevelt, who became president following McKinley's assassination, appointed a Filipino governor to head the provincial government. Meanwhile, Americans bought up the best land and invested heavily in the island's sugar economy.

The conquest of the Philippines, which remained a U.S. colony until 1946, evoked for its proponents the vision of empire. The Philippines joined Hawai'i as yet another stepping-stone for U.S. merchants en route to China. At the end of the Spanish-American War, the United States advanced its interests in the Caribbean to include Puerto Rico, ceded by Spain, and eventually the Virgin Islands of St. Thomas, St. John, and St. Croix, purchased from Denmark in 1917. The acquisition of Pacific territories, including Guam, marked the emergence of the United States as a global colonial power.

Once again, Josiah Strong proclaimed judgment over an era. His famous treatise *Expansion* (1900) roundly defended American overseas involvements. Many began to wonder, however, whether the United States could become an empire without sacrificing its democratic spirit, and to ask whether the subjugated people were really so fortunate under the rule of the United States. (See Communities *in* Conflict.)

"UNCLE SAM TEACHES THE ART OF SELF-GOVERNMENT" "Uncle Sam Teaches the Art of Self-Government," editorial cartoon, 1898. Expressing a popular sentiment of the time, a newspaper cartoonist shows the rebels as raucous children who constantly fight among themselves and need to be brought into line by Uncle Sam. The Filipino leader, Emilio Aguinaldo, appears as a dunce for failing to learn properly from the teacher. The two major islands where no uprising took place, Puerto Rico and Hawai'i, appear as passive but exotically dressed women, ready to learn their lessons.

Library of Congress (Photoduplication).

Communities *in* Conflict

Two Sides of Anti-Imperialism

"What we have to face is the question whether we should embark upon the difficult and dangerous policy of undertaking the government of alien races."

Industrialist Andrew Carnegie (1835–1919) gave generously to help finance the Anti-Imperialist League from its formation until his death. He also served as a vice president of the league. His position on American expansion was complex, arising out of his opinion that some peoples were incapable of assimilation into a democratic society. For example, Carnegie reluctantly agreed with the annexation of Hawai'i, in part because the islands were only thinly settled and, therefore, could absorb more advanced "races," including American immigrants. Strongly opposed to acquiring the Philippines, he made an offer to President McKinley to purchase the islands from the United States, after which he would restore governance to the Filipinos. McKinley rejected this offer, ensuring Carnegie's alliance with the anti-imperialists.

His statement was originally published in August 1898, when U.S. forces were invading the Philippines and Americans were debating what to do with the Spanish colonies.

The widow of a prominent businessman and throughout her life a committed reformer, Josephine Shaw Lowell (1843–1905) also opposed the Spanish-American War. Like Carnegie, she denounced the annexation of the Philippines and was a leader of the Anti-Imperialist League, serving as a vice president from 1901 to 1905. Lowell wrote her impassioned protest after the outbreak of Filipino resistance against American rule, but before the U.S. Army completed its bloody subjugation of the islands.

- **Are these two arguments contradictory or complementary? Is there more to Carnegie's objection to imperialism than racism? Is Lowell correct in arguing that some wars can be not only just but also morally elevating?**

Andrew Carnegie, Anti-Imperialist: America Cannot Absorb Alien Populations (August 1898)

Is the Republic, the apostle of Triumphant Democracy, of the rule of the people, to abandon her political creed and endeavor to establish in other lands the rule of the foreigner over the people, Triumphant Despotism?

Is the Republic to remain one homogeneous whole, one united people, or to become a scattered and disjointed aggregate of widely separated and alien races?

Is she to continue the task of developing her vast continent until it holds a population as great as that of Europe, all Americans, or to abandon that destiny to annex, and to attempt to govern, other far distant parts of the world as outlying possessions, which can never be integral parts of the Republic? . . .

There are two kinds of national possessions, one colonies, the other dependencies. In the former we establish and reproduce our own race. Thus Britain has peopled Canada and Australia with English-speaking people, who have naturally adopted our ideas of self-government.

With dependencies it is otherwise. The most grievous burden which Britain has upon her shoulders is that of India, for there it is impossible for our race to grow. The child of English-speaking parents must be removed and reared in Britain. The British Indian official must have long respites in his native land. India means death to our race. The characteristic feature of a dependency is that the acquiring power cannot reproduce its own race there.

If we could establish colonies of Americans, and grow Americans in any part of the world now unpopulated and unclaimed by any of the great powers, and thus follow the example of Britain, heart and mind might tell us that we should have to think twice, yea, thrice, before deciding adversely. Even then our decision should be adverse; but there is at present no such question before us. What we have to face is the question whether we should embark upon the difficult and dangerous policy of undertaking the government of alien races in lands where it is impossible for our own race to be produced. . . .

I am no "Little" American, afraid of growth, either in population or territory, provided always that the new territory be American, and that it will produce Americans, and not foreign races bound in time to be false to the Republic in order to be true to themselves. . . . The Philippines have about seven and a half millions of people, composed of races bitterly hostile to one another, alien races, ignorant of our language and institutions. Americans cannot be grown there. . . .

Source: Andrew Carnegie, "Distant Possessions: The Parting of the Ways," in *The Gospel of Wealth* (New York: Century Company, 1901), p. 151. Originally published in the *North American Review* (August 1898).

Josephine Shaw Lowell, Anti-Imperialist: America Must Not Wage Unjust Wars (ca. 1900)

I cannot speak on this subject without making a distinction between different kinds of wars.

A war which requires personal sacrifice, a war which makes a whole people place patriotism and public duty above private comfort and ease, which forces men and women out of self-indulgence, devotion to material wealth—such a war does not as a whole cause moral deterioration—but on the contrary, moral development in a nation.

Such a war was the Civil War in this country, forty years ago. . . .

The history of the introduction of the United States to the Philippine Islands is a disgraceful one. . . . In December, 1898 . . . the President of the United States proclaimed sovereignty over the Philippine Archipelago, this naturally aroused the anger of the Filipinos, who had been treasuring for six months or more the hope that the United States intended to help and protect their young republic against the attacks of other nations, and the feelings became more and more bitter, and finally culminated in a fight between the outposts of the two armies on February 4, 1899; and from that time, the United States devoted itself to the task of crushing out what was called the insurrection of the Filipinos.

That is, the United States, having obtained a foothold in a foreign country by professing friendship for the inhabitants, calls those inhabitants rebels because the people resist the invasion and try to defend their country. We direct our army to crush out all resistance. The Filipino people prefer death to subjugation, saying, as did Patrick Henry, the American patriot, "Give me liberty or give me death." Our unhappy army set to do such an un-American, such a wicked task, tried to obey orders, becomes gradually more and more cruel. . . .

It is incredible that the American people should have been so ignorant and so careless in regard to the great wrong which has been done in their name; but now at last we are awakening, we are beginning to realize the facts. . . . I said, that the liberties of the United States are at stake equally with the liberties of the Filipino people, for it is inevitable that should we willingly become the tyrant of these helpless millions, should we turn our backs so completely upon the principles which have made this country a world power, molding and influencing the character of all governments of the world during the past hundred and twenty-five years, as to make it possible for us to do such a thing our moral deterioration is so rapid, our conscience must become so hardened in the process, our love of liberty so absolutely dead, that, we should become fit subjects for a tyranny ourselves.

Source: "Moral Deterioration Following War," ca. 1900, reprinted in *The Philanthropic Work of Josephine Shaw Lowell: Containing a Biographical Sketch of Her Life*, collected by William Rhinelander Stewart (New York: Macmillan Co., 1911), pp. 466–470.

20.5.5 Critics of Empire

No mass movement formed to forestall U.S. expansion, but distinguished figures like Mark Twain, Andrew Carnegie, William Jennings Bryan, Grover Cleveland, and Harvard philosopher William James voiced their opposition strongly. Fearing that imperialism threatened the democratic principles grounded in the right to self-governance, a small group of prominent Bostonians organized the Anti-Imperialist League in June 1898. Most members supported American economic expansion. Carnegie, for one, aggressively sought foreign markets for his steel, most aggressively in Russia. But he, like most others, advocated free trade rather than political domination as a means to promote U.S. interests abroad. All strongly opposed the annexation of new territories, including Hawai'i and the Philippines. Within a year, the league claimed approximately 100 branches.

The *National Labor Standard* expressed its common hope that all those "who believe in the Republic against Empire should join," but individual members offered many reasons, including racist reasons, for opposing U.S. imperialism. A few outspoken anti-imperialists, such as former Illinois governor John Peter Altgeld, openly toasted Filipino rebels as heroes. Others, such as Samuel Gompers, a league vice president, felt no sympathy for conquered peoples and simply wanted to prevent colonized nonwhites from immigrating to the United States and "inundating" American labor.

Military leaders and staunch imperialists did not distinguish between racist and non-racist anti-imperialists. They called all dissenters "unhung traitors" and demanded their arrest. Newspaper editors accused universities of harboring antiwar professors, although college students as a group were enthusiastic supporters of the war.

Within the press, which overwhelmingly supported the Spanish-American War, the voices of opposition appeared primarily in African American and labor papers. The *Indianapolis Recorder* asked rhetorically in 1899, "Are the tender-hearted expansionists in the United States Congress really actuated by the desire to save the Filipinos from self-destruction or is it the worldly greed for gain?" The *Railroad Telegrapher* similarly commented, "The wonder of it all is that the working people are willing to lose blood and treasure in fighting another man's battle."

Most Americans put aside their doubts and welcomed the new era of imperialism. Untouched by the private tragedies of dead or wounded American soldiers or the mass destruction of civilian society in the Philippines, the vast majority could approve of Theodore Roosevelt's defense of armed conflict; "No triumph of peace is quite so great as the supreme triumphs of war."

Conclusion

The conflicts marking the last quarter of the nineteenth century that pitted farmers, workers, and the proprietors of small businesses against powerful national interests had offered Americans an important moment of democratic promise. By the end of the century, however, the rural and working-class campaigns to retain a large degree of self-government in their communities had been defeated, their organizations destroyed, their autonomy eroded. The rise of a national governing class and its counterpart, the large bureaucratic state, established new rules of behavior, new sources of prestige, and new rewards for the most successful citizens.

The nation would eventually pay a steep price for the failure of democratic reform. Regional antagonisms, nativist movements against the foreign-born, and, above all, deepening racial tensions blighted American society. As the new century opened, progressive reformers moved to correct flaws in government while accepting the framework of a corporate society and its overseas empire. So, too, did the majority of citizens who shared their president's pride in expansion.

William Jennings Bryan made another bid for the presidency in 1900 on a strong anti-imperialist platform and was roundly defeated at the polls. The dream of Queen Lili'uokalani for an independent Hawai'i was likewise crushed, although in 1993, a century after her overthrow, President William Clinton signed a joint congressional resolution apologizing for the "alleged role the United States had played" in her deposing. But in 1900, Americans would find the widening divisions in their own society difficult—if not impossible—to overcome.

Key Terms

Interstate Commerce Commission (ICC) A commission established by the 1887 law that expanded federal power over business by prohibiting pooling and discriminatory rates by railroads. p. 457

Pendleton Civil Service Reform Act A law passed in 1883 that reformed the spoils system by prohibiting government workers from making political contributions and creating the Civil Service Commission to oversee their appointment on the basis of merit rather than politics. p. 458

Populism A mass movement of the 1890s formed on the basis of the Southern Farmers' Alliance and other reform organizations. p. 459

Grange The National Grange of the Patrons of Husbandry, a national organization of farm owners formed after the Civil War. p. 459

Granger laws State laws enacted in the Midwest in the 1870s that regulated rates charged by railroads, grain elevator operators, and other middlemen. p. 459

Southern Farmers' Alliance The largest of several organizations that formed in the post-Reconstruction South to advance the interests of beleaguered small farmers. p. 460

Woman's Christian Temperance Union (WCTU) Women's organization whose members visited schools to educate children about the evils of alcohol, addressed prisoners, and blanketed men's meetings with literature. p. 462

Coxey's Army A protest march of unemployed workers, led by Populist businessman Jacob Coxey, demanding inflation and a public works program during the depression of the 1890s. p. 464

protective association Organizations formed by mine owners in response to the formation of labor unions. p. 464

Sherman Silver Purchase Act An 1890 act that directed the Treasury to increase the amount of currency coined from silver mined in the West and also permitted the U.S. government to print paper currency backed by the silver. p. 466

free silver Philosophy that the government should expand the money supply by purchasing and coining all the silver offered to it. p. 466

nativism Favoring the interests and culture of native-born inhabitants over those of immigrants. p. 468

Jim Crow laws Segregation laws that became widespread in the South during the 1890s. p. 468

Segregation A system of racial control that separated the races, initially by custom but increasingly by law, during and after Reconstruction. p. 468

Plessy v. Ferguson Supreme Court decision holding that Louisiana's railroad segregation law did not violate the Constitution as long as the railroads or the state provided equal accommodations. p. 468

Grandfather clauses Rules that required potential voters to demonstrate that their grandfathers had been eligible to vote; used in some Southern states after 1890 to limit the black electorate. p. 468

CHRONOLOGY

Pendleton Act passed	**1883**
	1887 Interstate Commerce Commission created
National Farmers' Alliance formed	**1889**
	1890 Sherman Silver Purchase Act / McKinley Tariff enacted
Populist (People's) Party formed / Homestead strike	**1892**
	1893 Financial panic and depression
"Coxey's Army" marches on Washington, D.C. / Pullman strike and boycott	**1894**
	1896 *Plessy v. Ferguson* upholds segregation / William McKinley defeats William Jenning Bryan for president
Hawai'i is annexed / Spanish-American War begins	**1898**

Chapter 21
Urban America and the Progressive Era 1900–1917

NINETEENTH AMENDMENT ADOPTED Suffragettes hold a victory jubilee, 1920. Elated women wave American flags and blow noisemakers.

Library of Congress.

 ## Contents and Focus Questions

21.1 **The Origins of Progressivism**
What were the social and intellectual roots of progressive reform?

21.2 **Progressive Politics in Cities and States**
How did progressives try to redefine the role of the government in American life?

21.3 **Social Control and Its Limits**
How did tensions between social justice and social control divide progressives?

21.4 **Challenges to Progressivism**
What groups challenged the progressive vision of politics?

21.5 **Women's Movements and Black Activism**
What new forms of activism emerged among the working class, women, and African Americans?

21.6 **National Progressivism**
What role did Theodore Roosevelt envision the federal government playing in national life?

American Communities

The Henry Street Settlement House: Women Settlement House Workers Create a Community of Reform

A shy and frightened young girl appeared in the doorway of a weekly home-nursing class for women on Manhattan's Lower East Side. The teacher beckoned her to come forward. Tugging on the teacher's skirt, the girl pleaded in broken English for the teacher to come home with her. "Mother," "baby," "blood," she kept repeating. The teacher gathered up the sheets that were part of the interrupted lesson in bed making. The two hurried through narrow, garbage-strewn, foul-smelling streets, then groped their way up a pitch-dark, rickety staircase. They reached a cramped, two-room apartment, home to an immigrant family of seven and

481

several boarders. There, in a vermin-infested bed, encrusted with dried blood, lay a mother and her newborn baby. The mother had been abandoned by a doctor because she could not afford his fee.

The teacher, Lillian Wald, recalled this scene as her baptism by fire and the turning point in her life. Born in 1867, Wald had enjoyed a comfortable upbringing in a middle-class German Jewish family in Rochester. Despite her parents' objections, she moved to New York City to become a professional nurse. Resentful of the disdainful treatment nurses received from doctors, and horrified by the inhumane conditions at a juvenile asylum where she worked, Wald determined to find a way of caring for the sick in their neighborhoods and homes. With nursing school classmate Mary Brewster, Wald rented a fifth-floor walk-up apartment on the Lower East Side and established a visiting nurse service. The two provided professional care in the home to hundreds of families for a nominal fee of 10 to 25 cents. They also offered each family they visited information on basic health care, sanitation, and disease prevention. In 1895, philanthropist Jacob Schiff generously donated a red brick Georgian house on Henry Street as a new base of operation.

The Henry Street Settlement stood in the center of perhaps the most overcrowded neighborhood in the world, New York's Lower East Side. Roughly 500,000 people were packed into an area only as large as a midsized Kansas farm. Population density was about 500 per acre, roughly four times the figure for the rest of New York City, and far more concentrated than even the worst slums of London or Calcutta. A single city block might have as many as 3,000 residents. Home for most Lower East Siders was a small tenement apartment that might include paying boarders squeezed in alongside the immediate family. Residents were mostly recent immigrants from southern and eastern Europe: Jews, Italians, Germans, Greeks, Hungarians, and Slavs. Men, women, and children toiled in the garment shops, small factories, retail stores, breweries, and warehouses that were found on nearly every street.

The Henry Street Settlement became a model for a new kind of reform community composed essentially of college-educated women who encouraged and supported one another in a wide variety of humanitarian, civic, and political activities. These included support for organized labor, campaigns for better sanitation and more parks, lobbying state legislatures for tougher laws regulating tenement construction and factory safety, and pushing for women's rights. Settlement house living arrangements closely resembled those in the dormitories of such new women's colleges as Smith, Wellesley, and Vassar. Like these colleges, the settlement house was

an "experiment," but one designed, in settlement house pioneer Jane Addams's words, "to aid in the solution of the social and industrial problems which are engendered by the modern conditions of urban life." Unlike earlier moral reformers, who tried to impose their ideas from outside, settlement house residents lived in poor communities and worked for immediate improvements in the health and welfare of those communities. Yet, as Addams and others repeatedly stressed, the college-educated women were beneficiaries as well. The settlement house allowed them to preserve a collegial spirit, satisfy the desire for service, and apply their academic training.

With its combined moral and social appeal, the settlement house movement attracted many educated young women and grew rapidly. There were 6 settlement houses in the United States in 1891, some 74 in 1897, more than 200 by 1900, and more than 400 by 1910. Few women made settlement work a career, but those who did typically chose not to marry, and most lived together with female companions. As the movement flourished, settlement house residents called attention to the plight of the poor and fostered respect for different cultural heritages in countless articles and lectures. Leaders of the movement, including Jane Addams, Lillian Wald, and Florence Kelley, emerged as influential political figures during the progressive era.

The settlement house movement embodied the impulses toward social justice and civic engagement that were hallmarks of the progressive movement. But in a broader sense, the progressive era was defined by struggles over the true meaning of American democracy. If there was growing agreement that Americans needed to address the excesses of industrial growth and rapid urbanization, there was less consensus over precisely how. As progressive activism spread from reform communities like settlement houses, to city halls and statehouses, and finally to the national stage of the White House and Congress, Americans experimented with new approaches to urgent problems. How might the power of government be used to restrain corporate excess and improve the lives of children, industrial laborers, and others in need of protection? Could the machinery of democracy be reformed to make politics less corrupt and more responsive to the needs of ordinary citizens? Did the calls to social action mean that full citizenship rights would be extended to African Americans, women, and new immigrants? What were the most effective ways to expose social problems and appeal to the public conscience?

During the first two decades of the twentieth century, millions of Americans identified themselves as "progressives" and most, like Lillian Wald, were first drawn to causes and campaigns

New York City

rooted in their local communities. But many soon saw that confronting the grim realities of an urban and industrial society required national and even global strategies for pursuing reform. It was no cliché for Wald to say, as she did on many occasions, "The whole world is my neighborhood." By the time America entered World War I in 1917, despite its contradictions, the progressive movement had reshaped the political and social landscape of the entire nation.

21.1 The Origins of Progressivism

What were the social and intellectual roots of progressive reform?

Between the 1890s and World War I, a large and diverse number of Americans claimed the political label "progressive." Progressives could be found in all classes, regions, and races. They shared a fundamental belief that America needed a new social consciousness to cope with the problems brought on by the enormous rush of economic and social change in the post-Civil War decades. Yet **progressivism** was no unified movement with a single set of principles. It is best understood as a varied collection of reform communities, often fleeting, uniting citizens in a host of political, professional, and religious organizations, some of which were national in scope.

Progressivism flowered in the soil of several key issues: ending political corruption, bringing more businesslike methods to governing, and offering a more compassionate legislative response to the excesses of industrialism. As a national movement, progressivism reached its peak in 1912, when the four major presidential candidates all ran on some version of a progressive platform. This last development was an important measure of the extent to which local reform movements, like the Henry Street Settlement, and new intellectual currents had captured the political imagination of the nation.

21.1.1 Unifying Themes

Three basic attitudes underlay the various progressive crusades and movements. The first was anger over the excesses of industrial capitalism and urban growth. Unlike Populist-era reformers, who were largely rural and small-town oriented, progressives focused their energies on the social and political ills experienced by Americans in factories, mines, and cities. At the same time, progressives shared an essential optimism about the ability of citizens to improve social and economic conditions. They were reformers, not revolutionaries, who believed in using the democratic institutions available to them—the vote, the courts, the legislature—to address social problems. If those political processes were found to be corrupt or undemocratic, they would have to be reformed as well.

Second, progressives emphasized social cohesion and common bonds as a way to understand how modern society and economics actually worked. They largely rejected the ideal of individualism that had informed nineteenth-century economic and political theory. For progressives, poverty and success hinged on more than simply individual character; the economy was more than merely a sum of individual calculations. For progressives, society's problems were structural rather than just the result of individual failures.

Third, progressives believed in the need for citizens to intervene actively, both politically and morally, to improve social conditions. They looked to convert personal outrage into civic activism and to mobilize public opinion in new ways. Progressives thus called for expansion of the legislative and regulatory powers of the state. They moved away from the nineteenth-century celebration of minimal government as the surest way to allow all Americans to thrive.

Progressive rhetoric and methods drew on two distinct sources of inspiration. One was evangelical Protestantism, particularly the late-nineteenth-century social gospel movement. Social gospelers emphasized both the capacity and the duty of Christians to purge the world of poverty, inequality, and economic greed. Many progressive activists with roots in the evangelical tradition adapted the old emphasis on individual salvation into a new social activism more focused on finding the common good. A second strain of progressive thought looked to natural and social scientists to develop rational measures for improving the human condition. They believed that experts trained in statistical analysis, engineering, and the sciences could make government and industry more efficient and set new standards for personal behavior. Progressivism thus offered an uneasy combination of social justice and social control, a tension that would characterize American reform for the rest of the twentieth century. (See Table 21.1.)

21.1.2 New Journalism: Muckraking

Changes in journalism helped fuel a new reform consciousness by drawing the attention of millions to urban poverty, political corruption, the plight of industrial workers, and immoral business practices. As early as 1890, journalist Jacob Riis had shocked the nation with his landmark book

Table 21.1 CURRENTS OF PROGRESSIVISM

	Key Figures	Issues
Local Communities	Jane Addams, Lillian Wald, Florence Kelley, Frederic C. Howe, Samuel Jones	• Improving health, education, welfare in urban immigrant neighborhoods • Child labor, eight-hour day • Celebrating immigrant cultures • Reforming urban politics • Municipal ownership/ regulation of utilities
State	Robert M. La Follette, Hiram Johnson, Al Smith	• Limiting power of railroads, other corporations • Improving civil service • Direct democracy • Applying academic scholarship to human needs
National	James K. Vardaman, Hoke Smith, Theodore Roosevelt, Woodrow Wilson	• Disfranchisement of African Americans • Trust-busting • Conservation and western development • National regulation of corporate and financial excesses • Reform of national banking
Intellectual/ Cultural	Jacob Riis, Lincoln Steffens, Ida Tarbell, Upton Sinclair, S. S. McClure John Dewey, Louis Brandeis, Edwin A. Ross	• Muckraking • Education reform • Sociological jurisprudence • Empowering "ethical elite"

How the Other Half Lives, a portrait of New York City's poor. Riis's book included a remarkable series of photographs he had taken in tenements, lodging houses, sweatshops, and saloons. These striking pictures, combined with Riis's analysis of housing patterns in the slums, had a powerful impact on a whole generation of urban reformers. (See SEEING History.)

Within a few years, magazine journalists turned to uncovering the seamier side of American life. The key innovator was S. S. McClure, a young midwestern editor who in 1893 started America's first large-circulation magazine, *McClure's*. Charging only a dime for his monthly, McClure effectively combined popular fiction with articles on science, technology, travel, and recent history. He attracted a new readership among the urban middle class through aggressive subscription and promotional campaigns, as well as newsstand sales. By the turn of the century, *McClure's* and several imitators—*Munsey's, Cosmopolitan, Collier's, Everybody's,* and the *Saturday Evening Post*—had circulations in the hundreds of thousands. Making extensive use of photographs and illustrations, these cheap upstarts soon far surpassed older, more staid and expensive magazines such as *The Atlantic Monthly* and *Harper's* in circulation.

In 1902, McClure began hiring talented reporters to write detailed accounts of the nation's social problems. Lincoln Steffens's series *The Shame of the Cities* (1903) revealed the widespread graft at the center of American urban politics. Ida Tarbell, in her *History of the Standard Oil Company* (1904), thoroughly documented how John D. Rockefeller

SEEING History

Photographing Poverty in the Slums of New York

Jacob A. Riis was a 20-year-old Danish immigrant when he arrived in New York City in 1870. After several years wandering the country as a casual laborer, he returned to New York and began a career as a reporter covering the police beat. By the early 1880s, Riis found himself drawn to report on perhaps the most overwhelming and rapidly worsening problem in the city: the deteriorating conditions of tenement house life. As he accompanied city police and Board of Health employees in their inspections of sanitary conditions, Riis's reports on the tenement districts reflected a keen outrage and new sense of purpose. Part of the story could be reduced to staggering statistics. By 1880, more than 600,000 New Yorkers lived in 24,000 tenements, each of which housed anywhere from four to several score families. Overcrowding kept getting worse, as in one Mulberry Street tenement that housed nearly 200 people in small apartments meant for 20 families. Thousands of buildings

HOME OF AN ITALIAN RAGPICKER IN NEW JERSEY STREET

Jacob A. Riis/Getty Images.

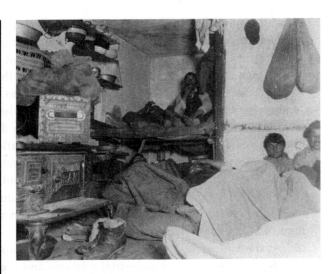

FIVE CENTS A SPOT

Jacob A. Riis/Getty Images.

had terrible sanitary conditions, with seriously defective plumbing, and often no ventilation or sewer connections. "It was upon my midnight trips with the sanitary police," he recalled, "that the wish kept cropping up in me that there were some way of putting before the people what I saw there."

In 1888, Riis taught himself the rudiments of photography, using the new "flash powder" technology to take pictures where there was no natural light. He shot many of these photographs in the dead of the night, taking his subjects by surprise. Other photographs were carefully staged to ensure maximum emotional impact on the middle- and upper-class audience Riis was trying to reach. Riis converted his photographs into "lantern slides," which could be projected as large images before audiences. He spent two years touring the country, presenting an illustrated lecture called "The Other Half: How It Lives and Dies in New York" to churches and reform groups, appealing to the conscience and Christian sympathy of his listeners. Newspapers reviewed Riis's slide lecture as both an "entertainment" and a new philanthropic campaign. In 1890, he published his landmark book, *How the Other Half Lives: Studies Among the Tenements*, illustrated with his photographs. The use of photography would become a key element for reform crusades in the progressive era and beyond.

- **Here are two Riis photographs, "Home of an Italian Ragpicker" and "Five Cents a Spot." What visual information does each communicate about tenement life? How do they differ in their depiction of New York City's immigrant poor? How do you imagine Riis set up the scene for each of these photographs?**

ruthlessly squeezed out competitors with unfair business practices. Ray Stannard Baker wrote detailed portraits of life and labor in Pennsylvania coal towns.

McClure's and other magazines discovered that "exposure journalism" paid off handsomely in terms of increased circulation. The middle-class public responded to this new combination of factual reporting and moral exhortation. A series such as Steffens's fueled reform campaigns that swept individual communities. Between 1902 and 1908, magazines were full of articles exposing insurance scandals, patent medicine frauds, and stock market swindles. Upton Sinclair's 1906 novel *The Jungle*, a socialist tract set among Chicago packinghouse workers, exposed the filthy sanitation and abysmal working conditions in the stockyards and the meatpacking industry. In an effort to boost sales, Sinclair's publisher devoted an entire issue of a monthly magazine it owned, *World's Work*, to articles and photographs that substantiated Sinclair's devastating portrait.

Muckraking crusades could take many forms. In the 1890s, the young African American newspaper editor Ida B. Wells set out to investigate an upsurge in lynchings around the city of Memphis. She paid special attention to the common white defense of lynching—that it was a necessary response to attempts by black men to rape white women. Her 1895 pamphlet *The Red Record* showed that the vast majority of black lynching victims had not even been accused of sexual transgression. Instead, Wells found that lynching was primarily a brutal device to eliminate African Americans who competed with white businesses or who had become too prosperous or powerful.

In 1906, David Graham Phillips, in a series for *Cosmopolitan* called, "The Treason of the Senate," argued

YOUNG FEMALE FACTORY WORKER Lewis Hine, one of the pioneers of documentary photography, made this evocative 1908 portrait of a young spinner in a North Carolina cotton mill. She earned 48 cents a day. The National Child Labor Committee hired Hine to help document and publicize the widespread employment of children in industrial occupations. "These pictures," Hine wrote, "speak for themselves and prove that the law is being violated."

Everett Collection Inc/Alamy Stock Photo.

that many conservative U.S. senators were no more than mouthpieces for big business. President Theodore Roosevelt, upset by Phillips's attack on several of his friends and supporters, coined a new term when he angrily denounced Phillips and his colleagues as "muckrakers" who "raked the mud of society and never looked up." Partly due to Roosevelt's outburst, the muckraking vogue began to wane. But muckraking had demonstrated the potential for mobilizing public opinion on a national scale.

21.1.3 Intellectual Trends Promoting Reform

On a deeper level than muckraking, early twentieth-century thinkers challenged several core ideas in American intellectual life. Their new theories of education, law, economics, and society provided effective tools for reformers. The emergent fields of the social sciences—sociology, psychology, anthropology, and economics—emphasized observation of how people actually lived and behaved in their communities. Progressive reformers linked the systematic analysis of society and the individual characteristics of these new fields of inquiry to the project of improving the material conditions of Americans.

Significantly, many of these intellectual currents transcended national boundaries. American progressives engaged in running dialogues with European counterparts who also contended with crafting effective and rational responses to the needs of overcrowded cities, impoverished industrial workers, and unresponsive political systems. Jane Addams's original inspiration for the Hull House settlement in Chicago had come when she visited Toynbee Hall in London. Housing reformers in Glasgow and Manchester, as well as workmen's compensation reformers in Berlin and old-age insurance experts in Copenhagen, provided important international forums for progressives in the United States and around the world. Despite their national differences, progressives around the world searched for new ways to reinforce social bonds in the modern era.

Sociologist Lester Frank Ward, in his pioneering work *Dynamic Sociology* (1883), offered an important critique of **Social Darwinism**, the orthodox theory that attributed social inequality to natural selection and the "survival of the fittest." Ward argued that the conservative social theorists responsible for Social Darwinism, such as Herbert Spencer and William Graham Sumner, had wrongly applied evolutionary theory to human affairs. They had confused organic evolution with social evolution. Nature's method was genetic: unplanned, involuntary, automatic, and mechanical. By contrast, civilization had been built on successful human intervention in the natural processes of organic evolution.

Philosopher John Dewey criticized the excessively rigid and formal approach to education found in most American schools. Dewey advocated developing what he called "creative intelligence" in students, which could then be put to use in improving society. Schools ought to be "embryonic communities," miniatures of society, where children were encouraged to participate actively in different types of experiences. By cultivating imagination and openness to new experiences, schools could develop creativity and the habits required for systematic inquiry. Dewey's belief that education was the "fundamental method of social progress and reform" inspired generations of progressive educators.

At the University of Wisconsin, John R. Commons founded the new field of industrial relations and organized a state industrial commission that became a model for other states. Working closely with Governor Robert M. La Follette, Commons and his students helped draft pioneering laws in worker compensation and public utility regulation. Another Wisconsin faculty member, economist Richard Ely, argued that the state was "an educational and ethical agency whose positive aim is an indispensable condition of human progress." He rejected the doctrine of laissez-faire as merely "a tool in the hands of the greedy." Ely believed the state must intervene directly to help solve public problems. Like Commons, Ely worked with Wisconsin lawmakers to apply his expertise in economics to reforming the state's labor laws.

Progressive legal theorists began challenging the conservative view of constitutional law that had dominated American courts. Since the 1870s, the Supreme Court had interpreted the Fourteenth Amendment (1868) as a guarantee of broad rights for corporations. That amendment, which prevented states from depriving "any person of life, liberty, or property, without due process of law," had been designed to protect the civil rights of African Americans against violations by the states. But the Court, led by Justice Stephen J. Field, used the due process clause to strike down state laws regulating business and labor conditions. The Supreme Court and state courts had thus made the Fourteenth Amendment a bulwark for big business and a foe of social welfare measures.

The most important dissenter from this view was Oliver Wendell Holmes, Jr. A scholar and Massachusetts judge, Holmes believed the law had to take into account changing social conditions. And courts should take care not to invalidate social legislation enacted democratically. After his appointment to the Supreme Court in 1902, Holmes wrote a number of notable dissents to conservative court decisions overturning progressive legislation. Criticizing the majority opinion in *Lochner v. New York* (1905), in which the Court struck down a state law setting a 10-hour day for bakers, Holmes insisted that the Constitution "is not intended to embody a particular theory."

Before the late 1930s, Holmes's pragmatic view of the law seldom convinced a majority of the Court. But his views influenced a generation of lawyers who began practicing what came to be called sociological jurisprudence. In *Muller v. Oregon* (1908), the Court upheld an Oregon law limiting the maximum hours for working women, finding that the liberty of contract "is not absolute." Noting that, "woman's physical structure and the performance of maternal functions place her at a disadvantage," the Court found that "the physical well-being of woman becomes an object of public interest and care." Louis Brandeis, the state's attorney, amassed statistical, sociological, and economic data, rather than traditional legal arguments, to support his arguments. The "Brandeis Brief" became a common strategy for lawyers defending the constitutionality of progressive legislation.

21.1.4 The Female Dominion

In the 1890s, the settlement house movement had begun to provide an alternative to traditional concepts of private charity and humanitarian reform. Settlement workers found they could not transform their neighborhoods without confronting a host of broad social questions: chronic poverty, overcrowded tenement houses, child labor, industrial accidents, public health. They soon discovered the need to engage the political and cultural life of the larger community. As on Henry Street, college-educated, middle-class women were a key vanguard in the crusade for social justice.

Jane Addams founded one of the first settlement houses, Hull House, in Chicago in 1889, after years of struggling to find work and a social identity equal to her talents. A member of one of the first generations of American women to attend college, Addams was a graduate of Rockford College. Many educated women were dissatisfied with the life choices conventionally available to them: early marriage or the traditional female professions of teaching, nursing, and library work. Settlement work provided an attractive alternative. Hull House was located in a rundown slum area of Chicago. It had a day nursery, a dispensary for medicines and medical advice, a boardinghouse, an art gallery, and a music school. Addams often spoke of the "subjective necessity" of settlement houses. By this she meant that they gave young, educated women a way to satisfy their powerful desire to connect with the real world. "There is nothing after disease, indigence and guilt," she wrote, "so fatal to life itself as the want of a proper outlet for active faculties."

Lillian Wald and her allies convinced the New York Board of Health to assign a nurse to every public school in the city. They lobbied the board of education to create the first school lunch programs. They persuaded the city to set up municipal milk stations to ensure the purity of milk. Henry Street also pioneered tuberculosis treatment and prevention. Its leaders became powerful advocates for playground construction, improved street cleaning, and tougher housing inspection. The settlement's Neighborhood Playhouse became an internationally acclaimed center for innovative theater, music, and dance. Lillian Wald became a national figure—an outspoken advocate of child labor legislation and woman suffrage and a vigorous opponent of American involvement in World War I. She offered Henry Street as a meeting place to the National Negro Conference in 1909, out of which emerged the National Association for the Advancement of Colored People (NAACP).

Social reformer Florence Kelley helped direct the support of the settlement house movement behind groundbreaking state and federal labor legislation. Arriving at Hull House in 1891, Kelley found what she described as a "colony of efficient and intelligent women." In 1893, she wrote a report detailing the dismal conditions in sweatshops and the effects of long hours on the women and children who worked in them. This report became the basis for landmark legislation in Illinois that limited women to an eight-hour workday, barred children under 14 from working, and abolished tenement labor. Illinois governor John Peter Altgeld appointed Kelley as chief inspector for the new law. In 1895, Kelley published *Hull House Maps and Papers*, the first scientific study of urban

JANE ADDAMS A portrait of the young Jane Addams, probably taken around the time she founded Hull House in Chicago, in 1889.

poverty in America. Moving to the Henry Street Settlement in 1898, Kelley served as general secretary of the new National Consumers' League. With Lillian Wald, she established the New York Child Labor Committee and pushed for the creation of the U.S. Children's Bureau, established in 1912. Its director, the first woman to head a federal bureau, was Julia Lathrop, another alumna of Hull House.

New female-dominated occupations, such as social work, public health nursing, and home economics, allowed women to combine professional aspirations with the older traditions of moral reform, especially those centered on child welfare. The new professionalism, in turn, sustained reform commitments and a female dominion that simultaneously expanded the social welfare function of the state and increased women's public authority and influence.

Kelley, Addams, Wald, Lathrop, and their circle consciously used their power as women to reshape politics in the progressive era. Electoral politics and the state were historically male preserves, but female social progressives turned their gender into an advantage. Activists like Kelley used their influence in civil society to create new state powers in the service of social justice. "Women's place is Home," wrote reformer Rheta Childe Dorr, "but Home is not contained within the four walls of an individual home. Home is the community."

21.2 Progressive Politics in Cities and States

How did progressives try to redefine the role of the government in American life?

Progressive reformers poured much of their zeal and energy into local political battles. In cities and states across the nation, progressive politicians became a powerful force, often balancing the practical need for partisan support with nonpartisan appeals to the larger citizenry. Although their motives and achievements were mixed, progressives were united in their attacks on corruption in government, in emphasizing the need to rein in corporate power, and in calls for more activist city and state governments.

21.2.1 The Urban Machine

By the turn of the century, Democratic Party machines, usually dominated by first- and second-generation Irish, controlled the political life of most large American cities. The keys to machine strength were disciplined organization and the delivery of essential services to both immigrant communities and business elites. The successful machine politician viewed his work as a business, and he accumulated his capital by serving people who needed assistance. Recent immigrants in particular faced frequent unemployment, sickness, and discrimination. In exchange for votes, machine politicians offered their constituents a variety of services. These included municipal jobs, intervention with legal problems, and food and coal during hard times.

For those who did business with the city, staying on the machine's good side was simply another business expense. In exchange for valuable franchises and city contracts, businessmen routinely bribed machine politicians and contributed liberally to their campaign funds. George Washington Plunkitt, a stalwart of New York's Tammany Hall machine, good-naturedly defended what he called "honest graft": making money from inside information on public improvements. "It's just like lookin' ahead in Wall Street or in the coffee or cotton market. . . . I seen my opportunities and I took 'em."

The machines usually had close ties to organized prostitution and gambling, as well as more legitimate commercial entertainments. Many machine figures began as saloonkeepers, and liquor dealers and beer brewers provided important financial support for organizations. Vaudeville and burlesque theater, boxing, horse racing, and professional baseball were other urban enterprises with economic and political links to machines. On New York City's Lower East Side, where the Henry Street Settlement was located, Timothy D. "Big Tim" Sullivan embodied the popular machine style. Big Tim, who had risen from desperate poverty, remained enormously popular with his constituents until his death in 1913. Critics charged that Sullivan controlled the city's gambling and made money from prostitution. His real fortune came through his investments in vaudeville and the early movie business. Sullivan, whose district included the largest number of immigrants and transients in the city, provided shoe giveaways and free Christmas dinners to thousands every winter. To help pay for these and other charitable activities, he informally taxed the saloons, theaters, and restaurants in the district.

In the early twentieth century, to expand their base of support, political machines in the Northeast began concentrating more on passing welfare legislation beneficial to working-class and immigrant constituencies. In this way, machine politicians often allied themselves with progressive reformers in state legislatures. In New York, for example, Tammany Hall figures such as Robert Wagner, Al Smith, and Big Tim Sullivan worked with middle-class progressive groups to pass child labor laws, factory safety regulations, worker compensation plans, and other efforts to make government more responsive to social needs. As Jewish and Catholic immigrants

"BIG TIM" SULLIVAN Timothy D. "Big Tim" Sullivan, the popular and influential Democratic Party machine boss of the Bowery and Lower East Side districts of New York City, ca. 1901.

Daniel J. Czitrom.

expanded in number and proportion in the city population, urban machines also began to champion cultural pluralism, opposing prohibition and immigration restrictions and defending the contributions made by new ethnic groups in the cities.

21.2.2 Progressives and Urban Reform

Political progressivism originated in the cities. It was both a challenge to the power of machine politics and a response to deteriorating urban conditions. City governments, especially in the Northeast and industrial Midwest, seemed hardly capable of providing the basic services needed to sustain large populations. For example, an impure water supply left Pittsburgh with one of the world's highest rates of death from typhoid, dysentery, and cholera. Most New York City neighborhoods rarely enjoyed street cleaning, and playgrounds were nonexistent. "The challenge of the city,"

Cleveland progressive Frederic C. Howe wrote in 1906, "has become one of decent human existence."

Reformers placed much of the blame for urban ills on the machines and looked for ways to restructure city government. The "good government" movement, led by the National Municipal League, fought to make city management a nonpartisan, even nonpolitical process by bringing the administrative techniques of large corporations to cities. Reformers revised city charters in favor of stronger mayoral power and expanded use of appointed administrators and career civil servants. They drew up blueprints for model charters, ordinances, and zoning plans designed by experts trained in public administration.

Business and professional elites became the biggest boosters of structural reforms in urban government. In the summer of 1900, a hurricane in the Gulf of Mexico unleashed a tidal wave on Galveston, Texas. To cope with this disaster, leading businessmen convinced the state legislature to replace the mayor-council government with a small board of commissioners. Each commissioner was elected at large, and each was responsible for a different city department. Under this plan, voters could more easily identify and hold accountable those responsible for city services. By 1917, nearly 500 cities, including Houston, Oakland, Kansas City, Denver, and Buffalo, had adopted the commission form of government.

Progressive politicians who focused on the human problems of the industrial city championed a different kind of reform, one based on changing policies rather than the political structure. In Cleveland, for example, wealthy businessman Thomas L. Johnson served as mayor from 1901 to 1909. He emphasized both efficiency and social welfare. His popular program included lower streetcar fares, public baths, milk and meat inspection, and an expanded park and playground system.

21.2.3 Statehouse Progressives

On the state level, progressives focused on two major reform themes that sometimes coexisted uneasily. On the one hand, they looked to make politics more open and accessible by pushing through procedural reforms. The *direct primary*, for example, promised to take the selection of electoral candidates out of the smoke-filled backrooms of party bosses and put it in the hands of party voters. In 1902, Oregon was the first state to adopt two other reforms: the *initiative*, the popular power to initiate legislation, and the *referendum*, the right to a popular vote on proposed legislation. Several states also adopted a related reform, the "Australian," or secret ballot, which took the mechanics of ballot printing and distribution from the parties and made it the responsibility of the government. California and other states also established the *recall*: the power to remove elected officials from office. And in 1913, the states and Congress ratified the Seventeenth Amendment, shifting the selection of U.S. senators from the state legislatures to direct election by voters. On the other hand, progressive activists sought to remove some decisions from the electoral process entirely. They believed that judgments about railroad regulations, improving a city's sewer system, or establishing tax rates might best be made by informed, unbiased experts appointed to boards and commissions charged with setting policy.

In Wisconsin, Republican dissident Robert M. La Follette forged a coalition of angry farmers, small businessmen, and workers with his fiery attacks on railroads and other large corporations. Leader of the progressive faction of the state Republicans, "Fighting Bob" won three terms as governor (1900–1906), and then served as a U.S. senator until his death in 1925. As governor, he pushed through tougher corporate tax rates, a direct primary, an improved civil service code, and a railroad commission designed to regulate freight charges. La Follette used faculty experts at the University of Wisconsin to help research and write his bills. Other states began copying the "Wisconsin Idea," the application of academic scholarship and theory to the needs of the people. In practice, La Follette's railroad commission accomplished far less than progressive rhetoric claimed. It essentially represented special interests— commercial farmers and businessmen seeking reduced shipping rates. Ordinary consumers did not see lower passenger fares or reduced food prices. And, as commissioners began to realize, the national reach of the railroads limited the effectiveness of state regulation.

In New York, Theodore Roosevelt won the governor's race in 1898, propelled by his fame as a Spanish-American War hero. Although supported by the Republican Party machine, Roosevelt embraced the progressive view that the people's interest ought to be above partisan politics, and he used his personal popularity with voters to assert independence from party leaders. As governor, he held frequent press conferences to communicate more directly with voters and gain support for progressive legislation. Roosevelt's administration strengthened the state's civil service system, set wage and hour standards for state employees, raised teachers' salaries, and placed a franchise tax on corporations controlling public utilities. Roosevelt also championed progressive conservation measures by expanding New York's forest preserves and reforming the fish and game service, thus anticipating his strong support of environmental regulation as president.

Western progressives targeted railroads, mining and timber companies, and public utilities for reform. Large corporations such as Pacific Gas and Electric and the Southern Pacific Railroad had amassed enormous wealth and political influence. They were able to corrupt state legislatures and charge consumers exorbitant rates. An alliance between middle-class progressives and working-class voters reflected growing disillusionment with the ideology of individualism that had helped pave the way for the rise of the big corporation. In 1910, California elected progressive attorney Hiram Johnson governor, and he then pushed through laws regulating utilities and child labor, mandating an eight-hour day for workingwomen, and providing a state-worker compensation plan.

In the South, progressives organized to control both greedy corporations and "unruly" citizens. Citizen groups, city boards of trade, and newspapers pressed reluctant legislators to use state power to regulate big business. Between 1905 and 1909, nearly every southern state moved to regulate railroads by mandating lower passenger and freight rates. Southern progressives also directed their energies at the related problems of child labor and educational reform. In 1900, at least one-quarter of all southern cotton mill workers were between the ages of 10 and 16, and many worked more than 60 hours per week. Led by reform-minded ministers Edgar Gardner Murphy and Alexander McKelway and drawing on the activism of white club women, reformers attacked child labor by focusing on the welfare of children and their mothers and emphasizing the degradation of "Anglo Saxons." In 1903, Alabama and North Carolina enacted the first state child labor laws, setting 12 as a minimum age for employment. But the laws were weakened by many exemptions and an absence of provisions for enforcement, as lawmakers also heard the loud complaints from parents and mill owners who resented the efforts of reformers to limit their choices.

But southern progressivism was for white people only. Indeed, southern progressives believed that the disenfranchisement of black voters and the creation of a legally segregated public sphere were necessary preconditions for political and social reform. With African Americans removed from political life, white southern progressives argued, the direct primary system of nominating candidates would give white voters more influence. Between 1890 and 1910, southern states passed a welter of statutes specifying poll taxes, literacy tests, and property qualifications with the explicit goal of preventing voting by blacks. This systematic disenfranchisement of African American voters stripped black communities of any political power. To prevent the disenfranchisement of poor white voters under these laws, states established so-called understanding and grandfather clauses. Election officials had discretionary power to decide whether an illiterate person could understand and reasonably interpret the Constitution when read to him. Unqualified white men were also registered if they could show that their grandfathers had voted.

Southern progressives supported the push toward a fully segregated public sphere. Between 1900 and 1910, southern states strengthened Jim Crow laws requiring separation of races in restaurants, streetcars, beaches, and theaters. Schools were separate but hardly equal. A 1916 Bureau of Education study found that per capita expenditures for education in southern states averaged $10.32 a year for white children and $2.89 for black children. And African American teachers received far lower salaries than their white counterparts. The legacy of southern progressivism was thus closely linked to the strengthening of the legal and institutional guarantees of white supremacy.

Contradictions in the progressive approach to political reform were not limited to the South. Undermining party control of voting and elections may also have weakened politicians' incentives to get out the vote. Greater reliance on city commissions and other experts meant less in the way of promised favors for voters, which may also have made voters less interested in elections. Tightening up on residency requirements and voter registration rules in the cities cut into turnout in immigrant and ethnic neighborhoods. The effort to make politics more open, nonpartisan, and voter friendly also led, ironically, to a decline in voter participation and interest around the country. Whereas in the 1890s, voter participation in national elections was routinely close to 90 percent, by World War I that figure had fallen to barely 60 percent, where it would stay for most of the rest of the century.

21.3 Social Control and Its Limits

How did tensions between social justice and social control divide progressives?

Many middle- and upper-class Protestant progressives feared that immigrants and large cities threatened the stability of American democracy. They worried that alien cultural practices were disrupting what they viewed as traditional American morality. Edward A. Ross's landmark work *Social Control* (1901), a book whose title became a key phrase in progressive thought, argued that society needed an "ethical elite" of citizens "who have at heart the general welfare and know what kinds of conduct will promote this welfare." Progressives often believed they had a mission to frame laws and regulations for the "benefit" of immigrants, industrial workers, and African Americans. These efforts at social control usually required some form of coercion. This was the moralistic and frequently xenophobic side of progressivism, and it provided a powerful source of support for the regulation of drinking, prostitution, leisure activities, and schooling.

21.3.1 The Prohibition Movement

During the last two decades of the nineteenth century, the Woman's Christian Temperance Union (WCTU) had grown into a powerful mass organization. The WCTU appealed especially to women angered by men who used alcohol and then abused their wives and children. It directed most of its work toward ending the production, sale, and consumption of alcohol. Local WCTU chapters put their energy into nontemperance activities as well, including homeless shelters, Sunday schools, prison reform, child nurseries, and woman suffrage. The WCTU thus provided women with a political forum in which they could fuse their traditional moral posture as guardians of the home with broader public concerns. By 1911, the WCTU, with a quarter million members, was the largest women's organization in American history.

Other **temperance groups** had a narrower focus. The Anti-Saloon League, founded in 1893, began by organizing local-option campaigns in which rural counties and small towns banned liquor within their geographical limits. It drew much of its financial support from local businessmen, who saw a link between closing a community's saloons and increasing the productivity of workers. The league was a one-issue pressure group that played effectively on antiurban and anti-immigrant prejudice. League lobbyists hammered away at the close connections among saloon culture, liquor dealers, brewers, and big-city political machines.

The battle to ban alcohol revealed deep ethnic and cultural divides within America's urban communities. Opponents of alcohol were generally "pietists," who viewed the world from a position of moral absolutism. These included native-born, middle-class Protestants associated with evangelical churches, along with some old-stock Protestant immigrant denominations. Opponents of **prohibition** were generally "ritualists" with less arbitrary notions of personal morality. These were largely new-stock, working-class Catholic and Jewish immigrants, along with some Protestants, such as German Lutherans. (See Communities *in* Conflict.)

21.3.2 The Social Evil

Many of the same reformers who battled the saloon and drinking also engaged in efforts to eradicate prostitution. Crusades against "the social evil" had appeared at intervals throughout the nineteenth century, but they reached a new level of intensity between 1895 and 1920. In part, this new sense of urgency stemmed from the sheer growth of cities and the greater visibility of prostitution in red-light districts and neighborhoods. Antiprostitution campaigns epitomized the diverse makeup and mixed motives of so

Communities *in* Conflict

Debating Prohibition in Progressive-Era Ohio

"You will see that the liquor traffic is asking fathers of Ohio to 'give me your boys.'"

Should the manufacture and sale of alcoholic beverages be made illegal? The State of Ohio had long been one of the most intense battlegrounds over this controversial issue. The Woman's Christian Temperance Union had been founded in Cleveland in 1874, and the Anti-Saloon League was organized in Oberlin in 1893. Both groups quickly gained national followings. In 1909, the League established new national headquarters in Westerville, Ohio, a small city that strongly supported prohibition. But Ohio also had a large and well-organized brewery industry. Beer was by far the most popular alcoholic beverage among Americans, and the brewery industry was the most profitable sector of the alcohol business. German Americans dominated among brewers and maintained close ties to the large German American communities in cities like Cincinnati.

In 1908, the Anti-Saloon League and its allies succeeded in getting a law passed by the Ohio legislature granting counties a "local option" to ban the alcohol trade. As the "drys" set their sights on a statewide prohibition law, the brewers, working closely with German American community groups, organized a counterattack that featured lobbyists and a sophisticated propaganda campaign to mobilize the influence and votes of "wets." The brewers also tried to reform their industry by reducing the number of saloons and ensuring that saloonkeepers were citizens of "good character." With Ohioans closely divided between "wet" and "dry" views, both sides put an enormous amount of money into campaigns aimed at influencing public opinion. Well-financed interest-group campaigns of this type were a distinctively new feature of progressive-era politics. After losing statewide referendums in 1915 and 1917, the Anti-Saloon League spearheaded a narrow victory in 1918, finally achieving statewide prohibition in Ohio. National prohibition would follow in 1920 with the ratification of the Eighteenth Amendment to the Constitution.

Percy Andreae was a leading lobbyist for the brewery industry. James A. White was the head of the Ohio Anti-Saloon League and organizer of the Ohio Dry Federation, an umbrella group of prohibitionist forces. Here are their arguments.

- **What arguments does Andreae use to undermine the prohibitionist appeal, particularly with respect to religious belief? How does the Ohio Dry Federation make its case in this ad? Why do you think it emphasized this strategy over other prohibitionist objections to the alcohol trade?**

Percy Andreae: "Behind the Mask of Prohibition" (1915)

I have met many active prohibitionists, both in this and in other countries, all of them thoroughly in earnest. In some instances I have found that their allegiance to the cause of prohibition took its origin in the fact that some near relative or friend had succumbed to over-indulgence in liquor. In one or two cases the man himself had been a victim of this weakness, and had come to the conclusion, firstly that every one else was constituted as he was, and, therefore, liable to the same danger; and secondly, that unless every one were prevented from drinking, he would not be secure from the temptation to do so himself.

This is one class of prohibitionists. The other, and by far the larger class, is made up of religious zealots, to whom prohibition is a word having at bottom a far wider application than that which is generally attributed to it. The liquor question, if there really is such a question per se, is merely put forth by them as a means to an end, an incidental factor in a fight which has for its object the supremacy of a certain form of religious faith. The belief of many of these people is that the Creator frowns upon enjoyment of any and every kind, and that he has merely endowed us with certain desires and capacities for pleasure in order to give us an opportunity to please Him by resisting them. They are, of course, perfectly entitled to this belief, though some of us may consider it eccentric and somewhat in the nature of a libel on the Almighty. But are they privileged to force that belief on all their fellow beings? That, in substance, is the question that is involved in the present-day prohibition movement. . . .

If there is any one who doubts the truth of this statement, let me put this to him: How many Roman Catholics are prohibitionists? How many Jews, the most temperate race on earth, are to be found in the ranks of prohibition? Or Lutherans? Or German Protestants generally? What is the proportion of Episcopalians to that of Methodists, Baptists and Presbyterians, and the like, in the active prohibition army? The answers to these questions will, I venture to say, prove conclusively the assertion that the fight for prohibition is synonymous with the fight of a certain religious sect, or group of religious sects, for the supremacy of its ideas.

Temperance and self-control are convertible terms. Prohibition, or that which it implies, is the direct negation of the term self-control. In order to save the small percentage of men who are too weak to resist their animal desires, it aims to put chains on every man, the weak and the strong alike. And if this is proper in one respect, why not in all respects? Yet, what would one think of a proposition to keep all men locked up because a certain number have a propensity to steal? Theoretically, perhaps, all crime or vice could be stopped by chaining us all up as we chain up a wild animal, and only allowing us to take exercise under proper supervision and control. But while such a measure would check crime, it would not eliminate the criminal. . . .

Prohibition, though it must cause, and is already causing, incalculable damage, may never succeed in this country; but that which is behind it, as the catapults and the cannon were behind the battering rams in the battles of olden days, is certain to succeed unless timely measures of prevention

are resorted to; and if it does succeed, we shall witness the enthronement of a monarch in this land of liberty compared with whose autocracy the autocracy of the Russian Czar is a mere trifle. The name of this monarch is Religious Intolerance.

Source: Percy Andreae, *The Prohibition Movement in Its Broader Bearings upon Our Social, Commercial, and Religious Liberties* (1915), www.druglibrary .org/schaffer/alcohol.

Prohibitionist James A. White: "Give Me Your Boy" (1918)

Take away the "camouflage" with which the Liquor Traffic tries to disguise itself and [a] sinister figure . . . stands revealed.

Take away the smooth phrases and cunning twists of the Liquor Traffic's appeal For Permission to continue its career—get right down to naked truth and you will see that the liquor traffic is asking fathers of Ohio to "give me your boys."

WHAT WILL THE SALOON DO FOR THE BOYS? Is its purpose to inspire them with greater ambitions; to teach them clean morals, to avoid bad habits, to become better men and citizens, better husbands and fathers?

You know the saloon does nothing FOR boys, but appalling harm TO them.

Its prosperity depends on the number of VICTIMS it entraps.

Men in the liquor traffic are not blind to its evils.

Many distillers will not allow THEIR OWN SON to drink intoxicants; many brewers forbid the use of intoxicants to their sons; many saloonists don't drink the stuff they sell;

they won't hire drinking bartenders and they bar their sons from the saloons.

Still, they ask you to give YOUR son for the sake of the money they can make out of him. They ask you to approve temptation of your son to become a drunkard.

They ask you to vote to MAKE DRUNKARDS out of thousands of Ohio's boys.

Are you with them? Are YOU for the Booze Huns or for the boys?

There can be no neutrality in this fight. Failure to vote "yes" on prohibition on November 5th is silent approval of the liquor traffic's record and misdeeds.

You must be either for the BEST INTERESTS of your state, your nation and humanity—or you must be for the ENEMY liquor traffic, which works AGAINST the best interest of the state, the nation and humanity.

Vote "Yes" for Prohibition November 5th

Source: Ohio Dry Federation (1918), http://ehistory.osu.edu/osu/sources.

---

much progressive reform. Male business and civic leaders joined forces with feminists, social workers, and clergy to eradicate "commercialized vice."

Between 1908 and 1914, exposés of the "white slave traffic" became a national sensation. Dozens of books, articles, and motion pictures alleged an international conspiracy to seduce and sell girls into prostitution. Most of these materials exaggerated the practices they attacked. They also made foreigners, especially Jews and southern Europeans, scapegoats for the sexual anxieties of native-born whites. In 1910, Congress passed legislation that permitted the deportation of foreign-born prostitutes or any foreigner convicted of procuring or employing them. That same year, the Mann Act made it a federal offense to transport women across state lines for prostitution or other "immoral purposes."

Reformers had trouble believing that any woman would freely choose to be a prostitute; such a choice was antithetical to conventional notions of female purity and sexuality. Nor could they understand how many women engaged in casual prostitution, especially during economic hard times. But for wage-earning women, prostitution was a rational choice in a world of limited opportunities.

Maimie Pinzer, a prostitute, summed up her feelings in a letter to a wealthy female reformer: "I don't propose to get up at 6:30 to be at work at 8 and work in a close, stuffy room with people I despise, until dark, for $6 or $7 a week! When I could, just by phoning, spend an afternoon with some congenial person and in the end have more than a week's work could pay me." The anti-vice crusades succeeded in closing down many urban red-light districts and larger brothels, but the streetwalker and call girl, who were more vulnerable to harassment and control by policemen and pimps, replaced them. Rather than eliminating prostitution, reform efforts transformed the organization of the sex trade.

21.3.3 The Redemption of Leisure

Progressives faced a thorny issue in the growing popularity of commercial entertainment. For large numbers of working-class adults and children, leisure meant time and money spent at vaudeville and burlesque theaters, amusement parks, dance halls, and motion picture houses. For many cultural traditionalists, the flood of new urban commercial amusements posed a grave threat. As with prostitution, urban progressives sponsored a host of recreation and amusement surveys detailing the situation in their individual cities. One distinctively progressive response was the Playgrounds Movement. Los Angeles created the nation's first urban Department of Playgrounds in 1904, and proponents nationwide saw municipal playgrounds as a way to offer free, healthy, outdoor recreation for city children.

By 1908, movies had become the most popular form of cheap entertainment in America. One survey estimated that 11,500 movie theaters attracted 5 million patrons each day. For 5 or 10 cents, "nickelodeon" theaters offered programs that might include a slapstick comedy, a western, a travelogue, and a melodrama. Early movies were most popular in the tenement and immigrant districts of big cities and with children. As the films themselves became more sophisticated and as "movie palaces" began to replace cheap storefront theaters, the new medium attracted a large middle-class clientele as well.

Progressive reformers seized the chance to help regulate the new medium as a way of improving the commercial recreation of the urban poor. In 1909, New York City movie producers and exhibitors joined with the reform-minded People's Institute to establish the voluntary National Board of Censorship (NBC). A revolving group of civic activists reviewed new movies and passed them, suggested changes, or condemned them. Local censoring committees all over the nation subscribed to the Board's weekly bulletin. They aimed at achieving what John Collier of the NBC called "the redemption of leisure." By 1914 the NBC was reviewing 95 percent of the nation's film output, beginning an era of industry self censorship designed to make movies more attractive to the middle class and to women.

21.3.4 Standardizing Education

Along with reading, writing, and mathematics, schools inculcated patriotism, piety, and respect for authority. Progressive educators looked to the public school primarily as an agent of "Americanization." Elwood Cubberley, a leading educational reformer, expressed the view that schools could be the vehicle by which immigrant children could break free of the parochial ethnic neighborhood. "Our task," he argued in *Changing Conceptions of Education* (1909), "is to break up these groups or settlements, to assimilate and amalgamate these people as a part of our American race, and to implant in their children, so far as can be done, the Anglo-Saxon conception of righteousness, law and order, and popular government."

The most important educational trends in these years were the expansion and bureaucratization of the nation's public school systems. Children began school earlier and stayed there longer. Kindergartens spread rapidly in large cities. They presented, as one writer put it in 1903, "the earliest opportunity to catch the little Russian, the little Italian, the little German, Pole, Syrian, and the rest and begin to make good American citizens of them." By 1918, every state had some form of compulsory school attendance. High schools also multiplied, extending the school's influence beyond the traditional grammar school curriculum. In 1890, only 4 percent of the nation's youth between 14 and 17 were enrolled in school; by 1930, the figure was 47 percent.

This trend reflected a growing belief that schools should be comprehensive, multifunctional institutions. To support vocational training in high schools, the Smith-Hughes Act of 1917 provided federal grants and set up a Federal Board for Vocational Education.

21.4 Challenges to Progressivism

What groups challenged the progressive vision of politics?

While most progressive reformers had roots in Protestantism and the middle-class professions, other Americans vigorously challenged their political vision. Organized workers often invoked progressive rhetoric and ideals but for quite different, sometimes radical ends. The Industrial Revolution, which had begun transforming American life and labor in the nineteenth century, reached maturity in the early twentieth century. The world of the industrial worker included large manufacturing towns in New England; barren mining settlements in the West; primitive lumber and turpentine camps in the South; steelmaking and coal-mining cities in Pennsylvania and Ohio; and densely packed immigrant ghettos from New York to San Francisco, where workers toiled in garment-trade sweatshops.

All these industrial workers shared the need to sell their labor for wages in order to survive. At the same time, differences in skill, ethnicity, and race proved powerful barriers to efforts at organizing trade unions that could bargain for improved wages and working conditions. So, too, did the economic and political power of the large corporations that dominated much of American industry. These years also saw many labor struggles that created effective trade unions or laid the groundwork for others. Industrial workers became a force in local and national politics, adding a chorus of insistent voices to the calls for social justice.

21.4.1 The New Global Immigration

The first two decades of the twentieth century saw a profound transformation in both the size and scope of immigration, as more than 14.5 million people from all over the world made their way to the United States. In the nineteenth century, much of the overseas migration had come from the industrial districts of northern and western Europe. By contrast, roughly 60 percent of early-twentieth-century immigrants came from southern and eastern Europe. Unlike their predecessors, nearly all the new Italian, Polish, Hungarian, Jewish, and Greek immigrants lacked industrial skills. They thus entered the bottom ranks of factories, mines, mills, and sweatshops; by the eve of World War I, close to 60 percent of the industrial labor force was foreign born (See Map 21.1).

These new immigrants had been driven from their European farms and towns by several forces, including the undermining of subsistence farming by commercial agriculture; a falling death rate that brought a shortage of land; and religious and political persecution.

American corporations also sent agents to recruit cheap labor. Except for Jewish immigrants, a majority of whom fled virulent anti-Semitism in Russia and Poland, most newcomers planned on earning a stake and then returning home. Hard times in America forced many back to Europe. In the depression year of 1908, for example, more Austro-Hungarians and Italians left than entered the United States.

The decision to emigrate usually occurred through social networks—people linked by kinship, personal acquaintance, and work experience. These "chains," extending from places of origin to specific destinations in the United States, helped immigrants cope with the considerable risks entailed by the long and difficult journey. A study conducted by the U.S. Immigration Commission in 1909 found that about 60 percent of the immigrants of that time had their passage arranged by immigrants already in America.

Map 21.1 IMMIGRATION TO THE UNITED STATES, 1901–1920

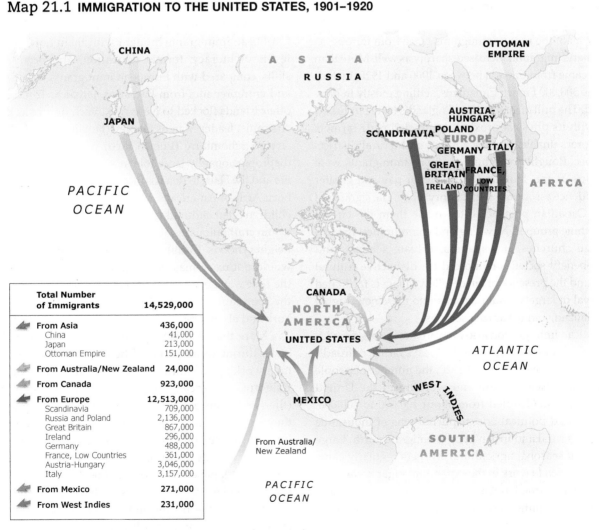

Total Number of Immigrants	14,529,000
From Asia	436,000
China	41,000
Japan	213,000
Ottoman Empire	151,000
From Australia/New Zealand	24,000
From Canada	923,000
From Europe	12,513,000
Scandinavia	709,000
Russia and Poland	2,136,000
Great Britain	867,000
Ireland	296,000
Germany	488,000
France, Low Countries	361,000
Austria-Hungary	3,046,000
Italy	3,157,000
From Mexico	271,000
From West Indies	231,000

Adapted from *Historical Statistics of the United States*, Volume 1, Part A Population, Chapter Ad, International Migration (NY, 2006, Millennial Edition).

Immigrant communities used ethnicity as a collective resource for gaining employment in factories, mills, and mines. One Polish steelworker recalled how the process operated in the Pittsburgh mills: "Now if a Russian got his job in a shear department, he's looking for a buddy, a Russian buddy. He's not going to look for a Croatian buddy. And if he sees the boss looking for a man he says, 'Look, I have a good man,' and he's picking out his friends." Specialization of work by ethnic origin was quite common throughout America's industrial communities.

The low-paid, backbreaking work in basic industry became nearly the exclusive preserve of the new immigrants. In 1907, of the 14,359 common laborers employed at Pittsburgh's U.S. Steel mills, 11,694 were eastern Europeans. For 12-hour and 7-day weeks, two-thirds of these workers made less than $12.50 a week; one-third made less than $10.00. One-third of the immigrant steelworkers were single, and among married men who had been in the country less than five years, about two-thirds reported that their wives were still in Europe. Workers with families generally supplemented their incomes by taking in single men as boarders.

Not all of the recent immigrants came from Europe, as hemispheric migration increased sharply as well. More than 900,000 came from Canada between 1900 and 1920, including some 300,000 French Canadians, settling mostly in New England. The pull of jobs in New England's textile industry, along with its physical proximity, attracted male farmers and laborers unable to make a living in the rural districts of Québec. Roughly one-third of female immigrants were domestic servants looking for the higher pay and greater independence associated with factory labor. The significant French Canadian presence often made them the largest single ethnic group in New England communities. French-language churches, newspapers, private schools, and mutual-benefit societies reinforced the distinctive cultural milieu, and the presence of kin or fellow villagers facilitated the arrival of largely rural migrants into these new, highly industrialized, and urbanized settings.

Mexican immigration also grew in these years, providing a critical source of labor for the West's farms, railroads, and mines. Between 1900 and 1920, the number of people of Mexican descent living and working in the United States nearly quadrupled from about 100,000 to 400,000. Economic and political crises spurred tens of thousands of Mexico's rural and urban poor to emigrate north. Large numbers of seasonal agricultural workers regularly came up from Mexico to work in the expanding sugar beet industry and then returned. But a number of substantial resident Mexican communities also emerged in the early twentieth century.

Throughout Texas, California, New Mexico, Arizona, and Colorado, western cities developed *barrios*, distinct communities of Mexicans. Mexican immigrants attracted by jobs in the smelting industry made El Paso the most thoroughly Mexican city in the United States. In San Antonio, Mexicans worked at shelling pecans, becoming perhaps the most underpaid and exploited group of workers in the country. By 1910, San Antonio contained the largest number of Mexican immigrants of any city. In southern California, labor agents for railroads recruited Mexicans to work on building new interurban lines around Los Angeles.

The Caribbean-born population of the United States grew significantly as well; approximately 230,000 immigrants from that region arrived between 1900 and 1920. Bahamian farm laborers and Cuban cigar workers, for example, established small but permanent communities in South Florida in the early 1900s. New York City soon became the most popular destination for Caribbean immigrants, attracting tens of thousands who passed through Ellis Island in search of better-paying jobs and career opportunities. By 1930, almost one-quarter of black Harlem was of Caribbean origin, and as much as one-third of all of New York's black professionals and business owners came from the ranks of Caribbean immigrants. These early Caribbean immigrants brought with them notably higher levels of literacy, formal education, and occupational skills, compared with European immigrants. Professionals and entrepreneurs from Barbados, Jamaica, Trinidad, and other islands flocked to New York. Such figures as the Pan Africanist leader Marcus Garvey (Jamaica) and the scholar Arturo Schomburg (Puerto Rico) would come to play a disproportionately large role in African American political life and the Harlem Renaissance of the 1920s. Yet, like native-born African Americans, Caribbean immigrants and their children often endured racial discrimination in their efforts to join craft unions, establish credit with banks, or integrate neighborhoods. Caribbean migration to the United States would not reach mass levels until after World War II, but the first wave of early-twentieth-century immigrants laid the foundation for Afro-Caribbean communities in New York and elsewhere.

More than 200,000 Japanese also entered the United States during these decades. The vast majority were young men working as contract laborers in the West, mainly in California. American law prevented Japanese immigrants (the *Issei*) from obtaining American citizenship because they were not white. This legal discrimination, along with informal exclusion from many occupations, forced the Japanese to create niches for themselves within local economies. Most Japanese settled near Los Angeles, where they established small communities centered on fishing, truck farming, and the flower and nursery business. In 1920, Japanese farmers produced 10 percent of the dollar volume of California agriculture on 1 percent of the farm acreage. By 1930, over 35,000 *Issei* and their children (the *Nisei*) lived in Los Angeles.

ELLIS ISLAND Newly landed European immigrant families arriving at Ellis Island in New York City, ca., 1907.

Archive Pics/Alamy Stock Photo.

21.4.2 Urban Ghettos

In large cities, new immigrant communities took the form of densely packed ghettos. By 1920, immigrants and their children constituted almost 60 percent of the populations of cities over 100,000. They were an even larger percentage in major industrial centers such as Chicago, Pittsburgh, Philadelphia, and New York. The sheer size and dynamism of these cities made the immigrant experience more complex than in smaller cities and more isolated communities. Workers in the urban garment trades toiled for low wages and suffered layoffs, unemployment, and poor health. But conditions in the small, labor-intensive shops of the clothing industry differed significantly from those in the large-scale, capital-intensive industries like steel.

New York City had become the center of both Jewish immigration and America's huge ready-to-wear clothing industry. The city's Jewish population was 1.4 million in 1915, almost 30 percent of its inhabitants. In small factories, lofts, and tenement apartments, some 200,000 people—most of them Jews, some of them Italian—worked in the clothing trades. Most of the industry operated on the grueling piece-rate, or task, system, in which manufacturers and subcontractors paid individuals or teams of workers to complete a certain quota of labor within a specific time.

The garment industry was highly seasonal. A typical workweek was 60 hours, with 70 common during the busy season. But there were long stretches of unemployment in slack times. Often forced to work in cramped, dirty, and badly lit rooms, garment workers strained under a system in which time equaled money. Morris Rosenfeld, a presser of men's clothing who wrote Yiddish poetry, captured the feeling:

> *The tick of the clock is the boss in his anger*
> *The face of the clock has the eye of a foe*
> *The clock—I shudder—Dost hear how it draws me?*
> *It calls me "Machine" and it cries to me "Sew!"*

In November 1909, two New York garment manufacturers responded to strikes by unskilled women workers by hiring thugs and prostitutes to beat up pickets. The strikers won the support of the Women's Trade Union League, a group of sympathetic female reformers that included Lillian Wald, Mary Dreier, and prominent society figures. The Uprising of the 20,000, as it became known, swept through the Garment District, in New York City. The strikers demanded union recognition, better wages, and safer and more sanitary conditions. They drew support from thousands of suffragists, trade unionists, and sympathetic middle-class women as well. Class differences might be bridged by the bonds of sisterhood, as several wealthy society women, including Anne Morgan, daughter of banker J. P. Morgan, offered financial assistance. Hundreds of strikers were arrested, and many were beaten by police. After three cold months on the picket line, the strikers returned to work without union recognition. But the International

Ladies Garment Workers Union (ILGWU), founded in 1900, did gain strength and negotiated contracts with some of the city's shirtwaist makers. The strike was an important breakthrough in the drive to organize unskilled workers into industrial unions.

On March 25, 1911, the issues raised by the strike took on new urgency when a fire raced through three floors of the Triangle Shirtwaist Company. As the flames spread, workers found themselves trapped by exit doors that had been locked from the outside. Fire escapes were too narrow, and too weak to withstand the heat. Within half an hour, 146 people, mostly young Jewish women, had been killed by smoke or had leaped to their deaths. In the bitter aftermath, women progressives led by Florence Kelley and Frances Perkins of the National Consumers' League joined with Tammany Hall leaders Al Smith, Robert Wagner, and Big Tim Sullivan to create a New York State Factory Investigation Commission. Under Perkins's vigorous leadership, the commission conducted an unprecedented round of public hearings and on-site inspections, leading to a series of state laws that dramatically improved safety conditions and limited the hours for working women and children.

21.4.3 Company Towns

Immigrant industrial workers and their families often established their communities in a company town, where

TRIANGLE SHIRTWAIST FIRE New York City police set up this makeshift morgue to help identify victims of the disastrous Triangle Shirtwaist Company fire, March 25, 1911. Unable to open the locked doors of the sweatshop and desperate to escape from smoke and flames, many of the 146 who died had leaped eight stories to their death.

Bettmann/Getty Images.

a single large corporation was dominant. Cities such as Lawrence, Massachusetts, Gary, Indiana, and Butte, Montana revolved around the industrial enterprises of Pacific Woolen, U.S. Steel, and Anaconda Copper, respectively. Workers had little or no influence over the economic and political institutions of these cities. In the more isolated company towns, residents often had no alternative but to buy their food, clothing, and supplies at company stores, usually for exorbitantly high prices. They did maintain some community control in other ways. Family and kin networks, ethnic lodges, saloons, benefit societies, churches and synagogues, and musical groups affirmed traditional forms of community in a setting governed by individualism and private capital.

On the job, modern machinery and industrial discipline meant high rates of injury and death. A 1910 study of work accidents revealed that nearly a fourth of all new steelworkers were killed or injured each year. Mutual aid associations, organized around ethnic groups, offered some protection through cheap insurance and death benefits.

In steel and coal towns, women not only maintained the household and raised the children, but they also boosted the family income by taking in boarders, sewing, and laundry. Many women also tended gardens and raised chickens, rabbits, and goats. Their produce and income helped reduce dependence on the company store. Working-class women felt the burdens of housework more heavily than their middle-class sisters. Pump water, indoor plumbing, and sewage disposal were often available only on a pay-as-you-go basis. The daily drudgery endured by working-class women far outlasted the "man-killing" shifts worked by their husbands. Many women struggled with the effects of their husbands' excessive drinking and faced early widowhood.

The adjustment for immigrant workers was not so much a process of assimilation as it was one of adaptation and resistance. Work habits and Old World cultural traditions did not always mesh with factory discipline. A Polish wedding celebration might last three or four days. A drinking bout following a Sunday funeral might cause workers to celebrate "St. Monday" and not show up for work. Most immigrants were far more concerned with job security than with upward mobility. As new immigrants became less transient and more permanently settled in company towns, they increased their involvement in local politics and union activity.

The power of large corporations in the life of company towns was most evident among the mining communities of the West, as was violent labor conflict. The Colorado Fuel and Iron Company (CFI) employed roughly half of the 8,000 coal miners who labored in that state's mines. In mining towns such as Ludlow and Trinidad, the CFI thoroughly dominated the lives of miners and their families.

"The miner," one union official observed, "is in this land owned by the corporation that owns the homes, that owns the boarding houses, that owns every single thing there is there . . . not only the mines, but all the grounds, all the buildings, all the places of recreation, as well as the school and church buildings." By the early twentieth century, new immigrants, such as Italians, Greeks, Slavs, and Mexicans, composed a majority of the population in these western mining communities.

In September 1913, the United Mine Workers led a strike in the Colorado coalfields, calling for improved safety, higher wages, and recognition of the union. Thousands of miners' families moved out of company housing and into makeshift tent colonies provided by the union. In October, Governor Elias Ammons ordered the Colorado National Guard into the tense strike region to keep order. By spring, the strike had bankrupted the state, forcing the governor to remove most of the troops. The coal companies then brought in large numbers of private mine guards who were extremely hostile toward the strikers. On April 20, 1914, a combination of guardsmen and private guards surrounded the largest of the tent colonies at Ludlow, where more than a thousand mine families lived. A shot rang out (each side accused the other of firing), and a pitched battle ensued that lasted until the poorly armed miners ran out of ammunition. At dusk, the troops burned the tent village to the ground, routing the families and killing 14, 11 of them children. Enraged strikers attacked mines throughout southern Colorado in an armed rebellion that lasted 10 days, until President Woodrow Wilson ordered the U.S. Army into the region. News of the Ludlow Massacre shocked millions and aroused widespread protests and demonstrations against the policies of Colorado Fuel and Iron and its owner, John D. Rockefeller, Jr.

21.4.4 Competing Visions of Unionism: The AFL and the IWW

Following the depression of the 1890s, the American Federation of Labor (AFL) emerged as the strongest and most stable organization of workers. Samuel Gompers's strategy of recruiting skilled labor into unions organized by craft had paid off. Union membership climbed from under 500,000 in 1897 to 1.7 million by 1904. Most of this growth took place in AFL affiliates in coal mining, the building trades, transportation, and machine shops. The national unions—the United Mine Workers of America, the Brotherhood of Carpenters and Joiners, the International Association of Machinists—represented workers of specific occupations in collective bargaining. Trade autonomy and exclusive jurisdiction were the ruling principles within the AFL.

The strength of craft organization also gave rise to weakness. Each trade looked mainly to the welfare of its own, and many explicitly barred women and African Americans from membership. There were some important exceptions. The United Mine Workers of America (UMWA) followed a more inclusive policy, recruiting both skilled underground pitmen and the unskilled aboveground workers. The UMWA even tried to recruit strikebreakers brought in by coal operators. With 260,000 members in 1904, the UMWA became the largest AFL affiliate.

AFL unions had a difficult time holding on to their gains. Economic slumps, technological changes, and aggressive counterattacks by employer organizations could be devastating. Trade associations using management-controlled efficiency drives fought union efforts to regulate output and shop practices. The National Association of Manufacturers (NAM), a group of smaller industrialists founded in 1903, launched an **open shop** campaign to eradicate unions altogether. "Open shop" was simply a new name for a workplace where unions were not allowed. Unfriendly judicial decisions also hurt organizing efforts. Not until the 1930s and New Deal legislation would unions be able to count on legislative and legal protections for collective bargaining and the right to strike.

Some workers developed more radical visions of labor organizing. In the harsh and isolated company towns of Idaho, Montana, and Colorado, miners suffered from low wages, poor food, and primitive sanitation, as well as injuries and death from frequent cave-ins and explosions. The Western Federation of Miners (WFM) had gained strength in the metal mining regions of the West by leading several strikes marred by violence. In 1899, during a strike in the silver mining district of Coeur d'Alene, Idaho, the Bunker Hill and Sullivan Mining Company had enraged the miners by hiring armed detectives and firing all union members. Desperate miners retaliated by destroying a company mill with dynamite. Idaho's governor declared martial law and obtained federal troops to enforce it. In a pattern that would become familiar in western labor relations, the soldiers served as strikebreakers, rounding up hundreds of miners and imprisoning them for months in makeshift bullpens.

In response to the brutal realities of labor organizing in the West, most WFM leaders embraced socialism and industrial unionism. In 1905, leaders of the WFM, the Socialist Party, and various radical groups gathered in Chicago to found the Industrial Workers of the World (IWW). The IWW charter proclaimed bluntly, "The working class and the employing class have nothing in common. . . . Between these two classes a struggle must go on until the workers of the world unite as a class, take possession of the earth and the machinery of production, and abolish the wage system." William D. "Big Bill" Haywood, an imposing, one-eyed hard-rock miner, emerged as the most influential and flamboyant spokesman for the IWW, or **Wobblies**, as they were called. Haywood, a charismatic speaker and effective organizer, regularly denounced the AFL for its conservative emphasis on organizing skilled workers by trade. He insisted that the IWW would exclude no one from its ranks. The Wobblies concentrated their efforts on miners, lumberjacks, sailors, "harvest stiffs," and other casual laborers.

The IWW briefly became a force among eastern industrial workers, tapping the rage and growing militancy of immigrants and the unskilled. In 1909, an IWW-led steel strike at McKees Rocks, Pennsylvania, challenged the power of U.S. Steel. In the 1912 "Bread and Roses" strike in Lawrence, Massachusetts, IWW organizers turned a spontaneous walkout of textile workers into a successful struggle for union recognition. Wobbly leaders such as Haywood, Elizabeth Gurley Flynn, and Joseph Ettor used class-conscious rhetoric and multilingual appeals to forge unity among the ethnically diverse Lawrence workforce of 25,000.

The IWW failed to establish permanent organizations in the eastern cities, but it remained a force in the lumber camps, mines, and wheat fields of the West. In spite of its militant rhetoric, the IWW concerned itself with practical gains. "The final aim is revolution," said one Wobbly organizer, "but for the present let's see if we can get a bed to sleep in, water enough to take a bath in and decent food to eat." But when the United States entered World War I, the Justice Department used the IWW's anticapitalist rhetoric and antiwar stance to crush it.

21.4.5 Rebels in Bohemia

During the 1910s, a small but influential community of painters, journalists, poets, social workers, lawyers, and political activists coalesced in the New York City neighborhood of Greenwich Village. These cultural radicals, nearly all of middle-class backgrounds and hailing from provincial American towns, shared a deep sympathy toward the struggles of labor, a passion for modern art, and an affinity for socialism and anarchism. Unlike most progressives, however, especially those from small towns and the nation's hinterlands, the "Village **bohemians**," particularly the women among them, challenged accepted middle-class morality and assumptions. They rejected the double standard of Victorian sexual morality, challenged traditional marriage and sex roles, advocated birth control, and experimented with homosexual relations. They became a powerful national symbol for rebellion and the merger of political and cultural radicalism.

The term "bohemian" referred to anyone who had artistic or intellectual aspirations and who lived with disregard

for conventional rules of behavior. Other American cities, notably Chicago at the turn of the century, had supported bohemian communities. But the Village scene was unique, if fleeting. The neighborhood offered cheap rents, studio space, and good ethnic restaurants, and it was close to the exciting political and labor activism of Manhattan's Lower East Side. The worldview of the Village's bohemian community found expression in *The Masses*, a monthly magazine founded in 1911 by socialist critic Max Eastman, who was also its editor. "The broad purpose of *The Masses*," wrote John Reed, one of its leading writers, "is a social one—to everlastingly attack old systems, old morals, old prejudices—the whole weight of outworn thought that dead men have saddled upon us." For some, Greenwich Village offered a chance to experiment with sexual relationships

PATERSON STRIKE POSTER Publicity poster for the 1913 pageant, organized by John Reed and other Greenwich Village radicals, supporting the cause of striking silk workers in Paterson, New Jersey. This poster drew on aesthetic styles associated with the Industrial Workers of the World, typically including a heroic, larger-than-life image of a factory laborer.

or work arrangements. For others, it was an escape from small-town conformity, or a haven for like-minded artists and activists. Yet the Village bohemians were united in their search for a new sense of community. Intellectuals and artists, as well as workers, feeling alienated from the rest of society, sought shelter in the collective life and close-knit social relations of the Village community. The Village bohemia lasted only a few years, a flame snuffed out by the chill political winds accompanying America's entry into World War I. Yet for decades, Greenwich Village remained a mecca for young men and women searching for alternatives to conventional ways of living.

21.5 Women's Movements and Black Activism

What new forms of activism emerged among the working class, women, and African Americans?

Like working-class radicals, politically engaged women and African American activists often found themselves at odds with more moderate and mainstream progressive reformers. They contested both gender and racial assumptions inherited from the nineteenth century. Some progressives supported the challenges in one or both of these spheres. They helped shape an agenda for social justice that would echo throughout the rest of the twentieth century. Women were at the forefront of several campaigns, such as the settlement house movement, prohibition, suffrage, and birth control. Millions of others took an active role in new women's associations that combined self-help and social mission. These organizations gave women a place in public life, increased their influence in civic affairs, and nurtured a new generation of female leaders.

In fighting racial discrimination, African Americans had a more difficult task. As racism gained ground in the political and cultural spheres, black progressives fought defensively to prevent the rights they had secured during Reconstruction from being further undermined. Still, they managed to produce leaders, ideas, and organizations that would have a long-term impact on American race relations.

21.5.1 The New Woman

The settlement house movement discussed in the opening of this chapter was just one of the new avenues of opportunity opened to progressive-era women. A steady proliferation of women's organizations attracted growing numbers of educated, middle-class women. With more men working in offices, more children attending school, and family size declining, the middle-class home was emptier. At the same time, more middle-class women were graduating from high

school and college. In 1870, only 1 percent of college-age Americans had attended college, about 20 percent of them women; by 1910, about 5 percent of college-age Americans attended college, but the proportion of women among them had doubled to 40 percent.

Single-sex clubs brought middle-class women into the public sphere by celebrating the distinctive strengths associated with women's culture: cooperation, uplift, service. By 1900, the General Federation of Women's Clubs boasted 150,000 members, and by World War I, it claimed to represent more than a million women. The women's club movement combined an earlier focus on self-improvement and intellectual pursuits with newer benevolent efforts on behalf of working women and children. The Buffalo Union, for example, sponsored art lectures for housewives and classes in typing, stenography, and bookkeeping for young working women. It also maintained a library, set up a "noon rest" downtown where women could eat lunch, and ran a school for training domestics.

For many middle-class women, the club movement provided a new kind of female-centered community. Club activity often led members to participate in other civic ventures, particularly "child-saving" reforms, such as child labor laws and mothers' pensions. Some took up the cause of working-class women, fighting for protective legislation and offering aid to trade unions. As wives and daughters of influential and well-off men in their communities, club women had access to funds and could generate support for projects they undertook.

Other women's associations made even more explicit efforts to bridge class lines between middle-class homemakers and working-class women. The National Consumers' League (NCL), started in 1898 by Maud Nathan and Josephine Lowell, sponsored a "white label" campaign in which manufacturers who met safety and sanitary standards could put NCL labels on their food and clothing. Under the dynamic leadership of Florence Kelley, the NCL took an even more aggressive stance by publicizing labor abuses in department stores and lobbying for maximum-hour and minimum-wage laws in state legislatures. In its efforts to protect home and housewife, worker and consumer, the NCL embodied the ideal of "social housekeeping."

21.5.2 Birth Control

The phrase "birth control," coined by Margaret Sanger around 1913, described her campaign to provide contraceptive information and devices for women. Sanger had seen her own mother die at age 49 after bearing 11 children. In 1910, Sanger was a 30-year-old nurse and housewife living with her husband and three children in a New York City suburb. Excited by a socialist lecture she had attended, she convinced her husband to move to the city, where she threw herself into the bohemian milieu. She became an organizer for the IWW, and in 1912, she wrote a series of articles on female sexuality for a socialist newspaper.

When postal officials confiscated the paper for violating obscenity laws, Sanger left for Europe to learn more about contraception. She returned to New York determined to challenge the obscenity statutes with her own magazine, the *Woman Rebel*. Sanger's journal celebrated female autonomy, including the right to sexual expression and control over one's body. "Women cannot be on an equal footing with men," she argued, "until they have full and complete control over their reproductive function." When she distributed her pamphlet *Family Limitation*, postal inspectors confiscated copies and she found herself facing 45 years in prison. In October 1914, she fled to Europe again. In her absence, anarchist agitator Emma Goldman and many women in the Socialist Party took up the cause.

An older generation of feminists had advocated "voluntary motherhood," or the right to say no to a husband's sexual demands. The new birth control advocates embraced contraception as a way of advancing sexual freedom for middle-class women, as well as responding to the misery of those working-class women who bore numerous children while living in poverty.

Sanger returned to the United States in October 1915. After the government dropped the obscenity charges, she embarked on a national speaking tour. In 1916, she again defied the law by opening a birth control clinic in a working-class neighborhood in Brooklyn and offering birth control information without a physician present. Arrested and jailed, she gained more publicity for her crusade. Opponents of birth control accused her of undermining the family and traditional morality. But many thousands of women, desperate for help in understanding their bodies and planning their families, responded positively to Sanger's efforts. In 1921 she founded the American Birth Control League, later renamed Planned Parenthood. Within a few years, birth control leagues and clinics could be found in every major city and most large towns in the country.

21.5.3 Racism and Accommodation

At the turn of the century, four-fifths of the nation's 10 million African Americans still lived in the South, where most eked

MARGARET SANGER AND ETHEL BYRNE A supportive crowd surrounds birth control pioneer Margaret Sanger and her sister Ethel Byrne as they leave the Court of Special Services in New York City in 1917. Police had recently closed Sanger's first birth control clinic in the immigrant neighborhood of Brownsville, and Sanger herself had spent a month in jail.

Bettmann/Getty Images.

out a living working in agriculture. In the cities, most blacks were relegated to menial jobs, but a small African American middle class of entrepreneurs and professionals gained a foothold by selling services and products to the black community. They all confronted a racism that was growing in both intensity and influence in American politics and culture. White racism came in many variants and had evolved significantly since slavery days. The more virulent strains, influenced by Darwin's evolutionary theory, held that blacks were a "degenerate" race, genetically predisposed to vice, crime, and disease and destined to lose the struggle for existence with whites.

African Americans also endured a deeply racist popular culture that made hateful stereotypes of black people a normal feature of political debate and everyday life. Benjamin Tillman, a U.S. senator from South Carolina, denounced the African American as "a fiend, a wild beast, seeking whom he may devour." In northern cities "coon songs," based on gross caricatures of black life, were extremely popular in theaters and as sheet music. As in the antebellum minstrel shows, these songs reduced African Americans to creatures of pure appetite—for food, sex, alcohol, and violence. Southern progressives articulated a more moderate racial philosophy. They also assumed the innate inferiority of blacks, but they believed that black progress was necessary to achieve the economic and political progress associated with a vision of the New South. Their solution to the "race problem" stressed paternalist uplift.

Amid this political and cultural climate, Booker T. Washington won recognition as the most influential black leader of the day. Born a slave in 1856, Washington was educated at Hampton Institute in Virginia, one of the first freedmen's schools devoted to industrial education. In 1881, he founded Tuskegee Institute, a black school in Alabama devoted to industrial and moral education. He became the leading spokesman for racial accommodation, urging blacks to focus on economic improvement and self-reliance, as opposed to political and civil rights. In an 1895 speech delivered at the Cotton States Exposition in Atlanta, Washington outlined the key themes of accommodationist philosophy. "Cast down your buckets where you are," Washington told black people, meaning they should focus on improving their vocational skills as industrial workers and farmers. "In all things that are purely social," he told attentive whites, "we can be as separate as the fingers, yet one as the hand in all things essential to mutual progress."

Washington's message won him the financial backing of leading white philanthropists and the respect of progressive whites. His widely read autobiography, *Up from Slavery* (1901), stands as a classic narrative of an American self-made man. Written with a shrewd eye toward cementing his support among white Americans, it stressed the importance of learning values such as frugality, cleanliness, and personal morality. Washington also gained a large following among African Americans, especially those who aspired to business success. With the help of Andrew Carnegie, he founded the National Negro Business League to preach the virtue of black business development in black communities.

Washington also had a decisive influence on the flow of private funds to black schools in the South. Publicly, he insisted that "agitation of questions of social equality is the extremest folly." Privately, Washington also spent money and worked behind the scenes trying to halt disfranchisement and segregation. He offered secret financial support, for example, for court cases that challenged Louisiana's grandfather clause, the exclusion of blacks from Alabama juries, and railroad segregation in Tennessee and Georgia.

21.5.4 Racial Justice, the NAACP, and Black Women's Activism

Washington's focus on economic self-help remained deeply influential in African American communities long after his death in 1915. But alternative black voices challenged his racial philosophy while he lived. In the early 1900s, scholar and activist W. E. B. Du Bois provided a significant alternative to Washington's leadership. A product of the black middle class, Du Bois had been educated at Fisk University and Harvard, where in 1895 he became the first African American to receive a PhD. His book *The Philadelphia Negro* (1899) was a pioneering work of social science that refuted racist stereotypes by, for example, discussing black contributions to that city's political life and describing the wide range of black business activity. In *The Souls of Black Folk* (1903), Du Bois declared prophetically that "the problem of the twentieth century is the problem of the color line." Through essays on black history, culture, education, and politics, Du Bois explored the concept of "double consciousness." Black people, he argued, would always feel the tension between an African heritage and their desire to assimilate as Americans. *Souls* represented the first published effort to embrace African American culture as a source of collective black strength and something worth preserving.

Du Bois criticized Booker T. Washington's philosophy for its acceptance of "the alleged inferiority of the Negro." The black community, Du Bois argued, must fight for the right to vote, for civic equality, and for higher education for the "talented tenth" of their youth. In 1905, Du Bois and editor William Monroe Trotter brought together a group of educated black men to oppose Washington's conciliatory views. The **Niagara Movement** protested legal segregation, the exclusion of blacks from labor unions, and the curtailment of voting and other civil rights. Discrimination they encountered in Buffalo, New York, prompted the men to move their meeting to Niagara Falls, Ontario. "Any discrimination based simply on race or color is barbarous," they declared. "Persistent manly agitation is the way to liberty."

The Niagara movement failed to generate much change. But in 1909, many of its members, led by Du Bois, attended a National Negro Conference held at the Henry Street Settlement in New York. The group included a number of white progressives sympathetic to the idea of challenging Washington's philosophy. A new interracial organization emerged from this conference, the **National Association for the Advancement of Colored People**. Du Bois, the only black officer of the original NAACP, founded and edited *The Crisis*, the organization's monthly journal.

For the next several decades, the NAACP would lead struggles to overturn legal and economic barriers to equal opportunity.

The disenfranchisement of black voters in the South severely curtailed African American political influence. In response, African American women created new strategies to challenge white supremacy and improve life in their communities. Founded in 1900, the Women's Convention of the National Baptist Convention, the largest black denomination in the United States, offered African American women a new public space to pursue reform work and "racial uplift." They organized settlement houses and built playgrounds; they created daycare facilities and kindergartens; they campaigned for women's suffrage, temperance, and advances in public health. In effect, they transformed church missionary societies into quasi–social service agencies. Using the motto "Lifting as We Climb," the National Association of Colored Women Clubs by 1914 boasted 50,000 members in 1,000 clubs nationwide.

NIAGARA MOVEMENT In July 1905, a group of African American leaders met in Niagara Falls, Ontario, to protest legal segregation and the denial of civil rights to the United State's black population. This portrait was taken against a studio backdrop of the falls. In 1909, the leader of the Niagara movement, W. E. B. Du Bois (second from right, middle row), founded and edited *The Crisis*, the influential monthly journal of the National Association for the Advancement of Colored People.

Schomburg Center, NYPL/Art Resource, NY.

21.6 National Progressivism

What role did Theodore Roosevelt envision the federal government playing in national life?

The progressive impulse had begun at local levels and percolated up. Some state progressive leaders, such as Robert La Follette of Wisconsin and Hiram Johnson of California, achieved national influence as they pushed Progressive forces in both major political parties to take a more aggressive stance on the reform issues of the day. On the presidential level, both Republican Theodore Roosevelt and Democrat Woodrow Wilson laid claim to the progressive mantle—a good example of how progressivism animated many perspectives. In their pursuit of reform agendas, both significantly reshaped the office of the president. As progressivism moved to Washington, nationally organized interest groups and public opinion began to rival the influence of the old political parties in shaping the political landscape.

21.6.1 Theodore Roosevelt and Presidential Activism

The assassination of William McKinley in 1901 made 42-year-old Theodore Roosevelt the youngest man to ever hold the office of president. Roosevelt viewed the presidency as a "bully pulpit"—a platform from which he could exhort Americans to reform their society—and he aimed to make the most of it.

In New York, his friend Jacob Riis, the muckraking journalist, took him on tours of the city's tenement districts and

ROOSEVELT HUNTS TRUSTS This 1909 cartoon by Clifton Berryman depicts President Theodore Roosevelt slaying those trusts he considered "bad" for the public interest, while restraining those whose business practices he considered "good" for the economy. The image also plays on TR's well-publicized fondness for big-game hunting.

Historical/Getty Images.

converted Roosevelt to progressivism. In 1897, Roosevelt went to Washington as assistant secretary of the navy, and during the Spanish-American War he won national fame as leader of the Rough Rider regiment in Cuba. Upon his return, he was elected governor of New York, and then in 1900, vice president of the United States.

Roosevelt was a uniquely colorful figure, a shrewd publicist, and a creative politician. His three-year stint as a rancher in the Dakota Territory, his fondness for hunting and nature study, and his passion for scholarship, which resulted in 10 books before he became president, all set "TR" apart from most of his upper-class peers. Roosevelt preached the virtues of "the strenuous life," and he believed that educated and wealthy Americans had a special responsibility to serve, guide, and inspire those less fortunate. He also believed the United States was at a crossroads that required the national state to play a more active role in curbing the power of wealthy industrialists.

Roosevelt made key contributions to national progressivism and to changing the office of the president. He knew how to inspire and guide public opinion. He stimulated discussion and aroused curiosity like no one before him. In 1902, Roosevelt demonstrated his unique style of activism when he personally intervened in a bitter dispute in the anthracite coal industry. Using public calls for conciliation, a series of White House meetings, and private pressure on the mine owners, Roosevelt secured an arbitrated settlement that won better pay and working conditions for the miners but without recognition of their union. Roosevelt also pushed for efficient government as the solution to social problems. Unlike most nineteenth-century Republicans, who had largely ignored economic and social inequalities, Roosevelt frankly acknowledged them. Administrative agencies run by experts, he believed, could find rational solutions that would satisfy everyone.

21.6.2 Trust-Busting and Regulation

One of the first issues Roosevelt faced was growing public concern with the rapid business consolidations taking place in the American economy. In 1902, he directed the Justice Department to begin a series of prosecutions under the **Sherman Antitrust Act**. The first target was the Northern Securities Company, a huge merger of transcontinental railroads brought about by financier J. P. Morgan. The deal would have created a giant holding company controlling nearly all the long-distance rail lines from Chicago to California. In *Northern Securities v. United States* (1904), the Court held that the stock transactions constituted an illegal combination in restraint of interstate commerce.

This case established Roosevelt's reputation as a "trust-buster." During his two terms, the Justice Department filed 43 cases under the Sherman Antitrust Act to restrain or dissolve business monopolies. These included actions against the so-called tobacco and beef trusts and the Standard Oil Company. Roosevelt viewed these suits as necessary to publicize the issue and assert the federal government's ultimate authority over big business. But he did not really believe in the need to break up large corporations. "Trust-busting" might be good politics, but unlike many progressives, who were nostalgic for smaller companies and freer competition, Roosevelt accepted centralization as a fact of modern economic life. Indeed, many of the legal cases against trusts were dropped after business executives met privately with Roosevelt in the White House. What was most important, in TR's view, was to insist on the right and power of the federal government to rein in excessive corporate behavior.

After easily defeating Democrat Alton B. Parker in the 1904 election, Roosevelt felt more secure in pushing for regulatory legislation. In 1906, Roosevelt responded to public pressure for greater government intervention and, overcoming objections from a conservative Congress, signed three important measures into law. The **Hepburn Act** strengthened the Interstate Commerce Commission

(ICC), established in 1887 as the first independent regulatory agency, by authorizing it to set maximum railroad rates and inspect financial records. The other two laws passed in 1906 also expanded the regulatory power of the federal government. The battles surrounding these reforms demonstrate how progressive measures often attracted supporters with competing motives. The **Pure Food and Drug Act** established the Food and Drug Administration (FDA), which tested and approved drugs before they went on the market. The Meat Inspection Act (passed with help from the shocking publicity surrounding Upton Sinclair's muckraking novel *The Jungle*) empowered the Department of Agriculture to inspect and label meat products. In both of these cases, supporters hailed the new laws as providing consumer protection against adulterated or fraudulently labeled food and drugs.

Regulatory legislation found advocates among American big business as well. Large meatpackers such as Swift and Armour strongly supported stricter federal regulation as a way to drive out smaller companies that could not meet tougher standards. The new laws also helped American packers compete more profitably in the European export market by giving their meat the official seal of federal inspectors. Large pharmaceutical manufacturers similarly supported new regulations that would eliminate competitors and patent medicine suppliers. Thus, these reforms won support from large corporate interests that viewed stronger federal regulation as a strategy for consolidating their economic power. Progressive-era expansion of the nation-state had its champions among—and benefits for—big business as well as American consumers.

21.6.3 The Birth of Environmentalism

As a naturalist and outdoorsman, Theodore Roosevelt also believed in the need for government regulation of the natural environment. He worried about the destruction of forests, prairies, streams, and the wilderness. The conservation of forest and water resources, he argued, was a national problem of vital import. In 1905, he created the U.S. Forest Service and named conservationist Gifford Pinchot to head it. Pinchot recruited a force of forest rangers to manage the reserves. By 1909, total timber and forest reserves had increased from 45 million to 195 million acres, and more than 80 million acres of mineral lands had been withdrawn from public sale.

On the broad issue of managing America's natural resources, the Roosevelt administration took the middle ground between preservation and unrestricted commercial development. But other voices championed a more radical vision of conservation, emphasizing the preservation of wilderness lands against the encroachment of commercial exploitation. The most influential and committed

of these was John Muir, an essayist and founder of the modern environmentalist movement. Muir made a passionate and spiritual defense of the inherent value of the American wilderness. "Climb the mountains and get their good tidings," he advised. "Nature's peace will flow into you as the sunshine into the trees." Muir served as first president of the Sierra Club, founded in 1892 to preserve and protect the mountain regions of the West Coast as well as Yellowstone National Park in Wyoming, Montana, and Idaho.

A bitter, drawn-out struggle over new water sources for San Francisco revealed the deep conflicts between conservationists, represented by Pinchot, and preservationists, represented by Muir. After a devastating earthquake in 1906, San Francisco sought federal approval to dam and flood the spectacular Hetch Hetchy Valley, located 150 miles from the city in Yosemite National Park. The project promised to ease the city's chronic freshwater shortage and to generate hydroelectric power. Conservationists and their urban progressive allies argued that developing Hetch Hetchy would be a victory for the public good over greedy private developers, since the plan called for municipal control of the water supply. To John Muir and the Sierra Club, Hetch Hetchy was a "temple" threatened with destruction by the "devotees of ravaging commercialism." Congress finally approved the reservoir plan in 1913; utility and public development triumphed over the preservation of nature.

Although they lost the battle for Hetch Hetchy, the preservationists gained much ground in the larger campaign of alerting the nation to the dangers of a vanishing wilderness. They began to use their own utilitarian rationales, arguing that national parks would encourage economic growth through tourism and provide Americans with a healthy escape from urban and industrial areas. In 1916, the preservationists obtained their own bureaucracy in Washington with the creation of the National Park Service.

The Newlands Reclamation Act of 1902 represented another important victory for the conservation strategy of Roosevelt and Pinchot. With the goal of turning arid land into productive family farms through irrigation, the act established the Reclamation Bureau within the Department of the Interior and provided federal funding for dam and canal projects. But in practice, the bureau did more to encourage the growth of large-scale agribusiness and western cities than of small farming. The Roosevelt Dam on Arizona's Salt River, along with the 40-mile Arizona Canal, helped develop the Phoenix area. The Imperial Dam on the Colorado River diverted water to California's Imperial and Coachella Valleys. The Newlands Act established a growing federal presence in managing water resources, the critical issue in twentieth-century western development.

WILLIAM ROBINSON LEIGH'S *GRAND CANYON* "The Grand Canyon fills me with awe," said President Theodore Roosevelt when he first visited in 1903. "Do nothing to mar its grandeur, sublimity and loveliness. You cannot improve on it. But what you can do is to keep it for your children, your children's children, and all who come after you, as the one great sight which every American should see." It became part of the National Parks Service in 1919.

21.6.4 The Election of 1912: A Four-Way Race

In 1908, Roosevelt kept his promise to retire after a second term. He chose Secretary of War William Howard Taft as his successor. Taft easily defeated Democrat William Jennings Bryan in the 1908 election. During Taft's presidency, the gulf between "insurgent" progressives and the "stand pat" wing split the Republican Party wide open. Compared with Roosevelt, the reflective and judicious Taft brought a much more restrained concept of the presidency to the White House. He supported some progressive measures, including the constitutional amendment legalizing a graduated income tax (ratified in 1913), safety codes for mines and railroads, and the creation of a federal Children's Bureau (1912). But in a series of bitter political fights involving tariff, antitrust, and conservation policies, Taft alienated Roosevelt and many other progressives.

After returning from an African safari and a triumphant European tour in 1910, Roosevelt threw himself back into national politics. He directly challenged Taft for the Republican Party leadership. In a dozen bitter state presidential primaries (the first ever held), Taft and Roosevelt fought for the nomination. Although Roosevelt won

most of these contests, the old guard still controlled the national convention and renominated Taft in June 1912. Roosevelt's supporters stormed out, and in August, the new Progressive Party nominated Roosevelt and Hiram Johnson of California as its presidential ticket. Roosevelt's "New Nationalism" presented a vision of a strong federal government, led by an activist president, regulating and protecting the various interests in American society. The platform called for woman suffrage, the eight-hour day, prohibition of child labor, minimum-wage standards for working women, and stricter regulation of large corporations.

The Democrats chose Governor Woodrow Wilson of New Jersey as their candidate. Although not nearly as well known nationally as Taft and Roosevelt, Wilson had built a strong reputation as a reformer. The son of a Virginia Presbyterian minister, Wilson spent most of his early career in academia. After teaching history and political science at several schools, he became president of Princeton University in 1902, and in 1910 he won election as New Jersey's governor, running against the state Democratic machine. Wilson declared himself and the Democratic Party to be the true progressives. Viewing Roosevelt rather than Taft as his main rival, Wilson contrasted his **New Freedom** campaign with Roosevelt's New Nationalism. Crafted largely by progressive lawyer Louis Brandeis, Wilson's platform was far more ambiguous than Roosevelt's. The New Freedom emphasized restoring conditions of free competition and equality of economic opportunity. Wilson did favor a variety of progressive reforms for workers, farmers, and consumers. But Wilson argued against allowing the federal government to become as large and paternalistic as Roosevelt advocated. "What this country needs above everything else," Wilson declared, "is a body of laws which will look after the men who are on the make rather than the men who are already made."

Socialist Party nominee Eugene V. Debs offered the fourth and most radical choice to voters. The socialists had more than doubled their membership since 1908, to exceed 100,000. By 1912, more than a thousand socialists

held elective office in 33 states and 160 cities, including 56 mayors and one congressman. The party's 1912 platform called for collective ownership of all large-scale industry and all means of transportation and communication. It demanded shorter working hours, an end to child labor, and the vote for women. An inspiring orator who drew large and sympathetic crowds wherever he spoke, Debs proved especially popular in areas with strong labor movements and populist traditions. He wrapped his socialist message in an apocalyptic vision. Socialists would "abolish this monstrous system and the misery and crime which flow from it. "Debs and the socialists also took credit for pushing both Roosevelt and Wilson further toward the left. Both the Democratic and Progressive Party platforms contained proposals that had been considered extremely radical only 10 years earlier.

In the end, the divisions in the Republican Party gave the election to Wilson. (See Map 21.2.) Even though he won with only 42 percent of the popular vote, Wilson swept the electoral college with 435 votes to Roosevelt's 88 and Taft's 8, giving him the largest electoral majority up to that time. In several respects, the election of 1912 was the first "modern" presidential race. It featured the first direct primaries, challenges to traditional party loyalties, an issue-oriented campaign, and a high degree of interest-group activity.

21.6.5 Woodrow Wilson's First Term

As president, Wilson followed Roosevelt's lead in expanding the activist dimensions of the office. He became more responsive to pressure for a greater federal role in regulating business and the economy. This increase in direct lobbying—from hundreds of local and national reform groups, Washington-based organizations, and the new Progressive Party—was itself a new and defining feature of the era's political life. With the help of a Democratic-controlled Congress, Wilson pushed through a significant battery of reform proposals.

The **Underwood-Simmons Act of 1913** substantially reduced tariff duties on a variety of raw materials and manufactured goods, including wool, sugar, agricultural machinery, shoes, iron, and steel. Taking advantage of the newly ratified **Sixteenth Amendment**, which gave Congress the power to levy taxes on income, it also imposed the first graduated tax (up to 6 percent) on personal incomes. The **Federal Reserve Act** that same year restructured the nation's banking and currency system. It created 12 Federal Reserve Banks, regulated by a central board in Washington. Member banks were required to keep a portion of their cash reserves in the Federal Reserve Bank of their district. By raising or lowering the percentage of reserves required, "the Fed" could either discourage or encourage credit expansion

PRESIDENTIAL CANDIDATES, 1912 This political cartoon, drawn by Charles Jay Budd, appeared on the cover of *Harper's Weekly*, September 28, 1912. It employed the imagery of autumn county fairs to depict voters as unhappy with their three choices for president. Note that the artist did not include the fourth candidate, socialist Eugene V. Debs, who was often ignored by more conservative publications such as *Harper's*.

Harvard University, The Houghton Library Reading Room.

Map 21.2 THE ELECTION OF 1912

Numbers on states represent Electoral Votes.	Electoral Vote (%)	Popular Vote (%)
WOODROW WILSON (W) (Democrat)	435 (82)	6,296,547 (42)
Theodore Roosevelt (R) (Progressive)	88 (17)	4,118,571 (27)
William Taft (T) (Republican)	8 (1)	3,486,720 (23)
Eugene Debs (Socialist)	—	900,672 (6)

The split within the Republican Party allowed Woodrow Wilson to become only the second Democrat since the Civil War to be elected president. Eugene Debs's votes were the highest ever polled by a socialist candidate.

by member banks. By giving central direction to banking and monetary policy, the Federal Reserve Board diminished the power of large private banks.

Wilson also supported the **Clayton Antitrust Act of 1914**, which replaced the old Sherman Act of 1890 as the nation's basic antitrust law. The Clayton Act reflected the growing political clout of the American Federation of Labor. It exempted unions from being construed as illegal combinations in restraint of trade, and it forbade federal courts from issuing injunctions against strikers. But Wilson adopted the view that permanent federal regulation was necessary for checking the abuses of big business. The **Federal Trade Commission (FTC)**, established in 1914, sought to give the federal government the same sort of regulatory control over corporations that the ICC had over railroads. Wilson believed a permanent federal body like the FTC would provide a method for corporate oversight superior to the erratic and time-consuming process of legal trust-busting.

On social issues, Wilson proved more cautious in his first two years. His initial failure to support federal child labor legislation and rural credits to farmers angered many progressives. A Southerner, Wilson also issued an executive order that instituted legal segregation in federal employment, requiring African Americans to work separately from white employees in government offices around Washington, D.C. As the reelection campaign of 1916 approached, Wilson worried about defections from the labor and social justice wings of his party. He proceeded to support a rural credits act providing government capital to federal farm banks, as well as federal aid to agricultural extension programs in schools. He also came out in favor of a worker compensation bill for federal employees, and he signed the landmark Keating-Owen Act, which banned children under 14 from working in enterprises engaged in interstate commerce. Although it covered less than 10 percent of the nation's 2 million working children, the new law established a minimum standard of protection and put the power of federal authority behind the principle of regulating child labor. But by 1916, the dark cloud of war in Europe had already begun to cast its long shadow over progressive reform.

Conclusion

In her memoirs, Lillian Wald summarized the growth of the Henry Street Settlement she founded in 1895 as a home health and visiting nurse service on New York's Lower East Side. "Our experience in one small East Side section," she recalled in 1934, "a block perhaps, has led to a next contact, and a next, in widening circles, until our community relationships have come to include the city, the state, the national government, and the world at large."

Much the same could be said of the progressive movement. What had begun as a series of interlocking, sometimes contradictory reform initiatives had come to redefine Americans' relationship to government itself. Cities and state legislatures routinely made active interventions to improve the lives of their citizens. Real advances had been made through a range of social legislation covering working conditions, child labor, minimum wages, and worker compensation. Social progressives, too, had discovered the power of organizing into extraparty lobbying groups, such as the National Consumers' League and the National American Woman Suffrage Association. The national government had become the focus of political power and reform energy. The president was expected to provide leadership in policymaking, and new federal bureaucracies exerted more influence over the day-to-day lives of Americans.

Yet many progressive reforms had uneven or unintended consequences. The tensions between fighting for social justice and the urge toward social control remained unresolved. The emphasis on efficiency, uplift, and rational administration often collided with humane impulses to aid the poor, the immigrant, the slum dweller. The large majority of African Americans, blue-collar workers, and urban poor remained untouched by federal assistance programs. The drive for a more open and democratic political process, in particular, had the effect of excluding some people from voting while including others. For African Americans, progressivism largely meant disenfranchisement from voting altogether. Stricter election laws made it more difficult for third parties to get on the ballot. Voting itself steadily declined after 1916.

Overall, party voting became a less important form of political participation. Interest-group activity, congressional and statehouse lobbying, and direct appeals to public opinion gained currency as ways of influencing government. Business federations and individual trade associations were among the most active groups pressing their demands on government. Political action often shifted from legislatures to the new administrative agencies and commissions created to deal with social and economic problems. Popular magazines and journals grew significantly in both number and circulation, becoming more influential in shaping and appealing to national public opinion.

America's entry into World War I effectively drained the energy out of progressive reform. The progressive movement, however, with all its contradictions and internal tensions, had profoundly changed the landscape of American political and social life.

Key Terms

Progressivism A national movement focused on a variety of reform initiatives, including ending corruption, a more business like approach to government, and legislative responses to industrial excess. p. 483

Muckraking Journalism exposing economic, social, and political evils, so named by Theodore Roosevelt for its "raking the muck" of American society. p. 485

Social Darwinism The application of Charles Darwin's theory of biological evolution to society, holding that the fittest and wealthiest survive, the weak and the poor perish, and government action is unable to alter this "natural" process. p. 486

Referendum Submission of a law, proposed or already in effect, to a direct popular vote for approval or rejection. p. 489

Temperance groups Groups dedicated to reducing the sale and consumption of alcohol. p. 491

Prohibition A ban on the production, sale, and consumption of liquor, achieved temporarily through state laws and the Eighteenth Amendment. p. 491

Open shop Factory or business employing workers regardless of whether they are union members; in practice, such a business usually refuses to hire union members and follows antiunion policies. The name for a workplace where unions were not allowed. p. 499

Wobblies Popular name for the members of the Industrial Workers of the World (IWW). p. 500

Bohemian Artistic individual who lives with disregard for the conventional rules of behavior. p. 500

Niagara Movement African American group organized in 1905 to promote racial integration, civil and political rights, and equal access to economic opportunity. p. 504

National Association for the Advancement of Colored People Organization cofounded by W. E. B. Du Bois in 1910 dedicated to restoring African American political and social rights. p. 504

Sherman Antitrust Act The first federal antitrust measure, passed in 1890; sought to promote economic competition by prohibiting business combinations in restraint of trade or commerce. p. 505

Hepburn Act An act that strengthened the Interstate Commerce Commission (ICC) by authorizing it to set maximum railroad rates and inspect financial records. p. 505

Pure Food and Drug Act An act that established the Food and Drug Administration (FDA), which tested and approved drugs before they went on the market. p. 506

New Freedom Woodrow Wilson's 1912 program for limited government intervention in the economy to restore competition by curtailing the restrictive influences of trusts and protective tariffs, thereby providing opportunities for individual achievement. p. 507

Underwood-Simmons Act of 1913 Reform law that lowered tariff rates and levied the first regular federal income tax. p. 508

Sixteenth Amendment Authorized a federal income tax. p. 508

Federal Reserve Act The 1913 law that revised banking and currency by extending limited government regulation through the creation of the Federal Reserve System. p. 508

Clayton Antitrust Act of 1914 Replaced the old Sherman Act of 1890 as the nation's basic antitrust law. It exempted unions from being construed as illegal combinations in restraint of trade, and it forbade federal courts from issuing injunctions against strikers. p. 509

Federal Trade Commission (FTC) Government agency established in 1914 to provide regulatory oversight of business activity. p. 509

CHRONOLOGY

Jane Addams founds Hull House in Chicago	**1889**
	1890 Jacob Riis publishes *How the Other Half Lives*
Robert M. La Follette elected governor of Wisconsin	**1900**
	1901 Theodore Roosevelt succeeds the assassinated William McKinley as president
Industrial Workers of the World is founded in Chicago	**1905**
	1906 Congress passes Pure Food and Drug Act and Meat Inspection Act and establishes Food and Drug Administration
Uprising of 20,000 garment workers in New York City helps organize unskilled workers into unions National Association for the Advancement of Colored People (NAACP) is founded	**1909**
	1912 Democrat Woodrow Wilson wins presidency, defeating Republican William H. Taft, Progressive Theodore Roosevelt, and Socialist Eugene V. Debs
Sixteenth Amendment, legalizing a graduated income tax, is ratified Seventeenth Amendment, shifting the selection of U.S. senators to direct election by voters, is ratified	**1913**

Chapter 22
The United States in the Era of the Great War 1901–1920

AMERICAN TROOPS AT SOUTHAMPTON EMBARKING FOR FRANCE This 1917 painting by Thomas Derrick captures the departure of American troops for the Western Front.

Snark/Art Resource, NY.

 ## Contents and Focus Questions

American Communities

The American Expeditionary Force in France

At 5:30 A.M. on September 26, 1918, some 600,000 soldiers of the American Expeditionary Force (AEF) headed into the dense gray fog on a 20-mile front between the Meuse River and the Argonne Forest in northern France. The biggest and costliest American operation of World War I had begun. In sheer size and scale, the Meuse-Argonne offensive dwarfed anything an American army had ever attempted. The number of American soldiers involved exceeded the total of Union and Confederate soldiers who had fought at Gettysburg. American commander General John J. Pershing aimed to overwhelm the undermanned and dispirited German lines with massive numbers and swift movement, and thereby force a German surrender. To be sure, elements of the AEF had seen action in several earlier battles, but in most of those engagements Americans had fought under British or French command. Pershing hoped to put a distinctively American stamp on ending the war with the Meuse-Argonne offensive.

The individual infantryman, however, had little time or use for grand strategy. Each man carried a rifle and bayonet, steel helmet, and gas mask, along with 250 rounds of ammunition. His two days of "iron rations" consisted of two cans of corned beef, six boxes of hard crackers, and a quart canteen of water.

The American thrust quickly stalled as the Germans put up fierce resistance with well-placed machine gun nests and artillery batteries, spread out amidst a ghostly landscape littered with abandoned trenches, tangled barbed-wire fences, water-filled craters, and dead and mangled bodies everywhere. The scene was nothing like the storybooks of war, recalled Lieutenant Maury Maverick. "There were no bugles, no flags, no drums, and as far as we knew, no heroes . . . I have never read in any military history a description of the high explosives that break overhead. There is a great swishing scream, a smash-bang, and it seems to tear everything loose from you. The intensity of it simply enters your heart and brain and tears every nerve to pieces." After America's entry into the European conflict in April 1917, millions of Americans traded their civilian clothes for a uniform, creating a new kind of community of soldiers in a modern mechanized army. The Wilson administration had acted swiftly to mobilize the nation's economy and civilian population. The Selective Service Act required the registration and classification for military service of all men between ages 21 and 35, and by war's end in November 1918, some 24 million men had registered for the draft, and another 2 million had volunteered. The numbers were there, but the looming question remained: Could the nation create a cohesive, efficient, and mass fighting force where none had existed before? In 1917, one out of five soldiers was born in another country and overall illiteracy rates ran as high as 25 percent. Nearly 400,000 African Americans would enter the armed forces, but they faced rigid segregation and deep prejudice against their fitness to fight.

Despite the extraordinary differences of region, class, education, and ethnicity, the **doughboys**, as AEF members were affectionately called (for the doughnut shaped uniform buttons), shared a great deal of common experiences. For many, the journey to training camp represented their first substantial trip away from home. "The military tent where they all sleep side by side," Theodore Roosevelt predicted,

"will rank next to the public schools among the great agents of democratization." Many progressives saw the army as a field for continuing social reform and education. In training camps, the War Department mounted a vigorous campaign against venereal disease, and the scientific discussions of sex to which recruits were subjected in lectures, pamphlets, and films were surely a first for the vast majority. Accepting military discipline was new to most as well, and it often rubbed against traditional American notions of freedom and independence.

By the summer of 1918, when most American soldiers traveled to France, the carnage across Europe was no secret; nor was the grim reality of death associated with machine guns, tanks, and trench warfare. The blizzard of posters, films, war bond drives, and other propaganda activities coordinated by the Committee on Public Information (CPI) mostly avoided this side of war. Instead, the CPI emphasized appeals to patriotism, manhood, heroism, and the fight for democracy. Many doughboys also carried with them vague and often romantic notions of what to expect on the battlefield—images of war shaped by their grandfathers' stories about the Civil War or romantic accounts of medieval knights.

Their experiences in the Meuse-Argonne offensive brought those doughboys face-to-face with the very different reality of mass mechanized killing. Rather than the swift victory General Pershing had hoped for, the campaign turned into a slow, sometimes chaotic slog. Between September 25 and the Armistice ending the fighting on November 11, each day claimed an average of more than 550 Americans dead, with a total of 26,000 Americans killed in the campaign. For many, the worst horror was artillery bombardment, with unseen enemy guns lobbing high explosives that could instantly turn a group of men into unrecognizable piles of flesh. The men endured sleep deprivation, hunger, and lice, and they could never get dry. Behind the front, American inexperience with such a large-scale operation created enormous logistical problems. Huge traffic jams made it difficult to evacuate the wounded to hospitals and led to severe shortages of rations, water, and ammunition. Discipline frequently broke down, with as many as 100,000 stragglers wandering in the rear areas, unable or unwilling to rejoin their units. Meanwhile, a lethal influenza outbreak, part of the worldwide pandemic that would claim more than 20 million lives, swept through the AEF in France, afflicting 100,000 doughboys and killing about 10,000 of them.

Many AEF men would long remember their brief time in France as a life-changing high point of their lives, and for some it achieved a mythic significance. Revulsion at the horrors of warfare often coexisted with strong feelings of camaraderie, as expressed by one of the most celebrated doughboys, Sergeant Alvin York. A religious pacifist who had originally sought conscientious objector status, the

Tennessee sharpshooter received the Medal of Honor for single-handedly eliminating an entire German machine gun battalion and taking 132 prisoners. War, York recalled, "turns you into a mad fightin' animal, but it also brings out something else, something I jes don't know how to describe, a sort of tenderness and love for the fellows fightin' with you."

America's emergence as a global power required mass mobilization of the armed forces and created a new community of veterans. In early 1919, encouraged by some senior officers, a group of AEF veterans founded the American Legion, "to preserve the memories and incidents of our association in the great war . . . to consecrate and sanctify our comradeship."

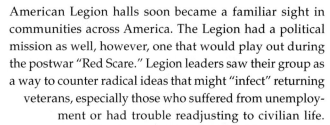

Verdun

American Legion halls soon became a familiar sight in communities across America. The Legion had a political mission as well, however, one that would play out during the postwar "Red Scare." Legion leaders saw their group as a way to counter radical ideas that might "infect" returning veterans, especially those who suffered from unemployment or had trouble readjusting to civilian life.

The American Legion would commemorate the war, celebrate sacrifice, and honor the dead, all in the name of promoting "100 Per Cent Americanism" and fighting against "dangerous" socialists and other radical groups. As much a political lobby as a veterans' organization, the American Legion would extend the memory and life of the AEF community well into the twentieth century.

22.1 Becoming a World Power

How did the United States use military power as a component of foreign policy under Roosevelt, Taft, and Wilson?

In the first years of the new century, the United States pursued a more vigorous and aggressive foreign policy than it had in the past. In addition to its newfound imperial presence in Asia, the United States marked out the Western Hemisphere as a site for establishing American hegemony. Presidents Theodore Roosevelt, William Howard Taft, and Woodrow Wilson all contributed to "progressive diplomacy," in which commercial expansion was backed by a growing military presence in the hemisphere. This policy reflected a view of world affairs that stressed the links between ensuring American commercial expansion and a foreign policy couched in terms of moralism, order, and a special, even God-given role for the United States. By 1917, when the United States entered the Great War, the nation was just as complicit in building empire as were the European states and Japan.

22.1.1 Roosevelt: The Big Stick

Theodore Roosevelt left a strong imprint on the nation's foreign policy. Like many of his class and background, "TR" took for granted the superiority of Protestant Anglo-American culture and the goal of spreading its values and influence. He believed that to maintain and increase its economic and political stature, America must be militarily strong. In 1900, Roosevelt summarized his activist views, declaring, "I have always been fond of the West

African proverb, 'Speak softly and carry a big stick, you will go far.'"

Roosevelt brought the "big stick" approach to disputes in the Caribbean region. Since the 1880s, several British, French, and American companies had pursued plans for building a canal across the Isthmus of Panama, thereby connecting the Atlantic and Pacific oceans. The canal was a top priority for Roosevelt, and he tried to negotiate a leasing agreement with Colombia, of which Panama was a province. When the Colombian Senate rejected a final American offer in the fall of 1903, Roosevelt invented a new strategy. A combination of native forces and foreign promoters associated with the canal project plotted a revolt against Colombia. Roosevelt kept in touch with at least one leader of the revolt, Philippe Bunau-Varilla, and the president let him know that U.S. warships were steaming toward Panama.

On November 3, 1903, just as the USS *Nashville* arrived in Colón harbor, the province of Panama declared itself independent of Colombia. The United States immediately recognized the new Republic of Panama. Less than two weeks later, Bunau-Varilla, serving as a minister from Panama, signed a treaty granting the United States full sovereignty in perpetuity over a 10-mile-wide canal zone. America guaranteed Panama's independence and agreed to pay it $10 million initially and an additional $250,000 a year for the Canal Zone.

The Panama Canal was a triumph of modern engineering and gave the United States a tremendous strategic and commercial advantage in the Western Hemisphere. It took eight years to build and cost hundreds of workers their lives. Several earlier attempts to build a canal in the region had failed, but with better equipment and a vigorous campaign against disease, the United States succeeded. In 1914,

"THE WORLD'S CONSTABLE" This 1905 cartoon portraying President Theodore Roosevelt, "The World's Constable," appeared in *Judge* magazine. In depicting the president as a strong but benevolent policeman bringing order in a contentious world, the artist Louis Dalrymple drew on familiar imagery from Roosevelt's earlier days as a New York City police commissioner.

after $720 million in construction costs, the first merchant ships sailed through the canal.

"The inevitable effect of our building the Canal," wrote Secretary of State Elihu Root in 1905, "must be to require us to police the surrounding premises." Roosevelt agreed. He was especially concerned that European powers might step in if America did not. To prevent armed intervention by the Europeans, in 1904 Roosevelt proclaimed what became known as the **Roosevelt Corollary** to the Monroe Doctrine. "Chronic wrongdoing, or an impotence which results in a general loosening of the ties of civilized society," the statement read, justified "the exercise of an international police power" anywhere in the hemisphere. Roosevelt and later presidents cited the corollary to justify armed intervention in the internal affairs of Cuba, Haiti, the Dominican Republic, Nicaragua, and Mexico.

With the outbreak of the Russo-Japanese War in 1904, Roosevelt worried about the future of the **Open Door** trade and investment policy in Asia. A total victory by Russia or Japan could upset the balance of power in East Asia and threaten American business enterprises there. He became especially concerned after the Japanese scored a series of military victories over Russia and began to loom as a dominant power in East Asia. Roosevelt mediated a settlement of the Russo-Japanese War at Portsmouth, New

Hampshire, in 1905 (for which he was awarded the 1906 Nobel Peace Prize). In this settlement, Japan won recognition of its dominant position in Korea and consolidated its economic control over Manchuria. Yet repeated incidents of anti-Japanese racism in California kept American-Japanese relations strained. In 1906, for example, the San Francisco school board, responding to nativist fears of a "yellow peril," ordered the segregation of Japanese, Chinese, and Korean students. Japan angrily protested. In 1907, in the so-called Gentlemen's Agreement, Japan agreed not to issue passports to Japanese male laborers looking to immigrate to the United States, and Roosevelt promised to fight anti-Japanese discrimination. He then persuaded the San Francisco school board to exempt Japanese students from the segregation ordinance.

Roosevelt did not want these conciliatory moves to be interpreted as weakness. He thus built up American naval strength in the Pacific, and in 1908, he sent battleships to visit Japan in a muscle-flexing display of sea power. In that same year, the two burgeoning Pacific powers reached a reconciliation. The Root-Takahira Agreement affirmed the "existing status quo" in Asia, mutual respect for territorial possessions in the Pacific, and the Open Door trade policy in China. From the Japanese perspective, the agreement recognized Japan's colonial dominance in Korea and southern Manchuria.

22.1.2 Taft: Dollar Diplomacy

Roosevelt's successor, William Howard Taft, believed he could replace the militarism of the big stick with the more subtle and effective weapon of business investment. Taft and his secretary of state, corporate lawyer Philander C. Knox, followed a strategy (called "dollar diplomacy" by critics) in which they assumed that political influence would follow increased U.S. trade and investment. As Taft explained in 1910, he advocated "active intervention to secure for our merchandise and our capitalists opportunity for profitable investment."

Overall American investment in Central America grew rapidly, from $41 million in 1908 to $93 million by 1914. Most of this money went into railroad construction, mining, and plantations. The United Fruit Company alone owned about 160,000 acres of land in the Caribbean by 1913. But dollar diplomacy ended up requiring military support. The Taft administration sent the navy and the Marines to intervene in political disputes in Honduras and Nicaragua, propping up factions pledged to protect American business interests. A contingent of U.S. Marines remained in Nicaragua until 1933. The economic and political structures of Honduras and Nicaragua were controlled by both the dollar and the bullet. (See Map 22.1.)

In China, Taft and Knox pressed for a greater share of the pie for U.S. investors. They gained a place for U.S. bankers in the European consortium, building the massive new Hukuang Railway in southern and central China. But Knox blundered by attempting to "neutralize" the existing railroads in China. He tried to secure a huge international loan for the Chinese government that would allow it to buy up all the foreign railways and develop new ones. Both Russia and Japan, which had fought wars over their railroad interests in Manchuria, resisted this plan. Knox's "neutralization" scheme, combined with U.S. support for the Chinese Nationalists in their 1911 revolt against the ruling Manchu dynasty, prompted Japan to sign a new friendship treaty with Russia. The Open Door to China was now effectively closed, and American relations with Japan began a slow deterioration that ended in war 30 years later.

22.1.3 Wilson: Moralism and Intervention in Mexico

Right after he took office in 1913, President Woodrow Wilson observed that, "it would be the irony of fate if my administration had to deal chiefly with foreign affairs." His political life up to then had centered on achieving progressive reforms in the domestic arena. As it turned out, Wilson had to face international crises from his first day in office. He brought to foreign affairs a set of fundamental principles that combined a moralist's faith in American democracy with a realist's understanding of the power of international commerce. He believed that American economic expansion, accompanied by democratic principles and Christianity, was a civilizing force in the world.

Wilson, like most corporate and political leaders of the day, emphasized foreign investments and industrial exports as the keys to the nation's prosperity. He believed that the United States, with its superior industrial efficiency, could achieve supremacy in world commerce if artificial barriers to free trade were removed. He championed and extended the Open Door principles of John Hay, advocating strong diplomatic and military measures "for making ourselves supreme in the world from an economic point of view." Wilson often couched his vision of a dynamic, expansive American capitalism in terms of a moral crusade. As he put it in a speech to a congress of salesmen, "[Since] you are Americans and are meant to carry liberty and justice and the principles of humanity wherever you go, go out and sell goods that will make the world more comfortable and more happy, and convert them to the principles of America." Yet he quickly found that the complex realities of power politics could interfere with moral vision.

Wilson's policies toward Mexico, which foreshadowed the problems he would encounter in World War I, best illustrate his difficulties. The 1911 Mexican Revolution had overthrown the brutally corrupt dictatorship of Porfirio Díaz, and popular leader Francisco Madero had won wide support by promising democracy and economic reform for millions of landless peasants. But the U.S. business community was nervous about the future of its investments, which in the previous generation had come to dominate the Mexican economy. By 1910, American companies owned over one-quarter—130 million acres—of Mexico's land, including more than half of its coastlines and border areas. A handful of American mining companies had led the way in exploiting Mexican natural resources, using high capitalization, advanced technology, and sophisticated marketing networks to win control of roughly four-fifths of the gold, silver, and copper extracted from Mexican mines.

Wilson at first gave his blessing to the revolutionary movement, expressed regret over the Mexican-American War of 1846–1848, and disavowed any interest in another war. But right before he took office, Wilson was stunned when Madero was ousted and murdered by his chief lieutenant, General Victoriano Huerta. Other nations, including Great Britain and Japan, recognized the Huerta regime, but Wilson refused. An armed faction opposed to Huerta, known as the Constitutionalists and led by Venustiano Carranza, emerged in northern Mexico. Both sides rejected an effort by Wilson to broker a compromise between them. Carranza,

Map 22.1 THE UNITED STATES IN THE CARIBBEAN, 1865–1933

An overview of U.S. economic and military involvement in the Caribbean during the late nineteenth and early twentieth centuries. Victory in the Spanish-American War, the Panama Canal project, and rapid economic investment in Mexico and Cuba all contributed to a permanent and growing U.S. military presence in the region.

an ardent nationalist, pressed for the right to buy U.S. arms, which he won in 1914. Wilson also isolated Huerta diplomatically by persuading the British to withdraw their support in exchange for American guarantees of English property interests in Mexico.

Huerta stubbornly remained in power. In April 1914, Wilson used a minor insult to U.S. sailors in Tampico as an excuse to invade Mexico. American naval forces bombarded and then occupied Veracruz, the main port through which Huerta received arms shipments. Nineteen Americans and 126 Mexicans died in the battle, which brought the United States and Mexico close to war, and provoked anti-American demonstrations in Mexico and throughout Latin America. Wilson accepted the offer of the ABC Powers—Argentina, Brazil, and Chile—to mediate the dispute. Huerta rejected a plan for him to step aside in favor of a provisional government. In August, however, Carranza managed to overthrow Huerta. Playing to nationalist sentiment, Carranza also denounced Wilson for his intervention.

HUMANITY
NEUTRAL RIGHTS
INTERNATIONAL LAW

The Class in Reading and Writing
Kirby in the New York World

WOODROW WILSON AND AMERICA'S ROLE IN THE WORLD This political cartoon comments approvingly on Woodrow Wilson's foreign policy idealism. By depicting Wilson as a school teacher giving lessons to children, the image captures the paternalistic view of the world held by many American policymakers.

WS Collection/Alamy Stock Photo.

As war loomed in Europe, Mexico's revolutionary politics continued to frustrate Wilson. For a brief period, Wilson threw his support behind Francisco "Pancho" Villa, Carranza's former ally, who led a rebel army of his own in northern Mexico. But Carranza's forces dealt Villa a major setback in April 1915. In October, when its attention was focused on the war in Europe, the Wilson administration recognized Carranza as Mexico's de facto president. Meanwhile, Villa, feeling betrayed, turned on the United States and tried to provoke a crisis that might draw the United States into war with Mexico. In 1916, Villa led several raids in Mexico and across the border into the United States that killed a few dozen Americans. The man once viewed by Wilson as a fighter for democracy was now dismissed as a dangerous bandit.

In March 1916, enraged by Villa's defiance, Wilson dispatched General John J. Pershing and an army that eventually numbered 15,000 to capture him. For a year, Pershing's troops chased Villa in vain, penetrating 300 miles into Mexico. The invasion made Villa a symbol of national resistance in Mexico, and his army grew from 500 men to 10,000

by the end of 1916. Villa's effective hit-and-run guerrilla tactics kept the U.S. forces at bay.

Skirmishes between American forces and Carranza's army brought the two nations to the brink of war again in June 1916. Although Wilson prepared a message to Congress asking permission for American troops to occupy all of northern Mexico, he never delivered it. There was fierce opposition to war with Mexico throughout the United States. Perhaps more important, mounting tensions with Germany caused Wilson to hesitate. Wilson thus accepted negotiations by a face-saving international commission.

Wilson's attempt to guide the course of Mexico's revolution left a bitter legacy of suspicion and distrust in Mexico. It also suggested the limits of a foreign policy tied to a moral vision rooted in the idea of American exceptionalism. **Militarism** and **imperialism**, Wilson had believed, were hallmarks of the old European way. American liberal values—rooted in capitalist development, democracy, and free trade—were the wave of the future. Wilson believed the United States could lead the world in establishing a new international system based on peaceful commerce and political stability. In both the 1914 invasion and the 1916 punitive expedition, Wilson declared that he had no desire to interfere with Mexican sovereignty. But in both cases, that is exactly what he did. The United States, he argued, must actively use its enormous moral and material power to create the new order. That principle would soon engage America in Europe's bloodiest war and its most momentous revolution.

22.2 The Great War

Why did most Americans oppose U.S. involvement in World War I in 1914?

World War I—or the Great War, as it was originally called—took an enormous human toll on an entire generation of Europeans. At the war's start in August 1914, both sides had confidently predicted a quick victory. Instead, the killing dragged on for more than four years and, in the end, transformed the old power relations and political map of Europe. The United States entered the war reluctantly, and American forces played a supporting, rather than a central, role in the military outcome.

22.2.1 The Guns of August

Only a complex and fragile system of alliances had kept the European powers at peace with each other since 1871. Two great competing camps had evolved by 1907: the Triple Alliance (also known as the **Central Powers**), which included Germany, Austria-Hungary, and Italy; and the Triple Entente (also known as the **Allies**), which included Great

Britain, France, and Russia. At the heart of this division was the competition between Great Britain, long the world's dominant colonial and commercial power, and Germany, which had powerful aspirations for an empire of its own. The alliance system managed to keep small conflicts from escalating into larger ones for most of the late nineteenth and early twentieth centuries. But its inclusiveness was also its weakness: The alliance system threatened to entangle many nations in any war that did erupt. On June 28, 1914, Archduke Franz Ferdinand, heir to the throne of the unstable Austro-Hungarian Empire, was assassinated in Sarajevo, Bosnia. The archduke's killer was a Serbian nationalist who believed the Austro-Hungarian province of Bosnia ought to be annexed to neighboring Serbia. Germany gave Austria-Hungary a blank check to stamp out the Serbian threat, and the Serbians in turn asked Russia for help.

That summer both sides began mobilizing their armies, and by early August they had exchanged declarations of war. Germany invaded Belgium and prepared to move across the French border. At the beginning, most Europeans supported the war effort, believing there would be quick and glorious victories. Appeals to nationalist sentiment and glory overcame even the anti-war socialists, who had long fought to transcend national boundaries in their political work. After the German armies were stopped at the River Marne in September, however, the war settled into a long, bloody stalemate. New and grimly efficient weapons, such as the machine gun and the tank, and the horrors of trench warfare meant unprecedented casualties for all involved. In northern France and Poland, and on the Italian front, the fighting killed 5 million people during the next two and a half years. Allied campaigns waged against German colonies in Africa and against the Ottoman Empire in the Middle East reflected the global nature of the war, as did the British and French dependence on colonial troops from India and Africa.

22.2.2 American Neutrality

The outbreak of war in Europe shocked Americans. President Wilson issued a formal proclamation of neutrality. In practice, powerful cultural, political, and economic factors made the impartiality advocated by Wilson impossible. The U.S. population included many ethnic groups with close emotional ties to the Old World. Out of a total population of 92 million in 1914, about one-third were "hyphenated" Americans, either foreign-born or having one or both parents who were immigrants. Strong support for the Central Powers could be found among the 8 million German Americans, as well as the 4 million Irish Americans, who shared their ancestral homeland's historical hatred of English rule. On the other side, many Americans were at least mildly pro-Allies due to cultural and language bonds

with Great Britain and the tradition of Franco-American friendship.

Both sides bombarded the United States with vigorous propaganda campaigns. The British effectively exploited their bonds of language and heritage with Americans. Reports of looting, raping, and the killing of innocent civilians by German troops circulated widely in the press. Many of these atrocity stories were exaggerated, but verified German actions—the invasion of neutral Belgium, submarine attacks on merchant ships, and the razing of towns—lent them credibility. Wartime propaganda highlighted the terrible human costs of the war and, thus, strengthened the conviction that America should stay out of it.

Economic ties between the United States and the Allies were perhaps the greatest barrier to true neutrality. Early in the war, Britain imposed a blockade on all shipping to Germany. The United States, as a neutral country, might have insisted on the right of non-belligerents to trade with both sides, as prescribed by international law. In practice, although Wilson protested the blockade, he wanted to avoid antagonizing Britain and disrupting trade between the United States and the Allies. Trade with Germany all but ended, while trade with the Allies increased dramatically. As war orders poured in from Britain and France, the value of American trade with the Allies shot up from $824 million in 1914 to $3.2 billion in 1916. By 1917, loans to the Allies—primarily from private American banks—exceeded $2.5 billion, compared with loans to the Central Powers of only $27 million. As America's annual export trade jumped from $2 billion in 1913 to nearly $6 billion in 1916, the nation enjoyed a great economic boom and the United States became neutral in name only.

22.2.3 Preparedness and Peace

In February 1915, Germany declared the waters around the British Isles to be a war zone, a policy that it would enforce with unrestricted submarine warfare. All enemy shipping would be subject to surprise submarine attack. Neutral powers were warned that the problems of identification at sea put their ships at risk. The United States issued a sharp protest to this policy, calling it "an indefensible violation of neutral rights," and threatened to hold Germany accountable.

On May 7, 1915, a German U-boat sank the British liner *Lusitania* off the coast of Ireland. Among the 1,198 people who died were 128 American citizens. The *Lusitania* was, in fact, secretly carrying war materials, and passengers had been warned about a possible attack. Wilson nevertheless denounced the sinking as illegal and inhuman, and the American press loudly condemned the act as barbaric. An angry exchange of diplomatic notes led Secretary of State

William Jennings Bryan to resign in protest against a policy he thought too warlike.

Tensions heated up again in March 1916 when a German U-boat torpedoed the *Sussex*, an unarmed French passenger ship, injuring four Americans. President Wilson threatened to break off diplomatic relations with Germany unless it abandoned its submarine warfare. He won a temporary diplomatic victory when Germany promised that all vessels would be visited prior to attack. But the crisis also prompted Wilson to begin preparing for war. In June 1916, Congress passed the National Defense Act, which more than doubled the size of the regular army to 220,000 and integrated the state National Guards under federal control. In August, Congress passed a bill that dramatically increased spending for new battleships, cruisers, and destroyers.

Not all Americans supported these preparations for battle, and opposition to military buildup found expression in scores of American communities. As early as August 29, 1914, 1,500 women clad in black had marched down New York's Fifth Avenue in the Woman's Peace Parade. Out of this gathering evolved the American Union against Militarism, which lobbied against the **preparedness** campaign and against intervention in Mexico. Antiwar feeling was especially strong in the South and Midwest. A group of 30 to 50 House Democrats, led by majority leader Claude Kitchin of North Carolina, stubbornly opposed Wilson's military buildup. Jane Addams, Lillian D. Wald, and many other prominent progressive reformers spoke out for peace.

Wilson acknowledged the active opposition to involvement in the war by adopting the winning slogan "He Kept Us Out of War" in the 1916 presidential campaign. He made a point of appealing to progressives of all kinds, stressing his support for the eight-hour day and his administration's efforts on behalf of farmers. The war-induced prosperity no doubt helped him to defeat conservative Republican Charles Evans Hughes.

22.2.4 Safe for Democracy

By the end of January 1917, Germany's leaders had decided against a negotiated peace settlement, placing their hopes instead in a final decisive offensive against the Allies. On February 1, 1917, with the aim of breaking the British blockade, Germany declared unlimited submarine warfare, with no warnings, against all neutral and belligerent shipping. This strategy went far beyond the earlier, more limited use of the U-boat. The decision was made with full knowledge that it might bring America into the conflict. In effect, German leaders were gambling that they could destroy the ability of the Allies to fight before the United States would be able to effectively mobilize manpower and resources.

Wilson was indignant and disappointed. He still hoped for peace, but Germany had made it impossible for him to preserve his twin goals of U.S. neutrality and freedom of the seas. Reluctantly, Wilson broke off diplomatic relations with Germany and called on Congress to approve the arming of U.S. merchant ships. On March 1, the White House shocked the country when it made public a recently intercepted coded message, sent by German foreign secretary Arthur Zimmermann to the German ambassador in Mexico. The Zimmermann note proposed that an alliance be made between Germany and Mexico if the United States entered the war. Zimmermann suggested that Mexico take up arms against the United States and receive in return the "lost territory in New Mexico, Texas, and Arizona." The note caused a sensation and became a very effective propaganda tool for those who favored U.S. entry into the war.

Revelation of the Zimmermann note stiffened Wilson's resolve. He issued an executive order in mid-March, authorizing the arming of all merchant ships and allowing them to shoot at submarines. In that month, German U-boats sank seven U.S. merchant ships, with a heavy death toll. Anti-German feeling increased, and thousands took part in pro-war demonstrations in New York, Boston, Philadelphia, and other cities. Wilson finally called a special session of Congress to ask for a declaration of war.

On April 2, before a packed and very quiet assembly, Wilson made his case. He reviewed the escalation of submarine warfare, which he called "warfare against mankind," and said that neutrality was no longer feasible or desirable. The conflict was not merely about U.S. shipping rights, Wilson argued. He employed highly idealistic language to make the case for war, reflecting his deeply held belief that America had a special mission as the world's most enlightened and advanced nation:

> It is a fearful thing to lead this great peaceful people into war, into the most terrible and disastrous of all wars, civilization itself seeming to be in the balance. But the right is more precious than peace, and we shall fight for the things which we have always carried nearest to our hearts—for democracy, for the right of those who submit to authority to have a voice in their own governments, for the rights and liberties of small nations, for a universal dominion of right by such a concert of free peoples as shall bring peace and safety to all nations and make the world itself at last free.

In effect, Wilson wrapped together American commercial and diplomatic interests in the language of universal principles like freedom of the seas and neutral rights. The Senate adopted the war resolution 82 to 6, the House 373 to 50. Wilson's eloquent speech won over not only the Congress, but also most of the press, and even his bitterest political critics, such as Theodore Roosevelt. On April 6, President Wilson signed the declaration of war. All that remained was to win over the American public.

22.3 American Mobilization

How did the federal government try to change public opinion about U.S. involvement in World War I?

The overall public response to Wilson's war message was enthusiastic. Most newspapers, religious leaders, state legislatures, and prominent public figures endorsed the call to arms. The Wilson administration was less certain about the feelings of ordinary Americans and their willingness to fight in Europe. It therefore took immediate steps to strengthen public support for the war effort, to place a legal muzzle on anti-war dissenters, and to establish a universal military draft. War mobilization was, above all, a campaign to unify the country.

22.3.1 Selling the War

Just a week after signing the war declaration, Wilson created the **Committee on Public Information (CPI)** to organize public opinion. Its civilian chairman, the journalist and reformer George Creel, quickly transformed the CPI into a sophisticated and aggressive agency for promoting the war. To sell the war, Creel adapted techniques from the emerging field of public relations. He enlisted more than 150,000 people to work on a score of CPI committees. They produced more than 100 million pieces of literature—pamphlets, articles, books—that explained the causes and meaning of the war. Across the nation, a volunteer army of 75,000 "Four Minute Men" gave brief patriotic speeches before stage and movie shows. The CPI also created posters, slides, newspaper advertising, and films to promote the war. It called upon movie stars such as Charlie Chaplin, Mary Pickford, and Douglas Fairbanks to help sell war bonds at huge rallies. Famous journalists like the muckraker Ida Tarbell and well-known artists like Charles Dana Gibson were recruited. Many popular entertainers injected patriotic themes into their work as well, such as when Broadway composer George M. Cohan wrote the rousing pro-war anthem "Over There," sung by the great opera tenor Enrico Caruso. (See SEEING History.)

The CPI led an aggressively negative campaign against all things German. Posters and advertisements depicted the Germans as Huns, bestial monsters outside the civilized world. German music and literature, indeed the German language itself, were deemed suspect and were banished from the concert halls, schools, and libraries of many communities. Many restaurants offered "liberty cabbage" and "liberty steaks" instead of sauerkraut and hamburgers. The CPI also urged ethnic Americans to abandon their Old World ties, to become "unhyphenated Americans." The CPI's push for conformity soon

NAVY RECRUITING POSTER James Montgomery Flagg's Navy recruiting poster from 1918 combined appeals to patriotism, the opportunity to "make history," and traditional images depicting liberty as a woman.

Library of Congress (Photoduplication).

encouraged thousands of local, sometimes violent campaigns of harassment against German Americans, radicals, and peace activists.

22.3.2 Fading Opposition to War

By defining the call to war as a great moral crusade, President Wilson won over many Americans who had been reluctant to go to war. In particular, many liberals and progressives were attracted to the possibilities of war as a positive force for social change. Although some progressives—notably Senator Robert M. La Follette of Wisconsin—continued to oppose the war, many more identified with President Wilson's definition of the war as an idealistic crusade to defend democracy, spread liberal principles, and redeem European decadence and militarism.

The writer and cultural critic Randolph Bourne was an important, if lonely, voice of dissent among intellectuals.

SEEING History

Selling War

The Committee on Public Information (CPI), chaired by the progressive Denver journalist George Creel, oversaw the crucial task of mobilizing public opinion for war. Creel employed the most sophisticated sales and public relations techniques of the day to get Americans behind the war effort. The CPI created a flood of pamphlets, billboards, and news articles; sent volunteer "Four Minute Men" to make hundreds of thousands of patriotic speeches in movie theaters between reels; sponsored government-funded feature films depicting life on the front lines; and staged celebrity-studded rallies to promote the sale of war bonds. CPI writers and artists worked closely with government agencies such as the Food Administration and the Selective Service, as well as private organizations like the YMCA and the Red Cross, in creating patriotic campaigns in support of the war. The Division of Pictorial Publicity, headed by the popular artist Charles Dana Gibson, churned out posters and illustrations designed to encourage military enlistment, food conservation, war bond buying, and contributions for overseas victims of war.

The posters generally defined the war as a clear struggle between good and evil, in which American democracy and freedom opposed German militarism and despotism. Artists used a wide range of visual themes to illustrate these stark contrasts. World War I posters drew upon traditional ideas about gender differences (men as soldiers, women as nurturers), but they also illustrated the new wartime expectations of women working outside the home in support of the war effort. Appeals to American patriotism cutting across lines of ethnic and religious difference were common, as was the demonizing of the German enemy. And just as the wartime economy blurred the boundaries between public and private enterprises, businesses adapted patriotic appeals to their own advertising.

Creel aptly titled the memoir of his war experience *How We Advertised America*. These three images illustrate the range of World War I propaganda posters.

- **How would you contrast the different kinds of patriotic appeals made by Pershing's Crusaders, Americans All, and And They Thought We Couldn't Fight? Which of these posters do you think makes the most compelling case for supporting the war? How do the artists portray gender differences as part of a visual strategy for winning the war?**

SELLING WAR

Left: Library of Congress, Middle: swim ink 2 llc/Getty Images, Right: Library of Congress.

A former student of John Dewey's at Columbia University, Bourne wrote a series of anti-war essays warning of the disastrous consequences for reform movements of all kinds. He was particularly critical of "war intellectuals" who were so eager to shift their energies to serving the war effort. "War is essentially the health of the State," Bourne wrote, and he accurately predicted sharp infringements on political and intellectual freedoms.

The Woman's Peace Party, founded in 1915 by feminists opposed to the preparedness campaign, dissolved.

Most of its leading lights—Florence Kelley, Lillian D. Wald, and Carrie Chapman Catt—threw themselves into volunteer war work. Catt, leader of the huge National American Woman Suffrage Association (NAWSA), believed that supporting the war might help women win the right to vote. She joined the Women's Committee of the Council of National Defense and encouraged suffragists to mobilize women for war service of various kinds. A few lonely feminist voices, such as Jane Addams, continued steadfastly to oppose the war effort. But war work proved very popular among activist middle-class women. It gave them a leading role in their communities—selling bonds, coordinating food conservation drives, and working for hospitals and the Red Cross.

22.3.3 "You're in the Army Now"

When war was declared, there were only about 200,000 men in the army. Traditionally, the United States had relied on volunteer forces organized at the state level. But volunteer rates after April 6 were lower than they had been for the Civil War or the Spanish-American War, reflecting the softness of pro-war sentiment. The administration thus introduced the **Selective Service Act**, which provided for the registration and classification for military service of all men between ages 21 and 35. On June 5, 1917, nearly 10 million men registered for the draft. There was scattered organized resistance, but overall, registration records offered evidence of national support. By the end of the war, some 24 million men had registered. Of the 2.8 million men eventually called up for service, about 340,000, or 12 percent, failed to show up.

The vast, polyglot army posed unprecedented challenges of organization and control. But progressive elements within the administration also saw opportunities for pressing reform measures, especially for the one-fifth of U.S. soldiers born in another country. Army psychologists gave the new Stanford-Binet intelligence test to all recruits and were shocked to find illiteracy rates as high as 25 percent. The low test scores among recent immigrants and rural African Americans undoubtedly reflected the cultural biases embedded in the tests and a lack of proficiency in English for many test takers. After the war, intelligence testing became a standard feature of America's educational system.

The recruits themselves took a more lighthearted view, while singing the army's praises:

> Oh, the army, the army, the democratic army,
>
> They clothe you and feed you because the army needs you
>
> Hash for breakfast, beans for dinner, stew for suppertime,
>
> Thirty dollars every month, deducting twenty-nine.
>
> Oh, the army, the army, the democratic army,
>
> The Jews, the Wops, and the Dutch and Irish Cops,
>
> They're all in the army now!

22.3.4 Racism in the Military

President Wilson claimed the war would make the world "safe for democracy," and his idealistic rhetoric struck a chord with most African Americans. For them the war presented the chance to demonstrate their patriotism while also striking a blow against racial injustice. Delegates at an NAACP convention in 1917 urged "colored fellow citizens to join heartily in this fight for eventual world liberty . . . to enlist in the army." W. E. B. Dubois wrote prowar editorials in *The Crisis,* advising blacks to "forget our special grievances and close our ranks shoulder to shoulder with our white fellow citizens."

Yet African Americans who served found severe limitations in the U.S. military. They were organized into totally segregated units, barred entirely from the Marines and the Coast Guard, and largely relegated to working as cooks, laundrymen, stevedores, and the like in the army and navy. Thousands of black soldiers endured humiliating, sometimes violent treatment, particularly from southern white officers. African American servicemen faced hostility from white civilians as well, North and South, and often were denied service in restaurants and admission to theaters near training camps. The ugliest incident occurred in Houston, Texas, in August 1917. Black infantrymen, incensed over continual insults and harassment by local whites, seized weapons from an armory and killed 17 civilians. The army executed 30 black soldiers and imprisoned 41 others for life, denying any of them a chance for appeal.

More than 350,000 African Americans eventually served in the armed forces during WW I. Some 200,000 were sent to France, but only about one in five saw combat, as opposed to two out of three white soldiers. American black combat units served with distinction in various divisions of the French army. The French government awarded the Croix de Guerre to the all-black 369th U.S. Infantry regiment, and 171 officers and enlisted men were cited individually for exceptional bravery in action. African American soldiers by and large enjoyed a friendly reception from French civilians as well. The contrast with their treatment at home would remain a sore point with these troops upon their return to the United States.

22.3.5 Americans in Battle

President Wilson appointed General Pershing, recently returned from pursuing Pancho Villa in Mexico, as commander of the AEF. Pershing insisted that the AEF maintain its own identity, distinct from that of the French and British armies. He was also reluctant to send American troops into battle before they had received at least six months' training. Not until early 1918 did AEF units reach the front in large numbers; eight months later, the war was over. (See Map 22.2.)

The prospective arrival of millions of American troops forced the Germans to mount their largest offensive of the war in the spring of 1918. They hoped to end the war decisively before the American arrived. But after early victories the offensive stalled, and the steady flow of fresh American troops took its toll on the morale of the exhausted Germans. Nearly all the AEF's battles with the German army took place in the war's final two months. More than 26,000 Americans died in the single battle of the Meuse-Argonne, almost half of all those killed in combat.

By the time the guns went silent on November 11, some 2 million men had served in the AEF. Overall some 53,000 Americans had died in battle, with 206,000 wounded. Another 63,000 died from diseases, mainly influenza. These figures paled in comparison with the millions lost by the European nations. Yet the American contribution to winning the war was substantial, and both the Allies and the Germans attested to the bravery and enthusiasm that American soldiers displayed on the front. Shortly after the Armistice, German General Paul von Hindenburg asserted that the balance between the two sides "was broken by the American troops." Without them the war might have continued as a stalemate.

Map 22.2 THE WESTERN FRONT, 1918

American units saw their first substantial action in late May, helping to stop the German offensive at the Battle of Cantigny. By September, more than 1 million American troops were fighting in a counteroffensive campaign at St. Mihiel, the largest single American engagement of the war.

367th INFANTRY REGIMENT, 77th DIVISION African American officers of the 367th Infantry Regiment, 77th Division, pose with a girl in France, 1918. Nicknamed the "Buffalos," a reference to the black "buffalo soldiers" who had served in the U.S. Army during the late-nineteenth-century campaigns against Indians, this was one of only two army units that commissioned African American officers.

MPI/Getty Images.

22.3.6 The Russian Revolution, the Fourteen Points, and Allied Victory

Since early 1917, the turmoil of the Russian Revolution had changed the climate of both foreign affairs and domestic politics. The repressive and corrupt regime of Czar Nicholas II was overthrown in March 1917 by a coalition of forces demanding change. The new provisional government vowed to keep Russia in the fight against Germany. But the war had taken a terrible toll on Russian soldiers and civilians, and had become very unpopular. The radical **Bolsheviks**, led by V. I. Lenin, gained a large following by promising "peace, land, and bread," and they began plotting to seize power. The Bolsheviks followed the teachings of German revolutionary Karl Marx, emphasizing the inevitability of class struggle and the replacement of capitalism by communism. In November 1917, the Bolsheviks took control of the Russian government.

Although sympathetic to the March revolution overthrowing the czar, President Wilson refused to recognize the authority of the Bolshevik regime. Bolshevism represented a threat to the liberal-capitalist values that Wilson believed to be the foundation of America's moral and material power. Thus, in January 1918, Wilson outlined American war aims, known as the **Fourteen Points**, in a speech before Congress. He wanted to counter a fierce Bolshevik campaign to discredit the war as a purely imperialist venture, their sensational publication of secret treaties that the czar had signed with the Allies, and their revelations about annexationist plans across Europe. In effect, Wilson's response to the Bolsheviks was the opening shot of the Soviet-American Cold War that would dominate so much of American domestic politics and foreign affairs for the remainder of the century.

As a blueprint for peace, the Fourteen Points contained three main elements. First, Wilson offered a series of specific proposals for setting postwar boundaries in Europe and creating new countries out of the collapsed Austro-Hungarian and Ottoman empires. The key idea here was the right of all peoples to "national self-determination." Second, Wilson listed general principles for governing international conduct, including freedom of the seas, free trade, open covenants instead of secret treaties, reduced armaments, and mediation for competing colonial claims. Third, and most important, Wilson called for a **League of Nations** to help implement these principles and resolve future disputes. The Fourteen Points offered a plan for world order deeply rooted in the liberal progressivism long associated with Wilson. The plan reflected a faith in efficient government and the rule of law as means for solving international problems. It advocated a dynamic democratic capitalism as a middle ground between Old World autocracy and revolutionary socialism.

In March 1918, to the dismay of the Allies, the new Bolshevik government followed through on its promise and negotiated a separate peace with Germany, the Treaty of Brest-Litovsk. Russia's defection made possible a massive shift of German troops to the Western Front. In the early spring of 1918, the Germans launched a major offensive that brought them within 50 miles of Paris. In early June, about 70,000 AEF soldiers helped the French stop the Germans in the battles of Château-Thierry and Belleau Wood. In July, Allied forces led by Marshal Ferdinand Foch of France began a counteroffensive designed to defeat Germany once and for all. American reinforcements began flooding the ports of Liverpool in England and Brest and Saint-Nazaire in France. The "doughboys" (a nickname for soldiers dating back to Civil War-era recruits who joined the army for the money) streamed in at a rate of over 250,000 a month. By September, General Pershing had more than 1 million Americans in his army.

In late September 1918, the AEF took over the southern part of a 20-mile front in the Meuse-Argonne offensive. In seven weeks of fighting, U.S. soldiers used more ammunition than the entire Union army had in the four years of the Civil War. The Germans, exhausted and badly outnumbered, began to fall back and look for a cease-fire. On November 11, 1918, the war ended with the signing of an armistice.

The massive influx of American troops and supplies no doubt hastened the end of the war. About two-thirds of the U.S. soldiers saw at least some fighting, but even they managed to avoid the horrors of the sustained trench warfare that had marked the earlier years of the war. For most Americans at the front, the war experience was a mixture of fear, exhaustion, and fatigue. Their time in France would remain a decisive moment in their lives. American casualty figures—120,000 dead from both combat and disease, and roughly 200,000 wounded—awful as they were, paled against the estimated casualties (killed and wounded) suffered by the European nations: 9 million for Russia, more than 6 million for Germany, nearly 5 million for France, and more than 2 million each for Great Britain and Italy.

22.4 Over Here

How did the war affect American economic and political life?

In one sense, World War I can be understood as the ultimate progressive crusade: an opportunity to expand the powers of the federal government in order to win the war. Nearly all the reform energy of the previous two decades turned toward that central goal. The federal government played a larger role than ever in managing and regulating the wartime economy. Planning, efficiency, scientific analysis, and cooperation were key principles for government agencies and large volunteer organizations. Although much of the regulatory spirit was temporary, the war experience started some important and lasting organizational trends in American life.

22.4.1 Organizing the Economy

In the summer of 1917, President Wilson established the **War Industries Board (WIB)** as a clearinghouse for industrial mobilization to support the war effort. The WIB proved a major innovation in expanding the regulatory power of the federal government. Given broad authority over the conversion of industrial plants to wartime needs and the manufacture of war materials, the WIB had to balance price controls against war profits. Only by ensuring a fair rate of return on investment could it encourage stepped-up production. The WIB eventually handled 3,000 contracts worth $14.5 billion with various businesses.

In August 1917, Congress passed the Food and Fuel Act, authorizing the president to regulate the production and distribution of the food and fuel necessary for the war effort. To lead the Food Administration (FA), Wilson appointed Herbert Hoover, a millionaire engineer who had already won fame for directing a program of war relief for Belgium. He became one of the best-known figures of the war administration. Hoover imposed price controls on certain agricultural commodities, such as sugar, pork, and wheat. These were purchased by the government and then sold to the public through licensed dealers. The FA also raised the purchase price of grain, so that farmers would increase production. Hoover stopped short of imposing mandatory food rationing, preferring to rely on persuasion, high prices, and voluntary controls.

Hoover's success, like George Creel's at the CPI, depended on motivating hundreds of thousands of volunteers in thousands of American communities. The FA directed patriotic appeals for "Wheatless Mondays, Meatless Tuesdays, and Porkless Thursdays." These efforts resulted in a sharp cutback in the consumption of sugar and wheat as well as a boost in the supply of livestock. The resultant increase in food exports helped sustain the Allied war effort.

The enormous cost of fighting the war, roughly $33 billion, required unprecedented government expenditures. The tax structure shifted dramatically as a result. Taxes on incomes and profits replaced excise and customs levies as the major source of revenue, as the number of Americans who paid income tax grew from 437,000 in 1916 to 4,425,000 in 1918. The bulk of war financing came from government borrowing, especially in the form of the popular **Liberty Bonds** sold to the American public. Bond drives became highly organized patriotic campaigns that ultimately raised a total of $23 billion for the war effort. The administration also used the new Federal Reserve Banks to expand the money supply, making borrowing easier. The federal debt jumped from $1 billion in 1915 to $20 billion in 1920.

"FOOD WILL WIN THE WAR" A Food Administration poster blended a call for conservation of wheat with an imaginative patriotic appeal for recent immigrants to support the war effort.

World History Archive/Alamy Stock Photo.

22.4.2 The Government-Business Partnership

Overall, the war meant expansion and high profits for American business. Total capital expenditure in U.S. manufacturing jumped from $600 million in 1915 to $2.5 billion in 1918. Corporate profits as a whole nearly tripled between 1914 and 1919, and many large businesses did much better than that. Annual prewar profits for U.S. Steel, for example, had averaged $76 million; in 1917, they were $478 million. The total value of farm produce rose from $9.8 billion in 1914 to $21.3 billion by 1918. Expanded farm acreage and increased investment in farm machinery led to a jump of 20 percent to 30 percent in overall farm production.

The most important and long-lasting economic legacy of the war was the organizational shift toward corporatism in American business. The wartime need for efficient management, manufacturing, and distribution could be met only via a greater reliance on the productive and marketing power of large corporations. Never before had business and the federal government cooperated so closely. Entire industries (such as radio manufacturing) and economic sectors (such as agriculture and energy) were organized, regulated, and subsidized. War agencies used both public and private power—legal authority and voluntarism—to hammer out and enforce agreements. Here was the genesis of the modern bureaucratic state.

Some Americans worried about the wartime trend toward a greater federal presence in their lives. As the *Saturday Evening Post* noted, "All this government activity will be called to account and reexamined in due time." Although many aspects of the government-business partnership proved temporary, some institutions and practices grew stronger in the postwar years. Among these were the Federal Reserve Board, the income tax system, the Chamber of Commerce, the Farm Bureau, and the growing horde of lobbying groups that pressed Washington for special-interest legislation.

22.4.3 Labor and the War

Organized labor's power and prestige, though by no means equal to those of business or government, clearly grew during the war. The expansion of the economy, combined with army mobilization and a decline in immigration from Europe, caused a growing wartime labor shortage. As the demand for workers intensified, the federal government was forced to recognize that labor would have to be more carefully tended to than in peacetime. For the war's duration, working people generally enjoyed higher wages and a better standard of living. Trade unions, especially those affiliated with the American Federation of Labor (AFL), experienced a sharp rise in membership. In effect, the government took in labor as a junior partner in the mobilization of the economy.

Samuel Gompers, president of the AFL, emerged as the leading spokesman for the nation's trade union movement. An English immigrant and a cigar maker by trade, Gompers had rejected the socialism of his youth for a philosophy of "business unionism." Gompers pledged the AFL's patriotic support for the war effort, and in April 1918, President Wilson appointed him to the National War Labor Board (NWLB). During 1917, the nation had seen thousands of strikes involving more than a million workers. Wages were usually at issue, reflecting workers' concerns with spiraling inflation and higher prices. The NWLB, cochaired by labor attorney Frank Walsh and former president William Howard Taft, acted as a kind of supreme court for labor, arbitrating disputes and working to prevent disruptions in production. The great majority of these interventions resulted in improved wages and reduced hours of work. Most important, the NWLB supported the right of workers to organize unions and furthered the acceptance of the eight-hour day for war workers—central aims of the labor movement. AFL unions gained more than a million new members during the war, and overall union membership rose from 2.7 million in 1914 to more than 5 million by 1920.

The war also brought widespread use of federal troops under the War Department's new "public utilities" doctrine, under which any private business remotely connected to war production was defined as a public utility. An influx of federal troops poured into lumber camps, coal districts, mining towns, and rail junctions across the nation, as employers requested help in guarding against threatened strikes or alleged "sabotage" by militant workers. Wartime conditions often meant severe disruptions and discomfort for America's workers as well. Overcrowding, rapid workforce turnover, and high inflation rates were typical in war-boom communities. In Bridgeport, Connecticut, for example, a center for small-arms manufacturing, the population grew by 50,000 in less than a year.

WOMEN MUNITIONS WORKERS Women workers at the Midvale Steel and Ordnance Company in Pennsylvania, 1918. Wartime labor shortages created new opportunities for more than 1 million women to take high-wage manufacturing jobs, like the women shown here. The opportunities proved temporary, however, and with the war's end, nearly all of these women lost their jobs. By 1920, the number of women employed in manufacturing was lower than it had been in 1910.

In the Southwest, the demand for wartime labor temporarily eased restrictions against the movement of Mexicans into the United States. The Immigration Act of 1917, requiring a literacy test and an $8 head tax, had cut Mexican immigration nearly in half, down to about 25,000 per year. But employers complained of severe shortages of workers. Farmers in Arizona's Salt River Valley and in southern California needed hands to harvest grain, alfalfa, cotton, and fruit. El Paso's mining and smelting industries, Texas's border ranches, and southern Arizona's railroads and copper mines insisted they depended on unskilled Mexican labor as well.

Responding to these protests, in June 1917, the Department of Labor suspended the immigration law for the duration of the war and negotiated an agreement with the Mexican government permitting some 35,000 Mexican contract laborers to enter the United States. Pressure from southwestern employers kept the exemptions in force until 1921, well after the end of the war, demonstrating the growing importance of cheap Mexican labor to the region's economy.

If the war boosted the fortunes of the AFL, it also spelled the end for more radical elements of the U.S. labor movement. The Industrial Workers of the World (IWW), unlike the AFL, had concentrated on organizing unskilled workers into all-inclusive industrial unions. The Wobblies denounced capitalism as an unreformable system based on exploitation, and they opposed U.S. entry into the war. The IWW had grown in 1916 and 1917, gaining strength among workers in several areas crucial to the war effort: copper mining, lumbering, and wheat harvesting. In September 1917, the Wilson administration responded to appeals from western business leaders for a crackdown on the Wobblies. Justice Department agents, acting under the broad authority of the recently passed **Espionage Act**, swooped down on IWW offices in more than 60 towns and cities, arresting more than 300 people and confiscating files. The mass trials and convictions that followed broke the back of America's radical labor movement and marked the beginning of a powerful wave of political repression.

22.4.4 Women at Work

For many of the 8 million women already in the labor force, the war meant a chance to switch from low-paying jobs, such as domestic service, to higher-paying industrial employment. About a million women joined the labor force for the first time. Of the estimated 9.4 million workers directly engaged in war work, some 2.25 million were women. Female munitions plant workers, train engineers, drill-press operators, streetcar conductors, and mail carriers became a common sight around the country. World War I also marked the first time that women were mobilized directly into the armed forces. More than 16,000 women served overseas with the AEF in France, where most worked as nurses, clerical workers, telephone operators, and canteen operators. Another 12,000 women served stateside in the navy and U.S. Marine Corps, and tens of thousands of civilian women were employed in army offices and hospitals. But the war's impact on women was greatest in the broader civilian economy.

In response to the widened range of female employment, the Labor Department created the Women in Industry Service (WIS). Directed by Mary Van Kleeck, a longtime progressive activist and expert on women's labor, the service advised employers on using female employees and formulated general standards for the treatment of women workers. The WIS represented the first attempt by the federal government to take a practical stand on improving working conditions for women. Its standards included the eight-hour day, equal pay for equal work, a minimum wage, the prohibition of night work, and the provision of rest periods, meal breaks, and restroom facilities. Although these standards had no legal force, they were accepted nonetheless as goals by nearly every group concerned with improving the conditions of working women.

At war's end, women lost nearly all their defense-related jobs. Wartime women railroad workers, for example, were replaced by returning servicemen, through the application of laws meant to protect women from hazardous conditions. But the war accelerated female employment in fields already dominated by women. By 1920, more women who worked outside the home did so in white-collar occupations—as telephone operators, secretaries, and clerks, for example—than in manufacturing or domestic service. The new awareness of women's work led Congress to create the Women's Bureau in the Labor Department, which continued the WIS wartime program of education and investigation through the postwar years.

22.4.5 Woman Suffrage

The presence of so many new female wageworkers, combined with the highly visible volunteer work of millions of middle-class women, helped finally to secure the vote for women. Volunteer war work—selling bonds, saving food, organizing benefits—was popular among housewives and clubwomen. Until World War I, the fight for woman suffrage had been waged largely within individual states. Western states and territories had led the way. Various forms of woman suffrage became law in Wyoming in 1869, followed by Utah (1870), Colorado (1893), and Idaho (1896). Rocky Mountain and Pacific Coast states did not have the sharp ethnocultural divisions between

Catholics and Protestants that hindered suffrage efforts in the East. For example, the close identification in the East between the suffrage and prohibition movements led many Catholic immigrants and German Lutherans to oppose the vote for women, because they feared it would lead to prohibition.

The U.S. entry into the war provided a unique opportunity for suffrage groups to shift their strategy to a national campaign for a constitutional amendment granting the vote to women. The most important of these groups was the National American Woman Suffrage Association (NAWSA). Before 1917, most American suffragists had opposed the war. Under the leadership of Carrie Chapman Catt, the NAWSA threw its support behind the war effort and doubled its membership to 2 million. Catt gambled that a strong show of patriotism would help clinch the century-old fight to win the vote for women. She encouraged suffragists to support the war effort through volunteer work and by taking jobs left vacant by soldiers. She pressed President Wilson to support a constitutional amendment. If it failed, she wrote him, "it will take the heart out of thousands of women" and undercut their support for the war. The fight for democracy, she argued, must begin at home, and she urged passage of the woman suffrage amendment as a "war measure."

At the same time, more militant suffragists, led by the young Quaker activist Alice Paul, injected new energy and more radical tactics into the movement. Dissatisfied with the NAWSA's conservative strategy of quiet lobbying and orderly demonstrations, Paul left the organization in 1916. She joined forces with western women voters to form the National Woman's Party. Borrowing from English suffragists, this party pursued a more aggressive and dramatic strategy of agitation. Paul and her supporters picketed the White House, publicly burned President Wilson's speeches, and condemned the president and the Democrats for failing to produce an amendment. In one demonstration, they chained themselves to the White House fence and, after their arrest, went on a hunger strike in jail. The militants generated a great deal of publicity and sympathy.

Although some in the NAWSA objected to these tactics, Paul's radical approach helped make the NAWSA position more acceptable to Wilson. In 1917, the president urged Congress to pass a woman suffrage amendment as "vital to the winning of the war." The House did so in January 1918 and a more reluctant Senate approved it in June 1919. Another year of hard work was spent convincing the state legislatures. In August 1920, Tennessee gave the final vote needed to ratify the Nineteenth Amendment to the Constitution, finally making woman suffrage legal nationwide.

WOMAN VOTER The confident bearing and direct gaze of this woman voter, depicted on a 1920 cover of *Leslie's Illustrated Weekly*, suggest how the historic achievement of woman suffrage reinforced images of the "New Woman."

The Art Archive/REX/Shutterstock.

22.4.6 Prohibition

Another reform effort closely associated with women's groups triumphed at the same time. The movement to eliminate alcohol from American life had attracted many Americans, especially women, since before the Civil War. Temperance advocates saw drinking as the source of many of the worst problems faced by the working class, including family violence, unemployment, and poverty. By the early twentieth century, the Woman's Christian Temperance Union, with a quarter-million members, had become the single largest women's organization in American history. With so many breweries bearing German names, the movement benefited as well from the strong anti-German feeling of the war years. Outlawing beer and whiskey would also help to conserve precious grain, prohibitionists claimed.

The moral fervor that accompanied America's entry into the war provided a crucial boost to the cause. In 1917, a coalition of progressives and rural fundamentalists in Congress pushed through a constitutional amendment providing for a national ban on alcoholic drinks. The Eighteenth Amendment was ratified by the states in January 1919 and became the law of the land one year later. Although Prohibition would create a host of problems in the postwar years, especially as a stimulus for the growth of organized crime, many Americans—particularly native-born Protestants—considered it a worthy moral reform.

22.4.7 Public Health and the Influenza Pandemic

Wartime mobilization brought deeper government involvement with public health issues, especially in the realms of sex hygiene, child welfare, and disease prevention. The rate of venereal disease among draftees was as high as 6 percent in some states, presenting a potential manpower problem for the army. In April 1917, the War Department mounted a vigorous campaign against venereal disease, which combined suppression of prostitution near army camps with an aggressive campaign of sex education for the troops. The campaign attracted the energies of progressive-era sex reformers—social hygienists and antivice crusaders. Under the direction of Raymond Fosdick and the Commission on Training Camp Activities, the military educated troops on the dangers of contracting syphilis and gonorrhea. Venereal disease rates for soldiers declined by more than 300 percent during the war.

The wartime boost to government health work continued into the postwar years. The Children's Bureau, created in 1912 as a part of the Labor Department, undertook a series of reports on special problems growing out of the war: the increase in employment of married women, the finding of daycare for children of working mothers, and the growth of both child labor and delinquency. In 1917, Julia C. Lathrop, chief of the bureau and a veteran of the settlement house movement, proposed a plan to institutionalize federal aid to the states for protection of mothers and children. Congress finally passed the Maternity and Infancy Act in 1921, appropriating over $1 million a year to be administered to the states by the Children's Bureau. In the postwar years, clinics for prenatal and obstetrical care grew out of these efforts and greatly reduced the rate of infant and maternal mortality and disease.

The disastrous influenza pandemic of 1918–1919 offered the most serious challenge to national public health during the war years. It was part of a global scourge that

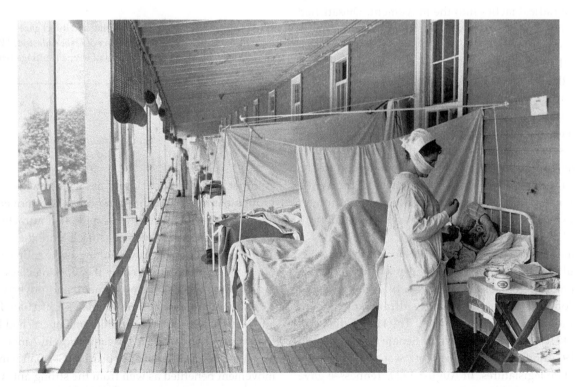

GLOBAL INFLUENZA PANDEMIC A nurse takes a patient's pulse in the influenza ward at Walter Reed Hospital, Washington, D.C., November 1, 1918. Intensified by the crowded conditions on the battlefield, in training camps, and on troop ships, the influenza pandemic killed more than half a million Americans and some 21 million people worldwide.

Library of Congress/Getty Images.

originated in South China, then spread to the Philippines and moved across the United States, over to Europe, and then back with returning troops. Wartime conditions—large concentrations of people in military camps, on transport ships, and at the front—made its impact especially devastating. With no cure for the lethal combination of the "flu" and respiratory complications (mainly pneumonia), the pandemic killed more than 21 million people worldwide. Few Americans paid attention to the disease until it swept through military camps and eastern cities in September 1918 and killed roughly 550,000 Americans in 10 months. Most victims were young adults between the ages of 20 and 40. Congress appropriated $1 million to the Public Health Service to combat and suppress the epidemic, but it offered no money for research. Much of the care for the sick and dying came from Red Cross nurses and volunteers working in local communities across the nation. With a war on, and the nation focused on reports from the battlefront, even a public health crisis of this magnitude went relatively unnoticed.

22.5 Repression and Reaction

What steps did the federal government take to suppress the antiwar movement?

World War I exposed and intensified many of the deepest social tensions in American life. On the local level, vigilantes increasingly took the law into their own hands to punish those suspected of disloyalty. The push for national unity led the federal government to crack down on a wide spectrum of dissenters. The war inflamed racial hatred, and the worst race riots in the nation's history exploded in several cities. At war's end, a newly militant labor movement briefly asserted itself in mass strikes around the nation. Over each of these developments loomed the 1917 Bolshevik Revolution in Russia. Radicals around the world had drawn inspiration from what looked like the first successful revolution against a capitalist state. Many conservatives worried that similar revolutions were imminent. From 1918 through 1920, the federal government directed a repressive antiradical campaign that had crucial implications for the nation's future.

22.5.1 Muzzling Dissent: The Espionage and Sedition Acts

The Espionage Act of June 1917 became the government's key tool for the suppression of anti-war sentiment. It set severe penalties (up to 20 years' imprisonment and a $10,000 fine) for anyone found guilty of aiding the enemy, obstructing recruitment, or causing insubordination in the armed forces. The act also empowered the postmaster general to exclude from the mails any newspapers or magazines he thought treasonous. Within a year, the mailing rights of 45 newspapers and magazines had been revoked. These included several anti-British and pro-Irish publications, as well as such leading journals of American socialism as the Kansas-based *Appeal to Reason*, which had enjoyed a prewar circulation of half a million, and *The Masses*.

To enforce the Espionage Act, the government had to increase its overall police and surveillance machinery. Civilian intelligence was coordinated by the newly created Bureau of Investigation in the Justice Department. This agency was reorganized after the war as the Federal Bureau of Investigation (FBI). In May 1918, the **Sedition Act**, an amendment to the Espionage Act, outlawed "any disloyal, profane, scurrilous, or abusive language intended to cause contempt, scorn, contumely, or disrepute" to the government, Constitution, or flag.

These acts became a convenient vehicle for striking out at socialists, pacifists, radical labor activists, and others who resisted the patriotic tide. The most celebrated prosecution came in June 1918, when federal agents arrested Eugene V. Debs in Canton, Ohio, after he gave a speech defending anti-war protesters. Sentenced to 10 years in prison, Debs defiantly told the court: "I have been accused of having obstructed the war. I admit it. Gentlemen, I abhor war. I would oppose the war if I stood alone." Debs served 32 months in federal prison before being pardoned by President Warren G. Harding on Christmas Day, 1921.

The Supreme Court upheld the constitutionality of the acts in several 1919 decisions. In *Schenck v. United States*, the Court unanimously ruled that Congress could restrict speech if the words "are used in such circumstances and are of such a nature as to create a clear and present danger." The decision upheld the conviction of Charles Schenck for having mailed pamphlets urging potential army inductees to resist conscription. In *Debs v. United States*, the Court affirmed Debs's guilt for his antiwar speech in Canton, even though he had not explicitly urged violation of the draft laws. Finally, in *Abrams v. United States*, the Court upheld Sedition Act convictions of four Russian immigrants who had printed pamphlets denouncing American military intervention in the Russian Revolution. The nation's highest court thus endorsed the severe wartime restrictions on free speech.

In many western communities, local vigilantes used the superpatriotic mood to settle scores with labor organizers and radicals. In July 1917, for example, 2,000 armed vigilantes swept through the mining town of Bisbee, Arizona, acting on behalf of the Phelps-Dodge mining company and local businessmen. They wanted to break an IWW-led strike that had crippled Bisbee's booming copper industry. The IWW's vocal opposition to the war made it vulnerable to charges of disloyalty. The vigilantes seized miners in their homes, on the street, and in restaurants and stores, delivering an ultimatum that any miner who refused to return to work would be deported. Some 1,400 miners were forced at gunpoint onto a freight train, which took them to Columbus, New Mexico, where they were dumped in the desert.

In thousands of other instances, government repression and local vigilantes reinforced each other. The American Protective League, founded with the blessing of the Justice Department, mobilized 250,000 self-appointed "operatives" in more than 600 towns and cities. Members of the league, mostly businessmen, bankers, and former policemen, spied on their neighbors and staged a series of well-publicized "slacker" raids on antiwar protesters and draft evaders. Many communities, inspired by Committee on Public Information campaigns, sought to ban the teaching of the German language in their schools or the performance of German music in concert halls.

22.5.2 The Great Migration and Racial Tensions

Economic opportunity brought on by war prosperity triggered a massive migration of rural black Southerners to northern cities. From 1914 to 1920, between 300,000 and 500,000 African Americans left the rural South for the North. Chicago's black population increased by 65,000, or 150 percent; Detroit's by 35,000, or 600 percent. Acute labor shortages led northern factory managers to recruit black migrants to the expanding industrial centers. The Pennsylvania Railroad alone drew 10,000 black workers from Florida and Georgia. Black workers eagerly left low-paying jobs as field hands and domestic servants for the chance at relatively high-paying work in meatpacking plants, shipyards, and steel mills. (See Table 22.1.)

Kinship and community networks were crucial in shaping what came to be called the **Great Migration**. The networks spread news about job openings, urban residential districts, and boardinghouses in northern cities. Black clubs, churches, and fraternal lodges in southern

THE GREAT MIGRATION This southern African American family is shown arriving in Chicago around 1910. Black migrants to northern cities often faced overcrowding, inferior housing, and a high death rate from disease. But the chance to earn daily wages of $6 to $8 (the equivalent of a week's wages in much of the South), as well as the desire to escape persistent racial violence, kept the migrants coming.

Chicago History Museum/Getty Images.

Table 22.1 **THE GREAT MIGRATION: BLACK POPULATION GROWTH IN SELECTED NORTHERN CITIES, 1910–1920**

Northern Cities	1910		1920		
	No.	Percent	No.	Percent	Percent Increase
New York	91,709	1.9%	152,467	2.7%	66.3%
Chicago	44,103	2.0	109,458	4.1	148.2
Philadelphia	84,459	5.5	134,229	7.4	58.9
Detroit	5,741	1.2	40,838	4.1	611.3
St. Louis	43,960	6.4	69,854	9.0	58.9
Cleveland	8,448	1.5	34,451	4.3	307.8
Pittsburgh	25,623	4.8	37,725	6.4	47.2
Cincinnati	19,739	5.4	30,079	7.5	53.2

DATA SOURCE: U.S. Department of Commerce.

communities frequently sponsored the migration of their members, as well as return trips to the South. Single African American women often made the trip first, because they could more easily obtain steady work as maids, cooks, and laundresses. Relatively few African American men actually secured high-paying skilled jobs in industry or manufacturing. Most had to settle for such low-paying occupations as construction laborer, teamster, janitor, or porter.

Rigid residential segregation of African Americans laid the foundation for the sprawling segregated ghettoes characteristic of twentieth-century northern cities. Shut out of white neighborhoods by a combination of custom and law (such as restrictive covenants forbidding homeowners to sell to nonwhites), African American migrants found themselves forced to squeeze into less desirable and all-black neighborhoods. In 1920, for example, approximately 85 percent of Chicago's 110,000 black citizens lived within a narrow strip roughly three miles long and a quarter-mile wide. The city's South Side ghetto—surrounded on all sides by railroad tracks—had been born.

The persistence of lynching and other racial violence in the South no doubt contributed to the Great Migration, but racial violence was not limited to the South. On July 2, 1917, in East St. Louis, Illinois, a ferocious mob of whites attacked African Americans, killing at least 200. Before this riot, some of the city's manufacturers had steadily recruited black labor as a way to keep local union demands down. Unions had refused to allow black workers as members, and politicians had cynically exploited white racism in appealing for votes. In Chicago, on July 27, 1919, antiblack rioting broke out on a Lake Michigan beach. For two weeks, white gangs hunted African Americans in the streets and burned hundreds out of their homes. Twenty-three African Americans and 15 whites died, and more than 500 were injured. In 1921, the bloodiest race riot of all took place in Greenwood, a thriving African American neighborhood in Tulsa, Oklahoma. A group of armed blacks, many of them army veterans, confronted a white mob intent on lynching a young African American accused of rape. The next day, whites invaded the Greenwood district, burned it to the ground, and murdered some 300 African Americans. (See Communities *in* Conflict.)

Communities *in* Conflict

Race Riot in Tulsa, 1921

One of the worst race riots in American history took place in Tulsa, Oklahoma, in the late spring of 1921. A series of oil discoveries during the previous decade had transformed Tulsa from a small frontier town into a booming industrial center with about 70,000 people. The new oil wealth attracted thousands of white newcomers seeking high-wage job in oil fields, refineries, gas works, and related industries. It was a magnet as well for rural African Americans looking to improve their lot, and the thriving black community of Greenwood, across the railroad tracks just north of downtown, grew to roughly 10,000 by World War I. Blacks were excluded from jobs in the oil fields, but many prospered working as chauffeurs, butlers, porters, and domestic servants for Tulsa's white community by day before returning to their homes in Greenwood at night. A flourishing black middle class included realtors, doctors, lawyers, and teachers, and Greenwood enjoyed a national reputation as one of the wealthiest African American communities in the country, sometimes called "the Black Wall Street." Yet Tulsa's oil business suffered from the deep postwar recession; unemployment was high, with over half the industry shut down. Hard times fueled white resentment of black success.

On May 31, Dick Rowland, a young African American boot-black, was arrested for allegedly assaulting a white teenaged girl, Sarah Page, in an office building elevator. It is not clear exactly what happened between them, or if they knew each other. An inflammatory article and editorial in the local newspaper brought hundreds of whites to the courthouse, some of whom talked openly of lynching Rowland. Just a few months earlier, a white murder suspect had been dragged from his jailhouse and lynched by a large mob. This evening, fearing for young Rowland's safety, a group of armed African Americans, many of them World War I veterans, arrived at the courthouse and offered to help the sheriff protect his prisoner. The sheriff politely declined their assistance and urged them to go home. The sight of armed blacks enraged whites crowded around the courthouse, and many went home and returned with guns. After a tense standoff, some shots were exchanged and both sides suffered casualties. The black contingent, badly outnumbered and fearing a bloodbath, hurriedly made its way back to Greenwood. All through the night wild rumors about a "Negro uprising" spread throughout Tulsa, as the sheriff began deputizing hundreds of whites.

At dawn on June 1 a group of roughly 5,000 armed white men marched across the railroad tracks into Greenwood. Moving in small groups, they methodically ransacked black homes and businesses, stole cash and valuables, spread kerosene, and torched the buildings. Small groups of armed blacks resisted as long as they could, but they were no match for the thousands of white "deputies" and National Guardsmen, all of whom joined in the attack. Some of the city's whites, particularly in a few churches, helped to hide or protect black Tulsans. By late morning, Greenwood was a smoking ruin, as over 35 city blocks had been burned to the ground. African Americans were removed from their homes at gunpoint, lined up on streets with hands in the air, and forced to march out of Greenwood. Eventually some 6,000 blacks were corralled into a nearby fairground.

As many as 300 blacks lost their lives in the riot, but the invasion of Greenwood was less about mass killing than the racist urge to physically and spiritually destroy a black community. In this respect it resembled nearly all of the race riots of this era. For decades, the story of the riot was largely covered up and forgotten. In 1997 Oklahoma created the Tulsa Race Riot Commission, and its report four years later called for reparations to survivors and their descendants. The state legislature refused to offer reparations, but it did establish a college scholarship fund for descendants of Greenwood residents. The first document reproduces the first news coverage of Rowland's arrest. The second offers excerpts from an oral history done with a black survivor of the riot. The third comes from an analysis of the riot written by Walter White, assistant secretary for the NAACP, who witnessed the riot himself while on a fact-finding tour about lynching.

- **How did the language in the *Tulsa Tribune's* coverage reflect racial stereotypes of the day? How might it have inflamed white public opinion? What do Kinney White's reminiscences reveal about black life in Greenwood? How does Walter White attempt to contextualize the riot in the American economic and political climate after World War I?**

"Nab Negro for Attacking Girl in Elevator," *Tulsa Tribune*, May 31, 1921

A Negro delivery boy who gave his name to the public as "Diamond Dick," but who has been identified as Dick Rowland, was arrested on South Greenwood avenue this morning by Officers Carmichael and Pack, charged with attempting to assault the 17 year old white elevator operator girl in the Drexel Building early yesterday.

He will be tried in municipal court this afternoon on a state charge.

The girl said she noticed the negro a few minutes before the attempted assault looking up and down the hallway on the third floor of the Drexel Building as if to see if there was anyone in sight but thought nothing of it at the time.

A few minutes later, he entered the elevator she claimed, and attacked her, scratching her hands and face and tearing her clothes. Her screams brought a clerk from Renberg's store to her assistance and the negro fled. He was captured and identified this morning by both the girl and the clerk, police say.

Rowland denied that he tried to harm the girls, but admitted he put his hand on her arm when she was alone.

Tenants of the Drexel Building said the girl was an orphan who works as an elevator girl to pay her way through business college.

Source: *Tulsa Tribune*, May 31, 1921.

Kinney Booker, Oral History of a Survivor (Born 1913; Interviewed in 1998)

At the time of the Tulsa Race Riot of 1921, my parents, my brother, sister, and I lived at 320 North Hartford. We had a lovely home, owned by my parents, filled with beautiful furniture including a grand piano. That beautiful home with the elegant furnishings, and all our clothes and personal belongings were burned up during the riot. . . . I have had to fight bitter feelings about the way blacks were treated then. They did not have opportunities to develop their talents to their fullest extent. My Dad was a mechanical genius. He could have been another Thomas Edison if he had had a chance. America did not nurture its black citizens then. But that's another story. Now back to the day of the riot.

Early on the morning of June 1, 1921, My parents were awakened by the sounds of shooting, the smell of fire, and the noise of fleeing blacks running past the house. My Dad had awakened us children and sent us to the attic with our mother. We could hear what was going on below in the house. We heard Dad pleading with mobsters who had broken into our house.

We could hear him begging, 'Please don't set my house on fire. Please don't burn my house.' But, of course, that is exactly what they did. We could smell the smoke. Dad pretended to leave the house and when the mobsters left after they had sprayed our house with gasoline or kerosene and set it on fire, Dad returned and rushed to the attic and rescued us. We joined the fleeing black refugees who were trying

to get out of Tulsa to the safety of the countryside. What a pitiful bunch we were. In our nightclothes . . . barefoot . . . electric lines falling down around us . . . smouldering relics of once beautiful homes . . . the sight and smell of death and destruction all around us, there we were, men, women, children running like frightened animals fleeing a forest fire. We saw things that day that no human eye should ever see. My little sister's comment sears my soul to this day. She asked me, 'Kinney, is the world on fire?' I replied, 'I don't think so, but we're in a lot of trouble!' And, oh Lord, we black people of Tulsa were certainly in a lot of trouble that day. My family and the people who were fleeing with us were captured by the Guards and taken to a detention center, Convention Hall (now the Brady Theater).

After the riot, Dad rebuilt us a nice house, but to us, it was never as fine as that first house, and we sure did miss the elegant furnishings we had in that first house, especially that grand piano.

Source: Oral history interview with Kinney Booker, Tulsa, May 30, 1998. Interview done as part of the Report by the Oklahoma Commission to Study the Tulsa Race Riot of 1921 (2001). Original on deposit at Oklahoma Historical Society.

Walter White, "The Eruption of Tulsa," *The Nation*, June 15, 1921

What are the causes of the race riot that occurred in such a place? First, the Negro in Oklahoma has shared in the sudden prosperity that has come to many of his white brothers, and there are some colored men there who are wealthy. This fact has caused a bitter resentment on the part of the lower order of whites, who feel that these colored men, members of an "inferior race," are exceedingly presumptuous in achieving greater economic prosperity than they who are members of a divinely ordered superior race.

One of the charges made against the colored men in Tulsa is that they were "radical." Questioning the whites more closely regarding the nature of this radicalism, I found it means that Negroes were uncompromisingly denouncing "Jim-Crow" [railroad] cars, lynching, peonage; in short, were asking that the Federal constitutional guaranties of "life, liberty, and the pursuit of happiness" be given regardless of color. The Negroes of Tulsa and other Oklahoma cities are pioneers; men and women who have dared, men and women who have had the initiative and the courage to pull up stakes in other less-favored States and face hardship in a newer one for the sake of greater eventual progress. That type is

ever less ready to submit to insult. Those of the whites who seek to maintain the old white group control naturally do not relish seeing Negroes emancipating themselves from the old system.

What is America going to do after such a horrible carnage—one that for sheer brutality and murderous anarchy cannot be surpassed by any of the crimes now being charged to the Bolsheviki in Russia? How much longer will America allow these pogroms to continue unchecked? There is a lesson in the Tulsa affair for every American who fatuously believes that Negroes will always be the meek and submissive creatures that circumstances have forced them to be during the past three hundred years. Dick Rowland was only an ordinary bootblack with no standing in the community. But when his life was threatened by a mob of whites, every one of the 15,000 Negroes of Tulsa, rich and poor, educated and illiterate, was willing to die to protect Dick Rowland. Perhaps America is waiting for a nationwide Tulsa to wake her. Who knows?

Source: *The Nation*, 112 (June 29, 1921): 909–910.

African Americans had supported the war effort as faithfully as any group. In 1917 most African Americans, despite a segregated army and discrimination in defense industries, thought the war might improve their lot. Black disillusionment with the war grew quickly, however, as did a newly militant spirit. A heightened sense of race consciousness and

activism was evident among black veterans and the growing black communities of northern cities. Taking the lead in the fight against bigotry and injustice, in 1919 the NAACP held a national conference on lynching. By 1919 membership in the NAACP had reached 60,000 and the circulation of its journal, *The Crisis*, exceeded half a million.

22.5.3 Labor Strife

The relative labor peace of 1917 and 1918 dissolved after the armistice. In 1919 alone, more than 4 million American workers were involved in some 3,600 strikes. This unprecedented strike wave had several causes. Most of the modest wartime wage gains were wiped out by spiraling inflation and high prices for food, fuel, and housing. With the end of government controls on industry, many employers withdrew their recognition of unions. Difficult working conditions, such as the 12-hour day in steel mills, were still routine in some industries.

Several of the postwar strikes received widespread national attention. They seemed to be more than simple economic conflicts, and they provoked deep fears about the larger social order. In February 1919, a strike in the shipyards of Seattle, Washington, over wages escalated into a general citywide strike involving 60,000 workers. The local press and Mayor Ole Hanson denounced the strikers as revolutionaries. Hanson effectively ended the strike by requesting federal troops to occupy the city. In September, Boston policemen went out on strike when the police commissioner rejected a citizens' commission study that recommended a pay raise. Massachusetts Governor Calvin Coolidge called in the National Guard to restore order and won a national reputation by crushing the strike. The entire police force was fired.

The biggest strike took place in the steel industry and involved some 350,000 steelworkers. Centered in several midwestern cities, the strike lasted from September 1919 to January 1920. The major demands were union recognition, the eight-hour day, and wage increases. The steel companies used black strikebreakers and armed guards to keep the mills running. Elbert Gary, president of U.S. Steel, directed a sophisticated propaganda campaign that branded the strikers as revolutionaries. Public opinion turned against the strike and condoned the use of state and federal troops to break it. The failed steel strike proved to be the era's most bitter and devastating defeat for organized labor.

22.6 An Uneasy Peace

How can we explain Woodrow Wilson's failure to win the peace?

The armistice of November 1918 ended the fighting on the battlefield, but the war continued at the peace conference. In the old royal Palace of Versailles near Paris, delegates from 27 countries spent five months hammering out a settlement. Yet neither Germany nor Russia was represented. The proceedings were dominated by leaders of the "Big Four": David Lloyd George (Great Britain), Georges Clemenceau (France), Vittorio Orlando (Italy), and Woodrow Wilson (United States). President Wilson saw the peace conference as a historic opportunity to project his domestic liberalism onto the world stage. The stubborn realities of power politics would frustrate Wilson at Versailles and lead to his most crushing defeat at home.

22.6.1 Peacemaking and the Specter of Bolshevism

Even before November 1918, the Allies struggled with how to respond to the revolutionary developments in Russia. British and French leaders wanted to help counterrevolutionary forces overthrow the new Bolshevik regime. And President Wilson refused to recognize the authority of the Bolsheviks. Bolshevism represented a threat to the liberal-capitalist values that Wilson believed to be the foundation of America's moral and material power, and that provided the basis for the Fourteen Points. At the same time, however, Wilson at first resisted British and French pressure to intervene in Russia, citing his commitment to national **self-determination** and noninterference in other countries' internal affairs.

By August 1918, as the Russian political and military situation became increasingly chaotic, Wilson agreed to British and French plans for sending troops to Siberia and northern Russia. Meanwhile, Japan poured troops into Siberia and northern Manchuria in a bid to control the commercially important Chinese Eastern and Trans-Siberian railways. After the Wilson administration negotiated an agreement that placed these strategic railways under international control, the restoration and protection of the railways became the primary concern of American military forces in Russia. Wilson's idealistic support for self-determination had succumbed to the demands of international power politics. Eventually, some 15,000 American troops served in northern and eastern Russia, with some remaining until 1920.

The Allied armed intervention widened the gulf between Russia and the West. In March 1919, Russian Communists established the Third International, or Comintern. Their call for a worldwide revolution deepened Allied mistrust, and the Paris Peace Conference essentially ignored the new political reality posed by the Russian Revolution.

22.6.2 Wilson in Paris

Wilson arrived in Paris with the United States delegation in January 1919. He believed the Great War revealed the bankruptcy of diplomacy based on alliances and the "balance of power." He believed that peacemaking, based on

SIGNING OF THE TREATY OF VERSAILLES
Woodrow Wilson, Georges Clemenceau, and
David Lloyd George are among the central figures
depicted in John Christen Johansen's *Signing of the
Treaty of Versailles.* The gathered statesmen appear
dwarfed by their surroundings.

National Portrait Gallery, Smithsonian Institution/Art Resource, NY.

the framework put forward in his Fourteen Points, meant an opportunity for America to lead the rest of the world toward a new vision of international relations. The most controversial element, both at home and abroad, would prove to be the League of Nations. The heart of the League Covenant, Article X, called for collective security as the ultimate method of keeping the peace; "The members of the League undertake to respect and preserve as against external aggression the territorial integrity and existing political independence of all Members."

Despite Wilson's devotion to "open covenants," much of the negotiating in Paris was in fact done in secret among the Big Four. The ideal of self-determination found limited expression. The independent states of Austria, Hungary, Poland, Yugoslavia, and Czechoslovakia were carved out of the homelands of the defeated Central Powers. The Allies resisted Wilson's call for independence for the colonies of the defeated nations. A compromise mandate system of protectorates gave the French and British control of parts of the old German and Turkish empires in Africa and western Asia. Japan won control of former German

colonies in China. Among those trying, but failing, to influence the treaty negotiations were the 60-odd delegates to the first Pan African Congress, held in Paris at the same time as the peace talks. The group included Americans W. E. B. Du Bois and William Monroe Trotter as well as representatives from Africa and the West Indies. All were disappointed with the failure of the peace conference to grant self-determination to thousands of Africans living in former German colonies.

Another disappointment for Wilson came with the issue of war guilt. He had strongly opposed the extraction of harsh economic reparations from the Central Powers. But the French and British insisted on making Germany pay. The final treaty contained a clause attributing the war to "the aggression of Germany," and a commission later set German war reparations at $33 billion. Bitter resentment in Germany over the punitive treaty helped sow the seeds for the Nazi rise to power in the 1930s.

The final treaty was signed on June 28, 1919, in the Hall of Mirrors at the Palace of Versailles. The Germans had no choice but to accept its harsh terms. President

Wilson had been disappointed by the endless compromising of his ideals, no doubt underestimating the stubborn reality of power politics in the wake of Europe's most devastating war. He had nonetheless won a commitment to the League of Nations, the centerpiece of his plan, and he was confident that the American people would accept the treaty.

22.6.3 The Treaty Fight

Preoccupied with peace conference politics in Paris, Wilson had neglected politics at home. His troubles had started earlier when Republicans captured both the House and the Senate in the 1918 elections. Wilson then made a tactical error by including no prominent Republicans in the U.S. peace delegation. He therefore faced a variety of tough opponents to the treaty he brought home.

Wilson's most extreme enemies in the Senate were a group of about 16 **irreconcilables** who were opposed to a treaty in any form. Some were isolationist progressives, such as Republicans Robert M. La Follette of Wisconsin and William Borah of Idaho, who opposed the League of Nations as steadfastly as they opposed American entry into the war. Others were racist xenophobes like Democrat James Reed of Missouri. He objected, he said, to submitting questions to a tribunal "on which a nigger from Liberia, a nigger from Honduras, a nigger from India, and an unlettered gentleman from Siam, each have votes equal to the great United States of America."

The less dogmatic but more influential opponents were led by Republican Henry Cabot Lodge of Massachusetts, powerful majority leader of the Senate. They had strong reservations about the League of Nations, especially the provisions for collective security should a member nation be attacked. Lodge argued that this provision impinged on congressional authority to declare war and placed unacceptable restraints on the nation's ability to pursue an independent foreign policy. He proposed a series of amendments that would have weakened the League. Wilson refused to compromise, motivated in part by the long-standing hatred he and Lodge felt toward each other.

In September, Wilson set out on a speaking tour across the country to drum up support for the League and the treaty. The strain took its toll. On September 25, after speaking in Pueblo, Colorado, Wilson collapsed from exhaustion. His doctor canceled the rest of the trip. A week later, back in Washington, the president suffered a stroke that left him partially paralyzed. With Wilson badly incapacitated, his wife Edith and his doctor exercised significant decision-making authority, and they reinforced his refusal to agree to any amendments on the Treaty and the League Covenant. In November, Lodge brought the treaty out of committee

for a vote, having appended to it 14 reservations—that is, recommended changes. A bedridden Wilson stubbornly refused to compromise and instructed Democrats to vote against the Lodge version of the treaty. On November 19, Democrats joined with the "irreconcilables" to defeat the amended treaty, 39 to 55.

Wilson refused to budge. In January, he urged Democrats to either stand by the original treaty or vote it down. The 1920 election, he warned, would be "a great and solemn referendum" on the whole issue. In the final vote, on March 19, 1920, 21 Democrats broke with the president and voted for the Lodge version, giving it a majority of 49 to 35. But this was seven votes short of the two-thirds needed for ratification. As a result, the United States never signed the **Treaty of Versailles**, nor did it join the League of Nations. The absence of the United States weakened the League and made it more difficult for the organization to realize Wilson's dream of a peaceful community of nations.

22.6.4 The Red Scare

Revolutionary changes taking place in Russia became an important backdrop for domestic politics. In the United States, it became common to blame socialism, the IWW, trade unionism in general, and even racial disturbances on foreign radicals and alien ideologies. The accusation of Bolshevism became a powerful weapon for turning public opinion against strikers and political dissenters of all kinds. In truth, by 1919, the American radicals were already weakened and badly split. In the spring of 1919, a few extremists mailed bombs to prominent business and political leaders. That June, simultaneous bombings in eight cities killed two people and damaged the residence of U. S. Attorney General A. Mitchell Palmer. With public alarm growing, state and federal officials began a coordinated campaign to root out subversives and their alleged Russian connections.

Palmer used the broad authority of the 1918 Alien Act, which enabled the government to deport any immigrant found to be a member of a revolutionary organization prior to or after coming to the United States. In a series of raids in late 1919, Justice Department agents in 11 cities arrested and roughed up several hundred members of the IWW and the Union of Russian Workers. Little evidence of revolutionary intent was found, but 249 people were deported, including prominent anarchists Emma Goldman and Alexander Berkman. In early 1920, some 6,000 people in 33 cities, including many U.S. citizens and non-Communists, were arrested and herded into prisons and bullpens. Again, no evidence of a grand plot was found, but another 600 aliens were deported. The Palmer raids had a ripple effect around the nation, encouraging other repressive measures against radicals. In New York, the state assembly refused to seat five duly elected Socialist Party members.

Palmer's popularity had waned by the spring of 1920, when it became clear that his predictions of revolutionary uprisings were wildly exaggerated. A report prepared by a group of distinguished lawyers questioned the legality of the attorney general's tactics. As part of the resistance to Palmer's policies, a group of progressive activists formed the American Civil Liberties Union (ACLU) in 1920. Its founders included Clarence Darrow, Felix Frankfurter, Jane Addams, Helen Keller, and John Dewey. For progressives dispirited by the wartime political repression, the ACLU offered a new political front stressing the militant defense of civil liberties just when they seemed most fragile.

The **Red Scare** left an ugly legacy: wholesale violations of constitutional rights, deportations of hundreds of innocent people, fuel for the fires of nativism and intolerance. Business groups, such as the National Association of Manufacturers, found "Red-baiting" to be an effective tool in postwar efforts to keep unions out of their factories. Indeed, the government-sanctioned Red Scare reemerged later in the century as a powerful political force. In many communities, local vigilantes invoked the threat of Bolshevism and used the superpatriotic mood to settle scores with labor organizers and radicals.

The Red Scare took its toll on the women's movement as well. Before the war, many suffragists and feminists had maintained ties and shared platforms with socialist and labor groups. But the calls for "100 percent Americanism" during and after the war destroyed the fragile alliances that had made a group such as the NAWSA so powerful. Hostility to radicalism marked the political climate of the 1920s, and this atmosphere narrowed the political spectrum for women activists.

22.6.5 The Election of 1920

Woodrow Wilson had wanted the 1920 election to be a "solemn referendum" on the League of Nations and his conduct of the war. Ill and exhausted, Wilson did not run for reelection. A badly divided Democratic Party compromised on Governor James M. Cox of Ohio as its candidate. A proven vote-getter, Cox distanced himself from Wilson's policies, which had come under withering attack from many quarters.

The Republicans nominated Senator Warren G. Harding of Ohio. A political hack, the handsome and genial Harding had virtually no qualifications to be president, except that he looked like one. Harding's campaign was vague and elusive about the Versailles Treaty and almost everything else. He struck a chord with the electorate in calling for a retreat from Wilsonian idealism. "America's present need," he said, "is not heroics but healing; not nostrums but normalcy; not revolution but restoration."

The notion of a "return to normalcy" proved very attractive to voters weary of the war, inflation, big government, and social dislocation. Harding won the greatest landslide in history to that date, carrying every state outside the South and taking the popular vote by 16 million to 9 million. Republicans retained their majorities in the House and Senate as well. Socialist Eugene V. Debs, still a powerful symbol of the dream of radical social change, managed to poll 900,000 votes from jail. The overall vote repudiated Wilson and the progressive movement. Americans seemed eager to pull back from moralism in public and international controversies. Yet many of the economic, social, and cultural changes wrought by the war would accelerate during the 1920s. In truth, there could never be a "return to normalcy."

Conclusion

The global impact of the Great War, including the change in the United States's place in relation to the rest of the world, was profound. Although the casualties and social upheavals endured by the European powers might seem to dwarf the price paid by the United States, the war created economic, social, and political dislocations that helped reshape American life long after Armistice Day. The ability to raise and deploy the massive American Expeditionary Force overseas so quickly had proved decisive to ending the fighting. The government's direct intervention in every aspect of the wartime economy was unprecedented, and wartime production needs contributed to a "second industrial revolution" that transformed the economy in the decade following the war. Republican administrations invoked the wartime partnership between government and industry to justify an aggressive peacetime policy fostering cooperation between the state and business. Although the United States would not join the League of Nations, the war turned the United States into a major global force: The world's new leading creditor nation would now also take its place as a powerful commercial and industrial engine in the global economy.

Patriotic fervor and the exaggerated threat of Bolshevism were used to repress radicalism, organized labor, feminism, and the entire legacy of progressive reform. The wartime measure of national prohibition evolved into perhaps the most contentious social issue of peacetime. Sophisticated use of sales techniques, psychology, and propaganda during the war helped define the newly powerful advertising and public relations industries of the 1920s. The growing visibility of immigrants and African Americans, especially in the nation's cities, provoked a xenophobic and racist backlash in the politics of the 1920s. More than anything else, the desire for "normalcy" reflected the deep anxieties evoked by America's wartime experience.

Key Terms

doughboys Nickname for soldiers after the doughnut shaped buttons on their uniforms. p. 514

Roosevelt Corollary President Theodore Roosevelt's policy asserting U.S. authority to intervene in the affairs of Latin American nations; an expansion of the Monroe Doctrine. p. 516

Open Door American policy of seeking equal trade and investment opportunities in foreign nations or regions. p. 516

Militarism The tendency to see military might as the most important and best tool for the expansion of a nation's power and prestige. p. 519

imperialism The policy and practice of exploiting nations and peoples for the benefit of an imperial power either directly, through military occupation and colonial rule, or indirectly, through economic domination of resources and markets. p. 519

Central Powers Germany and its World War I allies in Austria-Hungary, Italy, Turkey, and Bulgaria. p. 519

Allies In World War I, Britain, France, Russia, and other belligerent nations fighting against the Central Powers, not including the United States. p. 519

preparedness Military buildup in preparation for possible U.S. participation in World War I. p. 521

Committee on Public Information (CPI) Government agency during World War I that sought to shape public opinion in support of the war effort through newspapers, pamphlets, speeches, films, and other media. p. 522

Selective Service Act The law establishing the military draft for World War I. p. 524

Bolsheviks Members of the Communist movement in Russia that established the Soviet government after the 1917 Russian Revolution. p. 526

Fourteen Points Goals outlined by Woodrow Wilson for war. p. 526

League of Nations International organization created by the Versailles Treaty after World War I to ensure world stability. p. 527

War Industries Board (WIB) The federal agency that reorganized industry for maximum efficiency and productivity during World War I. p. 527

Liberty Bonds Interest-bearing certificates sold by the U.S. government to finance the American World War I effort. p. 528

Espionage Act Law whose vague prohibition against obstructing the nation's war effort was used to crush dissent and criticism during World War I. p. 530

Sedition Act Broad law restricting criticism of America's involvement in World War I or its government, flag, military, taxes, or officials. p. 533

Great Migration The mass movement of African Americans from the rural South to the urban North, spurred especially by new job opportunities during World War I and the 1920s. p. 534

Self-determination The right of a people or a nation to decide on its own political allegiance or form of government without external influence. p. 538

irreconcilables Group of U.S. senators adamantly opposed to ratification of the Treaty of Versailles after World War I. p. 540

Treaty of Versailles The treaty ending World War I and creating the League of Nations. p. 540

Red Scare Post-World War I public hysteria over Bolshevik influence in the United States directed against labor activism, radical dissenters, and some ethnic groups. p. 541

CHRONOLOGY

United States obtains Panama Canal rights	**1903**
	1914 — U.S. forces invade Mexico / World War I begins in Europe
Wilson is reelected	**1916**
	1917 — United States declares war on Central Powers (April) / Espionage Act is passed (June)
Armistice ends war (November)	**1918**
	1919 — Eighteenth Amendment (Prohibition) is ratified / Versailles Treaty is signed in Paris
Senate rejects Versailles Treaty and League of Nations / Nineteenth Amendment (Woman Suffrage) is ratified	**1920**

Chapter 23
The Twenties 1920–1929

"CITY ACTIVITIES WITH DANCE HALL" Thomas Benton Hart's "City Activities with Dance Hall" is part of a series of murals entitled *America Today* that explores a variety of aspects of American life.

Image copyright © The Metropolitan Museum of Art. Image source/Art Resource, NY.

 Contents and Focus Questions

American Communities

The Movie Audience and Hollywood: Mass Culture Creates a New National Community

Inside midtown Manhattan's magnificent new Roxy Theater, a sellout crowd eagerly settled in for opening night. Outside, thousands of fans cheered wildly at the arrival of movie stars such as Charlie Chaplin, Gloria Swanson, and Harold Lloyd. A squadron of smartly uniformed ushers guided patrons under a five-story-tall rotunda to some 6,200 velvet-covered seats. The audience marveled at the huge gold-and-rose-colored murals, classical statuary, plush carpeting, and Gothic-style windows. Suddenly,

545

light flooded the orchestra pit and 110 musicians began playing "The Star-Spangled Banner." A troupe of 100 performers took the stage, dancing ballet numbers and singing old southern melodies such as "My Old Kentucky Home" and "Swanee River." Congratulatory telegrams from President Calvin Coolidge and other dignitaries flashed on the screen. Finally, the evening's feature presentation, *The Love of Sunya*, starring Swanson, began. Samuel L. "Roxy" Rothapfel, the theater's designer, had realized his grand dream—to build "the cathedral of the motion picture." As film pioneer Marcus Loew put it, "We sell tickets to theaters, not movies." Every large community boasted at least one opulent movie theater. Houston's Majestic was built to represent an ancient Italian garden; it had a ceiling made to look like an open sky, complete with stars and cloud formations. The Tivoli in Chicago featured French Renaissance decor; Grauman's Egyptian in Los Angeles re-created the look of a pharaoh's tomb; and Albuquerque's Kimo drew inspiration from Navajo art and religion.

The remarkable popularity of motion pictures, and later radio, forged a new kind of community. People who may have had little in common in terms of ethnicity, background, or geographic location found themselves part of a virtual community of movie fans. Hollywood films also achieved a global popularity that represented the cultural side of America's newfound influence in the world. The Webb-Pomerene Act of 1918 proved a boon for the global expansion of Hollywood film, as it exempted export associations from antitrust laws, allowing them to form cartels, fix prices, and engage in other trade practices that would have been barred at home. Hollywood movies soon emerged as one of the most widely circulated American commodities in the world, behind only Gillette razor blades and Ford automobiles. Producers found strong allies in the federal government, which touted the connections between the export of Hollywood movies and the growth of American trade around the world. "Trade follows the film," as one Commerce Department report put it, with movies supplying "an animated catalogue for ideas of dress, living, and comfort."

Hollywood's emergence might be thought of as part of a broader "second industrial revolution" that modernized industrial production and greatly expanded the availability of consumer goods in the postwar years. The studios concentrated on producing big-budget feature films designed for mass audiences, with the "star system" providing the industry's version of product branding. The economies of large-scale production allowed studios to sign popular actors to long-term contracts and invest heavily in their salaries and promotion. The stars themselves had to be willing to sacrifice their privacy in order to promote their "celebrity" status. Movie stars like Chaplin, Mary Pickford, Rudolph Valentino, Swanson, and Douglas Fairbanks became popular idols as much for their highly publicized private lives as for their roles on-screen. Many accumulated great wealth, becoming the nation's experts on how to live well. They built luxurious mansions in a variety of architectural styles, and outfitted them with swimming pools, tennis courts, golf courses, and lavish gardens. Americans embraced the culture of celebrity, voraciously consuming fan magazines, gossip columns, and news of the stars. Indeed, during the 1920s, there was a tight connection between celebrity and the rapid growth of new networks of mass culture—movies, radio, advertising, musical recordings, and big-time sports.

If the movies created a new kind of virtual community of fans in the 1920s, the town of Hollywood itself was also a new kind of American community. A suburb of Los Angeles that had barely existed in 1890, Hollywood was an alluring alternative to the East Coast cities where movies had been born. Its reliably sunny and dry climate was ideal for year-round filming. Its unique surroundings offered a perfect variety of scenic locations—mountains, desert, ocean—and downtown Los Angeles was only an hour away. Land was cheap and plentiful, and because Los Angeles was the leading nonunion, open-shop city in the country, so was labor. It lured the young and cosmopolitan with the promise of upward mobility and a new way of life.

Most of the top studio executives were Jewish immigrants from eastern and central Europe. In contrast to most Americans, who hailed from rural areas or small towns, more than half of Hollywood's writers, directors, editors, and actors were born in cities with populations over 100,000. Two-thirds of its performers were under 35, and three-fourths of its actresses were under 25. More than 90 percent of its writers (women made up one-third to one-half of this key group) had attended college or worked in journalism. Hollywood films celebrating the pleasures of leisure, consumption, and personal freedom redefined American cultural values in the 1920s. But the community that cranked them out was far from typically American.

Ordinary Americans found it easy to identify with movie stars despite their wealth and status. Unlike industrialists or politicians, stars had no social authority over large groups of employees or voters. They, too, had to answer to a boss, and most had risen from humble beginnings. But above all, Hollywood, like the movies it churned out, represented for millions of Americans new possibilities: freedom, material success, upward mobility, and the chance to remake one's very identity. By the end of the decade, the Hollywood "dream factory" had helped forge a national community whose collective aspirations and desires were increasingly defined by those possibilities, even if relatively few Americans realized them during the 1920s. And around the world, Hollywood movies became the preeminent version of the American way of life.

Of course, Hollywood films offered nothing near an accurate reflection of the complexities of American society. As American culture became increasingly defined by an urban-based mass media that claimed the entire nation for its audience, resentment toward and resistance against the new popular culture was widespread. Movies celebrated prosperity, new technologies, and expanded consumerism, but these

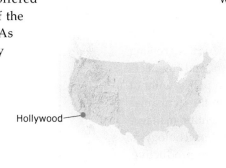

Hollywood

were by no means shared equally among Americans in the decade following World War I. While Hollywood films touted the promise of the modern, and the potential for people to remake themselves, tenacious belief in the old-fashioned verities of prewar America fueled some of the strongest political and cultural currents of the decade.

23.1 Postwar Prosperity and Its Price

What factors combined to produce postwar prosperity in the United States?

Republican Warren G. Harding won the presidency in 1920, largely thanks to his nostalgic call for a "return to normalcy." In the decade following the end of World War I, however, the American economy underwent profound structural changes that guaranteed life would never be "normal" again. The 1920s saw an enormous increase in the efficiency of production, a steady climb in real wages, a decline in the length of the average employee's workweek, and a boom in consumer-goods industries. Americans shared unevenly in the postwar prosperity, and by the end of the decade, certain basic weaknesses in the economy helped to bring on the worst depression in American history. Yet overall, the nation experienced crucial transformations in how it organized its business, earned its living, and enjoyed its leisure time.

23.1.1 The Second Industrial Revolution

The prosperity of the 1920s rested on what historians have called the "second industrial revolution" in American manufacturing, in which technological innovations made it possible to increase industrial output without expanding the labor force. Electricity replaced steam as the main power source for industry in those years, making possible the replacement of older machinery with more efficient and flexible electric machinery. In 1914, only 30 percent of the nation's factories were electrified; by 1929, 70 percent relied on the electric motor rather than the steam engine.

Much of the newer, automatic machinery could be operated by unskilled and semiskilled workers, and it boosted the overall efficiency of American industry. Thus, in 1929, the average worker in manufacturing produced

roughly three-quarters more per hour than the average in 1919. The machine industry itself, particularly the manufacture of electrical machinery, led in productivity gains, enjoying one of the fastest rates of expansion. It employed more workers than any other manufacturing sector—some 1.1 million in 1929—supplying not only a growing home market but 35 percent of the world market as well.

During the late nineteenth century, heavy industries such as machine tools, railroads, iron, and steel had pioneered mass-production techniques. These industries manufactured what economists call producer-durable goods. In the 1920s, modern mass-production techniques were increasingly applied to newer consumer-durable goods—automobiles, radios, washing machines, and telephones—permitting firms to make large profits while keeping prices affordable. Other consumer-based industries, such as canning, chemicals, synthetics, and plastics, began to change the everyday lives of millions of Americans. With more efficient management, greater mechanization, intensive product research, and ingenious sales and advertising methods, the consumer-based industries helped to nearly double industrial production in the 1920s.

The watchword for all this was efficiency, a virtue that progressives had emphasized in their pre-war efforts to improve urban life and the mechanics of government itself. But efficiency became an obsession for American businessmen, who thought it defined modernity as well. American success in mechanization and the mass production of consumer goods evoked admiration and envy in much of the industrialized (and industrializing) world.

23.1.2 The Modern Corporation

In the late nineteenth century, individual entrepreneurs such as John D. Rockefeller in oil and Andrew Carnegie in steel had provided a model for success. They maintained both corporate control (ownership) and business leadership (management) in their enterprises. In the 1920s, a managerial revolution increasingly divorced ownership of corporate stock from the everyday control of businesses. (See Figure 23.1.) The new corporate ideal was to be found in men such as Alfred P. Sloan of General Motors and Owen D. Young of the Radio Corporation of America. A growing class of salaried executives, plant managers, and engineers formed a new elite, who made corporate policy without themselves having a controlling interest in the companies for which they worked. They stressed scientific management and the latest theories of behavioral psychology in their effort to make their workplaces more productive, stable, and profitable. (See Figure 23.2.) Modern managers also brought a more sophisticated understanding of global markets to their management. Exploiting overseas markets, especially in Europe, became a key element in corporate strategy, especially for car manufacturers, chemical companies, and businesses engaged in the new world of modern mass media.

During the 1920s, the most successful corporations were those that led in three key areas: the integration of production and distribution, product diversification, and the expansion of industrial research. Until the end of World War I, for example, the chemical manufacturer Du Pont had specialized in explosives such as gunpowder. After the war, Du Pont moved aggressively into the consumer market with a diverse array of products. The company created separate but integrated divisions that produced and distributed new fabrics (such as rayon), paints, dyes, and celluloid products (such as artificial sponges). The great electrical manufacturers—General Electric and Westinghouse— similarly transformed themselves after the war. Previously

Figure 23.1 STOCK MARKET PRICES, 1921–1932

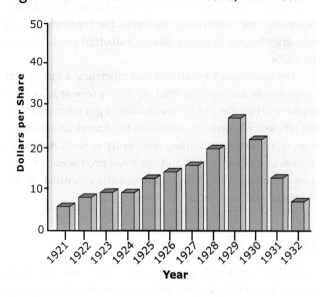

Common stock prices rose steeply during the 1920s. Although only about 4 million Americans owned stocks during the period, "stock watching" became something of a national sport.

Figure 23.2 CONSUMER DEBT, 1920–1931

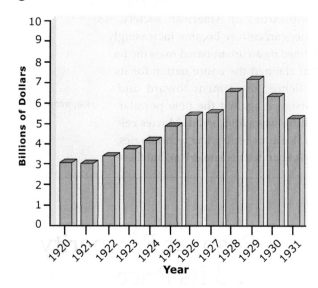

The expansion of consumer borrowing was a key component of the era's prosperity. These figures do not include mortgages or money borrowed to purchase stocks. They reveal the great increase in "installment buying" for such consumer-durable goods as automobiles and household appliances.

concentrating on lighting and power equipment, they diversified into household appliances like radios, washing machines, and refrigerators.

By 1929, the 200 largest corporations owned nearly half the nation's corporate wealth—that is, physical plant, stock, and property. Half the total industrial income—revenue from sales of goods—was concentrated in 100 corporations. Oligopoly—the control of a market by a few large producers—became the norm. Four companies packed almost three-quarters of all American meat. Another four rolled nine out of every ten cigarettes. National chain grocery stores, clothing shops, and pharmacies began squeezing out local neighborhood businesses. One grocery chain alone, the Great Atlantic and Pacific Tea Company (A&P), accounted for 10 percent of all retail food sales in America. A&P won out over thousands of older "mom-and-pop" grocery stores partly by selling its stores as "clean" and "modern," with no haggling over prices. These changes meant that Americans were increasingly members of national consumer communities, buying the same brands all over the country, as opposed to locally produced goods.

23.1.3 Welfare Capitalism

The wartime gains made by organized labor, and the active sympathy shown to trade unions by government agencies such as the National War Labor Board (NWLB), troubled most corporate leaders. Shortly after the war's end, largely as a result of pressure from business leaders, the Wilson administration dismantled the NWLB and other mechanisms aimed at mediation of labor disputes. To challenge the power and appeal of trade unions and collective bargaining, large employers aggressively promoted a variety of new programs designed to improve worker well-being and morale while also fending off unionization. These schemes, collectively known as **welfare capitalism**, became a key part of corporate strategy in the 1920s.

Welfare work in auto factories, textile mills, and other manufacturing plants was often guided by the new science of personnel management. Many plant managers and personnel departments consciously worked to improve safety conditions, provide medical services, and establish sports and recreation programs for workers. Employers hoped such measures would encourage workers to identify personally with the company and would discourage complaints on the job. Companies sponsored recreation in many forms, such as baseball teams, skating rinks, picnics, track meets, and dances. Welfare work might also include reading rooms for workers, short rest breaks, and social workers to listen to any problems arising on the job. Another approach encouraged workers to acquire property through stock-purchase plans or, less frequently, home-ownership plans. By 1927, 800,000 employees had more than $1 billion invested in more than 300 companies. Other programs offered workers insurance policies covering accidents, illness, old age, and death. By 1928, some 6 million workers had group insurance coverage valued at $7.5 billion.

Large corporations mounted an effective antiunion campaign in the early 1920s called "the American plan," as an alternative to trade unionism and the class antagonism associated with European labor relations. Backed by powerful business lobbies such as the National Association of Manufacturers and the Chamber of Commerce, campaign leaders called for the **open shop**, in which no employee would be compelled to join a union. In effect, an "open shop" meant that no known union member would be hired. If a union existed, nonmembers would still get whatever wages and rights the union had won—a policy that put organizers at a disadvantage in signing up new members.

The open shop undercut the gains won in a union shop, where new employees had to join an existing union, or a closed shop, where employers agreed to hire only union members. As alternatives, large employers such as U.S. Steel and International Harvester began setting up company unions. Their intent was to substitute largely symbolic employee representation in management conferences for the more confrontational process of collective bargaining. These management strategies contributed to a sharp decline in the ranks of organized labor. Total union membership dropped from about 5 million in 1920 to 3.5 million in 1926. A large proportion of the remaining union members were concentrated in the skilled crafts of the building and printing trades. A conservative and timid union leadership was

A&P ADVERTISEMENT The A&P grocery chain expanded from 400 stores in 1912 to more than 15,000 by the end of the 1920s, making it a familiar sight in communities across America. A&P advertisements, like this one from 1929, emphasized cleanliness, order, and the availability of name-brand goods at discount prices.

Fotosearch/Getty Images.

also responsible for the trend. William Green, who became president of the American Federation of Labor after the death of Samuel Gompers in 1924, showed no real interest in getting unorganized workers, such as those in the growing mass-production industries of automobiles, steel, and electrical goods, into unions.

Welfare capitalism succeeded in undercutting union strength, but it could not solve the chronic problems faced by industrial workers: seasonal unemployment, low wages, long hours, and unhealthy factory conditions. Indeed, corporate policy reinforced economic insecurity for millions of workers and advanced growing income inequality. The failure of the 1920s' economy to distribute gains in productivity more equally would help set the stage for the Great Depression of the 1930s.

23.1.4 The Auto Age

In their classic community study *Middletown* (1929), sociologists Robert and Helen Lynd noted the dramatic impact of the car on the social life of residents of Muncie, Indiana. "Why on earth do you need to study what's changing this country?" asked one lifelong Muncie resident in 1924. "I can tell you what's happening in just four letters: A-U-T-O!" This remark hardly seems much of an exaggeration today. No other single development matched the impact of the postwar automobile explosion on the way Americans worked, lived, and played. The auto industry offered the clearest example of the rise to prominence of consumer durables. During the 1920s, America made approximately 85 percent of all the world's passenger cars. By 1929, the motor vehicle industry was the most productive in the United States in terms of value. In that year, the industry added 4.8 million new cars to the more than 26 million—roughly one for every five people—already on American roads.

This extraordinary new industry had mushroomed in less than a generation. Its great pioneer, Henry Ford, had shown how the use of a continuous assembly line could drastically reduce the number of worker hours required to produce a single vehicle. Ford revolutionized the factory shop floor with new, custom-built machinery, such as the engine-boring drill press and the pneumatic wrench, and a more efficient layout. "Every piece of work in the shop moves," Ford boasted. In 1913, it took 13 hours to produce 1 automobile. In 1914, at his sprawling new Highland Park assembly plant just outside Detroit, Ford's system finished 1 car every 90 minutes. By 1925, cars were rolling off his assembly line at the rate of 1 every 10 seconds.

FORD ASSEMBLY LINE Assembly line workers at the Ford Motor Company, Highland Park, Michigan, dropping an engine into a Model T, c. 1920. During the 1920s Henry Ford achieved the status of folk hero, as his name became synonymous with the techniques of mass production. Ford cultivated a public image as the heroic genius of the auto industry, greatly exaggerating his personal achievements.

Bettmann/Getty Images.

In 1914, Ford startled American industry by inaugurating a new wage scale: $5 for an eight-hour day. This was roughly double the going pay rate for industrial labor, and a shorter workday as well. In defying the conventional economic wisdom of the day, Ford acted less out of benevolence than out of shrewdness. He understood that workers were consumers as well as producers, and the new wage scale helped boost sales of Ford cars. It also reduced the high turnover rate in his labor force and increased worker efficiency. Roughly two-thirds of the labor force at Ford consisted of immigrants from southern and eastern Europe. By the early 1920s, Ford also employed about 5,000 African Americans, more than any other large American corporation. Ford's mass-production system and economies of scale permitted him to progressively reduce the price of his cars, bringing them within the reach of millions of Americans. The famous Model T, thoroughly standardized and available only in black, cost just under $300 in 1924—about three months' wages for the best-paid factory workers.

By 1927, Ford had produced 15 million Model Ts. But by then, the company faced stiff competition from General Motors (GM), which had developed an effective new marketing strategy. Under the guidance of Alfred P. Sloan, GM organized into separate divisions, each of which appealed to a different market segment. Cadillac, for example, produced GM's most expensive car, which was targeted at the wealthy buyer; Chevrolet produced its least expensive model, which was targeted at working-class and lower-middle-class buyers. The GM business structure, along with its attempts to match production with demand through sophisticated market research and sales forecasting, became a widely copied model for other large American corporations. Both Ford and GM also pushed the idea of purchasing cars on credit, thus helping to make "installment buying" an underpinning of the new consumer culture.

The auto industry provided a large market for makers of steel, rubber, glass, and petroleum products. It stimulated public spending for good roads and extended the housing boom to new suburbs. Showrooms, repair shops, and gas stations appeared in thousands of communities. New small enterprises, from motels to billboard advertising to roadside diners, sprang up as motorists took to the highway. Automobiles widened the experience of millions of Americans. They made the exploration of the world outside the local community easier and more attractive. The automobile made leisure, in the sense of getting away from the routines of work and school, a more regular part of everyday life. It undoubtedly also changed the courtship practices of America's youth. Young people took advantage of the car to gain privacy and distance from their parents, and many had their first sexual experiences in automobiles.

Cancel distance & conquer weather

The woman who drives her own Ford Closed Car is completely independent of road and weather conditions in any season.

It enables her to carry on all those activities of the winter months that necessitate travel to and fro—in

or out of town. Her time and energy are conserved; her health is protected, no matter how bitterly cold the day, or how wet and slushy it is underfoot.

A Ford Sedan is always comfortable—warm and snug in winter, and in summer with ventilator and windows open wide, as cool and airy as an open car.

This seasonal comfort is combined with fine looks and Ford dependability; no wonder there is for this car so wide and ever-growing a demand.

FORD MOTOR COMPANY, DETROIT, MICHIGAN

TUDOR SEDAN, $580   ·:·   FORDOR SEDAN, $660
COUPE, $520   ∴   ALL PRICES F. O. B. DETROIT

CLOSED CARS

FORD ADVERTISEMENT Until 1924, Henry Ford had disdained national advertising for his cars. But as General Motors gained a competitive edge by making yearly changes in style and technology, Ford was forced to pay more attention to advertising. This ad was directed at "Mrs. Consumer," combining appeals to female independence and motherly duties.

Fotosearch/Getty Images.

23.1.5 Cities and Suburbs

Cars also promoted urban and suburban growth. The U.S. Census for 1920 was the first in American history in which the proportion of the population that lived in urban places (those with 2,500 or more people) exceeded the proportion of the population living in rural areas. More revealing of urban growth was the steady increase in the number of big cities. In 1910, there were 60 cities with more than 100,000 inhabitants; in 1920, there were 68; and by 1930, there were 92. During the 1920s, New York grew by 20 percent, to nearly 7 million, whereas Detroit, home of the auto industry, doubled its population, to nearly 2 million.

Cities promised business opportunity, good jobs, cultural richness, and personal freedom. They attracted millions of Americans, white and black, from small towns and farms, as well as immigrants from abroad. Immigrants were drawn to cities by the presence there of family and people of like background in already-established ethnic communities. In a continuation of the Great Migration that began during World War I, roughly 1.5 million African Americans from the rural South migrated to cities in search of economic opportunities during the 1920s, doubling the black populations of New York, Chicago, Detroit, and Houston.

Houston offers a good example of how the automobile shaped an urban community. In 1910, it was a sleepy railroad town that served the Texas Gulf coast and interior, with a population of about 75,000. The enormous demand for gasoline and other petroleum products helped transform the city into a busy center for oil refining. Its population soared to 300,000 by the end of the 1920s. Abundant cheap land and the absence of zoning ordinances, combined with the availability of the automobile, pushed Houston to expand horizontally rather than vertically. It became the archetypal decentralized, low-density city, sprawling miles in each direction from downtown and thoroughly dependent on automobiles and roads for its sense of community.

Suburban communities grew at twice the rate of their core cities, also thanks largely to the automobile boom. Undeveloped land on the fringes of cities became valuable real estate. Grosse Pointe, near Detroit, and Elmwood Park, near Chicago, grew more than 700 percent in 10 years. Long Island's Nassau County, just east of New York City, tripled in population. All the new "automobile suburbs" differed in important ways from earlier suburbs built along mass transit lines. The car allowed for a larger average lot size and, in turn, lower residential density.

23.2 The State, the Economy, and Business

How and why did the Republican Party dominate politics in the 1920s?

Throughout the 1920s, a confident Republican Party dominated national politics, certain that it had ushered in a "new era" in American life. A new and closer relationship between the federal government and American business became the hallmark of Republican policy in both domestic and foreign affairs during the administrations of three successive Republican presidents: Warren G. Harding (1921–23), Calvin Coolidge (1923–29), and Herbert Hoover (1929–33). Republicans never tired of claiming that the business-government partnership their policies promoted was responsible for the nation's economic prosperity.

23.2.1 Harding and Coolidge

Handsome, genial, and well spoken, Warren Harding may have looked the part of a president—but acting like one was another matter. Harding was a product of small-town Marion, Ohio, and the machine politics in his native state. Republican Party officials had made a point of keeping Senator Harding, a compromise choice, as removed from the public eye as possible in the 1920 election. Harding understood his own limitations. He sadly told one visitor to the White House shortly after taking office, "I knew that this job would be too much for me."

Harding surrounded himself with a close circle of friends, the "Ohio gang," delegating to them a great deal of administrative power. The president often conducted business as if he were in the relaxed, convivial, and masculine confines of a small-town saloon. In the summer of 1923, Harding began to get wind of the scandals for which his administration is best remembered. Soon after Harding's death from a heart attack later that year, a series of congressional investigations revealed a deep pattern of corruption. Attorney General Harry M. Daugherty had received bribes from violators of the Prohibition statutes. He had also failed to investigate graft in the Veterans Bureau, where Charles R. Forbes had pocketed a large chunk of the $250 million spent on hospitals and supplies. The worst affair was the Teapot Dome scandal involving Interior Secretary Albert Fall. Fall received hundreds of thousands of dollars in payoffs when he secretly leased navy oil reserves in Teapot Dome, Wyoming, and Elk Hills, California, to two private oil developers. He eventually became the first cabinet officer ever to go to jail.

The Harding administration's legacy was not all scandal. Andrew Mellon, an influential Pittsburgh banker, served as secretary of the treasury under all three Republican presidents of the 1920s. One of the richest men in America, and a leading investor in the Aluminum Corporation of America and Gulf Oil, Mellon believed government ought to be run on the same conservative principles as a corporation. He was a leading voice for trimming the federal budget and cutting taxes on incomes, corporate profits, and inheritances. These cuts, he argued, would free up capital for new investment and, thus, promote general economic growth. Mellon's program sharply cut taxes both for higher-income brackets and for businesses. By 1926, a person with an income of $1 million a year paid less than a third of the income tax paid in 1921.

When Calvin Coolidge succeeded to the presidency, he seemed to most people the temperamental opposite of Harding. Born and raised in rural Vermont, elected governor of Massachusetts, and coming to national prominence only through the 1919 Boston police strike (see Chapter 22), "Silent Cal" was the quintessential New England Yankee. Taciturn, genteel, and completely honest, Coolidge believed in the least amount of government possible. He spent only four hours a day at the office. His famous aphorism, "After all, the chief business of the American people is business" perfectly captured the core philosophy of the Republican new era. He was in awe of wealthy men such as Mellon, and he thought them best suited to make society's key decisions.

Coolidge easily won election on his own in 1924. He benefited from the general prosperity and from the contrast he provided with the disgraced Harding. Coolidge defeated little-known Democrat John W. Davis, the compromise choice of a party badly divided between its rural and urban wings. Also running was Progressive Party candidate Robert M. La Follette of Wisconsin, who mounted a reform campaign that attacked economic monopolies and called for government ownership of utilities. In his full term, Coolidge showed most interest in reducing federal spending, lowering taxes, and blocking congressional initiatives. He saw his primary function as clearing the way for American businessmen. They, after all, were the agents of the era's unprecedented prosperity.

23.2.2 Herbert Hoover and the "Associative State"

The most influential figure of the Republican new era was Herbert Hoover, who as secretary of commerce dominated the cabinets of Harding and Coolidge before becoming president himself in 1929. A successful engineer, administrator, and politician, Hoover had earned an enviable reputation as wartime head of the U.S. Food Administration and director general of relief for Europe. He effectively embodied the belief that enlightened business, encouraged and informed by the government, would act in the public interest. In the modern industrial age, Hoover believed, the government needed only to advise private citizens' groups about what national or international polices to pursue. "Reactionaries and radicals," he wrote in *American Individualism* (1922), "would assume that all reform and human advance must come through government. They have forgotten that progress must come from the steady lift of the individual and that the measure of national idealism and progress is the quality of idealism in the individual."

Hoover thus fused a faith in old-fashioned individualism with a strong commitment to the progressive possibilities offered by efficiency and rationality. Unlike an earlier generation of Republicans, Hoover wanted not just to create a favorable climate for business but also to actively assist the business community. He spoke of creating an "associative state," in which the government would encourage voluntary cooperation among corporations, consumers, workers, farmers, and small businessmen. This became the central occupation of the Department of Commerce under Hoover's leadership. The Bureau of Standards, for example, set engineering specifications for key American industries such as machine tools and automobiles. The Bureau also helped standardize the styles, sizes, and designs of many consumer products, such as canned goods and refrigerators.

Hoover actively encouraged the creation and expansion of national trade associations. By 1929, there were about 2,000 of them. At industrial conferences organized by the Commerce Department, government officials explained the advantages of mutual cooperation in figuring prices and costs and then publishing the information. The idea was to improve efficiency by reducing competition. To some, this practice violated the spirit of antitrust laws, but in the 1920s, the Justice Department's Antitrust Division took a very lax view of its responsibility. In addition, the Supreme Court consistently upheld the legality of trade associations. The government thus provided an ideal climate for the concentration of corporate wealth and power. The trend toward large corporate trusts and holding companies had been well under way since the late nineteenth century, but it accelerated in the 1920s. By 1929, the 200 largest American corporations owned almost half the total corporate wealth and about a fifth of the total national wealth. Concentration was particularly strong in manufacturing, retailing, mining, banking, and utilities.

23.2.3 War Debts, Reparations, Keeping the Peace

Rejection of the Treaty of Versailles and the League of Nations did not mean disengagement from the rest of the globe. The United States emerged from World War I as the strongest economic power in the world. The war transformed it from the world's leading debtor nation to its most important creditor. European governments owed the U.S. government about $10 billion in 1919. In the private sector, the war ushered in an era of expanding American investment abroad. As late as 1914, foreign investments in the United States were about $3 billion more than the total of American capital invested abroad. By 1919, that situation was reversed: America had $3 billion more invested abroad than foreigners had invested in the United States. By 1929, the surplus was $8 billion. New York replaced London as the center of international finance and capital markets. Yet America's postwar policies included a great contradiction: protectionism. The rest of the world owed the United States billions of dollars, but high tariffs on both farm products and manufactured goods made it much more difficult for debtor nations to repay from profits from exports.

During the 1920s, war debts and reparations were the most divisive issues in international economics. In France and Great Britain, which both owed the United States large amounts in war loans, many concluded that the Uncle Sam who had offered assistance during wartime was really a loan shark in disguise. In turn, many Americans viewed Europeans as ungrateful debtors. As President Coolidge acidly remarked, "They hired the money, didn't they?" In 1922, the U.S. Foreign Debt Commission negotiated an agreement with the debtor nations that called for them to repay $11.5 billion over a 62-year period. But by the late 1920s, the European financial situation had become so desperate that the United States agreed to cancel a large part of these debts. Continued insistence by the United States that the Europeans pay at least a portion of the debt fed anti-American feeling in Europe and isolationism at home.

The Germans believed that war reparations, set at $33 billion by the Treaty of Versailles, not only unfairly punished the losers of the conflict but, by saddling their civilian economies with such massive debt, also deprived them of the very means to repay. In 1924, Herbert Hoover and Chicago banker Charles Dawes worked out a plan to aid the recovery of the German economy. The Dawes Plan reduced Germany's debt, stretched out the repayment period, and arranged for American bankers to lend funds to Germany. These measures helped stabilize Germany's currency and allowed it to make reparations payments to France and Great

Britain. The Allies, in turn, were better able to pay their war debts to the United States.

In addition to the Dawes Plan and the American role in naval disarmament, the United States joined the league-sponsored World Court in 1926 and was represented at numerous league conferences. In 1928, with great fanfare, the United States and 62 other nations signed the Pact of Paris (better known as the Kellogg-Briand Pact, for U.S. Secretary of State Frank B. Kellogg and French Foreign Minister Aristide Briand, who initiated it), which grandly and naively renounced war in principle. Peace groups, such as the Woman's Peace Party and the Quaker-based Fellowship of Reconciliation, hailed the pact for formally outlawing war. Critics charged that the Kellogg-Briand Pact was essentially meaningless because it lacked powers of enforcement and relied solely on the moral force of world opinion. Within weeks of its ratification, the U.S. Congress had appropriated $250 million for new battleships.

23.2.4 Global Commerce and U.S. Foreign Policy

Throughout the 1920s, Secretary of State Charles Evans Hughes and other Republican leaders pursued policies designed to expand American economic activity abroad. They understood that capitalist economies must be dynamic; they must expand their markets if they are to thrive. The focus must be on friendly nations and on investments that would help foreign citizens buy American goods. Toward this end, Republican leaders urged close cooperation between bankers and the government as a strategy for expanding American investment and economic influence abroad. Throughout the 1920s, investment bankers routinely submitted loan projects to Hughes and Secretary of Commerce Hoover for informal approval, thus reinforcing the close ties between business investment and foreign policy.

American oil, autos, farm machinery, and electrical equipment supplied a growing world market. Much of this expansion took place through the establishment of branch plants overseas by American companies. America's overall direct investment abroad increased from $3.8 billion in 1919 to $7.5 billion in 1929. Leading the American domination of the world market were General Electric, Ford, and Monsanto Chemical. American oil companies, with the support of the State Department, also challenged Great Britain's dominance in the oil fields of the Middle East and Latin America, forming powerful cartels with English firms.

The strategy of maximum freedom for private enterprise, backed by limited government advice and assistance, significantly boosted the power and profits of American overseas investors. But in Central and Latin America, in particular, aggressive U.S. investment also fostered chronically underdeveloped economies, dependent on a few staple crops (sugar, coffee, cocoa, bananas) grown for export. American investments in Latin America more than doubled between 1924 and 1929, from $1.5 billion to over $3.5 billion. A large part of this money went to taking over vital mineral resources, such as Chile's copper and Venezuela's oil. The growing wealth and power of U.S. companies made it more difficult for these nations to grow their own food or diversify their economies. United States economic dominance in the hemisphere also hampered the growth of democratic politics by favoring autocratic, military regimes that could be counted on to protect U.S. investments.

23.2.5 Weakened Agriculture, Ailing Industries

Amid prosperity and progress, there were large pockets of the country that lagged behind. Advances in real income and improvements in the standard of living for workers and farmers were uneven at best. In 1920, some 32 million Americans still lived on farms, out of a total population of 106 million. Yet during the 1920s, the farm sector failed to share in the general prosperity. The years 1914–1919 had been a kind of golden age for the nation's farmers. Increased wartime demand, along with the devastation of much of European agriculture, had led to record-high prices for many crops. When the war ended, however, American farmers began to suffer from a chronic worldwide surplus of such farm staples as cotton, hogs, and corn.

In the South, farmers' dependency on "King Cotton" deepened, as the region lagged further behind the rest of the nation in both agricultural diversity and standard of living. Cotton acreage expanded, as large and heavily mechanized farms opened up new land in Oklahoma, west Texas, and the Mississippi-Yazoo delta. In most of the South, from North Carolina to east Texas, small one- and two-mule cotton farms, most under 50 acres, still dominated the countryside. With few large urban centers and inadequate transportation, even those southern farmers who had access to capital found it extremely difficult to find reliable markets for vegetables, fruit, poultry, or dairy products. The number of white tenant farmers increased by 200,000 during the 1920s, while black tenantry declined slightly as a result of the Great Migration. Some 700,000 southern farmers, roughly half white and half black, still labored as sharecroppers. Modern conveniences such as electricity, indoor plumbing, automobiles, and phonographs remained far beyond the reach of the great majority of southern farmers. Widespread rural poverty, poor diet, and little access to capital meant the world of southern agriculture had changed very little since the days of the populist revolt in the 1890s.

The most important initiatives for federal farm relief were the McNary-Haugen bills, a series of complicated measures designed to prop up and stabilize farm prices. The basic idea, borrowed from the old populist proposals of the

1890s, was for the government to purchase farm surpluses and either store them until prices rose or sell them on the world market. President Coolidge viewed these measures as unwarranted federal interference in the economy and vetoed the McNary-Haugen Farm Relief bill of 1927 when it finally passed Congress. American farmers hoping to export produce abroad also suffered from the high tariffs imposed by European countries trying to protect their own devastated economies.

To be sure, some farmers thrived. Improved transportation and chain supermarkets allowed for a wider and more regular distribution of such foods as oranges, lemons, and fresh green vegetables. Citrus, dairy, and truck farmers in particular profited from the growing importance of national markets. Wheat production jumped more than 300 percent during the 1920s. Across the plains of Kansas, Nebraska, Colorado, Oklahoma, and Texas, wheat farmers brought the methods of industrial capitalism to the land. They hitched disc plows and combined harvester-threshers to gasoline-powered tractors, tearing up millions of acres of grassland to create a vast wheat factory. With prices averaging above $1 per bushel over the decade, mechanized farming created a new class of large-scale wheat entrepreneurs on the plains. Ida Watkins, the "Wheat Queen" of Haskell County, Kansas, made a profit of $75,000 from her 2,000 acres in 1926. Hickman Price needed 25 combines to harvest the wheat on his Plainview, Texas, farm—34,500 acres stretching over 54 square miles. But when the disastrous dust storms of the 1930s rolled across the grassless plains, the long-range environmental impact of destroying so much native vegetation became evident.

Overall, per capita farm income remained well below what it had been in 1919, and the gap between farm and nonfarm income widened. By 1929, the average income per person on farms was $223, compared with $870 for nonfarm workers. By the end of the decade, hundreds of thousands had quit farming altogether for jobs in mills and factories. And fewer farmers owned their land. In 1930, 42 percent of all farmers were tenants, compared with 37 percent in 1919.

Large sectors of American industry also failed to share in the decade's general prosperity. As oil and natural gas gained in importance, America's coal mines became a less important source of energy. A combination of shrinking demand, new mining technology, and a series of losing strikes reduced the coal labor force by one-quarter. The United Mine Workers, perhaps the strongest AFL union in 1920, with 500,000 members, had shrunk to a membership of 75,000 by 1928. Economic hardship was widespread in many mining communities dependent on coal, particularly in Appalachia and the southern Midwest. Those miners who did work earned lower hourly wages.

In textiles, shrinking demand and overcapacity (too many factories) were chronic problems. The women's fashions of the 1920s generally required less material than had

earlier fashions, and competition from synthetic fibers such as rayon depressed demand for cotton textiles. To improve profit margins, textile manufacturers in New England and other parts of the Northeast began a long-range shift of operations to the South, where nonunion shops and substandard wages became the rule. Older New England manufacturing centers such as Lawrence, Lowell, Nashua, Manchester, and Fall River were hard hit by this shift. The center of the American textile industry shifted permanently to the Piedmont region of North and South Carolina. By 1933, factories there employed nearly 70 percent of the workers in the industry.

23.3 The New Mass Culture

How did the new mass media reshape American culture?

New communications media remade American culture in the 1920s, and much of the new mass culture was exported to the rest of the economically developed world. The phrase "Roaring Twenties" captures the explosion of image- and sound-making machinery that came to dominate so much of American life. Movies, radio, new kinds of journalism, the recording industry, and a more sophisticated advertising industry were deeply connected with the new culture of consumption. They also encouraged the parallel emergence of celebrity as a defining element in modern life. As technologies of mass impression, the media established national standards and norms for much of our culture—habit, dress, language, sounds, and social behavior. Cultural traditionalists both in America and abroad found these new norms deeply disturbing, and the 1920s saw powerful collisions between newer and older values. To be sure, most working-class families had only limited access to the world of mass consumption—and many had only limited interest in it. But the new mass culture helped redefine the ideal of "the good life" and made the images, if not the substance, of it available to a national community.

23.3.1 Movie-Made America

The early movie industry, centered in New York and a few other big cities, had made moviegoing a regular habit for millions of Americans, especially immigrants and the working class. They flocked to cheap, storefront theaters, called nickelodeons, to watch short westerns, slapstick comedies, melodramas, and travelogues. By 1914, there were about 18,000 "movie houses" showing motion pictures, with more than 7 million daily admissions and $300 million in annual receipts. With the shift of the industry westward to Hollywood, movies entered a new phase of business expansion.

SEEING History

Creating Celebrity

A common definition for "celebrity" is one who is famous for being famous. Although politics, the arts, science, and the military have produced famous people for centuries, the celebrity is a twentieth-century phenomenon, one closely linked to the emergence of modern forms of mass media. In the 1920s, Hollywood's "star system," along with tabloid newspapers and the new profession of public relations, created the modern celebrity. Film producers were at first wary of identifying screen actors by name, but they soon discovered that promoting popular leading actors would boost the box office for their movies. The use of "close-ups" in movies and the fact that screen images were literally larger than life distinguished the images of film actors from, say, stage performers or opera singers.

Fans identified with their favorites in contradictory ways. Stars like Charlie Chaplin and Mary Pickford were like royalty, somehow beyond the realm of ordinary mortals. Yet audiences were also curious about the stars' private lives. Film studios took advantage of this curiosity by carefully controlling the public image of their stars through press releases, planting stories in newspapers, and carefully managing interviews and public appearances. Theda Bara, for example, one of

the biggest female stars of the 1920s, was best known for her "vamp" roles depicting sexually aggressive and exotic women. According to the publicity from Fox Pictures, she was of Egyptian background, offspring of "a sheik and a princess, given in mystic marriage to the Sphinx, fought over by nomadic tribesmen, clairvoyant, and insatiably lustful." In truth, Theodosia Goodman was born and raised in Cincinnati, the daughter of middle-class Jewish parents, and became a stage actress after two years of college. By the 1920s, film stars were essentially studio-owned-and-operated commodities, requiring enormous capital investment. And the new media universe of newspapers, magazines, radio, movies, and advertising was held together by the public fascination with, and the commercial power of, celebrities.

- **What visual themes strike you as most powerful in the accompanying images? How do they compare—in contrasts and parallels—with celebrity images of today?**

- **Why do you think male stars such as Valentino and Fairbanks were so often portrayed as exotic foreigners? How did these posters convey a more open and accepting attitude toward sexuality?**

CREATING CELEBRITY

Left: Everett Collection, Middle: Christie's Images/Bridgeman Images, Right: Everett Collection.

Large studios such as Paramount, Fox, Metro-Goldwyn-Mayer (MGM), Universal, and Warner Brothers dominated the business with longer and more expensively produced movies—feature films. These companies were founded and controlled by immigrants from Europe, all of whom had a talent for discovering and exploiting changes in popular tastes. Adolph Zukor, the Hungarian-born head of Paramount, had been a furrier in New York City. Warsaw-born Samuel Goldwyn, a founder of MGM, had been a glove salesman. William Fox, of Fox Pictures, born in Hungary and raised in New York, began as a garment cutter in Brooklyn. Most of the immigrant moguls had started in the business by buying or managing small movie theaters before beginning to produce films.

Each studio combined the three functions of production, distribution, and exhibition, and each controlled hundreds of movie theaters around the country. The era of silent films ended when Warner Brothers scored a huge hit in 1927 with *The Jazz Singer*, starring Al Jolson, which successfully introduced sound. New genres—musicals, gangster films, and screwball comedies—soon became popular. To maintain their hold on European markets, the major studios established production facilities abroad that used foreign actors for the "dubbing" of American films into other languages. The higher costs associated with "talkies" also increased the studios' reliance on Wall Street investors and banks for working capital.

At the heart of Hollywood's success was the star system and the accompanying cult of celebrity, both of which help define American popular culture to this day. For many in the audience, there was only a vague line separating the on-screen and off-screen adventures of the stars. Studio publicity, fan magazines, and gossip columns reinforced this ambiguity. Film idols, with their mansions, cars, parties, and private escapades, became the national experts on leisure and consumption. Their movies generally emphasized sexual themes and celebrated youth, athleticism, and the liberating power of consumer goods. Young Americans in particular looked to movies to learn how to dress, wear their hair, talk, or kiss.

Many Americans, however, particularly in rural areas and small towns, worried about Hollywood's impact on traditional sexual morality. They attacked the permissiveness associated with Hollywood life, and many states created censorship boards to screen movies before allowing them to be shown in theaters. To counter growing calls for government censorship, Hollywood's studios came up with a plan to censor themselves. In 1922, they hired Will Hays to head the Motion Picture Producers and Distributors of America. Hays was just what the immigrant moguls needed. An Indiana Republican, an elder in the Presbyterian Church, and former postmaster general under President Harding, he personified midwestern Protestant respectability. As the movie industry's czar, Hays lobbied against censorship laws, wrote pamphlets defending the movie business, and began setting guidelines for what could and could not be depicted on the screen. He insisted that movies be treated like any other industrial enterprise, because he understood the relationship between Hollywood's success and the growth of the nation's consumer culture.

23.3.2 Radio Broadcasting

In the fall of 1920, Westinghouse executive Harry P. Davis noticed that amateur broadcasts from the garage of an employee had attracted attention in the local Pittsburgh press. A department store advertised radio sets capable of picking up these "wireless concerts." Davis converted this amateur station to a stronger one at the Westinghouse main plant. Beginning with the presidential election returns that November, station KDKA offered regular nightly broadcasts that were probably heard by only a few hundred people. Radio broadcasting, begun as a service for selling cheap radio sets left over from World War I, would soon sweep the nation.

The "radio mania" of the early 1920s was a response to the new possibilities offered by broadcasting. Before KDKA, wireless technology had been of interest only to the military, the telephone industry, and a few thousand "ham" (amateur) operators who enjoyed communicating with each other. By 1923, nearly 600 stations had been licensed by the Department of Commerce, and about 600,000 Americans had bought radios. Early programs included live popular music, the playing of phonograph records, talks by college professors, church services, and news and weather reports. For millions of Americans, especially in rural areas and small towns, radio provided a new and exciting link to the larger national community of consumption.

Who would pay for radio programs? In the early 1920s, owners and operators of radio stations included radio equipment manufacturers, newspapers, department stores, state universities, cities, ethnic societies, labor unions, and churches. But by the end of the decade, commercial (or "toll") broadcasting emerged as the answer. The dominant corporations in the industry—General Electric, Westinghouse, Radio Corporation of America (RCA), and American Telephone and Telegraph (AT&T)—settled on the idea that advertisers would foot the bill for radio. Millions of listeners might be the consumers of radio shows, but sponsors were to be the customers. Sponsors advertised directly or indirectly to the mass audience through such shows as the *Eveready Hour*, the *Ipana Troubadours*, and the *Taystee Loafers*. AT&T leased its nationwide system of telephone wires to allow the linking of many stations into powerful radio networks, such as the National Broadcasting Company (NBC) in 1926 and the Columbia Broadcasting System (CBS) in 1928. The rise of network radio squeezed out many of the stations and programs aimed at ethnic communities or broadcast in languages other than English, thus promoting a more homogenized culture.

NBC and CBS led the way in creating popular radio programs that relied heavily on older cultural forms. The variety show, hosted by vaudeville comedians, became network radio's first important format. Radio's first truly national hit, *The Amos 'n' Andy Show* (1928), was a direct descendant of nineteenth-century "blackface" minstrel entertainment. Radio did more than any previous medium to publicize and commercialize once-isolated forms of American music such as country-and-western, blues, and jazz. Broadcasts of baseball and college football games proved especially popular. In 1930, some 600 stations were broadcasting to more than 12 million homes with radios, or roughly 40 percent of American families. By that time, all the elements that characterize the present American system of broadcasting—regular daily programming paid for and produced by commercial advertisers, national networks carrying shows across the nation, and mass ownership of receiver sets in American homes—were in place.

Radio broadcasting created a national community of listeners, just as motion pictures created one of viewers. Like movies, it also transcended national boundaries. Broadcasting had a powerful hemispheric impact. In both Canada and Mexico, governments established national broadcasting systems to bolster cultural and political nationalism. Yet American shows—and advertising—continued to dominate Canadian airwaves. Large private Mexican radio stations were often started in partnership with American corporations such as RCA, as a way to create demand for receiving sets. Language barriers limited the direct impact of U.S. broadcasts, but American advertisers became the backbone of commercial radio in Mexico. Radio broadcasting thus significantly amplified the influence of American commercialism throughout the hemisphere.

23.3.3 New Forms of Journalism

A new kind of newspaper, the tabloid, became popular in the postwar years. The *New York Daily News*, founded in 1919 by Joseph M. Patterson, was the first to develop the tabloid style. Its folded-in-half page size made it convenient to read on buses or subways. With a terse, lively reporting style that emphasized sex, scandal, and sports, *Daily News* circulation reached 400,000 in 1922 and 1.3 million by 1929. This success spawned a host of imitators in New York and elsewhere. New papers like the *Chicago Times* and the *Los Angeles Daily News* brought the tabloid style to cities across America, while some older papers, such as the *Denver Rocky Mountain News*, also adopted the new format. The circulation of existing dailies was little affected. Tabloids had instead discovered an audience of millions who had never read newspapers before. Most of these new readers

were poorly educated working-class city dwellers, many of whom were immigrants or children of immigrants.

The tabloid's most popular new feature was the gossip column, invented by Walter Winchell, who began writing his column "Your Broadway and Mine" for the *New York Daily Graphic* in 1924. Winchell described the secret lives of public figures with a distinctive, rapid-fire, slangy style that made the reader feel like an insider. He chronicled the connections among high society, show business stars, powerful politicians, and the underworld. By the end of the decade, scores of newspapers "syndicated" Winchell's column, making him the most widely read—and imitated—journalist in America. The tight connection between tabloid journalism and celebrity culture continues to this day.

Journalism followed the larger economic trend toward consolidation and merger. Newspaper chains like Hearst, Gannett, and Scripps-Howard flourished during the 1920s, producing a more standardized kind of journalism that could be found anywhere in the country. There were sizable increases in the number of these chains and in the percentage of total daily circulation that was chain-owned. By the early 1930s, the Hearst organization alone controlled 26 dailies in 18 cities, accounting for 14 percent of the nation's newspaper circulation. One of every four Sunday papers sold in America was owned by the Hearst group.

23.3.4 Advertising Modernity

A thriving advertising industry both reflected and encouraged the growing importance of consumer goods in American life. Previously, advertising had been confined mostly to staid newspapers and magazines and offered little more than basic product information. The most creative advertising was usually for dubious products, such as patent medicines. The successful efforts of the government's Committee on Public Information, set up to "sell" World War I to Americans, suggested that new techniques using modern communication media could convince people to buy a wide range of goods and services. As a profession, advertising reached a higher level of respectability, sophistication, and economic power in American life during the 1920s.

The larger ad agencies moved toward a more scientific approach by sponsoring market research and welcoming the language of psychology to their profession. Behavioral psychologists like John B. Watson argued that all human behavior could be shaped (or manipulated) by careful study and application of stimulus and response. Watson left his post at Harvard University for an executive position at the J. Walter Thompson advertising agency. The writings of Viennese psychoanalyst Sigmund Freud, especially his emphasis on the irrational in human behavior and the power of the sex

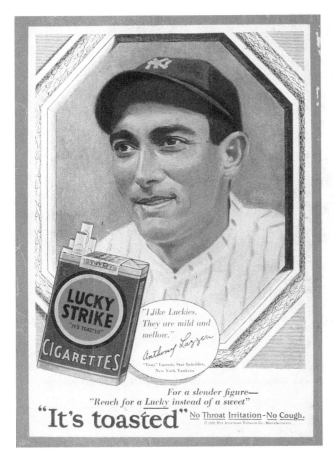

LUCKY STRIKE ADVERTISEMENT A 1928 advertisement for Lucky Strike cigarettes featured the image of baseball player Tony Lazzeri. Paid celebrity endorsements for consumer goods became a common practice in the post–WWI years. Tobacco companies were among the most aggressive purveyors of this new advertising strategy.

drive, were widely popularized in American magazines and universities. Advertisers began focusing on the needs, desires, and anxieties of the consumer, rather than on the qualities of the product. "There are certain things that most people believe," noted one ad agency executive in 1927. "The moment your copy is linked to one of those beliefs, more than half your battle is won."

Ad agencies and their clients invested extraordinary amounts of time, energy, and money trying to discover and, to some extent, shape those beliefs. Leading agencies such as Lord and Thomas in Chicago and J. Walter Thompson in New York combined knowledge gained from market research and consumer surveys with carefully prepared ad copy and graphics to sell their clients' wares. High-powered ad campaigns made new products like Fleischmann's Yeast, Kleenex, and Listerine household names across the country. Above all, advertising celebrated consumption itself as a positive good. In this sense, the new advertising ethic was a therapeutic one, promising that products would contribute to the buyer's physical, psychic, or emotional well-being.

Advertisers of the 1920s targeted women as never before. Research revealed that women were often the key decision makers for purchasing consumer durable goods, especially those associated with reducing household chores: refrigerators, vacuum cleaners, and washing machines. Advertisements increasingly appealed directly to working women buying make-up, clothing, phonographs, and automobiles. Advertisers helped define greater consumption by women as a fundamental component of the new consumer culture.

23.3.5 The Phonograph and the Recording Industry

Like radio and movies, the phonograph came into its own as a popular entertainment medium in the 1920s. Originally marketed in the 1890s, early phonographs used wax cylinders that could both record and replay. But the sound quality was poor, and the cylinders were difficult to handle. The convenient permanently grooved disc recordings introduced around World War I were eagerly snapped up by the public, even though the discs could not be used to make recordings at home. The success of records transformed the popular music business, displacing both cylinders and sheet music as the major source of music in the home. Dance crazes such as the foxtrot, tango, and grizzly bear, done to complex ragtime and Latin rhythms, boosted the record business tremendously. Dixieland jazz, which recorded well, also captured the public's fancy in the early 1920s, and records provided the music for new popular dances like the Charleston and the black bottom. In 1921, more than 200 companies produced some 2 million records, and annual record sales exceeded $100 million.

Record sales declined toward the end of the decade, due to competition from radio. But in a broader cultural sense, records continued to transform American popular culture. Record companies discovered lucrative regional and ethnic markets for country music, which appealed primarily to white Southerners, and blues and jazz, which appealed primarily to African Americans. Country musicians like the Carter Family and Jimmie Rodgers, and blues singers like Blind Lemon Jefferson, Ma Rainey, and Bessie Smith, had their performances put on records for the first time. Their records sold mainly in specialized "hillbilly" and "race" markets. Yet they were also played over the radio, and millions of Americans began to hear musical styles and performers previously isolated from the general population. Jazz records by such African American artists as Louis Armstrong and Duke Ellington found a wide audience overseas as well, and jazz emerged as a uniquely American cultural form with broad appeal around the globe. The combination of records and radio started an extraordinary cross-fertilization of American musical styles that continues to this day.

LOUIS ARMSTRONG AND HIS HOT FIVE This 1926 publicity photo shows Louis Armstrong and his Hot Five just after they made the historic recordings that established Armstrong as the most influential jazz soloist of the era. Armstrong also had a huge impact as a singer, and his popularity extended to all racial groups.

Louis Armstrong's Hot Five/Getty Images.

23.3.6 Sports and Celebrity

During the 1920s, spectator sports enjoyed an unprecedented growth in popularity and profitability. As radio, newspapers, magazines, and newsreels exhaustively documented their exploits, athletes took their place alongside movie stars in defining a new culture of celebrity. Big-time sports, like the movies, entered a new corporate phase. Yet it was the athletes themselves, performing extraordinary feats on the field and transcending their often-humble origins, who attracted millions of new fans. The image of the modern athlete—rich, famous, glamorous, and often a rebel against social convention—came into its own during the decade.

Major League Baseball had more fans than any other sport, and its greatest star, George Herman "Babe" Ruth, embodied the new celebrity athlete. Aided by the new "live ball," Ruth's prodigious home-run hitting completely changed baseball strategy and attracted legions of new fans to the sport. Ruth was a larger-than-life character off the field as well. In New York, media capital of the nation, newspapers and magazines chronicled his enormous appetites—for food, whiskey, expensive cars, and big-city nightlife. He hobnobbed with politicians, movie stars, and gangsters, and he regularly visited sick children in hospitals.

Ruth became the first athlete avidly sought by manufacturers for celebrity endorsement of their products.

Ruth's impact helped the game recover from the serious public relations disaster of the "Black Sox" scandal. In 1919, eight members of the poorly paid Chicago White Sox had become involved in a scheme to "throw" the World Series in exchange for large sums of money from gamblers. Although they were acquitted in the courts, baseball commissioner Judge Kenesaw Mountain Landis, looking to remove any taint of gambling from the sport, banned the accused players for life.

Baseball attendance exploded during the 1920s, reaching a one-year total of 10 million in 1929. The attendance boom prompted urban newspapers to increase their baseball coverage, and the larger dailies featured separate sports sections. The best sportswriters, such as Grantland Rice, Heywood Broun, and Ring Lardner, brought a poetic sensibility to descriptions of the games and their stars. William K. Wrigley, owner of the Chicago Cubs, discovered that by letting local radio stations broadcast his team's games, the club could win new fans, especially among housewives.

Among those excluded from Major League Baseball were African Americans, who had been banned from the game by an 1890s "gentleman's agreement" among owners.

BABE RUTH Babe Ruth, baseball's biggest star, at bat in the 1920s. Ruth's home run hitting revolutionized the game and made him perhaps the best-known celebrity in America.

Sueddeutsche Zeitung Photo/Alamy Stock Photo.

During the 1920s, black baseball players and entrepreneurs developed a world of their own, with several professional and semiprofessional leagues catering to expanding African American communities in cities. The largest of these was the Negro National League, organized in 1920 by Andrew "Rube" Foster. Black ball clubs also played exhibitions against, and frequently defeated, teams of white major leaguers. African Americans had their own baseball heroes, such as Josh Gibson and Satchel Paige, who no doubt would have been stars in the major leagues if not for racial exclusion.

The new media configuration of the 1920s created heroes in other sports as well. Radio broadcasts and increased journalistic coverage made college football a big-time sport. Teams like Notre Dame, located in sleepy South Bend, Indiana, but coached by the colorful Knute Rockne, could gain a wide national following. The center of college football shifted from the old elite schools of the Ivy League to the big universities of the Midwest and Pacific Coast, where most of the players were second-generation Irish, Italians, and Slavs. Athletes such as boxers Jack Dempsey and Gene Tunney, tennis players Bill Tilden and Helen Wills, golfer Bobby Jones, and swimmers Gertrude Ederle and Johnny Weissmuller became household names who brought legions of new fans to their sports.

23.3.7 A New Morality?

Movie stars, radio personalities, sports heroes, and popular musicians became the elite figures in a new culture of celebrity defined by the mass media. They were the model for achievement in the new age. Great events and abstract issues were made real through movie close-ups, radio interviews, and tabloid photos. The new media relentlessly created and disseminated images that are still familiar today: Babe Ruth trotting around the bases after hitting a home run; the wild celebrations that greeted Charles Lindbergh after he completed the first solo transatlantic airplane flight in 1927; the smiling gangster Al Capone, bantering with reporters who transformed his criminal exploits into important news events.

Images do not tell the whole story, however. Consider one of the most enduring images of the "Roaring Twenties," the flapper. She was usually portrayed on-screen, in novels, and in the press as a young, sexually aggressive woman with bobbed hair, rouged cheeks, and short skirt. She loved to dance to jazz music, enjoyed smoking cigarettes, and drank bootleg liquor in cabarets and dance halls. She could also be competitive, assertive, and a good pal. As writer Zelda Fitzgerald put it in 1924: "I think a woman gets more happiness out of being gay, light-hearted, unconventional, mistress of her own fate. . . . I want [my daughter] to be a flapper, because flappers are brave and gay and beautiful."

Was the flapper a genuine representative of the 1920s? Did she embody the "new morality" that was so widely discussed and chronicled in the media of the day? The flapper certainly did exist, but she was neither as new nor as widespread a phenomenon as the image would suggest. The delight in sensuality, personal pleasure, and rhythmically complex dance and music had long been key elements of subcultures on the fringes of middle-class society: bohemian enclaves, communities of political radicals, African American ghettos, working-class dance halls. In the 1920s, these activities became normative for a growing number of white middle-class Americans, including women. Jazz, sexual experimentation, heavy makeup, and cigarette smoking spread to college campuses.

Several sources, most of them rooted in earlier years, can be found for the increased sexual openness of the 1920s. Troops in the armed forces during World War I had been exposed to government-sponsored sex education.

New psychological and social theories like those of Havelock Ellis, Ellen Key, and Freud stressed the central role of sexuality in human experience, maintaining that sex is a positive, healthy impulse that, if repressed, could damage mental and emotional health. The pioneering efforts of Margaret Sanger in educating women about birth control had begun before World War I. (See Chapter 21.) In the 1920s, Sanger campaigned vigorously—through her journal *Birth Control Review*, in books, and on speaking tours—to make contraception freely available to all women.

Sociological surveys also suggested that genuine changes in sexual behavior began in the prewar years among both married and single women. Katherine Bement Davis's pioneering study of 2,200 middle-class women, carried out in 1918 and published in 1929, revealed that most used contraceptives and described sexual relations in positive terms. A 1938 survey of 777 middle-class females found that among those born between 1890 and 1900, 74 percent were virgins before marriage; for those born after 1910, the figure dropped to 32 percent. Women born after the turn of the century were twice as likely to have had premarital sex as those born before 1900. The critical change took place in the generation that came of age in the late teens and early twenties. By the 1920s, male and female "morals" were becoming more alike.

The emergence of homosexual subcultures also reflected the newly permissive atmosphere of the postwar years. Although such subcultures had been a part of big-city life since at least the 1890s, they had been largely confined to working-class saloons associated with the urban underworld. By the 1920s, the word "homosexual" had gained currency as a scientific term for describing romantic love between women or between men, and middle-class enclaves of self-identified homosexuals took root in cities like New York, Chicago, and San Francisco. Often organized around speakeasies, private clubs, tearooms, and masquerade balls, these venues also attracted heterosexual tourists and those looking to experiment with their sexuality, as well as homosexuals, for whom they served as important social centers. Even if these enclaves provided some sense of community and safety for homosexuals, the repressive shadow of the larger culture was never far away. Psychologists of the era, with Freud in the lead, condemned "perversion" as a mental illness and counseled the need for a "cure."

THE "NEW WOMAN" A woman in a man's shirt and necktie poses for an advertisement for ladies' golf attire. Her boyish, almost androgynous look reflects one way that notions of the "new woman" intersected with the worlds of fashion and advertising.

Everett Collection Historical/Alamy Stock Photo.

23.4 Modernity and Traditionalism

What explains the backlash against social and cultural change in the 1920s?

One measure of the profound cultural changes of the 1920s was the hostility and opposition expressed toward them by large sectors of the American public. Deep and persistent tensions, with ethnic, racial, and geographical overtones, characterized much of the decade's politics. The postwar Red Scare had given strength to the forces of antiradicalism in politics and traditionalism in culture. Resentments over the growing power of urban culture—on full display in Hollywood movies and modern advertising, and over the airwaves—were very strong in rural and small-town America. Several trends and mass movements reflected this anger and the longing for a less complicated past.

23.4.1 Prohibition

The Eighteenth Amendment, banning the manufacture, sale, and transportation of alcoholic beverages, took effect in January 1920. Prohibition was the culmination of a long campaign that associated drinking with the degradation of working-class family life and the worst evils of urban politics. Supporters, a coalition of women's temperance groups, middle-class progressives, and rural Protestants, hailed the new law as "a noble experiment." It became clear rather quickly that enforcing the new law would be extremely difficult. The **Volstead Act** of 1919 established a federal

Prohibition Bureau to enforce the Eighteenth Amendment. Yet the bureau was severely understaffed, with only about 1,500 agents to police the entire country.

The public demand for alcohol, especially in the big cities, led to widespread lawbreaking. Drinking was such a routine part of life for so many Americans that "bootlegging" quickly became a big business. Illegal stills and breweries, as well as liquor smuggled in from Canada, supplied the needs of those Americans who continued to drink. Nearly every town and city had at least one "speakeasy," where people could drink and enjoy music and other entertainment. Local law enforcement personnel, especially in the cities, were easily bribed to overlook these illegal establishments. By the early 1920s, many eastern states no longer made even a token effort at enforcing the law.

Liquor continued to be illegal, so Prohibition gave an enormous boost to violent organized crime. The profits to be made in the illegal liquor trade dwarfed those of the traditional sources of criminal income—gambling, prostitution, and robbery. The pattern of organized crime in the 1920s closely resembled the larger trends in American business: Smaller operations gave way to larger and more complex combinations. Successful organized crime figures, like Chicago's Al "Scarface" Capone, became celebrities in their own right and received heavy coverage in the mass media. Capone himself shrewdly used the business rhetoric of the new era to defend himself: "Everybody calls me a racketeer. I call myself a businessman. When I sell liquor it's bootlegging. When my patrons serve it on a silver tray on Lake Shore Drive, it's hospitality."

Organized crime, assisted by its huge profits from liquor, also made significant inroads into legitimate businesses, labor unions, and city government, especially in large cities. By the time Congress and the states ratified the Twenty-first Amendment in 1933, repealing Prohibition, organized crime was a permanent feature of American life. Prohibition did, in fact, significantly reduce per capita consumption of alcohol. In 1910, annual per capita consumption stood at 2.6 gallons; in 1934, the figure was less than 1 gallon.

Yet among young people, especially college students, the excitement associated with speakeasies and lawbreaking contributed to increased drinking during Prohibition.

23.4.2 Immigration Restriction

Sentiment for restricting immigration, which had been growing since the late nineteenth century, reached its peak immediately after World War I. Barriers against Asian immigrants were already in place with the Chinese Exclusion Act of 1882 and the so-called Gentleman's Agreement with Japan in 1907. The movement to curb European immigration reflected the growing preponderance after 1890 of "new immigrants"—those from southern and eastern Europe—over the immigrants from northern and western Europe, who had predominated before 1890. Between 1891 and 1920, roughly 10.5 million immigrants arrived from southern and eastern Europe. This was nearly twice as many as arrived during the same years from northern and western Europe. (See Figure 23.3.)

The "new immigrants" were mostly Catholic and Jewish, and they were darker-skinned than the "old immigrants." To many old-stock Americans, they seemed more exotic, more foreign, and less willing and able to assimilate

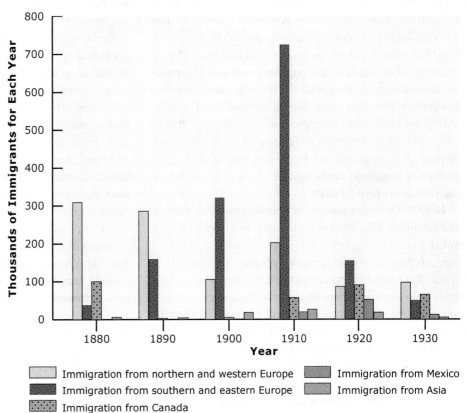

Figure 23.3 IMMIGRATION TRENDS TO THE UNITED STATES BY CONTINENT/ REGION, 1880–1930

Legend:
- Immigration from northern and western Europe
- Immigration from southern and eastern Europe
- Immigration from Canada
- Immigration from Mexico
- Immigration from Asia

Based on (1949) *Historical statistics of the United States, 1789-1945: a supplement to the Statistical abstract of the United States, Part 1.* United States. Bureau of the Census, U.S. Govt. Printing Office.

the nation's political and cultural values. They were also relatively poorer, more physically isolated in the nation's cities, and less politically strong than earlier immigrants. In the 1890s, the anti-Catholic American Protective Association called for a curb on immigration, and by exploiting the economic depression of that decade, it reached a membership of 2.5 million. In 1894, a group of prominent Harvard graduates, including Senator Henry Cabot Lodge (R-Massachusetts) and John Fiske, founded the Immigration Restriction League, providing an influential forum for the fears of the nation's elite. The league used newer scientific arguments, based on a flawed application of Darwinian evolutionary theory and genetics, to support its call for immigration restriction. The new immigration, Lodge argued, "is bringing to the country people whom it is very difficult to assimilate and who do not promise well for the standard of civilization in the United States."

Theories of scientific racism, which had become more popular in the early 1900s, reinforced anti-immigrant bias and distorted genetic theory to argue that America was committing "race suicide." Eugenicists, who enjoyed considerable vogue in those years, held that heredity determined almost all of a person's capacities and that genetic inferiority predisposed people to crime and poverty. Such pseudoscientific thinking sought to explain historical and social development solely as a function of "racial" differences.

Against this background, the war and its aftermath provided the final push for the restriction of European immigration. The "100 percent American" fervor of the war years fueled nativist passions. So did the Red Scare of 1919–1920, which linked foreigners with Bolshevism and radicalism of all kinds in the popular mind-set. The postwar depression coincided with the resumption of massive immigration, bringing much hostile comment on the relationship between rising unemployment and the new influx of foreigners. The American Federation of Labor proposed stopping all immigration for two years. Sensational press coverage of organized crime figures, many of them Italian or Jewish, also played a part.

In 1921, Congress passed the **Immigration Act**, setting a maximum of 357,000 new immigrants each year. Quotas limited annual immigration from any European country to 3 percent of the number of its natives counted in the 1910 U.S. Census. But restrictionists complained that the new law still allowed too many southern and eastern Europeans in, especially since the northern and western Europeans did not fill their quotas. The Reed-Johnson National Origins Act of 1924 revised the quotas to 2 percent of the number of foreign-born counted for each nationality in the census for 1890, when far fewer southern or eastern Europeans were present in the United States. The maximum total allowed each year was also cut to 164,000. A *Los Angeles Times* headline expressed both the fundamental premise and flawed science of the new law: "Nordic Victory Is Seen in Drastic Restrictions."

The 1924 National Origins Act in effect limited immigration to white Europeans eligible for immigration by country of origin (nationality), while it divided the rest of the world into "colored races" (black, mulatto, Chinese, and Indian) who were ineligible for immigration. These new restrictions dovetailed with two recent Supreme Court decisions, *Ozawa v. United States* (1922) and *United States v. Thind* (1923), in which the Court held that Japanese and Asian Indians, respectively, were unassimilable aliens and racially ineligible for U.S. citizenship. By the 1920s, American law had thus created the peculiar new racial category of "Asian" and codified the principle of racial exclusion in immigration and naturalization law.

23.4.3 The Ku Klux Klan

If immigration restriction was resurgent nativism's most significant legislative expression, a revived Ku Klux Klan (KKK) was its most effective mass movement. The original Klan had been formed in the Reconstruction South as an instrument of white racial terror against newly freed slaves. (See Chapter 17.) It had died out in the 1870s. The new Klan, born in Stone Mountain, Georgia, in 1915, was inspired by D. W. Griffith's racist spectacle *The Birth of a Nation*, a film released in that year depicting the original KKK as a heroic organization. The new Klan patterned itself on the secret rituals and antiblack hostility of its predecessor, and until 1920, it was limited to a few local chapters in Georgia and Alabama.

When Hiram W. Evans, a dentist from Dallas, became imperial wizard of the Klan in 1922, he transformed the organization. Evans hired professional fund-raisers and publicists, and directed an effective recruiting scheme that paid a commission to sponsors of new members. The Klan advocated "100 percent Americanism" and "the faithful maintenance of White Supremacy." It staunchly supported the enforcement of Prohibition, and it attacked birth control and Darwinism. The new Klan made a special target of the Roman Catholic Church, labeling it a hostile and dangerous alien power and claiming that their allegiance to the Pope made Catholics unfit for citizenship.

The new Klan also presented itself as the righteous defender of the embattled traditional values of small-town Protestant America. Ironically, to build its membership rolls, it relied heavily on the publicity, public relations, and business techniques associated with modern urban culture. By 1924, the new Klan counted more than 3 million members across the country. Its slogan, "Native, White, Protestant Supremacy," proved especially attractive in the Midwest and South, including many cities. Klansmen boycotted businesses, threatened families, and sometimes resorted to violence—public whippings, arson, and lynching—against their chosen enemies. The Klan's targets sometimes included white Protestants accused of sexual promiscuity, blasphemy, or drunkenness, but most victims were African Americans,

Catholics, and Jews. Support for Prohibition enforcement probably united Klansmen more than any single issue.

On another level, the Klan was a popular social movement, a defensive bastion against forces of modernity. Many members were more attracted by the Klan's spectacular social events and its efforts to reinvigorate community life than by its attacks on those considered outsiders. Perhaps a half-million women joined the Women of the Ku Klux Klan, and women constituted nearly half of the Klan membership in some states. Klanswomen drew on family and community traditions, such as church suppers, kin reunions, and gossip campaigns, to defend themselves and their families against what they saw as corruption and immorality. The Klan's power was strong in many communities precisely because it fit so comfortably into the everyday life of white Protestants.

At its height, the Klan also became a powerful force in Democratic Party politics, and it had a strong presence among delegates to the 1924 Democratic National Convention. The Klan began to fade in 1925, when its former Indiana leader, Grand Dragon D. C. Stephenson, was indicted for the abduction, kidnapping, and murder of a young white woman. One of the Klan's most powerful national figures, Stephenson was found guilty, destroying much of the Klan's reputation for upholding the law and protecting white womanhood. With one of its most famous leaders disgraced and in jail, the new Klan rapidly lost members and influence.

23.4.4 Fundamentalism in Religion

Paralleling political nativism in the 1920s was the growth of religious fundamentalism. In many eastern Protestant churches, congregations focused less on religious practice and worship than on progressive social and reform activities in the larger community. By the early 1920s, a fundamentalist revival had developed in reaction to these tendencies, particularly in the South and Midwest. The fundamentalists emphasized a literal reading of the Bible, and they rejected the tenets of modern science as inconsistent with the revealed word of God. Fundamentalist publications and Bible colleges flourished, particularly among southern Baptists.

One special target of the fundamentalists was the theory of evolution, first set forth by Darwin in his landmark work *The Origin of Species* (1859). Based around fossil evidence, evolutionary theory suggested that, over time, many species had become extinct and new ones had emerged through the process of natural selection. These ideas directly contradicted the account in the Book of Genesis of one fixed creation. Although most Protestant clergymen had long since found ways of blending the scientific theory with their theology, fundamentalists launched an attack on the teaching of Darwinism in schools and universities. By 1925, five southern state legislatures had passed laws restricting the teaching of evolution.

A young biology teacher, John T. Scopes, deliberately broke the Tennessee law prohibiting the teaching of Darwinism in 1925, in order to challenge it in court. The resulting trial that summer in Dayton, a small town near Chattanooga, drew international attention to the controversy. Scopes's defense team included attorneys from the American Civil Liberties Union and Clarence Darrow, the most famous trial lawyer in America. The prosecution was led by William Jennings Bryan, the old Democratic standard-bearer who had thrown himself into the fundamentalist and antievolutionist cause. Held in a circus atmosphere in sweltering heat, the trial attracted thousands of reporters and partisans to Dayton and was broadcast across the nation by the radio. (See Communities *in* Conflict.)

THE REVIVED KU KLUX KLAN The Royal Riders of the Red Robe and the Ladies of the Invisible Empire, branch groups of the Ku Klux Klan (KKK), at a night gathering, 1918. The revived Klan was a powerful presence in scores of American communities during the early 1920s, especially among native-born white Protestants, who feared cultural and political change. In addition to preaching "100 percent Americanism," local Klan chapters also served a social function for members and their families.

Hulton Archive/Getty Images.

Communities *in* Conflict

The Scopes Trial in Dayton, Tennessee

"The case has [become] a battle-royal between unbelief . . . and the defenders of the Christian faith."

The 1925 trial of John T. Scopes, a Tennessee high school science teacher arrested for teaching evolution, captured national attention. Scopes's guilt was never challenged, even by his defense team; the state's antievolution statute itself was on trial. Tennessee's case was argued by William Jennings Bryan, the aging stalwart of Populism, three-time Democratic presidential nominee, and hero to the growing legion of rural and small-town evangelical Christians. The defense, financed by the American Civil Liberties Union, was led by Chicago attorney Clarence Darrow, a religious skeptic and a labor and criminal defense lawyer long associated with radical causes.

The most electrifying moment of the trial came when Darrow put Bryan on the stand as an expert witness on the Bible. Although the judge expunged the testimony from the record, the wide press coverage proved embarrassing to Bryan and perhaps unfairly cemented his reputation as an antimodern rube. Bryan's criticism of Darwinian theory was in fact more sophisticated than his critics acknowledged. Bryan in particular objected to the use of evolutionary doctrine as scientific justification for Social Darwinism, such as when eugenicists argued for selectively breeding human beings. After Bryan's

testimony, Darrow, wanting to have the last word, asked the judge to instruct the jury to bring in a guilty verdict, thus making closing arguments unnecessary. The first excerpt is from the closing argument Bryan never had a chance to give. When Bryan died three days after the trial, H. L. Mencken, a reporter for the *Baltimore Sun* and Bryan's most caustic critic, wrote a final assessment of "The Great Commoner," from which the second excerpt originates.

The clash between Bryan and Mencken embodied many of the profound cultural tensions that defined the 1920s. Today's conflicts over the teaching of "creationism" and "intelligent design," disputes over the authority of state and local boards to set curricula or choose textbooks, and discussions about the relevance of First Amendment protections in schools all echo the sharp clashes heard in 1925.

- **How does Bryan link his critique of science and scientific thinking to recent world events?**

- **Why, in Bryan's view, does public school education require a Christian component?**

- **From Mencken's perspective, how did Bryan exploit evangelical Christianity for political purposes?**

- **Do you think Mencken's view has merit?**

William Jennings Bryan's Undelivered Speech to the Jury

Science is a magnificent force, but it is not a teacher of morals. It can perfect machinery, but it adds no moral restraints to protect society from the misuse of the machine. It can also build gigantic intellectual ships, but it constructs no moral rudders for the control of storm tossed human vessels. It not only fails to supply the spiritual element needed but some of its unproven hypotheses rob the ship of its compass and thus endanger its cargo. In war, science has proven itself an evil genius; it has made war more terrible than it ever was before. Man used to be content to slaughter his fellowmen on a single plane—the earth's surface. Science has taught him to go down into the water and shoot up from below and to go up into the clouds and shoot down from above, thus making the battlefield three times as bloody as it was before; but science does not teach brotherly love. Science has made war so hellish that civilization was about to commit suicide; and now we are told that newly discovered instruments of destruction will make the cruelties of the late war seem trivial in comparison with the cruelties of wars that may come in the future. If civilization is to be saved from the wreckage threatened by intelligence not consecrated by love,

it must be saved by the moral code of the meek and lowly Nazarene. His teachings, and His teachings, alone, can solve the problems that vex the heart and perplex the world. . . .

It is for the jury to determine whether this attack upon the Christian religion shall be permitted in the public schools of Tennessee by teachers employed by the state and paid out of the public treasury. This case is no longer local, the defendant ceases to play an important part. The case has assumed the proportions of a battle-royal between unbelief that attempts to speak through so-called science and the defenders of the Christian faith, speaking through the legislators of Tennessee. It is again a choice between God and Baal; it is also a renewal of the issue in Pilate's court. . . .

Again force and love meet face to face, and the question, "What shall I do with Jesus?" must be answered. A bloody, brutal doctrine—Evolution—demands, as the rabble did nineteen hundred years ago, that He be crucified. That cannot be the answer of this jury representing a Christian state and sworn to uphold the laws of Tennessee. Your answer will be heard throughout the world; it is eagerly awaited by a praying multitude. If the law is nullified, there will be rejoicing wherever God is repudiated, the savior scoffed at and the Bible ridiculed. Every unbeliever of every kind and degree will be happy. If, on the other hand, the law is upheld and the religion of the school children protected, millions of Christians will call you blessed and, with hearts full of gratitude to God, will sing again that grand old song of triumph: "Faith of our fathers, living still, In spite of dungeon, fire and sword; O how our hearts beat high with joy Whene'er we hear that glorious word—Faith of our fathers—Holy faith; We will be true to thee till death!"

Source: William Jennings Bryan, *Bryan's Last Speech: Undelivered Speech to the Jury in the Scopes Trial.* Oklahoma City: Sunlight Publishing Society, 1925.

H. L. Mencken in the *Baltimore Evening Sun* (July 27, 1925)

One day it dawned on me that Bryan, after all, was an evangelical Christian only by sort of afterthought—that his career in this world, and the glories thereof, had actually come to an end before he ever began whooping for Genesis. So I came to this conclusion: that what really moved him was a lust for revenge. The men of the cities had destroyed him and made a mock of him; now he would lead the yokels against them. Various facts clicked into the theory, and I hold it still. The hatred in the old man's burning eyes was not for the enemies of God; it was for the enemies of Bryan.

Thus he fought his last fight, eager only for blood. It quickly became frenzied and preposterous, and after that pathetic. All sense departed from him. He bit right and left, like a dog with rabies. He descended to demagogy so dreadful that his very associates blushed. His one yearning was to keep his yokels heated up—to lead his forlorn mob against the foe. That foe, alas, refused to be alarmed. It insisted upon seeing the battle as a comedy. Even Darrow, who knew better, occasionally yielded to the prevailing spirit. Finally, he lured poor Bryan into a folly almost incredible.

I allude to his astounding argument against the notion that man is a mammal. I am glad I heard it, for otherwise I'd never believe it. There stood the man who had been thrice a candidate for the Presidency of the Republic—and once, I believe, elected—there he stood in the glare of the world, uttering stuff that a boy of eight would laugh at! The artful Darrow led him on: he repeated it, ranted for it, bellowed it in his cracked voice. A tragedy, indeed! He came into life a hero, a Galahad, in bright and shining armor. Now he was passing out a pathetic fool.

But what of his life? Did he accomplish any useful thing? Was he, in his day, of any dignity as a man, and of any value to his fellow-men? I doubt it. Bryan, at his best, was simply a magnificent job-seeker. The issues that he bawled about usually meant nothing to him. He was ready to abandon them whenever he could make votes by doing so, and to take up new ones at a moment's notice. For years he evaded Prohibition as dangerous; then he embraced it as profitable. At the Democratic National Convention last year he was on both sides, and distrusted by both. In his last great battle there was only a baleful and ridiculous malignancy. If he was pathetic, he was also disgusting.

Bryan was a vulgar and common man, a cad undiluted. He was ignorant, bigoted, self-seeking, blatant and dishonest. His career brought him into contact with the first men of his time; he preferred the company of rustic ignoramuses. It was hard to believe, watching him at Dayton, that he had traveled, that he had been received in civilized societies, that he had been a high officer of state. He seemed only a poor clod like those around him, deluded by a childish theology, full of an almost pathological hatred of all learning, all human dignity, all beauty, all fine and noble things. He was a peasant come home to the dung-pile. Imagine a gentleman, and you have imagined everything that he was not.

Source: *Baltimore Sun.* All Rights Reserved.

The Scopes "monkey trial"—so called because fundamentalists trivialized Darwin's theory into a claim that humans were descended from monkeys—became one of the most publicized and definitive moments of the decade. Scopes's guilt was never in question. The jury convicted him quickly, although the verdict was later thrown out on a technicality. The struggle over the teaching of evolution continued in an uneasy stalemate; state statutes were not repealed, but prosecutions for teaching evolution ceased. Fundamentalism, a religious creed and a cultural defense against the uncertainties of modern life, continued to have a strong appeal for millions of Americans.

23.5 Promises Postponed

Which Americans were less likely to share in postwar prosperity and why?

The prosperity of the 1920s was unevenly distributed and enjoyed across America. Older progressive reform movements that had pointed out inequities faltered in the conservative political climate. But the new era did inspire a range of critics deeply troubled by unfulfilled promises in American life. Feminists sought to redefine their movement in the wake of the suffrage victory. Mexican immigration to the United States shot up, and in the burgeoning Mexican

American communities of the Southwest and Midwest, economic and social conditions were very difficult. African Americans, bitterly disappointed by their treatment during and after the Great War, turned to new political and cultural strategies. Many American intellectuals found themselves deeply alienated from the temper and direction of modern American society.

23.5.1 Feminism in Transition

The achievement of suffrage removed the central issue that had given cohesion to the disparate forces of female reform activism. In addition, female activists of all persuasions found themselves swimming against a national tide of hostility to political idealism. During the 1920s, the women's movement split into two main wings over a fundamental disagreement about female identity. Should activists stress women's differences from men—their vulnerability and the double burden of work and family—and continue to press for protective legislation, such as laws that limited the length of the workweek for women? Or should they emphasize the ways that women were like men—sharing similar aspirations—and push for full legal and civil equality?

In 1920, the National American Woman Suffrage Association reorganized itself as the **League of Women Voters**. The league represented the historical mainstream of the suffrage movement, those who believed that the vote for women would bring a nurturing sensibility and a reform vision to American politics. This view was rooted in politicized domesticity, the notion that women had a special role to play in bettering society: improving conditions for working women, abolishing child labor, humanizing prisons and mental hospitals, and serving the urban poor. Most League members continued working in a variety of reform organizations, and the League itself concentrated on educating the new female electorate, encouraging women to run for office, and supporting laws for the protection of women and children.

A newer, smaller, and more militant group was the National Woman's Party (NWP), founded in 1916 by combative suffragist Alice Paul. The NWP downplayed the significance of suffrage and argued that women were still subordinate to men in every facet of life. The NWP opposed protective legislation for women, claiming that such laws reinforced sex stereotyping and prevented women from competing with men in many fields. Largely representing the interests of professional women and businesswomen, the NWP focused on passage of a brief Equal Rights Amendment (ERA) to the Constitution, introduced in Congress in 1923. Written by Paul, the amendment stated simply: "Men and women shall have equal rights throughout the United States and every place subject to its jurisdiction. Congress shall have power to enforce this article by appropriate legislation."

Much of the older generation of women reformers opposed the ERA as elitist, arguing that far more women benefited from protective laws than were injured by them. Mary Anderson, director of the Women's Bureau in the Department of Labor, argued that "[w]omen who are wage earners, with one job in the factory and another in the home, have little time and energy left to carry on the fight to better their economic status. They need the help of other women and they need labor laws." ERA supporters countered that maximum-hours laws and laws prohibiting women from night work prevented women from getting many lucrative jobs. M. Carey Thomas, president of Bryn Mawr College, defended the ERA with language reminiscent of laissez-faire: "How much better by one blow to do away with discriminating against women in work, salaries, promotion and opportunities to compete with men in a fair field with no favour on either side."

Most women's groups did not think there was a "fair field." Positions solidified. The League of Women Voters, the National Consumers' League, and the Women's Trade Union League opposed the ERA. ERA supporters generally stressed individualism, competition, and the abstract language of "equality" and "rights." ERA opponents emphasized the grim reality of industrial exploitation and the concentration of women workers in low-paying jobs in which they did not compete directly with men. ERA advocates dreamed of the labor market as it might be, one in which women might have the widest opportunity. Anti-ERA forces looked at the labor market as it was, insisting it was more important to protect women from existing exploitation. The NWP campaign failed to get the ERA passed by Congress, but the debates it sparked would be echoed during the feminist movement of the 1970s, when the ERA became a central political goal of a resurgent feminism.

A small number of professional women made real gains in the fields of real estate, banking, and journalism. The press regularly announced new "firsts" for women, such as Amelia Earhart's 1928 airplane flight across the Atlantic. Anne O'Hare McCormick won recognition as the "first lady of American journalism" for her reporting and editorial columns in the *New York Times*. In 1900, less than 18 percent of employed women worked in clerical, managerial, sales, and professional areas. By 1930, the number was 44 percent. But studies showed that most of these women were clustered in the low-paying areas of typing, stenography, bookkeeping, cashiering, and sales clerking. Men still dominated in the higher-paid and managerial white-collar occupations.

The most significant, if limited, victory for feminist reformers was the 1921 **Sheppard-Towner Act**, which established the first federally funded health care program, providing matching funds for states to set up prenatal and child health care centers. These centers also provided public health nurses for house calls. Although hailed as a genuine reform breakthrough, especially for women in rural and isolated communities, the act aroused much opposition. Many Republicans, including President Harding, had supported it as a way to curry favor with newly enfranchised women voters. Their support faded when it became clear that there was little "gender gap" in voting patterns. The NWP disliked Sheppard-Towner for its assumption that all women were mothers. Birth control advocates such as Margaret Sanger complained that contraception was not part of the program. The American Medical Association (AMA) objected to government-sponsored health care and to nurses who functioned outside the supervision of physicians. By 1929, largely as a result of intense AMA lobbying, Congress cut off funds for the program.

23.5.2 Mexican Immigration

While immigration restriction sharply cut the flow of new arrivals from Europe, the 1920s also brought a dramatic influx of Mexicans to the United States. Mexican immigration, which was not included in the immigration laws of 1921 and 1924, had picked up substantially after the outbreak of the Mexican Revolution in 1911, when politically inspired violence and economic hardships provided incentives to cross the border to *El Norte*. According to the U.S. Immigration Service, an estimated 459,000 Mexicans entered the United States between 1921 and 1930, more than double the number for the previous decade. (See Figure 23.4.)

The primary pull was the tremendous agricultural expansion occurring in the American Southwest. Irrigation

and large-scale agribusiness had begun transforming California's Imperial and San Joaquin valleys from arid desert into lucrative fruit and vegetable fields. Cotton pickers were needed in the vast plantations of Lower Rio Grande Valley in Texas and the Salt River Valley in Arizona. The sugar beet fields of Michigan, Minnesota, and Colorado attracted many Mexican farmworkers. American industry had also begun recruiting Mexican workers, first to fill wartime needs and later to fill the gap left by the decline in European immigration.

The new Mexican immigration appeared more permanent than previous waves—that is, more and more newcomers stayed—and, like other immigrants, more were attracted to cities. This was partly the unintended consequence of new policies designed to make immigration more difficult. As the Border Patrol (established in 1924) made border crossing more difficult (through head taxes, visa fees, literacy tests, and document checks), what had once been a two-way process for many Mexicans became a one-way migration. Permanent communities of Mexicans in the United States grew rapidly. By 1930, San Antonio's Mexican community accounted for roughly 80,000 people out of a total population of a quarter million. Around 100,000 Mexicans lived in central and east Los Angeles, including 55,000 who attended city schools. Substantial Mexican communities also flourished in midwestern cities such as Chicago, Detroit, Kansas City, and Gary. Many of the immigrants alternated between agricultural and factory jobs, depending on the seasonal availability of work.

Racism and local patterns of residential segregation confined most Mexicans to barrios. Housing conditions were generally poor, particularly for recent arrivals who were forced to live in rude shacks without running water or electricity. Disease and infant mortality rates were much higher than average, and most Mexicans worked at low-paying, unskilled jobs and received inadequate health care. Legal restrictions passed by states and cities made it difficult for Mexicans to enter teaching, legal, and other professions. Mexicans were routinely banned from local public works projects as well. Many felt a deep ambivalence about applying for American citizenship. Loyalty to the Old Country was strong, and many cherished dreams of returning to live out their days in Mexico.

Nativist efforts to limit Mexican immigration were thwarted by the lobbying of powerful agribusiness interests. The Los Angeles Chamber of Commerce typically employed racist stereotyping in its arguments to keep the borders open. Mexicans, it claimed, were naturally suited for agriculture, "due to their crouching and bending habits . . . while the white is physically unable to adapt himself to them."

Mutual aid societies—*mutualistas*—became key social and political institutions in the Mexican communities of the Southwest and Midwest. They provided death benefits and widows' pensions for members and also served as centers

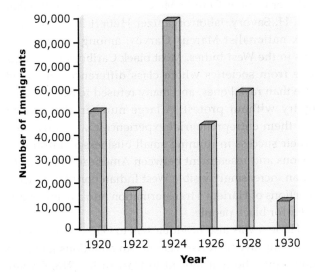

Figure 23.4 **MEXICAN IMMIGRATION TO THE UNITED STATES IN THE 1920S**

Many Mexican migrants avoided official border-crossing stations so they would not have to pay visa fees. Thus, these official figures probably underestimated the true size of the decade's Mexican migration. As the economy contracted with the onset of the Great Depression, immigration from Mexico dropped off sharply.

MEXICAN AMERICAN BARBER OUTSIDE OF HIS SHOP IN SAN ANTONIO During the 1920s, San Antonio's Mexican population doubled from roughly 40,000 to more than 80,000, making it the second largest *colonia* in *El Norte* after Los Angeles. This barber was one of many small businessmen serving the city's growing Mexican American community.

Harry Ransom Center.

of resistance to civil rights violations and discrimination. In 1928, the Federation of Mexican Workers Unions formed in response to a large farm labor strike in the Imperial Valley of California. A group of middle-class Mexican professionals in Texas organized the League of United Latin American Citizens (LULAC) in 1929. The founding of these organizations marked only the beginnings of a long struggle to bring economic and social equality to Mexican Americans.

23.5.3 The "New Negro"

The Great Migration spurred by World War I showed no signs of letting up during the 1920s, and African American communities in northern cities grew rapidly. By far the largest and most influential of these communities was New York City's Harlem. Previously a residential suburb, Harlem began attracting middle-class African Americans in the prewar years. After the war, heavy black migration from the South and the Caribbean encouraged real estate speculators and landlords to remake Harlem as an exclusively black neighborhood. (See Map 23.1.)

Harlem emerged as the demographic and cultural capital of black America, but its appeal transcended national borders, as mass migration from the Caribbean helped reshape the community. Between 1900 and 1930, some 300,000 West Indians emigrated to the United States, roughly half of whom settled in New York City. By the late 1920s, about one-quarter of Harlem's population had been born in Jamaica, Barbados, Trinidad, the Bahamas, or another part of the Caribbean. Some of the leading cultural, business, and political figures of the era—poet Claude McKay, newspaper publisher P. M. H. Savory, labor organizer Hubert Harrison, and black nationalist Marcus Garvey, among others—had roots in the West Indies. Most black Caribbean migrants came from societies where class differences mattered more than racial ones, and many refused to accept racial bigotry without protest. A large number also carried with them entrepreneurial experience that contributed to their success in running small businesses. Intraracial tensions and resentment between American-born blacks and an increasingly visible West Indian population were reflections of Harlem's transformation into a hemispheric center for black people.

Harlem was also headquarters to Garvey's Universal Negro Improvement Association. An ambitious Jamaican immigrant who had moved to Harlem in 1916, Garvey created a mass movement that stressed black economic self-determination and unity among the black communities of the United States, the Caribbean, and Africa. With colorful parades and rallies, and a central message affirming pride in black identity, Garvey attracted as many as a million

Map 23.1 BLACK POPULATION, 1920

Although the Great Migration had drawn hundreds of thousands of African Americans to the urban North, the southern states of the former Confederacy still remained the center of the African American population in 1920.

members worldwide. Garvey's best-publicized project was the Black Star Line, a black-owned and black-operated fleet of ships that was to link people of African descent around the world. But insufficient capital and serious financial mismanagement resulted in the spectacular failure of the enterprise. In 1923, Garvey was found guilty of mail fraud in his fund-raising efforts; he later went to jail and was subsequently deported to England. Despite the disgrace, Harlem's largest newspaper, the *Amsterdam News*, explained Garvey's continuing appeal to African Americans: "In a world where black is despised, he taught them that black is beautiful. He taught them to admire and praise black things and black people."

The demand for housing in this restricted geographical area led to skyrocketing rents, but most Harlemites held low-wage jobs. This combination produced extremely overcrowded apartments, unsanitary conditions, and the rapid deterioration of housing stock. Disease and death rates were abnormally high. Yet Harlem also boasted a large middle-class population and supported a wide array of churches, theaters, newspapers and journals, and black-owned businesses. It became a mecca, as poet and essayist James Weldon Johnson wrote, for "the curious, the adventurous, the enterprising, the ambitious, and the talented of the entire

Negro world." Poet Langston Hughes expressed the excitement of arriving in the community in 1921; "I can never put on paper the thrill of the underground ride to Harlem. I went up the steps and out into the bright September sunlight. Harlem! I stood there, dropped my bags, took a deep breath and felt happy again."

Harlem was the political and intellectual center for what writer Alain Locke called the "New Negro." Locke was referring to a new spirit in the work of black writers and intellectuals, an optimistic faith that encouraged African Americans to develop and celebrate their distinctive culture. This faith was the common denominator uniting the disparate figures associated with the **Harlem Renaissance**. "We younger Negro artists who create," Hughes declared in 1926, "now intend to express our individual dark-skinned selves without fear or shame. If white people are pleased, we are glad. If they are not, it doesn't matter. We know we are beautiful. And ugly too."

The assertion of cultural independence resonated in the works of a wide range of cultural figures. The deeply felt, down-home blues singing of Bessie Smith moved black audiences wherever she sang, especially those who were recent migrants to cities. Smith's record sales kept the young Columbia Records company afloat in the 1920s. Paul Robeson, an

All-American football player at Rutgers University and graduate of Columbia Law School, became an international star of stage and concert hall, where he regularly included his versions of African American folk songs and spirituals. Robeson also offered outspoken support for civil rights campaigns and the labor movement. Novelist and anthropologist Zora Neale Hurston consistently wove black folk culture into her novels, and portrayed brutal racial struggles in the American South honestly and openly. An array of black essayists—James Weldon Johnson; Jesse Fauset; Countee Cullen—explored themes of racial conflict, identity, and the responsibilities of African American artists to their larger community. Increasingly, these appeared in mainstream newspapers and magazines. Most black intellectuals agreed with Johnson when he wrote in 1927 that, "nothing can go farther to destroy race prejudice than the recognition of the Negro as a creator and contributor to American civilization."

There was a political side to the "New Negro" as well. The newly militant spirit that black veterans had brought home from World War I matured and found expression in a variety of ways in the Harlem of the 1920s. New leaders and movements began to appear alongside established organizations like the National Association for the Advancement of Colored People. A. Philip Randolph began a long career as a labor leader, socialist, and civil rights activist in these years, editing the *Messenger* and organizing the Brotherhood of Sleeping Car Porters, which grew into the single largest African American labor union.

Through the new mass media of radio and phonograph records, millions of Americans now listened and danced to a distinctively African American music, as jazz began to enter the cultural mainstream. Jazz found wildly enthusiastic fans in European capitals like Berlin and Paris, and noted classical composers such as Maurice Ravel and Igor Stravinsky treated it as a serious art form. The best jazz bands of the day, led by artists such as Duke Ellington, Fletcher Henderson, Cab Calloway, and Louis Armstrong, often had their performances broadcast live from such Harlem venues as the Cotton Club and Small's Paradise. These clubs themselves were rigidly segregated, however. Black dancers, singers, and musicians provided the entertainment, but no African Americans were allowed in the audience. Chronicled in novels and newspapers, Harlem became a potent symbol to white America of the ultimate good time. The average Harlemite never saw the inside of a nightclub. For the vast majority of Harlem residents, working menial jobs for low wages and forced to pay high rents, the day-to-day reality was depressingly different.

23.5.4 Alienated Intellectuals

War, Prohibition, growing corporate power, and the deep currents of cultural intolerance troubled many intellectuals in the 1920s. Some felt so alienated from the United States that they left to live abroad. In the early 1920s, Gertrude Stein, an American expatriate writer living in Paris, told the young novelist Ernest Hemingway, "All of you young people who served in the war, you are a lost generation." The phrase "the lost generation" was widely adopted as a label for American writers, artists, and intellectuals of the postwar era. Yet it is difficult to generalize about so diverse a community. For one thing, living abroad attracted only a handful of American writers. Alienation and disillusion with American life were prominent subjects in the literature and thought of the 1920s, but artists and thinkers developed these themes in very different ways.

The mass slaughter of World War I provoked revulsion and a deep cynicism about the heroic and moralistic portrayal of war so popular in the nineteenth century. Hemingway and fellow novelist John Dos Passos, who both served at the front as ambulance drivers, depicted the war and its aftermath in world-weary and unsentimental tones. The search for personal moral codes that would allow one to endure life with dignity and authenticity was at the center of Hemingway's fiction. In the taut, spare language of *The Sun Also Rises* (1926) and *A Farewell to Arms* (1929), he questioned idealism, abstractions, and large meanings. As Jake Barnes, the wounded war hero of *The Sun Also Rises*, explained, "I did not care what it was all about. All I wanted to know was how to live it."

Hemingway and F. Scott Fitzgerald were the most influential novelists of the era. Fitzgerald joined the army during World War I but did not serve overseas. His work celebrated the youthful vitality of the "Jazz Age" (a phrase he coined) but was also deeply distrustful of the promises of American prosperity and politics. His first novel, *This Side of Paradise* (1920), won a wide readership around the country with its exuberant portrait of a "new generation," "dedicated more than the last to the fear of poverty and the worship of success; grown up to find all Gods dead, all wars fought, all faiths in man shaken." Fitzgerald's finest work, *The Great Gatsby* (1925), written in the south of France, depicted the glamorous parties of the wealthy, while evoking the tragic limits of material success.

At home, many American writers engaged in sharp attacks on small-town America and what they viewed as its provincial values. Essayist H. L. Mencken, caustic editor of the *American Mercury*, heaped scorn on fundamentalists, Prohibition, and nativists, while ridiculing what he called the "American booboisie." Fiction writers also skewered small-town America, achieving commercial and critical success in the process. Sherwood Anderson's *Winesburg, Ohio* (1919) offered a spare, laconic, pessimistic, yet compassionate view of Middle America. He had a lasting influence on younger novelists of the 1920s.

The most popular and acclaimed writer of the time was novelist Sinclair Lewis. In a series of novels satirizing small-town life, such as *Main Street* (1920) and especially *Babbitt* (1922), Lewis affectionately mocked his characters. His treatment of the central character in *Babbitt*—George Babbitt of Zenith—also had a strong element of self-mockery, because Lewis could offer no alternative set of values to Babbitt's crass self-promotion, hunger for success, and craving for social acceptance. In 1930, Lewis became the first American author to win the Nobel Prize for literature.

In the aftermath of the postwar Red Scare, American radicalism found itself on the defensive throughout the 1920s. But one *cause célèbre* did attract a great deal of support from intellectuals. In 1921, two Italian American immigrants, Nicola Sacco and Bartolomeo Vanzetti, were tried and convicted for murder in the course of robbing a shoe factory in South Braintree, Massachusetts. Neither Sacco, a shoemaker, nor Vanzetti, a fish peddler, had a criminal record, but both had long been active in militant anarchist circles, labor organizing, and antiwar agitation. Their trial took place amidst an intense atmosphere of nativist and antiradical feeling, and both the judge and prosecuting attorney engaged in clearly prejudicial conduct toward the defendants. A six-year struggle to save Sacco and Vanzetti following the trial failed, despite attracting support from a broad range of liberal intellectuals, including Harvard law professor and future Supreme Court justice Felix Frankfurter. The two men were finally executed in 1927, and for many years, their case would remain a powerful symbol of how the criminal justice system could be tainted by political bias and anti-immigrant fervor.

Another side of intellectual alienation was expressed by writers critical of industrial progress and the new mass culture. The most important of these were a group of poets and scholars centered around Vanderbilt University in Nashville, Tennessee, collectively known as the Fugitives. They included Allen Tate, John Crowe Ransom, Donald Davidson, and Robert Penn Warren, all of whom invoked traditional authority, respect for the past, and older agrarian ways as ideals to live by. The Fugitives attacked industrialism and materialism as modern-day ills. Self-conscious Southerners, they looked to the antebellum plantation-based society as a model for a community based on benevolence toward dependents (such as black people and women) and respect for the land. Their book of essays, *I'll Take My Stand* (1930), was a collective manifesto of their ideas.

Not all intellectuals, of course, were critics of modern trends. Some, like the philosopher John Dewey, retained much of the prewar optimism and belief in progress. But many others, such as Walter Lippmann and Joseph Wood Krutch, articulated a profound uneasiness with the limits of material growth. In his 1929 book *A Preface to Morals*, the urbane and sophisticated Lippmann expressed doubts about the moral health of the nation. Modern science and technological advances could not address more cosmic questions of belief. The erosion of old religious faiths and moral standards, along with the triumph of the new mass culture, had left many people with nothing to believe.

23.5.5 The Election of 1928

The presidential election of 1928 served as a kind of national referendum on the Republican new era. It also revealed just how important ethnic and cultural differences had become in defining American politics. The contest reflected many of the deepest tensions and conflicts in American society in the 1920s: native-born versus immigrant; Protestant versus Catholic; Prohibition versus legal drinking; small-town life versus the cosmopolitan city; fundamentalism versus modernism; traditional sources of culture versus the new mass media. (See Map 23.2.)

The 1928 campaign featured two politicians who represented profoundly different sides of American life. Al Smith, the Democratic nominee for president, was a pure product of New York City's Lower East Side. Smith came from a background that included Irish, German, and Italian ancestry, and he was raised as a Roman Catholic. He rose

Map 23.2 THE ELECTION OF 1928

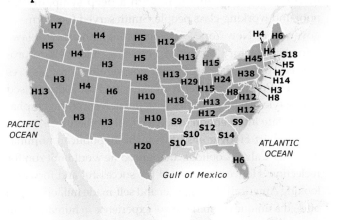

Numbers on states represent Electoral Votes.	Electoral Vote (%)	Popular Vote (%)
HERBERT HOOVER (H) (Republican)	444 (82)	21,391,993 (58.2)
Alfred E. Smith (S) (Democrat)	87 (17)	15,016,169 (40.9)
Norman Thomas (Socialist)	—	267,835 (0.7)
Other parties (Socialist Labor, Prohibition)	—	62,890 (0.2)

Although Al Smith managed to carry the nation's 12 largest cities, Herbert Hoover's victory in 1928 was one of the largest popular and electoral landslides in the nation's history.

AL SMITH AND HERBERT HOOVER
Clifford K. Berryman's 1928 political cartoon interpreted that year's presidential contest along sectional lines. It depicted the two major presidential contenders as each setting off to campaign in the regions where their support was weakest. For Democrat Al Smith, that meant the West, and for Republican Herbert Hoover, the East.

Library of Congress (Photoduplication).

through the political ranks of New York's Tammany Hall machine. A personable man with a deep sympathy for poor and working-class people, Smith served four terms as governor of New York, pushing through an array of laws reforming factory conditions, housing, and welfare programs. Two of his closest advisers were the progressives Frances Perkins and Belle Moskowitz. Smith thus fused older-style machine politics with the newer reform emphasis on state intervention to solve social problems.

Herbert Hoover easily won the Republican nomination after Calvin Coolidge announced he would not run for reelection. Hoover epitomized the successful and forward-looking American. An engineer and self-made millionaire, he offered a unique combination of experience in humanitarian war relief, administrative efficiency, and pro-business policies. Above all, Hoover stood for a commitment to voluntarism and individualism as the best method for advancing the public welfare. He was one of the best-known men in America, and he promised to continue Republican control of national politics.

Smith himself quickly became the central issue of the campaign. His sharp New York accent, jarring to many

Americans who heard it over the radio, marked him clearly as a man of the city. So did his brown derby and fashionable suits, as well as his promise to work for the repeal of Prohibition. As the first Roman Catholic nominee of a major party, Smith also drew a torrent of anti-Catholic bigotry, especially in the South and Midwest. Nativists and Ku Klux Klansmen shamelessly exploited old anti-Catholic prejudices and intimidated participants in Democratic election rallies. But Smith was also attacked from more respectable quarters. Bishop James Cannon, head of the Southern Methodist Episcopal Church, insisted that "no subject of the Pope" should be permitted to occupy the White House. For his part, Smith ran a largely conservative race. He appointed John Raskob, a Republican vice president of General Motors, to manage his campaign and tried to outdo Hoover in his praise for business. He avoided economic issues such as the unevenness of the prosperity, the plight of farmers, and the growing unemployment. Democrats remained regionally divided over Prohibition, Smith's religion, and the widening split between rural and urban values. Hoover did not have to do much, other than take credit for the continued prosperity.

Hoover polled 21 million votes to Smith's 15 million, and carried the electoral college 444 to 87, including New York State. Even the solid South, reliably Democratic since the Civil War, gave five states to Hoover—a clear reflection of the ethnocultural split in the party. Yet the election offered important clues to the future of the Democrats. Smith was more successful in the big cities of the North and East than any other Democrat in modern times. He outpolled Hoover in the aggregate vote of the nation's 12 largest cities and carried 6 of them, thus pointing the way to the Democrats' future dominance with urban, northeastern, and ethnic voters.

Conclusion

America's big cities, if not dominant politically, now defined the nation's cultural and economic life as never before. With Hollywood movies leading the way, the new mass media brought cosmopolitan entertainment and values to the remotest small communities. The culture of celebrity knew no geographic boundaries. New consumer-durable goods associated with mass-production techniques—automobiles, radios, telephones, household appliances—were manufactured largely in cities. The advertising and public relations companies that sang their praises were also distinctly urban enterprises. Even with the curtailing of European immigration, big cities attracted a kaleidoscopic variety of migrants: white people from small towns and farms, African Americans from the rural South and Caribbean, Mexicans from across the border, and intellectuals and professionals looking to make their mark.

Many Americans, of course, remained deeply suspicious of postwar cultural and economic trends. The partisans of Prohibition, members of the Ku Klux Klan, and religious fundamentalists usually found themselves on the defensive against what they viewed as alien cultural and economic forces centered in the cities. Large sectors of the population did not share in the era's prosperity. But the large numbers who did—or at least had a taste of good times—ensured Republican political dominance throughout the decade. Thus, America in the 1920s balanced dizzying change in the cultural and economic realms with conservative politics. The reform crusades that attracted millions during the progressive era were a distant memory. Political activism was no match for the new pleasures promised by technology and prosperity.

Key Terms

welfare capitalism A paternalistic system of labor relations emphasizing management responsibility for employee well-being. p. 549

open shop Factory or business employing workers regardless of whether they are union members; in practice, such a business usually refuses to hire union members and follows antiunion policies. p. 549

Volstead Act The 1919 law defining the liquor forbidden under the Eighteenth Amendment and giving enforcement responsibilities to the Prohibition Bureau of the Department of the Treasury. p. 562

Immigration Act A 1921 act setting a maximum of 357,000 new immigrants each year. p. 564

League of Women Voters League formed in 1920 advocating for women's rights, among them the right for women to serve on juries and equal pay laws. p. 568

Sheppard-Towner Act The first federal social welfare law, passed in 1921, providing federal funds for infant and maternity care. p. 568

Harlem Renaissance A new African American cultural awareness that flourished in literature, art, and music in the 1920s. p. 571

CHRONOLOGY

Prohibition takes effect	**1920**
	1921 First immigration quotas are established by Congress
	Sheppard-Towner Act establishes first federally funded health care program
Equal Rights Amendment is first introduced in Congress	**1923**
	1924 Reed-Johnson Immigration Act tightens quotas established in 1921
	Calvin Coolidge elected to full term as president
Henry Ford's Highland Park assembly plant achieves pace completing one Model T every ten seconds	**1925**
Scopes trial pits religious fundamentalism against modernity	
	1926 National Broadcasting Company establishes first national radio network
Warner Brothers produces *The Jazz Singer*, the first feature-length motion picture with sound	**1927**
	1928 Herbert Hoover defeats Al Smith for the presidency

Chapter 24

The Great Depression and the New Deal 1929–1940

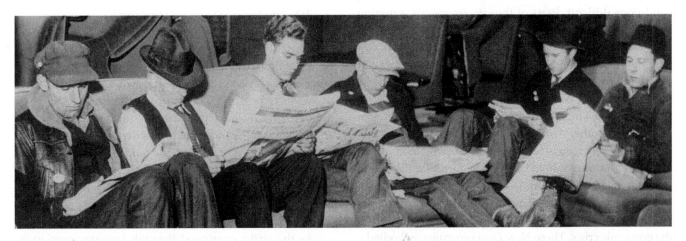

SIT-DOWN STRIKE On December 30, 1936, workers at the GM Fisher body plant in Flint, Michigan, took over the plant and staged a sit-down strike.

Bettmann/Getty Images.

⌄ Contents and Focus Questions

24.1 Hard Times
What were the causes of the Great Depression, and what were its consequences?

24.2 FDR and the First New Deal
What was the First New Deal?

24.3 Left Turn and the Second New Deal
How did the Second New Deal differ from the First New Deal?

24.4 The New Deal in the South and West
How did the New Deal expand the scope of the federal government in the South and West?

24.5 The Limits of Reform
What were the limits of the New Deal's reforms, and what legacy did they leave?

24.6 Depression-Era Culture
How did the Great Depression affect American cultural life during the 1930s?

American Communities

Sit-Down Strike at Flint: Automobile Workers Organize a New Union

In the gloomy evening of February 11, 1937, 400 tired, unshaven, but very happy strikers marched out of the sprawling automobile factory known as Fisher Body Number 1 in Flint, Michigan. Most carried American flags and small bundles of clothing. A makeshift banner on top of the plant announced "Victory Is Ours." A wildly cheering parade line of a thousand supporters greeted the strikers at the gates. Shouting with joy, honking horns, and singing songs, they marched to two other factories to greet other emerging strikers. After 44 days, the great Flint sit-down strike was over.

Flint was the heart of production for General Motors, the largest corporation in the world. In 1936, GM's net profits had reached $285 million, and its total assets were $1.5 billion. Originally a center for lumbering and then for carriage making, Flint had boomed with the auto industry during the 1920s. Thousands of migrants streamed into the city, attracted by assembly-line jobs averaging about $30 a week. By 1930, Flint's population had grown to about 150,000 people, 80 percent of whom depended on work at General Motors. A severe housing shortage made living conditions difficult. Parts of the city resembled a mining camp, with workers living in tar-paper shacks, tents, and even railroad cars.

The Great Depression hit Flint very hard. Employment at GM fell from a 1929 high of 56,000 to fewer than 17,000 in 1932. As late as 1938, close to half the city's families were receiving some kind of emergency relief. By that time, as in thousands of other American communities, Flint's private and county relief agencies had been overwhelmed by the needs of the unemployed and their families. Two new national agencies based in Washington, D.C., the Federal Emergency Relief Administration and the Works Progress Administration, had replaced local sources of aid during the economic crisis. These New Deal programs embodied a new federal approach to providing relief and employment to American communities unable to cope with the enormity of mass unemployment.

The United Automobile Workers (UAW) came to Flint in 1936, seeking to organize GM workers into one industrial union. The previous year, Congress had passed the **National Labor Relations Act** (also known as the Wagner Act), which made union organizing easier by guaranteeing the right of workers to join unions and bargain collectively. The act established the National Labor Relations Board to oversee union elections and prohibit illegal antiunion activities by employers. But the obstacles to labor organizing were still enormous.

Unemployment was high, and GM had maintained a vigorous antiunion policy for years. By the fall of 1936, the UAW had signed up only a thousand members. The key moment came with the seizure of two Flint GM plants by a few hundred auto workers on December 30, 1936. The idea was to stay in the factories until strikers could achieve a collective bargaining agreement with General Motors. "We don't aim to keep the plants or try to run them," explained one sit-downer to a reporter, "but we want to see that nobody takes our jobs. We don't think we're breaking the law, or at least we don't think we're doing anything really bad."

A new and daring tactic—the sit-down strike—gained popularity among American industrial workers during the 1930s. In 1936, there were 48 sit-downs involving nearly 90,000 workers, and in 1937 some 400,000 workers participated in 477 sit-down strikes. Sit-downs expressed the militant exuberance of the rank and file. As one union song of the day put it:

When they tie the can to a union man,

Sit down! Sit down!

When they give him the sack they'll take him back,

Sit down! Sit down!

When the speed up comes, just twiddle your thumbs,

Sit down! Sit down!

When the boss won't talk don't take a walk,

Sit down! Sit down!

The Flint strikers carefully organized themselves into what one historian called "the sit-down community." Each plant elected a strike committee and appointed its own police chief and sanitary engineer. No alcohol was allowed, and strikers were careful not to destroy company property. Committees were organized for food preparation, recreation, sanitation, education, and contact with the outside. A Women's Emergency Brigade—the strikers' wives, mothers, and daughters—provided crucial support preparing food and maintaining militant picket lines.

As the strike continued through January, support in Flint and around the nation grew. Overall production in the GM empire dropped from 53,000 vehicles per week to 1,500. Reporters and union supporters flocked to the plants. On January 11, in the so-called Battle of Running Bulls, strikers and their supporters clashed violently with Flint police and private GM guards. Michigan governor Frank Murphy, sympathetic to the strikers, brought in the National Guard to protect them. He refused to enforce an injunction obtained by GM to evict the strikers. In the face of determined unity by the sit-downers, GM gave in and recognized the UAW as the exclusive bargaining agent in all 60 of its factories.

The strike was perhaps the most important in American labor history, sparking a huge growth in union membership in the automobile and other mass-production industries. Out of the tight-knit, temporary community of the sit-down strike emerged a looser yet more permanent kind of community: a powerful, nationwide trade union of automobile workers. The national UAW, like other new unions in the mass-production industries, was composed of locals around the country. The permanent community of unionized auto workers won significant improvements in wages, working conditions, and benefits. Locals also became influential in the political and social lives of their larger communities—industrial cities such as Flint, Detroit, and Toledo.

More broadly, the Flint sit-down embodied the new political and economic dynamics of Depression-era America. Workers, farmers, and consumers hard hit by the worst economic catastrophe in U.S. history called for a more activist federal government to relieve suffering and offer greater economic security for Americans. In response, a rejuvenated Democratic Party, led by President Franklin D. Roosevelt and in solid control of Congress, created the New Deal, an ambitious collection of measures designed to promote relief, recovery, and reform. With the 1935 National Labor Relations Act, the New Deal encouraged labor organizing by legally assuring the right to union membership for the first time in American history. A newly militant and aggressive labor movement in turn became a critical component of the "New Deal coalition" that kept Democrats in power. Organized labor provided crucial support for many of the social welfare initiatives associated with the New Deal throughout the 1930s and beyond: federal relief, a Social Security system, public works projects, new standards regulating minimum wages and maximum hours, and Washington-based efforts to improve the nation's housing. By the late 1930s, conservative resistance would limit the scope of New Deal reforms. But in communities around the nation, labor unions inspired by the Flint sit-down reached unprecedented levels of popularity and influence in economic and political life. Nationally, they would remain a crucial component of the New Deal political coalition, and a key power broker in the Democratic Party, for decades to come.

Flint

24.1 Hard Times

What were the causes of the Great Depression, and what were its consequences?

No twentieth-century event more profoundly affected American life than the **Great Depression**—the worst economic crisis in American history. Statistics tell only part of the story of a slumping economy, mass unemployment, and swelling relief rolls. Even today, the emotional and psychological toll of those years has left what one writer called an "invisible scar" on the lives and memories of millions of American families.

24.1.1 Underlying Weaknesses of the 1920s Economy

It would be oversimple to say that the 1929 stock market collapse "caused" the Great Depression. Signs of deep economic weakness had already begun to surface amid the general prosperity of the 1920s. First, workers and consumers received too small a share of the enormous increases in labor productivity. Between 1923 and 1929, manufacturing output per worker-hour increased by 32 percent, while wages rose only 8 percent. Gains in wages and salaries were extremely uneven. While workers in newer industries such as automobiles and electrical manufacturing enjoyed pay increases, those in textiles and coal mining watched their wages fall. Moreover, the rise in productivity itself had encouraged overproduction in many industries, and the farm sector had never been able to regain the prosperity of the World War I years. (See Chapter 23.)

To be sure, Americans overall in the 1920s had more money to spend on cars, telephones, radios, washing machines, canned goods, and other consumer goods. Child labor was in decline, and more Americans than ever graduated from high school. But economic insecurity was still a brutal fact of life for millions of families, especially in rural communities. Most industrial workers endured regular bouts of unemployment and seasonal layoffs. The two-day weekend and paid vacations were largely unknown. Eighty percent of the nation's families had no savings at all, and an old age spent in poverty was far more likely for the average worker than "retirement." The most important weakness in the economy was the extremely unequal distribution of income, yielding the greatest concentration of wealth in the nation's history. (See Table 24.1.)

Table 24.1 **DISTRIBUTION OF TOTAL FAMILY INCOME AMONG VARIOUS SEGMENTS OF THE POPULATION, 1929–44 (IN PERCENTAGES)**

Year	Poorest Fifth	Second-Poorest Fifth	Middle Fifth	Second-Wealthiest Fifth	Wealthiest Fifth	Wealthiest 5 Percent
1929		12.5	13.8	19.3	54.4	30.0
1935–36	4.1	9.2	14.1	20.9	51.7	26.5
1941	4.1	9.5	15.3	22.3	48.8	24.0
1944	4.9	10.9	16.2	22.2	45.8	20.7

Source: Adapted from U.S. Bureau of the Census, *Historical Statistics of the United States, Colonial Times to 1970*, Bicentennial Edition (Washington, DC: U.S. Government Printing Office, 1975), 301.

24.1.2 The Bull Market and the Crash

Stock trading in the late 1920s captured the imagination of the broad American public. The stock market resembled a sporting arena; millions followed stock prices as avidly as they did the exploits of Babe Ruth or Jack Dempsey. Business leaders and economists as much as told Americans that it was their duty to buy stocks. John J. Raskob, chairman of the board of General Motors, wrote an article for the *Ladies' Home Journal* titled "Everybody Ought to Be Rich." A person who saved $15 each month and invested it in good common stocks would, he claimed, have $80,000 within 20 years.

During the bull market of the 1920s, stock prices increased at roughly twice the rate of industrial production. By the end of the decade, stocks that once had been bought mainly on the basis of their earning power, which was passed on to stockholders in the form of dividends, came to be purchased only for the resale value after their prices rose. In 1928 alone, for example, the price of Radio Corporation of America stock shot up from $85 per share to $420; Chrysler stock more than doubled, from $63 to $132.

TAIL HOLT

WALL STREET BEAR MARKET Rollin Kirby's 1929 cartoon depicts an individual investor losing his money as he clings to a bear running down Wall Street. The bear symbolizes an atmosphere of panic selling and heavy losses, the opposite of a "bull" market, in which investor confidence spurs buying and faith in the future.

Everett Collection Historical/Alamy Stock Photo.

Yet only about 3 million Americans—out of a total population of 120 million—owned any stocks at all. Many of these stock buyers had been lured into the market through easy-credit margin accounts, which allowed investors to purchase stocks with a small down payment (as low as 10 percent), borrowing the rest from a broker and using the shares as collateral on the loan. Just as installment plans had stimulated the automobile and other industries, "buying on the margin" brought new customers to the stock market. Investment trusts, similar to today's mutual funds, attracted many new investors with promises of high returns. Corporations found that lending excess capital to stockbrokers was more profitable than investing in new technologies. All these factors fed an expansive and optimistic atmosphere on Wall Street.

Although often portrayed as a one- or two-day catastrophe, the Wall Street crash of 1929 was actually a steep slide. The bull market peaked in early September, and prices drifted downward. As expectations of an endless boom began to melt, the market had to decline. On Monday, October 28, the Dow Jones Industrial Average lost 38 points—13 percent of its value. The next day—"Black Tuesday," October 29—the bottom fell out. Over 16 million shares, more than double the previous record, were traded as panic selling took hold. For many stocks, no buyers were available at any price.

The situation worsened. The market's fragile foundation of credit, based on the margin debt, quickly crumbled. Many investors with margin accounts had to sell when stock values fell. Since the shares themselves represented the security for their loans, more money had to be put up to cover the loans when prices declined. By mid-November, about $30 billion in the market price of stocks had been wiped out. Stocks listed on the New York Times index lost half their value in 10 weeks.

The stock market crash undermined the confidence, investment, and spending of businesses and the well-to-do. Manufacturers cut production and began laying off workers, which brought further declines in consumer spending, and so another round of production cutbacks ensued. A spurt of consumer spending might have checked this downward spiral, but consumers had less to spend as industries laid off workers and reduced work hours. With a shrinking market for products, businesses feared to expand. A large proportion of the nation's banking funds had been tied to the speculative bubble. Many banks began to fail as anxious depositors withdrew their funds, which were uninsured, costing thousands of families all their savings. And an 86 percent plunge in agricultural prices between 1929 and 1933, compared with a decline in agricultural production of only 6 percent, brought terrible suffering to America's farmers.

24.1.3 Mass Unemployment

At a time when unemployment insurance did not exist and public relief was completely inadequate, the loss of a job could mean economic catastrophe for workers and their families. Massive unemployment across America became the most powerful sign of a deepening depression. In 1930, the Department of Labor estimated that roughly 9 percent of the labor force was out of work. By 1933, 12.6 million workers—over one-quarter of the labor force—were without jobs. (Other sources put the figure that year above 16 million, or nearly one out of every three workers.) No statistics tell us how long people were unemployed or how many Americans found only part-time work.

Many Americans, raised believing that they were responsible for their own fate, blamed themselves for their failure to find work. Journalists and social workers

WHITE ANGEL BREADLINE, SAN FRANCISCO, 1933 Dorothea Lange captured the lonely despair of unemployment in *White Angel Breadline, San Francisco, 1933*. During the 1920s, Lange had specialized in taking portraits of wealthy families, but by 1932, she could no longer stand the contradiction between her portrait business and "what was going on in the street." She said of this photograph of unemployed men waiting for free bread, "There are moments such as these when time stands still and all you can do is hold your breath and hope it will wait for you."

Art Resource, NY.

noted the common feelings of shame and guilt expressed by the unemployed. One jobless Houston woman told a relief caseworker, "I'm just no good, I guess. I've given up ever amounting to anything. It's no use." One despondent Pennsylvania man asked a state relief agency, "Can you be so kind as to advise me as to which would be the most human way to dispose of my self and family, as this is about the only thing that I see left to do."

Nathan Ackerman, a psychiatrist who went to Pennsylvania to observe the impact of prolonged unemployment on coal miners, found an enormous sense of "internal distress":

> They hung around street corners and in groups. They gave each other solace. They were loath to go home because they were indicted, as if it were their fault for being unemployed. A jobless man was a lazy good-for-nothing. The women punished the men for not bringing home the bacon, by withholding themselves sexually. . . . These men suffered from depression. They felt despised, they were ashamed of themselves. They cringed, they comforted one another. They avoided home.

Unemployment upset the psychological balance in many families by undermining the traditional authority of the male breadwinner. Women, because their labor was cheaper than men's, found it easier to keep jobs. Female clerks, secretaries, maids, and waitresses earned much less than male factory workers, but their jobs were more likely to survive hard times. Pressures on those lucky enough to have a job increased as well. Anna Novak, a Chicago meat packer, recalled the degrading harassment at the hands of foremen, "You could get along swell if you let the boss slap you on the behind and feel you up. God, I hate that stuff, you don't know!" Men responded in a variety of ways to unemployment. Some withdrew emotionally; others became angry or took to drinking.

A few committed suicide. In 1934, one Chicago social worker summed up the strains she found in families; "Fathers feel they have lost their prestige in the home; there is much nagging, mothers nag at the fathers, parents nag at the children. Children of working age who earn meager salaries find it hard to turn over all their earnings and deny themselves even the greatest necessities and as a result leave home." Fear of unemployment and a deep desire for security marked the Depression generation.

24.1.4 Hoover's Failure

The enormity of the Great Depression overwhelmed traditional—and meager—sources of relief. In most communities across America, these sources were a patchwork of private agencies and local government units, such as towns, cities, or counties. They simply lacked the money, resources, and staff to deal with the worsening situation. In large urban centers like Detroit and Chicago, unemployment approached 50 percent by 1932. Smaller communities could not cope either. For the year 1932, one West Virginia coal-mining county with 1,500 unemployed miners had only $9,000 to meet relief needs.

There was great irony, as well as tragedy, in President Hoover's failure to respond to human suffering. During World War I, he had effectively administered Belgian war relief abroad and won wide praise for his leadership of the Food Administration at home. As a leader of the progressive wing of the Republican Party, Hoover had long championed a kind of cooperative individualism that relied upon public-spirited citizens. Although he felt real personal anguish over the hardships people suffered, he lacked the political skill to demonstrate his compassion in public. Failing to face the facts of the Depression, Hoover worried more about undermining individual initiative than providing actual relief for victims. He ignored all mounting evidence to the contrary when he claimed, in his 1931 State of the Union Address, "Our people are providing against distress from unemployment in true American fashion by magnificent response to public appeal and by action of the local governments."

Hoover's plan for recovery centered on restoring business confidence. His administration's most important institutional response to the Depression was the Reconstruction Finance Corporation (RFC), established in early 1932 and based on the War Finance Corporation of the World War I years. The RFC was designed to make government credit available to ailing banks, railroads, insurance companies, and other businesses, thereby stimulating economic activity. The key assumption here was that the problem was one of supply (for businesses) rather than demand (from consumers). Given the public's low purchasing power, most businesses were not interested in obtaining loans for expansion. The RFC managed to save numerous banks and other businesses from going under, but its approach did not hasten recovery. Hoover was loath to use the RFC to make direct grants to states, cities, or individuals. In July 1932, congressional Democrats pushed through the Emergency Relief Act, which authorized the RFC to lend $300 million to states that had exhausted their own relief funds. Hoover grudgingly signed the bill, but less than $30 million was actually given out by the end of 1933.

Two other federal actions—in each case, the opposite of what should have been done—worsened the situation.

First, the Federal Reserve, whose policies of low interest rates and easy credit in the late 1920s helped fuel the speculative boom in stock buying, tightened credit sharply. That caused interest rates to spike, putting heavy pressure on the nation's banking system, especially the smaller banks on which farmers, merchants, and local businessmen relied. Without any state or federal insurance, more than 5,000 rural banks and ethnic group-oriented savings and loans institutions failed between 1929 and 1932, and more than 9 million depositors lost their savings. Second, in 1930 Congress passed (and Hoover signed) the Smoot-Hawley Tariff, raising import duties to their highest

HOOVERVILLE As many as 20,000 former soldiers and their families converged on Washington in the summer of 1932, during the depths of depression, to support legislation advancing the bonus payment promised to World War I veterans. The "Bonus Army" built this "Hooverville" on Anacostia Flats, in Washington, D.C., in June 1932. U.S. Army troops burned it down when they suppressed the veterans' protest the following month.

Everett Collection Inc/Alamy Stock Photo.

levels in American history. Supporters, including the president, claimed that this would protect American farmers from global competition and raise farm prices. Other nations responded by raising their own tariffs, which caused world trade to decline steeply, thus exacerbating the economic collapse.

24.1.5 A Global Crisis and the Election of 1932

By 1931, the Depression had spread not only across the United States but also throughout the world, a sign of how interdependent the global economy had become. The immediate problem was the highly unstable system of international finance. The 1919 peace settlement had saddled Germany with $33 billion in war reparations, owed largely to Great Britain and France. The United States loaned money to the British and French during the war, and American banks loaned large sums to Germany in the 1920s. Germany used these loans to pay reparations to the British and French, who in turn used these reparations to repay their American debts. The 1929 stock market crash put an end to American loans for Germany, thus removing a critical link in the international cash flow. When Germany then defaulted on its reparations, Great Britain and France in turn stopped paying what they owed to this country. As German banks collapsed and unemployment swelled, nervous European investors sold their American stocks, depressing the stock market even further. Great Britain and several other European nations also abandoned the gold standard and devalued (lowered) their currency relative to the dollar. This made American goods more difficult to sell abroad, further dampening production at home. With many nations also raising their tariffs to protect national industries, international trade slowed to a crawl. The total volume of global trade declined from about $36 billion in 1929 to roughly $12 billion by 1932. American banks, badly hurt by both domestic depositors clamoring for their money and the foreign withdrawal of capital, began failing in record numbers. In 1931 alone, 2,294 U.S. banks failed, double the number that had collapsed in 1930.

By 1932, the desperate mood of many Americans was finding expression in direct, sometimes violent protests that were widely covered in the press. On March 7, communist organizers led a march of several thousand Detroit auto workers and unemployed in Dearborn. Ford-controlled police fired tear gas and bullets, killing 4 demonstrators and seriously wounding 50 others. Desperate farmers in Iowa organized the Farmers' Holiday Association, aimed at raising prices by refusing to sell produce. In August, some 1,500 farmers dumped milk and other perishables into ditches.

The spring of 1932 also saw the **Bonus Army** begin descending on Washington, D.C. This protest took its name from Congress's promise in 1924 to pay every veteran of World War I a $1,000 bonus—in the form of a bond that would not mature until 1945. The veterans who were gathering in Washington demanded immediate payment of the bonus in cash. By summer, they and their families numbered around 20,000 strong and were camping out all over the capital city. The House passed a bill for immediate payment, but when the Senate refused to agree, most of the downcast veterans left. At the end of July, U.S. troops, led by Army Chief of Staff General Douglas MacArthur, forcibly evicted the remaining 2,000 veterans. The spectacle of these unarmed and unemployed men, the heroes of 1918, being driven off by bayonets and bullets provided the most disturbing evidence yet of the failure of Hoover's administration.

In 1932, Democrats nominated Franklin D. Roosevelt, governor of New York, for the presidency. Roosevelt's acceptance speech stressed the need for reconstructing the nation's economy. "I pledge you, I pledge myself," he said, "to a new deal for the American people." Roosevelt's plans for recovery were vague and contradictory. He frequently attacked Hoover for reckless and extravagant spending and accused him of concentrating too much power in Washington, but he also spoke of the need for government to meet "the problem of underconsumption" and to help in "distributing wealth and products more equitably." Above all, Roosevelt stressed, "the country demands bold, persistent experimentation." Hoover bitterly condemned Roosevelt's ideas as a "radical departure" from the American way of life. The Democratic victory was overwhelming. Roosevelt carried 42 states, taking the Electoral College 472 to 59 and the popular vote by about 23 million to 16 million. Democrats won big majorities in

both the House and the Senate. The stage was set for FDR's "new deal." (See Map 24.1.)

Map 24.1 THE ELECTION OF 1932

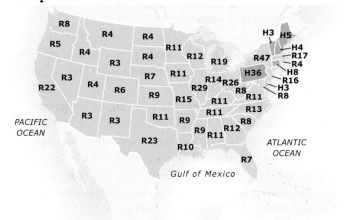

Numbers on states represent Electoral Votes.	Electoral Vote (%)	Popular Vote (%)
FRANKLIN D. ROOSEVELT (R) (Democrat)	472 (89)	22,809,638 (57)
Herbert Hoover (H) (Republican)	59 (11)	15,758,901 (40)
Minor parties	—	1,153,306 (3)

Democrats owed their overwhelming victory in 1932 to the popular identification of the Depression with the Hoover administration. Roosevelt's popular vote was about the same as Hoover's in 1928, and FDR's Electoral College margin was even greater.

24.2 FDR and the First New Deal

What was the First New Deal?

No twentieth-century president had a greater impact on American life and politics than did Franklin Delano Roosevelt (FDR). To a large degree, the New Deal was a product of his astute political skills and the sheer force of his personality. The only president ever elected to four terms, FDR would loom as the dominant personality in American political life through 12 years of depression and global war.

24.2.1 FDR the Man

Franklin Delano Roosevelt was born in 1882 in Dutchess County, New York, where he grew up an only child, secure and confident, on his aristocratic family's vast estate. Roosevelt's education at private schools, Harvard, and Columbia Law School reinforced his aristocratic family's sense of civic duty. In 1905, he married his distant cousin, Anna Eleanor Roosevelt, a niece of President Theodore Roosevelt. He was elected as a Democrat to the New York State Senate in 1910, served as assistant secretary of the navy from 1913 to 1920, and was nominated for vice president by the Democrats in the losing 1920 campaign.

In the summer of 1921, Roosevelt was stricken with polio; he was never to walk again without support. His illness proved the turning point in his life. The wealthy aristocrat, for whom everything had come relatively easily, now personally understood the meaning of struggle and hardship. Elected governor of New York in 1928, Roosevelt served two terms and won a national reputation for reform. As governor, he instituted unemployment insurance, strengthened child labor laws, enacted tax relief for farmers, and provided pensions for the old. As the Depression hit the state, he slowly increased public works.

24.2.2 "The Only Thing We Have to Fear": Restoring Confidence

In the first days of his administration, Roosevelt conveyed a sense of optimism and activism that helped restore the badly shaken confidence of the nation. "First of all," he told Americans in his Inaugural Address on March 4, 1933, "let me assert my firm belief that the only thing we have to fear is fear itself." The very next day, as people lined up to pull savings out of failing banks and hoarded cash under their mattresses, he issued an executive order calling for a four-day "bank holiday" to stop the collapse of the country's financial system. Contemporary investigations had revealed a disquieting pattern of stock manipulation, illegal loans to bank officials, and tax evasion that helped erode public confidence in the banking system.

The new Congress was not scheduled to convene until the end of 1933, but Roosevelt convened a special session to deal with the banking crisis, unemployment aid, and farm relief. On March 12, he broadcast his first **fireside chat** to explain the steps he had taken to meet the financial emergency. These radio broadcasts became a standard part of Roosevelt's political technique, bringing a new personal intimacy to his efforts to inform and sway the public. They proved enormously successful. By reaching directly into people's homes, the fireside chats gave courage to ordinary Americans and communicated a genuine sense of compassion from the White House.

Congress immediately passed the **Emergency Banking Relief Act**, which gave the president broad discretionary powers over all banking transactions and foreign exchange. It authorized healthy banks to reopen only under licenses from the Treasury Department and provided for greater federal authority in managing the affairs of failed banks. By the end of March, about half the country's banks, holding about 90 percent of the nation's deposits, were open for business again. The bank crisis had passed.

Roosevelt assembled a group of key advisers, the "brains trust," to counsel him in the White House. The key

ROOSEVELT INAUGURATION, 1933 This *New Yorker* magazine cover depicted an ebullient Franklin D. Roosevelt riding to his 1933 inauguration in the company of a glum Herbert Hoover. This drawing typified many mass media images of the day, contrasting the different moods and temperaments of the new president and the defeated incumbent.

Franklin D. Roosevelt Library.

figures included two economists, Rexford G. Tugwell and Adolf A. Berle, and the attorneys Felix Frankfurter and Samuel Rosenman. They gave conflicting advice. Some advocated fiscal conservatism to restore confidence in the dollar; others pushed for central planning to manage the economy. But the "brain trusters" shared a basic belief in expert-directed government-business cooperation. Structural economic reform, they argued, must accept the modern reality of large corporate enterprise based on mass production and distribution.

24.2.3 The Hundred Days

From March to June 1933—"the Hundred Days"—FDR pushed through Congress an extraordinary amount of Depression-fighting legislation. Roosevelt's enormous political skill—as a power broker, as a coalition builder, and as a communicator with the American public—was crucial.

CCC POSTER A recruitment poster represents the Civilian Conservation Corps (CCC) as much more than simply an emergency relief measure, stressing character building and the opportunity for self-improvement. By the time the CCC expired in 1942, it had become one of the most popular of all the New Deal programs.

Library of Congress (Photoduplication).

What came to be called the **New Deal** was no unified program to end the Depression but rather an improvised series of reform and relief measures, some of which completely contradicted each other. Still, all the New Deal programs were united by the fundamental goals of relief, reform, and recovery.

Five measures were particularly important and innovative. The Civilian Conservation Corps (CCC), established in March as an unemployment relief effort, provided work for jobless young men in protecting and conserving the nation's natural resources. Road construction, reforestation, flood control, and national park improvements were some of the major projects performed in work camps across the country. CCC workers received room and board and $30 each month, up to $25 of which had to be sent home to dependents. By the time the program was phased out in 1942, more than 2.5 million youths had worked in some 1,500 CCC camps.

In May, Congress authorized $500 million for the Federal Emergency Relief Administration (FERA). Half the money went as direct relief to the states; the rest was distributed on the basis of a dollar of federal aid for every three dollars of state and local funds spent for relief. This system of outright federal grants differed significantly from Hoover's loans-only approach. Establishment of work relief projects, however, was left to state and local governments. To direct this massive undertaking, FDR tapped Harry Hopkins, a streetwise former New York City social worker driven by a deep moral passion to help the less fortunate and an impatience with bureaucracy. Hopkins would emerge as the key figure administering New Deal relief programs.

The Agricultural Adjustment Administration (AAA) was set up to provide immediate relief to the nation's farmers. The AAA established a new federal role in agricultural planning and price setting. It established parity prices for basic farm commodities, including corn, wheat, hogs, cotton, rice, and dairy products. The concept of parity pricing was based on the purchasing power that farmers had enjoyed during the prosperous years of 1909–1914. That period became the benchmark for setting the "floor"—that is, minimum—prices for farm commodities. The AAA also incorporated the principle of subsidy, whereby farmers received benefit payments in return for reducing acreage or otherwise cutting production where surpluses existed. New taxes on food processing would pay for these programs.

The AAA raised total farm income and was especially successful in pushing up the prices of wheat, cotton, and corn. It had some troubling side effects, however. Landlords often failed to share their AAA payments with tenant farmers, and they frequently used benefits to buy tractors and other equipment that displaced sharecroppers. Many Americans were disturbed, too, by the sight of surplus crops, livestock, and milk being destroyed while millions went hungry.

The **Tennessee Valley Authority (TVA)** proved to be one of the most unique and controversial projects of the New Deal era. It had its origins in the federal government's effort during World War I to build a large hydroelectric power complex and munitions plant on the Tennessee River at Muscle Shoals, Alabama. During the 1920s, Republican Senator George W. Norris of Nebraska had led an unsuccessful fight to provide for permanent government operation of the Muscle Shoals facilities on behalf of the area's population. The TVA, an independent public corporation, built dams and power plants, produced cheap fertilizer for farmers, and, most significantly, brought cheap electricity for the first time to thousands of people in six southern states. Denounced by some as a dangerous step toward socialism, the TVA stood for decades as a model of how careful government planning could dramatically improve the social and economic welfare of an underdeveloped region.

On the very last of the Hundred Days, Congress passed the National Industrial Recovery Act, the closest attempt yet to a systematic plan for economic recovery. It had two main parts. The National Recovery Administration (NRA) sought to stimulate production and competition in business by means of industrial codes regulating prices, output, and trade practices. In theory, each industry would be self-governed by a code hammered out by representatives of business, labor, and the consuming public. Once approved by the NRA in Washington, led by General Hugh Johnson and symbolized by the distinctive Blue Eagle stamp, the codes would have the force of law. In practice, almost all the NRA codes were written by the largest firms in any given industry; labor and consumers got short shrift. The sheer administrative complexities involved with code writing and compliance made a great many people unhappy with the NRA's operation. Overall, the NRA looked to business and industry leaders to find a way to recovery.

Finally, the Public Works Administration (PWA), led by Secretary of the Interior Harold Ickes, authorized $3.3 billion for the construction of roads, public buildings, and other projects. The idea was to provide jobs and thus stimulate the economy through increased consumer spending. A favorite image for this kind of spending was "priming the pump." Just as a farmer had to prime a pump with water before it could draw more water from the well, the government had to prime the economy with jobs for the unemployed. Eventually the PWA spent more than $4.2 billion building roads, schools, post offices, bridges, courthouses, and other public buildings around the country. In thousands of communities today, these structures remain the most tangible reminders of the New Deal era.

During the Hundred Days and the months immediately following, Congress passed other legislation that would have important long-range effects. The Glass-Steagall Act created the Federal Deposit Insurance Corporation (FDIC), which provided protection to individual depositors by guaranteeing accounts with balances of up to $5,000 in case of bank failure. Congress also established the Securities and Exchange Commission (SEC) to regulate stock exchanges and brokers, require full financial disclosures, and curb the speculative practices that had contributed to the 1929 crash. The 1934 National Housing Act, aimed at stimulating residential construction and making home financing more affordable, set up the Federal Housing Administration (FHA). The FHA insured loans made by banks and other private lenders for home building and home buying. (See Table 24.2.)

24.2.4 Roosevelt's Critics, Right and Left

From the beginning, the New Deal had loud and powerful critics on the right who complained bitterly that FDR had

Table 24.2 KEY LEGISLATION OF THE FIRST NEW DEAL ("HUNDRED DAYS," MARCH 9 TO JUNE 16, 1933)

Legislation	Purpose
Emergency Banking Relief Act	Enlarged federal authority over private banks Government loans to private banks
Civilian Conservation Corps	Unemployment relief Conservation of natural resources
Federal Emergency Relief Administration	Direct federal money for relief, funneled through state and local governments
Agricultural Adjustment Administration	Federal farm aid based on parity pricing and subsidy
Tennessee Valley Authority	Economic development and cheap electricity for Tennessee Valley
National Industrial Recovery Act	Self-regulating industrial codes to revive economic activity
Public Works Administration	Federal public works projects to increase employment and consumer spending

overstepped the traditional boundaries of government action. From the left came angry cries that Roosevelt had not done nearly enough.

Pro-Republican newspapers and the American Liberty League, a group of conservative businessmen organized in 1934, vehemently attacked the administration for what they considered its attack on property rights, the growing welfare state, and the alleged decline of personal liberty. In the 1934 election, however, Democrats crushed their right-wing critics and—counter the losses that incumbent parties usually suffer at midterm—increased their majorities in both houses of Congress.

Some of Roosevelt's staunchest early supporters turned critical. Father Charles E. Coughlin, a Catholic priest in suburban Detroit, attracted a huge national radio audience of 40 million listeners with passionate sermons attacking Wall Street, international bankers, and "plutocratic capitalism." Coughlin at first supported Roosevelt and the New Deal, and he tried to build a close personal relationship with the president. But by 1934 the ambitious Coughlin, frustrated by his limited influence on the administration, began attacking FDR. Roosevelt was a tool of special interests, he charged, who wanted dictatorial powers. New Deal policies were part of a communist conspiracy, threatening community autonomy with centralized federal power. Coughlin finally broke with FDR and founded the National Union for Social Justice. In 1936 the Coughlin-dominated Union Party nominated William Lemke, an obscure North Dakota congressman, to run for president. Lemke polled only 900,000 votes, but Coughlin continued his biting attacks on Roosevelt through 1940.

More troublesome for Roosevelt were the vocal and popular movements on the left. These found the New Deal too timid. In California, the well-known novelist and socialist Upton Sinclair entered the 1934 Democratic primary for governor by running on a program he called EPIC ("End Poverty in California"). He proposed a monthly pension of $50 for all poor people over age 60 and championed a government-run system of "production for use" (rather than profit) workshops for the unemployed. Sinclair shocked local and national Democrats by winning the primary easily. He lost a close general election only because the Republican candidate received heavy financial and tactical support from wealthy Hollywood studio executives and frightened regular Democrats. Another Californian, Francis E. Townsend, a retired dentist, won a large following among senior citizens with his Old Age Revolving Pension plan. He called for payments of $200 per month to all people over 60, provided all the money was spent within 30 days. The pensions would be financed by a national 2 percent tax on commercial transactions. This plan managed to attract a nationwide following of more than 3 million by 1936. But Townsend's plan was essentially regressive, since it proposed to tax all Americans equally, regardless of their income.

Huey Long, Louisiana's flamboyant backcountry orator, posed the greatest potential threat to Roosevelt's leadership. Long had captured Louisiana's governorship in 1928 by attacking the state's entrenched oil industry and calling for a radical redistribution of wealth. In office, he significantly improved public education, roads, medical care, and other public services, winning the loyalty of the state's poor farmers and industrial workers. Elected to the U.S. Senate in 1930, Long came to Washington with national ambitions. He at first supported Roosevelt, but in 1934, his own presidential ambitions and his impatience with the pace of New Deal measures led to a break with FDR.

Long organized the Share Our Wealth Society. Its purpose, he thundered, "was to break up the swollen fortunes of America and to spread the wealth among all our people." Limiting the size of large fortunes, Long promised, would mean a homestead worth $5,000 and a $2,500 annual income for everyone. A secret poll in the summer of 1935 stunned the Democratic National Committee by showing that Long might attract 3 million or 4 million votes for president. Although Long's economics were fuzzy, his "Every Man a King" slogan touched a deep popular nerve. Only his assassination that September by a political enemy of his corrupt political machine prevented Long's third-party candidacy, which might have proved disastrous for FDR.

In the nation's workplaces and streets, a rejuvenated and newly militant labor movement also loomed as a force to be reckoned with. Unemployed Councils, organized largely by the Communist Party in industrial cities, held marches and rallies demanding public works projects and relief payments. Section 7a of the National Industrial Recovery Act required that workers be allowed to bargain collectively with employers through representatives of their own choosing. Although this provision of the NIRA was not enforced, it did help raise expectations and sparked union organizing. Almost 1.5 million workers took part in some 1,800 strikes in 1934.

Employers continued to resist unionization, often with violence and the help of local and state police. In Minneapolis, a local of the International Brotherhood of Teamsters won a bloody strike against the combined opposition of the union's own national officials, vehemently antiunion employers, and a brutal city police force. Violence against strikers helped unite the city's working classes. The Minneapolis Central Labor Union was prepared to support a general strike, and the funeral of a striker shot by police drew 100,000 people. In San Francisco in 1934, a general strike in support of striking members of the International Longshoremen's Association (ILA) effectively shut down the city. Employer use of strikebreakers and violent intimidation prompted an outpouring of support for the ILA from the city's working class, as well as from many shopkeepers and middle-class professionals. When the ILA accepted government arbitration, it won on its main issue—control over the hiring halls on the waterfront. In both Minneapolis and San Francisco, workers had demonstrated the power of labor solidarity and mass protest.

24.3 Left Turn and the Second New Deal

How did the Second New Deal differ from the First New Deal?

The popularity of Coughlin, Sinclair, Townsend, and Long suggested Roosevelt might be losing electoral support among workers, farmers, the aged, and the unemployed. In addition, FDR had to contend with a conservative Supreme Court that did not share the public's enthusiasm for the New Deal. In May 1935, in *Schecter v. United States*, the Court found the NRA unconstitutional in its entirety. In early 1936, ruling in *Butler* v. *United States*, the Court invalidated the AAA, declaring it an unconstitutional attempt at regulating agriculture. The Court was composed mostly of Republican appointees, 6 of them over 70. Looking toward the 1936 election and eager for a popular mandate, Roosevelt and his closest advisers responded by turning left and offering new social-reform programs. These programs had three major goals: strengthening the national commitment to creating jobs; providing security against old age, unemployment, and illness; and improving housing conditions and clearing slums. What came to be called "the Second Hundred Days" marked the high point of progressive lawmaking in the New Deal. (See Table 24.3.)

Table 24.3 KEY LEGISLATION OF THE SECOND NEW DEAL (1935–1938)

Legislation	Purpose
Emergency Relief Appropriation Act (1935)	Large-scale public works program for the jobless (included Works Progress Administration)
Social Security Act (1935)	Federal old-age pensions and unemployment insurance
National Labor Relations Act (1935)	Federal guarantee of right to organize trade unions and collective bargaining
Resettlement Administration (1935)	Relocation of poor rural families Reforestation and soil erosion projects
National Housing Act (1937)	Federal funding for public housing and slum clearance
Fair Labor Standards Act (1938)	Federal minimum wage and maximum hours

24.3.1 The Second Hundred Days

In April 1935, the administration pushed through Congress the Emergency Relief Appropriation Act, which allocated $5 billion for large-scale public works programs for the jobless. New Deal economists argued that each government dollar spent had a multiplier effect, pumping two or three dollars into the depressed gross domestic product. Over the next 7 years, the Works Progress Administration, under Harry Hopkins's leadership, oversaw the employment of more than 8 million Americans on a vast array of construction projects: roads, bridges, dams, airports, and sewers. Among the most innovative WPA programs were community service projects that employed thousands of jobless artists, musicians, actors, and writers.

The landmark Social Security Act of 1935 provided for old-age pensions and unemployment insurance. A payroll tax on workers and their employers created a fund from which retirees received monthly pensions after age 65. Payment size depended upon how much employees and their employers had contributed over the years. The unemployment compensation plan established a minimum weekly payment and a minimum number of weeks during which those who lost jobs could collect. The Social Security Board administered this complex system of federal-state cooperation. The original law failed to cover domestics and farm workers, many of whom were Latinos and African Americans. It also made no provisions for casual laborers or public employees. The old-age pensions were quite small at first, as little as $10 a month. And to collect unemployment, one had to have first lost a job. But the law, which has since been amended many times, established the crucial principle of federal responsibility for America's most vulnerable citizens.

Roosevelt and congressional New Dealers called for new legislation to strengthen labor's right to organize after the Supreme Court, in May 1935, ruled the National Industrial Recovery Act unconstitutional, including its provisions protecting union organizing. In July 1935, Congress passed the National Labor Relations Act, often called the Wagner Act for its chief sponsor, Democratic Senator Robert F. Wagner of New York. The new law had far-reaching implications for American politics and the economy. For the first time, the federal government guaranteed the right of American workers to join or form independent labor unions and bargain collectively for improved wages, benefits, and working conditions. The National Labor Relations Board would conduct secret-ballot elections in shops and factories to determine which union, if any, workers desired as their sole bargaining agent. The law also defined and prohibited unfair labor practices by employers, including firing workers for union activity. The Wagner Act, described as the "Magna Carta for labor," quickly proved a boon to union growth, especially in previously unorganized industries such as automobiles, steel, and textiles. It set the stage for the sit-down strike in Flint and for General Motors's eventual acceptance of union labor in its factories.

Finally, the Resettlement Administration (RA) produced one of the most utopian New Deal programs, one designed to create new kinds of model communities. Established by executive order and led by key brain truster Rexford G. Tugwell, the RA helped destitute farm families relocate to more productive areas. It granted loans for purchasing land and equipment, and it directed reforestation and soil erosion projects, particularly in the hard-hit Southwest. Due to lack of funds and poor administration, however, only about 1 percent of the projected 500,000 families were actually moved.

Tugwell, one of the New Deal's most ardent believers in planning, was more successful in his efforts at creating model greenbelt communities combining the best of urban and rural environments. "My idea," he wrote, "is to go just outside centers of population, pick up cheap land, build a whole community and entice people into it." Though his vision was only partially fulfilled, several of these communities—such as Greenhills, near Cincinnati, and Greendale, near Milwaukee—still thrive.

24.3.2 Labor's Upsurge: Rise of the CIO

The Wagner Act greatly facilitated union organizing and galvanized the moribund labor movement. In 1932, only 2.8 million workers were union members, a half million fewer than in 1929 and more than 2 million fewer than in 1920. Yet by 1942, unions claimed more than 10.5 million members, nearly a third of the total non-agricultural work force. This remarkable turnaround was one of the key events of the Depression era. The growth in the size and power of the labor movement permanently changed the work lives and economic statuses of millions, as well as the national and local political landscapes.

At the core of this growth was a series of dramatic successes in the organization of workers in large-scale, mass-production industries, such as those producing automobiles, steel, rubber, electrical goods, and textiles. Workers in these fields had largely been ignored by the conservative, craft-conscious unions that dominated the American Federation of Labor. At the 1935 AFL convention, a group of more militant union officials, led by John L. Lewis (of the United Mine Workers) and Sidney Hillman (of the Amalgamated Clothing Workers), formed the Committee for Industrial Organization (CIO). Their goal was to organize mass-production workers by industry rather than by craft. They emphasized the need for opening the new unions to all, regardless of a worker's level of skill. And they differed from nearly all old-line AFL unions by calling for the inclusion of black and women workers.

Lewis was the key figure in the CIO. The gruff son of a Welsh miner, Lewis was articulate, ruthless, and very ambitious. He saw the new legal protection given by the Wagner Act as a historic opportunity. But despite the passage of the Act—whose constitutionality was unclear until 1937—Lewis knew that establishing permanent unions in the mass-production industries would be a bruising battle. He committed the substantial resources of the United Mine Workers to a series of organizing drives, focusing first on the steel and auto industries. Many CIO organizers were communists or radicals of other persuasions, and their dedication, commitment, and willingness to work within disciplined organizations proved invaluable in the often dangerous task of creating industrial unions. Of the roughly 200 full-time organizers on the payroll of the Steel Workers Organizing Committee in 1937, almost a third were members of the Communist Party.

Militant rank-and-file unionists were often ahead of Lewis and other CIO leaders. The sit-down strike—refusing to work but staying in the factory to prevent "scab" workers from taking over—emerged as a popular tactic among rubber and auto workers. After the dramatic breakthrough in the Flint sit-down strike at General Motors, membership in CIO unions grew rapidly. In eight months, membership in the United Automobile Workers alone soared from 88,000 to 400,000. CIO victories in the steel, rubber, and electrical industries followed, but often at a very high cost. One bloody example of the perils of union organizing was the 1937 Memorial Day Massacre in Chicago. In a field near the struck Republic Steel Mill in South Chicago, police fired into a crowd of union supporters, killing 10 workers and wounding scores more.

Overall, the success of the CIO's organizing drives was remarkable. In 1938 CIO unions, now boasting nearly 4 million members, withdrew from the AFL and reorganized themselves as the Congress of Industrial Organizations. Ahead lay many hard battles organizing workers in such nonunion bastions as the Ford Motor Company and the textile plants of the South. But for the first time ever, the labor movement had gained a permanent place in the nation's mass-production industries. Organized labor took its place as a key power broker in Roosevelt's New Deal and the national Democratic Party. Frances Perkins, FDR's secretary of labor and the nation's first woman cabinet member, captured the close relationship between the new unionism and the New Deal; "Programs long thought of as merely labor welfare, such as shorter hours, higher wages, and a voice in the terms of conditions of work, are really essential economic factors for recovery."

POLICE ATTACK STRIKING WORKERS
On Memorial Day 1937, Chicago policemen used guns, clubs, and tear gas against a crowd of 1,000 striking workers and their families near Republic Steel on the city's southeast side. Ten workers were killed and another 60 were badly injured in this notorious example of the violence many union organizing campaigns faced.

CARL LINDE/AP Images.

24.3.3 The New Deal Coalition at High Tide

Did the American public support Roosevelt and his New Deal policies? Both major political parties looked forward to the 1936 elections as a national referendum, and the campaign itself was an exciting and hard-fought contest. Very few political observers predicted its lopsided result. The Republicans nominated Governor Alfred M. Landon of Kansas, who had gained attention by surviving the Democratic landslide of 1934. His campaign served as a lightning rod for all those, including many conservative Democrats, who were dissatisfied with Roosevelt and the direction he had taken.

Roosevelt attacked the "economic royalists" who denied that government "could do anything to protect the citizen in his right to work and his right to live." At the same time, FDR was careful to distance himself from radicalism. "It was this administration," he declared, "which saved the system of private profit and free enterprise after it had been dragged to the brink of ruin." As Roosevelt's campaign crossed the country, his advisers were heartened by huge and enthusiastic crowds, especially in large cities like Chicago and Pittsburgh. Still, the vast majority of the nation's newspapers endorsed Landon. And a widely touted "scientific" poll by the *Literary Digest* forecast a Republican victory in November.

Election day erased all doubts. Roosevelt carried every state but Maine and Vermont, polling 61 percent of the popular vote. Democrats increased their substantial majorities in the House and Senate as well. The *Literary Digest*, it turned out, had drawn the sample for its poll from people whose addresses were listed in telephone directories and car registration records, thus omitting the poorer Americans who had no telephones or cars—and who supported Roosevelt. In 1936 the Democrats drew millions of new voters into the political process and at the same time forged a new coalition of voters that would dominate national politics for two generations.

This **New Deal coalition**, as it came to be known, included white Southern Democrats, ethnic groups who supported big-city political machines, unionized workers (including those being organized by the CIO), and many Depression-hit farmers. Black voters in the North and West, long affiliated with the Republicans as "the party of Lincoln," went Democratic in record numbers. (Of course, blacks were largely barred from voting in the South.)

The Great Depression was by no means over. But the New Deal's active response to the nation's misery, particularly its bold initiatives in 1935, had obviously struck a powerful chord with the American electorate. Roosevelt was especially popular among first- and second-generation Catholics and Jews, and the New Deal drew enthusiastic support from millions in the ethnic working class who had never bothered with politics. As one Slovak worker in Chicago's stockyards put it, "Our people did not know anything about the government until the Depression years. In my neighborhood, I don't remember anyone voting." The severity of the Great Depression had overwhelmed the ethnically based support networks—mutual benefit societies, immigrant banks, and religious charities—that had traditionally helped so many to survive hard times. Working-class voters in large cities like New York, Chicago, Detroit, and Philadelphia increasingly took credit for putting and keeping Democrats in power locally and nationally—and their attitudes toward politics changed. The federal government no longer seemed so remote or irrelevant to their lives. Popular federal programs like Social Security, the WPA, and Home Owners Loan Corporation mortgages changed the consciousness of a generation of the ethnic working class. In exchange for their votes, they now looked to the state—especially the federal government—for relief, protection, and help in achieving the American dream.

24.4 The New Deal in the South and West

How did the New Deal expand the scope of the federal government in the South and West?

The New Deal had its most profound impact in the South and the West. Federal farm programs moved southern agriculture away from its longtime dependence upon sharecropping and tenant farming and helped reorganize it around new patterns of wage labor and agribusiness. New Deal dam building and power projects introduced electricity to millions of rural southerners, transforming their lives. New Deal programs reshaped western agriculture, created new sources of water and energy, and changed Indian policy. From Great Plains farming communities to Pacific Coast cities, federal subsidy and management became an integral part of western life. In the process, the New Deal helped propel both the South and the West into the modern era and laid the groundwork for the postwar "Sunbelt."

24.4.1 Modernizing Southern Farming and Landholding

In 1930, less than half of all southern farmers owned their own land; over three-quarters of the region's African American farmers and nearly half its white farmers were sharecroppers or tenants. Few of these earned any cash income at all; those who did averaged about $100 annually. The continued dominance of a few crops—mainly cotton and tobacco—had only intensified the Depression by glutting the market and keeping crop prices at rock bottom. The Agricultural Adjustment Administration succeeded in boosting prices by paying farmers to "plow under"— take their land out of production. Particularly in the South, however, these federal subsidies went overwhelmingly to large landowners, who controlled local county committees charged with administering AAA programs. Most planters did not share these payments with sharecroppers and tenants, and individual protest was usually futile.

The Southern Tenant Farmers Union (STFU), founded in 1934, fought both landlords and AAA policies. Active in six southern states and composed of about 30,000 tenant farmers (more than half of them black), the STFU protested evictions, called strikes to raise farm labor wages, and challenged landlords to give tenants their fair share of subsidy payments. The STFU drew national attention to the plight of sharecroppers and tenant farmers, but it failed to influence national farm policy.

New Deal policies helped destroy the old sharecropping and tenant system largely by helping landowners prosper. Those farmers who had access to government funds were able to diversify their crops, consolidate holdings, and work their land more efficiently with labor-saving machinery such as tractors and mechanical harvesters. Mechanized farming and government-subsidized reductions of cultivated land cut the demand for labor and increased evictions. Uprooted tenants, sharecroppers, and day laborers found themselves on the road in search of work; many thousands migrated to cities and towns.

No New Deal initiative had a greater impact on southern communities than electrification. In the early 1930s, only about 3 percent of rural Southerners had access to electric power and, hence, to household appliances and farm machinery. The Tennessee Valley Authority and the Rural Electrification Administration (REA) helped millions of southern households move into the modern era by making electricity available for the first time. The TVA built 16 dams across some 800 miles of the Tennessee River basin, bringing flood control and electric power to hundreds of thousands of families in seven southern states. It also significantly reduced consumer electric rates in many cities and towns by providing a cheaper alternative to private utilities. By 1944, the TVA was the largest power producer in the United States. If rural life was still harsh, electrification allowed farm families to enjoy radio, electric lights, and conveniences that other Americans had long taken for granted.

24.4.2 An Environmental Disaster: The Dust Bowl

An ecological and economic catastrophe of unprecedented proportions struck the southern Great Plains in the mid-1930s. The region had suffered several drought years in the early 1930s. Such dry spells occurred regularly, in roughly 20-year cycles. But this time, the parched earth

became swept up in violent dust storms, the likes of which had never been seen before. The dust storms were largely the consequence of years of stripping the landscape of its natural vegetation. During World War I, wheat brought record-high prices on the world market, and for the next 20 years Great Plains farmers turned the region into a vast wheat factory.

The wide flatlands of the Great Plains were especially suited to mechanized farming, and gasoline-powered tractors, disc plows, and harvester-thresher combines increased productivity enormously. As wheat prices fell in the 1920s, farmers broke still more land to make up the difference with increased production. Great Plains farmers had created an ecological time bomb that exploded when drought returned in the early 1930s. With native grasses destroyed to grow wheat, there was nothing left to prevent soil erosion. Dust storms blew away tens of millions of acres of rich topsoil, and tens of thousands of farm families left the region. The hardest-hit regions were western Kansas, eastern Colorado, western Oklahoma, the Texas Panhandle, and eastern New Mexico—areas that a Denver journalist named the "Dust Bowl." (See Map 24.2.)

Map 24.2 THE DUST BOWL, 1935–1940

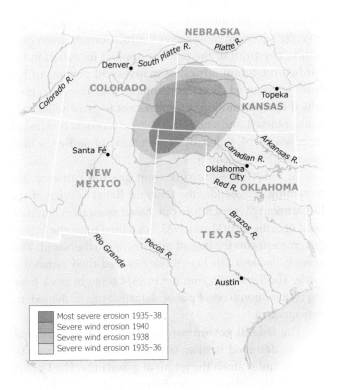

This map shows the extent of the Dust Bowl in the southern Great Plains. Federal programs designed to improve soil conservation, water management, and farming practices could not prevent a mass exodus of hundreds of thousands out of the Great Plains.

Black blizzards of dust a mile and a half high rolled across the landscape, darkening the sky and whipping the earth into great drifts of dust that settled over hundreds of miles. Dust storms made it difficult for humans and livestock to breathe, and destroyed crops and trees over vast areas. Dust storms turned day into night, terrifying those caught in them. "Dust pneumonia" and other respiratory infections afflicted thousands, and many travelers found themselves stranded in automobiles and trains unable to move. The worst storms occurred in the early spring of 1935. A Garden City, Kansas, woman gave an account of her experience for the *Kansas City Times*:

> All we could do about it was just sit in our dusty chairs, gaze at each other through the fog that filled the room and watch that fog settle slowly and silently, covering everything—including ourselves—in a thick, brownish gray blanket. When we opened the door swirling whirlwinds of soil beat against us unmercifully. The door and windows were all shut tightly, yet those tiny particles seemed to seep through the very walls. It got into cupboards and clothes closets; our faces were as dirty as if we had rolled in the dirt; our hair was gray and stiff and we ground dirt between our teeth.

Many thousands of Great Plains farm families were given direct emergency relief by the Resettlement Administration. Other federal assistance included crop and seed loans, moratoriums on loan payments, and temporary WPA jobs. In most Great Plains counties, from one-fifth to one-third of the families applied for relief; in the hardest-hit communities, as many as 90 percent of the families received direct government aid. The AAA paid wheat farmers millions of dollars not to grow what they could not sell and encouraged the diversion of acreage from soil-depleting crops like wheat to soil-enriching crops such as sorghum.

To reduce the pressure from grazing cattle on the remaining grasslands, the Drought Relief Service of the Department of Agriculture purchased more than 8 million head of cattle in 1934 and 1935. For a brief time, the federal government was the largest cattle owner in the world. This agency also lent ranchers money to feed their remaining cattle. The Taylor Grazing Act of 1934 brought stock grazing on 8 million acres of public domain lands under federal management.

The federal government also pursued longer-range policies designed to alter land-use patterns, reverse soil erosion, and nourish the return of grasslands. The Department of Agriculture, under Secretary Henry A. Wallace, sought to change farming practices. The spearhead for this effort was the Soil Conservation Service (SCS), which conducted research into controlling wind and water erosion, set up demonstration projects, and offered technical assistance, supplies, and equipment to farmers engaged in conservation work on farms and ranches. The SCS pumped additional federal funds into the Great Plains and created a new rural organization, the soil conservation district, which administered conservation regulations locally.

By 1940 the acreage subject to blowing in the Dust Bowl area of the southern Plains had been reduced from roughly 50 million acres to less than 4 million acres. In the face of the Dust Bowl disaster, New Deal farm policies had restricted market forces in agriculture. But the return of regular rainfall and the outbreak of World War II led many farmers to abandon the techniques that the SCS had taught them to accept. Wheat farming expanded and farms grew as farmers once again pursued commercial agriculture with little concern for its long-term effects on the land.

While large landowners and ranchers reaped sizable benefits from AAA subsidies and other New Deal programs in the southern Plains, tenant farmers and sharecroppers received very little. In the cotton lands of Texas, Oklahoma, Missouri, and Arkansas, thousands of tenant and sharecropper families were forced off the land. They became part of a stream of roughly 300,000 people, disparagingly called "Okies," who migrated to California in the 1930s. California migrants included victims of the Dust Bowl, but the majority were blue-collar workers and small businessmen looking to improve their economic lot. California suffered from the Depression along with the rest of the nation, but it still offered more jobs, higher wages, and higher relief payments than the states of the southern Plains. Most Okies could find work only as poorly paid agricultural laborers in the fertile San Joaquin Valley and Imperial Valley districts. There they faced discrimination and scorn as "poor white trash" while they struggled to create communities amid the squalor of migrant labor camps. Only with the outbreak of World War II and the pressing demand for labor were migrants able to significantly improve their situation.

Mexican farm laborers faced stiff competition from Dust Bowl refugees. By the mid-1930s Mexicans no longer dominated California's agricultural workforce. In 1936 an estimated 85 percent to 90 percent of the state's migratory workers were white Americans, as compared with less than 20 percent before the Depression. Mexican farm worker families who managed to stay employed in California, Texas, and Colorado saw their wages plummet. Southwestern communities, responding to racial hostility from unemployed whites and looking for ways to reduce their welfare burden, campaigned to deport Mexicans and Mexican Americans. Employers, private charities, and the Immigration and Naturalization Service joined in this effort. Authorities made little effort to distinguish citizens from aliens; most of the children they deported had been born in the United States and were citizens. Los Angeles County had the most aggressive campaign, using boxcars to ship out more than 13,000 Mexicans between 1931 and 1934. The hostile climate convinced thousands more to leave

YEARS OF DUST

RESETTLEMENT ADMINISTRATION
Rescues Victims
Restores Land to Proper Use

"YEARS OF DUST" This 1936 poster by the artist and photographer Ben Shahn served to publicize the work of the Resettlement Administration, which offered aid to destitute farm families hit hard by the Dust Bowl. Shahn's stark imagery here was typical of the documentary aesthetic associated with Depression-era art and photography.

Pictorial Press Ltd/Alamy Stock Photo.

voluntarily. Overall, over 400,000 left the United States during the decade. Some Mexican deportees crossed the border with a melancholy song on their lips:

After being exploited

In these lands of the north

Now they are being thrown out

For not having a passport.

24.4.3 Water Policy

The New Deal ushered in the era of large-scale water projects, designed to provide irrigation and cheap power and to prevent floods. The long-range impact of these undertakings on western life was enormous. The key government agency in this realm was the Bureau of Reclamation of the Department of the Interior, established in 1902. The Bureau's original responsibility had been to construct dams and irrigation works and thereby to encourage the growth of small farms throughout the arid regions of the West. Until the late 1920s, its efforts had been of little consequence. Its fortunes changed when its focus shifted to building huge multipurpose dams designed to control entire river systems. (See Map 24.3.)

The first of these projects was the Boulder Dam (later renamed the Hoover Dam). The dam, actually begun during the Hoover administration, was designed to harness the Colorado River, the wildest and most isolated of the major western rivers. Its planned benefits included flood prevention, the irrigation of California's Imperial Valley, the supplying of domestic water for southern California, and the generation of cheap electricity for Los Angeles and southern Arizona. Hoover, however, had opposed the public power aspect of the project, arguing that the government ought not to compete with private utility companies. This position was contrary to that of most Westerners, who believed cheap public power was critical for development. Roosevelt's support for government-sponsored power projects was a significant factor in his winning the political backing of the West in 1932 and subsequent election years.

Boulder Dam was completed in 1935 with the help of funds from the Public Works Administration. Its total cost was $114 million, which was to be offset by the sale of the hydroelectric power it generated. Los Angeles and neighboring cities built a 259-mile aqueduct, costing $220 million, to channel water to their growing populations. Lake Mead, created by construction of the dam, became the world's largest artificial lake, extending 115 miles up the canyon and providing a popular new recreation area. The dam's irrigation water helped make the Imperial Valley, covering over 500,000 acres, one of the most productive agricultural districts in the world.

The success of Boulder Dam transformed the Bureau of Reclamation into a major federal agency with huge resources at its disposal. In 1938 it completed the All-American Canal—an 80-mile channel connecting the Colorado River to the Imperial Valley, with a 130-mile branch to the Coachella Valley. The canal cost $24 million to build and carried a flow of water equal to that of the Potomac River. More than a million acres of desert land were opened up to the cultivation of citrus fruits, melons, vegetables, and cotton. Irrigation districts receiving water promised to repay, without interest, the cost of the canal over a 40-year period. This interest-free loan was in effect a huge government subsidy to the private growers who benefited from the canal.

In 1935 the Bureau began the giant Central Valley Project (CVP). The Central Valley, stretching through the California interior, is a 500-mile oblong watershed with an average width of 125 miles. The idea was to bring water from the Sacramento River in the north down to the arid lands of the larger San Joaquin Valley in the south. Completed in 1947, the project eventually cost $2.3 billion. The CVP stored water and transferred it to the

Map 24.3 THE NEW DEAL AND WATER

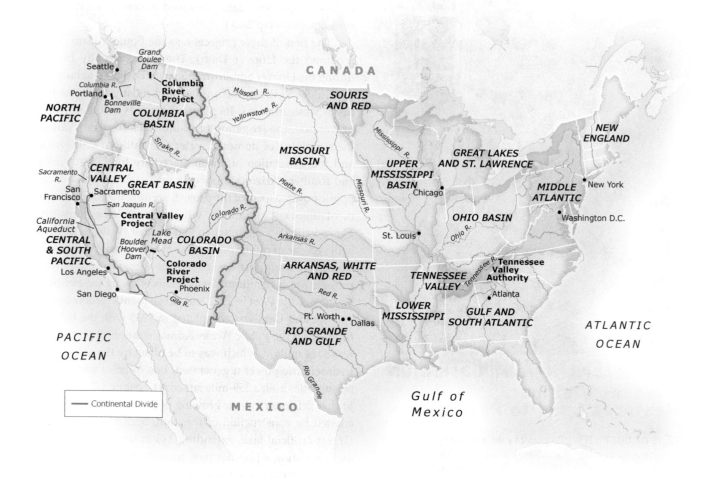

This map illustrates U.S. drainage areas and the major large-scale water projects begun or completed by federal agencies in them during the New Deal. By providing irrigation, cheap power, flood control, and recreation areas, these public works had a historically unprecedented impact on America's western communities.

drier southern regions of the state. It also provided electricity, flood control, and municipal water. The federal government, local municipalities, and buyers of electric power paid most of the cost, and the project proved a boon to large-scale farmers in the Sacramento and San Joaquin river valleys.

The largest power and irrigation project of all was Grand Coulee Dam, northwest of Spokane, Washington. Completed in 1941, it was designed to convert the power of the Columbia River into cheap electricity and to irrigate previously uncultivated land, thereby stimulating economic development in the Pacific Northwest. The construction of Grand Coulee employed tens of thousands of workers and pumped millions of dollars into the region's badly depressed economy. Between 1933 and 1940, Washington state ranked first in per capita federal expenditures. In the longer run, Grand Coulee provided the cheapest electricity in the United States and helped attract new manufacturing

to a region previously dependent on the export of raw materials, such as lumber and metals.

These technological marvels and the new economic development they stimulated were not without an environmental and human cost. Grand Coulee and smaller dams nearby reduced the Columbia River, long a potent symbol of the western wilderness, to a string of lakes. Spawning salmon could no longer run the river above the dam. In California, the federal guarantee of river water made a relative handful of large farmers fabulously wealthy. But tens of thousands of farmworkers, mostly of Mexican descent, labored in the newly fertile fields for very low wages, and pesticides undermined their health. The Colorado River, no longer emptying into the Pacific, began to build up salt deposits, making its water increasingly unfit for drinking or irrigation. Water pollution in the form of high salinity continues to plague the 2,000-mile river to this day.

Communities *in* Conflict

Californians Face the Influx of "Dust Bowl" Migrants

During the 1930s, between 300,000 and 400,000 Americans left Oklahoma, Texas, Arkansas, and Missouri for California. Like westward pioneers of old, they sought a better life. In the depths of the Depression, however, most found only a shortage of work, low wages, and housing in tent camps or shacks. Many of these migrants were victims of the Dust Bowl disaster, but others were Depression-hit town and city dwellers attracted by stories of opportunity in California. The new migration was most visible in rich agricultural areas, such as the San Joaquin Valley, about 100 miles from Los Angeles.

The state was largely hostile to poor newcomers. California's 1933 Indigent Act made it a crime to bring people with no visible means of support into the state, and dozens were prosecuted for helping relatives move to California. In 1936, the Los Angeles Police Department set up a border patrol, known as the "Bum Blockade," to turn back "undesirables" trying to enter the city limits. But the plight of the migrants also received widespread publicity and support in works like John Steinbeck's 1939 novel, *The Grapes of Wrath*; the evocative photographs of Dorothea Lange; and the reporting of journalists like Carey McWilliams and Paul Taylor. Most of this publicity focused on the problems faced by white families, who increasingly replaced the Mexicans, Filipinos, and single males who had traditionally worked the seasonal harvest.

A feature piece in the *Los Angeles Times* on July 21, 1937, offers a harrowing but sympathetic account of life among the roughly 50,000 migrant workers in the San Joaquin Valley. The focus is on the poor conditions endured by the migrants, as well as where they have come from. The opposing excerpt reflects the views of the California Citizens' Association, one of several conservative groups that saw the migrants as a growing peril to California's economy and social stability. In 1941, after a challenge to the Indigent Act by the American Civil Liberties Union, the U.S. Supreme Court ruled in *Edwards v. California* that states had no power to restrict migration by poor people or any other American citizens.

- **How do these two accounts differ in their perceptions of who the migrants are and of their motives for coming to California? How do they understand the meaning of "citizenship"?**

- **Do you find any correlations between these two documents and the contemporary debates over "illegal immigration" to the United States?**

"Squatter Army Wages Grim Battle for Life"

Human squalor—a picture of approximately 50,000 persons driven to California by dust storms, drought, ill health and debts—awaits the visitor looking beyond the roadside today in the San Joaquin Valley. A new chapter in American history is being written here. A battle for life, for food, health, homes and security is being waged by these hordes of transient indigents.

Within an hour the skeptic must admit he has seen disease, privation, filth and threats of epidemics. But he also must admit that he is seeing a fight for a home similar to that of the pioneers in the South and Middle West in the last century. These people are not hoboes. They are not tramps. They are not foreigners. They are men destroyed financially in the Middle West and Southwest. Many are the cotton belt "white trash" but they are Americans.

Whether one visits the Federal Resettlement Administration's camps at Shafter and Arvin or the huddles of migrant indigents beside the roads throughout Kern county, one almost is struck dumb with sympathy. Ranchers have provided eighty-six camps, ranging in size from a few dirty tents and tin shacks to the seventy-one bunkhouses, tents, trailer houses, railroad box and refrigerator cars on the Digiorgio farms near Alvin. The Digiorgio layout includes separate quarters for Americans, Filipinos, and Mexicans. But most camps throughout the county are populated by white Americans.

There is no starvation—yet. Despite Works Progress Administration, State Relief Administration, and Kern County Welfare Department rules to care first for permanent residents, these transients do occasionally receive financial aid and hospitalization. But funds are almost totally lacking to aid them adequately. The men pick fruit and chop cotton. They earn an average of $2.75 to $3 a day. But they work, at the most, only half the days of the year. They must follow the crops throughout the San Joaquin Valley, and meantime their wives and children are falling prey to disease. Most camps have no baths, no showers, poor plumbing.

San Joaquin Valley growers welcome the indigents. Some have even advertised in the Southwestern States, inviting them, the workers say. As M.W. Skelton, Kern county welfare and county relief administration director, explains: "The growers prefer the migratory workers to permanent residents. The relief client may feel that if he doesn't like his job he can go back on the dole. The out-of-State workers must stay on the job."

What will happen next winter? Everyone is afraid to answer. Relief officials pray for Federal funds. Ranchers want more adequate camps. Police hope a crime wave will not break out. But no one can predict without a prayer.

Source: From Ray Zeman and *Los Angeles Times* Staff, "Squatter Army Wages Grim Battle for Life," in the *Los Angeles Times*, July 21, 1937. Copyright © 1937 by the *Los Angeles Times*. Used with permission.

Thomas McManus, California Citizens' Associations: California "Indigents Peril"

The Federal government is responsible for hundreds of thousands of indigents coming to this State. They stay here a year—then they are citizens, adding their burden of relief to the State. The State Relief Administration relief fund is near exhaustion. If this keeps up it will break down entirely the security of citizens of this State.

It has been necessary for manufacturers and employers of the State to meet this influx. The result has been a breaking down of our wage standards. These indigents are willing to work for from one-third to one-sixth of the wage scale throughout the State—anything to get food and anything to stay here long enough to gain citizenship in the State.

We've kept the wage scales high here. As a result, indigents can come here, get on WPA, and make more than they ever made in their lives in their home sectors. Our wage scales in WPA are two or three times as large as they are where these people come from.

It is up to us to defend our legitimate California people—we can care for them with old age pensions and relief, but certainly we can't take care of the indigents of other states.

Our program is to save California jobs for Californians—if the Federal government is going to spend moneys for them let them spend where they live and keep them there. We have plenty of native youth in this State growing up who need the jobs there are here—we don't need relief chiselers from other States coming here chiseling the jobs of Californians.

24.4.4 A New Deal for Indians

The New Deal brought important changes and some limited improvements to the lives of Indians. In 1933 some 320,000 Indian people, belonging to about 200 tribes, lived on reservations. Most were in Oklahoma, Arizona, New Mexico, and South Dakota. Indian people suffered from the worst poverty of any group in the nation and an infant mortality rate twice that of the white population. The incidence of alcoholism and other diseases, such as tuberculosis and measles, was much higher on the reservations than off. Half of all those on reservations were landless, forced to rent or live with relatives. The Bureau of Indian Affairs (BIA), oldest of the federal bureaucracies in the West, had a long history of corruption and mismanagement. The BIA had for years tried to assimilate Indians through education and had routinely interfered with Indian religious affairs and tribal customs. In 1928 the Merriam Report, prepared by the Institute for Government Research, had offered a scathing and widely publicized critique of BIA mismanagement. But the Hoover administration made no effort to reform the agency.

In 1933, Roosevelt appointed John Collier to bring change to the BIA. Collier had deep roots in progressive-era social work and community organizing in eastern big-city slums. During the 1920s he had become passionately interested in Indian affairs after spending time in Taos, New Mexico. He became involved with the struggle of the Pueblo Indians to hold on to their tribal lands, and he had served as executive secretary of the American Indian Defense Association. As the new BIA head, Collier pledged to "stop wronging the Indians and to rewrite the cruel and stupid laws that rob them and crush their family lives." Collier brought a reformer's zeal to his new job, and he quickly demonstrated his bureaucratic skills. He halted the sale of Indian lands, obtained emergency conservation work for 77,000 Indians under the CCC program, and secured millions of dollars in PWA funds to finance Indian day schools on the reservations. He also fired incompetent and corrupt BIA officials and insisted that those who remained respect tribal customs.

Most importantly, Collier became the driving force behind the Indian Reorganization Act (IRA) of 1934. The IRA reversed the allotment provisions of the Dawes Severalty Act of 1887, which had weakened tribal sovereignty by shifting the distribution of land from tribes to individuals. (See Chapter 18.) The new legislation permitted the restoration of surplus reservation lands to tribal ownership, and it allocated funds to purchase additional lands and for economic development. At its heart, the IRA sought to restore tribal structures by making the tribes instruments of the federal government. Any tribe that ratified the IRA could then elect a tribal council that would enjoy federal recognition as the legal tribal government. In this way, Collier argued, tribes would be "surrounded by the protective guardianship of the federal government and clothed with the authority of the federal government." He fought first to get the legislation through a reluctant Congress, which—uneasy with reversing the long-standing policy of Indian assimilation—insisted on many changes to Collier's original plan.

The more difficult battle involved winning the approval of the Indian peoples. Collier's efforts to win acceptance of the IRA met with mixed results on the reservations. Linguistic barriers made it nearly impossible for some tribes to fully assess the plan. The Papagos of southern Arizona, for example, had no words for "budget" and "representative." Their language made no distinction among the terms "law," "rule," "charter," and "constitution," and they used the same word for "president," "reservation agent," "king," and "Indian commissioner." In all, 181 tribes organized governments under the IRA, while 77 tribes rejected it.

The Navajos—the nation's largest tribe, with over 40,000 members—rejected the IRA, illustrating some of the contradictions embedded in federal policy. The Navajo refusal came as a protest against the BIA's forced reduction of their livestock, part of a soil conservation program. The government blamed Navajo sheep for the gullying and erosion that threatened to fill in Lake Mead and make Boulder Dam inoperable. But the hundreds of thousands of sheep in the Navajos' herds were central to their economy and society. They used sheep for barter, to pay religious leaders, and as their primary source of meat.

The Navajos believed the erosion stemmed not from overgrazing but from lack of sufficient water and inadequate acreage on the reservation. Howard Gorman, a Navajo political leader, angrily responded to Collier's last-minute personal appearance before the tribal council; "This thing, the thing you said that will make us strong, what do you mean by it? We have been told that not once but many times this same thing, and all it is is a bunch of lies. . . . You're wasting your time coming here and talking to us." Facing loss of half their sheep, Navajos took their anger out on Collier, rejecting the reorganization plan.

Under Collier, the BIA became much more sensitive to Indian cultural and religious freedom. The number of Indian people employed by the BIA itself increased from a few hundred in 1933 to more than 4,600 in 1940. Collier trumpeted the principle of Indian political autonomy, a radical idea for the day. In practice, however, both the BIA and Congress regularly interfered with reservation governments, especially in money matters. For the long run, Collier's most important legacy was the reassertion of the status of Indian tribes as semisovereign nations. In 1934, a Department of the Interior lawyer, Nathan Margold, wrote a legal opinion that tribal governments retained all their original powers—their "internal sovereignty"—except when these were specifically limited by acts of Congress. Decades later, U.S. courts would uphold the Margold opinion, leading to a significant restoration of tribal rights and land to Indian peoples of the West.

24.5 The Limits of Reform

What were the limits of the New Deal's reforms, and what legacy did they leave?

In his second Inaugural Address, Roosevelt emphasized that much remained to be done to remedy the effects of the Depression. Tens of millions of Americans were still denied the necessities for a decent life. "I see one-third of a nation ill-housed, ill-clad, ill-nourished," the president said. With his stunning electoral victory, the prospects for

further social reform seemed bright. Yet by 1937, the New Deal was in retreat. A rapid political turnaround over the next two years put continuing social reform efforts on the defensive. And even the most innovative programs, such as Social Security and the Wagner Act, too often reflected and in some cases deepened the racial inequality of 1930s America.

24.5.1 Court Packing

FDR and his advisers were frustrated by several Supreme Court rulings declaring important New Deal legislation unconstitutional. In May 1935, in *Schecter v. United States,* the Court found the National Recovery Administration unconstitutional in its entirety. The grounds included excessive delegation of legislative power to the executive branch and the regulation of business that was intrastate, as opposed to interstate or national, in character. In early 1936, ruling in *Butler v. United States,* the Court invalidated the Agricultural Adjustment Administration, declaring it an unconstitutional attempt at regulating agriculture. The Court was composed mostly of Republican appointees, 6 of whom were over 70. Roosevelt looked for a way to get more friendly judges on the high court.

In February 1937, FDR asked Congress for legislation that would expand the Supreme Court from 9 to a maximum of 15 justices. The president would be empowered to make a new appointment whenever an incumbent judge failed to retire upon reaching age 70. Roosevelt argued that age prevented justices from keeping up with their workload, but few people believed this logic. Newspapers almost unanimously denounced FDR's "court-packing bill."

Even more damaging was the determined opposition from a congressional coalition of conservatives and outraged New Dealers. The president gamely fought on, disingenuously insisting that his purpose was simply to reduce the workload of elderly Supreme Court justices. As the battle dragged on through the spring and summer, FDR's claims weakened. Conservative justice Willis Van Devanter announced plans to retire, giving Roosevelt the chance to make his first Court appointment.

More important, the Court—possibly influenced by FDR's landslide reelection—upheld the constitutionality of some key laws from the Second New Deal, including the Social Security Act and the National Labor Relations Act. At the end of August, FDR backed off from his plan and accepted a compromise bill that reformed lower-court procedures but left the Supreme Court untouched. FDR lost the battle for his judiciary proposal, but he may have won the war for a more responsive Court. Still, the political price was very high. The Court fight badly weakened Roosevelt's relations with Congress. Many more conservative Democrats now felt free to oppose further New Deal measures.

24.5.2 The New Deal and Race

"The Negro was born in Depression," recalled Clifford Burke, a black man interviewed decades after the 1930s. "It only became official when it hit the white man." Long near the bottom of the American economic ladder, African Americans suffered disproportionately through the difficult days of the 1930s. The old saying among black workers that they were "last hired, first fired" was never more true than during times of high unemployment. With jobs made scarce by the Depression, even traditional "Negro occupations"—domestic service, cooking, janitorial work, elevator operating—were coveted. One white clerk in Florida expressed a widely held view among white Southerners when he defended a lynch mob attack on a store with black employees; "A nigger hasn't got no right to have a job when there are white men who can do the work and are out of work."

Overall, the Roosevelt administration made little overt effort to combat the racism and segregation entrenched in American life. That would have been politically impossible, even if FDR had been inclined to challenge it. (He was not.) White Southerners dominated the Democratic Party in Congress. They held nearly half of the seats in both the House and Senate and, due to their seniority, chaired most of the important committees. FDR needed Southern Democrats to move forward, and that meant accepting their resolute commitment to white supremacy. Thus, under the guise of liberal reform, many New Deal programs excluded African Americans and Latinos by design, and some deepened institutional racism in American life.

The Agricultural Adjustment Administration, for example, vested authority to distribute federal relief funds to farmers in the state and local officials. When local AAA committees in the South reduced acreage and production to boost prices, thousands of black sharecroppers and farm laborers were forced off the land. Both the Social Security Act and the Wagner Act excluded agricultural and domestic laborers (two-thirds of black workers in the South) from their provisions. The Civilian Conservation Corps at first did not accept African Americans, and later established separate camps for them. The NRA labor codes tolerated lower wages for black workers doing the same jobs as white workers. African Americans could not get jobs with the TVA. In Atlanta, relief payments for black clients averaged $19.29 per month, compared with $32.66 for white clients.

African Americans understood well how the realities of Democratic Party politics severely limited the New Deal's benefits for people of color. In 1936 a diverse group of African American attorneys, labor leaders, academics, and civil rights activists founded the National Negro Congress (NNC). They focused on, as a conference title put it, "The Position of the Negro in Our National Economic Crisis." The NNC mobilized grassroots efforts to press for more attention to civil rights issues and the plight of black workers. Though it fell short of its grand ambition to build a black-led, interracial movement for social justice, the NNC provided a crucial link between the earlier work of the NAACP and the post-WWII civil rights struggle.

Some limited gains were made. President Roosevelt issued an executive order in 1935 banning discrimination in WPA projects. In the cities, the WPA, paying minimum wages of $12 a week, enabled thousands of African Americans to survive. Between 15 percent and 20 percent of all WPA employees were black people, although African Americans made up less than 10 percent of the nation's population. The Public Works Administration, under Harold Ickes, constructed a number of integrated housing complexes and employed more than its fair share of black workers in construction.

FDR appointed several African Americans to second-level positions in his administration. This group became known as "the Black Cabinet." Mary McLeod Bethune, an educator who rose from a sharecropping background to found Bethune-Cookman College, proved a superb leader of the Office of Minority Affairs in the National Youth Administration. Her most successful programs substantially reduced black illiteracy. Harvard-trained Robert Weaver advised the president on economic affairs and in 1966 became the first black cabinet member when he was appointed secretary of housing and urban development. Yet Roosevelt himself was diffident about advancing civil rights. Typically, he spoke out against lynching in the South, but unlike his wife, Eleanor, he refused to support legislation making it a federal crime. Nor would he risk alienating white Southerners by working for long-denied voting rights for African Americans in the South.

Hard times were especially trying for Mexican Americans as well. As the Great Depression drastically reduced the demand for their labor, they faced massive layoffs, deepening poverty, and deportation. During the 1930s over 400,000 Mexican nationals and their children returned to Mexico, often coerced by local officials unwilling to provide them with relief but happy to offer train fare to border towns. Many native-born Americans argued that deporting Mexicans could reduce unemployment for U.S. citizens. But these claims reflected deep racial prejudice inflamed by the economic crisis. In Detroit, deportations reduced the size of that city's thriving Mexican *colonia* from 15,000 to 3,000 by 1933. In Los Angeles, where 100,000 Mexicans constituted the largest *colonia* in the Unites States, fully one-third became *repatriados*.

For those who stayed, the New Deal programs did little to help. The AAA benefited large growers, not stoop laborers. Mexican American farm laborers found themselves excluded from the National Labor Relations Act and the

Social Security Act. The Federal Emergency Relief Administration and the Works Progress Administration did, at first, provide relief and jobs to the needy irrespective of citizenship status. But after 1937, the WPA eliminated aliens from eligibility, causing great hardship for thousands of Mexican families. Both mass repatriation and New Deal public works programs would have profound long-term implications for Mexican American communities. By World War II, *colonias* would be increasingly dominated by the American-born second generation, rather than those born in Mexico. And since only citizens and aliens who had begun the process of naturalization were eligible for public works jobs, these programs motivated more Mexican immigrants to become U.S. citizens.

The New Deal record for racial minorities was mixed at best. African Americans, especially in the cities, benefited from New Deal relief and work programs, though this assistance was not colorblind. Black industrial workers made inroads into labor unions affiliated with the CIO. The New Deal made no explicit attempt to attack the deeply rooted patterns of racism and discrimination in American life. The deteriorating economic and political conditions faced by Mexicans and Mexican Americans resulted in a mass reverse exodus. Yet by 1936, for the first time ever, a majority of black voters had switched their political allegiance to the Democrats—concrete evidence that they supported the directions taken by FDR's New Deal.

24.5.3 The Women's Network

The Great Depression and the New Deal brought some significant changes for women in American economics and politics. Most women continued to perform unpaid domestic labor within their homes, work that was not covered by the Social Security Act. A growing minority, however, also worked for wages and salaries outside the home. Women represented 24.3 percent of all workers in 1930; by 1940, 25.1 percent of the workforce was female. There was also an increase in married working women as a result of hard times. Between 1930 and 1940 the proportion of married women among the female workforce jumped from 28.8 percent to 35 percent. Jobs in which men predominated, such as in construction and heavy industry, were hardest hit by the Depression. In contrast, secretarial work, sales, and other areas long associated with women's labor were less affected. But sexual stereotyping still routinely forced women into low-paying and low-status jobs.

The New Deal brought a measurable, if temporary, increase in women's political influence. For those women associated with social reform, the New Deal opened up possibilities to effect change. A "women's network," linked by personal friendships and professional connections, made its presence felt in national politics and government. Most of the women in this network had long been active in movements promoting suffrage, labor law reform, and welfare programs.

Eleanor Roosevelt became a powerful political figure in her own right, actively using her prominence as First Lady to fight for the liberal causes she believed in. She revolutionized the role of the political wife by taking a position involving no institutional duties and turning it into a base for independent action. Privately, she enjoyed great influence with her husband, and her support for a cause could give it instant credibility. She worked behind the scenes with a wide network of women professionals and reformers whom she had come to know in the 1920s. She was a strong supporter of protective labor legislation for women, and her overall outlook owed much to the social reform tradition of the women's movement. "When all is said and done," she wrote in *It's Up to the Women* (1933), "women are different from men. They are equal in many ways, but they cannot refuse to acknowledge their differences. . . . Their physical functions in life are different and perhaps in the same way the contributions which they are to bring to the spiritual side of life are different."

One of Eleanor Roosevelt's first public acts as First Lady was to convene a White House Conference on the Emergency Needs of Women in November 1933. She helped Ellen Woodward, head of women's projects in the Federal Emergency Relief Administration, find jobs for 100,000 women, ranging from nursery school teaching to sewing. Roosevelt worked vigorously for antilynching legislation, compulsory health insurance, and child labor reform, and she fought racial discrimination in New Deal relief programs. She saw herself as the guardian of "human values" within the administration, a buffer between Depression victims and government bureaucracy. She frequently testified before legislative committees, lobbied her husband privately and the Congress publicly, and wrote a widely syndicated newspaper column.

Eleanor Roosevelt's closest political ally was Molly Dewson. A longtime social worker and suffragist, Dewson wielded a good deal of political clout as director of the Women's Division of the national Democratic Party. Under her leadership, women for the first time played a central role in shaping the party platform and running election campaigns. Dewson proved a tireless organizer, traveling to cities and towns around the country and educating women about Democratic policies and candidates. Her success impressed the president, and he relied on her judgment in recommending political appointments. Dewson placed more than a hundred women in New Deal positions.

Perhaps Dewson's most important success came in persuading FDR to appoint Frances Perkins secretary of labor—the first woman cabinet member in U.S. history.

A graduate of Mount Holyoke College and a veteran activist for social welfare and reform, Perkins had served as FDR's industrial commissioner in New York before coming to Washington. As labor secretary, Perkins embodied the gains made by women in appointive offices. Her department was responsible for creating the Social Security Act and the Fair Labor Standards Act of 1938, both of which incorporated protective measures long advocated by women reformers. Perkins defined feminism as, "the movement of women to participate in service to society." Yet despite the best efforts of the "women's network," women never constituted more than 19 percent of those employed by work relief programs, even though they made up 37 percent of the unemployed.

New Deal agencies opened up spaces for scores of women in the federal bureaucracy. These women were concentrated in Perkins's Labor Department, the FERA and WPA, and the Social Security Board. In addition, the social work profession, which remained roughly two-thirds female in the 1930s, grew enormously in response to the massive relief and welfare programs. In sum, although

ELEANOR ROOSEVELT AT WPA NURSERY SCHOOL Eleanor Roosevelt visiting a Works Progress Administration nursery school for African Americans in Des Moines, Iowa, in 1936. Mrs. Roosevelt was more outspoken than the president in championing the rights of African Americans and labor, and she actively used her prestige as First Lady in support of social justice causes.

Everett Collection Inc/Alamy Stock Photo.

the 1930s saw no radical challenges to existing male and female roles, working-class women and professional women held their own and managed to make some gains.

24.5.4 The Roosevelt Recession and the Ebbing of the New Deal

The nation's economy had improved significantly by 1937. Unemployment had declined to *only* 14 percent (9 million people), farm prices had improved to 1930 levels, and industrial production was slightly higher than the 1929 mark. Economic traditionalists, led by Secretary of the Treasury Henry Morgenthau, called for reducing the federal deficit, which had grown to more than $4 billion in fiscal year 1936. Roosevelt, always uneasy about the growing national debt, called for large reductions in federal spending, particularly in WPA and farm programs. Federal Reserve System officials, worried about inflation, tightened credit policies.

Rather than stimulating business, the retrenchment brought about a steep recession. The stock market collapsed in August 1937, and industrial output and farm prices plummeted. Most alarming was the big increase in unemployment. By March 1938, the jobless rate hovered around 20 percent, with more than 13 million people looking for work. As conditions worsened, Roosevelt began to blame the "new depression" on a "strike of capital," claiming businessmen had refused to invest because they wanted to hurt his prestige. In truth, the administration's own severe spending cutbacks were more responsible for the decline.

The blunt reality was that even after five years, the New Deal had not brought about economic recovery. Throughout 1937 and 1938, the administration drifted. Roosevelt received conflicting advice on the economy. Some advisers, suspicious of the reluctance of business to make new investments, urged a massive antitrust campaign against monopolies. Others urged a return to the strategy of "priming the economic pump" with more federal spending. Emergency spending bills in the spring of 1938 pumped new life into the WPA and the PWA. But Republican gains in the 1938 congressional elections (80 seats in the House, 7 in the Senate) made it harder than ever to get new reform measures through.

There were a couple of important exceptions. The 1938 Fair Labor Standards Act established the first federal minimum wage (25 cents an hour) and set a maximum workweek of 44 hours for all employees engaged in interstate commerce. The National Housing Act of 1937, also known as the Wagner-Steagall Act, funded public housing construction and slum clearance and provided rent subsidies for low-income families. But by and large, by 1938, the reform whirlwind of the New Deal was over.

24.6 Depression-Era Culture

How did the Great Depression affect American cultural life during the 1930s?

The Great Depression profoundly affected American culture, as it did all other aspects of national life. Yet contradictory messages coexisted, sometimes within the same novel or movie. With American capitalism facing its worst crisis in history, radical expressions of protest and revolution became more frequent. But there were also strong celebrations of individualism; nostalgia for a simpler, rural past; and many attempts to define American core virtues.

24.6.1 A New Deal for the Arts

The Depression hit America's writers, artists, and teachers just as hard as it did blue-collar workers. In 1935, the WPA allocated $300 million for the unemployed in these fields. Over the next four years, Federal Project No. 1, an umbrella agency covering writing, theater, music, and the visual arts, offered work to desperate unemployed artists and intellectuals, enriched the cultural lives of millions, and left a substantial artistic and cultural legacy. Nearly all these works were informed by the "documentary impulse," a deep desire to record and communicate the experiences of ordinary Americans.

At its height, the Federal Writers Project employed 5,000 writers on a variety of programs. Most notably, it produced a popular (and still useful) series of state and city guidebooks. The 150-volume *Life in America* series, for example, included valuable oral histories of former slaves, studies of ethnic and Indian cultures, and pioneering collections of American songs and folk tales. Work on the Writers Project helped many American writers to survive, to hone their craft, and later to achieve prominence—among them Ralph Ellison, Richard Wright, Margaret Walker, John Cheever, Saul Bellow, and Zora Neale Hurston. Novelist Anzia Yezierska recalled a strong spirit of camaraderie among the writers; "Each morning I walked to the Project as light-hearted as if I were going to a party." The Federal Theater Project (FTP) reached as many as 30 million Americans with its productions, expanding the audience for theater beyond the regular patrons of the commercial stage. Among its most successful productions were T. S. Eliot's *Murder in the Cathedral*, Maxwell Anderson's *Valley Forge*, and Orson Welles's version of *Macbeth* with an all-black cast.

The parallel Federal Music Project, under Nikolai Sokoloff of the Cleveland Symphony Orchestra, employed 15,000 musicians and financed hundreds of thousands of low-priced public concerts by touring orchestras. The Composers' Forum Laboratory commissioned new works by important young American classical composers. Among the struggling painters, later world-famous, who received government assistance through the Federal Art Project (FAP) were Willem de Kooning, Jackson Pollock, and Louise Nevelson. The FAP employed painters and sculptors to teach studio skills and art history in schools, churches, and settlement houses. It also commissioned artists to paint hundreds of murals on the walls of post offices, meeting halls, courthouses, and other government buildings.

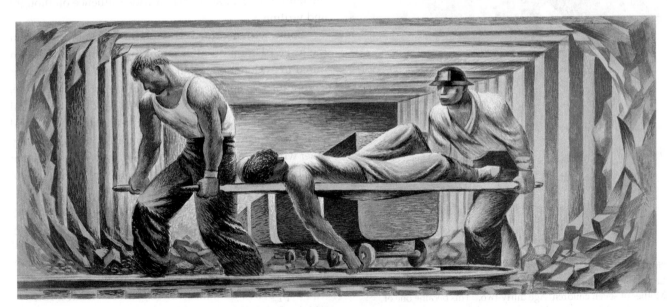

MINE RESCUE Fletcher Martin painted *Mine Rescue* (1939) in the Kellogg, Idaho, post office. The work was part of a Treasury Department program that employed unemployed artists to beautify government buildings. The mural was eventually removed under pressure from local citizens who worried that it might upset those who had lost loved ones in mine accidents.

Smithsonian American Art Museum, Washington, DC/Art Resource, NY.

24.6.2 The Documentary Impulse

During the 1930s, an enormous number of artists, novelists, journalists, photographers, and filmmakers tried to document the devastation wrought by the depression in American communities. They also depicted people's struggles to cope with, and reverse, hard times. Mainstream mass media, such as *Life* magazine, with its photo essays and "March of Time" newsreels, also adapted this stance.

The "documentary impulse" became a prominent style in 1930s cultural expression. The most direct and influential expression of the documentary style was the photograph. In 1935, Roy Stryker, chief of the Historical Section of the Resettlement Administration, gathered a remarkable group of photographers to help document the work of the agency. Stryker encouraged them to photograph whatever caught their interest, even if the pictures had no direct connection with RA projects. These photographers, including Dorothea Lange and Walker Evans, left the single most significant visual record of the Great Depression. They traveled through rural areas, small towns, and migrant labor camps, and they produced

"MIGRANT MOTHER" The original caption for this 1936 Dorothea Lange photograph read, "Destitute pea pickers in California. Mother of seven children. Age thirty-two." This became one of the most widely circulated images produced by the Farm Security Administration. Lange's popular photograph, also known as "Migrant Mother," soon became a universal symbol of suffering and poverty.

Library of Congress (Photoduplication).

powerful images of despair and resignation, of hope and resilience. Stryker believed that the faces of the subjects were most memorable. "You could look at the people," he wrote, "and see fear and sadness and desperation. But you saw something else, too. A determination that not even the depression could kill. The photographers saw it—documented it." (See SEEING History.)

That double vision, combining a frank portrayal of pain and suffering with a faith in the possibility of overcoming disaster, could be found in many other cultural works of the period. John Steinbeck's *The Grapes of Wrath* (1939), soon made into an acclaimed film, sympathetically portrayed the hardships of Oklahoma Dust Bowl migrants on their way to California. "We ain't gonna die out," Ma Joad asserts near the end of the book. "People is goin' on—changing' a little, maybe, but goin' right on." Many writers interrupted their work to travel around the country and discover the thoughts and feelings of ordinary people. "With real events looming larger than any imagined happenings," novelist Elizabeth Noble wrote, "documentary films and still photographs, reportage and the like have taken the place once held by the grand invention."

24.6.3 Waiting for Lefty

For some, capitalism itself was responsible for the Great Depression. Relatively few Americans became communists or socialists in the 1930s (at its height, the Communist Party of the United States had perhaps 100,000 members), and many of these remained active for only a brief time. Yet Marxist analysis, with its emphasis on class conflict and the failures of capitalism, had a wide influence on thought and writing.

Some writers joined the Communist Party, seeing in the Soviet Union an alternative to an American system mired in exploitation, racial inequality, and human misery. Communist writers sought to radicalize art and literature, and celebrated collective struggle rather than individual achievement. Granville Hicks, an editor of the radical magazine *The New Masses*, flatly declared, "If there is any other working interpretation of the apparent chaos than that which presents itself in terms of the class struggle, it has not been revealed."

A more common pattern for intellectuals, especially young ones, was brief flirtation with communism. Many African American writers, attracted by the Communist Party's militant opposition to lynching, job discrimination, and segregation, briefly joined the party or found their first supportive audiences there. These included Richard Wright, Ralph Ellison, and Langston Hughes. Playwrights and actors associated with New York's influential Group Theater were often part of the Communist Party orbit in those years. One production of the group, Clifford Odets's *Waiting for Lefty* (1935), depicted a union-organizing drive among taxi drivers. At the climax, someone yells that the organizer Lefty (for whom everyone has been waiting) has been killed by the police, and the audience joins the actors in shouting "Strike!" A commercial and political success, it offered perhaps the most celebrated example of radical, politically engaged art.

Left-wing influence reached its height after 1935, during the "Popular Front" period. Alarmed by the rise of fascism in Europe (see Chapter 25), communists around the world followed the Soviet line of aligning with liberals and other antifascists. Some 3,000 American men and women volunteered for the Abraham Lincoln Brigade—organized by the Communist Party—to fight in the Spanish Civil War on the republican side against the fascists led by Francisco Franco. The Lincoln Brigade's sense of commitment and sacrifice appealed to millions of Americans sympathetic to the republican cause. At home, the American Communist Party adopted the slogan "Communism is

SEEING History

Documenting Hard Times in Black and White and Color

Between 1935 and 1942, photographers working for the Farm Security Administration (FSA) created a remarkable pictorial record of Depression life. The photography project had a political goal as well: to prod New Deal agricultural policy into providing greater support for the poorest agricultural workers. The photographers thus took aim at social, economic, and racial inequalities within American agriculture. They worked under difficult conditions. On the road for months, they worked in harsh weather, often eating bad food and staying in primitive accommodations, trying to capture the lives of subjects suspicious of their motives. Their unexposed film had to be processed in Washington, so the photographers never knew what they had shot until they received prints weeks later.

Many FSA photographs were published in newspapers and popular magazines as part of the agency's campaign to win public support for a greater federal role in building more migrant worker camps. Some of these photographs, such as those by Dorothea Lange and Walker Evans, have become among the most widely circulated images in the history of the medium. Even though Lange's *Migrant Mother* became a kind of universal symbol of suffering, its context and social-science origins have been lost. Her original caption simply read, "Destitute pea pickers in California. Mother of seven children. Age thirty-two."

In 1939, some FSA photographers began using new 35-mm Kodachrome film to make color slides. Unlike black-and-white prints, color slides were neither easily made nor reproducible in newspapers and magazines. Black-and-white images also seemed to offer a starker, more "realistic" documentation of poverty; many thought color photos too cheery. FSA photographers produced some 164,000 black-and-white images and only about 1,600 in color. Photographs like Russell Lee's, however, remind us that people lived lives in color, even during the Depression.

- **How does Lee's portrait of the homesteader couple compare to Lange's portrait of the Migrant Mother as a document of rural life in the Great Depression? Are there differences beyond black and white and color?**

DOCUMENTING HARD TIMES IN BLACK AND WHITE AND COLOR

Left and right: Library of Congress (Photoduplication).

Twentieth-Century Americanism," and Communists proclaimed strong support of Roosevelt's New Deal (which before they had denounced). Their influence became especially strong within the labor movement as Communists and other radicals, known for their dedication and effectiveness, played a leading role in the difficult CIO unionizing drives in the auto, steel, and electrical industries. The radical presence was also strong within certain WPA arts projects. A decade later, many young idealists who came into the Communist Party orbit, no matter how briefly, would pay a heavy price.

24.6.4 Raising Spirits: Film, Radio, and the Swing Era

Despite the Depression, the mass-culture industry expanded enormously during the 1930s. If mass culture offered little in the way of direct responses to the economic and social problems of the day, it nonetheless played a more integral role than ever in shaping the rhythms and desires of the nation's everyday life.

Toward the end of the 1920s, the coming of "talking pictures" helped make movies the most popular entertainment form of the day. More than 60 percent of Americans attended one of the nation's 20,000 movie houses each week, and millions followed the lives and careers of movie stars more avidly than ever. With so many movies being churned out by Hollywood studios for so many fans, it is difficult to generalize about the cultural impact of individual films. Moviegoing itself, usually enjoyed with friends, family, or a date, was perhaps the most significant development of all.

At the same time, the movie studios themselves, responding to pressure from the Roman Catholic Church and other advocates of traditional morality, instituted a more stringent Production Code in 1933. For the next three decades, American filmmakers had to work within very narrow parameters of what was acceptable to depict onscreen. The code required unambiguous depictions of good triumphing over evil and a straitlaced treatment of sex.

It is too easy to dismiss movies as mere escapism. The more interesting question is, what were people escaping to? Several film genres proved enormously popular during the 1930s. Gangster films did very well in the early Depression years. *Little Caesar* (1930), starring Edward G. Robinson, and *Public Enemy* (1931), with James Cagney, set the standard. They all depicted violent criminals brought to justice by society—but along the way they gave audiences a vicarious exposure to the pleasures of wealth, power, and lawbreaking. Social disorder could also be treated comically, as in such Marx Brothers films as *Duck Soup* (1933) and *A Night at the Opera* (1935). Mae West's popular comedies, such as *She Done Him Wrong* (1933) and *I'm No Angel* (1933), made people laugh by subverting expectations about sex roles. West was

an independent woman, not afraid of pleasure. When Cary Grant asked her, "Haven't you ever met a man who could make you happy?" she replied, "Sure, lots of times."

Movie musicals offered audiences extravagant song-and-dance spectacles, as in Busby Berkeley's *Gold Diggers of 1933* and *42nd Street* (1933). "Screwball comedies" featured sophisticated, fast-paced humor and usually paired popular male and female stars: Clark Gable and Claudette Colbert in *It Happened One Night* (1934), and Katharine Hepburn and Cary Grant in *Bringing Up Baby* (1938). A few movies, notably from the Warner Brothers studio, tried to offer a more "socially conscious" view of Depression-era life. These included *I Am a Fugitive from a Chain Gang* (1932), *Wild Boys of the Road* (1933), and *Black Legion* (1936).

By and large, Hollywood avoided social or political controversy. Some 1930s filmmakers expressed highly personal visions of core American values. Two who succeeded in capturing both popular and critical acclaim were Walt Disney and Frank Capra. By the mid-1930s, Disney's animated cartoons had become moral tales that stressed keeping order and following the rules. The Mickey Mouse cartoons and the full-length features, such as *Snow White and the Seven Dwarfs* (1937), pulled back from the fantastic stretching of time and space in earlier cartoons. Capra's comedies, such as *Mr. Deeds Goes to Town* (1936) and *You Can't Take It with You* (1938), idealized a small-town America with close families and comfortable homes. Although Capra's films dealt with contemporary problems more than most—unemployment, government corruption, economic monopoly—he made no critique of the social and economic system. Rather, he seemed to suggest that most of the country's ills could be solved if only its leaders learned the old-fashioned values of "common people"—kindness, loyalty, and charity.

Radio broadcasting emerged as the most powerful medium of communication in the home, profoundly changing the rhythms and routines of everyday life. In 1930, roughly 12 million American homes (40 percent of the total) had radio sets; by the end of the decade, 90 percent had them. Advertisers dominated the structure and content of American radio, forming a powerful alliance with the two large networks, the National Broadcasting Company (NBC) and the Columbia Broadcasting System (CBS). The Federal Communications Commission (FCC), established in 1934, continued long-standing policies that favored commercial broadcasting over other arrangements, such as municipal or university programming. By 1937 NBC and CBS controlled about 90 percent of the wattage in the American broadcasting industry. Nearly all network shows were produced by advertising agencies.

The Depression actually helped radio expand. An influx of talent arrived from the weakened worlds of vaudeville, ethnic theater, and the recording industry. The well-financed networks offered an attractive outlet to advertisers seeking a national audience. Radio programming achieved a regularity and professionalism absent in the 1920s, making it much easier for a listener to identify a show with its sponsor. Companies with national distribution paid thousands of dollars an hour to networks; by 1939 annual radio advertising revenues totaled $171 million.

Much of network radio was based on older cultural forms. The variety show, hosted by comedians and singers and based on the old vaudeville format, was the first important style. It featured stars like Eddie Cantor, Ed Wynn, Kate Smith, and Al Jolson, who constantly plugged the sponsor's product. The use of a studio audience recreated the human interaction so necessary in vaudeville. The popular comedy show *Amos 'n' Andy* adapted the minstrel "blackface" tradition to the new medium. White comedians Freeman Gosden and Charles Correll used only their two voices to invent a world of stereotyped African Americans for their millions of listeners.

The spectacular growth of the daytime serial, or soap opera, dominated radio drama. Aimed mainly at women working in the home, these serials alone constituted 60 percent of all daytime shows by 1940. Soaps such as *Ma Perkins*, *Helen Trent*, and *Clara Lou and Em* revolved around strong, warm female characters who provided advice and strength to weak, indecisive friends and relatives. Action counted very little; the development of character and relationships was all-important. Contemporary studies found that the average soap opera fan regularly tuned in to six or more different series. Evening radio dramas included thrillers such as *Inner Sanctum* and *The Shadow*, which emphasized crime and suspense. These shows made great use of music and sound effects to sharpen their impact.

In the late 1930s serious drama bloomed briefly, independent of commercial sponsorship, at CBS's Columbia Workshop. Archibald MacLeish's *Fall of the City*, a parable about fascism, and Orson Welles's *War of the Worlds*, a super-realistic adaptation of the H. G. Wells classic, proved the persuasive power of radio. Welles's show convinced many who tuned in that a Martian invasion was actually under way. Radio became a key factor in politics as well, as President Roosevelt showed early on with his popular "fireside" chats.

Radio news arrived in the 1930s, showing the medium's potential for direct and immediate coverage of political events. Network news and commentary shows multiplied rapidly. Complex political and economic issues and the impending European crisis (see Chapter 25) fueled a news hunger among Americans. A 1939 survey found that 70 percent of Americans relied on the radio as their prime source of news. Yet commercial broadcasting, dominated by big sponsors and large radio manufacturers, failed to cover politically controversial events such as labor struggles. The most powerful station in the country, WLW in Cincinnati, refused to even mention strikes on the air. NBC routinely canceled programs it feared might undermine "public confidence and faith."

One measure of radio's cultural impact was its role in popularizing jazz. Before the 1930s, jazz was heard largely among African Americans and a small coterie of white fans. Regular broadcasts of live performances exposed a broader public to the music. So did radio disc jockeys who played jazz records on their shows. Bands led by black artists such as Duke Ellington and Count Basie began to enjoy reputations outside of traditional jazz centers like Chicago, Kansas City, and New York.

TWENTY CENT MOVIE Reginald Marsh, *Twenty Cent Movie*, 1936. Marsh documented the urban landscape of the 1930s with great empathy, capturing the city's contradictory mix of commercialism, optimism, energy, and degradation. The popularity of Hollywood films and their stars reached new heights during the Great Depression.

SuperStock/Glow Images.

Benny Goodman became the key figure in the "swing era," largely through radio exposure. Goodman, a white, classically trained clarinetist, had been inspired by African American bandleaders Fletcher Henderson and Don Redman, who created big-band arrangements that combined harmonic call-and-response patterns with breaks for improvised solos. Goodman purchased a series of these arrangements, smoothing out the sound but keeping the strong dance beat. His band's late-Saturday-night broadcasts began to attract attention, and in 1935, at the Palomar Ballroom in Los Angeles, made the breakthrough that established his enormous popularity. When his band started playing, the young crowd, primed by radio broadcasts, roared its approval and began to dance wildly. Goodman's music was perfect for doing the jitterbug or lindy hop, dances borrowed from African American culture. As the "King of Swing," Goodman helped make big-band jazz a hit with millions of teenagers and young adults from all backgrounds. In the late 1930s, big-band music by artists like Goodman, Ellington, and Basie accounted for the majority of million-selling records.

Millions of Americans no doubt used mass culture as a temporary escape from their problems, but the various meanings they drew from movies, radio, and popular music were by no means monolithic. In most communities, Americans—especially young people—identified more closely than ever with the national communities forged by modern media.

Conclusion

Although American capitalism and democracy survived the cataclysm of the Great Depression, the New Deal failed in its central mission. It was never able to bring full economic recovery or end the scourge of mass unemployment. Only the economic boom that accompanied World War II would do that. Far from being the radical program its conservative critics charged, the New Deal did little to alter fundamental property relations or the distribution of wealth. Indeed, most of its programs largely failed to help the most powerless groups in America—migrant workers, tenant farmers and sharecroppers, African Americans, and other minorities.

But the New Deal profoundly changed many areas of American life. Overall, it radically increased the role of the federal government in American lives and communities, creating a new kind of liberalism defined by an activist state. Social Security, unemployment insurance, and federal relief programs established at least the framework for a welfare state. For the first time, the federal government guaranteed the rights of workers to join trade unions, and it set standards for minimum wages and maximum hours worked. The national government now took responsibility for assisting the elderly with their retirement. The FDIC and the SEC established important new federal rules protecting individuals from financial ruin and unregulated stock markets. Western and southern communities in particular were transformed through federal intervention in water, power, and agricultural policies. In politics, the New Deal established the Democrats as the majority party. Some version of the Roosevelt New Deal coalition would dominate the nation's political life for another three decades.

While the New Deal aided some previously unrecognized groups—the poor, the elderly, and the industrial working class—it did little to challenge racial and gender discrimination. Some of the more ambitious programs, such as those centered around subsidizing the arts and building model communities, enjoyed only brief success. Other reform proposals, such as national health insurance, never got off the ground. Conservative counterpressures, especially after 1937, limited what could be changed. Still, the New Deal did more than strengthen the presence of the national government in people's lives. It also fed expectations that the federal presence would intensify. Washington became a much greater center of economic regulation and political power, and the federal bureaucracy grew in size and influence. With the coming of World War II, the direct role of national government in shaping American communities would expand beyond the dreams of even the most ardent New Dealer.

Key Terms

Great Depression The nation's worst economic crisis, extending through the 1930s, producing unprecedented bank failures, unemployment, and industrial and agricultural collapse. p. 579

Bonus Army Gathering of unemployed veterans of World War I in Washington in 1932 demanding payment of service bonuses not due until 1945. p. 583

fireside chat One of a series of speeches broadcast nationally over the radio in which President Franklin D. Roosevelt explained complex issues and programs in plain language, as though his listeners were gathered around the fireside with him. p. 584

Emergency Banking Relief Act 1933 act which gave the president broad discretionary powers over all banking transactions and foreign exchange. p. 584

New Deal The collection of economic and political policies of the Roosevelt administration in the 1930s. p. 585

Tennessee Valley Authority (TVA) Federal regional planning agency established to promote conservation, produce electric power, and encourage economic development in seven Southern states. p. 585

National Labor Relations Act Act establishing federal guarantee of right to organize trade unions and collective bargaining. p. 578

New Deal coalition Alliance that included traditional-minded white Southern Democrats, big-city political machines, industrial workers of all races, trade unionists, and many Depression-hit farmers. p. 590

CHRONOLOGY

1929	Stock market crash
1932	Bonus Army marches on Washington / Franklin D. Roosevelt elected president
1933	Roughly 13 million workers unemployed / The "Hundred Days" legislation of the First New Deal
1934	Mass deportations of Mexican nationals
1935	Boulder Dam completed / Committee for Industrial Organization (CIO) established / Dust storms turn the southern Great Plains into the Dust Bowl / Social Security Act and National Labor Relations Act
1936	Roosevelt defeats Alfred M. Landon in reelection landslide / Sit-down strike begins at General Motors plants in Flint, Michigan
1937	Roosevelt's "court-packing" plan weakens him politically / "Roosevelt recession" begins
1938	Fair Labor Standards Act establishes the first federal minimum wage

Chapter 25
World War II 1941–1945

FDR REVIEWS TROOPS President Franklin Delano Roosevelt reviews helmeted soldiers standing at attention.

Library of Congress (Photoduplication).

 ## Contents and Focus Questions

American Communities

Los Alamos, New Mexico

On Monday, July 16, 1945, the first atomic bomb exploded in a brilliant flash visible in three states. The heat generated by the blast was four times the temperature at the center of the sun, and the light produced rivaled that of nearly 20 suns. Even 10 miles away, people felt a strong surge of heat. The giant fireball ripped a crater a half mile wide in the ground, fusing the desert sand into glass. The shock wave blew out windows in houses more than 200 miles away. The blast killed every living creature—squirrels, rabbits, snakes,

plants, and insects—within a mile, and the smells of death lingered for nearly a month.

Very early that morning, Ruby Wilkening had driven to a nearby mountain ridge, where she joined several other women waiting for the blast. Wilkening worried about her husband, a physicist, who was already at the Trinity test site. No one knew exactly what to expect, not even the scientists who developed the bomb.

The Wilkenings were part of a unique community of scientists who had been marshaled for war. President

Franklin D. Roosevelt had inaugurated a small nuclear research program in 1939. Then, after the United States entered World War II in 1941, the president released resources to create the Manhattan Project under the direction of the Army Corps of Engineers. By December 1942, a team headed by Italian-born Nobel Prize winner Enrico Fermi had produced the first chain reaction in uranium. Now the mission was to build the atomic bomb.

In March 1943, the government moved the key researchers and their families to Los Alamos, a remote and sparsely populated region in New Mexico. Some researchers and their families lived in a former boys' preparatory school until new houses could be built; others doubled up in rugged log cabins or at nearby ranches. Despite the chaos, outstanding American and European scientists eagerly signed up for this top-secret project. Most were young and quite a few were recently married. Many couples began their families at Los Alamos, producing a boom of nearly 1,000 babies between 1943 and 1949.

The scientists and their families formed an exceptionally close-knit community, united by the need for secrecy and their shared antagonism toward their army guardians. The military atmosphere was oppressive. Homes and laboratories were cordoned off by barbed wire and patrolled by military police. Security personnel followed the scientists whenever they left Los Alamos. All outgoing mail was censored, and residents could not let even their closest relatives know where they were. Well-known scientists commonly worked under aliases, and code names were used for such terms as *atom*, *bomb*, and *uranium fission*. Children were registered without surnames at nearby public schools. Even automobile accidents, weddings, and deaths went unreported.

A profound urgency motivated the research team, which included refugees from Nazi Germany and Fascist Italy and a large proportion of Jews. The premier scientists were all men, although nearly 100 women worked in subordinate jobs in the scientific and technical sectors. Other women filled mainly administrative and clerical positions or provided medical and educational support services for the community. The director of the project, California physicist J. Robert Oppenheimer, promoted a collegial élan that offset the military style of commanding general Leslie Groves. Just 38, "Oppie" personified the idealism that helped the community of scientists overcome whatever moral reservations they held about placing such a potentially terrible weapon in the hands of the government.

The unprecedented scientific mobilization at Los Alamos mirrored changes occurring throughout American society as the nation rallied behind the war effort. Sixteen million men and women left home for military service and nearly as many moved to take advantage of wartime jobs. In becoming what Roosevelt called "a great arsenal of democracy," the American economy quickly and fully recovered from the Great Depression. Several states in the South and Southwest experienced huge surges in population. California alone grew by 2 million people, a large proportion of them from Mexico. Many broad social changes with roots in earlier times—such as the economic expansion of the West, the erosion of farm tenancy among black people in the South and white people in Appalachia, and the increasing employment of married women—accelerated during the war. The events of the war eroded old communities, created new ones like Los Alamos, and transformed nearly all aspects of American society.

Although the transition to wartime was far from smooth, the United States emerged from World War II far stronger than its European and Russian allies, who bore the brunt of the fighting. Indeed, the nation emerged strong enough to claim a new role as the world's leading superpower.

Los Alamos

25.1 The Coming of World War II

What steps did Roosevelt take in the late 1930s to prepare the United States for war?

The worldwide depression helped to undermine a political order that had been shaky since World War I. Political unrest spread across Europe and Asia as international trade dropped by as much as two-thirds and unemployment rose. Demagogues played on national and racial hatreds, fueled by old resentments and current despair, and offered solutions in the form of territorial expansion by military conquest. Although the majority of Americans opposed foreign entanglements, overseas events pulled the nation steadily toward war.

25.1.1 The Shadows of War across the Globe

Two major threats to peace gathered force in the 1930s in East Asia and in Central Europe. In September 1931, the imperial army of Japan seized Manchuria from China and established a puppet government. When the League of Nations objected, Japan simply quit the League. A full-scale Japanese invasion of China proper followed in 1937, and the world watched in horror the Rape of Nanking (today, Nanjing)—the destruction of what was then China's capital and the slaughter of as many as 300,000 Chinese men, women, and children. Within a year, Japan controlled most of coastal China.

In Europe, fanatical and tyrannical fascist leaders were taking power—first in Italy and later in Germany. "We have buried the putrid corpse of liberty," boasted Italy's fascist dictator, Benito Mussolini, in the 1920s. In Germany, nationalist resentment over the Treaty of Versailles fueled Adolf Hitler's National Socialist (Nazi) movement with its racist doctrine of "Aryan" supremacy that condemned nonwhites and Jews as "degenerate races." In January 1933, Hitler became chancellor, with the backing of leading industrialists but only about one-third of voters. With his brown-shirted storm troopers ruling the streets, he quickly destroyed opposition parties and made himself absolute dictator of the strongest nation in Central Europe. Renouncing the disarmament provisions imposed by the Versailles peace treaty, Hitler began to rebuild Germany's armed forces. No European powers opposed him.

Soon enough, Mussolini and Hitler began to act on their imperial visions. In 1935, Italy conquered Ethiopia and turned the African nation into a colony. In 1936, Hitler occupied the formerly demilitarized Rhineland region. In the Spanish Civil War that broke out later that year, Italy and Germany both supported General Francisco Franco's fascist rebels against the democratic republican regime. In November, Germany and Italy forged an alliance, the Rome-Berlin Axis. Hitler now prepared to implement his plan to secure *Lebensraum*—living space for the "Aryan" populations—which demanded expansion into neighboring countries.

In 1938, Hitler annexed Austria and then turned toward Czechoslovakia, the one remaining democracy in Central Europe, which Britain and France had pledged to assist. War seemed imminent. But Britain and France surprised the world by agreeing, at Munich on September 30, 1938, to allow Germany to annex the Sudetenland—the German-speaking parts of Czechoslovakia. Accepting this "appeasement," Hitler pledged that he would make no more territorial demands. Within six months, Nazi troops poured into the country, and Hitler seized the rest of Czechoslovakia in March 1939.

By then, much of the world was aware of the horror of Hitler's racist regime. On the night of November 9, 1938, Nazi storm troopers rounded up Jews, beating them mercilessly and murdering an untold number. In this coordinated pogrom, which came to be known as *Kristallnacht*, the "Night of Broken Glass," the attackers smashed windows of Jewish shops, ransacked Jewish homes, and burned synagogues. The Nazi government expropriated Jewish property and excluded Jews from all but the most menial jobs. Pressured by Hitler, his allies Hungary and Italy also enacted laws curtailing the civil rights of Jews.

25.1.2 Roosevelt Readies for War

FDR's instincts were to stand with other threatened democracies, but he knew that the American public and many members of Congress were strongly isolationist. In 1935, Congress passed the first of five Neutrality Acts to deter entanglements in future foreign wars. It required the president to embargo the sale and shipment of munitions to all belligerents. As late as 1937, nearly 70 percent of Americans responding to a Gallup poll agreed that U.S. involvement in World War I had been a mistake. Although this sentiment continued to resonate in Congress, Roosevelt managed to secure $1 billion in appropriations to enlarge the navy.

In the fall of 1939, war broke out in Europe. In August, Germany and the Soviet Union—hitherto mortal enemies—had stunned the world by signing a nonaggression pact. A week later, on September 1, Hitler invaded Poland. Within days, Poland's allies, Great Britain and France, declared war on Germany. After Soviet troops joined the invasion on September 17, Hitler and Stalin divided Poland between them. Soviet forces also attacked Finland and seized the tiny Baltic republics.

Hitler began a crushing offensive against Western Europe in April 1940. In a **blitzkrieg** (lightning war), fast-moving columns of German tanks supported by air power struck first at Denmark and Norway and soon thereafter conquered Holland, Belgium, and Luxembourg. Hitler's army, joined at the last minute by the Italians, then easily overran France in June 1940. When Britain refused to negotiate, Hitler launched the Battle of Britain. Nazi bombers pounded cities while U-boats tried to cut off incoming supplies. The Royal Air Force delivered Nazi Germany its first major defeat in the war.

Even after Germany, Italy, and Japan formed the **Axis powers** alliance on September 27, 1940, and pledged to "stand by and co-operate with one another" for the next 10 years, the American public desperately hoped to stay out of the war. Roosevelt invoked the **Neutrality Act of 1939**, which permitted the sale of arms to Britain, France, and China, and affirmed his position; "All aid to the Allies short of war." But by May 1940, while France was collapsing, he had already begun to transfer surplus U.S. warships and equipment to Britain. Then, in September, while the Battle of Britain raged, Roosevelt and Congress enacted the nation's first peacetime military draft, which sent 1.4 million young men to army training camps by July 1941.

FDR could not yet admit the inevitability of U.S. involvement—especially in 1940, an election year. After he defeated Wendell L. Willkie, a Republican from Indiana,

Roosevelt moved more aggressively to aid hard-pressed Great Britain. In his annual message to Congress in early 1941, he proposed a bill allowing the president to sell, exchange, or lease arms to any country whose defense he judged vital to U.S. security. Passed in March 1941, the **Lend-Lease Act** made Great Britain the first beneficiary of massive aid.

In August 1941, Roosevelt met secretly on a warship off Newfoundland with Winston Churchill, the embattled British prime minister. Roosevelt evaded Churchill's pleas to enter the war—he knew that Congress and the American public still hoped to stay out—but the two leaders outlined common goals for the postwar world in what was called the **Atlantic Charter**, a lofty proclamation calling for all peoples to live in freedom from fear, want, and tyranny. The Atlantic Charter also set the terms for the postwar international order, including free trade, self-determination for all nations occupied during the war, the end to territorial seizures, and disarmament.

The European war widened. Having conquered the Balkans, Hitler broke the Nazi-Soviet Pact and, in June 1941, 3.2 million German troops invaded the Soviet Union. Roosevelt sent Lend-Lease supplies to the Soviets and ordered U.S. warships to "sink on sight" any lurking German submarines. The result was an undeclared and unpublicized naval war between the United States and Nazi Germany on the North Atlantic.

25.1.3 Pearl Harbor

Throughout 1940 and 1941, Americans watched with dread the widening European struggle; meanwhile, war also escalated in East Asia. Anticipating trouble in the Pacific, in May 1940 Roosevelt transferred the Pacific fleet from its California bases to a forward position at Pearl Harbor in Hawai'i.

Both the United States and Japan were playing for time. Roosevelt wanted to bank resources to fight Germany (the greater danger, he thought); Japan's leaders gambled that America's preoccupation with Europe might allow them to conquer all Southeast Asia, the oil-rich Dutch East Indies (today, Indonesia). Lacking petroleum, Japan was desperate to obtain a reliable source for oil. When Japan occupied French Indochina in July 1941, Roosevelt moved from economic sanctions, which had been in place for several months, to freezing Japanese assets in the United States and cutting off its oil supplies.

War with Japan looked more likely. The Japanese military decided to hit the Americans with a knock-out blow that would give them time to seize Southeast Asia and the western Pacific. But American intelligence had broken the Japanese secret diplomatic code, and the president knew that Japan was preparing to strike somewhere, most likely the Philippines. By the end of November, all American Pacific forces were put on high alert.

On December 7, 1941, Japan struck the Pacific fleet at Pearl Harbor. Within two hours, Japanese bombers destroyed nearly 200 American planes and badly damaged the fleet; more than 2,400 Americans were killed and nearly 1,200 wounded. (Fortunately, the U.S. carriers were spared, being out to sea on the morning of the attack.) That same day, Japan bombed U.S. bases on the Philippines, Guam, and Wake Island and attacked the British fleet and colonies in East Asia.

On December 8, declaring the attack on Pearl Harbor "a date which will live in infamy," Roosevelt asked Congress for a declaration of war against Japan. With only one dissenting vote—by pacifist Jeannette Rankin of Montana, who had voted against U.S. entry into World War I in 1917—Congress agreed. On December 11, Germany and Italy declared war on the United States. World War II had begun for Americans.

25.2 The Great Arsenal of Democracy

What were the economic consequences of the war for the United States?

In December 1940, Roosevelt told Americans in a radio "fireside chat" that the nation must become the "great arsenal of democracy," and by the time the United States entered the war, the U.S. economy had already geared up for military purposes. After Pearl Harbor, the federal government poured unprecedented energy and money into wartime production and assigned a huge army of experts to manage it. During the next three years, the economic machinery that had failed during the 1930s was running at full speed. Defense spending would spark the greatest economic boom in the history of any nation. Suddenly, it seemed, the Great Depression ended.

25.2.1 Mobilizing for War

Less than two weeks after the Pearl Harbor attack, Roosevelt signed the **War Powers Act of 1941**, emergency legislation that established a precedent for executive authority that would endure long after the war's end. Under the new law, the president could reorganize the federal government and create new agencies, censor all news and information and abridge civil liberties, seize foreign-owned property, and even award government contracts without competitive bidding.

Roosevelt promptly used his authority to create special wartime agencies. At the top of his agenda was a massive reorganization of the economy, to be managed by an alphabet soup of new agencies. For example, the Supply Priorities and Allocation Board (SPAB) oversaw the use of

FDR ADDRESSES CONGRESS On the day after the attack on Pearl Harbor, President Franklin D. Roosevelt addressed a joint session of Congress and asked for an immediate declaration of war against Japan. The resolution passed with one dissenting vote, and the United States entered World War II.

ASSOCIATED PRESS.

scarce materials and resources vital to the war. The Office of Price Administration (OPA) used price controls to check inflation. The National War Labor Board (NWLB) mediated labor-management disputes. The War Manpower Commission (WMC) directed the mobilization of military and civilian services. Overseeing this massive transformation from peacetime to wartime production was the War Production Board (WPB). Then, in May 1943, Roosevelt created the Office of War Mobilization (OWM) to coordinate operations among all these agencies.

Several new agencies took on the responsibility of creating propaganda to promote a war that was being fought 3,000 miles away. Although Pearl Harbor brought an outpouring of rage against Japan, the government nevertheless fanned patriotic fires and tried to shape public opinion. In June 1942, the president created the Office of War Information (OWI) to engage the press and radio and film industries in selling the war to the American people, as well as to publish leaflets for the armed services and to flood enemy ranks with subversive propaganda. Domestic propaganda also fueled the selling of war bonds. Polls showed, however, that most Depression-stung Americans bought war bonds—$185.7 billion worth by war's end—mainly to invest safely, to counter inflation, and to save for postwar purchases.

The federal government sponsored various measures to prevent acts of treason. The U.S. attorney general

authorized wiretapping in cases of espionage or sabotage, but the Federal Bureau of Investigation (FBI) also used it extensively—and illegally—for domestic surveillance. The Joint Chiefs of Staff created the Office of Strategic Services (OSS) to assess enemy military strength, gather intelligence, and conduct foreign espionage, and engaged leading social scientists to plot psychological warfare.

In mid-1942, Roosevelt established an agency that would prove vital to the Allied victory and change the way science was conducted in the United States. The Office of Scientific Research and Development (OSRD) brought together government, business, and scientific leaders to coordinate military research. The OSRD developed better radar and early-warning systems, more effective medicines and pesticides, and improved weapons.

With the creation of these new agencies, the size of the federal government increased many times over its New Deal level, and the government spent twice as much during the war as it had during its entire history up to then. The number of federal employees nearly quadrupled, from a little over 1 million in 1940 to nearly 4 million by the war's end.

The New Deal itself, however, withered away. In 1942, Roosevelt announced that "Dr. New Deal" had yielded to "Dr. Win the War." With the Depression over and chronic unemployment giving way to acute labor shortages, FDR's administration directed all its resources toward securing the planes, ships, guns, and food—and the war workers—required for victory. Moreover, the 1942 elections weakened the New Deal coalition by unseating many liberal Democrats while sending 55 new and mostly conservative Republicans to Congress. Republicans quashed proposals to extend the social programs instituted during the 1930s. One by one, New Deal agencies vanished.

25.2.2 Organizing the War Economy

Victory would ultimately depend less on military prowess and superior strategy than on the ability of the United States to outproduce its enemies. The nation enjoyed incomparable advantages: freedom from bombing and invasions, a huge industrial base, abundant natural resources, and a civilian population large enough to swell both its labor force and its armed forces. First, however, the entire civilian

BUY WAR BONDS

"BUY WAR BONDS" The U.S. government issued war bonds to help finance World War II. The War Finance Committee oversaw the sale of these savings bonds, and the War Advertising Council promoted them to the general public. Together, these two agencies produced the largest volume of advertising in American history. By the end of the war, more than 85 million Americans—nearly half the population—had purchased more than $185 billion in bonds.

N.C. Wyeth/Alamy Stock Photo

economy had to be both expanded and transformed for the production of arms and other military supplies.

Even before Pearl Harbor, by the summer of 1941, the federal government was pouring vast sums into defense production. Six months after the attack, allocations topped $100 billion for equipment and supplies, which exceeded what American firms had produced in all previous wars. Facing war orders too large to fill, American industries were primed for all-out production. Once-idle factories operated around the clock, seven days a week. "Something is happening," announced *Time* magazine, "that Adolf Hitler does not understand . . . it is the miracle of production."

Defense production transformed entire regions. The impact was strongest in the West, the major staging area for the war in the Pacific. California got 10 percent of all federal funds, and by 1944 Los Angeles was the nation's second-largest manufacturing center, only slightly behind Detroit. The South benefited from having 60 of the army's 100 new military camps, and its textile factories hummed: The army alone required nearly 520 million pairs of socks and 230 million pairs of pants. Much of the South's share-cropping and tenant-farming populations migrated into well-paid urban industrial jobs, and unprecedented profits poured into southern businesses.

Across the nation, the rural population decreased by almost 20 percent, and American farmers could not keep up with rising demand for milk, potatoes, fruits, and sugar. The war speeded the development of large-scale and mechanized crop production, including the first widespread use of chemical fertilizers and pesticides. By 1945, farm income had doubled, but thousands of small farms had disappeared.

Much like large-scale commercial agriculture, many big businesses did well during the war. Military contracts allowed huge profits. The government provided low-interest loans and even direct subsidies for the expansion of facilities, with generous tax write-offs for retooling. The 100 largest corporations, which manufactured 30 percent of all goods in 1940, garnered 70 percent of all war and civilian contracts and the bulk of war profits. On the other hand, many small businesses closed.

25.2.3 New Workers

The wartime economy required an unprecedented number of new workers. The *bracero* program, negotiated by the United States and Mexico in 1942, brought more than 200,000 Mexicans into the United States for short-term employment, mainly as farm and railroad workers. Sioux and Navajos were hired in large numbers to build ordnance depots and military training centers. African Americans secured in just four years a greater variety of jobs than they had in the seven decades since the Civil War. They joined white workers in defense industries—in iron and steel plants, shipyards and aircraft factories, and numerous government agencies. The number of black workers rose from 2.9 million to 3.8 million.

The war most dramatically altered the wage-earning patterns of women. The female labor force grew by more than 50 percent, reaching 19.5 million in 1945. The rate of growth proved especially high for white women over 35, and for the first time married women became the majority of female wage earners. The employment rate changed comparatively little for African American women; fully 90 percent had been in the labor force in 1940. However, many black women left domestic service for higher-paying industrial jobs.

Neither government nor industry rushed to recruit women. Well into the summer of 1942, the Department of War advised businesses to hold back from hiring women "until all available male labor in the area had first been employed." Likewise, neither government nor industry expected women to stay in their jobs when the war ended. "Rosie the Riveter" appeared in posters and advertisements as the model female citizen, but only "for the duration." (See SEEING History.)

Compared with the Great Depression, when married women were barred from many jobs, World War II

WOMEN IN THE DEFENSE INDUSTRY Facing a shortage of workers and increased production demands, the War Manpower Commission and the Office of War Information conducted a campaign to recruit women into the labor force. Women were encouraged to "take a job for your husband/son/brother" and to "keep the world safe for your children." Higher wages also enticed many women to take jobs in factories. In this photograph, a woman is shown working on an airplane engine.

Library of Congress.

Table 25.1 STRIKES AND LOCKOUTS IN THE UNITED STATES, 1940–1945

	Number of Strikes	Number of Workers Involved	Number of Man-Days Idle	Percent of Total Employed
1940	2,508	576,988	6,700,872	2.3
1941	4,288	2,362,620	23,047,556	8.4
1942	2,968	839,961	4,182,557	2.8
1943	3,752	1,981,279	13,500,529	6.9
1944	4,956	2,115,637	8,721,079	7.0
1945	4,750	3,467,000	38,025,000	12.2

Source: Data from "Work Stoppages Caused by Labor-Management Disputes in 1945," *Monthly Labor Review*, May 1946, p. 720.

ultimately opened up new fields. The number of women automobile workers jumped from 29,000 to 200,000, and that of women electrical workers from 100,000 to 374,000. In some defense plants, women made up nearly half the labor force, although a small percentage of them landed one of the better-paying skilled positions. Nevertheless, recruiters used conventional gender stereotypes to attract women and to reassure the public. Where once housewives sewed curtains for their kitchens, they now produced silk parachutes. Their skill with a vacuum cleaner supposedly translated into riveting on huge ships. The majority of women workers, however, enjoyed the opportunity to work in unfamiliar settings, such as manufacturing plants. Polled near the end of the war, 75 percent said they wanted to keep working, preferably at the same jobs.

Although the war generated 17 million new jobs, the economic gains were not evenly distributed. Wages increased by as much as 50 percent, but never as fast as profits or prices. This widely reported disparity produced one of the most turbulent periods in American labor history. (See Table 25.1.) More workers went on strike in 1941, before the United States entered the war, than in any previous year except 1919. A long, brutal union drive at Ford Motor Company's enormous River Rouge plant made the United Auto Workers (UAW) one of the most powerful labor organizations in the world. Total union membership increased from 10.5 million to 14.7 million, with the women's share alone rising from 11 to 23 percent. Unions also enrolled 1,250,000 African Americans, twice the prewar number.

Once the United States entered the war, the major unions patriotically agreed to no-strike pledges for the duration. Nevertheless, rank-and-file union members sporadically staged illegal "wildcat" strikes. The most dramatic, a walk-out of more than a half million coal miners in 1943 led by the rambunctious John L. Lewis, withstood the attacks of the government and the press. Roosevelt repeatedly ordered the mines seized, only to find, as Lewis retorted, that coal could not be mined with bayonets. The Democratic-majority Congress passed the first federal antistrike bill, over Roosevelt's veto, giving the government the power to seize and run war industries threatened by strikes and establishing criminal penalties for union leaders. And yet the strikes reached a level greater than in any other four-year period in American history.

Union leaders negotiated shorter hours, higher wages, and seniority rules, and helped to build union membership to a new height. When the war ended, nearly 30 percent of all non-agricultural workers were union members.

25.3 The Home Front

What major changes occurred in American society as a consequence of wartime mobilization?

Alone among the major combatants, the homelands of the United States and Canada were neither invaded nor bombed, except for remote Pearl Harbor. On the U.S. mainland, most civilians—unless they had loved ones serving in the armed forces or relocated to distant parts—experienced the war

SEEING History

Norman Rockwell's "Rosie, the Riveter"

During his long career as an artist-illustrator, Norman Rockwell painted 47 covers for the popular family magazine *The Saturday Evening Post*, all venerating various aspects of American life. "Rosie, the Riveter" appeared on the cover of the magazine's May 29, 1943, issue and virtually enshrined women's contributions to the war effort. The *Post* donated the original painting to the U.S. Department of the Treasury, which took "Rosie" on a national tour to get Americans to buy war bonds.

Now an iconic image, Rosie was modeled on a real-life woman, a telephone operator in Vermont. Rockwell took advantage of his artistic license by making Rosie older and more muscular than his slight 19-year-old model—who was quite surprised when she finally saw the portrait! There is no doubt, though, that Rockwell captured the spirit of wartime patriotism. The self-confident Rosie takes obvious pride in her work, keeping her riveter on her ample lap even during lunchtime. A halo encircles her head, and the American flag waves in the background. To seal the message, Rockwell shows Rosie crushing Hitler's autobiography, *Mein Kampf*, under her penny loafer.

Despite calling attention to Rosie's impressive biceps, Rockwell nevertheless attended to the small details that assure viewers that his defense worker has lost none of her femininity. Like most other women in the 1940s, she wears lipstick and rouge, and polishes her nails. She also keeps a lace hanky and compact in the pocket of her overalls and wears a necklace—albeit one of merit buttons—around her neck. Moreover, Rockwell does not show Rosie riveting but instead eating a ham sandwich that she undoubtedly made at home.

Rockwell's painting, beloved during World War II, became even more popular with the rise of the women's liberation movement in the late 1960s, and remains to this day an emblem of women's strength and determination. In May 2002, Sotheby's auctioned the original canvas for more than $4.9 million.

- **In what ways does Rockwell's painting convey ideals related to gender roles during the war?**

NORMAN ROCKWELL'S "ROSIE THE RIVETER"

Terry Smith Images/Alamy Stock Photo.

---

mainly in terms of inconveniences: rationing, long workdays, and a sharp increase in income taxes. Nevertheless, Americans were not immune to the social upheavals that accompany war.

25.3.1 Families in Wartime

"Economic conditions were ripe for a rush to the altar," quipped one social scientist. The wartime boom sent personal incomes surging, providing many young couples with sufficient resources to set up separate households for the first time since the depression struck. Even before the U.S. entry into the war, men and women rushed into marriage, despite (or maybe because of) wartime uncertainties.

After Pearl Harbor, while the United States geared up for combat, the prospect of wartime separation pushed many young men and women into marriage. Then, too, before 1942 married men were deferred from the draft. The marriage rate peaked in 1946—but by then divorces were also setting records.

Housing shortages were acute and rents were high. With apartments scarce, taxi drivers (for an extra fee) became up-to-the-minute guides to vacancies. Landlords were free to discriminate against families with children—and, even more so, against racial minorities.

Wartime wages made many Americans eager to stock up on consumer goods, including a few luxuries, but they soon discovered that even supplying a household was difficult.

YOUNG COUPLES APPLY FOR MARRIAGE LICENSES Students at Officers' Training School at Northwestern University, who were not allowed to marry until they were commissioned as ensigns, apply for marriage licenses in Chicago, August 20, 1943, shortly before graduation. These young couples helped the marriage rate skyrocket during World War II.

Louis Armstrong's Hot Five/Getty Images.

Shopping had to be squeezed in between long work hours. Rationing required extra planning for purchasing meat, cheese, sugar, milk, coffee, gasoline, and shoes. One homemaker said she and her friends referred to butter as "twenty-four karat gold." Illegal black markets flourished despite the high prices charged for scarce or rationed goods.

Many women found it nearly impossible to manage both a demanding job and a household. This dual responsibility contributed to high turnover and absentee rates in factories. Caring for small children became a major problem. Wartime employment or military service often separated husbands and wives, leaving children in the care of only one parent. Although the War Manpower Commission estimated that as many as 2 million children needed some form of child care, federally funded daycare centers served less than 10 percent of defense workers' children. In most communities, the limited facilities sponsored by industry or municipal governments could not keep up with the growing number of "latchkey" children.

Juvenile delinquency rose. With employers relaxing minimum age requirements, many teenagers quit school for high-wage factory jobs. Runaways drifted from city to city, finding temporary work at wartime plants or military installations. Urban gangs spawned brawling, prostitution, and automobile thefts for joy rides. To curb this trend, the U.S. Office of Education and the Children's Bureau sponsored a back-to-school campaign and appealed to employers to hire only older workers. Many communities responded to the problem by opening Teen Canteens, which offered young people a safe and above-board place for recreation.

Public health improved greatly. Forced to forgo medical care during the Great Depression, many Americans spent large portions of their wartime paychecks on doctors, dentists, and prescription drugs. Even more important were the medical benefits provided to the more than 16 million men inducted into the armed forces and their dependents. Nationally, incidences of communicable diseases dropped considerably, the infant death rate fell by more than a third, and life expectancy increased by three years. In the South and Southwest, however, racism and poverty combined to halt or even reverse these trends. These regions continued to have the nation's highest infant and maternal mortality rates.

25.3.2 The Internment of Japanese Americans

No families suffered more from wartime dislocations than Japanese Americans who were interned for the duration. After Pearl Harbor, military officials feared an invasion of the mainland and suspected Japanese Americans of secret disloyalty. On December 8, 1941, the federal government froze the financial assets of those born in Japan, called Issei, who had been barred from U.S. citizenship. Meanwhile, in the name of national defense, a coalition of politicians, patriotic organizations, business groups, and military officials called for the removal of all Americans of Japanese descent from Pacific coastal areas. Although a State Department intelligence report certified their loyalty, Japanese Americans—two-thirds of them American-born citizens—became the largest ethnic group singled out for legal sanction.

Accusations of sedition against Japanese Americans, however bogus, unleashed deep racial prejudices. Headlines freely blared the word *Jap*, while political cartoonists and the popular culture employed blatant racial stereotypes. "The very fact that no sabotage has taken place to date," an army report suggested, with twisted logic, "is a disturbing and confirming indication that action will be taken."

On February 19, 1942, Roosevelt signed Executive Order 9066, which banned more than 120,000 Japanese American men, women, and children from designated military areas, mainly in California, but also in Oregon, Washington, and southern Arizona. The army prepared for forced evacuation, rounding up and removing Japanese Americans from communities where they had lived and worked, sometimes for generations.

During the spring of 1942, Japanese American families received one week's notice to close up their businesses and homes. Told to bring only what they could carry, they were then transported to one of the 10 internment camps managed by the War Relocation Authority. The guarded camps were located as far away as Arkansas, although the majority had been set up in the remote desert areas of Utah, Colorado,

JAPANESE AMERICANS FACE INTERNMENT More than 110,000 Japanese Americans were interned during World War II, some for up to four years.

American Photo Archive/Alamy Stock Photo.

Idaho, Arizona, Wyoming, and California. By August, virtually every West Coast resident with at least one Japanese grandparent had been interned.

The Japanese American Citizens League charged that "racial animosity," not military necessity, motivated the internment policy. Despite the complaints of the American Civil Liberties Union and several church groups, the Supreme Court in *Korematsu v. United States* (1944) upheld the constitutionality of relocation on grounds of national security. By this time a program of gradual release was in place, although the last center did not close until March 1946. In protest, nearly 6,000 Japanese Americans renounced their U.S. citizenship. Japanese Americans had lost homes and businesses valued at $500 million in what many historians judge as being the worst violation of American civil liberties during the war. Not until 1988 did Congress vote to award each of the 60,000 surviving victims reparations of $20,000 and a public apology.

25.3.3 "Double V": Victory at Home and Abroad

Throughout the war, African American activists conducted a "Double V" campaign, mobilizing not only for Allied victory but also for their own rights as citizens. "The army is about to take me to fight for democracy," one Detroit resident said, "but I would as leave fight for democracy right here." Black activists demanded, at a minimum, fair housing and equal employment opportunities, laying the foundation for the postwar civil rights movement.

Even before the United States entered the war, the foremost black labor leader—A. Philip Randolph, president of both the Brotherhood of Sleeping Car Porters and the National Negro Congress—began to mobilize against discrimination. At a planning meeting in Chicago, a black woman proposed sending African Americans to Washington, D.C., in order to "get some action from the White House." Under Randolph's leadership, African Americans across the country began to prepare for a "great rally" of no fewer than 100,000 people at the Lincoln Memorial on the Fourth of July.

Eager to stop the March on Washington movement, Roosevelt met with Randolph, who proposed an executive order "making it mandatory that Negroes be permitted to work in [defense] plants." On June 25, 1941, Roosevelt gave in to Randolph's ultimatum and issued Executive Order 8802, banning discrimination in defense industries and government. The president later appointed a Fair Employment Practices Committee to hear complaints and redress grievances. Randolph called off the march

but remained determined, along with other black leaders encouraged by this victory, to "shake up white America."

Several civil rights organizations formed during wartime to fight discrimination and Jim Crow, including segregation in the armed forces. The interracial Congress of Racial Equality (CORE), formed by pacifists in 1942, staged sit-ins at Chicago, Detroit, and Denver restaurants that refused to serve African Americans. Membership in the NAACP, which fought discrimination in defense plants and the armed forces, grew from 50,000 in 1940 to 450,000 in 1946. Demonstrators marched with placards that read: "Are you for Hitler's Way or the American Way?" The Supreme Court ruling in *Smith v. Albright* (1944) overturning the legality of "white primaries" used in southern states to exclude black voters was another major victory paving the way for future civil rights struggles.

Despite these advances, racial conflict intensified during the war. Approximately 1.2 million African Americans left the rural South to take wartime jobs, and they faced not only serious housing shortages but also whites intent on keeping them out of their own jobs and neighborhoods. "Hate strikes" broke out in defense plants across the country when African Americans were hired or upgraded to "white" positions. Violence reigned in many communities where African Americans attempted to relocate. In February 1942, when black families prepared to move into new federally funded apartments in Detroit, a mob of 700 armed white protesters halted the moving vans and burned a cross on the project's grounds. After two months of struggle, and with the protection of 1,100 city and state police and 1,600 members of the Michigan National Guard, six black families became the first to move into the Sojourner Truth Housing Project, named for the famous abolitionist.

Racial violence reached its wartime peak during the summer of 1943, when 274 conflicts broke out in nearly 50 cities. In Detroit, where the black population had grown by more than a third since the beginning of the war, 25 blacks and 9 whites were killed and more than 700 were injured. In Harlem, a riot claimed the lives of six African Americans. In several southern cities, and especially at military training centers, race riots targeted African Americans, and the rate of lynching increased during the war years.

MR. PREJUDICE This painting is by Horace Pippin, a self-taught African American artist who began painting as therapy for an injury suffered while serving with the U.S. Army's 369th Colored Infantry Regiment during World War I. It is one of a series drawn during World War II illustrating the contradiction between the principles of liberty and justice, for which Americans were fighting abroad, and the reality of racial prejudice at home.

The Philadelphia Museum of Art/Art Resource, NY.

25.3.4 Zoot Suit Riots

On the night of June 4, 1943, sailors poured into nearly 200 cars and taxis to drive through the streets of East Los Angeles in search of Mexican Americans dressed in "zoot suits." The sailors assaulted their victims at random, even chasing one youth into a movie theater and stripping him of his clothes while the audience cheered. Riots broke out and continued for five days.

Two communities had collided with tragic results. The sailors had only recently been uprooted from their hometowns and regrouped under the strict discipline of boot camp. Now awaiting deployment overseas, they came face to face with Mexican American teenagers wearing long-draped coats, pegged pants, pocket watches with oversized chains, and big floppy hats. To the sailors, the zoot suit signaled defiance and a lack of patriotism.

The zoot-suiters, however, represented less than 10 percent of the Hispanic community's youth. More than 300,000 Mexican Americans were serving in the armed forces—often in the most hazardous branches, the paratroopers and Marine Corps. Many others were employed in war industries in Los Angeles, which had become home to the nation's largest Mexican American community.

Military and civilian authorities eventually contained the zoot suit riots by ruling several sections of Los Angeles off-limits to military personnel, and the city council passed legislation making the wearing of a zoot suit in public a criminal offense. Many Mexican Americans expressed concern about their personal safety; some feared that after the government rounded up the Japanese, they would be the next group sent to internment camps.

25.3.5 Popular Culture and "The Good War"

Compared with their European allies, Americans felt the impact of the war only indirectly in their everyday activities. Food shortages, long hours in the factories, and even fear for loved ones abroad did not take away all the pleasures of full employment and prosperity. With money in their pockets, a dramatic change from the Depression years, Americans spent freely at vacation resorts, country clubs, racetracks, nightclubs, dance halls, and movie theaters. Sales of books skyrocketed, and spectator sports attracted huge and diverse audiences.

Baseball changed for the duration. Although President Roosevelt encouraged the major leagues to contribute to morale by continuing to play, more than 500 professional players joined the armed forces. With the loss of crowd-pleasing stars such as Joe DiMaggio, Ted Williams, Yogi Berra, and Stan Musial, attendance dwindled. The minor leagues, with more than 5,000 players gone, nearly collapsed. To fill the gap, Philip K. Wrigley, the owner of the Chicago Cubs, promoted the All-American Girls Baseball League. In 1943, the Racine Belles of Wisconsin won the league championship. The women's professional league proved so successful that it did not disband until 1954. Only in 1947 did Jackie Robinson break the "color barrier" in professional baseball. The Negro leagues nevertheless flourished during the war, game attendance swelled by African Americans earning good wages in wartime industries.

Popular music proved more accommodating, and somewhat eased the sharpening racial divisions of the neighborhood and the workplace. Transplanted southern musicians,

U-BOAT PRISONER This poster advertises a feature film produced during World War II, in 1944, that portrays the bravery and heroism of an American merchant seaman captured by the Nazis. Entertaining as well as inspiring, movies such as "U-Boat Prisoner" presented movie viewers —90 million per week during World War II—with vivid images of both the horror and glory of wartime and helped to rally support for the war and the troops fighting abroad.

Everett Collection, Inc./Alamy Stock Photo.

black and white, brought their regional styles to northern cities. "Country" and "rhythm & blues" not only won new audiences but also inspired musicians to crisscross old boundaries. Musicians of the war years "made them steel guitars cry and whine," Ray Charles recalled. They also paved the way musically for the emergence of rock and roll a decade later.

Hollywood mobilized, as one screenwriters group explained, "to build morale" and to "stimulate . . . initiative and responsibility." With military cooperation, wartime movies encouraged Americans to think well of all the Allies—including the Soviet Union. Several films, such as *Tender Comrade*, plugged pro-Soviet views that would be abruptly reversed in the postwar years. Other films such as the Oscar-winning *Since You Went Away* portrayed the loyalty and resilience of American families with servicemen stationed overseas. Frank Capra directed the government-sponsored *Why We Fight*, a series of documentaries to explain the war's aims to soldiers.

The wartime spirit infected even the juvenile world of comics. Their climbing sales spawned a proliferation of patriotic superheroes such as the Green Lantern, Batman, and Captain America. Wonder Woman used her super strength to fight crime and the Nazis. Even Bugs Bunny put on a uniform and fought sinister-looking enemies.

The fashion industry also did its part. Production of nylon stockings was halted because the material was needed for parachutes; to save cotton and woolen fabric for the production of uniforms, women's skirts were shortened, while the War Production Board encouraged cuffless "Victory Suits" for men. Executive Order M-217 restricted the colors of shoes manufactured during the war to "black, white, navy blue, and three shades of brown." For many civilians, including civil defense volunteers and Red Cross workers, wearing a uniform demonstrated patriotism, and padded shoulders and straight lines became popular among fashion-conscious men and women. Women employed in defense plants wore slacks, often for the first time in their lives.

Much of this war fervor was spontaneous, but the government did all it could to encourage self-sacrificing patriotism. The Office of War Information screened all popular music, movies, radio programs, and advertisements to ensure that everyone got the message: Only the collective effort of all Americans could preserve democracy at home and save the world from fascism.

By the mid-1940s, popular culture had helped to shape a collective memory of World War II as "the good war," the standard by which the nation's subsequent wars would be judged. It also played an important part in bringing diverse and sometimes antagonistic communities together, not only in support of the war but also as steadfast consumers of mass entertainment.

25.4 Men and Women in Uniform

How did military service during World War II change the lives of American men and women?

World War II mobilized 16.4 million Americans into the armed forces. Although only 34 percent of men who served in the army saw combat—the majority during the final year of the war—the experience had a powerful impact on nearly everyone. Whether working in the steno pool at Great Lakes Naval Training Center in northern Illinois or slogging through mud with rifle in hand in the Philippines, many men and women saw their lives reshaped in unpredictable ways. For those who survived, the war often proved to be the defining experience of their lives.

25.4.1 Creating the Armed Forces

Neither the army nor the navy was prepared for the scale of combat World War II entailed. Before 1939, when the European war broke out, most of the 200,000 men in the armed forces patrolled the Mexican border or occupied colonial possessions. Only the U.S. Marine Corps, which had been planning since the 1920s to seize the western Pacific from Japan in the event of war, was ready to fight.

On October 16, 1940, National Registration Day, all men between 21 and 36 had to register for military service. After the United States entered the war, the draft age was lowered to 18, and local boards were instructed to choose the youngest first.

The draft law exempted those "who by religious training or belief" opposed war. About 25,000 conscientious objectors served in non-combatant roles in the military services; another 12,000 performed "alternative service." Approximately 6,000 men were jailed for refusing to register for the draft.

One-third of the men examined by the Selective Service were rejected. Surprising numbers were refused induction as physically unfit. For the first time, men were screened for "neuropsychiatric disorders or emotional problems," and approximately 1.6 million were rejected for that reason. At a time when only one American in four graduated from high school, many conscripts were turned away as functionally illiterate.

A shortage of officers during World War I had prompted a huge expansion of the Reserve Officer Training Corps (ROTC) on many campuses, but the army still fell short. Racing to make up for this deficiency, new, specialized schools opened for officer candidates. In 1942, in a 17-week training period, these schools produced more than 54,000 platoon leaders. Closer in sensibility to the civilian population, these new officers matched the military style preferred by General Dwight D. Eisenhower, the supreme commander of the Allied forces in Europe.

Most GIs (short for "government issue") had little contact with high-ranking officers and instead forged bonds with the men in their own combat units and with their company commanders. Proud to serve in the "best-dressed, best-fed, best-equipped army in the world," the majority of these citizen-soldiers responded less to patriotic idealism than to the desire "to get the task done" and return as soon as possible to home and family.

25.4.2 Women Enter the Military

In 1942, the U.S. Congress approved a bill forming the Women's Army Auxiliary Corps (WAAC), later changed to Women's Army Corps (WAC). Other bills, passed a short time later, established a women's division of the navy (WAVES), the Women's Air Force Service Pilots, and the Marine Corps Women's Reserve.

Overall, more than 350,000 women served in World War II, two-thirds of them in the WAC and WAVES. As a group, they were better educated and more skilled—although paid less—than the average enlisted man. However, military policy prohibited women from supervising male workers, even in desk jobs.

Barred from combat, women were not necessarily protected from danger. Nurses accompanied troops into combat, treated men under fire, and dug their own foxholes. More than 1,000 women flew planes, although not in combat missions. Others worked as photographers and cryptanalysts. The vast majority remained far from battlefronts, however. Stationed mainly within the United

WAC RECRUITS New recruits to the Women's Army Corps (WAC) pick up their clothing "issue" (allotment). These volunteers served in many capacities, from nursing men in combat to performing clerical and communication duties "stateside" (within the United States). Approximately 140,000 women served in the WAC during World War II.

National Archives and Records Administration.

States, most women worked in familiar jobs, serving in administration, communications, clerical, or health care facilities.

The WAC and WAVES were subject to both hostile commentary and bad publicity. The overwhelming majority of soldiers believed that most WACs were prostitutes; the War Department itself, fearing "immorality" among women in the armed forces, closely monitored their conduct and established much stricter rules for women than for men.

25.4.3 Old Practices and New Horizons

The Selective Service Act specified that, "there shall be no discrimination against any person on account of race or color." The draft did bring hundreds of thousands of young black men into the army, and African Americans enlisted at a rate 60 percent above their proportion of the general population. By 1944, black soldiers represented 10 percent of the army's troops, and overall approximately 1 million African Americans served in the armed forces during World War II. The army, however, channeled black recruits into segregated, poorly equipped units, commanded by white officers. The majority of African Americans served mainly in construction or stevedore work.

Only toward the end of the war, when the shortage of infantry neared a crisis, were African Americans permitted to rise to combat status. The all-black 761st Tank Battalion, the first African American armored unit, served 183 days in action without relief. Despite the very small number of African Americans admitted to the Air Force, the 99th Pursuit Squadron, trained at the new base in Tuskegee,

Alabama, earned high marks in action against the feared German Luftwaffe. Even the Marine Corps and the Coast Guard agreed to end their historic exclusion of African Americans, although they recruited and promoted only a small number.

The ordinary black soldier, sailor, or Marine encountered discrimination everywhere. Even the blood banks kept blood segregated by race (although a black physician, Dr. Charles Drew, had invented the process for storing plasma). The year 1943 marked the peak of unrest, with violent confrontations between blacks and whites breaking out at military installations, especially in the South, where the majority of African American soldiers were stationed. Toward the end of the war, to improve morale among black servicemen, the army relaxed its policy of segregation, mainly in recreational facilities.

The army also grouped Japanese Americans into segregated units, sending most to fight far from the Pacific Theater. Better educated than the average soldier, many **Nisei** soldiers who knew Japanese served stateside as interpreters and translators. When the army decided to create a Nisei regiment, more than 10,000 volunteers stepped forward, although only one in five was accepted. The Nisei 442nd fought heroically in Italy and France and became the most decorated regiment in the war.

Despite segregation, the armed forces ultimately pulled many Americans out of their separate communities. Many Jews and other second-generation European immigrants, for example, described their military stint as an "Americanizing" experience. For the first time in their lives, many Indian peoples left reservations, as approximately 25,000 served in the armed forces. In the Pacific war, Navajo "code talkers" used their native language (a complex, unwritten language unknown to the Japanese) to transmit information from the front lines and also improved their English in special classes. For many African Americans, military service provided a bridge to postwar civil rights agitation.

Many homosexuals also discovered a wider world in the service. Despite rules barring them from the military, most slipped through at the induction centers. Moreover, the emotional pressures of wartime, especially the fear of death, encouraged close friendships, and homosexuals in the military often found more room than in civilian life to express their sexual orientation openly.

Most veterans looked back on World War II, with all its dangers and discomforts, as the greatest experience they ever knew. As *The New Republic* predicted in 1943, they met other Americans from every part of the country and recognized for the first time in their lives "the bigness and wholeness of the United States." The army itself promoted such expectations. *Twenty-Seven Soldiers* (1944), a government-produced film for the troops, showed Allied soldiers of several nationalities all working together in harmony.

25.4.4 The Medical Corps

By the time the war ended, nearly 500,000 Americans had died in military actions. Although the European Theater produced the most casualties, the Pacific held grave dangers beyond enemy fire. For soldiers in hot, humid jungles, malaria, typhus, diarrhea, and dengue fever posed the most common threat to their lives. For the 25th Infantry Division, which landed in Guadalcanal in 1943 the malaria-carrying mosquito proved a deadlier enemy than Japanese forces.

The prolonged stress of combat also took a toll in "battle fatigue"—the official army term for combat stress or what would today be called posttraumatic stress. More than 1 million soldiers suffered at one time or another from debilitating psychiatric symptoms, and the army rushed to care for these casualties. At the beginning of the war, only 35 psychiatrists worked in the army; by war's end more than 2,500 psychiatrists and clinical psychologists were affiliated with military hospitals. Their patients suffered not from individual weakness, the psychiatrists concluded, but from the stress and anxiety caused by long stints on the front lines. In 1944, the army set a cap of eight months in combat. When replacements were available, a rotation system relieved exhausted soldiers.

To care for sick and wounded soldiers, the army employed a variety of medical personnel. In basic training, soldiers received first aid instruction, and they went into battle with bandages to treat minor wounds. For anything more serious they needed the physicians and medics who went to the front lines. During the war, the army

MEDICS ON A D-DAY LANDING BEACH During World War II, combat medics served on the front lines of battle. They could not provide extensive treatment to wounded soldiers, but instead worked to stabilize them in preparation for evacuation to a field hospital. Rarely doctors or nurses themselves, they had received special training in trauma care and first aid to stop bleeding, apply bandages, and administer sedatives such as morphine. Medics were identified by the Red Cross symbol on their uniforms or helmets.

Everett Collection, Inc./Alamy Stock Photo.

enlisted nearly 50,000 physicians, for the first time including 83 women. The Army Medical Corps set up makeshift tent hospitals, where physicians pioneered advanced surgical techniques. They also used the new "wonder drugs" developed during the war. Without penicillin and other antibiotics, many wounded soldiers would have died, as they did in earlier wars. Overall, fewer than 4 percent of all soldiers who received medical care died from their injuries. Much of the success in treatment came from the use of blood plasma, which reduced the often-lethal effect of shock from severe bleeding.

Grateful for the care of skilled surgeons, many soldiers nevertheless named medics the true heroes of the battle-front. Thirty to 40 medics were attached to each infantry battalion, and under fire they gave emergency first aid and, equally important, quickly transported the wounded away from the front line. The medics moved the injured soldier to the aid station and, if necessary, the field hospital.

In the military hospitals, including the field hospitals at the front lines, American nurses gave the bulk of care to recovering soldiers. Like medics, army nurses went first to training centers in the United States, learning how to dig foxholes and dodge bullets before being sent overseas. By 1945, approximately 56,000 women, including 500 African American women, were on active duty in the Army Nurse Corps, staffing medical facilities in every theater of the war. The army granted its nurses officers' commissions, including full retirement privileges, and provided free nursing education until 1948.

25.5 The World at War

What were the main elements of the Allied war strategy?

Almost until the end of 1942, from the Atlantic to deep in Russia, Hitler and his allies controlled most of continental Europe and continued to pound Great Britain from the air. A German army also swept across North Africa and almost took the Suez Canal from the British.

In the Pacific and East Asia, the situation was just as dire. Just two hours after the attack on Pearl Harbor, Japanese planes struck the main U.S. airbase in the Philippines and demolished half the warplanes commanded by General Douglas MacArthur. Japanese troops soon conquered the entire Philippines. The Japanese easily overran Britain's Southeast Asian colonies, the Dutch East Indies, and the entire western Pacific. Although China officially joined the Allies, Japanese forces on the Chinese mainland remained on the offensive. (See Map 25.1.) Roosevelt called the news "all bad," and his military advisors predicted a long fight to victory.

The Allies did enjoy several important advantages: America's vast natural resources and a skilled workforce with sufficient reserves to accelerate the production of weapons and ammunitions; the determination of millions of antifascists throughout Europe and Asia; and the capacity of the Soviet people to endure immense losses and hardships. Slowly at first, but then with quickening speed, these advantages came into play.

25.5.1 Soviets Halt Nazi Drive

Unlike World War I, which was fought with poison gas and machine-gun fire by armies largely immobilized in trenches, World War II was a war of offensive maneuvers punctuated by surprise attacks. Its chief weapons—tanks and planes lined up on land, and aircraft carriers and submarines at sea—combined mobility and concentrated firepower. Also important were artillery and explosives, which according to some estimates accounted for more than 30 percent of casualties. Major improvements in communication systems, mainly two-way radio transmission and radio-telephony that permitted commanders to stay in contact with division leaders, played a decisive role throughout the war.

From the beginning of the European war in 1939, Hitler had used these methods to seize the advantage, purposefully striking terror among stricken populations of Western Europe as he routed opposing armies. The Royal Air Force, however, fought the Luftwaffe to a standstill in the Battle of Britain, frustrating Hitler's hopes of invading England. By the spring of 1941, Hitler had turned his attention eastward, planning to conquer the Soviet Union. But he had to delay the invasion to rescue Mussolini, whose weak army faced defeat in North Africa and Greece. Not until June 22, 1941, six weeks behind schedule, did Hitler invade the Soviet Union.

Hitler's forces initially devastated the Red Army, killing or capturing nearly 3 million soldiers and leaving thousands to die from exposure or starvation. But the brutality of the Nazis kindled civilian resistance. The German army in Russia found its supply lines overextended and the brutal Russian winter just beginning, while Stalin was able to send every available resource to his troops concentrated just outside Moscow. The Red Army launched a massive counterattack, catching the frostbitten German troops off guard and driving them to retreat. Despite suffering his first major setback, Hitler remained fixed on conquering Russia.

In the decisive Battle of Stalingrad, which began in August 1942, Hitler met his nemesis. In that battle alone, the Soviets suffered more casualties than Americans did during the entire war. House-to-house fighting and a massive Red Army counterattack inflicted an even greater toll on the Nazis. Hitler ordered to his troops to die rather than surrender. In February 1943, the German Sixth Army, reduced to 100,000 starving men and overpowered by Soviet weaponry, at last gave up.

Already in retreat but plotting one last desperate attempt to halt the Red Army, the Germans threw most of their remaining armored vehicles into action at Kursk in July 1943. The clash quickly spiraled into the greatest tank battle in history, involving more than 2 million troops and 6,000 tanks. After another stunning defeat, the Germans had only one option left: to delay the advance of the Red Army toward their own homeland.

Meanwhile, the Soviet Union had begun to recover from its early losses, even as tens of millions of its people remained homeless and near starvation. Assisted by Lend-Lease, by 1942 the Soviets were outproducing Germany in many types of weapons and other supplies.

Soviet victories had turned the tide. The Soviet Union, not the Western Allies, bore by far the heaviest burden in halting the Nazi advance. The American and British people were grateful for this immense Soviet contribution, and the British and American governments found themselves under enormous pressure from Stalin to open a second front in the west.

25.5.2 The Allied Invasion of Europe

After Stalingrad, the Axis powers continued to lose ground. In the Pacific that summer, Japan's plans to invade Hawai'i and Australia were stopped by the U.S. Navy. Germany found itself far outstripped by the capacity of the United States to build submarines, landing craft, and amphibious vehicles. The German Luftwaffe, now outnumbered by the Allies, was increasingly limited to defensive action.

Against this backdrop, Roosevelt, Churchill, and their generals hammered out a strategy to defeat the Axis. They saw Japan as the lesser threat—one that for the moment should be contained rather than attacked. Germany, they agreed, must

Map 25.1 THE WAR IN EUROPE

The Allies remained on the defensive during the first years of the war, but by 1943 the British and Americans, with seemingly endless supplies of resources, had turned the tide.

be beaten first, which meant eventually invading from the west, while the Red Army advanced from the east.

But the Allies disagreed about where to attack Germany. Churchill and his generals wanted to strike through what he called "Europe's soft underbelly," the Mediterranean. The American generals favored a meticulously prepared assault through France.

In the end, Roosevelt and Churchill compromised: They would first send smaller armies into the Mediterranean, while gathering a huge Anglo-American invasion army in Britain. This strategy was set during the summer of 1942. In the desert near El Alamein, Egypt, British forces halted a major offensive by the German Afrika Korps, headed by General Erwin Rommel, and ultimately drove the Axis armies out of Egypt. Then, in November, American troops for the first time went into action in the European Theater by joining the British in **Operation Torch**, an invasion of Morocco and Algeria. In six months, French North Africa was cleared of Axis troops.

In January 1943, while the fighting raged in North Africa, Roosevelt and Churchill met at Casablanca, Morocco, and announced that they would accept nothing less than the unconditional surrender of their enemies. There would be no negotiations with the Axis powers. Stalin, who did not attend, criticized the policy, predicting that it, would only increase enemy determination to fight to the end and thereby prolong the war and swell the casualty list.

Allied aerial bombing was increasing the pressure on Germany. Some U.S. leaders believed that the B-17 Flying Fortress, "the mightiest bomber ever built," could win the war from the air without any western troops having to fight their way into Europe. The U.S. Army Air Corps (predecessor of the Air Force) described the B-17 as a "humane" weapon,

capable of hitting specific military targets while sparing civilians. That claim was nonsense. Especially when weather or darkness required bombardiers to sight with radar, they could not distinguish among industrial, military, and civilian targets, and even with the best available targeting, bombs might land anywhere within a nearly two-mile radius. Bombing missions over the Rhineland and the Ruhr took out many German factories while also costing tens of thousands of civilian lives.

Determined to break German resistance, the Royal Air Force redirected its main attack away from military targets to cities, fuel dumps, and transportation lines. Indiscriminate bombing practically leveled the great city of Hamburg, killing between 60,000 and 100,000 people and destroying 300,000 buildings. Sixty other cities were hit hard, leaving 20 percent of Germany's total residential area in ruins. Americans joined in the very worst air raid of the war—650,000 incendiary bombs dropped on Dresden in 1945, destroying eight square miles and killing perhaps 135,000 civilians. Dresden, famous for its architecture and art galleries, had no military value. This was terror bombing. Hitler had started it, but the Allies more than repaid in kind.

The Allied strategic air offensive succeeded in weakening the German economy. It also terrorized (and enraged) German civilians. Moreover, in trying to defend German cities and factories, the Luftwaffe sacrificed most of its remaining fighter planes and aircraft fuel. When the Allies invaded Western Europe in the summer of 1944, they enjoyed total air superiority.

Meanwhile, in the summer of 1943, the Allies continued their Mediterranean offensive by attacking southern Italy. On September 8, Italy surrendered. Hitler, however, sent

ALLIED BOMBING OF DRESDEN As part of the air war on Germany, Allied bombers launched a devastating attack on Dresden, a major economic center, in February 1945. Of the civilians who died, most from burns or smoke inhalation during the firestorm, a large number were women and children, refugees from the eastern front. The city was left in ruins.

Fred Ramage/Getty Images.

new divisions into northern and central Italy, stalling the Allied campaign. Almost until the end of the European war, a large Allied army was still bogged down on Italy's rugged terrain, battling a much smaller German force.

All across occupied Europe, resistance to the Nazis spread. Jews walled off in the Nazi-built Warsaw ghetto, realizing that they were marked for extermination, revolted in the summer of 1943 and fought to the death. Scattered revolts followed in the Nazi labor camps, where military prisoners of war and civilians were being worked on starvation rations. Underground fighters, known as partisans, resisted the Nazis from Norway to Greece and from Poland to France. Untrained and lightly armed, men, women, and children risked their lives to distribute anti-fascist propaganda, committed sabotage, rescued downed Allied bombers, and killed Nazi collaborators.

By early 1944, the United States and Britain had advanced the plans for **Operation Overlord**, a campaign to retake the Continent with a decisive counterattack through France. **D-Day**—the start of the Allied invasion—finally came on June 6, 1944, with General Eisenhower in command. Under heavy German machine-gun and mortar fire, wave after wave of American, British, Canadian, and Free French troops hit the Normandy beaches, the tides swelling with the dead and the wounded. Some 2,500 men died in the initial assault, many before they could fire a shot. Although the Germans responded slowly, at Omaha Beach they had prepared their defense almost perfectly, and the Americans who landed there had a particularly difficult time gaining a toehold. Within days, though, more than 175,000 Allied troops and 20,000 vehicles were battling the

Germans—the largest landing operation in history. Over the next six weeks, nearly 1 million more Allied soldiers came ashore. Not until mid-July did this invasion army finally break out of Normandy and drive into the French interior.

All eyes now turned to Paris. Allied bombers pounded roads, bridges, rail lines, and factories that were producing German munitions all around the French capital. With Free French and Allied troops, General Charles de Gaulle entered Paris on August 25 and announced a reconstituted French Republic. Belgium also fell swiftly to the liberators. But Allied troops had only reached a resting place between bloody battles, their supply lines stretched thin and German resistance stiffening.

By September 1944, Allied commanders were searching for a way to end the war quickly. They turned north, intending to strike through the Netherlands into Germany's industrial heartland. Faulty intelligence reports overlooked a well-armed German division at the Dutch town of Arnhem waiting to cut Allied paratroops to pieces. The Germans captured 6,000 Americans.

That winter, making a final, desperate effort to break the Allied momentum, Hitler sent his last reserves, a quarter million men, against Allied lines in Belgium's dense Ardennes forest. In this so-called **Battle of the Bulge**, the Germans surprised the Allied forces, but also exhausted their capacity for counterattack. After Christmas Day 1944, the Germans had to retreat into their own territory.

The end approached. In March 1945, discovery of a single intact bridge across the Rhine allowed the Allies to

D-DAY LANDING D-Day landing, June 6, 1944, marked the greatest amphibious maneuver in military history. Troop ships ferried Allied soldiers from England to Normandy beaches. Within a month, nearly 1 million men had assembled in France, ready to retake western and central Europe from German forces.

Library of Congress (Photoduplication).

roll into the heart of Germany, taking the heavily industrialized Ruhr Valley.

By that time, Soviet offenses were crushing the German army in the east. The Red Army had reached Warsaw in the midsummer of 1944, but then stood by while the anti-Russian Polish resistance rose up—only to be destroyed (along with most of the city) by the Nazis. While that tragedy unfolded, the Soviets occupied the Balkans and battled the Germans in Hungary. Only in January 1945 did the Red Army sweep across Poland and by April besiege Berlin, where Hitler had holed up.

The defense of Germany, now hopeless, had fallen into the hands of teenagers, terrified elderly men, and a few desperate Nazis.

25.5.3 The War in Asia and the Pacific

Six months after Pearl Harbor, the United States began regaining naval superiority in the central Pacific. The Americans had been supremely lucky that their aircraft carriers were out at sea during the Pearl Harbor attack; that luck was spectacularly demonstrated in the great naval battle of the Coral Sea on May 7–8, 1942, in which carrier-based American aircraft blocked a Japanese thrust at Australia. A month later, on June 4, the Japanese fleet converged on Midway Island, an outpost vital to American communications and to the defense of Hawai'i. There, the Americans had another lucky break; intelligence officers had broken the Japanese codes and thus knew when and where the attack would fall. Still separated by hundreds of miles of open sea, the Japanese and American carrier fleets clashed at long distance. Descending from the clouds, American warplanes sank four Japanese carriers and destroyed hundreds of planes, ending Japan's offensive threat to Hawai'i and the West Coast.

Even so, Japan controlled a vast arc of the western Pacific. That perimeter stretched from the outermost Aleutians (off Alaska) to northern New Guinea and the Solomon Islands (off Australia). Japan also dominated all of coastal China and the European colonies of Southeast Asia: Indochina, Malaya, present-day Indonesia, and Burma. (See Map 25.2.) In much of East Asia (except China), nationalistic and anticolonial sentiment played into Japanese hands at first. With only 200,000 troops, Japan easily overran Southeast Asia because so few people in the British, French, and Dutch colonies would fight for their imperial masters. Japan installed puppet governments in Burma and the Philippines, and independent Thailand became a Japanese ally. But the new Japanese empire proved terrifyingly cruel. Local nationalists from Indochina to the Philippines turned against the Japanese, forming guerrilla bands that harassed the invaders. In China, Japan's huge land army bogged down fighting both the Nationalist forces of Chiang Kai-shek and the Communist People's Liberation Army led by Mao Zedong.

Thus, in mid-1942, the war for the Pacific was still only beginning. Japanese commanders calculated that bitter fighting, with high casualties on both sides, would wear down the American military and public. The U.S. command, divided between MacArthur in the southwest Pacific and Admiral Chester Nimitz in the central Pacific, developed a strategy to strangle the Japanese import-dependent economy and to **island-hop** from one strategic outpost to another, closing in on the home islands.

In the Solomons and New Guinea, American and Australian ground troops began the counterattack. On Guadalcanal in the Solomons, U.S. Marines struck at one Japanese stronghold, and during a six-month struggle endured tropical diseases, dangerous parasites, food and ammunition shortages, and very high casualty rates against Japanese defenders who fought to the death. The Marines were reduced to eating roots and berries to stay alive. Finally, in February 1943, with strong supply lines secured by a string of costly naval battles, the Americans prevailed, proving that they could defeat Japanese forces in brutal jungle combat.

For the next two years, the U.S. Navy and Marine Corps opened a path to Japan, capturing a series of important Pacific atolls but bypassing others, helplessly stranding well-armed Japanese defenders. Tarawa in the Gilbert Islands was first of these assaults, in November 1943; it cost more than 1,000 U.S. Marine lives. In June 1944, simultaneously with the Normandy landings, the U.S. Navy inflicted crippling losses on the Japanese fleet in the Battle of the Philippine Sea. Then, in August 1944, the Americans took Guam, Saipan, and Tinian in the Mariana Islands, for the first time bringing the Japanese home islands within bomber range. And in October of that year, MacArthur led an American force of 250,000 to retake the Philippines. Trying to hold the islands, practically all that remained of the Japanese navy threw itself at the Americans in the Battle of Leyte Gulf, the largest naval battle in history. The United States gained control of the Pacific. While MacArthur mopped up operations in the Philippines—at a cost of 100,000 Filipino lives and leaving Manila devastated—the small but strategically important island of Iwo Jima, south of Japan, fell. Here, too, the American death toll was high; casualties were estimated at nearly 27,000.

Even bloodier was the struggle for Okinawa, an island 350 miles southwest of the Japanese home islands and the site of vital airbases. The invasion—the largest American amphibious operation in the Pacific war—began on April 1, 1945. Waves of Japanese *kamikaze* ("divine wind") pilots, flying suicide missions with a 500-pound bomb and only enough fuel for a one-way flight, met the Marines on the beaches. On Okinawa, more Americans died or were wounded than at Normandy. At the end of June, when the

Map 25.2 WAR IN THE PACIFIC

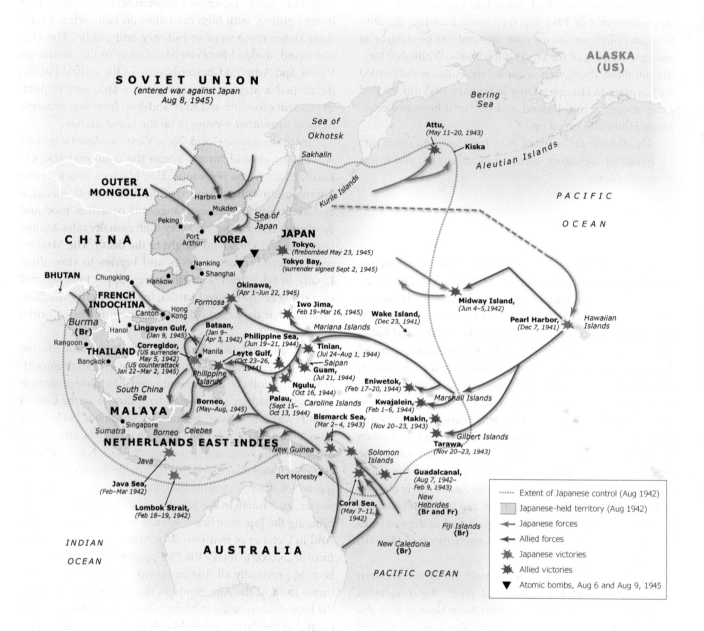

Across an ocean battlefield utterly unlike the European Theater, Allies battled Japanese troops near their homeland.

ghastly struggle ended, 140,000 Japanese were dead, including 42,000 civilians.

The war was over in Europe, and the Allies could concentrate on Japan alone. Tokyo and other Japanese cities were targeted by B-17s and new B-29s flying from Guam with devastating results. Massive fire bombings burned thousands of civilians alive in their mostly wooden or bamboo houses, and hundreds of thousands were left homeless. Meanwhile, U.S. submarines cut off the home islands from supplies on the East Asian mainland.

Japan could not hold out forever. Without a navy or air force, critically important oil, tin, rubber, and grain could not be transported to maintain its soldiers or feed its people. Great Britain and particularly the United States, however, pressed for a quick and unconditional surrender. They had special reasons to hurry. Earlier they had sought a commitment from the Soviet Union to invade Japan, but now they looked beyond the war, determined to prevent the Red Army from taking any Japanese-held territories.

These calculations, as well as chilling forecasts of the bloody cost of invading and subjugating the home islands, set the stage for unleashing the top-secret weapon that American scientists had been building: the atomic bomb. (See Communities *in* Conflict.)

Communities *in* Conflict

On Deploying the Atomic Bomb

"Atomic bombs are primarily a means for the ruthless annihilation of cities.

Although the scientists employed in the Manhattan Project embraced their assignment with fervor, they nevertheless thought deep and hard about the moral ramifications of their work. After the first test of the atomic bomb revealed its horrifying power, they began to discuss among themselves the necessary criteria for using a weapon of such deadly force. By May 1945, under J. Robert Oppenheimer's leadership, a "target committee" had outlined a list of conditions necessary to deploy the "gadget" (a code name for the atomic bomb) against Japan. A month later, small groups of scientists working on the Manhattan Project at the University of Chicago began to appeal to government officials, advising supreme caution in considering the use of the atomic bomb. They acknowledged "the military advantages and the saving of American lives" that deployment against Japan might bring, but warned that such gain "may be outweighed by the ensuing loss of confidence and wave of horror and repulsion, sweeping over the rest of the world, and perhaps dividing even the public opinion

at home." They also recommended that, rather than immediately deploying the bomb, the United States invite nations to witness a demonstration on a barren island or desert. Oppenheimer and Fermi, however, both disagreed and held firm to the letter of their assignment: to produce the bomb for military use. In secret correspondence, which is now declassified, two of the top scientists of the Manhattan Project map the opposing positions.

Leo Szilard (1898–1964), a Hungarian-born scientist, is said to have conceived of the idea of nuclear chain reaction, the process that in uranium provides the power for nuclear energy. In a letter to President Truman in July 1945, he warns against using the atomic bomb against Japan. The physicist Edward Teller (1908–2003), also Hungarian-born, worked closely with Fermi and Oppenheimer at Los Alamos. After the war, he promoted the development of a "super bomb," the hydrogen bomb, and ultimately convinced President Truman to fund the project as a bulwark against the Soviet Union. In his letter, he replies to Szilard's request.

- **What arguments did the scientists pose for and against the deployment of the atomic bomb?**

July 3, 1945: A Petition to the President of the United States

Discoveries of which the people of the United States are not aware may affect the welfare of this nation in the near future. The liberation of atomic power which has been achieved places atomic bombs in the hands of the Army. It places in your hands, as Commander-in-Chief, the fateful decision whether or not to sanction the use of such bombs in the present phase of the war against Japan.

We, the undersigned scientists, have been working in the field of atomic power for a number of years. Until recently we have had to reckon with the possibility that the United States might be attacked by atomic bombs during this war and that her only defense might lie in a counterattack by the same means. Today with this danger averted we feel impelled to say what follows:

The war has to be brought speedily to a successful conclusion and the destruction of Japanese cities by means of atomic bombs may very well be an effective method of warfare. We feel, however, that such an attack on Japan could not be justified in the present circumstances. We believe that the United States ought not to resort to the use of atomic

bombs in the present phase of the war, at least not unless the terms which will be imposed upon Japan after the war are publicly announced and subsequently Japan is given an opportunity to surrender.

If such public announcement gave assurance to the Japanese that they could look forward to a life devoted to peaceful pursuits in their homeland and if Japan still refused to surrender, our nation would then be faced with a situation which might require a re-examination of her position with respect to the use of atomic bombs in the war.

Atomic bombs are primarily a means for the ruthless annihilation of cities. Once they were introduced as an instrument of war it would be difficult to resist for long the temptation of putting them to such use.

The last few years show a marked tendency toward increasing ruthlessness. At present our Air Forces, striking at the Japanese cities, are using the same methods of warfare which were condemned by American public opinion only a few years ago when applied by the Germans to the cities of England. Our use of atomic bombs in this war would carry the world a long way further on this path of ruthlessness.

Atomic power will provide the nations with new means of destruction. The atomic bombs at our disposal represent only the first step in this direction and there is almost no limit to the destructive power which will become available in the course of this development. Thus a nation which sets the precedent of using these newly liberated forces of nature for purposes of destruction may have to bear the responsibility of opening the door to an era of devastation on an unimaginable scale.

In view of the foregoing, we, the undersigned, respectfully petition that you exercise your power as Commander-in-Chief to rule that the United States shall not, in the present phase of the war, resort to the use of atomic bombs.

Leo Szilard and 58 co-signers

Source: Box 70, *J. Robert Oppenheimer Papers*, Manuscript Division, Library of Congress, Washington, DC.

Teller's Response to Szilard

Dear Szilard:

Since our discussion I have spent some time thinking about your objections to an immediate military use of the weapon we may produce. I decided to do nothing; I should like to tell you my reasons.

First of all let me say that I have no hope of clearing my conscience. The things we are working on are so terrible that no amount of protesting or fiddling with politics will save our souls.

This much is true: I have not worked on the project for a very selfish reason and I have gotten mucsh (sic) more trouble than pleasure out of it. I worked because the problems interested me and I should have felt it a great restraint not to go ahead. I can not claim that I simply worked to do my duty. A sense of duty could keep me out of such work. It could not get me into the present kind of activity against my inclinations. If you should succeed in convincing me that your moral objections are valid, I should quit working. I hardly think that I should start protesting.

But I am not really convinced of your objections. I do not feel that there is any chance to outlaw any one weapon. If we have a slim chance of survival, it lies in the possibility to get rid of wars. The more decisive a weapon is the more surely it will be used in any real conflict and no agreements will help.

Our only hope is in getting the facts of our results before the people. This might help to convince everybody that the next war would be fatal. For this purpose actual combat use might even be the best thing.

And this brings me to the main point. The accident that we worked out this dreadful thing should not give us the responsibility of having a voice in how it is to be used. This responsibility must in the end be shifted to the people as a whole and that can be done only by making the facts known. This is the only cause for which I feel entitled in doing something: the necessity of lifting the secrecy at least as far as the broad issues of our work are concerned. My understanding is that this will be done as soon as the military situation permits it.

All this may seem to you quite wrong. I should be glad if you showed this letter to Eugene and to Franck who seem to agree with you rather than with me. I should like to have the advice of all of you whether you think it is a crime to continue to work. But I feel that I should do the wrong thing if I tried to say how to tie the little toe of the ghost to the bottle from which we just helped it to escape.

With best regards.
Yours,
E. Teller

Source: Box 70, *J. Robert Oppenheimer Papers*, Manuscript Division, Library of Congress, Washington, DC.

25.6 The Last Stages of War

How did the relationship among the Allies change once victory was in sight?

From the attack on Pearl Harbor until mid-1943, Roosevelt and his advisors had focused primarily on military strategy rather than on postwar plans. Once the defeat of Nazi Germany appeared in sight, they considered long-range objectives. Roosevelt wanted both to crush the Axis powers and to establish a system of collective security to avert another world war. He knew he could not succeed without the cooperation of the other key Allied leaders, Stalin and Churchill. In 1944 and early 1945, these "Big Three" met several times to hammer out the shape of postwar policy.

Although they did not expect to reach a final agreement, neither did they anticipate how quickly momentous global events would shake the foundation of their "Grand Alliance."

25.6.1 The Holocaust

As the war entered its final stages, the American public finally became aware of the full horror of Nazi atrocities. As part of a comprehensive plan for achieving Aryan superiority and the "final solution of the Jewish question," Hitler had ordered the systematic extermination of "racial enemies" and others deemed undesirable, including mentally and physically disabled German children and adults. The toll included some 6 million Jews, 250,000 Romany (Gypsies), and 60,000 homosexuals, all deemed enemies of the German Reich and its "master race." Gruesome "medical experiments" were also performed on Jews and Soviet prisoners of war. These policies had begun at the onset of Hitler's regime in 1933, and beginning in 1942 the Nazis initiated mass murder in death camps such as Auschwitz in Poland.

Throughout almost the entire war, the U.S. government released little information about what came to be known as the **Holocaust**. Although liberal magazines such as *The Nation* and small committees of intellectuals tried to call attention to what was happening in the Nazi death camps, major news media like the *New York Times* treated reports of genocide as minor news items. Leaders of the American Jewish community, however, had been petitioning the U.S. government since the mid-1930s to suspend immigration quotas that barred significant numbers of German Jews from taking refuge in the United States.

It was not until January 1944 that Roosevelt responded to pressure. Secretary of the Treasury Henry Morgenthau, Jr., the only Jew in the president's cabinet, presented a report on "one of the greatest crimes in history, the slaughter of the Jewish people in Europe," and charged the State Department with actually thwarting rescue efforts. Within a week, in part to avoid scandal, Roosevelt issued an executive order creating the War Refugee Board. Still, Roosevelt and the War Department refused to bomb rail lines leading to the Nazi death camps. Attempts to rescue civilians, according to the government, would divert resources from military operations.

The extent of Nazi depravity was finally revealed to Americans after the Allied liberation of the Nazi concentration camps in 1945. The Soviets liberated Auschwitz, the largest extermination camp, on January 27, now commemorated as International Holocaust Remembrance Day. In April, four American soldiers from the Sixth Armored Division liberated Buchenwald, which had already been taken over by Communist prisoners. Touring Ohrdruf concentration camp that same month, Eisenhower found barracks crowded with corpses and crematories still reeking of burned flesh. "I want every American unit not actually in the front lines to see this place," he ordered. "We are told that the American soldier does not know what he is fighting for. Now, at last, he will know what he is fighting against."

25.6.2 The Yalta Conference

In November 1944, Roosevelt was elected to a fourth term, defeating the moderately liberal Republican governor of New York, Thomas E. Dewey. Elected with FDR was a new vice president, a middle-of-the-road Missouri senator named Harry S. Truman. Unknown to the public, however, Roosevelt was now exhausted and gravely ill.

With the end of the war in sight, Roosevelt and other Allied leaders began to reassess their goals. The Atlantic Charter of 1941 had stated noble objectives for the world after the defeat of fascism: national self-determination, no territorial aggrandizement, equal access of all peoples to raw materials and collaboration for the improvement of economic opportunities, freedom of the seas, disarmament, and "freedom from fear and want." Now, four years later, Roosevelt realized that neither Great Britain nor the Soviet Union intended to abide by any code of conduct that compromised their national security or conflicted with their economic interests. In October 1944, Stalin and Churchill met secretly in Moscow and reached a new agreement, one projecting their respective spheres of influence in Eastern Europe.

BIG THREE AT YALTA This photograph was taken at the second wartime meeting of "the Big Three": British Prime Minister Winston Churchill, United States President Franklin D. Roosevelt, and Soviet Premier Joseph Stalin. These heads of government met at Yalta in Crimea to discuss Germany and to plan for the post-war reorganization of Europe. They agreed to the terms of unconditional surrender for Germany and accepted Stalin's pledge to enter the Asian war against Japan. Ill at the conference, President Roosevelt died just two months later.

In early February 1945, Roosevelt met with Churchill and Stalin at Yalta, a Crimean resort on the Black Sea. Although diplomats avoided the touchy phrase "spheres of influence," it was clear that this opportunistic principle guided all negotiations. Neither the United States nor Great Britain raised serious objections to Stalin's demand to retain the Baltic states and eastern Poland—booty from the time of the Nazi-Soviet pact—and to create an East European "buffer zone" protecting Russia against future German aggression. In return, Churchill insisted on restoring the British Empire in Asia, and the United States hoped to retain captured Pacific islands from which Japanese military resurgence could be checked. Roosevelt hoped to ease the harshness of these imperialistic goals by creating a global peacekeeping organization, the United Nations, and by using promises of postwar American economic aid to persuade Stalin to behave with restraint in countries, like Poland, that the Red Army was liberating and occupying. The biggest and most controversial item on the agenda at Yalta was the Soviet entry into the Pacific war. The Soviet Union had not declared war on Japan, and Roosevelt believed Soviet participation necessary for a timely Allied victory.

Roosevelt told Congress that the Yalta meeting had been a "great success," proof that the wartime alliance remained intact. Privately, however, he concluded that the outcome of the conference revealed that the Atlantic Charter, with its grand aspirations for the postwar world, had been nothing more than a "beautiful idea." The Yalta conference was, FDR's critics agreed, a diplomatic failure, with too much conceded to the Soviet Union, particularly the dominance of Eastern Europe.

The death of Franklin Roosevelt of a massive stroke on April 12, 1945, cast a dark shadow over all hopes for long-term, peaceful solutions to global problems. The president did not live to learn of Hitler's suicide in his Berlin bunker on April 30, 1945, or the unconditional surrender of Germany one week later, on May 8.

25.6.3 The Atomic Bomb

Roosevelt's death made Allied cooperation even more difficult. President Harry Truman, an honest, plainspoken politician from Kansas City, Missouri, lacked both foreign-policy experience and FDR's finesse and prestige. From July 17 to August 2, 1945, at Potsdam, just outside Berlin, he met with Stalin and prime minister Clement Atlee, Churchill's successor, to discuss the future of defeated and occupied Germany, the Soviet occupation of Eastern Europe, reparations and economic aid to rebuild a shattered Europe, and crucial details about organizing the United Nations. The Big Three clashed sharply over most of these issues, but they held fast in demanding the unconditional surrender of reeling but still-defiant Japan.

It was at Potsdam that Truman learned a closely guarded secret: that on July 16 the United States had successfully tested an atomic bomb in New Mexico. As a senator and as vice president, Truman had not been informed of the existence of the Manhattan Project; he first heard about it upon Roosevelt's death. Until the moment of the test, Truman had been pressing Stalin to make good his Yalta promise to enter the Pacific war three months after Germany's surrender—a deadline that would fall on August 8. The president was eager to get Soviet participation in what everyone said would be a horrendously bloody U.S. invasion of Japan, and indeed he did extract Stalin's promise to attack Japan on schedule. But then Secretary of War Henry L. Stimson received a cable: "Babies satisfactorily born." Truman and his advisers concluded that Soviet assistance was no longer needed to end the war.

HIROSHIMA On August 6, 1945, the U.S. Army Air Force dropped the first atomic bomb used in warfare and destroyed the city of Hiroshima, Japan. Between 70,000 and 80,000 people—30 percent of the city's population—were killed. Although much of the city was reduced to rubble, the Genbaku Dome, which is fortified by a metal framework, remained. After many discussions, Hiroshima's residents agreed to preserve the structure, which became the centerpiece of the Hiroshima Peace Memorial Park, a UNESCO World Heritage site since 1996.

Pictorial Press Ltd/Alamy Stock Photo.

On August 3, 1945, Japan announced its refusal to surrender. Its military leaders still pledged to fight to the death, and Japanese civilian politicians wanted Allied guarantees that the emperor, considered sacred, would keep his throne. Three days later, the B-29 bomber nicknamed *Enola Gay* dropped the five-ton uranium bomb that destroyed the Japanese city of Hiroshima. Instantly, some 40,000 people died; in the following weeks, 100,000 more perished from radiation poisoning or burns.

"This is not war, this is not even murder; this is pure nihilism . . . a crime against God which strikes at the very basis of moral existence." So wrote the Japanese *Nippon Times*. In the United States, several leading religious publications echoed this view. The *Christian Century* judged the use of the bomb as a "moral earthquake." Albert Einstein, whose physics provided the foundation for the Manhattan Project (but in which he had taken no part), said that the atomic bomb had changed everything—except the nature of man. The majority of troops serving in the Pacific Theater, in contrast, praised the decision to drop bombs as saving their lives.

Americans first heard of the atomic bomb on August 7, when the news reported the destruction and death it had brought to Hiroshima. But fears about the implications of the appalling new weapon were overwhelmed by an outpouring of relief: Japan surrendered—still not unconditionally—on August 14, several days after a second nuclear bomb destroyed Nagasaki, killing another 73,000 people.

Allied insistence on unconditional surrender and the decision to atom-bomb Japan remain two of the most controversial political and moral questions about the conduct of World War II. Although Truman insisted in his memoirs (written years later) that he gave the order so as to save "a half a million American lives" in ground combat, no such official estimate exists. An intelligence document of April 30, 1946, stated that "the dropping of the bomb was the pretext seized upon by all [American] leaders as the reason for ending the war, but [even if the bomb had not been used] the Japanese would have capitulated upon the entry of Russia into the war." There is no question, however, that the use of nuclear weapons did strengthen U.S. policymakers' hand. It certainly forced caution upon Stalin, soon to emerge as America's primary adversary. Truman and his advisers knew that their nation's atomic monopoly would not last, but they hoped that in the meantime the United States could play the leading role in building the postwar world.

Conclusion

The new tactics and weapons of World War II, such as massive air raids and the atomic bomb produced by the Los Alamos scientists, made warfare incomparably deadlier than before to both military and civilian populations. Between 40 million and 50 million people died in World War II—four times the number in World War I—and half the casualties were women and children. More than 405,000 Americans died, and more than 670,000 were wounded. Although slight compared with the casualties suffered by other Allied nations—more than 20 million Soviets died during the war—the human cost of World War II for Americans was second only to that of the Civil War.

Coming at the end of two decades of resolutions to avoid military entanglements, the war pushed the nation's leaders to the center of global politics and into risky military and political alliances that would not outlive the war. The United States emerged the strongest nation in the world, but in a world where the prospects for lasting peace appeared increasingly remote. If World War II raised the nation's international commitments to a new height, its impact on ordinary Americans was not so easy to gauge. Many new communities formed as Americans migrated in mass numbers to new regions that were booming as a result of the wartime economy. Enjoying a rare moment of full employment, many workers new to well-paying industrial jobs anticipated further advances against discrimination. Exuberant at the Allies' victory over fascism and the return of the troops, the majority were optimistic as they looked ahead.

Key Terms

blitzkrieg German war tactic in World War II (translating to "lightning war") involving the concentration of air and armored firepower to punch and exploit holes in opposing defensive lines. p. 610

Axis powers The opponents of the United States and its allies in World War II. p. 610

Neutrality Act of 1939 Permitted the sale of arms to Britain, France, and China. p. 610

Lend-Lease Act An arrangement for the transfer of war supplies, including food, machinery, and services, to nations whose defense was considered vital to the defense of the United States in World War II. p. 611

Atlantic Charter Statement of common principles and war aims developed by President Franklin Roosevelt and British Prime Minister Winston Churchill at a meeting in August 1941. p. 611

War Powers Act of 1941 An act that gave the U.S. president the power to reorganize the federal government and create new agencies; to establish programs censoring news and information; to abridge civil liberties; to seize foreign-owned property; and to award government contracts without bidding. p. 611

Nisei United States citizens born of immigrant Japanese parents. p. 621

Operation Torch The Allied invasion of Axis-held North Africa in 1942. p. 625

Operation Overlord United States and British invasion of France in June 1944. p. 626

D-Day June 6, 1944, the day of the first paratroop drops and amphibious landings on the coast of Normandy, France, in the first stage of Operation Overlord. p. 626

Battle of the Bulge German offensive in December 1944 that penetrated deep into Belgium (creating a "bulge"). Allied forces, while outnumbered, attacked from the north and south. By January 1945, the German forces were destroyed or routed, but not without some 77,000 Allied casualties. p. 626

island-hop The Pacific campaigns of 1944 that were the American naval versions of the *blitzkrieg*. p. 627

Holocaust The systematic murder of millions of European Jews and others deemed undesirable by Nazi Germany. p. 631

CHRONOLOGY

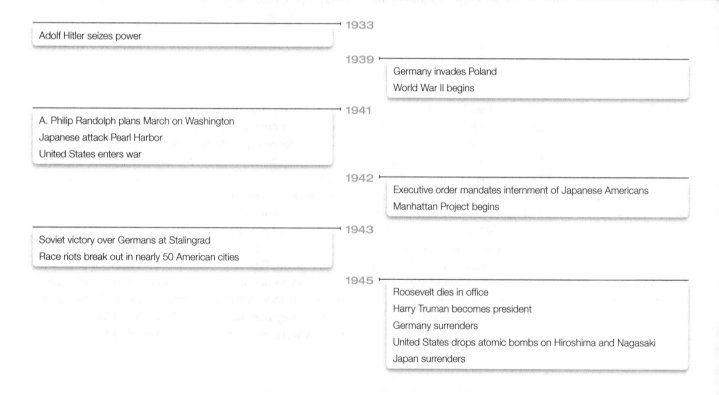

1933
Adolf Hitler seizes power

1939
Germany invades Poland
World War II begins

1941
A. Philip Randolph plans March on Washington
Japanese attack Pearl Harbor
United States enters war

1942
Executive order mandates internment of Japanese Americans
Manhattan Project begins

1943
Soviet victory over Germans at Stalingrad
Race riots break out in nearly 50 American cities

1945
Roosevelt dies in office
Harry Truman becomes president
Germany surrenders
United States drops atomic bombs on Hiroshima and Nagasaki
Japan surrenders

Chapter 26
The Cold War Begins 1945–1952

"KIDDE KOKOON" A family inside "Kidde Kokoon," an underground bomb shelter manufactured by Walter Kidde Nuclear Laboratories of Garden City, Long Island, 1955.

Library of Congress (Photoduplication).

 ## Contents and Focus Questions

American Communities

University of Washington, Seattle: Students and Faculty Face the Cold War

In May 1948, a philosophy professor at the University of Washington in Seattle answered a knock on his office door. Two state legislators, members of the state's Committee on Un-American Activities, entered. "Our information," they charged, "puts you in the center of a communist conspiracy."

The accused professor, Melvin Rader, had never been a communist. During the 1930s, alarmed by the rise of fascism, Rader had become a prominent political activist in his community. At one point, he served as president of the University of Washington Teacher's Union, which had formed during the upsurge of labor organizing during the New Deal. When invited to join the Communist Party, Rader bluntly refused.

Rader was caught up in a second Red Scare—the first had been that of 1919–1920 (see Chapter 22)—that curtailed free speech and political activity on campuses throughout the

United States. At some universities, such as Yale, the FBI set up camp with the consent of the college administration, spying on students and faculty, screening the credentials of job or scholarship applicants, and enticing students to report on friends or roommates. The University of Washington administration turned down the Physics Department's recommendation to hire J. Robert Oppenheimer, the famed atomic scientist and former director of Los Alamos Scientific Laboratory who had become a vocal opponent of the arms race.

Although one state legislator claimed that "not less than 150 members" of the University of Washington faculty were subversives, the state's Committee on Un-American Activities turned up just six Communist Party members. These six were hauled before the university's Faculty Committee on Tenure and Academic Freedom. Three were ultimately dismissed, while the other three were placed on probation.

What had provoked this paranoia? Instead of peace in the wake of World War II, "Cold War"—tense, icy relations but no outright fighting—prevailed between the United States and the Soviet Union. Uneasy wartime allies, the two superpowers now viewed each other as archenemies. Within the United States, the Cold War demanded pledges of absolute loyalty from citizens in every institution, from universities to unions and from the media to government itself.

Without the Cold War, this era might have been one of the most fruitful in the history of higher education. The Servicemen's Readjustment Act, popularly known as the G.I. Bill of Rights, passed by Congress in 1944, offered stipends covering tuition and living expenses to veterans attending vocational schools or college. By the 1947–1948 academic year, the federal government was subsidizing nearly half of all male college students. Between 1945 and 1950, 2.3 million students benefited from the G.I. Bill. At the University of Washington, the student population

Seattle

in 1946 had grown by 50 percent over its prewar peak of 10,000, with veterans representing two-thirds of the student body. A quickly expanded faculty taught into the evening to use classroom space efficiently. Meanwhile, the state legislature pumped in funds for the construction of new buildings, including dormitories and prefabricated units for married students.

The Cold War squelched much of that. FBI director J. Edgar Hoover testified that the college campuses were centers of "red propaganda." Due to "communistic" teachers and "communist-line textbooks," a senator wailed, thousands of parents sent "their sons and daughters to college as good Americans," only to see them return home "four years later as wild-eyed radicals."

These extravagant charges were far from true. The overwhelming majority of college graduates in the late 1940s and 1950s were conservative and conformist. Nevertheless, several states, including Washington, enacted or revived loyalty-security programs, obligating all state employees to swear in writing their loyalty to the United States and to disclaim membership in any subversive organization. Nationwide, approximately 200 "radical" faculty members were dismissed outright and many others were denied tenure. Thousands of students simply left school, dropped out of organizations, or changed friends after "visits" from FBI agents or interviews with administrators.

This tense, gloomy mood reversed the wave of optimism that had swept through America only a few years earlier. Victory in Japan (V-J) Day had escalated into two days of wild celebrations, ticker-tape parades, spontaneous dancing, and kisses for returning G.I.s. Americans, living in the richest and most powerful nation in the world, finally seemed to have gained the peace they had fought for and sacrificed to win. But peace proved fragile and elusive.

26.1 Global Insecurities at War's End

What steps did the United States take in the years following World War II to shape the economic and political future of Europe?

The war that had engulfed the world from 1939 to 1945 created an international interdependence that no country could ignore. Never before, not even at the end of World War I, had hopes been so strong for a genuine "community

of nations." But, as a 1945 opinion poll indicated, most Americans believed that prospects for a durable peace rested to a large degree on one factor: harmony between the two remaining superpowers, the United States and the Soviet Union.

26.1.1 Financing the Future

In 1941, Henry Luce, the publisher of *Time*, *Life*, and *Fortune* magazines, forecast the dawn of "the American Century." During the darkest days of World War II, he wrote that Americans must "accept wholeheartedly our duty and our opportunity as the most powerful and vital nation in the world and in consequence to assert upon the world the full impact of our influence, for such means as we see fit." After the bombing of Hiroshima, President Harry S. Truman underscored this message, pronouncing the United States "the most powerful nation in the world—the most powerful nation, perhaps, in all history."

Americans had good reason to be confident about their prospects for setting the terms of the postwar order. Unlike Great Britain, France, and the Soviet Union, the United States not only had escaped the ravages of the war, but had actually prospered. By June 1945, the capital assets of manufacturing had increased 65 percent over prewar levels to equal in value approximately half the entire world's goods and services.

Yet many Americans understood that it was the massive government spending to pay for the war rather than New Deal programs that had ended the spectre of the Great Depression. A stark question loomed: What would happen when wartime production ended and millions of troops returned home to claim jobs?

"We need markets—big markets—in which to buy and sell," answered Assistant Secretary of State for Economic Affairs Will Clayton. Just to maintain the current level of growth, the United States needed to export—to a war-ravaged world—a staggering $14 billion in goods and services. During the war, many business leaders had looked to the Soviet Union as a future customer. With that prospect vanishing, with potential Eastern European markets threatened, and with the enormous European colonies closed to American enterprise, U.S. business and government leaders pushed to integrate Western Europe, Latin America, and Asia into an international economy open to American trade and investment.

During the final stages of the war, President Franklin Roosevelt's advisers laid plans to secure U.S. primacy in the postwar global economy. In July 1944, representatives from 44 Allied nations met at Bretton Woods, New Hampshire, to work out the details of a new international financial system. They established the International Bank for Reconstruction and Development (the World Bank) and the **International Monetary Fund (IMF)**, two institutions designed to help rebuild war-torn Europe and Asia and to stabilize monetary exchanges among nations. The United States became the principal supplier of funds for the IMF and the World Bank (more than $7 billion to each) and thus, by determining the allocation of loans, could unilaterally reshape the global economy.

The Soviet Union participated at Bretton Woods, but Stalin later refused to ratify the agreements. Accepting World Bank and IMF aid would, Stalin believed, make the war-torn Soviet Union an economic colony of the capitalist West. By spurning this aid, the Soviet Union economically isolated itself and its East European satellites.

26.1.2 The Division of Europe

In the Atlantic Charter of 1941, the United States and Great Britain had proclaimed the right of all nations to self-determination and renounced claims to new territories as spoils of war. Before the war ended, though, Churchill, Stalin, and Roosevelt violated the charter by dividing Europe into spheres of influence. (See Chapter 25 and Map 26.1.)

For Roosevelt, that strategy had seemed compatible with ensuring world peace. FDR balanced his internationalist idealism with a belief that the United States was entitled to extraordinary influence in Latin America and the Philippines, and that other great powers might have similar privileges or responsibilities elsewhere. Roosevelt also recognized the diplomatic consequence of the brutal ground war that had been fought largely on Soviet territory: the Soviet Union's nonnegotiable demand for security along its western border.

From the earliest days of fighting Hitler, the Soviet Union was intent on reestablishing its 1941 borders. At the Potsdam Conference, held in the bombed-out Berlin suburb in July 1945, Stalin not only regained but also extended his territory, annexing eastern Poland with Western approval and the little Baltic nations without it. Soviet influence quickly became paramount in all East European countries that the Red Army had occupied. The question remained: Did Stalin aim to bring all of Europe into the communist domain?

BIG THREE AT POTSDAM Representatives of the "Big Three" nations—the Soviet Union, the United Kingdom, and the United States—gathered at Potsdam, Germany, near Berlin, from July 17 until August 2, 1945. This photograph shows Stalin, Truman, and Churchill as they begin to discuss the terms of peace and postwar arrangements. They concluded by issuing the "Potsdam Declaration," which demanded Japan's unconditional surrender.

Map 26.1 DIVIDED EUROPE

During the Cold War, Europe was divided into opposing military alliances, the North Atlantic Treaty Organization (NATO) and the Warsaw Pact (Communist bloc).

At the Potsdam Conference, when the wartime allies began to plan Germany's future, that question loomed over all deliberations. They decided to divide the conquered nation into four occupation zones, each temporarily ruled by one of the Allied nations. They could not agree on long-term plans, however.

After the war, continuing disagreements about the future of Germany darkened hopes for Soviet-American cooperation. By July 1946, Americans had begun to withhold reparations due to the Soviets from their occupation zone and began to grant amnesty to some former Nazis. Then, in December, the Americans and British merged their zones and invited France and the Soviet Union to join. France agreed; Stalin, fearing a resurgence of a united Germany, refused.

The United States and the Soviet Union were now at loggerheads. Twice in the twentieth century, Germany had invaded Russia, and the Soviet Union interpreted any moves toward German reunification as menacing. For their part, American policymakers, assuming Stalin to be aggressively expansionist, envisioned a united Germany as a bulwark against further Soviet encroachments.

26.1.3 The United Nations and Hopes for Collective Security

In addition to addressing the postwar financial order and the disposition of Germany, the Allies—pushed determinedly by FDR—discussed mechanisms for preventing future wars and promoting peace. In 1944 at the Dumbarton Oaks Conference in Washington, and again in April 1945 at San Francisco, the representatives worked to shape the United Nations (UN) as a world organization that would arbitrate disputes among member nations and stop aggressors—by force, if necessary. By 1946, the UN also planned for international control of atomic energy for peacetime use.

The terms of membership, however, limited the UN's ability to mediate disputes. Although all fifty nations that signed the UN charter voted in the General Assembly, only five (the United States, Great Britain, the Soviet Union, France, and China) served permanently on the Security Council, and each had absolute veto power over the Council's decisions. The primary goal of the UN—to maintain international peace and security—proved elusive.

The UN achieved its greatest success with its humanitarian programs. Its relief agency gave war-torn European and Asian countries billions of dollars for medical supplies, food, and clothing. The UN also dedicated itself to the high principles of the 1948 Universal Declaration of Human Rights, which owed much to Eleanor Roosevelt, one of the first delegates from the United States.

On other issues, however, the UN operated strictly along lines dictated by the emerging **Cold War**. The Western nations allied with the United States held the balance of power and controlled the admission of new members. For example, in 1949, when the Communists won the Chinese civil war (discussed later), the Western powers would block the new People's Republic from claiming China's UN seat, held by the defeated Nationalists in Taiwan. The sharpening division into East and West made negotiated settlements virtually impossible and the prospects for peace at best precarious.

26.2 The Policy of Containment

How did the Truman Doctrine shape U.S. postwar foreign policy?

In March 1946, in a speech delivered in Fulton, Missouri, Winston Churchill proclaimed the definitive end of wartime cooperation with the Soviet Union. With President Truman at his side, the former British prime minister solemnly intoned, "An iron curtain has descended across the [European] continent." He called directly upon the United States, standing "at this time at the pinnacle of world power," to recognize its "awe-inspiring accountability to the future" and, in alliance with Great Britain, to act vigorously to stop Soviet expansion beyond the Eastern bloc that it already had claimed.

Although Truman at first responded cautiously to Churchill's warning, his administration ultimately rose to the challenge. As a policy uniting military, economic, and diplomatic strategies, the "containment" of communism possessed a powerful ideological dimension—an "us-versus-them" division of the world into "freedom" and "slavery."

26.2.1 The Truman Doctrine

Many Americans believed that Franklin D. Roosevelt, had he lived, could have smoothed tensions between the Soviet Union and the United States. His successor sorely lacked FDR's diplomatic talent and experience. More comfortable with machine politicians than with polished New Dealers, Truman liked to talk tough and act defiantly. "I'm tired of babying the Soviets," he snapped.

Truman's policies regarding the Soviet Union were inconsistent. In the first years after the war, at times he attempted to be conciliatory. Among U.S. policymakers, however, an anti-Soviet consensus was growing, fed by perceptions that Stalin was taking a hard line. In February 1946, George F. Kennan, the nation's premier diplomat in

ELEANOR ROOSEVELT AT THE UNITED NATIONS In 1946, President Harry S. Truman appointed former First Lady Eleanor Roosevelt as the United States delegate to the United Nations. Deeply concerned with the fate of refugees after World War II, she agreed to chair its new Human Rights Commission. Roosevelt was instrumental in formulating the Universal Declaration of Human Rights, which promoted, in her words, "equal justice, equal opportunity, equal dignity without discrimination" for all people worldwide.

dealing with the Soviet Union, sent an 8,000-word "long telegram" from Moscow to the State Department, insisting that Soviet fanaticism made cooperation impossible. The Soviet Union intended to extend its realm not by military means alone, he explained, but by "subversion" within "free" nations. In the long run, Kennan predicted, the Soviet system would collapse from within, but until that happened the West should pursue a policy of containment.

A perceived crisis in the Mediterranean marked the turning point. On February 21, 1947, amid a civil war in Greece, Great Britain informed the U.S. State Department that it could no longer afford to prop up the anti-communist government there and announced its intention to withdraw all aid. Without U.S. intervention, Truman concluded, Greece, Turkey, and perhaps the entire oil-rich Middle East would fall under Soviet control. But, warned an influential Republican senator, Congress would not act unless the President "scare[d] hell out of the American people."

On March 12, 1947, the president made his case in a speech to Congress. Never naming the Soviet Union, he appealed for all-out resistance to a "certain ideology" wherever it appeared in the world. The preservation of peace and the freedom of all Americans depended, the president insisted, on containing communism.

Congress approved $400 million to aid Greece and Turkey, which helped conservative forces in those countries crush left-wing rebels. By dramatically opposing communism, Truman somewhat buoyed his sagging popularity and helped generate popular support for an anti-communist crusade at home and abroad.

The significance of what became known as the **Truman Doctrine** far outlasted events in the Mediterranean: The United States had declared its right to intervene to promote democracy and to save other nations from communism. (See Table 26.1.) It was now the responsibility of the United States, the White House insisted, to safeguard what was coming to be called the Free World by any means necessary. The Truman Doctrine had fused anti-Communism and internationalism into a strong foreign policy that redirected the United States away from its long-standing apprehension about foreign commitments.

26.2.2 The Marshall Plan

The Truman Doctrine complemented the European Recovery Program, commonly known as the Marshall Plan. Introduced in a commencement speech at Harvard University on June 5, 1947, by Secretary of State George C. Marshall,

Table 26.1 MAJOR COLD WAR POLICIES

Date	Policy	Provisions
1947	Truman Doctrine	Pledged the United States to the containment of communism in Europe and elsewhere; the foundation of Truman's foreign policy, this doctrine impelled the United States to support any nation whose stability was threatened by communism or the Soviet Union
1947	Federal Employees Loyalty and Security Program	Established by Executive Order 9835, this barred communists and fascists from federal employment and outlined procedures for investigating current and prospective federal employees
1947	Marshall Plan	Also known as the European Recovery Program, this U.S. program to aid war-torn Europe was a cornerstone in the U.S. use of economic policy to contain communism
1947	National Security Act	Established Department of Defense (to coordinate the three armed services), the National Security Council (to advise the president on security issues), and the Central Intelligence Agency (to gather and evaluate intelligence data)
1948	Smith-Mundt Act	Launched an overseas campaign of anti-Communist propaganda
1949	North Atlantic Treaty Organization (NATO)	A military alliance of 12 nations formed to deter possible aggression by the Soviet Union against Western Europe
1950	NSC-68	National Security Council Paper 68, calling for an expanded and aggressive U.S. defense policy, including greater military spending and higher taxes
1950	Internal Security Act (also known as the McCarran Act and the Subversive Activities Control Act)	Legislation providing for the registration of all communist and totalitarian groups and authorizing the arrest of suspect persons during a national emergency
1951	Psychological Strategy Board	Created to coordinate anti-Communist propaganda campaigns
1952	Immigration and Nationality Act (also known as McCarran Walter Immigration Act)	Reaffirmed the national origins quota system but tightened immigration controls, barring homosexuals and people considered subversive from entering the United States

the plan sought to reduce "hunger, poverty, desperation, and chaos" and to restore "the confidence of the European people in the economic future of their own countries and of Europe as a whole." Indirectly, the Marshall Plan aimed to turn back left-wing socialist and communist bids for votes in Western Europe. Not least, the plan was also designed to boost the U.S. economy by securing a European market for American goods.

Considered by many historians the most successful postwar U.S. diplomatic venture, the **Marshall Plan** improved the climate for a viable capitalist economy in Western Europe and, in effect, brought aid recipients into bilateral agreements with the United States. (See Table 26.1.) In addition, the United States and 17 Western European nations ratified the tariff-cutting General Agreement on Tariffs and Trade pact, thus opening all to U.S. trade and investment.

The Marshall Plan was costly to Americans. In its initial year, it accounted for 12 percent of the federal budget. But much of that aid was in the form of American-made goods, produced by American workers. In the European nations covered by the plan, industrial production increased by 35 percent between 1947 and 1952, living standards improved, and American consumer goods and the American lifestyle became familiar.

As Truman later acknowledged, the Marshall Plan and the Truman Doctrine were "two halves of the same walnut." The Marshall Plan drove a deeper wedge between the United States and the Soviet Union. Although invited to participate, Stalin denounced the plan for what it was—an American scheme to rebuild Germany and incorporate it into an anti-Soviet bloc. Soon after the announcement of the Marshall Plan, the Soviet Union tightened its grip in Eastern Europe.

26.2.3 The Berlin Crisis and the Formation of NATO

Within a year of the start of the Marshall Plan, the United States and Britain moved closer to the goal of economically integrating their occupation zones in Germany into the Western sphere of influence. A common currency was established for these zones. Stalin reacted on June 24, 1948, by halting all traffic to the Western occupation zones of Berlin, deep within Soviet-occupied eastern Germany. (See Map 26.1.)

The **Berlin blockade** created both a crisis and an opportunity for the Truman administration. With help from the Royal Air Force, the United States began an unprecedented around-the-clock airlift. "Operation Vittles" delivered nearly 2 million tons of supplies to West Berliners. Stalin finally relented and lifted the blockade in May 1949, clearing the way for the Western powers to merge their occupation zones into a single nation, the Federal Republic of Germany.

BERLIN AIRLIFT Located deep within Communist East Germany, West Berlin was suddenly cut off from the West when the Soviets blockaded all surface traffic in an attempt to take over the war-torn city. Between June 1948 and May 1949, British and U.S. pilots made 272,000 flights, dropping food and supplies to civilians. New York Times photographer Henry Ries captured what became an iconic image of German children watching the landing of a U.S. Douglas C-54 Skymaster, a four-engine transport carrier.

Everett Collection Historical/Alamy Stock Photo.

The Soviet Union countered by turning its zone into the communist-dominated German Democratic Republic.

The Berlin Crisis furthered cooperation between the United States and noncommunist Western European nations, and in April 1949 ten European nations, Canada, and the United States formed the **North Atlantic Treaty Organization (NATO)**, a mutual-defense pact in which "an armed attack against one or more of them . . . shall be considered an attack against them all." NATO complemented the Marshall Plan, strengthening economic ties among the member nations. (See Table 26.1.) It also deepened divisions between Eastern and Western Europe, making a permanent military mobilization on both sides almost inevitable.

Global implications flowed from the forging of the North Atlantic alliance. Several Western European allies ruled valuable but restive colonial empires. During the war, FDR had urged British and French leaders to start dismantling their empires. In 1947, a financially strapped Britain granted independence to India and Pakistan, and under U.S. pressure, the Dutch gave up Indonesia in 1949. The French, however, were determined to regain Indochina, lost to Japan before Pearl Harbor. (See Chapter 25.) Cold War anti-Communism now trumped traditional American anticolonialism. Because the most important fighter against France's attempt to reconquer Indochina was Vietnamese communist Ho Chi Minh, Truman decided that France deserved American support. The first seeds had been planted of what would eventually become an American commitment to fight communism in Vietnam.

The Truman administration took Latin America for granted and was satisfied when the right-wing dictators ruling much of that region proclaimed themselves staunchly anti-Communist. The most positive gesture that the United States made toward Latin American opinion was designating Puerto Rico a self-governing "commonwealth" in 1952. Beneath the surface, though, trouble was brewing for the United States throughout the hemisphere.

Between 1947 and 1949, the Truman administration had defined the policies that would shape the Cold War for decades to come. The Truman Doctrine explained the ideological basis of containment, not for just Europe but also around the globe; the Marshall Plan put into place its economic underpinnings in Western Europe; and NATO created the mechanisms for military defense. When NATO extended membership to a rearmed West Germany in May 1955, the Soviet Union responded by creating a counterpart, the Warsaw Pact, including East Germany.

26.2.4 Atomic Diplomacy

The containment policy depended on the ability of the United States to back its commitments through military force, and Truman invested his faith in the U.S. monopoly of atomic weapons. After 1945, the United States began to build an atomic stockpile and to conduct tests on remote Pacific islands.

Despite warnings to the contrary by leading scientists, U.S military analysts estimated it would take the Soviet Union up to ten years to produce an atomic bomb. However, as early as August 1949, the Soviet Union tested its own atomic bomb, and the arms race that scientists had feared since 1945 was under way. By the mid-1950s, both the United States and the Soviet Union were testing hydrogen bombs a thousand times more powerful than the weapons dropped on Hiroshima and Nagasaki in 1945. By the late 1950s, stockpiles of nuclear bombs were being supplemented by intercontinental ballistic missiles, a new and more effective delivery system for nuclear weapons. The United States and the Soviet Union had effected a policy known as mutual assured destruction, with each nation knowingly capable of obliterating the other and therefore forced to choose restraint.

The United States and the Soviet Union were firmly locked into the Cold War. The nuclear arms race risked global catastrophe, diverted economic resources, and fed public fears of impending doom. Despite the victory won by the Grand Alliance of World War II, the world had again divided into hostile camps.

26.3 Cold War Liberalism

How did the "Fair Deal" differ from the "New Deal"?

Truman linked the Soviet threat abroad to the need for a strong presidency at home. After succeeding FDR, the new president at first aspired to enlarge the New Deal, but soon settled on a modest domestic agenda to promote social welfare and an anti-isolationist, anti-Communist foreign policy. Fatefully, during his administration, domestic and foreign policy became increasingly entangled. Out of that entanglement emerged a distinctive brand of liberalism—Cold War liberalism.

26.3.1 "To Err Is Truman"

Within a year of assuming office, Harry Truman's poll ratings were among the lowest of any twentieth-century president. The responsibilities of reestablishing peacetime conditions seemed to overwhelm the new president. "To err is Truman," critics sneered.

The task of converting from a wartime to a peacetime economy was enormous. Truman faced millions of restless would-be consumers tired of rationing and eager to spend their wartime savings on shiny cars, new appliances, choice cuts of meat, and stylish clothing. The demand for consumer items rapidly outran supply, fueling inflation and a huge black market.

In 1945 and 1946, the country appeared ready to explode. While homemakers protested rising prices by boycotting neighborhood stores, industrial workers struck in unprecedented numbers. Employers, fearing a rapid decline to Depression-level profits, determined to slash wages; workers wanted a bigger cut of the huge war profits they had heard about. With nearly 4.6 million workers on picket lines, the new president was alarmed. In May 1946, Truman proposed to draft striking railroad workers. The usually conservative Senate killed this plan.

Congress defeated most of Truman's proposals to revive the New Deal. One week after Japan's surrender, the president introduced a 21-point program that included greater unemployment compensation, higher minimum wages, and housing assistance. Later he added national health insurance and atomic-energy legislation. Congress rejected most of these bills. Legislators did pass the Employment Act of 1946, but only with substantial modification of the original draft. The act did not guarantee full employment, only support for a business climate favorable to this goal. The act established the **Council of Economic Advisers**, experts who would counsel the president and formulate policies for maintaining employment, production, and purchasing power.

With the White House falling short on legislative accomplishments, Republicans asked voters: "Had enough?" At the mid-term elections, the voters answered and turned over both houses of Congress and many state capitols to Republicans. Symbolically repudiating FDR, Republican-dominated state legislatures ratified the Twenty-second Amendment, limiting future presidents to two terms.

The Republicans, dominant in Congress for the first time since 1931, mounted a counterattack on the New Deal, beginning with organized labor. Unions had peaked in size

POSTWAR STRIKES Police and strikers confront each other in Los Angeles during one of many postwar strikes in 1946. Employers wanted to cut wages, and workers refused to give up the higher living standard achieved during the war.

and prestige; membership topped 15 million and encompassed nearly 40 percent of all wage earners. Claiming that "Big Labor" had gone too far, the Eightieth Congress aimed at abolishing many practices legalized by the Wagner Act of 1935. (See Chapter 24.) The resultant **Taft-Hartley Act** of 1947, passed over Truman's veto, outlawed the closed shop, the secondary boycott, and the use of union dues for political activities; mandated an 80-day cooling-off period in the case of strikes affecting "national safety or health"; and required all union officials to swear that they were not communists. Truman himself would later invoke the act against strikers.

26.3.2 The 1948 Election

Harry Truman had considered some of Roosevelt's advisers "crackpots and the lunatic fringe." By 1946, he had forced out many of the remaining social planners who had staffed the Washington bureaus for more than a decade. Truman also fired Roosevelt's secretary of commerce and former vice president, Henry Wallace, for advocating a more conciliatory policy toward the Soviet Union.

Wallace, refusing to fade away, vowed to run against Truman for president. He pledged to expand New Deal programs by moving boldly to establish full employment, racial equality, and stronger unions. He also promised peace with the Soviet Union. As the 1948 election neared,

Wallace appeared a viable candidate on the new Progressive Party ticket.

Truman shrewdly repositioned himself. He deflated Wallace by branding him a tool of the communists and attacked congressional Republicans for their conservative agenda. He countered both Wallace and the Republicans by proposing federal funds for education, housing, and medical insurance. Summoning Congress back for a special session after the summertime political conventions of 1948, he dared it to enact its own legislation and—when it predictably failed to do so—lambasted the "do-nothing Congress."

Wallace and the Republican nominee, New York governor Thomas E. Dewey, had taken strong leads on civil rights, but Truman outflanked them. In July 1948, he issued executive decrees desegregating the armed forces and banning discrimination in the federal civil service. In response, some 300 southern delegates bolted from the Democratic National Convention and named a States' Rights (**Dixiecrat**) ticket, headed by the staunchly segregationist governor of South Carolina, J. Strom Thurmond. With the South looking as good as lost, with Wallace threatening to siphon off left-leaning Democrats, and with soothing Dewey heading the Republicans, Truman appeared doomed.

But "Give 'em Hell, Harry's" vigorous campaign slowly revived the New Deal coalition. Fear of Republicans—who had passed Taft-Hartley—won back the bulk of organized

IS THIS TOMORROW? Published in 1947, this full-color comic book appeared as one of many sensationalistic illustrations of the threat of the "commie menace" to Americans at home. Approximately 4 million copies of *Is This Tomorrow?* were printed, the majority distributed to church groups or sold for ten cents a copy.

Advertising Archive/Courtesy Everett Collection.

Map 26.2 THE ELECTION OF 1948

Numbers on states represent Electoral Votes.	Electoral Vote (%)	Popular Vote (%)
HARRY S. TRUMAN (T) (Democrat)	303 (57)	24,105,812 (49.5)
Thomas E. Dewey (D) (Republican)	189 (36)	21,970,065 (45.1)
Strom Thurmond (Th) (States' Rights)	39 (7)	1,169,063 (2.4)
Henry A. Wallace (Progressive)	—	1,157,172 (2.4)
Other candidates (Socialist, Prohibition, Socialist Labor, Socialist Workers)	—	272,713 (0.6)

Initially an unpopular candidate, Truman made a whistle-stop tour of the country by train to win 49.5 percent of the popular vote to Dewey's 45.1 percent. His was the fifth straight presidential victory for the Democratic Party, which also regained control of Congress.

labor, and Truman's decision in May 1948 to recognize immediately the new State of Israel kept many liberal Jews loyally Democratic. The success of the Berlin airlift buoyed the president's popularity, and on Election Day growing anti-Communist sentiment among liberals limited the Wallace vote to the extreme left. Meanwhile, Dewey tried to coast to victory by appearing bland and "presidential."

Polls predicted a Dewey victory—but the pollsters stopped taking samples several weeks before Election Day and so missed a late Democratic surge. Truman won the popular vote by a 5 percent margin, trouncing Dewey 303 to 189 in electoral votes. Democrats regained majorities in both houses of Congress. (See Map 26.2.)

26.3.3 The Fair Deal

"Every segment of our population and every individual has a right," Truman announced in January 1949, "to

expect from our Government a fair deal." Democratic congressional majorities would, he hoped, translate campaign promises into laws and expand the New Deal. But a powerful bloc of conservative southern Democrats and midwestern Republicans turned back his domestic agenda.

The National Housing Act of 1949 provided federally funded low-income housing. Congress also raised the minimum wage (from 40 cents per hour to 75 cents per hour) and brought an additional 10 million people under Social Security coverage. Otherwise, Truman made no headway. He and congressional liberals introduced a variety of bills to weaken southern racism, including a federal antilynching law, another outlawing poll taxes, and a third banning discrimination in interstate transportation. Southern-led filibusters killed them all, while conservative-dominated congressional committees bottled up his initiatives for national health insurance, federal aid for education, and a repeal or modification of Taft-Hartley.

"DEWEY DEFEATS TRUMAN" Harry Truman holds up a copy of the *Chicago Tribune* with headlines confidently and mistakenly predicting the victory of his Republican opponent, Thomas E. Dewey. An initially unpopular candidate, Truman made a whistle-stop tour of the country by train to win 49.5 percent of the popular vote to Dewey's 45.1 percent.

Everett Collection, Inc./Alamy Stock Photo.

Truman's greatest domestic achievement was to articulate the basic principles of Cold War liberalism, which would remain the northern Democratic agenda for decades to come. Truman's Fair Deal promoted bread-and-butter issues and economic growth. His administration insisted, therefore, on an ambitious program of expanded foreign trade, while relying on the federal government to encourage higher productivity. Equally important, Truman reshaped liberalism by making anti-Communism a key element in both foreign policy and domestic affairs.

26.4 The National Security State

How did concerns about national security lead to the abridgement of civil liberties?

The concept of a national security state developed during World War II, when the government promoted its responsibility to act to protect its citizens from several forms of crisis, such as military threats, natural disasters, and economic catastrophe. At the close of the war, the government emphasized its ability to avoid future war and, equally important, to repel external coercion, such as the dictates of a foreign, undemocratic government or encroachments on its territory. The imperative of national security destroyed old-fashioned isolationism, forcing the United States into unprecedented alliances such as NATO and into global leadership. "If we falter in our leadership," Truman warned, "we may endanger the peace of the world—and

we shall surely endanger the welfare of this nation." The acceptance of such responsibility demanded a substantial increase in the size of the federal government—in its military forces, surveillance agencies, and preparedness programs.

26.4.1 The National Security Programs

By the late 1940s, the Communist Party, U.S.A., was steadily losing ground. Nevertheless, anti-Communism now held center stage in domestic politics. FBI Director J. Edgar Hoover warned of "the diabolic machination of sinister figures engaged in un-American activities." The federal government, with help from the media, led the crusade, using the threat of communism to reorder its operation and to quell dissent. Security measures designed to keep the nation in a steady state of preparedness, readily justified during wartime, were now extended indefinitely and expanded.

On March 21, 1947, not two weeks after proclaiming the Truman Doctrine, the president signed **Executive Order 9835**, establishing a civilian loyalty program for all federal employees. The new Federal Employees Loyalty and Security Program (see Table 26.1) outlined procedures for investigating current and prospective federal employees. The loyalty review boards often asked employees about their opinions of the Soviet Union, the Marshall Plan, or NATO, and whether they would report fellow workers if they found out they were communists. Any employee could be dismissed merely on "reasonable grounds," including guilt by association (that is, knowing or being related to a "subversive" person), rather than on proof of disloyalty. Later amendments added homosexuals as potential security risks, on the grounds that they might be targeted by enemies for blackmail.

Many state and municipal governments enacted loyalty programs and required public employees, including teachers at all levels, to sign loyalty oaths. In all, some 6.6 million people underwent loyalty and security checks. An estimated 500 government workers were fired, and perhaps as many as 6,000 more chose to resign. Numerous private employers and labor unions also instituted loyalty programs.

In April 1947, Attorney General Tom C. Clark aided this effort by publishing a list of hundreds of potentially subversive organizations. The famous "Attorney General's List" effectively outlawed many political and social organizations, stigmatizing hundreds of thousands of individuals who had done nothing illegal. Church associations, civil rights organizations, musical groups, and even summer camps appeared on the list. Fraternal and social institutions, especially popular among aging Eastern European immigrants, were among the largest organizations destroyed. New York State, for example, legally dismantled the

International Workers' Order, which had provided insurance to nearly 200,000 immigrants and their families.

Other security measures were designed to keep the nation in a steady state of preparedness. The sweeping National Security Act, passed by Congress in July 1947, established the Department of Defense and the **National Security Council (NSC)** to administer and coordinate defense policies and advise the president. The new Department of Defense absorbed the War and Navy departments, bringing all the armed forces under a single cabinet-level secretary. Ties between the armed forces and the State Department grew closer as retired military officers routinely filled positions in the State Department and diplomatic corps. The act also created the National Security Resources Board (NSRB) to coordinate plans throughout the government "in the event of war" and, for the first time in American history, to maintain military preparedness in peacetime.

The Department of Defense and the NSRB also became the principal sponsors of scientific research during the first 10 years of the Cold War. Federal agencies tied to military projects supplied well over 90 percent of the funding for research in the physical sciences, much of it at major universities.

The **Central Intelligence Agency (CIA)** was another product of the National Security Act. With roots in the wartime Office of Strategic Services (OSS), the new CIA became a permanent operation devoted to collecting political, military, and economic information for intelligence assessments and conducting covert actions throughout the world. (It was barred from domestic intelligence gathering, which was the domain of its rival, the FBI.)

The national security state required a huge workforce. Before World War II, approximately 900,000 civilians worked for the federal government, about 10 percent of them in security work; by the beginning of the Cold War, nearly 4 million people were on the government's payroll, 75 percent of them in national security agencies.

National security absorbed increasingly large portions of the nation's resources. By the end of Truman's second term, defense allocations accounted for 10 percent of GNP, directly or indirectly employed hundreds of thousands of well-paid workers, and subsidized some of the nation's most profitable corporations. This vast financial outlay created the rationale for permanent, large-scale military spending and powerfully stimulated economic growth.

26.4.2 The Second Red Scare

The **House Committee on Un-American Activities (HUAC)**, since 1945 a permanent standing committee charged with investigating disloyalty and subversion, had the power to subpoena witnesses and to compel them to answer all questions or face contempt-of-Congress charges. In October 1947,

HUAC began hearings on communists and the Hollywood film industry. The mother of actress Ginger Rogers defended her daughter by saying that she had been duped into appearing in the 1943 pro-Soviet wartime film *Tender Comrade* and "had been forced" to read the subversive line "Share and share alike, that's democracy." HUAC encouraged such testimony by other "friendly witnesses," including actors Ronald Reagan and Gary Cooper. A small but prominent minority refused to cooperate with HUAC and became known as "unfriendly witnesses." A handful served prison sentences for refusing to "name names."

Hollywood studios would not employ any writer, director, or actor who refused to cooperate with HUAC. The resulting blacklist remained in effect until the 1960s and limited the production of films dealing with "controversial" social or political issues.

The labor movement also became a victim of this second Red Scare. Like the Hollywood film industry, a sizable portion of its leaders and members had affiliated with the Communist Party or supported liberal causes in the 1930s, and they emerged from their wartime experiences even more deeply committed to social justice. In 1947, the R.J. Reynolds Tobacco Company charged union activists who had organized against the company's racial discriminatory policy as pawns of Moscow. A year later, CIO president Philip Murray gave in to this pressure and decided to rid his organization of all communists. Soon, 11 unions representing more than a million workers were expelled.

HUAC also acted to identify spies and agents of espionage in the United States. In August 1948, *Time* magazine editor Whittaker Chambers appeared before HUAC to name Alger Hiss as a fellow communist in the Washington underground during the 1930s. Hiss, a former member of FDR's State Department, denied the charges and sued his accuser for slander. Chambers then revealed his trump card: a cache of films of secret documents that had been hidden in a hollowed-out pumpkin on his Maryland farm. He claimed that Hiss had passed them to him for transmission to the Soviet Union. The statute of limitations for espionage having run out, a federal grand jury in January 1950 instead convicted Hiss of perjury for denying he knew Chambers. He received two concurrent five-year prison terms. Hiss was released three and half years later proclaiming his innocence, a position he held throughout his life. Historians remain divided on the question of his spying.

The most dramatic spy case of the era involved Julius Rosenberg, a former government engineer, and his wife, Ethel, who were accused of conveying atomic secrets to Soviet agents during World War II. Although the Rosenbergs maintained their innocence to the end, in March 1951 a jury found them both guilty. They died in the electric chair on June 19, 1953. Documents declassified in the 1990s provided evidence of Julius (but not Ethel) Rosenberg's guilt.

26.4.3 McCarthyism

In a sensational Lincoln Day speech to the Republican Women's Club of Wheeling, West Virginia, on February 9, 1950, Republican Senator Joseph R. McCarthy of Wisconsin announced that the United States had been sold out by the "traitorous actions" of men holding important positions in the federal government. These men acted as part of a conspiracy, he charged, of 205 card-carrying Communists in the State Department. (See Communities *in* Conflict.)

McCarthy refused to reveal names because, in reality, he had none. Nevertheless, a few days later, he told persistent reporters, "I'm not going to tell you anything. I just want you to know I've got a pailful [of dirt] . . . and I'm going to use it where it does the most good." Although investigations uncovered not a single Communist in the State Department, McCarthy launched a flamboyant offensive against New Deal Democrats and the Truman administration for failing to defend the nation's security. He gave his name to the era: **McCarthyism**.

Behind the blitz of publicity, the previously obscure junior senator from Wisconsin had struck a chord. Communism seemed to many Americans to be much more than a military threat; it was nothing less than a demonic force undermining all basic values. It compelled patriots to prepare Americans even for atomic warfare: "Better Dead Than Red."

Civil rights organizations faced the worst persecution since the 1920s. But attacks on women's organizations and homosexuals, which cloaked deep fears about changing sexual mores, also took a huge toll. Aided by FBI reports, the federal government fired up to sixty homosexuals per month in the early 1950s. Dishonorable discharges from the U.S. armed forces for homosexuality, an administrative procedure without appeal, also increased dramatically.

McCarthy and his fellow Red-hunters eventually burned themselves out. During nationally televised congressional hearings in 1954, McCarthy not only failed to prove his wild charges of Communist infiltration of the Army but also, in the glare of television, appeared deranged. Cowed for four years, the Senate finally censured him for "conduct unbecoming a member."

JOSEPH McCARTHY The tables turned on Senator Joseph McCarthy (1908–1957) after he instigated an investigation of the U.S. Army for harboring Communists. A special congressional committee then investigated McCarthy for attempting to make the Army grant special privileges to his staff aide, Private David Schine. During the televised hearings, McCarthy discredited himself. In December 1954, the Senate voted to censure him, thus robbing him of his power. He died three years later.

Time & Life Pictures/Getty Images.

Communities *in* Conflict

Congress and the Red Scare

"Today we are engaged in a final, all-out battle between communistic atheism and Christianity."

Joseph McCarthy, the junior Republican senator from Wisconsin, stepped onto the national stage by pushing the second Red Scare into the highest levels of government. On February 9, 1950, at a Lincoln Day celebration in Wheeling, West Virginia, he took aim at President Truman's foreign policy. He charged Secretary of State Dean Acheson with harboring at least 205 "traitorous" Communists within his department. Two days later, McCarthy sent a letter to the president, revising downward the number of Communists employed by the State Department to 57. He nevertheless demanded a full investigation and predicted that hundreds more would turn up. He warned the president not to stall, for failure to act would "label the Democratic Party as being the bedfellow of international communism." He would give versions of his Wheeling speech, excerpted here, on many later occasions, never tiring of Red-baiting the Democrats.

One of the first critics to challenge McCarthy was Senator Margaret Chase Smith, a member of his own party. Smith (1897–1995) had served eight years in the House of Representatives before being elected to the Senate in 1948. She was the first woman elected to serve in both houses of Congress. On June 1, 1950, Smith read to the Senate a "Declaration of Conscience," which she had composed. She reviled the leaders of both parties for "lack of effective leadership," deplored the atmosphere of suspicion, and strongly denounced the mudslinging anti-Communist campaign. Six additional Republican senators signed her Declaration, although Smith and her allies refused to endorse a report later prepared by Democrats that defended the State Department against McCarthy's "fraudulent" charges.

- **What is the basis of Joseph McCarthy's charges, and why is he targeting the State Department?**

- **What is the basis of Margaret Chase Smith's response to McCarthy, and why is she criticizing a fellow Republican?**

Senator Joseph McCarthy Charges that Communists Riddle the State Department, Wheeling, West Virginia (February 9, 1950)

Today we are engaged in a final, all-out battle between communistic atheism and Christianity. The modern champions of communism have selected this as the time, and ladies and gentlemen, the chips are down—they are truly down. . . .

Ladies and gentlemen, can there be anyone tonight who is so blind as to say that the war is not on? Can there be anyone who fails to realize that the Communist world has said the time is now? . . . that this is the time for the show-down between the democratic Christian world and the communistic atheistic world? . . .

As one of our outstanding historical figures once said, "When a great democracy is destroyed, it will not be from enemies from without, but rather because of enemies from within." . . .

The reason why we find ourselves in a position of impotency is not because our only powerful potential enemy has sent men to invade our shores . . . but rather because of the traitorous actions of those who have been treated so well by this Nation. It has not been the less fortunate, or members of minority groups who have been traitorous to this Nation, but rather those who have had all the benefits that the wealthiest Nation on earth has had to offer . . . the finest homes, the finest college education and the finest jobs in government we can give.

This is glaringly true in the State Department. There the bright young men who are born with silver spoons in their mouths are the ones who have been most traitorous. . . . I have here in my hand a list of 205 . . . a list of names that were made known to the Secretary of State as being members of the Communist Party and who nevertheless are still working and shaping policy in the State Department. . . .

As you know, very recently the Secretary of State proclaimed his loyalty to a man guilty of what has always been considered as the most abominable of all crimes—being a traitor to the people who gave him a position of great trust—high treason. . . .

He has lighted the spark which is resulting in a moral uprising and will end only when the whole sorry mess of twisted, warped thinkers are swept from the national scene so that we may have a new birth of honesty and decency in government.

Source: Joseph McCarthy, "Speech at Wheeling, West Virginia, 9 February 1950." In Michael P. Johnson, ed., *Reading the American Past*, Vol. II (Boston: Bedford Books, 1998), 191–195. (The speech is also on several websites and freely available.)

Senator Margaret Chase Smith Announces Her Declaration of Conscience (June 1, 1950)

Mr. President, I would like to speak briefly and simply about a serious national condition. It is a national feeling of fear and frustration that could result in national suicide and the end of everything that we Americans hold dear. . . .

I speak as a Republican. I speak as a woman. I speak as a United States Senator. I speak as an American. . . .

I think that it is high time for the United States Senate and its Members to do some soul searching—for us to weigh our consciences—on the manner in which we are performing our duty to the people of America; on the manner in which we are using or abusing our individual powers and privileges.

I think that it is high time that we remembered that we have sworn to uphold and defend the Constitution. I think that it is high time that we remembered that the Constitution, as amended, speaks not only of the freedom of speech, but also of trial by jury instead of trial by accusation.

Whether it be a criminal prosecution in court or a character prosecution in the Senate, there is little practical distinction when the life of a person has been ruined.

Those of us who shout the loudest about Americanism in making character assassinations are all too frequently those who, by our own words and acts, ignore some of the basic principles of Americanism—

The right to criticize;

The right to hold unpopular beliefs;

The right to protest;

The right of independent thought.

The exercise of these rights should not cost one single American citizen his reputation or his right to a livelihood nor should he be in danger of losing his reputation or livelihood merely because he happens to know someone who holds unpopular beliefs. Who of us doesn't? Otherwise none of us could call our souls our own. Otherwise thought control would have set in.

The American people are sick and tired of being afraid to speak their minds lest they be politically smeared as "Communists" or "Fascists" by their opponents. Freedom of speech is not what it used to be in America. It has been so abused by some that it is not exercised by others. . . .

As a woman, I wonder how the mothers, wives, sisters, and daughters feel about the way in which members of their families have been politically mangled in Senate debate—and I use the word "debate" advisedly.

As a United States Senator, I am not proud of the way in which the Senate has been made a publicity platform for irresponsible sensationalism. . . .

I don't like the way the Senate has been made a rendezvous for vilification, for selfish political gain at the sacrifice of individual reputations and national unity. I am not proud of the way we smear outsiders from the floor of the Senate and hide behind the cloak of congressional immunity and still place ourselves beyond criticism on the floor of the Senate. . . .

Source: Margaret Chase Smith, *Declaration of Conscience*, ed. by William C. Lewis, Jr. (Garden City, NY: Doubleday & Company, Inc., 1972). (This Declaration is also on the website "American Rhetoric: Top 100 Speeches.")

26.5 The Cold War at Home

How did the Cold War shape mid-twentieth-century American culture?

As the Truman Doctrine revealed, the Cold War did not necessarily mean military confrontation. Nor was it defined exclusively by a quest for economic supremacy. The Cold War embodied the struggle of one "way of life" against another. It was, in short, a contest of values. If Americans were to guard their own society and rebuild the world along the same lines, they had to rededicate themselves to defending their birthrights: freedom and democracy.

26.5.1 An Age of Anxiety

The phrase came from a Pulitzer prize-winning poem by W.H. Auden that suggested to many readers the perilousness of the modern life. By the time Auden published his poem, in 1947, anxiety had surfaced as a major theme in American popular culture. *The Best Years of Our Lives* (1946), one of the most acclaimed Hollywood films of the era, followed three fictional veterans trying to readjust to civilian life. The former soldiers found that dreams of reunion with family and loved ones, which had sustained them through years of fighting, now seemed hollow. In some cases, their wives and children had become so self-reliant that the men had no clear function in the household; in other cases, the prospects for employment appeared dim. One veteran who had lost both arms was shunned by almost everyone. The feeling of community shared with wartime buddies dissipated, leaving only profound loneliness in a crass, selfish society.

The genre of *film noir* (French for "black film") deepened this postwar moodiness into a pessimistic aesthetic. American movies like *Out of the Past, Detour,* and *They Live by Night* told stories of relentless fate and ruthless betrayal. Their protagonists were loners running from a bad past, falsely accused of transgressions, or trapped into committing crimes. The high-contrast lighting of these black-and-white films accentuated the difficulty of distinguishing friend from foe.

Serious literature echoed these emotions and often vividly captured a sense of anxious alienation. Playwright Arthur Miller in *Death of a Salesman* (1949) sketched an exacting portrait of self-destructive individualism. Willy Loman, the play's hero, is obsessively devoted to his career in sales, but is nevertheless a miserable failure. Worse, he taught his sons to excel in personal presentation and style—the very methods prescribed by standard American success manuals—making them both shallow and materialistic. J. D. Salinger's novel *Catcher in the Rye* (1951) explored the mental anguish of a teenage boy estranged by his parents' psychological distance and materialism.

Cold War anxiety manifested itself in a flurry of unidentified flying object (UFO) sightings. Thousands of Americans imagined that a communist-like invasion from outer space was already under way, or hoped that superior creatures might arrive to show the way to world peace. The U.S. Air Force discounted "flying saucer" reports, but dozens of private researchers and faddists claimed to have been contacted by aliens. Hollywood fed these beliefs. In *The Invasion of the Body Snatchers* (1956), for example, a small town is captured by aliens who take over the minds of its

inhabitants when they fall asleep—a subtle warning against apathy toward the threat of communist "subversion." (See SEEING History.)

26.5.2 The Family as Bulwark

Many Americans found, as one writer put it, a "defense—an impregnable bulwark" against the era's anxieties in their family life. Postwar prosperity also encouraged young couples to marry younger and produce more children than at any time in the previous century. The Census Bureau predicted that the "baby boom" would be temporary. To everyone's surprise, the birthrate continued to grow at a record pace. (See Figure 26.1.)

Postwar prosperity also inaugurated a spending spree of trailblazing proportions. Consumer goods—automobiles, clothing, home appliances, paperback books—broke through their wartime barriers. By the time Truman left office, two-thirds of all American households claimed at

SEEING History

The Hollywood Film *Invasion, U.S.A.*

Invasion, U.S.A. was the first of the genre of Red-scare films to do well at the box office. Shot in just seven days and released by Columbia Pictures in 1952, the film opens by depicting a group of well-off Americans, drinking casually in a New York bar and showing no particular concern about the imminent threat to their nation. Suddenly, they hear the news of horrific

attacks by The Enemy. After atomic bombs fall and The Enemy approaches the nation's capital, they have all learned a potent lesson about complacency and begin to renounce their selfish ways. The group disperses, each character now understanding that freedom carries with it the price of vigilance.

The Enemy is never named, but Slavic accents and references to the "People's Government" that takes over Manhattan strongly suggest that the evildoers are Russian communists.

This still image from the film builds on the foundation of fear. Studio publicists also advised local movie theaters to promote the movie along the same line: "Dress a young man in full paratroop regalia and have him walk through the principal streets of town in advance of playdate with a sign on his back reading HERE'S HOW IT WOULD HAPPEN IF IT HAPPENED NOW! SEE COLUMBIA PICTURES' *INVASION, U.S.A.* AT THE STATE THEATER FRIDAY!" The studio also suggested that blasts by air raid sirens and the use of local Civil Defense workers would be good choices to advertise the film. Despite these fear-provoking messages, one reviewer pointed out that poor production quality—featuring stock footage from World War II—and stilted dialogue unintentionally made *Invasion, U.S.A.* the first film to make audiences laugh at the atomic bomb.

INVASION U.S.A.

Columbia TriStar/Getty Images.

- **How did Hollywood and other forms of mass media help to shape Cold War culture in the late 1940s and early 1950s?**

Figure 26.1 U.S. BIRTHRATE, 1930–1980

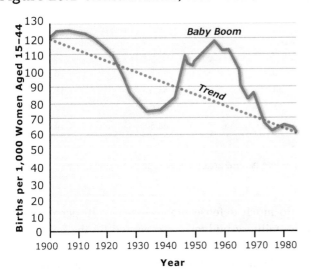

The bulge of the "baby boom," a leading demographic factor in the postwar economy, stands out for this 50-year period.

National Archives and Records Administration.

least one television set. For many Americans, purchasing power represented political power, a measure of democracy and U.S. global superiority. To a greater and greater extent, the "American way of life" was based on a consumer ideal that emphasized access to an array of material goods unavailable in communist countries.

These two trends—the baby boom and high rates of consumer spending—encouraged a major change in the middle-class family. Having worked during World War II, often in occupations traditionally closed to them, many women wished to continue in full-time employment. Reconversion to peacetime production forced the majority from their factory positions, but most women quickly returned, taking jobs at a faster rate than men and providing half the total growth of the labor force. By 1952, 2 million more wives worked than during the war. Gone, however, were the high-paying unionized jobs in manufacturing. Instead, most women found low-wage jobs in the expanding service sector: clerical work; health care and education; and restaurant, hotel, and retail services. Older women whose children were grown might work because they had come to value a job for its own sake. Younger women often worked out of "economic necessity"—that is, to maintain a middle-class standard of living that now required more than one income. Indeed, mothers of young children were the most likely to be employed. (See Table 26.2.)

Even though most women sought employment primarily to support their families, they ran up against

OFFICE IN A SMALL CITY Edward Hopper (1882–1967) was the best-known realist painter in the United States at mid-century. Many of his paintings portray the starkness and loneliness of American life, with cityscapes depicting empty streets or all-night restaurants where the few patrons sit at a distance from each other. This painting, owned by the Metropolitan Museum of Art in New York, expresses the mood of alienation associated with Cold War culture.

The Metropolitan Museum of Art/Art Resource, NY.

Table 26.2 DISTRIBUTION OF TOTAL PERSONAL INCOME AMONG VARIOUS SEGMENTS OF THE POPULATION, 1947–1970 (IN PERCENTAGES)*

Year	Poorest Fifth	Second-Poorest Fifth	Middle Fifth	Second-Wealthiest Fifth	Wealthiest Fifth	Wealthiest 5 Percent
1947	3.5	10.6	16.7	23.6	45.6	18.7
1950	3.1	10.5	17.3	24.1	45.0	18.2
1960	3.2	10.6	17.6	24.7	44.0	17.0
1970	3.6	10.3	17.2	24.7	44.1	16.9

Despite the general prosperity of the postwar era, the distribution of income remained essentially unchanged.

*Monetary income only.

Source: Adapted from U.S. Bureau of the Census, *Historical Statistics of the United States, Colonial Times to 1970*, Bicentennial ed. (Washington, DC.: U.S. Government Printing Office, 1975), p. 292.

popular opinion and expert advice urging them to go home. Polls registered resounding disapproval—by 86 percent of those surveyed—of a married woman working if jobs were scarce and her husband could support her. Noting that most Soviet women worked outside the home, many commentators appealed for a return to an imaginary "traditional" American family where men alone were breadwinners and women were exclusively homemakers. FBI director J. Edgar Hoover exhorted the nation's women to fight communism by fulfilling their "natural" role as "homemakers and mothers."

This campaign began on a shrill note. Ferdinand Lundberg and Marynia Farnham, in their best-selling *Modern Woman: The Lost Sex* (1947), attributed the "super-jittery age in which we live" to women's abandonment of the home to pursue careers. To counter this danger, they proposed federally funded psychotherapy to readjust women to their housewifely roles and cash subsidies to encourage them to bear more children. Articles in popular magazines, television shows, and high-profile experts chimed in with similar messages.

Patterns of women's higher education reflected this conservative trend. Having made slight gains during World War II, when college-age men were serving in the armed forces or working in war industries, women lost ground after the **G.I. Bill** created a huge upsurge in male enrollment. Women represented 40 percent of all college graduates in 1940, but only 25 percent a decade later.

26.5.3 Military-Industrial Communities in the American West

All regions of the United States felt the impact of the Cold War, but none so directly as the West. World War II defense spending had stimulated the western economy and encouraged a mass westward migration of people eager to find wartime jobs. Following the war, many cities successfully converted to peacetime production. It was the Cold War, however, by reviving defense funding, that gave the western economy its most important boost.

So much defense money—nearly 10 percent of the entire military budget—was poured by the federal government into California that the state's rate of economic growth between 1949 and 1952 outpaced that of the nation as a whole; nearly 40 percent came from aircraft manufacturing alone. Ten years later, an estimated one-third of all Los Angeles workers were employed by defense industries, particularly aerospace, and the absolute number of defense workers far exceeded that of the peak production years in World War II. The Bay Area also benefited economically from defense spending, and cities such as San Jose began their rise as a home to the nation's budding high-technology industry.

The Cold War pumped new life into communities that had grown up during World War II. Hanford, Washington, and Los Alamos, New Mexico—both centers of the **Manhattan Project**—employed more people in the construction of the Cold War nuclear arsenal than in the development of the atom bomb. New communities accompanied the growth of the U.S. military bases and training camps in the West. Many of these installations, as well as hospitals and supply depots, not only survived but expanded during the transition from the actual warfare of World War II to the threatened warfare of the Cold War. Between 1950 and 1953, approximately 20 western bases were reopened. California became at least a temporary home to more military personnel than any other state, and Texas was not far behind. The availability of public lands with areas of sparse population made western states especially attractive to military planners designing such dangerous and secretive installations as the White Sands Missile Range in the New Mexico desert.

Local politicians, real estate agents, and merchants usually welcomed these developments as sources of revenue and employment. There were, however, heavy costs for speedy and unplanned federally induced growth. To accommodate the new populations, the government poured money into new highway systems but did little for public transportation. Uncontrolled sprawl, traffic congestion, air pollution, and strains on limited water and energy resources all grew with the military-industrial communities in the West. For those populations living near nuclear testing grounds, environmental degradation complemented the ultimate threat to their own physical well-being: Over the next 40 years, cancer rates soared.

26.5.4 "The American Way"

Americans began to retreat from public displays of patriotism following the massive and spontaneous V-J Day celebrations, but soon new organizations, like the Freedoms Foundation of Valley Forge and the American Heritage Foundation, were joining the American Legion and the Chamber of Commerce in defining the "American way" in opposition to Soviet communism. These organizations sponsored events such as "freedom rallies" and "freedom fashion shows" to remind Americans of their nation's democratic values and commitment to free enterprise.

In Mosinee, Wisconsin, for example, the American Legion used political theater to inculcate the American way, orchestrating an imaginary communist coup in the small community. In 1950, on May Day (the traditional left-wing holiday), "Communist agents," followed by more than sixty reporters, forced the mayor and the chief of police from their homes and announced that the Council of People's Commissars had taken over the local government. Roadblocks were put up to prevent residents from escaping to "free" territory. The restaurants served only Soviet fare: black bread, potato soup, and coffee. The local *Mosinee Times* printed a special edition on pink stock under its new "Red Star" masthead. Citizens discovered that all private property had been confiscated and all constitutional rights annulled. Every adult was required "to contribute to the State four extra hours of labor without compensation." That evening, after a full day of communist indoctrination, the residents rallied in "Red Square" and declared an end to "Communist rule," and then raised the American flag and headed home singing "God Bless America." The national media all covered Mosinee's "Day under Communism."

Meanwhile, Attorney General Tom C. Clark—supported by Truman, private donors, and the American Heritage Foundation—was putting on the nation's rails the "Freedom Train." Carrying copies of the Bill of Rights, the Constitution, and the Emancipation Proclamation, the Freedom Train traveled to communities across the land, where local citizens viewed the displays.

Patriotic messages also permeated public education. Following guidelines set down by the Truman administration, teachers were to "strengthen national security through education" by designing their lesson plans to illustrate the superiority of the American democratic system over Soviet communism. In 1947, the federal Office of Education launched a "Zeal for Democracy" program for implementation by school boards nationwide. The program intended to "promote and strengthen democratic thinking and practice, just as the schools of totalitarian states have so

effectively promoted the ideals of their respective cultures." Meanwhile, in a national civil defense program, schoolchildren learned to "duck" under their desks and "cover" their heads in the event of a surprise Soviet nuclear attack.

Voices of protest were raised. The black poet Langston Hughes expressed his skepticism in verse, writing that he hoped the Freedom Train would carry no Jim Crow car. A brave minority of scholars protested infringements on academic freedom by refusing to sign loyalty oaths and by writing books pointing out the potential dangers of aggressively nationalistic foreign and domestic policies. But the chilling atmosphere made many individuals reluctant to express contrary opinions or ideas.

26.6 Stalemate for the Democrats

How did the Republicans win the presidency and control of Congress in 1952?

With Cold War tensions festering in Europe, neither the United States nor the Soviet Union would have predicted that events in Asia would bring them to the brink of a new world war. Yet in China, the most populous land on earth, Communists completed their seizure of power in late 1949, and a few months later, in June 1950, Communist armies threatened to conquer the Korean Peninsula.

Truman had considered Korea a major "ideological battleground" of Asia, and by 1950 had sought to implement his containment policies there. Convinced that the Soviet Union meant to "swallow up" all Asia through its influence in North Korea, the president bypassed congressional approval and sent American forces to conduct a "police action" against a "bunch of bandits" determined to jeopardize world peace. Within a few years, combat in Korea absorbed more than 1.8 million U.S. troops with no victory in sight. For Truman, the "loss" of China and the Korean stalemate proved political suicide, ending the 20-year Democratic lock on the presidency and the greatest era of reform in U.S. history.

26.6.1 Democratizing Japan and "Losing" China

At the close of World War II, the United States acted deliberately to secure Japan firmly within its sphere of influence. General Douglas MacArthur directed an interim Japanese government in a reconstruction program that included land reform, creation of independent trade unions, abolition of contract marriages, granting of woman suffrage, sweeping demilitarization, and eventually a constitutional democracy that renounced war as a sovereign right and barred communists from all posts. American leaders worked to rebuild the nation's economy along capitalist lines and integrate Japan, like West Germany, into an anti-Soviet bloc. Japan also housed huge U.S. military bases, placing U.S. troops and weapons on the doorstep of the Soviet Union's Asian rim.

China could not be handled so easily. After years of civil war, the pro-Western Nationalist government of Jiang Jeishi (Chiang Kai-shek) collapsed. Since World War II, the United States had been aiding Jiang's unpopular and corrupt regime, while warning him that without major reforms and a coalition with his political opponents, the Nationalists were heading for defeat. Jiang refused any concessions, and in the late 1940s the Truman administration cut off virtually all aid and then watched as Nationalist troops surrendered to the Communists, led by Mao Zedong. Abandoning the entire mainland, the defeated Nationalists fled to the island of Taiwan. On October 1, 1949, Mao proclaimed the People's Republic of China, and in February 1950, the Soviet Union and the People's Republic of China signed the Sino-Soviet Treaty of Friendship, Alliance, and Mutual Assistance.

China's "fall" to communism set off an uproar in the United States. The Asia First wing of the Republican Party, which saw the Far East rather than Europe as the primary target of U.S. trade and investment, blamed Truman for the "loss" of China. The president's adversaries, pointing to the growing menace of "international communism," called the Democrats the "party of treason."

26.6.2 The Korean War

At the end of World War II, the Allies had divided the Korean peninsula, surrendered by Japan, at the 38th Parallel. Although all Koreans hoped to reunite their nation under an independent government, the line between North and South hardened. While the United States backed the unpopular southern government of Syngman Rhee (the Republic of Korea), the Soviet Union sponsored a rival government in North Korea under Communist Kim Il-Sung. (See Map 26.3.)

On June 25, 1950, the U.S. State Department received a cablegram reporting an invasion of South Korea by the Communist North. Truman concluded that Stalin had provoked this "lawless action." If the United States failed to act, he warned, "the Soviets will keep right on going and swallow up one piece of Asia after another" and possibly move on to the Middle East and Europe. Truman sought the Security Council's approval to send troops to defend South Korea under the UN's collective-security provisions. With the Soviet delegate withdrawn as an act to protest the exclusion of China, the Security Council backed the U.S. request for intervention. Two-thirds of Americans polled approved the president's decision to send troops under MacArthur's command.

Military events seemed at first to justify the president's decision. Seoul, the capital of South Korea, fell to North Korean troops within weeks, and Communist forces pushed south, occupying most of the peninsula. The situation appeared grim until Truman authorized MacArthur to carry out an amphibious landing at Inchon, near Seoul, on September 15, 1950. With tactical brilliance and good fortune, the general's campaign not only halted the Communist drive, but also sent the North Koreans fleeing. By October, UN troops had retaken South Korea.

Basking in victory, the Truman administration could not resist the temptation to expand its war aims. The president decided to roll back the Communists beyond the 38th Parallel, uniting Korea as a showcase for democracy. China, not yet directly involved in the war, warned that crossing that dividing line would threaten its national security. Truman flew to Wake Island in the Pacific on October 15 to confer with MacArthur, who assured him of a speedy victory.

MacArthur had sorely miscalculated. Chinese troops massed along the Yalu River, the border between Korea and China. As the UN forces approached the Yalu, suddenly and without air support, a Chinese "human wave" attack began. MacArthur, who had foolishly divided his forces, suffered a crushing defeat. The Chinese drove the UN troops back into South Korea, where they regrouped south of the 38th Parallel. Finally, by the summer of 1951 a stalemate had been reached very near the old dividing line. Then, for the next 18 months, negotiations for an armistice dragged out amid heavy fighting.

MacArthur tried to convince Truman to prepare for a new invasion of Communist territory. Encouraged by strong support at home, and defying the American tradition of civilian control over the military, MacArthur publicly criticized the president's policy, calling for bombing supply lines in China and blockading the Chinese coast. Such actions would certainly have led to a Chinese-American war. Finally, on April 10, 1951, Truman fired MacArthur for insubordination.

26.6.3 The Price of National Security

The Korean conflict had profound implications for the use of executive power. By unilaterally instituting a peacetime draft in 1948 and ordering American troops into Korea without a declaration of war in 1950, Truman had bypassed congressional authority. Republican Senator Robert Taft called the president's actions "evidence of an 'imperial presidency' " that was guilty of "a complete usurpation" of checks and balances. For a while, Truman sidestepped such criticisms and their constitutional implications by declaring a national emergency and by carefully referring to the military deployment not as a U.S. "war" but as a UN-sanctioned "police action."

Map 26.3 THE KOREAN WAR

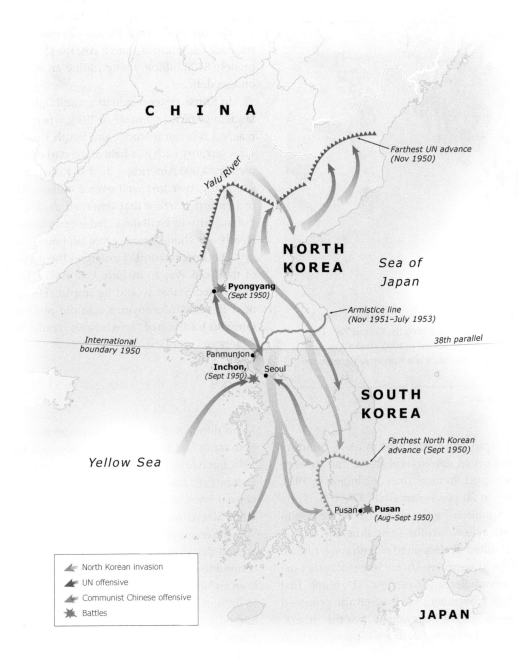

The intensity of battles underscored the strategic importance of Korea in the Cold War.

The president was acting at the prompting of **National Security Council Paper 68 (NSC-68)**, a sweeping declaration of Cold War policy submitted to Truman in April 1950. The lengthy, top-secret document defined the struggle between the United States and the Soviet Union as "permanent" and the era as one of "total war." The Soviet Union, the document declared, pledged itself to "a new fanatic faith, antithetical to our own," which required American citizens to sacrifice—"to give up some of the benefits which they have come to associate with their freedom"—to defend their way of life. NSC-68, in recommending "affirmative" containment, articulated the intellectual and psychological rationale behind U.S. national security policies, including massive defense spending, for the next 40 years.

Initially hesitant, after the outbreak of the Korean War, Truman accepted the policies outlined in NSC-68

KOREAN WAR REFUGEES Estimates run as high as 6 million for the number of civilian refugees during the Korean War. This American news photograph, published in 1950, shows American soldiers heading toward battle sites while Korean refugees move in the opposite direction.

Library of Congress (Photoduplication).

and agreed to a rapid and permanent military buildup. By the time the Korean conflict subsided, the defense budget had quadrupled, to more than $52 billion in 1953, or from 5 percent to 20 percent of GNP. The U.S. Army had grown to 3.6 million—6 times its size at the beginning of the "police action." At the same time, the federal government accelerated development of both conventional and nonconventional weapons. Its nuclear stockpile now included the thermonuclear hydrogen (or "H") bomb, first tested at full scale in November 1952. NSC-68 also proposed expensive "large-scale covert operations" for the "liberation" of communist-dominated countries, particularly in Eastern Europe.

The Korean War also provided the rationale to expand anti-Communist propaganda. At the end of World War II, Truman had taken steps to transform the Office of War Information into a peacetime program with a much smaller budget. However, by 1950, Congress had doubled the budget for anti-Communist programming, granting $3 million to revive the Voice of America, the shortwave international radio program that had been established in 1942. The new legislation also funded films, print media, cultural exchange programs, and exhibitions, and it created a foundation to disseminate anti-Communist propaganda throughout the world. By 1951, a massive "Campaign of Truth" was reaching 93 nations, and the Voice of America was broadcasting in 45 languages.

In his annual message to Congress in 1951, President Truman requested $115 million to fund these programs, but as the war in Korea bogged down, he managed to get only $85 million. In the end, the Korean conflict did nothing to roll back communism, and it cost the United States approximately $100 billion, inaugurating an era of huge federal budget deficits.

In Korea, peace negotiations and fighting proceeded in tandem until the summer of 1953, when a settlement was reached returning North and South Korea to almost the same territory each had held at the start of the war. Approximately 54,000 Americans died in Korea; North Korea and China together lost well over 2 million. True to patterns of modern warfare that emerged during World War II, the majority of civilians killed were women and children. Nearly a million Koreans were left homeless.

The Korean conflict enlarged the geographical range of the Cold War to include East Asia. "Red China" and the United States would be implacable enemies for the next 20 years. Moreover, Korea did much to establish an ominous tradition of "unwinnable" conflicts that left many Americans skeptical of official policy.

26.6.4 "I Like Ike": The Election of 1952

Korea dominated the election campaign of 1952. Truman's popularity had wavered continually since he took office in 1945, but it sank to an all-time low in the early 1950s shortly after he fired MacArthur. Thousands of letters and telegrams poured into Congress demanding Truman's impeachment, while MacArthur returned home to a hero's welcome.

The case against Truman widened. The Asia First lobby argued that if the president had aggressively turned back communism in China in the late 1940s, there would have been no "limited war" in Korea. Large-scale corruption came to light in Truman's administration, with several agencies allegedly dealing in 5-percent kickbacks on government contracts. Business and organized labor complained about price and wage freezes during the Korean War. A late-1951 Gallup poll showed the president's approval rating at 23 percent. In March 1952, Truman announced he would not run for reelection, even though he was constitutionally permitted another term.

Accepting political defeat and disgrace, Truman endorsed the uncharismatic governor of Illinois, Adlai E. Stevenson, Jr. Admired for his eloquence, wit, honesty, and intelligence, Stevenson offered no solutions to the conflict in Korea, the accelerating arms race, or the Cold War generally. Accepting the Democratic nomination, he candidly admitted that "the ordeal of the twentieth century is far from over."

The Republicans made the most of the Democrats' dilemma. Without proposing any sweeping answers of their own, they zeroed in on "K_1C_2"—Korea, Communism, and

CANDIDATE DWIGHT D. EISENHOWER Dwight D, Eisenhower entered the presidential campaign in 1952 promising "not to turn the clock back—ever." Unlike most Republicans, he supported much of the New Deal legislation, including Social Security and labor laws. Building on his stellar wartime reputation, he inspired confidence and spoke directly to the American people. He attracted large crowds while stopping in 45 states on his whistle-wind train tour. His 30-second television ads also convinced many voters to echo his "I like Ike" slogan at the ballot box. Eisenhower was elected by a landslide with 55.2 percent of the popular vote.

Everett Collection Historical/Alamy Stock Photo.

NIXON AND CHECKERS On September 23, 1952, Republican vice-presidential candidate Richard M. Nixon appeared on national television to defend himself against charges that he had taken illegal campaign contributions. This photograph shows him with one of those gifts, a black-and-white spotted cocker spaniel. He said, "And our little girl Tricia, the six year old, named it 'Checkers.' And you know, the kids, like all kids, love the dog, and I just want to say this, right now, that regardless of what they say about it, we're gonna keep it." This speech, which was simulcast on radio, won the hearts of many voters.

ASSOCIATED PRESS.

Corruption. When opinion polls showed retired General Dwight D. Eisenhower with an "unprecedented" 64 percent approval rating, they found in "Ike" the perfect candidate.

Eisenhower styled himself the voice of "modern Republicanism." He wisely avoided the negative impressions made in 1948 by Dewey, who had seemed as aggressive as Truman abroad and bent on repealing the New Deal at home. Eisenhower knew better: Voters wanted peace and a limited welfare state. He called New Deal reforms "a solid floor that keeps all of us from falling into the pit of disaster," and without going into specifics promised "an early and honorable" peace in Korea. Whenever he was tempted to address questions of finance or the economy, his advisers warned him: "The chief reason that people want to vote for you is because they think you have more ability to keep us out of another war."

Richard Nixon, Eisenhower's vice-presidential candidate, meanwhile waged a relentless and defamatory attack on "Adlai the Appeaser." Joe McCarthy chortled that with club in hand he might be able to make "a good American" of Stevenson. A month before the election, McCarthy went on network television with his requisite "exhibits" and "documents," purportedly showing that the Democratic presidential candidate had promoted communism at home and abroad. These outrageous charges kept the Stevenson campaign off balance.

The Republican campaign was itself not scandal-free: Nixon was caught accepting personal gifts from wealthy benefactors. On national television, he pathetically described his wife Pat's "good Republican cloth coat" and their struggling life, but then contritely admitted to indeed accepting one gift: a puppy named Checkers that his little daughters loved and that he refused to give back. The masterfully maudlin "Checkers Speech" defused the scandal without answering the most important charges. The speech also underscored how important television was becoming in molding voters' perceptions.

Soaring above the scandal, Eisenhower inspired voters as the peace candidate. Ten days before the election, he dramatically announced, "I shall go to Korea."

Eisenhower carried 55 percent of the vote and 39 states, bringing an unusually large harvest of voters in normally Democratic areas, such as the South, and in New York, Chicago, Boston, and Cleveland. Riding his coattails, the Republicans regained narrow control of Congress. The New Deal coalition—ethnic minorities, northern blacks, unionized workers, liberals, Catholics, Jews, and white southern conservatives—no longer commanded a majority.

Conclusion

In his farewell address, in January 1953, Harry Truman reflected, "I suppose that history will remember my term in office as the years when the 'cold war' began to overshadow our lives. I have hardly had a day in office that has not been dominated by this all-embracing struggle."

The election of Dwight Eisenhower helped to diminish the intensity of the country's dour mood without actually bringing a halt to the conflict. The new president pledged himself to liberate the world from communism by peaceful means rather than force. "Our aim is more subtle," he announced during his campaign, "more pervasive, more complete. We are trying to get the world, by peaceful means, to believe the truth." Increasing the budget of the CIA, Eisenhower took the Cold War out of the public eye by relying to a far greater extent than Truman on psychological warfare and covert operations.

"The Eisenhower Movement," wrote journalist Walter Lippmann, was a "mission in American politics" to restore a sense of community among the American people. In a larger sense, many of the issues of the immediate post-World War II years seemed to have been settled or put off for a distant future. The international boundaries of communism were frozen with the Chinese Revolution, the Berlin crisis, and now the Korean War. Meanwhile, at home, Cold War defense spending had become a permanent part of the national budget, an undeniable drain on tax revenues but an important element in the government contribution to economic prosperity. If the nuclear arms race remained a cause for anxiety, joined by more personal worries about the changing patterns of family life, a sense of relative security nevertheless spread. Prospects for world peace had dimmed, but the worst nightmares of the 1940s had eased as well.

Key Terms

International Monetary Fund (IMF) International organization established in 1945 to assist nations in maintaining stable currencies. p. 637

Cold War The political and economic confrontation between the Soviet Union and the United States that dominated world affairs from 1946 to 1989. p. 639

Truman Doctrine President Harry Truman's statement in 1947 that the United States should assist other nations that were facing external pressure or internal revolution. p. 640

Marshall Plan Secretary of State George C. Marshall's European Recovery Plan of June 5, 1947, committing the United States to help in the rebuilding of post-World War II Europe. p. 641

Berlin blockade 300-day Soviet blockade of land access to the U.S., British, and French occupation zones in Berlin, 1948–1949. p. 641

North Atlantic Treaty Organization (NATO) Alliance of 10 European countries, Canada, and the United States,

who together formed a mutual-defense pact in April 1949. p. 641

Council of Economic Advisers Board of three professional economists established in 1946 to advise the president on economic policy. p. 642

Taft-Hartley Act Federal legislation of 1947 that substantially limited the tools available to labor unions in labor-management disputes. p. 643

Dixiecrat States' Rights Democrats. p. 643

Executive Order 9835 Signed by Harry Truman in 1947 to establish a loyalty program requiring federal employees to sign loyalty oaths and undergo security checks. p. 645

National Security Council (NSC) The formal policymaking body for national defense and foreign relations, created in 1947 and consisting of the president, the secretary of defense, the secretary of state, and others appointed by the president. p. 646

Central Intelligence Agency (CIA) Agency established in 1947 that coordinates the gathering and evaluation of military and economic information on other nations. p. 646

House Committee on Un-American Activities (HUAC) Originally intended to ferret out pro-fascists, it later investigated "un-American propaganda" that attacked constitutional government. p. 646

McCarthyism Anti-Communist attitudes and actions associated with Senator Joe McCarthy in the early 1950s, including smear tactics and innuendo. p. 647

G.I. Bill Legislation passed in June 1944 that eased the return of veterans into American society by providing educational and employment benefits. p. 652

Manhattan Project Scientific research project during World War II specifically devoted to developing the atomic bomb. p. 652

National Security Council Paper 68 (NSC-68) Policy statement that committed the United States to a military approach to the Cold War. p. 655

CHRONOLOGY

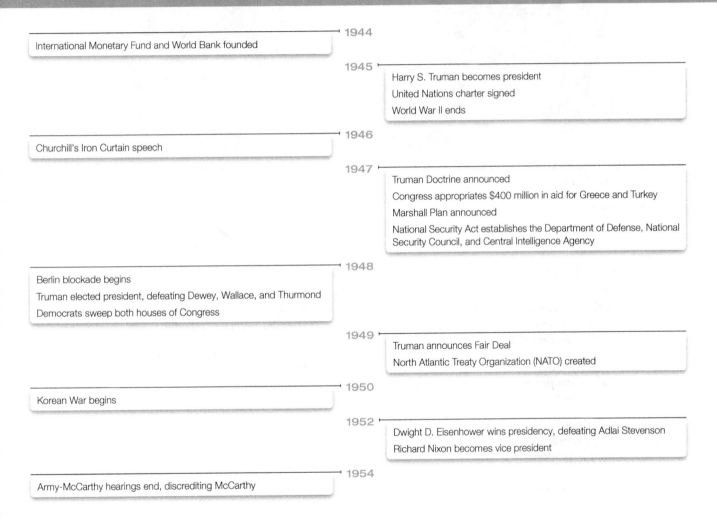

International Monetary Fund and World Bank founded	**1944**
	1945 Harry S. Truman becomes president
	United Nations charter signed
	World War II ends
Churchill's Iron Curtain speech	**1946**
	1947 Truman Doctrine announced
	Congress appropriates $400 million in aid for Greece and Turkey
	Marshall Plan announced
	National Security Act establishes the Department of Defense, National Security Council, and Central Intelligence Agency
Berlin blockade begins	**1948**
Truman elected president, defeating Dewey, Wallace, and Thurmond	
Democrats sweep both houses of Congress	
	1949 Truman announces Fair Deal
	North Atlantic Treaty Organization (NATO) created
Korean War begins	**1950**
	1952 Dwight D. Eisenhower wins presidency, defeating Adlai Stevenson
	Richard Nixon becomes vice president
Army-McCarthy hearings end, discrediting McCarthy	**1954**

Chapter 27
America at Mid-Century 1952–1963

ELVIS PRESLEY Elvis Presley, the King of Rock and Roll, performs on an outdoor stage before a wildly enthusiastic audience during the Mississippi State Fair in the early 1950s.

Hulton Archive/Getty Images.

 ## Contents and Focus Questions

American Communities

Popular Music in Memphis

The 19-year-old Mississippian peered nervously out over the large crowd at Overton Park, Memphis's outdoor amphitheater. He knew that people had come that hot, sticky July day in 1954 to hear the headliner, country music star Slim Whitman. Sun Records, a local Memphis label, had just released the unknown young man's first record, and it had begun to receive some airplay on local radio. He and his two bandmates had never played in a setting even remotely as large as this one. And their music defied categories: It wasn't black and it wasn't white; it wasn't pop and it wasn't country. But when he launched into his version of a black blues song called "That's All Right," the crowd went wild. "I came offstage," he later recalled, "and my manager told me that they was hollering because I was wiggling my legs. I went back out for an encore, and I did a little more, and the more I did, the wilder they went." Elvis Presley had arrived.

Elvis combined a hard-driving, rhythmic approach to blues and country music with a riveting performance style; as much as anyone, he defined the new music known as rock 'n' roll. An unprecedented cultural phenomenon, rock 'n' roll was made largely for and by teenagers. In communities all over America, rock 'n' roll brought teens together around jukeboxes, at sock hops, in cars, and at private parties. It also demonstrated the enormous consumer power of an emerging youth culture. Postwar teenagers would constitute the most affluent generation of young people in American history. Their ability and eagerness to buy records, phonographs, transistor radios, clothing, makeup, and even cars forced businesses and advertisers to recognize a new teen market. Their buying power helped define the affluent society of the postwar era.

Elvis Presley's life and career also personified many of the themes and tensions of postwar American life. Elvis was born in Tupelo, Mississippi, in 1935, but like many thousands of other poor rural whites, the Presley family moved to Memphis in 1949. Elvis's father found work in a munitions plant. The Presleys were poor enough to qualify for an apartment in Lauderdale Courts, a Memphis public housing project built during the New Deal. Located halfway between St. Louis and New Orleans on the Mississippi River, Memphis enjoyed healthy growth during World War II, with lumber mills, furniture factories, and chemical manufacturing supplementing the cotton market as sources of jobs and prosperity. Memphis also boasted a remarkable diversity of popular theater and music, including a large opera house, numerous brass bands, vaudeville and burlesque, minstrel shows, jug bands, and blues clubs. Like the rest of the South, Memphis was a legally segregated city; whites and blacks lived, went to school, and worked apart. But music—in live clubs and on the radio—was an important means of breaking through the barriers of racial segregation.

As a boy, Elvis turned to music for emotional release and spiritual expression. He soaked up the wide range of musical styles available in Memphis. The all-white Assembly of God Church his family attended featured a renowned hundred-voice choir. Elvis and his friends went to marathon all-night "gospel singings" at Ellis Auditorium, where they enjoyed the tight harmonies and emotional style of white gospel quartets. Elvis also drew from the sounds he heard on Beale Street, the main black thoroughfare of Memphis. In the postwar years, local black rhythm-and-blues artists like B. B. King, Junior Parker, and Muddy Waters attracted legions of black

and white fans with their emotional power and exciting showmanship. Elvis performed along with black contestants in amateur shows at Beale Street's Palace Theater. Nat D. Williams, a prominent black Memphis disc jockey and music promoter, recalled how black audiences responded to Elvis's unique style. "He had a way of singing the blues that was distinctive. He could sing 'em not necessarily like a Negro, but he didn't sing 'em altogether like a typical white musician. . . . Always he had that certain humanness about him that Negroes like to put in their songs." Elvis himself understood his debt to black music and black performers. "The colored folks," he told an interviewer in 1956, "been singing and playing it just like I'm doing now, man, for more years than I know. They played it like that in the shanties and in their juke joints and nobody paid it no mind until I goosed it up. I got it from them."

Dissatisfied with the cloying pop music of the day, white teenagers across the nation were increasingly turning to the rhythmic drive and emotional intensity of black rhythm and blues. They quickly adopted rock 'n' roll (the term had long been African American slang for dancing and sexual intercourse) as their music. But it was more than just music: It was also an attitude, a celebration of being young, and a sense of having something that adult authority could not understand or control. For millions of young people, rock 'n' roll was an expression of revolt against the conformity and blandness found in so many new postwar suburbs. When Sun Records sold Presley's contract to RCA Records in 1956, Elvis became an international star. Records like "Heartbreak Hotel," "Don't Be Cruel," and "Jailhouse Rock" shot to the top of the charts and blurred the old boundaries between pop, country, and rhythm and blues. His appearances on network television shows contributed to his enormous popularity and demonstrated the extraordinary power of this new medium of communication. Television helped Elvis attract legions of new fans despite—and partly because of—the uproar over his hip shaking, overtly sexual performance style.

In early 1958, at the height of his popularity, Elvis was drafted into the U.S. Army for a two-year hitch. The peacetime draft was a grim reminder for millions of American young men of the Cold War anxieties that hovered over the economic prosperity of the era. Even the most famous entertainer in the world could not escape them. Elvis did most of his service in Germany, a critical site of American and Soviet confrontation between 1948 and the early 1960s.

By helping to accustom white teenagers to the style and sound of black artists, Elvis established rock 'n' roll as an interracial phenomenon. The considerable adult opposition to rock 'n' roll

Memphis

revolved largely around fears of race mixing. To a remarkable degree, the new music anticipated and contributed to the collapse of segregation, at least in the realm of popular culture. Institutional racism would continue to plague the music business—many black artists were routinely cheated out of royalties and severely underpaid—but the music of postwar Memphis at least pointed the way toward the exciting cultural possibilities that could emerge from breaking down the barriers of race. It also gave postwar American

teenagers a newfound sense of community. In a broader sense, rock 'n' roll heralded a generational shift in American society. Just as Elvis's extraordinary popularity led the way for a new kind of music, in 1960 the nation elected John F. Kennedy, the youngest president in its history and a leader who came to symbolize youthful idealism. His assassination cut short the promise of the new frontier, but not before young people had established a crucial new presence in the nation's economy, culture, and political life.

27.1 Under the Cold War's Shadow

How did the Eisenhower administration's foreign policy differ from that of the Truman administration?

By the time Dwight D. Eisenhower—universally called "Ike"—entered the White House in 1953, the confrontation with communism was already providing the framework for America's relations with the world. Eisenhower developed new strategies for the containment of what he called "international communism," including a greater reliance on nuclear deterrence and aggressive use of the CIA for covert action. Yet Eisenhower also resolved to do everything possible to forestall an all-out nuclear conflict. Recognizing the limits of raw military power, he accepted a less-than-victorious end to the Korean conflict and avoided full military involvement in Indochina. Ironically, Eisenhower's promotion of high-tech strategic weaponry fostered what he called—disapprovingly—the military-industrial complex. By the time he left office in 1961, he felt compelled to warn the nation against excessive military spending. His Democratic successor, John F. Kennedy, would discover just how difficult it was to escape the Cold War framework.

27.1.1 The Eisenhower Presidency

Ike's landslide election victory in 1952 set the stage for the first full two-term Republican presidency since Ulysses S. Grant's. Eisenhower's experience in foreign affairs had been one of his most attractive assets as a presidential candidate. As he had promised during his campaign, in December 1952 Eisenhower traveled to Korea just after his election and spent three days at the front. He returned home determined to end the fighting. The death of Soviet leader Joseph Stalin in March 1953, along with the exhaustion of Chinese and North Korean forces, created conditions favorable for a truce. In July 1953, a cease-fire agreement—not a peace settlement—brought the fighting to an uneasy end, freezing the division of North and South Korea near the 38th Parallel.

Eisenhower's success in ending the Korean fighting set the tone for his administration and increased his popularity. As president, Eisenhower kept up anti-Communist Cold War rhetoric while persuading Americans to accept the East/West stalemate as a more-or-less permanent fact. At home, Ike became the reassuring symbol of moderation and stability in a nation worried by threats ranging from communism and nuclear war to a new depression.

A conservative vision of community lay at the core of Eisenhower's political philosophy. He saw America as a corporate commonwealth, similar to Herbert Hoover's "associative state" of a generation earlier. (See Chapter 23.) Eisenhower believed the industrial strife, high inflation, and fierce partisan politics of the Truman years could be corrected only through cooperation, self-restraint, and disinterested public service. As president, Eisenhower sought to limit New Deal trends that had expanded federal power, and he encouraged a voluntary—as opposed to a regulatory—government-business partnership. To him, social harmony and "the good life" at home were closely linked to maintaining a stable, American-led international order abroad. He was fond of the phrase "middle of the road." As he told reporters, "I feel pretty good when I'm attacked from both sides. It makes me more certain I'm on the right track." The majority of the American public agreed with Eisenhower's seemingly easygoing approach.

In running his White House staff and his administration, Eisenhower adapted the staff system with which he had effectively managed unwieldy Allied forces during World War II. His "hidden hand presidency" relied on letting the states and corporate interests guide domestic policy and the economy. He appointed nine businessmen—three with ties to General Motors—to his first cabinet. Former GM chief Charles Wilson, his secretary of defense, epitomized the administration's economic views when he famously told Congress, "What was good for our country was good for General Motors, and vice versa." He appointed men congenial to the corporate interests they were supposed to regulate to the Federal Trade Commission, the Federal Communications Commission, and the Federal Power Commission. Forty billion dollars' worth of

EISENHOWER CAMPAIGN HEADQUARTERS
Presidential contender Dwight D. Eisenhower hosts a group of Republican National Committee women at his campaign headquarters in 1952. Ike's status as America's biggest war hero, along with his genial public persona, made him an extremely popular candidate with voters across party lines.

Bettmann/Getty Images.

disputed offshore oil lands were transferred from the federal government to the Gulf states under the Submerged Lands Act of 1953, whose passage Eisenhower secured. This enhanced the presence of state governments and private companies in the oil business—and cost the Treasury billions in lost revenues.

At the same time, Eisenhower accepted the New Deal legacy of greater federal responsibility for social welfare. He rejected conservative Republican appeals to dismantle Social Security. His administration agreed to a modest expansion of Social Security and unemployment insurance, and small increases in the minimum wage. Ike also created the Department of Health, Education, and Welfare, appointing as its head the second woman in history to hold a cabinet position, Oveta Culp Hobby. In agriculture, Eisenhower continued to sustain farm prices—and the interests of agribusiness—by means of New Deal-style parity payments. Between 1952 and 1960, federal spending on agriculture jumped from about $1 billion to $7 billion, and government storage facilities bulged with surpluses.

Eisenhower, a fiscal conservative in Hoover's mold, hesitated to use fiscal policy (government spending) to pump up the economy when it twice went into recession: after the Korean war and again in 1958. In that year, though unemployment hit 7.5 percent, the administration refused to cut taxes or increase spending. Eisenhower feared inflation more than unemployment or poverty—and indeed, by the time he left office, he could boast that on his watch the average family's real wages (that is, factoring in inflation) had risen by 20 percent. With low inflation and steady, if modest, growth, the Eisenhower years were prosperous for most Americans. Long after he retired from public life,

Ike liked to remember his major achievement as "an atmosphere of greater serenity and mutual confidence."

27.1.2 The "New Look" in Foreign Affairs

The death of Stalin in 1953, just two months after Eisenhower's inauguration, brought an internal power struggle in the Soviet Union. It also opened up the prospects for a thaw in the Cold War, giving Eisenhower hope for peaceful coexistence between the two superpowers. Although Eisenhower recognized that the United States was engaged in a long-term struggle with the Soviet Union, he feared that permanent Cold War mobilization might overburden the American economy and create a "garrison state." He therefore pursued a high-tech, capital-intensive defense policy that emphasized America's qualitative advantage in strategic weaponry and sought cuts in the military budget. As a percentage of the federal budget, military spending fell from 66 percent to 49 percent during Eisenhower's two terms. Much of this saving was gained through increased reliance on nuclear weapons and long-range delivery systems, which were relatively cheaper than conventional forces.

Secretary of State John Foster Dulles gave shape to the "new look" in American foreign policy in the 1950s. A devout Presbyterian lawyer, Dulles brought to the job a strong sense of righteousness, an almost missionary belief in America's responsibility to preserve the Free World from godless, immoral communism. Dulles called not simply for "containing" communism, but for a "rollback." The key would be greater reliance on America's nuclear superiority.

As part of a new strategic doctrine, Dulles emphasized the capacity of the Strategic Air Command to inflict devastating destruction with thermonuclear H-bombs. This would be "massive retaliation . . . at times and places of our own choosing" to deter Soviet aggression.

The limits of a policy based on nuclear strategy became painfully clear when American leaders faced tense situations that offered no clear way to intervene without provoking full-scale war. When East Berliners rebelled against Communist rule in June 1953, Cold War hard-liners thought they saw the long-awaited moment for rollback. American agents had encouraged rebellion in East Berlin with implied promises of American support. It never came, and Soviet tanks crushed the uprising. But precisely how could the United States have responded? In the end, the United States did nothing except protest angrily. U.S. leaders faced the same dilemma in 1956 when Hungary revolted against Communist rule. The United States opened its gates to thousands of Hungarian refugees, but refused to intervene against Soviet tanks and troops. Eisenhower recognized that the Soviets would defend not just their own borders, but also their domination of Eastern Europe—by all-out war, if necessary.

Nikita Khrushchev, who had emerged as Stalin's successor, in 1955 withdrew Soviet troops from eastern Austria in a conciliatory gesture. This first real rollback had been achieved by negotiation and a spirit of common hope, not by threats or force. In 1958, Khrushchev, probing American intentions and hoping to redirect the Soviet economy toward the production of more consumer goods, unilaterally suspended nuclear testing. Khrushchev made a 12-day trip to America in 1959. If nothing else, such "summit" diplomacy offered a psychological thaw in the Cold War. In early 1960, Khrushchev called for another summit in Paris, to discuss German reunification and nuclear disarmament. Eisenhower prepared for a friendship tour of the Soviet Union.

All that collapsed in May 1960. The Soviets shot down an American U-2 spy plane gathering intelligence on nuclear facilities. Secret American surveillance and probes of Soviet air defenses had been going on for years—justified in American officials' eyes by Moscow's refusal to allow international inspections as part of any disarmament agreement. A deeply embarrassed Eisenhower at first denied the existence of U-2 flights, but then the Soviets produced the American pilot, who readily confessed. The summit collapsed when Eisenhower refused Khrushchev's demands for an apology and an end to spy flights. The U-2 incident demonstrated the limits of personal diplomacy in resolving the deep structural rivalry between the superpowers.

Eisenhower often provided a moderating voice on the issues of defense spending and missile development. The Soviet Union's dramatic launch of *Sputnik*, the first Earth-orbiting satellite, in October 1957 upset Americans'

NIKITA KHRUSHCHEV Soviet Premier Nikita Khrushchev enjoys a bite to eat during his tour of an Iowa farm in 1959. A colorful, earthy, and erratic man, Khrushchev loomed as the most visible human symbol of the Soviet Union for Americans. On this trip he called for Soviet-American friendship, yet he also boasted "We will bury you."

Bettmann/Getty Images.

precarious sense of security. This demonstration of Soviet technological prowess raised fears about Russian ability to deploy thermonuclear-tipped intercontinental ballistic missiles (ICBMs) against American cities. Critics attacked the Eisenhower administration for failure to keep up with the enemy. Senator Stuart Symington, a Missouri Democrat, bluntly warned, "Unless our defense policies are promptly changed, the Soviets will move from superiority to supremacy." In addition to huge increases in defense spending, some panic-stricken pundits urged a massive program to build fallout shelters for the entire population in case of nuclear attack.

Eisenhower rejected these radical responses. He knew from U-2 evidence that the Soviet Union in fact trailed far behind the United States in ICBM development, but he kept this knowledge secret so as not to reveal to the Soviets the sources of American intelligence. Instead of panicking before *Sputnik*, he held to a doctrine of "sufficiency": maintaining enough military strength to survive any attack and enough nuclear capability to deliver a massive counterattack. Two measures did emerge from Congress with Eisenhower's support: creation of the National Aeronautics and Space Administration (NASA) to coordinate space exploration and missile development, and the National Defense Education Act, which funneled more federal aid into science and foreign-language education. A bipartisan majority in Congress also voted to increase the military budget by another $8 billion, accelerating the arms race and bloating the defense sector of the economy.

27.1.3 Covert Action

A heavy reliance on covert CIA operations was the other side of Eisenhower's "new look" defense policy of threatening massive retaliation against America's foreign enemies. He had been an enthusiastic supporter of covert operations during World War II, and secret CIA-sponsored paramilitary operations became a key element of American foreign policy during his presidency. The CIA promised a cheap, quick, and quiet way to depose hostile or unstable regimes, or to prop up conservative governments under siege by indigenous radicals, reformers, or revolutionaries.

Eisenhower's new CIA chief was Allen Dulles, John Foster's brother and an important figure in the OSS, the CIA's World War II precursor. Under Dulles's command, the CIA far exceeded its mandate to collect and analyze information. All over the world, thousands of covert agents carried out operations that included making large, secret payments to friendly political parties (such as conservative Christian Democrats in Italy and Latin America) or to foreign trade unions that opposed the Communist Party.

Independence movements by now were shaking the European colonial empires throughout Asia and Africa, at the same time that dislike of U.S. hegemony was surging in Latin American. To the Eisenhower administration's alarm, the Soviet Union began winning influence in the "Third World," by appealing to allegedly common anti-imperialist solidarity and by offering modest foreign aid. Communists played only small roles in most Third World independence movements. But widespread anti-Western feelings in these lands were fanned by publicity about America's racial problems and by resentment against foreign investors' control of natural resources, including oil and mineral wealth. If emerging nations questioned U.S. regional security arrangements by opting for neutrality—or, worse, expropriated American property—the Eisenhower administration was apt to try covert countermeasures and military intervention.

27.1.4 Global Interventions

In Iran in 1953, the CIA produced a swift, major victory. The popular Iranian prime minister, Mohammed Mossadegh, had nationalized Britain's Anglo-Iranian Oil Company, and the State Department worried that this might set a precedent throughout the oil-rich Middle East. Kermit Roosevelt, the CIA chief in Iran, organized and financed opposition to Mossadegh within the Iranian army and on the streets of Teheran. This CIA-sponsored opposition movement drove Mossadegh from office and put in power an autocratic monarch (shah), Riza Pahlavi. The shah proved his loyalty to his American sponsors by renegotiating oil contracts, assuring American companies 40 percent of Iran's oil concessions. But U.S. identification with the shah's repressive regime in the long run created a groundswell of anti-Americanism among Iranians.

United States policy throughout the Middle East was complicated by the conflict between Israel and its Arab neighbors. Immediately after the United States and the Soviet Union recognized the newborn Jewish state in 1948, the Arab countries launched an all-out attack. Israel repulsed the attack, drove thousands of Palestinians from their homes, and seized territory considerably beyond the lines of the projected UN partition of Palestine into a Jewish and an Arab state. While the Arab world boycotted Israel economically and refused to recognize its right to exist, hundreds of thousands of Palestinians languished in squalid refugee camps. Yet most Americans supported the new Jewish state as a refuge for a people the Nazis had tried to exterminate in the Holocaust. Israel became a reliable U.S. ally in an unstable region.

Arab nationalism continued to vex American policymakers, culminating in the 1956 Suez Crisis. Egyptian president Gamal Abdel Nasser, a leading voice of Arab nationalism, dreamed of building the Aswan High Dam on the Nile to create more arable land and provide cheap electric power. To build the dam, he sought American and British economic aid. When negotiations broke down, Nasser turned to the Soviet Union for aid and announced he would nationalize the strategically vital—and British-controlled—Suez Canal. Eisenhower refused European appeals for help in forcibly returning the canal to the British. British, French, and Israeli forces then invaded Egypt in October 1956. The United States sponsored a UN cease-fire resolution demanding withdrawal of foreign forces. Yielding to this pressure and to Soviet threats, the British, French, and eventually Israeli forces withdrew. Eisenhower had won a major diplomatic battle through patience and pressure. The end of the crisis, however, brought no lasting peace to the troubled region. Arab nationalists continued to look primarily to the Soviet Union for support against Israel.

Guatemala saw the most publicized CIA intervention of the Eisenhower years. (See Map 27.1.) In that impoverished Central American country—where 2 percent of the population held 72 percent of all farmland, and the American-based United Fruit Company owned vast banana plantations—a fragile democracy took root in 1944. President Jácobo Arbenz Guzmán, elected in 1950, aggressively pursued land reform, encouraged the formation of trade unions, and tried to buy (at assessed value) enormous acreage that United Fruit owned but did not cultivate. The company demanded far more compensation for this land than Guatemala offered and, having powerful friends in the administration (CIA director Dulles had sat on United Fruit's Board of Directors), began lobbying intensively for U.S. intervention, linking land-reform programs to international communism. The CIA spent $7 million training Guatemalan dissidents in neighboring Honduras.

Map 27.1 THE UNITED STATES IN THE CARIBBEAN, 1948–1966

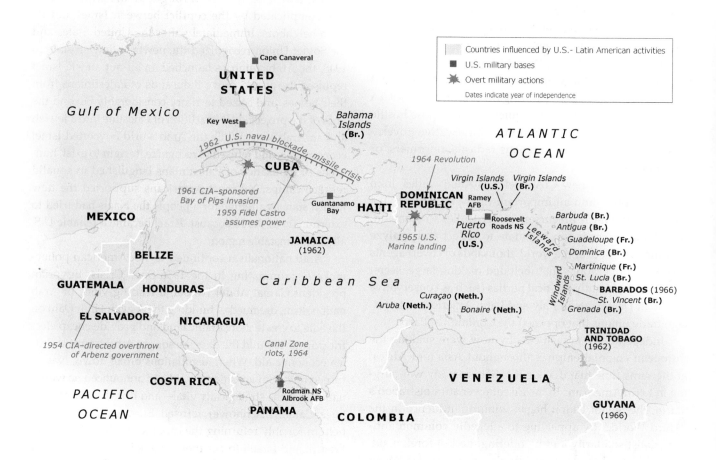

United States military intervention and economic presence grew steadily in the Caribbean following World War II. After 1960, opposition to the Cuban Revolution dominated U.S. Caribbean policies.

United States intervention began when the Navy stopped Guatemala-bound ships and seized their cargoes, and on June 14, 1954, the United States-trained antigovernment force invaded from Honduras. Guatemalans resisted by seizing United Fruit buildings, but U.S. Air Force bombing gave the invaders cover. Guatemala appealed in vain to the United Nations for help, while Eisenhower publicly denied any knowledge of CIA involvement. A newly appointed Guatemalan leader, Carlos Castillo Armas, flew to the Guatemalan capital in a U.S. Embassy plane. In the widespread terror that followed, unions were outlawed and thousands were arrested. United Fruit circulated photos of Guatemalans murdered by the invaders, mislabeling them "victims of communism." In 1957, Castillo Armas was assassinated, initiating a decades-long civil war between military factions and peasant guerrillas.

Vice President Nixon declared that the new Guatemalan government had earned "the overwhelming support

of the Guatemalan people"—a boast belied by events in Guatemala and by the resentment that the United States aroused throughout Latin America. In 1958, while Nixon made a "goodwill" tour of the region, angry mobs stoned his limousine in Caracas, Venezuela. U.S. actions had in fact triggered an anti-American backlash.

The global anti-Communist strategy that the Truman and Eisenhower administrations embraced led to American backing of France's desperate attempt to maintain its colonial empire in Indochina. (See Chapter 26.) From 1950 to 1954, the United States poured $2.6 billion in military aid (about three-quarters of the total French costs) and CIA assistance into the fight against the nationalist Vietminh movement, led by Communist Ho Chi Minh. When Vietminh forces surrounded 25,000 French troops at Dien Bien Phu in March 1954, France pleaded for direct American intervention. Secretary of State Dulles and Vice President Nixon, among others, called for using tactical nuclear weapons and U.S. ground troops to rescue the French. But Eisenhower, remembering Korea, refused. "I can conceive of no greater tragedy," he said, "than for the United States to become engaged in all-out war in Indochina."

Still, Eisenhower feared that the loss of one country to communism would inevitably lead to the loss of others. "You have a row of dominoes set up," he said, "and you knock over the first one and what will happen to the last one is the certainty that it will go over quickly." This so-called "domino theory" meant that the "loss" of Vietnam would threaten other Southeast Asian nations (Laos, Thailand, and the Philippines) and perhaps even India and Australia. After the French surrender at Dien Bien Phu, an international conference in Geneva established a cease-fire and a "temporary" division into a Communist northern state and a non-Communist southern state. National elections and reunification were promised in 1956. But the United States refused to sign the accord. Instead, the Eisenhower administration created the Southeast Asia Treaty Organization (SEATO), a NATO-like and United States-dominated security pact including the United States, Great Britain, France, Australia, New Zealand, Thailand, the Philippines, and Pakistan.

Ngo Dinh Diem, who quickly emerged as South Vietnam's president, was a former Japanese collaborator and a Catholic in a 90 percent Buddhist country. Supported by Eisenhower, Diem refused to permit the promised 1956 elections, knowing that the popular hero Ho Chi Minh would easily win. American economic and military aid, along with covert CIA activity, kept the increasingly isolated Diem in power. His corrupt and repressive policies alienated many peasants. By 1959, his Saigon regime faced a civil war against the thousands of peasants who were joining guerrilla bands to drive him out. Eisenhower's commitment of military advisers and economic aid to South Vietnam, based on Cold War assumptions, had laid the foundation for the Vietnam War of the 1960s.

27.2 The Affluent Society

How did postwar prosperity reshape American social and cultural life?

With the title of his influential book *The Affluent Society* (1958), economist John Kenneth Galbraith labeled postwar America. Galbraith observed that American capitalism had worked "quite brilliantly" in the years since World War II. But Americans, he argued, needed to spend less on personal consumption and devote more public funds to schools, medical care, culture, and social services. For most Americans, however, strong economic growth was the defining fact of the postwar period, and a fierce desire for consumer goods and the "good life" permeated American culture. The deeply held popular belief in the right to a continuously

expanding economy and a steadily rising standard of living—even against the backdrop of global Cold War anxieties—shaped American social and political life.

27.2.1 Subsidizing Prosperity

During the Eisenhower years, the federal government played a crucial role in subsidizing programs that helped millions of Americans achieve middle-class status. Federal aid helped people to buy homes, attend colleges and technical schools, and live in new suburbs. Much of this assistance expanded on programs begun during the New Deal and World War II. The Federal Housing Administration (FHA), established in 1934, extended the government's role in subsidizing the housing industry by insuring the lending institution against loss of principal in case the borrower fails to meet the terms and conditions of the mortgage. By putting "the full faith and credit" of the federal government behind residential mortgages, the FHA attracted new private capital into home building and revolutionized the industry. A typical FHA mortgage required less than 10 percent for a down payment and spread low-interest monthly payments over 30 years. In addition, homeowners benefited from the provision in the Internal Revenue Code (dating back to 1913) that allowed the deduction of all forms of interest payments from taxes. The mortgage interest deduction was the most important middle-class tax benefit for millions of postwar home buyers.

Yet FHA policies insured that postwar suburbs would be largely segregated communities. Builders were eager to leverage the FHA's guarantee of mortgages, which opened the flow of private capital from banks. But FHA approval of new suburban subdivisions required a commitment not to sell to African Americans. By 1950, the FHA and the Veterans Administration (which followed FHA guidelines) together were insuring half of all the nation's new mortgages. Bluntly, the FHA's Underwriting Manual warned, "If a neighborhood is to retain stability, it is necessary that properties shall continue to be occupied by the same social and racial classes." Thus, federal policy explicitly reinforced postwar racial and income segregation in the new suburbs.

Most suburbs were built as planned communities. One of the first, Levittown, opened in 1947 in Hempstead, on Long Island, on 1,500 acres of former potato fields. Developer William Levitt, who described his firm as "the General Motors of the housing industry," was the first entrepreneur to bring mass-production techniques to home building. All building materials were precut and prefabricated at a central factory, and then assembled on-site into houses by largely unskilled, nonunion labor. In this way, Levitt put up hundreds of identical houses each week. Eventually, Levittown encompassed more than 17,000 houses and 82,000 people. Yet in 1960 not one of Levittown's residents was

LEVITTOWN, NEW YORK An aerial view of 1950s tract houses in the suburban development of Levittown, New York. Mass-production techniques were key to providing affordable housing in the new postwar suburbs—but they required a "cookie cutter" approach to architecture, with little or no variation among the houses.

Hulton Archive/Getty Images.

African American, and owners who rented out their homes were told to specify that their houses would not be "used or occupied by any person other than members of the Caucasian race." (See Communities *in* Conflict.)

The 1944 Servicemen's Readjustment Act—the G.I. Bill of Rights—made an unprecedented impact on American life. In addition to educational grants, the act gave returning veterans low-interest mortgages and business loans, thus subsidizing suburban growth as much as the postwar expansion of higher education. Over 2 million enrolled in colleges and universities, and nearly 6 million received vocational and job training. Another 3 million got loans to run businesses and farms. By 1955, of the roughly 15.4 million military veterans of World War II, 12.4 million, or 78 percent, received some form of benefit from the law—affecting roughly one of every four American households. Yet not all veterans benefitted equally. Although African American and Latino vets were fully entitled to the same benefits as whites, they faced greater obstacles to enjoying them. Racial segregation and discrimination in higher education, as well as much lower high school graduation rates, left them less able to take advantage of education benefits. The common practice of "redlining" denied loans for housing in predominantly black or mixed-race neighborhoods. Racial prejudice among Veterans Administration officials also made it more difficult for veterans of color to fully collect benefits. As with many earlier New Deal programs, local discriminatory practices often undercut the federal promise of the G.I. Bill for African American and Latino veterans.

Another key boost to postwar growth, especially in suburbs, came from the National Interstate and Defense

Highways Act of 1956. It is significant that the program was sold to the country partly as a civil defense measure (supposedly to facilitate evacuating American cities in case of nuclear attack). The act originally authorized $32 billion to build a national interstate highway system. By 1972, the program had become the single largest public works program in American history, laying out 41,000 miles of highway at a cost of $76 billion. New taxes on gasoline, oil, tires, buses, and trucks paid for the program; the money was held in a Highway Trust Fund separately from general revenue. Federal subsidies for interstate highway construction stimulated both the automobile industry and suburb building, and helped transform the American landscape with motels, fast-food outlets, and other businesses servicing road-tripping Americans. The interstate also accelerated the decline of American mass transit and of many older cities. By 1970, the nation possessed the world's best roads—and one of the world's worst public transportation systems.

Cold War jitters also prompted the federal government to launch new initiatives to aid education. The Soviet launch of the *Sputnik* satellite in the fall of 1957 dealt a body blow to Americans' confidence in the superiority of their technology and education; officials, pundits, and educators alike worried that the country might be lagging behind the Soviets in training scientists and engineers. With bipartisan congressional backing, the Eisenhower administration pledged to strengthen support for educating American students in mathematics, science, and technology. The National Defense Education Act (NDEA) of 1958 allocated $280 million in grants—tied to matching grants from the states—for state universities to upgrade their science facilities.

Communities *in* Conflict

Integrating Levittown, Pennsylvania

"I really don't have any objections to colored people, but I don't think they ought to live in white neighborhoods."

The construction of mass-produced suburban communities represented a crucial shift in the lives of millions of postwar American families. The opportunity to own a new home—one that often came with brand new appliances such as refrigerators and ranges—proved enormously attractive. The availability of low-cost mortgages through the Federal Housing Administration (FHA) and the Veterans Administration (VA) provided a key boost into the middle-class world of home ownership. Builder William J. Levitt spearheaded this explosive expansion of suburbia by developing cheap prefabricated construction and creating Levittown, New York (with 17,500 homes on Long Island) and Levittown, Pennsylvania (with 15,500 homes just north of Philadelphia).

Racial segregation was built into many postwar suburbs as a result of federal policies. In order to gain FHA approval, and thus access to low-interest financing from banks, builders like Levitt submitted drawings, design specifications, and the proposed sale price to the agency. The FHA reviewed these and also required a commitment not to sell to African Americans before giving its approval. Levitt was blunt about his belief in the business necessity for all-white communities. "As a Jew," he said, "I have no room in my mind or heart for racial prejudice. But I have come to know that if I sell to a Negro family, then 90 to 95 percent of our white customers will not buy into the community. That is their attitude, not ours."

Levitt and other builders had no say over the resale of houses. In August 1957, William Myers, an African American veteran of World War II, purchased a home in Levittown, Pennsylvania. When he, his wife, and their three small children moved in, they sparked an angry and violent response from some of their neighbors. Unlike the Deep South, northern communities did not live under the rules of legal segregation. The opposition to integration in places like Levittown revealed that racial prejudice was by no means limited to the South. In 1959, the New Jersey Appellate Court, considering a discrimination lawsuit brought by two African Americans, ruled that a third Levittown being built in that state could not bar African Americans from purchasing homes. Incidents like the one described here were fairly widespread in northern suburbs, and they foreshadowed the fierce political and legal battles over de facto segregation that would become an important element of the civil rights movement.

A news account describes the opposition faced by the Myers family as they moved into Levittown. A more in-depth feature on the incident includes a variety of views expressed by members of the community.

- **What underlying assumptions about race relations do you find among white opponents to the integration of Levittown, Pennsylvania?**

- **How are economic arguments used to justify resistance to African Americans as neighbors?**

"Police Rout 400 at Negro's Home" (August 20, 1957)

Levittown, Pa.—State troopers armed with riot clubs broke up a disorderly crowd of 400 persons who had gathered here tonight to protest the purchase of a house by a Negro family.

The crowd, mostly teenagers, started to assemble at 6 P.M. near the home of Mr. and Mrs. William Myers Jr., the first Negroes to purchase a dwelling in this development. The Negro family moved into its home today in the Dogwood Hollow section of the 15,500 house development.

Despite an order barring the Dogwood Hollow section from all but residents and persons with business in the neighborhood, more people filtered into the area and the crowd numbered 400 at 9 P.M. There were derisive shouts and someone threw a stone, which struck a state trooper. Lieutenant M. J. Wicker [in charge of the state police contingent] announced over a loud speaker in a police car: "I will not tolerate this. I'll give you ten minutes to move out and go back to your homes."

The crowd refused to move and ten minutes later the police moved toward them. When the police used their clubs, poking and swinging, the crowd ran toward Haines Road, a block away. One man stopped to fight but was subdued and arrested. Some of the young girls in the group cried and there were shouts of "Gestapo" and "Is this Communist Russia?"

The crowd thinned and at 10:30 o'clock there were only 150 left.

The incident tonight was the latest of several protest meetings by the residents of the community. The meetings had been forbidden as illegal assemblages.

Mr. Myers, an equipment tester for a refrigeration concern in near-by Trenton, N.J. moved some furniture into the $11,000 house a week ago. The next evening, shortly after the Myerses had left, two windows in the living room were smashed by persons in a crowd of more than 300.

Gov. George M. Leader denounced the stone throwing and assigned the state police at the request of C. Leroy Murray, sheriff of Bucks County. Today, a newly formed citizens' group, the Levittown Betterment Committee, declared that it would continue to hold protest meetings in defiance of Mr. Murray's edict.

Earlier today, when the Myerses walked into their home carrying some suitcases, towels and other small articles, Mr. Myers said: "Now we're here to stay."

Reactions: "When a Negro Family Moved into a White Community" (August 30, 1957)

What happens when a Negro family buys a home and moves into a Northern community that has always had an all white population? This sprawling development of 16,000 homes just north of Philadelphia is finding out the hard way. It is a story of a peaceful community suddenly turned upside down by racial tension and unaccustomed turbulence.

Up till now, Levittown—with 55,000 residents—has been a quiet place. It was built between 1951 and 1955 by William J. Levitt, a real estate developer who also built the community of the same name on Long Island, N.Y.

No Negroes had ever lived in Levittown until August. Then William Myers, Jr., and his wife moved here from neighboring Bloomsdale Gardens, a racially integrated housing development. They are Negroes, parents of three small children.

Citizens committees—one favoring racial segregation for Levittown and another in favor of racial integration—quickly sprang up. The Levittown Betterment Association, formed among the Myerses' new neighbors, announced as its purpose the removal of the Negro family from the community by peaceful means. The Citizens' Committee for Levittown, composed of church and civic groups and backed by Quaker churchmen, appealed for an end to the violence and acceptance of the Myerses.

Almost overnight, Levittown residents whose principal concerns had been their homes and gardens and the cost of living found themselves on opposite sides of the fence in a king-sized row. Lewis Wechsler, who lives in the house next door, expresses one viewpoint. Of the Myerses he says: "They have a right to live here the same as any other American." Mr. Wechsler, a machinist, works in a plant across the Delaware River in Trenton, N.J.

James McDaniel, who lives on nearby Dogwood Drive, is one who doesn't like what has happened. A steelworker, he came north from Tennessee, and works in the big Fairless plant of U.S. Steel north of here. "We don't like Negroes living in the neighborhood," says Mr. McDaniel. "One family maybe is all right, but after one moves in others come. You hear a lot of talk among Negroes over at the plant that if the Myers family stays they'll move here, too. We don't like it, but there's nothing we can do about it legally."

George Bessam, a bachelor, also has a job at Fairless. What are his feelings on the racial storm that has struck Levittown? "I really don't have any objections to colored people, but I don't think they ought to live in white neighborhoods," he says. "A lot of people moved into Levittown from Philadelphia and other places for just one reason—to get away from colored people in their old neighborhoods. Now they're up against this—colored people moving into Levittown, too. I just don't think it ought to happen. And I think all this police stuff is terrible—people getting hit over the head by police clubs when they're just trying to see that they get their rights," adds Mr. Bessam.

Champney Bernauer lives with his family in Levittown's Willowood section. He's a salesman, is against Negroes moving into the community. "I know how I feel about this thing," he says, "but you couldn't print what I would have to say. Just say that I'm against it and I don't like it. What anyone can do about it, I don't know."

On the opposite side of the fence are the civic groups like the Citizens' Committee for Levittown, headed by Rev. Ray Harwick of Levittown's Evangelical and Reformed Church of the Reformation. "An overwhelming majority of our neighbors," the committee reports, "have been calmly accepting the Myerses move, regardless of whether they personally support or oppose the Myerses decision."

On taking up residence in his new home, Mr. Myers is quoted as having said he would try to be "a good neighbor." After all the trouble began, he is reported to have decided to stay put "if at all possible" and to have voiced the hope that he would be allowed to bring up his children in the community. "Pressure can't be any greater than it is now," he reportedly said.

The Levittown Betterment Association, which opposes the settling of the Myerses in the community, has indicated that it would try to raise the money to buy out the Negro family.

Real estate men say privately that Negroes never will be allowed in Levittown in any numbers. They point out that this community is one of low and medium-priced homes occupied for the most part by young couples just getting a start as homeowners. Such people, it is held, are touchy about things like property values, which they believe will drop precipitously when Negroes move into a neighborhood.

The NDEA also created low-interest loans for college students (who had to repay only half the amount if they went on to teach in elementary or secondary school after graduation), and fellowship support for graduate students planning to go into college and university teaching.

In a broader sense, the postwar economy floated on a sea of Cold War–justified military spending. At the height of the Korean War, defense expenditures swallowed up about half the federal budget, or 14 percent of GNP; military spending declined after Korea, but by 1960 defense contracts still constituted about 10 percent of GNP. That spending provided an enormous boost to defense-industry employers like Boeing and Douglas Aircraft and created hundreds of thousands of new jobs. New military bases, along with the growing aviation industry, spurred enormous economic and population growth across communities in southern California, around Seattle and Charleston, and on Long Island. Military spending, which many associated with high-paying jobs and prosperous communities, thus acquired enormous local political support and powerful patrons in Congress, all devoted to keeping federal contracts flowing into their districts.

27.2.2 Suburban Life

For millions of Americans, the Great Depression and World War II had meant squeezing into cramped apartments or run-down houses, often sharing space with relatives and boarders. Suburban home owning was irresistibly alluring for them, especially when home builders threw into the deal new appliances—gas ranges, refrigerators, washers, and dryers. Unquestionably, suburban living meant a huge improvement in material conditions for many postwar American families, and the suburban boom strengthened the domestic ideal of the nuclear family as the model for American life. The image of the perfect suburban wife— efficient, patient, always charming—permeated television, movies, and magazines. Suburban domesticity was usually presented as women's only path to happiness and fulfillment.

That glowing image often masked a stifling existence defined by housework, child care, and boredom. In the late 1950s, Betty Friedan, a wife, mother, and journalist, began a systematic survey of her Smith College classmates. She found "a strange discrepancy between the reality of our lives as women and the image to which we were trying to conform." Extending her research, in 1963 Friedan published her landmark book *The Feminine Mystique*, which gave voice to the silent frustrations of suburban women and helped to launch a new feminist movement.

For millions of suburban families, only two incomes could yield the middle-class life. The expansion of the female labor force—from 17 million in 1946 to 22 million in 1958—was a central economic fact of the post–World War II years. By 1960, 40 percent of women were employed full-time or part-time, and 30 percent of married women looked to supplement the family income and ensure a solidly middle-class standard of living. (See Figure 27.1.)

The powerful postwar rebirth of American religion was strongly associated with suburban living. In 1940, less than half the American population belonged to institutional churches; by the mid-1950s, nearly three-quarters called themselves church members, and a church-building boom was part of the nation's suburban expansion. Best-selling religious authors like the Presbyterian pastor Norman Vincent Peale and the Roman Catholic bishop Fulton J. Sheen (who also appeared on TV) offered a shallow blend of spiritual reassurance and "the power of positive thinking," stressing individual solutions to problems and opposing social or political activism. Billy Graham's

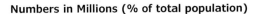

Figure 27.1 THE GROWTH OF THE SUBURBS, 1950–1970

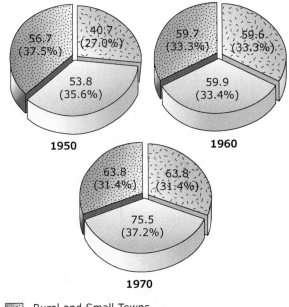

Numbers in Millions (% of total population)

1950

56.7 (37.5%) | 40.7 (27.0%) | 53.8 (35.6%)

1960

59.7 (33.3%) | 59.6 (33.3%) | 59.9 (33.4%)

1970

63.8 (31.4%) | 63.8 (31.4%) | 75.5 (37.2%)

▒ Rural and Small Towns
☐ Suburbs
⋮ Central Cities

Suburban growth, at the expense of older inner cities, was one of the key social trends in the 25 years following World War II. By 1970, more Americans lived in suburbs than in either inner cities or rural areas.

Adapted from U.S. Bureau of the Census, Current Censuses, 1930–1970 (Washington, DC: U.S. Government Printing Office, 1975).

hugely popular "Crusades for Christ" brought the religious revival to millions while warning of godless communism. Most popular religious writers emphasized the importance of belonging, of fitting in—an appeal that meshed perfectly with the conventional aspirations of suburban social life and with the ideal of family-centered domesticity.

California—so often the national trendsetter—came to embody postwar suburban life, centered on the automobile. Cars were a necessity for commuting to work. California led the nation in creating automobile-oriented facilities: motels ("motor hotels"), drive-in movies, drive-through fast-food eateries and banks, and parking-lot-encircled shopping malls. In Orange County, southeast of Los Angeles, the "centerless city" emerged as the dominant form of community. The experience of one resident there was typical; "I live in Garden Grove, work in Irvine, shop in Santa Ana, go to the dentist in Anaheim, my husband works in Long Beach, and I used to be the president of the League of Women Voters in Fullerton." (See Figure 27.2.)

Contemporary journalists, novelists, and social scientists fed the popular image of suburban life as essentially dull, conformist, and peopled exclusively by the educated

Figure 27.2 L.A. COUNTY POPULATION, 1920–1980

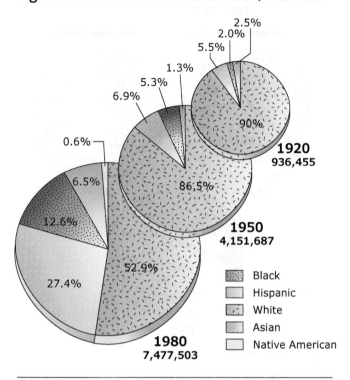

2.5%
2.0%
5.5%
1.3%
5.3%
6.9%
90%
1920
936,455

0.6%
6.5%
12.6%
86.5%
52.9%
27.4%
1950
4,151,687

Black
Hispanic
White
Asian
Native American

1980
7,477,503

middle class. John Cheever, for example, won the National Book Award for *The Wapshot Chronicle* (1957), a novel set in fictional Remsen Park, "a community of four thousand identical homes." Yet these writers (who were largely urban by birth and residence) tended to obscure the real class and ethnic differences among different suburban communities. Many new suburbs had a distinctively blue-collar cast. Milpitas, California, for example, grew up around a Ford auto plant about 50 miles outside San Jose. Its residents were blue-collar assembly-line workers and their families, not the stereotypical salaried, college-educated, white-collar employees. Self-segregation and zoning ordinances gave some new suburbs distinctively Italian, Jewish, or Irish ethnic identities, similar to older urban neighborhoods. For millions of new suburbanites, architectural and psychological conformity was an acceptable price to pay for the comforts of home ownership, a small plot of land, and a sense of security and status.

27.2.3 Organized Labor and the AFL-CIO

George Meany, the brusque, cigar-chomping head of the AFL, seemed the epitome of the modern labor boss. Originally a plumber, he had worked his way through the AFL bureaucracy and had played a leading role on the National War Labor Board during World War II. An outspoken

anti-Communist, Meany pushed the AFL closer to the Democratic Party but took pride in never having been on a strike or a picket line. Unions, he believed, must focus on improving the economic well-being of their members. Meany's counterpart in the CIO was Walter Reuther, originally a tool-and-die maker in the auto shops of Detroit. Reuther had come to prominence as a leader of the United Automobile Workers during the tumultuous organizing drives of the 1930s and 1940s. Reuther believed strongly that American unions ought to stand for something beyond the bread-and-butter needs of their members. His support of a broader social vision—including racial equality, aggressive union organizing, and expansion of the welfare state—reflected the more militant tradition of the CIO unions. Despite their differences, both Meany and Reuther believed a merger of their two organizations offered the best strategy for the labor movement. In 1955, the newly combined AFL-CIO brought some 12.5 million union members under one banner, with Meany as president and Reuther as director of the Industrial Union Department.

The merger marked the apex of trade union membership, and after 1955 its share of the labor market began a slow but steady decline. For millions of workers and their families in well-paying manufacturing jobs, union membership helped bring the trappings of middle-class prosperity: home ownership, higher education for children, travel, and a comfortable retirement. But the AFL-CIO showed little commitment to bringing unorganized workers into the fold. Scandals involving union corruption and racketeering hurt the labor movement's public image. In 1959, after highly publicized hearings into union corruption, Congress passed the **Landrum-Griffin Act**, which widened government control over union affairs and further restricted union use of picketing and secondary boycotts during strikes.

While union membership as a percentage of the total workforce declined, important growth did take place in new areas, reflecting a broader shift in the American workplace from manufacturing to service jobs. During the 1950s and 1960s, union membership among public sector employees—especially at the state and local levels—increased dramatically as millions of civil servants, postal employees, teachers, police, and firefighters joined unions for the first time.

27.2.4 Lonely Crowds and Organization Men

Perhaps the most ambitious and controversial critique of postwar suburban America was sociologist David Riesman's *The Lonely Crowd* (1950). Riesman argued that modern America had given birth to a new kind of character type, the "other-directed" man. Previously the nation had cultivated "inner-directed" people—self-reliant individualists who from early in life had internalized self-discipline and moral standards. By contrast, the "other-directed" person typical of the modern era was peer-oriented. Morality and ideals came from the overarching desire to conform. Americans, Riesman thought, were now less likely to take risks or act independently. Their thinking and habits had come to be determined by cues they received from the mass media.

Similarly, William H. Whyte's *Organization Man* (1956), a study of the Chicago suburb of Park Forest, offered a picture of people obsessed with fitting into their communities and jobs. In place of the old Protestant ethic of hard work, thrift, and competitive struggle, Whyte believed, middle-class suburbanites now strove mainly for a comfortable, secure niche in the system. They held to a new social ethic, he argued, "a belief in the group as the source of creativity; a belief in 'belongingness' as the ultimate need of the individual."

The most radical critic of postwar society, and the one with the most enduring influence, was Texas-reared sociologist C. Wright Mills. In *White Collar* (1951), Mills analyzed the job culture that typified life for middle-class salaried employees, office workers, and bureaucrats. "When white collar people get jobs," he wrote, "they sell not only their time and energy, but their personalities as well. They sell by the week or month their smiles and their kindly gestures, and they must practice the prompt repression of resentment and aggression." In *The Power Elite* (1956), Mills argued that a small, interconnected group of corporate executives, military men, and political leaders had come to dominate American society. The arms race in particular, pursued in the name of Cold War policies, had given an unprecedented degree of power to what President Eisenhower later termed the military-industrial complex.

27.2.5 The Expansion of Higher Education

American higher education grew explosively after the war, creating the system of post-secondary training that still exists. This expansion both reflected and reinforced other postwar social trends. The number of students enrolled in colleges and universities climbed from 2.6 million in 1950 to 3.2 million in 1960, and then more than doubled—to 7.5 million—by 1970, as the baby boomers (those born between 1946 and 1964) reached college age. Most of these new students attended greatly enlarged state university systems.

College students enjoyed a deferment from the draft, which normally faced young men soon after they finished high school. (If college graduates married and became fathers, or entered graduate or professional school, they could usually count on being deferred until they were past draft age, at 26.) In this sense, college marked an important class line in postwar America. Colleges and universities by and large accepted the values of postwar corporate culture. By the mid-1950s, 20 percent of all college graduates majored in business or similar fields.

A college degree opened a gateway to the middle class. It became a requirement for a whole range of expanding white-collar occupations in banking, insurance, real estate, advertising and marketing, and corporate management in general. Most administrators accommodated large business interests, which were well represented on university boards of trustees. Universities themselves were increasingly run like businesses, with administrators adopting the language of input-output, cost effectiveness, and quality control.

27.2.6 Health and Medicine

Dramatic improvements in medical care allowed many Americans to enjoy longer and healthier lives. New antibiotics such as penicillin, the "wonder drug" of World War II, became widely available to the general population. Federal support for research continued after the war with the reorganization of the National Institutes of Health in 1948.

Perhaps the most celebrated achievement of postwar medicine was the victory over poliomyelitis. Between 1947 and 1951, this disease, which usually crippled those it did not kill, struck an average of 39,000 Americans every year. In 1955, Jonas Salk pioneered the first effective vaccine against the disease, using a preparation of killed virus. A nationwide program of polio vaccination, later supplemented by the oral Sabin vaccine, virtually eliminated polio by the 1960s.

Yet access to "wonder drugs" and advanced medical techniques was not shared equally. More sophisticated treatments and expensive new hospital facilities sharply increased the costs of health care. Poor and many elderly Americans found themselves unable to afford modern medicine. Thousands of communities, especially in rural areas and small towns, lacked doctors and decent hospital facilities. The decline of the general practitioner—the family doctor—meant that fewer (and eventually no) physicians made house calls; for treatment, people went to hospital emergency rooms or outpatient clinics.

The American Medical Association (AMA), which certified medical schools, did nothing to increase the flow of new doctors. The number of physicians per 100,000 people actually declined between 1950 and 1960; doctors trained in other countries made up the shortfall. The AMA also lobbied hard against efforts to expand government responsibility for the public's health. President Truman had proposed national health insurance, to be run along the lines of Social Security, and President Eisenhower later proposed a program that would offer government assistance to private health insurance companies. Both proposals were denounced as "socialized medicine" by the AMA. Until 1965, with the advent of Medicare (for the elderly) and Medicaid (for the poor)—both of which it also opposed—the

AMA successfully fought any form of direct federal involvement in health care.

The growing prestige of science was not universally welcomed. In 1948, an Indiana University entomologist, Alfred Kinsey, published his landmark book on American sexuality, *Sexual Behavior in the Human Male*, followed five years later by *Sexual Behavior in the Human Female*. Based on personal interviews with thousands of subjects, Kinsey's books became best sellers—but offered a picture of American sexual behavior that many found shocking. He found, for example, that roughly half of American women had engaged in premarital sex and that some 10 percent of American men were homosexual. Overall Kinsey's work revealed that each new generation of young Americans was more sexually active than the preceding cohort, irrespective of class or gender. Many critics objected to what they saw as Kinsey's claim to objectivity and his reduction of sexual experience to statistics. Yet in the long run Kinsey's scientific approach helped to demystify sex and led to more openness about human sexuality.

27.3 Youth Culture

What larger trends were reflected in the youth culture of the 1950s?

The term "teenager," describing someone between 13 and 19, entered standard usage only at the end of World War II. According to the *Dictionary of American Slang*, the United States is the only country with a word for this age group and the only country to consider it "a separate entity whose influence, fads, and fashions are worthy of discussion apart from the adult world." During the 15 years after World War II, unprecedented attention was paid to America's adolescents. Adults expressed deep fears about everything from teenage sexuality and juvenile delinquency to young people's driving habits, hairstyles, and choice of clothing. At the same time, advertisers and businesses pursued the disposable income of America's affluent youth with a vengeance.

27.3.1 The Youth Market

Birthrates had accelerated gradually during the late 1930s and more rapidly during the war years. The children born in those years had by the late 1950s grown into the original teenagers, the older siblings of the celebrated baby boomers of 1946–64. They came of age in a society that, compared with that of their parents and the rest of the world, was uniquely affluent. Converging, the demographic growth of teens and the postwar economic expansion created an explosive and profitable youth market. Manufacturers and advertisers rushed to cash in on the special needs and desires of young consumers: cosmetics, clothing, radios and phonographs, and cars.

Life magazine summarized the new power of the youth market in 1959; "Counting only what is spent to satisfy their special teenage demands," the magazine reported, "the youngsters and their parents will shell out about $10 billion this year, a billion more than the total sales of GM." In addition, advertisers and market researchers found that teenagers often played a critical, if hard-to-measure, role as "secret persuaders" in a family's large purchase decisions. Specialized market research organizations, such as Eugene Gilbert & Company and Teen-Age Survey Incorporated, sprang up to serve business clients eager to attract teen consumers and instill brand loyalty.

To many parents, the emerging youth culture was a dangerous threat to their authority. One mother voiced this fear in a revealing, if slightly hysterical, letter to *Modern Teen* magazine:

> Don't you realize what you are doing? You are encouraging teenagers to write to each other, which keeps them from doing their school work and other chores. You are encouraging them to kiss and have physical contact before they're even engaged, which is morally wrong and you know it. You are encouraging them to have faith in the depraved individuals who make rock and roll records when it's common knowledge that ninety percent of these rock and roll singers are people with no morals or sense of values.

The special status of teenagers was also made apparent to the public by the increasing uniformity of public school education. In 1900, about one of every eight teenagers was in school; six out of eight were by the 1950s. Psychologists wrote guidebooks for parents, with titles like Dorothy Baruch's *How to Live with Your Teenager* (1953) and Paul Landis's *Understanding Teenagers* (1955). Traditional sources of adult authority and socialization—the marketplace, schools, child-rearing manuals, the mass media—all reinforced the notion of teenagers as a special community, united by age, rank, and status.

27.3.2 "Hail! Hail! Rock 'n' Roll!"

The demands of the new teen market, combined with structural changes in the postwar American mass media, reshaped the nation's popular music. As television broadcasting rapidly replaced radio as the center of family entertainment, people began using radios in new ways. There was a rapid rise in the production of car radios and portable transistor radios as listeners increasingly tuned them in for diversion from or an accompaniment to other activities. By 1956, some 2,700 AM radio stations were on the air across the United States, with about 70 percent of their broadcast time devoted to record shows.

In the recording industry, change was in the air. Small independent record labels led the way in aggressively recording African American rhythm-and-blues artists.

Atlantic Records, in New York, developed the most influential galaxy of artists, including Ray Charles, Ruth Brown, the Drifters, Joe Turner, LaVerne Baker, and the Clovers. Chess, in Chicago, had the blues-based singer-songwriter-guitarists Chuck Berry and Bo Diddley, as well as the "doo-wop" group the Moonglows. In New Orleans, Imperial recorded the veteran pianist-singer Fats Domino, while Specialty unleashed on the world the outrageous Little Richard. On radio, over jukeboxes, and in record stores, all these African American artists "crossed over," adding millions of white teenagers to their solid base of black fans. In 1954, the music trade magazine *Billboard* noted a trend among white teenagers; "The present generation has not known the rhythmically exciting dance bands of the swing era. It therefore satisfies its hunger for 'music with a beat' in modern r&b (rhythm and blues) groups."

The older, more established record companies had largely ignored black music. They responded to the new trend with slick, toned-down "cover" versions of rhythm and blues originals by white pop singers. These were invariably pallid, artistically inferior imitations. While African American artists began to enjoy newfound mass acceptance, there were limits to how closely white kids could identify with black performers. Racism, especially in so sexually charged an arena as musical performance, was a powerful force in American life. The major labels' superior promotional power, as well as institutional racism in the music business, ensured that white cover versions almost always outsold the black originals. At live shows, however, white and black teenagers often listened and danced together to the music of African American performers. Alan Freed, a white Cleveland disc jockey, popularized the term *rock 'n' roll* to describe the black rhythm and blues that he played on the air and promoted in live concerts before enthusiastic, racially mixed teen audiences.

The stage was thus set for the arrival of white rock 'n' roll artists who could exploit the new sounds and styles. As a rock 'n' roll performer and recording artist, Elvis Presley reinvented American popular music. His success challenged the old lines separating black music from white and pop from rhythm and blues or country. As a symbol of rebellious youth and as the embodiment of youthful sexuality, Elvis revitalized American popular culture. In his wake came a host of white rock 'n' rollers, many (like him) white Southerners: Jerry Lee Lewis, Buddy Holly, the Everly Brothers, and Roy Orbison. The greatest songwriter and most influential guitarist to emerge from this first "golden age of rock 'n' roll" was Berry, an African American from St. Louis who worked part-time as a beautician and house painter. With humor, irony, and passion, Berry proved especially adept at capturing the teen spirit. Composing hits around the trials and tribulations of school ("School Days"), young love ("Memphis"), and cars ("Maybellene"), Berry created music that defined what it meant to be young in postwar America.

"GO, JOHNNY, GO!" Poster advertising one of the many rock 'n' roll exploitation movies, churned out by Hollywood in an effort to capitalize on the new teenage music craze. Despite the fact that these movies had flimsy plots and were made on the cheap, fans jumped at the chance to see performances by rock 'n' roll stars, here including Chuck Berry, The Cadillacs, Ritchie Valens, and Jackie Wilson.

Everett Collection, Inc./Alamy Stock Photo.

27.3.3 Almost Grown

Teenage consumers remade into their own turf the landscape of popular music. The dollar value of annual record sales nearly tripled between 1954 and 1959, from $213 million to $603 million. New magazines aimed exclusively at teens flourished in the postwar years, focusing on the rituals, pleasures, and sorrows surrounding teenage courtship. Paradoxically, behavior patterns among white middle-class teenagers in the 1950s and early 1960s exhibited a new kind of youth orientation and at the same time a more pronounced identification with adults.

While parents were worrying about the separate world inhabited by their teenage children, many teens seemed determined to become adults as quickly as possible. Postwar affluence multiplied the number of two-car families, making it easier for 16-year-olds to win driving privileges formerly reserved for 18-year-olds. Girls began dating, wearing brassieres and nylon stockings, and using cosmetics at an earlier age than before—12 or 13 rather than 15 or 16. Several factors contributed to this trend, including a continuing decline in the age of menarche (first menstruation), the sharp drop in the age of marriage after World War II, and the precocious social climate of junior high schools (institutions that became widespread only after 1945). "Going steady," derived from the college custom of fraternity and sorority pinning, became commonplace among high schoolers. By the late 1950s, 18 had become the most common age at which American females married. Teenagers often felt torn between their identification with youth culture and pressures to assume adult responsibilities—a dilemma for which teen-oriented magazines, music, and movies routinely dispensed advice and sympathy.

27.3.4 Deviance and Delinquency

Many adults blamed rock 'n' roll for the apparent decline of parental control over teens. Much of the opposition to rock 'n' roll, particularly in the South, played on long-standing racist fears of white females being attracted to black music and black performers. The undercurrent beneath all this opposition was a deep anxiety over the more open expression of sexual feelings by both performers and audiences.

Paralleling the rise of rock 'n' roll was a growing concern with an alleged increase in juvenile delinquency. An endless stream of magazine articles, books, and newspaper stories asserted that criminal behavior among the nation's young was chronic. Gang fights, drug and alcohol abuse, car theft, and sexual offenses drew the most attention. The U.S. Senate established a special subcommittee on juvenile delinquency. Highly publicized hearings in 1955 and 1956 convinced much of the public that youthful criminals were terrorizing the country. Although crime statistics do suggest an increase in juvenile crime during the 1950s, particularly in the suburbs, the public perception of the severity of the problem was surely exaggerated.

In retrospect, the juvenile delinquency controversy tells us more about anxieties over family life and the erosion of adult authority than about crime patterns. Teenagers seemed more defined by and loyal to their peer culture than to their parents. A great deal of their music, speech, dress, and style seemed alien and threatening. The growing importance of the mass media in defining youth culture brought efforts to regulate or censor media forms believed to cause juvenile delinquency. In 1954, for example, psychiatrist Fredric Wertham published *Seduction of the Innocent*, arguing that crime comic books incited youngsters to criminal acts. Mass culture, he believed, could overwhelm the traditional influences of family, school, and religion. He led a highly publicized crusade that forced the comic book industry to adopt a code strictly limiting the portrayal of violence and crime.

As reactions to two of the most influential "problem youth" movies of the postwar era indicate, teens and their parents frequently interpreted depictions of youthful deviance in the mass media in very different ways. In *The Wild One* (1954), Marlon Brando played the crude, moody leader of a vicious motorcycle gang. Most adults thought of the film as a critique of mindless gang violence, but many teenagers identified with the Brando character, who, when asked, "What are you rebelling against?" coolly replied, "Whattaya got?" In *Rebel Without a Cause* (1955), James Dean, Natalie Wood, and Sal Mineo played emotionally troubled youths in an affluent California suburb. The movie suggests that parents can cause delinquency when they fail to conform to conventional roles—Dean's father does housework wearing an apron, and his mother is domineering.

Elvis, Brando, and Dean (who died in a car crash at the height of his popularity) were probably the most popular and widely imitated teen idols of the era. For most parents, they were vaguely threatening figures whose sexual energy and lack of discipline placed them outside the bounds of middle-class respectability. For teens, however, they offered an irresistible combination of rough exterior and sensitive core. They embodied, as well, the contradiction of individual rebellion versus the attractions of a community defined by youth.

27.4 Mass Culture and Its Discontents

How did television transform American culture?

No mass medium ever achieved such power and popularity as rapidly as television. The basic technology for broadcasting visual images with sound had been developed by the late 1930s, but World War II and corporate competition postponed television's introduction to the public until 1946. By 1960, nearly nine in ten American families owned at least one set, which was turned on an average of more than five

1950'S FAMILY WATCHING TELEVISION Manufacturers designed and marketed TV sets as living room furniture and emphasized their role in fostering family togetherness.

Pictorial Press Ltd/Alamy Stock Photo.

hours a day. Television reshaped leisure time and political life. It also helped create a new kind of national community defined by the buying and selling of consumer goods.

Dissident voices challenged the economic trends and cultural conformity of the postwar years. Academics, journalists, novelists, and poets offered a variety of works criticizing the overall direction of American life. These critics of what was dubbed "mass society" were troubled by the premium American culture put on conformity, status, and material consumption. Although a distinct minority, these critics were persistent. Many of their ideas and prescriptions would reverberate throughout the political and cultural upheavals of the 1960s and 1970s, and even into the "culture wars" of the 1980s and beyond.

27.4.1 Television: Tube of Plenty

Television was a radical change from radio, and its development as a mass medium was quicker and less chaotic. The three main television networks—NBC, CBS, and ABC—grew directly from radio corporations. The networks led the industry from the start, rather than following individual stations, as radio had done. Nearly all TV stations were affiliated with one or more of the networks; only a handful of independent stations struggled for survival.

Television not only depended on advertising, but it also transformed the advertising industry. The television business, like radio, was based on the selling of time to advertisers who wanted to reach the mass audiences tuning into specific shows. Radio had offered entire shows produced by and for single sponsors. But the higher costs of television production forced key changes. Sponsors left the production of programs to the networks, independent producers, and Hollywood studios.

Sponsors bought scattered time slots for spot advertisements instead of bankrolling an entire show. Ad agencies switched their creative energy to producing slick 30-second commercials rather than entertainment programs. A shift from broadcasting shows live to filming them opened up lucrative opportunities for reruns and exports. The total net revenue of the TV networks and their affiliated stations in 1947 was about $2 million; by 1957 it was nearly $1 billion.

The staple of network radio, the comedy-variety show, was now produced visually. The first great national TV hit, *The Milton Berle Show*, followed this format when it premiered in 1948. Radio stars such as Jack Benny, Edgar Bergen, George Burns and Gracie Allen, and Eddie Cantor switched successfully to television. Boxing, wrestling, roller derby, and other sporting events were also quite popular. For a brief time, original live drama flourished on writer-oriented shows such as *Goodyear Television Playhouse* and *Studio One*. In addition, early television featured an array of situation comedies with deep roots in radio and vaudeville.

Set largely among urban ethnic families, early shows like *I Remember Mama*, *The Goldbergs*, *The Life of Riley*, *Life with Luigi*, and *The Honeymooners* often featured working-class families struggling with the dilemmas posed by a consumer society. Most plots turned around comic tensions created and resolved by consumption: contemplating home ownership, going out on the town, moving to the suburbs, buying on credit, or purchasing a new car. Generational discord and the loss of ethnic identity were also common themes. To some degree, these early shows mirrored and spoke to the real dilemmas facing families that had survived the Great Depression and World War II and were trying to find their place in a prosperous consumer culture.

By the late 1950s, all the urban ethnic comedy shows were off the air. A new breed of situation comedies presented non-ethnic white, affluent, and insular suburban middle-class families. Shows like *Father Knows Best*, *Leave It to Beaver*, *The Adventures of Ozzie and Harriet*, and *The Donna Reed Show* epitomized the ideal suburban American family of the day. Their plots focused on genial crises, usually brought on by children's mischief or wives' inability to cope with money matters, but patiently resolved by

DAVY CROCKETT Fess Parker, the actor who starred as Davy Crockett in Walt Disney's popular television series, greets young fans at New York's Idlewild Airport in 1955. The series generated enormous sales of coonskin caps and other Crockett-inspired merchandise, demonstrating the extraordinary selling power of the new medium of television.

Bettmann/Getty Images.

kindly fathers. In retrospect, what is most striking about these shows is what is absent: Virtually unrepresented were politics, social issues, cities, white ethnic groups, African Americans, and Latinos.

Television also demonstrated a unique ability to create overnight fads and crazes across the nation. Elvis Presley's 1956 appearances on several network television variety shows, including those hosted by Milton Berle and Ed Sullivan, catapulted him from regional success to international stardom. A memorable example of TV's influence came in 1955 when Walt Disney produced a series of three one-hour shows on the life of frontier legend Davy Crockett. The tremendous success of the series instantly created a $300 million industry of Davy Crockett shirts, dolls, toys, and "coonskin" caps.

27.4.2 Television and Politics

Prime-time entertainment shows carefully avoided any references to the political issues of the day. Network executives bowed to the conformist climate created by the Cold War. Any hint of political controversy could scare off sponsors, ever wary of public protest. Anti-Communist crusaders set themselves up as private watchdogs, warning of alleged subversive influence in the broadcasting industry. Television and advertising executives responded by effectively blacklisting many talented individuals.

As in Hollywood, the Cold War chill severely restricted the range of political discussion on television. Any honest treatment of the conflicts in American society threatened the consensus mentality at the heart of the television business. Even public affairs and documentary programs were largely devoid of substantial political debate. An important exception was journalist Edward R. Murrow's *See It Now* on CBS—but that show was off the air by 1955. Television news did not come into its own until 1963, with the beginning of half-hour nightly network newscasts. Only then did television's extraordinary power to rivet the nation's attention during a crisis become clear.

Some of the ways that TV would alter the nation's political life were already emerging in the 1950s. Television made Democratic Senator Estes Kefauver of Tennessee a national political figure through live coverage of his 1951 Senate investigation into organized crime. In 1952, Republican vice presidential candidate Nixon's rambling, emotionally manipulative television appeal to voters—the famous "Checkers Speech" (see Chapter 26)—saved his career.

The 1952 election brought the first use of TV political advertising for presidential candidates. The Republican Party hired a high-powered ad agency, Batten, Barton, Durstine & Osborn (BBD&O), to create a series of short, sophisticated advertisements touting Ike. The BBD&O campaign saturated TV with 20-second Eisenhower spots for two weeks before Election Day. Ever since, television image-making—and the fund raising needed to pay for it—has been the single most important element in American electoral politics.

27.4.3 Culture Critics

Critics argued that the audiences for the mass media were atomized, anonymous, and detached. The media themselves had become omnipotent, capable of manipulating the attitudes and behavior of the isolated individuals in the mass. Many of these critics achieved great popularity themselves, suggesting that the public was deeply ambivalent about mass culture. One of the best-selling authors of the day was Vance Packard, whose 1957 exposé *The Hidden Persuaders* showed how advertisers exploited motivational research into the irrational side of human behavior. These critics undoubtedly overestimated the media's power. They ignored the preponderance of research suggesting that most people watched and responded to mass media in family, peer-group, and other social settings. The critics also missed the genuine vitality and creative brilliance to be found within mass culture: African American music; the films of Nicholas Ray, Elia Kazan, and Howard Hawks; the experimental television of Ernie Kovacs; and the madcap satire of teen-oriented *Mad* magazine.

Some of the sharpest dissents from the cultural conformity of the day came from a group of writers known collectively as the **Beats**. Led by the novelist Jack Kerouac and the poet Allen Ginsberg, the Beats shared a distrust of the American virtues of progress, power, and material gain. The Beats' sensibility celebrated spontaneity, friendship, jazz, open sexuality, drug use, and the outcasts of American society. Kerouac, born into and raised by a working-class French Canadian family in Lowell, Massachusetts, coined the term *beat* in 1948. It meant for him, "weariness with all the forms of the modern industrial state"—conformity, militarism, blind faith in technological progress. Kerouac's 1957 novel *On the Road*, chronicling the tumultuous adventures of Kerouac's circle of friends as they traveled by car back and forth across America, became the Beat manifesto.

Allen Ginsberg had grown up in New Jersey in an immigrant Jewish family. After being expelled from Columbia University, Ginsberg grew close to Kerouac and another writer, William Burroughs. At a 1955 poetry reading in San Francisco, Ginsberg read—actually, chanted—his epic poem *Howl* to a wildly enthusiastic audience. The poem captured perfectly the anger and anxiety of Ginsburg and many of his fellow Beats.

Howl became one of the best-selling poetry books in the history of publishing, and it established Ginsberg as an important new voice in American literature.

Beat writers received a largely antagonistic, even virulent reception from the literary establishment, and the mass media soon trivialized them. A San Francisco journalist coined the word *beatnik*, which by the late 1950s had become popularly associated with scruffy, bearded men and promiscuous women, all dressed in black, sporting sunglasses and berets, and acting rebellious and alienated. By challenging America's official culture, however, Beat writers foreshadowed the mass youth rebellion and counterculture of the 1960s.

27.5 The Coming of the New Frontier

How did the Cold War shape the Kennedy presidency?

In personality, temperament, and public image, no one could have less resembled Dwight Eisenhower—or, for that matter, the beatniks—than John Fitzgerald Kennedy. The handsome son of a prominent, wealthy Irish American diplomat, and married to a fashionable, trendsetting heiress, 42-year-old JFK embodied youth, excitement, and sophistication. As only the second Catholic candidate for president—the first was Al Smith in 1928—Kennedy ran under the banner of his self-proclaimed **New Frontier** His liberalism inspired idealism and hope in millions of young people at home and abroad, and his presidency seemed to embody the call for a new sense of national purpose beyond simply enjoying affluence. In foreign affairs, Kennedy generally followed, and in some respects deepened, the Cold War precepts that dominated postwar policymaking. But by the time of his assassination in 1963, he may have been veering away from the hard-line anti-Communist ideology he had earlier embraced.

27.5.1 The Election of 1960

John F. Kennedy's political career began in Massachusetts, which elected him to the U.S. House in 1946 and then the Senate in 1952. Kennedy won the Democratic nomination after a bruising series of primaries in which he defeated party stalwarts Hubert Humphrey of Minnesota and Lyndon B. Johnson of Texas. Vice President Richard M. Nixon, the Republican presidential nominee, had faithfully served the Eisenhower administration for eight years and was far better known than his younger opponent. The Kennedy campaign stressed its candidate's youth and his war-hero image. During his World War II tour of duty in the Pacific, Kennedy had bravely rescued one of his crew after their PT boat had been sunk. Kennedy's supporters made much

of his intellectual ability. JFK had won the Pulitzer Prize in 1957 for his book *Profiles in Courage*, which in fact had been written largely by his aides.

The 1960 election featured the first televised presidential debates. Political analysts have long argued over the impact of these four encounters, but agree that they moved television to the center of presidential politics, making image and appearance more critical than ever. Nixon, just recovering from illness, looked nervous, and heat from studio lights made his makeup run and his jowls look unshaven. Kennedy benefited from a confident manner, telegenic good looks, and less propensity to sweat. Both candidates emphasized foreign policy. Nixon defended the Republican record and stressed his maturity and experience. Kennedy hammered away at the alleged—but nonexistent—"missile gap" with the Soviet Union and promised executive leadership full of vigor. ("Vigah," he said in the Boston accent that became his trademark.)

Kennedy squeaked to victory (see Map 27.2), winning the popular vote by a little more than 100,000 out of nearly 69 million cast. By solemnly promising to keep church and state separate, he had countered residual anti-Catholic prejudice among conservative Protestants and suspicious liberals. Although his margin of victory was tiny, Kennedy was a glorious winner. Surrounding himself with prestigious Ivy League academics, Hollywood movie stars, and talented artists and writers, he imbued the presidency with

Map 27.2 THE ELECTION OF 1960

Numbers on states represent Electoral Votes.	Electoral Vote (%)	Popular Vote (%)
JOHN F. KENNEDY (K) (Democrat)	303 (56)	34,227,096 (49.7)
Richard M. Nixon (N) (Republican)	219 (41)	34,108,546 (49.5)
Harry F. Byrd (B) (Independent)	15 (3)	501,643 (0.7)

Kennedy's popular vote margin over Nixon was only a little more than 100,000, making this one of the closest elections in American history.

KENNEDY-NIXON PRESIDENTIAL DEBATE Presidential candidates John F. Kennedy and Richard M. Nixon during the second of four televised debates held during the 1960 election campaign. Moderator Frank McGee sits at a desk upstage, facing a panel of newsmen. Eighty-five million viewers watched at least one of the first-ever televised debates, which both reflected and increased the power of television in the electoral process.

Bettmann/Getty Images.

an aura of celebrity. The inauguration brought out a bevy of poets, musicians, and fashionably dressed politicians from around the world. The new administration promised to be exciting and stylish, a modern-day Camelot peopled by heroic young men and beautiful women. The new president's ringing inaugural address ("Ask not what your country can do for you—ask what you can do for your country") resonated through a whole generation of young Americans.

Just before Kennedy took office, President Eisenhower delivered a televised farewell address that included a stark and unexpected warning against what he called (coining a phrase) "the military-industrial complex." Throughout the 1950s, the small numbers of peace advocates in the United States had pointed to the ultimate illogic of Ike's "new look" in national-defense policy. Increasing reliance on nuclear weapons, they argued, did not strengthen national security—it threatened the entire planet with extinction. Peace advocates had demonstrated at military camps, nuclear-test sites, and missile-launching ranges, often getting arrested to make their point. Reports of radioactive fallout around the globe rallied a larger group of scientists and prominent intellectuals against further nuclear testing. Small but well-publicized actions protesting civil defense drills were led by groups such as National Committee for a Sane Nuclear Policy (SANE) and Women Strike for Peace in several big cities.

Eisenhower came to share some of the protesters' anxiety and doubts about the arms race, because he had found it difficult to rein in the "new look" system he helped create. Frustrated—and disturbed by the incoming Democrats' demands for increased military spending to close the "missile gap"—he used his farewell address to express alarm at the growing influence of a large military and defense-industry establishment. "We annually spend on military security more than the net income of all United States corporations," Eisenhower warned the country. "This conjunction of an immense military establishment and a large arms industry is new in the American experience. The total influence—economic, political, even spiritual—is felt in every city, every State house, every office of the Federal government. . . . Our toil, resources and livelihood are all involved; so is the very structure of our society."

The old soldier understood better than most the dangers of raw military force, and in later years, critics of American foreign policy and budget priorities would adapt the sentiments behind this language. Eisenhower's public posture of restraint and caution in foreign affairs accompanied an enormous expansion of American economic, diplomatic, and military strength. Yet the Eisenhower years also demonstrated the limits of power and intervention in a world that did not always conform to the simple dualistic assumptions of Cold War ideology.

27.5.2 New Frontier Liberalism

As president, Kennedy promised to revive the liberal domestic agenda, stalled since Truman's presidency. His New Frontier advocated such liberal programs as medical care for the elderly, greater federal aid for education and public housing, raising Social Security benefits and the minimum wage, and various antipoverty measures. Yet the thin margin of his victory and stubborn opposition by conservative southern Democrats in Congress made it difficult to achieve these goals. Congress blocked the administration's attempt to extend Social Security and unemployment benefits to millions of uncovered workers. Congress also failed to enact administration proposals for aid to public schools, mass-transit subsidies, and medical insurance for retired workers over 65.

There were a few New Frontier achievements: modest increases in the minimum wage (to $1.25 per hour), Social Security benefits, and $5 billion appropriated for public housing. The Manpower Retraining Act provided $435 million to train the unemployed. The Area Redevelopment Act provided federal funds for rural, depressed Appalachia. The Higher Education Act of 1963 offered aid to colleges for constructing buildings and upgrading libraries.

The Peace Corps was the New Frontier's best-publicized initiative. It sent thousands of mostly young men and women overseas for two-year stints to provide technical and educational assistance to underdeveloped Third World countries. Volunteers set up health care programs, helped villagers modernize farm technology, and taught English. As a force for change, the Peace Corps produced modest results, but it epitomized Kennedy's promise to provide opportunities for service for a new generation of idealistic young people.

Kennedy's Presidential Commission on the Status of Women, led by Eleanor Roosevelt, helped revive attention to women's rights issues. The Commission's 1963 report was the most comprehensive study of women's lives ever produced by the federal government. It documented the ongoing discrimination faced by American women in the workplace and in the legal system, as well as the inadequacy of social services such as daycare. It called for federally supported daycare programs, continuing-education programs for women, and an end to sex bias in Social Security and unemployment benefits. The **Equal Pay Act of 1963**, a direct result of the Commission's work, mandated equal wages for men and women employed in industries engaged in interstate commerce. Kennedy also directed executive agencies to prohibit sex discrimination in hiring and promotion. The work of the Commission contributed to a new generation of women's rights activism.

Kennedy took a more aggressive stance on stimulating economic growth and creating new jobs than had Eisenhower. The administration pushed lower business taxes through Congress, even at the cost of a higher federal deficit. The Revenue Act of 1962 encouraged new investment and plant renovation by easing tax depreciation schedules for businesses. Kennedy also gained approval for lower U.S. tariffs as a way to increase foreign trade. To help keep

inflation down, he intervened in the steel industry in 1961 and 1962, pressuring labor to keep its wage demands low and management to curb price increases.

A wholly new realm of government spending also won Kennedy's enthusiastic backing: the space program. The **National Aeronautics and Space Administration (NASA)** had been established in reaction to *Sputnik*, and in 1961, Kennedy pushed through a greatly expanded space program. Dramatically, he announced the goal of landing an American on the moon by the end of the decade. NASA eventually spent $33 billion before reaching this objective in 1969. This program of manned space flight—the *Apollo* missions, with their science fiction aura—appealed to the public.

Kennedy's longest-lasting achievement as president may have been his strengthening of the executive branch itself. He insisted on direct presidential control of details that Eisenhower had left to advisers and appointees. Moreover, under Kennedy the White House staff assumed many of the decision-making and advisory functions previously held by cabinet members. This arrangement increased Kennedy's authority, since these appointees, unlike cabinet secretaries, escaped congressional oversight and confirmation proceedings. White House aides lacked independent constituencies; their power derived solely from their ties to the president. Kennedy's aides—"the best and the brightest," he called them—dominated policymaking. Kennedy intensified a pattern whereby American presidents increasingly operated through small groups of fiercely loyal aides, often in secret.

27.5.3 Kennedy and the Cold War

During Kennedy's three years as president, his approach to foreign policy shifted from aggressive containment to efforts at easing U.S./Soviet tensions. Certainly when he first entered office, Kennedy and his chief aides saw their main task as confronting the Communist threat. In his first State of the Union Address, Kennedy told Congress that America must seize the initiative in the Cold War. The nation must "move outside the home fortress, and . . . challenge the enemy in fields of our own choosing." To head the State Department, Kennedy chose Dean Rusk, a conservative former assistant to Truman's secretary of state, Dean Acheson. Secretary of Defense Robert McNamara, a Republican and Ford executive, was determined to streamline military procedures and weapons buying; he typified the technical, cost-efficient, hyperrational approach to policymaking. These and other high officials believed, with Kennedy, that Eisenhower had timidly accepted stalemate when the Cold War could have been won.

Between 1960 and 1962, defense appropriations increased by nearly a third, from $43 billion to $56 billion.

JFK expanded Eisenhower's policy of covert operations, deploying the Army's elite Special Forces to supplement covert CIA operations against Third World guerrillas. These soldiers, fighting under the direct orders of the president, could provide "rapid response" to "brush-fire" conflicts where Soviet influence threatened American interests. The Special Forces, authorized by Kennedy to wear the green berets that gave them their unofficial name, reflected the president's desire to acquire greater flexibility, secrecy, and independence in the conduct of foreign policy.

But incidents in Southeast Asia showed there were limits to advancing American interests with covert actions and Green Berets. In Laos, the United States had ignored the 1954 Geneva agreement and installed a friendly, CIA-backed military regime, but it could not defeat Soviet-supported Pathet Lao guerrillas. The president had to arrange with the Soviets to neutralize Laos. In neighboring South Vietnam, a more difficult situation developed when Communist Vietcong guerrillas launched an insurgency against the United States-supported Diem regime. Kennedy began sending hundreds of Green Berets and other military advisers to bolster Diem. In May 1961, in response to North Vietnamese aid to the Vietcong, Kennedy ordered a covert action against Ho Chi Minh's northern regime that included sabotage and intelligence gathering.

Kennedy's approach to Vietnam reflected an analysis of the situation in that country by two aides, General Maxwell Taylor and Walt Rostow, who saw things solely through Cold War spectacles. "The Communists are pursuing a clear and systematic strategy in Southeast Asia," Taylor and Rostow concluded, ignoring the inefficiency, corruption, and unpopularity of the Diem government. By 1963, with Diem's army unable to contain the Vietcong rebellion, Kennedy had sent nearly 16,000 support and combat troops to South Vietnam. At that time, a wide spectrum of South Vietnamese society had joined the revolt against the hated Diem, including highly respected Buddhist monks and their students. Americans watched in horror as evening newscasts showed Buddhists burning themselves to death on the streets of Saigon—the ultimate protest against Diem's repressive rule. American press and television also reported the mounting casualty lists of U.S. forces in Vietnam. The South Vietnamese army, bloated by U.S. aid and weakened by corruption, continued to disintegrate. In the fall of 1963, American military officers and CIA operatives stood aside with approval as a group of Vietnamese generals toppled Diem, killing him and his top advisers. It was the first of many coups that racked the South Vietnamese government over the next few years.

In Latin America, where millions of impoverished peasants were forced to relocate to already-overcrowded cities, various revolutionary movements were also gaining ground—and Kennedy looked for ways to forestall them. In 1961, he unveiled the **Alliance for Progress**, a 10-year, $100 billion plan to spur economic development in Latin America. The United States committed $20 billion to the project, with the Latin nations responsible for the rest. The main goals included greater industrial growth and agricultural productivity, a more equitable distribution of income, and improved health and housing.

Kennedy saw the Alliance for Progress as a Marshall Plan that would benefit Latin America's poor and middle classes. It did help raise growth rates in Latin American economies. But the expansion in export crops and in consumption by the tiny upper class did little to aid the poor or encourage democracy. The United States hesitated to challenge the dictators and extreme conservatives who were its staunchly anti-Communist allies. Thus, the alliance soon degenerated into just another foreign-aid program, incapable of generating genuine social change.

27.5.4 The Cuban Revolution and the Bay of Pigs

The direct impetus for the Alliance for Progress was the 1959 Cuban Revolution, which loomed over Latin America—inspiring the left and alarming the right. The U.S. economic domination of Cuba, beginning with the Spanish-American War (see Chapter 20), had continued through the 1950s. American-owned businesses controlled all of Cuba's oil production, 90 percent of its mines, and roughly half of its railroads and sugar and cattle industries. Havana, the island's capital, was an attractive tourist center for Americans, but U.S. crime syndicates shared control—with dictator Fulgencio Batista—of the island's lucrative gambling, prostitution, and drug trades. As a response, in the early 1950s a peasant-based revolutionary movement, led by a middle-class student named Fidel Castro, began gaining strength in the rural districts and mountains outside Havana.

On New Year's Day 1959, after years of guerrilla war, the rebels entered Havana and, amid great public rejoicing, seized power. For a brief time, Castro seemed a hero in North America as well. The *New York Times* had conducted sympathetic interviews with Castro in 1958, while he was still fighting in Cuba's mountains. The CIA and President Eisenhower shared none of this exuberance. Castro's land-reform program, involving the seizure of acreage from the tiny minority that controlled much of the fertile land, threatened to set an example for other Latin American countries. Although Castro had not yet joined the Cuban Communist Party, he turned to the Soviet Union after the United States withdrew economic aid. He began to sell sugar to the Soviets and soon nationalized American-owned oil companies and other enterprises. Eisenhower established an economic boycott of Cuba in 1960 and then severed diplomatic relations.

Kennedy inherited from Eisenhower plans for a U.S. invasion of Cuba, including the secret arming and training of Cuban exiles. The CIA drafted the invasion plan, which was based on the assumption that a United States–led invasion would trigger a popular uprising and bring down Castro. Kennedy went along with the plan, but at the last moment decided not to supply Air Force cover for the invaders. On April 17, 1961, a ragtag army of 1,400 counter-revolutionaries led by CIA operatives landed at the **Bay of Pigs** on Cuba's southern coast. Castro's efficient and loyal army easily subdued them.

The debacle revealed that the CIA, blinded by Cold War assumptions, had failed to understand the Cuban Revolution. There was no popular uprising against Castro. An embarrassed Kennedy reluctantly took the blame for the disaster, and his administration was censured time and again by Third World delegates in the United Nations. American liberals criticized Kennedy for plotting Castro's overthrow, while conservatives blamed him for not supporting the invasion. Despite the failure, Kennedy remained committed to getting rid of Castro.

The botched invasion had strengthened Fidel's standing among the urban poor and peasants, already attracted by his programs of universal literacy and medical care. As Castro stifled internal opposition, many Cuban intellectuals and professionals fled to the United States. These middle-class émigrés would transform Miami from a

retirement resort into a bustling entrepreneurial center, but the growing Cuban presence in electoral-vote-rich Florida also created a powerful lobby for rigid anti-Castro U.S. policies. Even before the end of Kennedy's administration, the CIA's support for anti-Castro operations included at least eight attempts to assassinate Fidel, and the U.S. economic embargo against Cuba continues to this day.

27.5.5 The 1962 Missile Crisis

The aftermath of the Bay of Pigs led to the Cold War's most serious superpower confrontation: the **Cuban missile crisis** of October 1962. Frightened by U.S. belligerency, Castro asked Soviet Premier Khrushchev for military help. Khrushchev responded in the summer of 1962 by shipping to Cuba a large amount of sophisticated weaponry, including intermediate-range nuclear missiles capable of hitting Washington, D.C.; the Northeast; and the Midwest. In early October, American U-2 reconnaissance planes found camouflaged missile silos dotting the island. Several Kennedy aides and the Joint Chiefs of Staff demanded an immediate bombing of these missile sites, arguing that the Soviet move had decisively eroded the United States's strategic global advantage. The president and his advisers pondered their options in a series of tense meetings. Kennedy's aggressive attempts to exploit Cuba in the 1960 election and the Bay of Pigs disaster came back to haunt him: He worried that critics would accuse him of weakness in failing to stand up to the Soviets.

KENNEDY ADDRESSES THE NATION
Shoppers in an appliance store watch President John F. Kennedy deliver an address to the nation during the Cuban missile crisis in October 1962. Kennedy's presidency coincided with the emergence of television as the nation's dominant mass medium.

Ralph Crane/Getty Images.

Kennedy went on national television on October 22 to announce the discovery of the missile sites. He publicly demanded the removal of all missiles and proclaimed a naval "quarantine" of offensive military equipment shipped to Cuba. (This was actually a blockade; Kennedy avoided the word because a blockade is an act of war.) Requesting an emergency meeting of the UN Security Council, he promised that any missiles launched from Cuba would bring "a full retaliatory response upon the Soviet Union." For a grim week, Americans wondered whether the long-dreaded nuclear Armageddon was imminent. Eyeball to eyeball, each superpower waited for the other to blink. On October 26 and 27, Khrushchev blinked, ordering 25 Soviet ships off their course to Cuba, thus avoiding a challenge to the U.S. Navy.

Khrushchev offered to remove the missiles in return for a pledge from the United States not to invade Cuba and later added a demand for removal of American weapons from Turkey, which is as close to the Soviet Union as Cuba is to the United States. Secretly, Kennedy assured Khrushchev that the United States would dismantle its obsolete missiles in Turkey. On November 20, after weeks of delicate negotiations, Kennedy announced the withdrawal of Soviet missiles and bombers from Cuba. He also pledged to respect Cuban sovereignty and promised not to invade the island.

The crisis had passed. The Soviets, determined not to be intimidated again, began the largest weapons buildup in their history. For his part, Kennedy, perhaps chastened by this brush with nuclear disaster, made important gestures toward peaceful coexistence with the Soviets. In a June 1963 address at American University, Kennedy called for a rethinking of Cold War diplomacy. Both sides, he said, had been "caught up in a vicious and dangerous cycle in which suspicion on one side breeds suspicion on the other, and new weapons beget counterweapons."

Shortly after, Washington and Moscow set up a "hot line"—a direct phone connection to permit instant communication during times of crisis. More substantial was the **Limited Nuclear Test-Ban Treaty**, signed in August 1963 by the United States, the Soviet Union, and Great Britain. The treaty prohibited above-ground, outer-space, and underwater nuclear weapons tests, easing global anxieties about radioactive fallout. But underground testing continued to accelerate for years. The limited test ban was perhaps more symbolic than substantive, a psychological breakthrough in East-West relations after three particularly tense years.

By November 1963, the situation in South Vietnam was deteriorating; Diem's overthrow and murder in a United States-backed coup was symptomatic of U.S. failure to secure an anti-Communist alternative to Ho Chi Minh's revolutionary movement. Kennedy understood this. There are some indications that he was thinking of cutting losses, perhaps after winning reelection in 1964; there are other signs that he was preparing to escalate the U.S. commitment. Most likely, he meant to keep all options open. But we will never know what he would have done about Vietnam.

27.5.6 The Assassination of President Kennedy

The assassination of John F. Kennedy in Dallas on November 22, 1963, sent the entire nation into shock and mourning. Just 46 years old and president for only three years, Kennedy quickly ascended to martyrdom in the nation's consciousness. Millions had identified his strengths—intelligence, optimism, wit, charm, and coolness under fire—as those of American society. In life, Kennedy had helped put television at the center of American politics. In the aftermath of his death, television riveted a badly shocked nation. One day after the assassination, the president's accused killer, an obscure misfit named Lee Harvey Oswald, was himself gunned down before television cameras covering his arraignment in Dallas. Two days later, tens of millions watched the televised spectacle of Kennedy's funeral, trying to make sense of the brutal murder. (See SEEING History.) Although a special commission headed by Chief Justice Earl Warren found the killing to be the work of Oswald acting alone, many Americans doubted this conclusion. Kennedy's death gave rise to a host of conspiracy theories, none of which seems provable.

We will never know, of course, what Kennedy might have achieved in a second term. In his 1,037 days as president, he demonstrated a capacity to change and grow in office. Having gone to the brink during the missile crisis, he managed to launch new initiatives toward peaceful coexistence. At the time of his death, relations between the United States and the Soviet Union were more amicable than they had been at any time since the end of World War II. Much of the domestic liberal agenda of the New Frontier would be finally implemented by Kennedy's successor, Lyndon B. Johnson, who dreamed of creating a Great Society.

SEEING History

Televising a National Tragedy

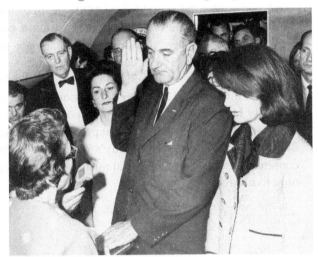

Historical/Getty Images.

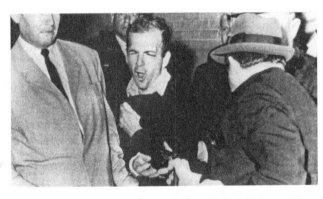

Pictorial Press Ltd/Alamy Stock Photo.

George Silk/Getty Images.

The assassination of President John F. Kennedy on Friday, November 22, 1963, marked the emerging power of television as a medium capable of focusing the entire nation's attention on an extraordinary news event.

Kennedy had traveled to Texas on November 21 to shore up popularity in a state crucial to his reelection hopes for 1964. Only local stations covered the presidential arrival and motorcade. But once the president had been shot and declared dead, the networks cut into regular programming, combining live coverage with videotape from local stations. The hasty inauguration of Vice President Lyndon B. Johnson aboard *Air Force One* was not televised, but widespread dissemination of still photos showed Americans how the constitutional process of succession proceeded side by side with the personal grief of the president's widow, Jacqueline Kennedy.

The next day, Saturday, audiences watched television coverage of world leaders arriving in Washington, D.C., for the presidential funeral. On Sunday, NBC offered live coverage of the accused assassin, Lee Harvey Oswald, being transferred from police custody to the county jail. Millions were stunned to suddenly see Jack Ruby, a shadowy Dallas underworld figure,

emerge from the crowd and shoot Oswald himself to death—the first nationally televised murder.

On Monday, November 25, virtually the entire nation watched Kennedy's televised funeral: the ceremony at the National Cathedral and the procession to Arlington National Cemetery. The images of the Kennedy family, especially five-year-old Caroline and three-year-old John Jr. saluting, lent a quiet dignity amid deep mourning. Critic Marya Mannes wrote of the four days of television coverage, "This was not viewing. This was total involvement. . . . I stayed before the set, knowing—as millions knew—that I must give myself over entirely to an appalling tragedy, and that to evade it was a treason of the spirit."

- **What strikes you as most powerful about these images from more than four decades ago?**

- **Can you think of any recent national events that have brought the nation together via television coverage?**

- **How has that coverage changed—or remained similar—in terms of both techniques and subjects covered?**

Conclusion

America in 1963 still enjoyed its postwar economic boom. To be sure, millions of Americans, particularly African Americans and Latinos, did not share in the good times. But millions had managed to reach the middle class since the early 1950s. An expanding economy, cheap energy, government subsidies, and dominance in the global marketplace had made the "the good life" available to more Americans than ever. The postwar "American dream" promised home ownership, college education, secure employment at decent wages, affordable appliances, and the ability to travel—for one's children if not for one's self. The nation's public culture—its schools, mass media, politics, advertising—presented a powerful consensus based on the idea that the American dream was available to all who would work for it.

The presidential transition of 1961—from grandfatherly war hero Dwight Eisenhower to charismatic young war hero Jack Kennedy—symbolized for many a generational shift as well. By 1963, young people had more influence than ever before in shaping the nation's political life, its media images, and its burgeoning consumer culture. Kennedy himself inspired millions of young Americans to pursue public service and to express their idealism. But even by the time of Kennedy's death, the postwar consensus and the conditions that nurtured it were beginning to unravel.

Key Terms

Landrum-Griffin Act A 1959 act that widened government control over union affairs and further restricted union use of picketing and secondary boycotts during strikes. p. 672

Beats A group of writers from the 1950s whose writings challenged American culture. p. 678

beatnik Term used to designate members of the Beats. p. 679

New Frontier John F. Kennedy's domestic and foreign policy initiatives, designed to reinvigorate a sense of national purpose and energy. p. 679

Equal Pay Act of 1963 Act that made it illegal for employers to pay men and women different wages for the same job. p. 681

National Aeronautics and Space Administration (NASA) Federal agency created in 1958 to manage American space flights and exploration. p. 681

Alliance for Progress Program of economic aid to Latin America during the Kennedy administration. p. 682

Bay of Pigs Site in Cuba of an unsuccessful landing by 1,400 anti-Castro Cuban refugees in April 1961. p. 683

Cuban missile crisis Crisis between the Soviet Union and the United States over the placement of Soviet nuclear missiles in Cuba. p. 683

Limited Nuclear Test-Ban Treaty Treaty signed by the United States, Great Britain, and the Soviet Union that outlawed nuclear testing in the atmosphere, in outer space, and underwater. p. 684

CHRONOLOGY

1952

Dwight Eisenhower elected president, defeating Adlai Stevenson

1954

Vietminh force French surrender at Dien Bien Phu

1956

Congress passes National Interstate and Defense Highway Act

Elvis Presley signs with RCA

1957

Soviet Union launches *Sputnik*, first Earth-orbiting satellite

Jack Kerouac publishes *On the Road*

1960

John F. Kennedy elected president, narrowly defeating Richard M. Nixon

1961

Bay of Pigs invasion of Cuba fails

1962

Cuban missile crisis brings United States and Soviet Union to brink of nuclear war

1963

Betty Friedan publishes *The Feminine Mystique*

President Kennedy is assassinated

Lyndon B. Johnson becomes president

Chapter 28

The Civil Rights Movement 1945–1966

MONTGOMERY TO SELMA MARCH, 1965 Dr. Martin Luther King Jr., addressing demonstrators in Montgomery, Alabama, March 26, 1965, at the end of the march for voting rights, begun 54 miles away in Selma.

AP Images.

∨ Contents and Focus Questions

American Communities

The Montgomery Bus Boycott: An African American Community Challenges Segregation

On December 1, 1955, Rosa Parks, a seamstress and well-known activist in the African American community of Montgomery, Alabama, was taken from a bus, arrested, and jailed for refusing to give up her seat to a white passenger.

Composing roughly half the city's 100,000 people, Montgomery's black community had long endured the humiliation of a strictly segregated bus system. Drivers could order a whole row of black passengers to stand for one white person. Black people had to pay their fares at the front of the bus, then step back outside and reenter through the rear door.

Protesting Parks's arrest, more than 30,000 African Americans answered a hastily organized call to boycott the city's buses. On the day of the boycott, a steady stream of cars and pedestrians jammed the streets around Holt Street Baptist Church. By early evening, a patient, orderly, and determined crowd of more than 5,000 African Americans packed the church and spilled over onto the sidewalks. Loudspeakers had to be set up for the thousands who could not squeeze inside. After a brief prayer and a reading from scripture, all attention focused on the 26-year-old minister, the Reverend Dr. Martin Luther King Jr., who rose to address the gathering. "We are here this evening," he began slowly, "for serious business. We are here in a general sense because first and foremost we are American citizens, and we are determined to apply our citizenship to the fullness of its means."

Sensing the crowd's expectant mood, Dr. King got down to specifics and described Parks's arrest. As he quickened his cadence and drew shouts of encouragement, he seemed to gather strength and confidence from the crowd. "You know, my friends, there comes a time when people get tired of being trampled over by the iron feet of oppression. There comes a time, my friends, when people get tired of being flung across the abyss of humiliation, when they experience the bleakness of nagging despair."

Even before Dr. King concluded, it was clear to all that the bus boycott would continue for more than just a day. The minister laid out the key principles that would guide the boycott—nonviolence, Christian love, and unity. His brief but stirring address created a powerful sense of communion. "If we are wrong, justice is a lie," he told the clapping and shouting throng. "And we are determined here in Montgomery to work and fight until justice runs down like water and righteousness like a mighty stream." Dr. King made his way out of the church amid waves of applause and rows of hands reaching out to touch him.

Dr. King's prophetic speech catapulted him into leadership of the Montgomery bus boycott—but he had not started what would become known simply as the Movement. When Rosa Parks was arrested, local activists with deep roots in the black protest tradition galvanized the community with the idea of a boycott. Parks herself had served for 12 years as secretary of the local NAACP chapter. She was a committed opponent of segregation and was thoroughly respected in the city's African American community. E. D. Nixon, president of the Alabama NAACP and head of the local Brotherhood of Sleeping Car Porters union, saw Parks's arrest as the right case on which to make a stand. It was Nixon who brought Montgomery's black ministers together on December 5 to coordinate an extended boycott of city buses. They formed the Montgomery Improvement Association (MIA) and chose Dr. King as their leader. Significantly, Parks's lawyer was Clifford Durr, a white liberal with a history of representing black clients.

His politically active wife, Virginia, for whom Parks worked as a seamstress, had been a longtime crusader against the poll tax, which prevented many blacks from voting. And two white ministers, Rev. Robert Graetz and Rev. Glenn Smiley, would offer important support to the MIA.

While Nixon organized black ministers, Jo Ann Robinson, an English teacher at Alabama State College, spread the word to the larger black community. Robinson led the Women's Political Council (WPC), an organization of black professional women founded in 1949. With her WPC allies, Robinson wrote, mimeographed, and distributed 50,000 copies of a leaflet telling the story of Parks's arrest and urging all African Americans to stay off city buses on December 5. They did. Now the MIA faced the more difficult task of keeping the boycott going. Success depended on providing alternate transportation for the 30,000–40,000 maids, cooks, janitors, and other black people who needed to get to work.

The MIA coordinated an elaborate system of carpools, using hundreds of private cars and volunteer drivers to provide as many as 20,000 rides each day. Many people walked. Local authorities, although shocked by the discipline and sense of purpose shown by Montgomery's African American community, refused to engage in serious negotiations. With the aid of the NAACP, the MIA brought suit in federal court against bus segregation in Montgomery. Police harassed boycotters with traffic tickets and arrests. White racists exploded bombs in the homes of Dr. King and Nixon. The days turned into weeks, then months, but still the boycott continued. All along, mass meetings in Montgomery's African American churches helped boost morale with singing, praying, and stories of individual sacrifice. The spontaneous remark of one elderly woman, refusing all suggestions that she drop out of the boycott on account of her age, became a classic refrain of the Movement; "My feets is tired, but my soul is rested."

The boycott reduced the bus company's revenues by two-thirds. In February 1956, city officials obtained indictments against King, Nixon, and 113 other boycotters under an old law forbidding hindrance to business without "just cause or legal excuse." A month later, King went on trial. A growing contingent of newspaper reporters and TV crews from around the country watched as the judge found King guilty, fined him $1,000, and released him on bond pending appeal. But on June 4, a panel of three federal judges struck down Montgomery's bus segregation ordinances as unconstitutional. On November 13, the Supreme Court affirmed the district court ruling. After 11 hard months and against all odds, the boycotters had won.

The boycotters' victory inspired a new mass movement for African American civil rights. A series of local struggles to dismantle segregation—in the schools of Little Rock, the department stores of Atlanta, the lunch counters of Greensboro, and the streets of Birmingham—would coalesce into a broad-based national movement at the center of American politics. By 1963, the massive March on Washington would win the endorsement of President John F. Kennedy, and his successor, Lyndon B. Johnson, would push through the landmark Civil Rights Act and Voting Rights Act.

The struggle to end legal segregation took root in scores of southern cities and towns. African American communities led these fights, developing a variety of tactics, leaders, and ideologies. With white allies, they engaged in direct-action protests such as boycotts, sit-ins, and mass civil disobedience, as well as strategic legal battles in state and federal courts. The Movement was not without its inner conflicts. Tensions between local campaigns and national civil rights organizations flared up regularly. Within African American communities, long-simmering distrust between the working classes and rural folk on the one hand and middle-class ministers, teachers, and businesspeople on the other sometimes threatened to destroy political unity. Generational conflicts pitted African American student activists against their elders. But overall, the civil rights movement created new social identities for African Americans, inspired a new "rights consciousness" among other minority groups, and profoundly changed American society.

Montgomery

28.1 Origins of the Movement

What were the legal and political origins of the African American civil rights struggle?

The civil rights movement arose out of the aspirations and community strength of African Americans. Its deepest roots lay in the historic injustices of slavery, racism, and segregation. African Americans' experiences during and immediately after World War II laid the foundation for the civil rights struggle of the 1950s and 1960s.

28.1.1 Civil Rights after World War II

Between 1939 and 1945, almost a million black men and women served in the armed forces. The discrepancy between fighting totalitarianism abroad and enduring segregation and racism in the military embittered many combat veterans and their families. Nearly 2 million African Americans worked in defense plants, and another 200,000 entered the federal civil service. Black union membership doubled, reaching more than 1.2 million. African American newspapers like the *Pittsburgh Courier* fought for the "Double V" campaign—victory over fascism abroad and over segregation at home. But wartime stress on national unity largely muted political protests. With the war's end, African Americans and their white allies determined to push ahead for full political and social equality.

The wartime boom spurred a mass northward migration of nearly a million black Southerners. Forty-three northern and western cities saw their black populations double during the 1940s. Although racial discrimination in housing and employment was by no means absent in northern cities, greater economic opportunities and political freedom continued to attract rural African Americans after the war. With the growth of African American communities in cities like New York, Chicago, and Detroit, black people gained significant influence in urban political machines. Within industrial unions such as the United Automobile Workers and the United Steel Workers, white and black workers learned the power of biracial unity in fighting for better wages and working conditions.

After the war, civil rights issues returned to the national political stage for the first time since Reconstruction. Black voters had already begun to switch their allegiance from the Republicans to the Democrats during the New Deal. A series of symbolic and substantive acts by the Truman administration solidified that shift. In 1946, Truman created a President's Committee on Civil Rights. Its 1947 report, *To Secure These Rights*, set out an ambitious program to end racial inequality: creating a permanent civil rights division in the Justice Department, protecting voting rights, passing antilynching legislation, and challenging laws that permitted segregated housing. Although he publicly endorsed nearly all these proposals, Truman introduced no legislation to make them law.

Truman and his advisers walked a political tightrope on civil rights. They understood that black voters in several key northern states would be pivotal in the 1948 election. At the same time, they worried about the loyalty of white southern Democrats adamantly opposed to changing the racial status quo. In July 1948, the president made his boldest move on behalf of civil rights, issuing an executive order ending segregation in the armed forces. Later that summer, when liberals forced the Democratic National Convention to adopt a strong civil rights plank, outraged southern delegates walked out and nominated Governor Strom Thurmond of South Carolina for president on a States' Rights ticket. Thurmond carried four southern states in the election. But even with the help of more than 70 percent of the northern black vote, Truman barely managed to defeat Republican Thomas E. Dewey in November. The deep split over race issues would continue to wrack the national Democratic Party for a generation.

Electoral politics was not the only arena for civil rights work. During the war, membership in the National Association for the Advancement of Colored People had mushroomed from 50,000 to 500,000. The NAACP conducted voter registration drives and lobbied against discrimination in housing and employment. Its Legal Defense and Education Fund, vigorously led by special counsel Thurgood Marshall, mounted several significant legal challenges to segregation laws. In *Morgan v. Virginia* (1946), the Supreme Court used the interstate-commerce clause to declare segregation on interstate buses unconstitutional. Other Supreme Court decisions struck down all-white election primaries, racially restrictive housing covenants, and the exclusion of blacks from law and graduate schools.

The NAACP's legal work demonstrated the potential for using federal courts in attacking segregation. Courts were one place where black people, using the constitutional language of rights, could make forceful arguments that could not be voiced in Congress or at political conventions. Federal enforcement of court decisions was often lacking, however. In 1947, a group of black and white activists tested compliance with the *Morgan* decision by traveling on a bus through the Upper South. This "Freedom Ride" was cosponsored by the Christian pacifist group Fellowship of Reconciliation (FOR) and its recent offshoot, the Congress of Racial Equality (CORE), which was devoted to interracial, nonviolent direct action. In North Carolina, several riders were arrested and sentenced to 30 days on a chain gang for refusing to leave the bus.

Two symbolic "firsts" raised black expectations and inspired pride. In 1947, Jackie Robinson broke the color barrier in Major League Baseball, winning Rookie of the Year honors with the Brooklyn Dodgers. Robinson's courage in the face of racist taunts from fans and players paved the way for the other black ballplayers who soon followed him into the big leagues. In 1950, United Nations diplomat Ralph Bunche won the Nobel Peace Prize for arranging the 1948 Arab-Israeli truce. Bunche, however, later declined an appointment as undersecretary of state because he did not want to subject his family to the humiliating segregation laws in Washington, D.C.

Cultural change could have political implications as well. In the 1940s, African American musicians created a new form of jazz that revolutionized American music and asserted a militant black consciousness. Although black musicians had pioneered swing and earlier styles of jazz, white bandleaders and musicians had reaped

CHARLIE PARKER AND MILES DAVIS Charlie Parker (alto sax) and Miles Davis (trumpet) with their group in 1947, at the Three Deuces Club in New York City. Parker and Davis were two creative leaders of the "bebop" movement of the 1940s. Working in northern cities, boppers reshaped jazz music and created a distinct language and style that were widely imitated by young people. They challenged older stereotypes of African American musicians by insisting that they be treated as serious artists.

PF-(bygone1)/Alamy Stock Photo.

most of the recognition and money. Black artists such as Charlie Parker, Dizzy Gillespie, Thelonius Monk, Bud Powell, and Miles Davis revolted against the standard big-band format of swing, preferring small groups and competitive jam sessions to express their musical visions. The new music, dubbed "bebop," demanded a much more sophisticated knowledge of harmony and melody, and featured more complex rhythms and extended improvisation than did previous jazz styles. The "boppers" insisted on independence from the white-defined norms of show business. Serious about both their music and the way it was presented, they refused to cater to white stereotypes of grinning, easygoing black performers.

28.1.2 The Segregated South

In the postwar South, still home to over half the nation's 15 million African Americans, the racial situation had changed little since the Supreme Court had sanctioned "separate but equal" segregation in *Plessy v. Ferguson* (See Chapter 20.) In practice, segregation meant separate but unequal. A tight web of state and local ordinances enforced strict separation of the races in schools, restaurants, hotels, movie theaters, libraries, restrooms, hospitals, and even cemeteries, and the facilities for black people were consistently inferior to those for whites. There were no black policemen in the Deep South and only a handful of black lawyers.

In the late 1940s, only about 10 percent of eligible southern black people voted, most of these in urban areas. A combination of legal and extralegal measures kept all but the most determined blacks disenfranchised. Poll taxes, all-white primaries, and discriminatory registration procedures reinforced the belief that voting was "the white man's business." African Americans who insisted on exercising their right to vote, especially in remote rural areas, faced physical violence—beatings, shootings, and lynchings. A former president of the Alabama Bar Association expressed a commonly held view when he declared, "No Negro is good enough and no Negro will ever be good enough to participate in making the law under which the white people of Alabama have to live."

Outsiders often noted that despite Jim Crow laws (see Chapter 20), contact between blacks and whites was ironically close. The majority of black Southerners worked on white-owned farms or in white households. One black preacher neatly summarized the nation's regional differences this way; "In the South, they don't care how close you get as long as you don't get too big; in the North, they don't care how big you get as long as you don't get too close." The South's racial code forced African Americans to accept, at least outwardly, social conventions that reinforced their low standing with whites. A black person did not shake hands with a white person, or enter a white home through the front door, or address a white person except formally. In these circumstances, survival and self-respect depended to a great degree on patience and stoicism. Black people learned to endure humiliation by keeping their thoughts and feelings hidden from white people.

The consequences of violating the code could be fatal. In the summer of 1955, Emmett Till, a 14-year-old African American boy from Chicago, was visiting relatives near Money, Mississippi. Leaving a store with some friends, Till spoke in an informal tone to the white wife of the store owner. Several days later, Till was kidnapped from his uncle's house in the middle of the night, and shortly thereafter his body was dragged out of the Tallahatchie River. Back in Chicago, Till's mother, Mamie Bradley, insisted on an open-casket funeral, and the photographs of his horribly mutilated body profoundly shocked African American readers of *Jet* magazine and other black publications around the country. No white publications carried these photos. Till's murderers were acquitted in a trial that attracted national attention and underlined the stark realities of southern segregation. It also reminded northern blacks that racist violence could touch their lives as well. In Bradley's words, "Two months ago I had a nice apartment in Chicago. I had a good job. I had a son. When something happened to the Negroes in the South I said, 'That's their business, not mine.' Now I know how wrong I was. The murder of my son has shown me that what happens to any of us, anywhere in the world, had better be the business of us all."

SEGREGATED SPACES Signs designating "White" and "Colored" restrooms, waiting rooms, entrances, benches, and even water fountains were a common sight in the segregated South. They were a constant reminder that legal separation of the races in public spaces was the law of the land.

Broad demographic and economic changes were also remaking the postwar South. On the eve of World War II, more than 40 percent of Southerners lived on farms; two-thirds of the South's 35 million people resided in places with fewer than 2,500 inhabitants. During the 1950s, tens of thousands of non-agricultural jobs were created in factories, mills, and office buildings across the region. More and more national corporations, attracted by the region's cheaper labor costs, began establishing a southern presence, and the region's towns and cities competed to lure them. A more highly mechanized agriculture and rapid industrialization pushed more Southerners, black and white, into cities and suburbs. By 1960, roughly half of all Southerners inhabited metropolitan districts and only 15 percent lived on farms.

28.1.3 *Brown v. Board of Education*

Since the late 1930s, the NAACP had chipped away at the legal foundations of segregation. Rather than making a frontal assault on the *Plessy* separate-but-equal rule, civil rights attorneys launched a series of suits seeking complete equality in segregated facilities. (See Table 28.1.) Their strategy was to make segregation so prohibitively expensive that the South would be forced to dismantle it. In the 1938 case *Missouri ex rel. Gaines v. Canada*, the Supreme Court ruled that the University of Missouri law school must either admit African Americans or build another, fully equal law school for them. NAACP lawyers pushed their arguments further, asserting that equality could not be measured simply by money or a school's facilities. In *McLaurin v. Oklahoma State Regents* (1950), the Court agreed with NAACP special counsel Thurgood Marshall's argument that regulations forcing a black law student to sit, eat, and study in areas apart from white students inevitably created a "badge of inferiority."

By 1951, Marshall had begun coordinating the NAACP's legal resources for a direct attack on the separate-but-equal doctrine, aiming to overturn *Plessy* and the constitutionality of segregation itself. For a test case, Marshall combined five lawsuits challenging segregation in public schools. One of these suits argued the case of Oliver Brown of Topeka, Kansas, who sought to overturn a state law permitting cities to maintain segregated schools. Topeka's ordinance, sanctioned by this law, forced Brown's eight-year-old daughter Linda to travel by bus to a black school even though she lived only three blocks from an all-white elementary school. The Supreme Court heard initial arguments on the cases, grouped together as *Brown v. Board of Education*, in December 1952. The *Brown* case offered an important reminder that segregation was not a purely southern phenomenon. Roughly 40 percent of America's 28 million schoolchildren attended legally segregated schools in the South and border states, while millions more were educated in northern communities where de facto segregation—created by discriminatory housing patterns and school districting—was the norm.

Table 28.1 LANDMARK CIVIL RIGHTS LEGISLATION, SUPREME COURT DECISIONS, AND EXECUTIVE ORDERS

Year	Decision, Law, or Executive Order	Significance
1938	*Missouri ex rel. Gaines v. Canada*	Required University of Missouri Law School either to admit African Americans or to build another fully equal law school
1941	Executive Order 8802 (by President Roosevelt)	Banned racial discrimination in defense industry and government offices; established Fair Employment Practices Committee to investigate violations
1946	*Morgan v. Virginia*	Ruled that segregation on interstate buses violated federal law and created an "undue burden" on interstate commerce
1948	Executive Order 9981 (by President Truman)	Desegregated the U.S. armed forces
1950	*McLaurin v. Oklahoma State Regents*	Ruled that forcing an African American student to sit, eat, and study in segregated facilities was unconstitutional because it inevitably created a "badge of inferiority"
1950	*Sweatt v. Painter*	Ruled that an inferior law school created by the University of Texas to serve African Americans violated their right to equal protection and ordered Herman Sweatt to be admitted to University of Texas Law School
1954	*Brown v. Board of Education of Topeka I*	Declared "separate educational facilities are inherently unequal," thus overturning *Plessy v. Ferguson* (1896) and the separate-but-equal doctrine as it applied to public schools
1955	*Brown v. Board of Education of Topeka II*	Ordered school desegregation to begin with "all deliberate speed," but offered no timetable
1957	Civil Rights Act	Created Civil Rights Division within the Justice Department
1964	Civil Rights Act	Prohibited discrimination in employment and most places of public accommodation on basis of race, color, religion, sex, or national origin; outlawed bias in federally assisted programs; created Equal Employment Opportunity Commission
1965	Voting Rights Act	Authorized federal supervision of voter registration in states and counties where fewer than half of voting-age residents were registered; outlawed literacy and other discriminatory tests in voter registration

In his brief before the Court, Marshall argued that separate facilities, by definition, denied black people their full rights as American citizens. Marshall used sociological and psychological evidence that went beyond standard legal arguments. For example, he cited the research of African American psychologist Kenneth B. Clark, who had studied the self-esteem of black children. Using black and white dolls and asking the children which they preferred, Clark illustrated how black children educated in segregated schools developed a negative self-image. When Chief Justice Fred Vinson died suddenly in 1953, President Dwight Eisenhower appointed California Governor Earl Warren to fill the post. After hearing further arguments, the Court remained divided on the issue of overturning *Plessy*. Warren, eager for a unanimous decision, patiently worked at convincing two holdouts. Using his political skills to persuade and achieve compromise, Warren urged his colleagues to affirm a simple principle as the basis for the decision.

On May 17, 1954, Warren read aloud the Court's unanimous decision. "Does segregation of children in public schools solely on the basis of race . . . deprive the children of the minority group of equal educational opportunities?" The chief justice paused. "We believe that it does." Warren made a point of citing several of the psychological studies of segregation's effects. He ended by directly addressing the constitutional issue. Segregation deprived the plaintiffs of the equal protection of the laws guaranteed by the Fourteenth Amendment. "We conclude that in the field of public education the doctrine of 'separate but equal' has no place. Separate educational facilities are inherently unequal. . . . Any language in *Plessy v. Ferguson* contrary to this finding is rejected."

African Americans and their liberal allies around the country hailed the decision and the legal genius of Thurgood Marshall. Marshall himself predicted that all segregated schools would be abolished within five years. Black newspapers were full of stories on the imminent dismantling of segregation. The *Chicago Defender* called the decision "a second emancipation proclamation." But the issue of enforcement soon dampened this enthusiasm. To gain a unanimous decision, Warren had to agree to let the Court delay for one year its ruling on how to implement desegregation. This second *Brown* ruling, handed down in May 1955, assigned responsibility for desegregation plans to local school boards. The Court left it to federal district judges to monitor compliance, requiring only that desegregation proceed "with all deliberate speed." Thus, although the Court had made a momentous and clear constitutional ruling, the need for compromise dictated gradual enforcement by unspecified means.

28.1.4 Crisis in Little Rock

Resistance to *Brown* took many forms. Most affected states passed laws transferring authority for pupil assignment to local school boards. This prevented the NAACP from bringing statewide suits against segregated school systems. Counties and towns created layers of administrative delays designed to stop implementation of *Brown*. Some school boards transferred public school property to new, all-white private "academies." State legislatures in Virginia, Alabama, Mississippi, and Georgia, resurrecting pre–Civil War doctrines, passed resolutions declaring their right to "interpose" themselves between the people and the federal government and to "nullify" federal laws. In 1956, 101 members of Congress from the former Confederate states signed the Southern Manifesto, urging their states to refuse compliance with desegregation. President Eisenhower declined to publicly endorse *Brown*, contributing to the southern resistance.

In Little Rock, Arkansas, the tense controversy over school integration became a test case of state versus federal power. A federal court ordered public schools to begin desegregation in September 1957, and the local school board made plans to comply. But Governor Orval Faubus, facing a tough reelection fight, decided to make a campaign issue out of defying the court order. He dispatched Arkansas National Guard troops to Central High School to prevent nine black students from entering. For three weeks, armed troops stood guard at the school. Screaming crowds, encouraged by Faubus, menaced the black students, beat up two black reporters, and chanted "Two, four, six, eight, we ain't going to integrate." Moderate whites opposed Faubus, fearing that his controversial tactics would make it harder to attract new businesses and investment capital to the city. Indeed, Little Rock's industrial recruitment efforts declined with the integration crisis, suggesting to southern

INTEGRATION IN LITTLE ROCK, ARKANSAS Elizabeth Eckford ignores the taunts of a hostile white crowd as she enters Central High School in Little Rock, Arkansas.

Bettmann/Getty Images.

moderates that militant resistance to integration could be bad for business.

At first, Eisenhower tried to intervene quietly, gaining Faubus's assurance that he would protect the nine black children. But when Faubus suddenly withdrew his troops, leaving the black students at the mercy of the white mob, Eisenhower had to move. On September 24, he placed the Arkansas National Guard under federal command and ordered a thousand paratroopers of the 101st Airborne Division of the U.S. Army to Little Rock. The nine black students arrived in a U.S. Army car. With fixed bayonets, the soldiers protected the students as they finally integrated Central High School. Eisenhower, the veteran military commander, justified his actions on the basis of upholding federal authority and enforcing the law. He also defended his intervention as crucial to national prestige abroad, noting the propaganda victory Faubus was handing the Communist world. (See SEEING History.) "Our enemies," the president argued, "are gloating over this incident and using it everywhere to misrepresent our whole nation."

SEEING History

Visualizing Civil Rights

Images from the front lines of the civil rights struggle were crucial to the evolution of "the Movement," and they could be used for very different purposes. They attracted local activists to the cause and helped to turn a regional battle into a national crusade. Photos of the racist violence that marked confrontations in Little Rock, on the Freedom Rides, and in Birmingham circulated widely in foreign newspapers, complicating the freedom-versus-tyranny narrative of Cold War-era policymakers.

The growth of the Movement also converged with the emergence of television as the dominant mass medium in American life. By 1957, some 85 percent of American homes watched TV at least five hours each day. To the nascent world of television news, the Movement offered dramatic confrontations, compelling visuals, and a sharp distinction between good and evil that resembled familiar forms like Hollywood westerns and coverage of the Cold War. But images could also provide a more intimate and human sense of what was at stake.

When Southern Christian Leadership Conference leaders planned the Birmingham campaign in the spring of 1963, they counted on a violent response from local authorities—and they got it. Images of demonstrators being attacked by police dogs or getting blasted by high-pressure water hoses circulated all over the globe.

Two years later, the SCLC looked to exploit the short temper and violent reputation of Sheriff Jim Clark when it brought its voting rights campaign to Selma, Alabama. As Andrew Young noted, "We're only saying to [Sheriff Clark] that if he still wants to beat heads he'll have to do it on Main Street, at noon, in front of CBS, NBC, and ABC television cameras." On March 7, 1965, when local police and Alabama state troopers attacked civil rights marchers on the Edmund Pettus Bridge, news cameras captured the searing moment. That night, ABC interrupted its premiere broadcast of the movie *Judgement at Nuremberg* with footage from Selma. The national outcry provided the final push for passage of the Voting Rights Act. As Selma's Mayor Joseph Smitherman later recalled, "I did not understand how big it was until I saw it on television."

- **How did compelling visual images help turn the civil rights movement from a regional struggle to a national one?**

- **Was the strategy of inciting violent reactions from its opponents hypocritical or cynical for a movement devoted to nonviolence?**

POLICE VIOLENCE IN THE FACE OF PROTEST

Left: Bill Hudson/ASSOCIATED PRESS, right: Everett Collection/Newscom.

As the first president since Reconstruction to use armed federal troops in support of black rights, Eisenhower demonstrated that the federal government could, indeed, protect civil rights. Unfazed, Governor Faubus kept Little Rock high schools closed during the 1958–59 academic year to prevent what he called "violence and disorder."

28.2 No Easy Road to Freedom, 1957–1962

How did student protesters and direct action shape the civil rights struggle in the South?

The legal breakthrough represented by the *Brown* decision heartened opponents of segregation everywhere. Most important, *Brown* demonstrated the potential for using the federal court system as a weapon against discrimination and as a means of protecting the full rights of citizenship. Yet widespread opposition to *Brown* showed the limits of a strictly legal strategy. Although they welcomed Eisenhower's intervention in Little Rock, civil rights activists noted his reluctance to endorse desegregation, suggesting that they could not rely on federal help. As the Montgomery bus boycott had proved, black communities would have to help themselves first.

28.2.1 Martin Luther King Jr. and the SCLC

When it ended with the Supreme Court decision in November 1956, the 381-day Montgomery bus boycott had made Martin Luther King Jr. a national figure. In January 1957, *Time* magazine put King on its cover; he was only the second African American ever to appear on NBC's *Meet the Press*. Speaking invitations poured in from universities and organizations all over the country.

King was an extraordinary and complex man. Born in 1929 in Atlanta, he enjoyed a middle-class upbringing as the son of a prominent Baptist minister. After graduating from prestigious Morehouse College, an all-black school, King earned a divinity degree at Crozer Theological Seminary in Pennsylvania and a PhD in theology from Boston University. In graduate school he was drawn to the Social Christianity of American theologian Walter Rauschenbusch, who insisted on connecting religious faith with struggles for social justice. Above all, King admired Mohandas Gandhi, a lawyer turned ascetic who had led a successful nonviolent resistance movement against British colonial rule in India. Gandhi taught his followers to confront authorities with a readiness to suffer in order to expose injustice and force those in power to end it. This tactic of nonviolent civil disobedience required discipline and sacrifice from its followers, who were sometimes called upon to lay their lives on the line against armed police and military forces. Crucially, King believed Gandhian nonviolence to be not merely a moral imperative but also a potent political strategy. A unique blend of traditional African American folk preacher and erudite intellectual, King used his passion and intelligence to help transform a community's pain into a powerful moral force for change. Two northern pacifists, Bayard Rustin of the War Resisters' League and Glenn Smiley of the Fellowship of Reconciliation, helped deepen King's commitment to the Gandhian philosophy.

King recognized the need to exploit the momentum of the Montgomery movement. In early 1957, with the help of Rustin and others, he brought together nearly 100 black ministers to found the **Southern Christian Leadership Conference (SCLC)**. The clergymen elected King president and his close friend, the Reverend Ralph Abernathy, treasurer. The SCLC called upon black people "to understand that nonviolence is not a symbol of weakness or cowardice, but as Jesus demonstrated, nonviolent resistance transforms weakness into strength and breeds courage in the face of danger."

But King and other black leaders also understood that the white South was no monolith. They believed white Southerners could be divided roughly into three groups: first, a tiny minority—often with legal training, social connections, and money—that might be counted on to help overthrow segregation; second, extreme segregationists who were willing and able to use violence and terror in defense of white supremacy; and third, a broad middle group who favored and benefited from segregation but were unwilling to take personal risks to prevent its destruction. In the battles to come, civil rights leaders made this nuanced view of the white South central to their larger political strategy. Extreme segregationists could be counted on to overreact, often violently, to civil rights campaigns, and thereby help to win sympathy and support for the cause. White moderates, especially in the business community, might be reluctant to initiate change, but they would try to distance themselves from the desperate violence of extremists and present themselves as pragmatic supporters of order and peace.

The SCLC gained support among black ministers, and King vigorously spread his message in speeches and writings. But the organization failed to generate the kind of mass, direct-action movement that had made history in Montgomery. Instead, the next great spark to light the fire of protest came from what seemed at the time a most unlikely source: black college students.

28.2.2 Sit-Ins: Greensboro, Nashville, Atlanta

On Monday, February 1, 1960, four black freshmen from North Carolina Agricultural and Technical College in Greensboro sat down at the whites-only lunch counter in

GREENSBORO SIT-IN The second day of the sit-in at the Greensboro, North Carolina, Woolworth lunch counter, February 2, 1960. From left: Ronald Martin, Robert Patterson, and Mark Martin. The Greensboro protest sparked a wave of sit-ins across the South, mostly by college students, demanding an end to segregation in restaurants and other public places.

Bettmann/Getty Images.

the nearby Woolworth store and politely ordered coffee and doughnuts. As the students had anticipated while planning the action in their dorm rooms, they were refused service. Although they could buy pencils or toothpaste, black people were not allowed to eat in Woolworth. But the four students stayed at the counter until closing time. Word of their actions spread quickly, and the next day they returned with more than two dozen supporters. On the third day, students occupied 63 of the 66 lunch counter seats. By Thursday, they had been joined by three white students from the Women's College of the University of North Carolina in Greensboro. Scores of sympathizers overflowed Woolworth's and started a sit-in down the street in S. H. Kress. On Friday, hundreds of black students and a few white sympathizers jammed the lunch counters.

The week's events put Greensboro in the national news. City officials, looking to end the protest, offered to negotiate in exchange for an end to demonstrations. White business leaders and politicians proved unwilling to change the racial status quo, however, and the sit-ins resumed on April 1. In response to the April 21 arrest of 45 students for trespassing, an outraged African American community organized a boycott of targeted stores that cut deeply into merchants' profits. Greensboro's leaders reluctantly gave in. On July 25, 1960, the first African American ate a meal at Woolworth.

The Greensboro sit-in sent a shock wave throughout the South. During the next 18 months, 70,000 people—most of them black students, a few of them white allies—participated in sit-ins against segregation in dozens of communities. More than 3,000 were arrested. African Americans had discovered a new form of direct-action protest, dignified and powerful, that white people could not ignore. The sit-in movement also transformed the

participants' self-image, empowering them psychologically and emotionally. Franklin McCain, one of the original four Greensboro students, later recalled a great feeling of soul cleansing; "I probably felt better on that day than I've ever felt in my life. Seems like a lot of feelings of guilt or what-have-you suddenly left me, and I felt as though I had gained my manhood, so to speak, and not only gained it, but had developed quite a lot of respect for it."

In Nashville, Reverend James Lawson, a northern-born black minister, had led workshops in nonviolent resistance since 1958. Lawson had served a jail term as a conscientious objector during the Korean War and had become active in the Fellowship of Reconciliation. He had also spent three years as a missionary in India, where he had learned close up the Gandhian methods of promoting social change. Lawson gathered around him a group of deeply committed black students from Fisk and Vanderbilt universities and other Nashville colleges. The psychological pressures were enormous. To be successful, practitioners of nonviolent resistance had to learn and practice strict self-control needed to resist lashing back at the angry crowds that would abuse them. Young activists there talked not only of ending segregation but also of creating a "Beloved Community" based on Christian idealism and Gandhian principles.

In the spring of 1960, more than 150 Nashville students were arrested in disciplined sit-ins aimed at desegregating downtown lunch counters. Lawson, who preached the need for sacrifice for the cause of justice, found himself expelled from the divinity school at Vanderbilt. Lawson and other veterans of the Nashville sit-ins, such as John Lewis, Diane Nash, and Marion Barry, would go on to play influential roles in the national civil rights movement. The Nashville group developed rules of conduct that became a model for protesters elsewhere; "Don't strike back or curse if abused. . . . Show yourself courteous and friendly at all times. . . . Report all serious incidents to your leader in a polite manner. Remember love and nonviolence."

The most ambitious sit-in campaign unfolded in Atlanta, the South's largest and wealthiest city, and home to the region's most powerful and prestigious black community. Students from Morehouse, Spelman, and the other all-black schools that made up Atlanta University took the lead. On March 15, 1960, 200 young black people staged a well-coordinated sit-in at restaurants in City Hall, the State Capitol, and other government offices. Police arrested and jailed 76 demonstrators that day, but the experience only strengthened the activists' resolve. Led by Julian Bond and Lonnie King, two Morehouse undergraduates, the students formed the Committee on an Appeal for Human Rights. Over the summer they planned a fall campaign of large-scale sit-ins at major Atlanta department stores and a boycott of downtown merchants. In October 1960, Martin Luther King Jr. and 36 students were arrested when they sat down in the all-white Magnolia Room restaurant in Rich's Department Store. As in Greensboro and Montgomery, the larger African American community in Atlanta supported the continuing sit-ins, picketing, and boycotts. The campaign stretched on for months, and hundreds of protesters went to jail. The city's business leaders finally relented in September 1961, and desegregation came to Atlanta.

28.2.3 SNCC and the "Beloved Community"

The sit-in movement pumped fresh energy into the civil rights cause, creating a new generation of activists and leaders. Mass arrests, beatings, and vilification in the southern white press only strengthened the resolve of those in the Movement. Students also had to deal with the fears of their families, many of whom had made great sacrifices to send them to college. John Lewis, a seminary student in Nashville, remembered his mother in rural Alabama pleading with him to "get out of that mess, before you get hurt."

The new student militancy also caused discord within black communities. The authority of local African American elites had traditionally depended on their influence and cooperation with the white establishment. Black lawyers, school principals, and businessmen had to maintain regular and cordial relations with white judges, school boards, and politicians. Student calls for freedom disturbed many community leaders worried about upsetting traditional patronage networks. Some black college presidents, pressured by trustees and state legislators, sought to moderate or stop the Movement altogether. The president of Southern University in Baton Rouge, the nation's largest black college, suspended 18 sit-in leaders in 1960 and

forced the entire student body of 5,000 to reapply so that "agitators" could be screened out.

An April 1960 conference of 120 black student activists in Raleigh, North Carolina, underlined the generational and radical aspects of the new movement. The meeting had been called by Ella Baker, executive director of the SCLC, to help the students assess their experiences and plan future actions. Fifty-five at the time, Baker had for years played an important behind-the-scenes role in the civil rights cause, serving as a community organizer and field secretary for the NAACP before heading the staff of the SCLC. She counseled the student activists to resist affiliating with any of the national civil rights organizations, and she also encouraged the trend toward group-centered leadership among the students.

With Baker's encouragement, the conference voted to establish a new group, the Student Nonviolent Coordinating Committee (SNCC, pronounced "Snick"). The strong influence of the Nashville students, led by James Lawson, could be found in the SNCC statement of purpose:

> We affirm the philosophical or religious ideal of nonviolence as the foundation of our purpose, the presupposition of our faith, and the manner of our action. Nonviolence as it grows from Judaic-Christian tradition seeks a social order of justice permeated by love. Integration of human endeavor represents the crucial first step towards such a society.

In the fall of 1960, SNCC established an organizational structure, a set of principles, and a new style of civil rights protest. The emphasis was on fighting segregation through direct confrontation, mass action, and civil disobedience. SNCC field-workers initiated and supported community-based actions around the South, working with and encouraging local activists. Many of these grassroots campaigners were African American women: sharecroppers, domestic workers, and teachers. Three-quarters of the first SNCC field-workers were younger than 22 years old. Leadership was vested in a nonhierarchical Coordinating Committee, but local groups were free to determine their own direction. SNCC people distrusted bureaucracy and structure; they stressed spontaneity and improvisation. A small but dedicated group of young white Southerners, inspired by SNCC's idealism and activism, joined the cause. Over the next few years SNCC was at the forefront of nearly every major civil rights battle.

28.2.4 The Election of 1960 and Civil Rights

The race issue was kept from center stage during the very close presidential campaign of 1960. As vice president, Richard Nixon had been a leading Republican voice for stronger civil rights legislation, whereas the Democratic nominee, Senator John F. Kennedy, had played virtually no role in the 1950s' congressional battles over civil rights. During the campaign, however, their roles reversed. Kennedy praised the sit-in movement as part of a revival of national reform spirit. While the Republican platform contained a strong civil rights plank, Nixon, eager to court southern white voters, minimized his own identification with the Movement. Republican conservatives, believing that the GOP might pick up southern electoral votes, pushed a States' Rights position, thus planting seeds for a reborn conservative movement in the 1960s.

In October, Martin Luther King Jr. was jailed after leading a demonstration in Atlanta and faced the strong possibility of being sent to a notorious state prison. Kennedy telephoned King's wife, Coretta Scott King, to reassure her and express his personal support. Senator Kennedy's brother and campaign manager Robert telephoned the judge in the case and angrily warned him that he had violated King's civil rights and endangered the national Democratic ticket. The judge released King soon afterward. News of this intervention did not gain wide attention in the white South, much to the relief of the Kennedys. But the Kennedy campaign effectively played up the story among black voters all over the country, using black churches as a grapevine. Kennedy won 70 percent of the black vote, which helped put him over the top in such critical states as Illinois, Texas, Michigan, and Pennsylvania and secure his narrow victory over Nixon. Many civil rights activists optimistically looked forward to a new president who would have to acknowledge his political debt to the black vote.

The very closeness of his victory constrained Kennedy on race. Democrats had lost ground in the House and Senate, and Kennedy had to worry about alienating conservative Southern Democrats who chaired key congressional committees. Passage of major civil rights legislation would be virtually impossible. The president did appoint some forty African Americans to high federal positions, including Thurgood Marshall to a federal appellate court. He also established a Committee on Equal Employment Opportunity, chaired by Vice President Lyndon B. Johnson, to fight discrimination in the federal civil service and in corporations that received government contracts.

Most significantly, the Kennedy administration sought to invigorate the Civil Rights Division of the Justice Department. The division had been created by the Civil Rights Act of 1957, which authorized the attorney general to seek court injunctions to protect people denied their right to vote. But the Eisenhower administration had made little use of this new power. Robert Kennedy, the new attorney general, began assembling a staff of brilliant and committed attorneys, headed by Washington lawyer Burke Marshall. Kennedy encouraged them to get out of Washington and into the field wherever racial troubles arose. In early 1961, when Louisiana school officials balked at a school desegregation

order, Robert Kennedy warned them that he would ask the federal court to hold them in contempt. When Marshall started court proceedings, the state officials gave in. The new, more aggressive mood at Justice could not solve the central political dilemma: how to move forward on civil rights without alienating Southern Democrats. Pressure from the newly energized southern civil rights movement soon revealed the true difficulty of that problem. The Movement would also provoke murderous outrage from white extremists determined to maintain the racial status quo. (See Map 28.1.)

28.2.5 Freedom Rides

In the spring of 1961, James Farmer, national director of CORE, announced plans for an interracial Freedom Ride through the South. The goal was to test compliance with court orders banning segregation in interstate travel and terminal accommodations. One of the founders of CORE in 1942, Farmer had worked for various pacifist and socialist groups and served as program director for the NAACP. He designed the Freedom Ride to induce a crisis, in the spirit of the sit-ins. "Our intention," Farmer declared, "was to provoke the southern authorities into arresting us and thereby prod the Justice Department into enforcing the law of the land." CORE received financial and tactical support from the SCLC and several NAACP branches. It also informed the Justice Department and the FBI of its plans but received no reply.

On May 4, seven blacks and six whites split into two interracial groups and left Washington, D.C., on public buses bound for Alabama and Mississippi. At first the two buses encountered only isolated harassment and violence as they headed south. But when one bus entered Anniston, Alabama, on May 14, an angry mob surrounded it, smashing windows and slashing tires. Six miles out of town, the tires went flat. A firebomb tossed through a window forced the passengers out. The mob then beat the Freedom Riders with blackjacks, iron bars, and clubs, and the bus burst into flames. A caravan of cars organized by the Birmingham office of the SCLC rescued the wounded. Another mob attacked the second bus in Anniston, leaving one Freedom Rider near death and permanently brain damaged.

The violence escalated. In Birmingham, a mob of 40 whites waited on the loading platform and attacked the bus that managed to get out of Anniston. Although police had been warned to expect trouble, they did nothing to stop the mob from beating the Freedom Riders with pipes and fists, nor did they make any arrests. FBI agents observed and took notes but did nothing. The remaining Freedom Riders decided to travel as a single group on the next lap, from Birmingham to Montgomery, but no bus would take them. Stranded and frightened, they reluctantly boarded a special flight to New Orleans arranged by the Justice Department. On May 17, the CORE-sponsored Freedom Ride disbanded.

Map 28.1 THE CIVIL RIGHTS MOVEMENT

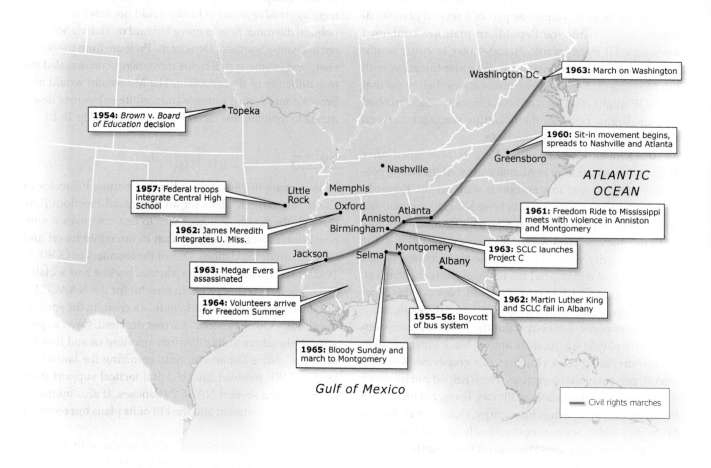

1963: March on Washington

Washington DC

1954: *Brown v. Board of Education* decision

Topeka

1960: Sit-in movement begins, spreads to Nashville and Atlanta

Greensboro

ATLANTIC OCEAN

• Nashville

1957: Federal troops integrate Central High School

Little Rock

• Memphis

Oxford

Atlanta

Anniston

Birmingham

1961: Freedom Ride to Mississippi meets with violence in Anniston and Montgomery

1962: James Meredith integrates U. Miss.

1963: SCLC launches Project C

Montgomery

Jackson

Selma

Albany

1963: Medgar Evers assassinated

1962: Martin Luther King and SCLC fail in Albany

1964: Volunteers arrive for Freedom Summer

1955–56: Boycott of bus system

1965: Bloody Sunday and march to Montgomery

Gulf of Mexico

Civil rights marches

Key battlegrounds in the struggle for racial justice in communities across the South.

That was not the end of the Freedom Rides. SNCC leaders in Atlanta and Nashville assembled a fresh group of volunteers to continue the trip. On May 20, 21 Freedom Riders left Birmingham for Montgomery. The bus station in the Alabama capital was eerily quiet and deserted as they pulled in. But when the passengers left the bus, a mob of several hundred whites rushed them, yelling "Get those niggers!" and clubbing people to the ground. James Zwerg, a white Freedom Rider from the University of Wisconsin, had his spinal cord severed. John Lewis, veteran of the Nashville sit-in movement, suffered a brain concussion. The mob indiscriminately beat journalists and clubbed John Siegenthaler, a Justice Department attorney sent to observe the scene. It took police more than an hour to halt the rioting. Montgomery's police commissioner later said, "We have no intention of standing guard for a bunch of troublemakers coming into our city."

The mob violence and the indifference of Alabama officials made the Freedom Ride front-page news around the country and throughout the world. Newspapers in

Europe, Africa, and Asia denounced the hypocrisy of the federal government. The Kennedy administration, preparing for the president's first summit meeting with Soviet Premier Nikita Khrushchev, saw the situation as a threat to the nation's global prestige. On May 21, an angry mob threatened to invade a support rally at Montgomery's First Baptist Church. A hastily assembled group of 400 U.S. marshals, sent by Robert Kennedy, barely managed to keep the peace. The attorney general called for a cooling-off period, but King, Farmer, and the SNCC leaders announced that the Freedom Ride would continue. A bandaged but spirited group of 27 Freedom Riders prepared to leave Montgomery for Jackson, Mississippi, on May 24. To avoid further violence, Robert Kennedy arranged a compromise through Mississippi Senator James Eastland. In exchange for a guarantee of safe passage through Mississippi, the federal government promised not to interfere with the arrest of the Freedom Riders in Jackson. This Freedom Ride and several that followed thus escaped violence. But more than 300 people were arrested that summer in Jackson on charges

ATTACKS ON THE FREEDOM RIDERS A Freedom Ride bus burns after being firebombed in Anniston, Alabama, May 14, 1961. After setting the bus afire, whites attacked the passengers fleeing the smoke and flames. Violent scenes like this one received extensive publicity in the mass media and helped compel the Justice Department to enforce court rulings banning segregation on interstate bus lines.

Library of Congress (Photoduplication).

of traveling "for the avowed purpose of inflaming public opinion." Sticking to a policy of "jail, no bail," Freedom Riders clogged the prison, where they endured beatings and intimidation by prison guards that went largely unreported in the press. Their jail experiences turned most of them into committed core leaders of the student movement.

The Freedom Rides exposed the ugly face of southern racism to the world and inspired grassroots activists around the South. But they also reinforced white resistance to desegregation and showed the limits of federal action against Jim Crow. Eventually the Justice Department did petition the Interstate Commerce Commission to issue clear rules prohibiting segregation on interstate carriers. At the end of 1962, CORE proclaimed victory in the battle against Jim Crow interstate travel. By creating a crisis, the Freedom Rides had forced the Kennedy administration to act. But they also revealed the unwillingness of the federal government to fully enforce the law of the land. The jailings and brutality experienced by Freedom Riders made clear to the civil rights community the limits of moral persuasion alone for effecting change.

28.2.6 The Albany Movement: The Limits of Protest

Where the federal government chose not to enforce the constitutional rights of black people, segregationist forces tenaciously held their ground, especially in the more remote

areas of the Deep South. One such place was Albany, a small city in southwest Georgia, where activists from SNCC, the NAACP, and other local groups formed a coalition known as the Albany Movement. For more than a year, beginning in October 1961, thousands of Albany's black citizens marched, sat in, and boycotted as part of a citywide campaign to integrate public facilities and win voting rights. More than a thousand people spent time in jail. In December, the arrival of Martin Luther King Jr. and the SCLC transformed Albany into a national symbol of the struggle.

The gains at Albany proved minimal. Local SNCC workers opposed the more cautious approach of NAACP officials, even though the more established organization paid many of the campaign's expenses. Albany Police Chief Laurie Pritchett shrewdly deprived the movement of the kind of national sympathy won by the Freedom Riders. Pritchett filled the jails with black demonstrators, kept their mistreatment to a minimum, and prevented white mobs from running wild. King himself was twice arrested in the summer of 1962, but Albany officials quickly freed him to avoid negative publicity. By late 1962, the Albany Movement had collapsed, and Pritchett proudly declared the city "as segregated as ever." Albany showed that mass protest without violent white reaction and direct federal intervention could not end Jim Crow.

In contrast to the failure at Albany, a successful battle to integrate the University of Mississippi reinforced the importance of federal intervention for guaranteeing African

American civil rights. In the fall of 1962, James Meredith, an Air Force veteran and a student at all-black Jackson State College, tried to register as the first black student at lily-white "Ole Miss." Defying a federal court order, Governor Ross Barnett personally blocked Meredith at the admissions office. When Barnett refused to assure Robert Kennedy that Meredith would be protected, the attorney general dispatched 500 federal marshals to the campus. Over the radio,

Barnett encouraged resistance to the "oppressive power of the United States," and an enraged mob of several thousand whites, many of them armed, laid siege to the campus on September 30. A night of violence left 2 people dead and 160 marshals wounded, 28 from gunfire. President Kennedy ordered 5,000 Army troops onto the campus to stop the riot. A federal guard remained to protect Meredith, who graduated the following summer. (See Communities *in* Conflict.)

Communities *in* Conflict

Showdown at Oxford: Integrating Ole Miss, 1962

Born in 1933, and raised and schooled in Mississippi, James Meredith served in the U.S. Air Force from 1951 to 1960. He attended Jackson State College for two years, but after being inspired by President John F. Kennedy's Inaugural Address, Meredith applied for admission to the all-white University of Mississippi in Oxford. With legal help from the NAACP, he sued the university after his application was denied. A federal district court ruled in June 1962 that the university must admit Meredith. Governor Ross Barnett vowed to prevent Meredith from registering for the fall 1962 semester, setting the stage for one of the most violent confrontations of the civil rights era. While negotiating with state officials, President Kennedy made a nationally televised address, appealing for law and order, and he sent 500 U.S. Marshals to protect Meredith.

By Sunday evening, September 30, 1962, a mob of several thousand white militants, many of them armed, had streamed onto the Oxford campus to prevent Meredith from entering the university. Heckling and jeering soon escalated to throwing bricks and bottles, and the marshals responded with tear gas as a full-fledged riot enveloped the campus that night. To protect the besieged marshals, President Kennedy ordered in thousands of regular Army troops, and he federalized units of the Mississippi National Guard. By dawn, 2 men lay dead, 28 marshals had been wounded by gunfire, and some 160 soldiers were injured.

After the federal military forces secured the campus Monday morning, Meredith registered and attended his first classes. Despite widespread harassment and ostracism from white students, Meredith completed his studies and graduated in June 1963 with a degree in political science. In later years, Meredith became an outspoken conservative who distanced himself from the civil rights struggle. But Oxford in the fall of 1962 had witnessed how the overwhelming force of the national government could confront massive white resistance in support of court-ordered integration.

The first document is the letter that Meredith wrote to Thurgood Marshall, head of the NAACP Legal Defense and Educational Fund, requesting legal assistance supporting his effort to attend the university. The second is from the address that Barnett delivered in September 1962 defending his refusal to allow Meredith admittance.

- **How does Meredith make his case to the NAACP for legal help? What does the letter's tone convey about Meredith as an individual?**

- **What legal, historical, and moral arguments does Barnett use to defend segregation as state policy? To what extent do you think his words encouraged armed resistance to integration?**

Letter from James Meredith to Thurgood Marshall, NAACP Legal Defense and Educational Fund, January 29, 1961

Dear Sir:

I am submitting an application for admission to the University of Mississippi. I am seeking entrance for the second semester which begins the 6th of February, 1961. I anticipate encountering some type of difficulty with the various agencies here in the state which are against my gaining entrance in the school. I discussed this matter with Mr. Evers, the Mississippi Field Secretary for the NAACP, and he suggested that I contact you and request legal assistance from your organization in the event it is needed for I am not financially able to fight a legal battle

against the state of Mississippi. I hope your decision on this request will be favorable. Below is a brief history of my background which might help you in reaching a decision.

I am a native Mississippian. All my elementary and secondary education was received in this state, except my last year of high school, which was completed in Florida. I spent nine years in the United States Air Force (1951-60), all of which were honorable. I have always been a "conscientious objector" to my "oppressed status" as long as I can remember. My long-cherished ambition has been to break the monopoly on rights and privileges held by the whites of the state of Mississippi.

My academic qualifications, I believe, are adequate. While in the Air Force, I successfully completed courses at four different schools conducting night classes. As an example, I completed 34 semester hours of work with the University of Maryland's Overseas Program. Of the twelve courses completed I made three A's and nine B's. I am presently enrolled at Jackson State College, here in Jackson. I have completed one quarter of work and I am now enrolled in a second quarter at Jackson. For the work completed I received one A, three B's and one C.

Finally, I am making this move in what I consider the interest of and for the benefit of: (1) my country, (2) my race, (3) my family, and (4) myself. I am familiar with the probable difficulties involved in such a move as I am undertaking and I am fully prepared to pursue it all the way to a degree from the University of Mississippi.

Sincerely yours,
J H MEREDITH

Source: John F. Kennedy Presidential Library and Museum
http://microsites.jfklibrary.org/olemiss/meredith/doc2.html

Governor Ross Barnett, Proclamation to the People of Mississippi, TV and Radio Broadcast, September 12, 1962

"The powers not delegated to the United States by the Constitution nor prohibited by it to the States are reserved to the States respectively or to the people." These are not my words. This is the tenth amendment to the Constitution of the United States.

Ladies and gentlemen, my friends and fellow Mississippians: I speak to you as your Governor in a solemn hour in the history of our great state and in our nation's history. I speak to you now in the moment of our greatest crisis since the War Between the States.

In the absence of constitutional authority and without legislative action, an ambitious federal government, employing naked and arbitrary power, has decided to deny us the right of self-determination in the conduct of the affairs of our sovereign state. Having long since failed in their efforts to conquer the indomitable spirit of the people of Mississippi and their unshakable will to preserve the sovereignty and majesty of our commonwealth, they now seek to break us physically with the power of force.

Even now as I speak to you tonight, professional agitators and the unfriendly liberal press and other trouble makers are pouring across our borders intent upon instigating strife among our people. Paid propagandists are continually hammering away at us in the hope that they can succeed in bringing about a division among us. Every effort is being made to intimidate us into submission to the tyranny of judicial oppression. The Kennedy Administration is lending the power of the federal government to the ruthless demands of these agitators. Thus we see our own federal government teamed up with a motley array of un-American pressure groups against us. This is the crisis we face today.

Principle is a little word. It is easy to speak and to spell and in print is easily overlooked, but it is a word that is tremendous in its import and meaning denoting respect and obedience to those fundamental and eternal truths that should be respected and form the way of life of all honest and right-thinking people. Expediency is for the hour; principles are for the ages. Principles are a passion for truth and right and justice, and as long as the rains descend and the winds blow, it is but folly to build upon the shifting sands of political expediency. It is better for one's blood to be poisoned than for him to be poisoned in his principles. So deep and compelling were the convictions and principles of our forefathers that they risked even death to establish this now desecrated Constitution as the American way of life and handed it to us in trust as our sacred heritage and for our preservation.

The day of expediency is past. We must either submit to the unlawful dictates of the federal government or stand up like men and tell them no. The day of reckoning has been delayed as long as possible. It is now upon us. This is the day, and this is the hour. Knowing you as I do, there is no doubt in my mind what the overwhelming majority of loyal Mississippians will do. They will never submit to the moral degradation, to the shame and the ruin which have faced all others who have lacked the courage to defend their beliefs.

I have made my position in this matter crystal clear. I have said in every county in Mississippi that no school in our state will be integrated while I am your Governor. I shall do everything in my power to prevent integration in our schools. I assure you that the schools will not be closed if this can possibly be avoided, but they will not be integrated if I can prevent it. As your Governor and Chief Executive of the sovereign State of Mississippi, I now call on every public official and every private citizen of our great state to join me . . .

Source: John F. Kennedy Presidential Library and Museum
http://microsites.jfklibrary.org/olemiss/controversy/doc2.html

28.3 The Movement at High Tide, 1963–1965

How did the civil rights movement intersect with national politics in the 1960s?

The tumultuous events of 1960–1962 convinced civil rights strategists that segregation could not be dismantled merely through orderly protest and moral persuasion. Only comprehensive civil rights legislation, backed by federal power, could guarantee full citizenship rights for African Americans. To build the national consensus needed for new laws, civil rights activists looked for ways to gain broader support for their cause. By 1963, their sense of urgency had led them to plan dramatic confrontations that would expose the violence and terror routinely faced by southern blacks. With the whole country—indeed, the whole world—watching, the Movement reached the peak of its political and moral power.

28.3.1 Birmingham

At the end of 1962, Martin Luther King Jr. and his SCLC allies decided to launch a new campaign against segregation in Birmingham, Alabama. Having failed in Albany, King and his aides looked for a way to shore up his leadership and inject new momentum into the freedom struggle. They needed a major victory. Birmingham, the most segregated big city in America, had a deep history of racial violence. African Americans endured total segregation in schools, restaurants, city parks, and department store dressing rooms. Although black people constituted more than 40 percent of the city's population, fewer than 10,000 of Birmingham's 80,000 registered voters were black.

Working closely with local civil rights groups led by the longtime Birmingham activist Reverend Fred Shuttlesworth, the SCLC carefully planned its campaign. The strategy was to fill the city jails with protesters, boycott downtown department stores, and enrage Public Safety Commissioner Eugene "Bull" Connor, a die-hard segregationist. In April, King arrived with a manifesto demanding an end to racist hiring practices and segregated public accommodations, and the creation of a biracial committee to oversee desegregation. Connor's police began jailing hundreds of demonstrators, including King himself, who defied a state court injunction against further protests. Held in solitary confinement for several days, King managed to write a response to a group of Birmingham clergy who had deplored the protests. King's "Letter from a Birmingham Jail" was soon widely reprinted and circulated as a pamphlet. It set out the key moral issues at stake, and scoffed at those who claimed the campaign was illegal and ill timed.

After King's release on bail, the campaign intensified. The SCLC kept up the pressure by recruiting thousands of Birmingham's young students for a "children's crusade." In early May, Connor unleashed high-powered water cannons, billy clubs, and snarling police dogs to break up demonstrations. Millions of Americans reacted with horror to the violent scenes from Birmingham shown on national television. Many younger black people, especially from the city's poor and working-class districts, began to fight back, hurling bottles and bricks at police. On May 10, mediators from the Justice Department negotiated an uneasy truce. The SCLC agreed to an immediate end to the protests. In exchange, businesses would desegregate and begin hiring African Americans over the next three months, and a biracial city committee would oversee desegregation of public facilities.

A few days after the announcement, more than a thousand robed Ku Klux Klansmen burned a cross in a park on the outskirts of Birmingham. When bombs rocked SCLC headquarters and the home of King's brother, a Birmingham minister, enraged blacks took to the streets and pelted police and firefighters with stones and bottles. President Kennedy ordered 3,000 Army troops into the city and prepared to nationalize the Alabama National Guard. The violence receded, and white businesspeople and politicians began to carry out the agreed-upon pact. But in September, a bomb killed four black girls in a Birmingham Baptist church, reminding the city and the world that racial harmony was still a long way off.

The Birmingham campaign and the other protests it sparked over the next seven months engaged more than 100,000 people and led to nearly 15,000 arrests. The civil rights community now drew support from millions of Americans, black and white, all inspired by the protesters and repelled by southern bigotry. At the same time, Birmingham changed the nature of black protest. The black unemployed and working poor who joined in the struggle brought a different perspective from that of the students, professionals, and members of the religious middle class who had dominated the Movement before Birmingham. They cared less about the philosophy of nonviolence and more about immediate gains in employment and housing and an end to police brutality.

28.3.2 JFK and the March on Washington

The growth of black activism and of white support convinced President Kennedy the moment had come to press for sweeping civil rights legislation. Continuing white resistance in the South also made clearer than ever the need for federal action. In June 1963, Governor George Wallace threatened to personally block the admission of two black students to the University of Alabama. Only the deployment of National Guard troops, placed under federal control by the president, ensured the students' safety and their peaceful admission into the university.

THE MARCH ON WASHINGTON Part of the huge throng of marchers at the historic March on Washington for "Jobs and Freedom," August 28, 1963. The size of the crowd, the stirring oratory and song, and the live network television coverage produced one of the most memorable political demonstrations in the nation's history.

Francis Miller/Getty Images.

On June 11, the president went on national television and offered his personal endorsement of the Movement. Reviewing the racial situation, Kennedy told the nation, "We face . . . a moral crisis as a country and a people. It cannot be met by repressive police action." Even more than was the case for Eisenhower at Little Rock, the realities of international Cold War politics pushed Kennedy toward support for civil rights. "Today we are committed to a worldwide struggle to promote and protect the rights of all who wish to be free. And when Americans are sent to Vietnam or West Berlin, we do not ask for whites only. . . . Are we to say to the rest of the world, and much more importantly, to each other, that this is a land of the free except for Negroes?" The next week, Kennedy asked Congress for a broad law that would ensure voting rights, outlaw segregation in public facilities, and bolster federal authority to deny funds for discriminatory programs. Knowing they would face a stiff fight from congressional conservatives, administration officials began an intense lobbying effort in support of the law. After three years of fence sitting, Kennedy finally committed his office and his political future to the civil rights cause.

Movement leaders lauded the president's initiative. Yet they understood that racial hatred still haunted the nation. Only hours after Kennedy's television speech, a gunman murdered Medgar Evers, leader of the Mississippi NAACP, outside his home in Jackson, Mississippi. To pressure Congress and demonstrate the urgency of their cause, a broad coalition of civil rights groups planned a massive, nonviolent **March on Washington**. The idea had deep roots in black protest. A. Philip Randolph, head of the Brotherhood of Sleeping Car Porters, had originally proposed such a march in 1941 to protest discrimination against blacks in defense industries. (See Chapter 25.) More than 20 years later, Randolph, along with his aide Bayard Rustin, revived the concept and convinced leaders of the major civil rights groups to support it.

The Kennedy administration originally opposed the march, fearing it would jeopardize support for the president's civil rights bill in Congress. As plans for the rally solidified, Kennedy reluctantly gave his approval. Leaders from the SCLC, the NAACP, SNCC, the Urban League, and CORE—the leading organizations in the civil rights community—put aside their tactical differences to forge a broad consensus for the event. John Lewis, the young head of SNCC, who had endured numerous brutal assaults, planned a speech that denounced the Kennedys as hypocrites. Lewis's speech enraged Walter Reuther, the white liberal leader of the United Auto Workers union, which had helped finance the march. Reuther threatened to turn off the loudspeakers he was paying for, believing Lewis's speech would embarrass the Kennedys. At the last moment, Randolph, the Movement's acknowledged elder statesman, convinced Lewis to tone down his remarks. "We've come this far," he implored. "For the sake of unity, change it."

On August 28, 1963, more than a quarter of a million people, including about 50,000 whites, gathered at the Lincoln Memorial to rally for "jobs and freedom." Union members, students, teachers, clergy, professionals, musicians, actors—Americans from all walks of life—joined the largest political assembly in the nation's history until that point. The sight of all those people holding hands and singing "We Shall Overcome," led by white folksinger Joan Baez, would not be easily forgotten, either by participants or by millions of television viewers. At the end of a long, exhilarating day of speeches and freedom songs, Martin Luther King Jr. provided the emotional climax. Combining the democratic promise of the Declaration of Independence with the religious fervor of his Baptist heritage, King stirred the crowd and the nation with his dream for America.

The following year, at age 35, King received the Nobel Peace Prize, which both solidified his reputation as the premier voice of the Movement and added greatly to his stature within mainstream American culture. The award also demonstrated the truly global impact of the Movement he led.

28.3.3 LBJ and the Civil Rights Act of 1964

An extraordinary demonstration of interracial unity, the March on Washington stood as the high-water mark in the struggle for civil rights. It buoyed the spirits of Movement leaders, as well as of liberals pushing the new civil rights bill through Congress. But the assassination of John F. Kennedy on November 22, 1963, in Dallas threw an ominous cloud over the whole nation and the civil rights movement in particular. Most African Americans probably shared the feelings of Coretta Scott King, who recalled her family's vigil, "We felt that President Kennedy had been a friend of the Cause and that with him as President we could continue to move forward. We watched and prayed for him."

Lyndon Baines Johnson (LBJ), Kennedy's successor, had never been much of a friend to civil rights. As a senator from Texas (1948–60, including six years as majority leader), Johnson had been one of the shrewdest and most powerful Democrats in Congress. Throughout the 1950s, he had worked to obstruct the passage and enforcement of civil rights laws. But as vice president he had ably chaired Kennedy's working group on equal employment. Even so, civil rights activists looked upon Johnson warily as he took over the Oval Office.

As president, Johnson realized that he faced a new political reality, created by the civil rights movement. Eager to unite the Democratic Party and prove himself as a national leader, he seized on civil rights as a golden political opportunity. Throughout the early months of 1964, the new president let it be known that he would brook no compromise on civil rights. Johnson exploited all his skills as a political insider to persuade key members of the House and Senate. Working with the president, the 15-year-old Leadership Conference on Civil Rights coordinated a sophisticated lobbying effort in Congress. Groups such as the NAACP, the AFL-CIO, the National Council of Churches, and the American Jewish Congress made the case for a strong civil rights bill. The House passed the bill in February by a 290 to 130 vote. The more difficult fight would be in the Senate, where a southern filibuster promised to block or weaken the bill. By June, however, Johnson's persistence had paid off. The southern filibuster collapsed.

On July 2, 1964, Johnson signed the Civil Rights Act of 1964. Every major provision had survived intact. This landmark law represented the most significant civil rights legislation since Reconstruction. It prohibited discrimination in most places of public accommodation; it banned discrimination in employment on the basis of race, color, religion, sex, or national origin; it outlawed bias in federally assisted programs; it authorized the Justice Department to institute lawsuits to desegregate public schools and other facilities; and it provided technical and financial aid to communities desegregating their schools. The act also created the Equal Employment Opportunity Commission (EEOC) to investigate and litigate cases of job discrimination.

There were important unintended consequences of this landmark legislation as well. It gave legal foundation to affirmative action policies and to the assertion of equal rights for women and non-black minorities. The EEOC, for example, became an important site for contesting both gender and racial discrimination in the workplace, receiving over 100,000 complaints a year by the 1970s. And on a political level, LBJ was perhaps more prescient than he realized when he commented after signing the bill that the Civil Rights Act "delivered the South to the Republican Party." It took real political courage for Johnson, a southern Democrat, to support the legislation as vigorously as he did, for the new law did indeed initiate a long-term political realignment that would transform the South from a solidly Democratic region to a solidly Republican one.

28.3.4 Mississippi Freedom Summer

While Johnson and his liberal allies won the congressional battle for the new civil rights bill, activists in Mississippi mounted a far more radical and dangerous campaign than any yet attempted in the South. In the spring of 1964, a coalition of workers led by SNCC launched the Freedom Summer project, an ambitious effort to register black voters and directly challenge the iron rule of segregation. Mississippi stood as the toughest test for the civil rights movement. It was the nation's poorest state and by most statistical measures the most backward, and it had remained largely untouched by the freedom struggle. African Americans constituted 42 percent of the state's population, but fewer than 5 percent could vote. A small white-planter elite controlled most of the state's wealth, and a long tradition of terror against black people maintained the racial caste system.

Bob Moses of SNCC and Dave Dennis of CORE planned Freedom Summer as a way of opening up this closed society. The project recruited more than 900 volunteers, mostly white college students, to aid in voter registration, teach in "freedom schools," and help build a "Freedom Party" as an alternative to Mississippi's all-white Democratic Party. Organizers expected violence, which was precisely why they wanted white volunteers. Dennis later explained their

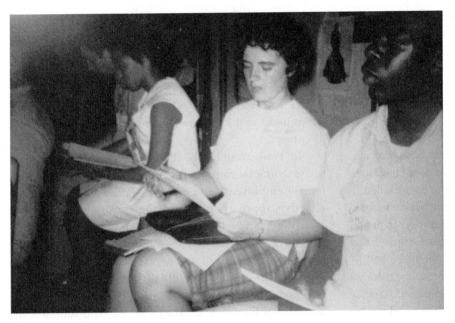

MISSISSIPPI FREEDOM SUMMER The organizers of Mississippi Freedom Summer actively recruited white college students, knowing that violence directed at white volunteers would draw national attention to the project.

Hyoung Chang/Getty Images.

reasoning; "The death of a white college student would bring on more attention to what was going on than for a black college student getting it. That's cold, but that was also in another sense speaking the language of this country." Mississippi authorities prepared for the civil rights workers as if expecting a foreign army, beefing up state highway patrols and local police forces.

On June 21, while most project volunteers were still training in Ohio, three activists disappeared in Neshoba County, Mississippi, where they went to investigate the burning of a black church that was supposed to serve as a freedom school. Six weeks later, after a massive search belatedly ordered by President Johnson, FBI agents discovered the bodies of the three—northern white students Michael Schwerner and Andrew Goodman, and a local black activist, James Chaney—buried in an earthen dam. Over the summer, at least three other civil rights workers died violently. Project workers suffered 1,000 arrests, 80 beatings, 35 shooting incidents, and 30 bombings of homes, churches, and schools.

Within the project, simmering problems tested the ideal of the Beloved Community. Black veterans of SNCC resented the affluent white volunteers, many of whom had not come to terms with their own racial prejudices. White volunteers, staying only a short time in the state, often found it difficult to communicate in the southern communities with local African Americans, wary of breaking old codes of deference. Sexual tensions between black male and white female volunteers also strained relations. A number of both black and white women, led by Ruby Doris Robinson, Mary King, and Casey Hayden, began to raise the issue of women's equality as a companion goal to racial equality. The day-to-day reality of violent

reprisals, police harassment, and constant fear took a hard toll on everyone.

The project did manage to rivet national attention on Mississippi racism, and it won enormous sympathy from northern liberals. Among their concrete accomplishments, the volunteers could point with pride to more than 40 freedom schools that brought classes in reading, arithmetic, politics, and African American history to thousands of black children. Some 60,000 black voters signed up to join the Mississippi Freedom Democratic Party (MFDP). In August 1964, the MFDP sent a slate of delegates to the Democratic National Convention looking to challenge the credentials of the all-white regular state delegation.

At the Democrats' Atlantic City convention, the idealism of **Freedom Summer** collided with the more cynical needs of the national Democratic Party. Concerned that Republicans might carry a number of southern states in November, President Johnson opposed seating the MFDP because he wanted to avoid a divisive floor fight. But before the convention opened, MFDP leaders and sympathizers gave dramatic testimony detailing the racism and brutality in Mississippi politics. "Is this America," asked Fannie Lou Hamer, "the land of the free and the home of the brave, where we are threatened daily because we want to live as decent human beings?" Led by Senator Hubert Humphrey, whom LBJ had already picked as his running mate, Johnson's forces offered a compromise that would have given the MFDP two token seats on the floor. Bitter over what they saw as a betrayal, the MFDP delegates turned the offer down. Within SNCC, the defeat of the MFDP intensified African American disillusionment with the Democratic Party and the liberal establishment.

28.3.5 Malcolm X and Black Consciousness

Frustrated with the limits of nonviolent protest and electoral politics, younger activists within SNCC found themselves increasingly drawn to the militant rhetoric and vision of Malcolm X, who since the early 1950s had been the preeminent spokesman for the black nationalist religious sect, the Nation of Islam (NOI). Founded in Depression-era Detroit by Elijah Muhammad, the NOI, like the followers of black-nationalist leader Marcus Garvey in the 1920s (see Chapter 23), aspired to create a self-reliant, highly disciplined, and proud community—a separate "nation" for black people. Elijah Muhammad preached a message of racial solidarity and self-help, criticized crime and drug use, and castigated whites as "blue-eyed devils" responsible for the world's evil. During the 1950s, the NOI (also called Black Muslims) successfully organized in northern black communities, appealing especially to criminals, drug addicts, and others on the margins of urban life. It operated restaurants, retail stores, and schools as models for black economic self-sufficiency.

The man known as Malcolm X had been born Malcolm Little in 1925 and raised in Lansing, Michigan. His father, a preacher and a follower of Marcus Garvey, was killed in a racist attack by local whites. In his youth, Malcolm led a life of petty crime, eventually serving a seven-year prison term for burglary. While in jail he educated himself and converted to the Nation of Islam. He took the surname "X" to symbolize his original African family name, lost through slavery. Emerging from jail in 1952, he became a dynamic organizer, editor, and speaker for the Nation of Islam. He spoke frequently on college campuses as well on the street corners of black neighborhoods like New York's Harlem. He encouraged his audiences to take pride in their African heritage and to consider armed self-defense rather than relying solely on nonviolence—in short, to break free of white domination "by any means necessary."

Malcolm ridiculed the integrationist goals of the civil rights movement. Black Muslims, he told audiences, do not want "to integrate into this corrupt society, but to separate from it, to a land of our own, where we can reform ourselves, lift up our moral standards, and try to be godly." In his best-selling *The Autobiography of Malcolm X* (1965), he admitted that his position was extremist. "The black race here in North America is in extremely bad condition. You show me a black man who isn't an extremist," he argued, "and I'll show you one who needs psychiatric attention."

In 1964, troubled by Elijah Muhammad's personal scandals (he faced paternity suits brought by two young female employees) and eager to find a more politically effective approach to improving conditions for blacks, Malcolm X broke with the Nation of Islam. He made the pilgrimage to Mecca, the Muslim holy city, where he met Islamic peoples of all colors and underwent a "radical alteration in my whole outlook about 'white' men." He returned to the United States as El-Hajj Malik El-Shabazz, abandoned his black separatist views, and founded the Organization of Afro-American Unity. Malcolm now looked for common ground with the civil rights movement, addressing a Mississippi Freedom Democrats rally in Harlem and meeting with SNCC activists. He stressed the international links between the civil rights struggle in America and the problems facing emerging African nations. On February 21, 1965, Malcolm X was assassinated while giving a speech in Harlem. His assailants were members of a New Jersey branch of the NOI, possibly infiltrated by the FBI.

SNCC leader John Lewis thought Malcolm X had been the most effective voice "to articulate the aspirations, bitterness, and frustrations of the Negro people," forming "a living link between Africa and the civil rights movement in this country." In his death, Malcolm X became a martyr for the idea that soon became known as Black Power. As much as anyone, he pointed the way to a new black consciousness that celebrated black history, black culture, African heritage, and black self-sufficiency.

28.3.6 Selma and the Voting Rights Act of 1965

Lyndon Johnson won election in 1964 by a landslide, capturing 61 percent of the popular vote. Of the 6 million black people who voted in the election—2 million more than in 1960—an overwhelming 94 percent cast their ballots for Johnson. Republican candidate Barry Goldwater managed to carry only his home state of Arizona and five Deep South states, where fewer than 45 percent of eligible black people could vote. With Democrats in firm control of both the Senate and the House, civil rights leaders believed the time was ripe for further legislative gains. There had already been some progress toward guaranteeing voting rights with the 1964 ratification of the Twenty-Fourth Amendment to the Constitution, outlawing the poll tax or any other tax as a condition of voting. Johnson and his staff began drafting

MALCOLM X Born Malcolm Little, Malcolm X (1925–1965) took the name "X" as a symbol of the stolen identity of African slaves. He emerged in the early 1960s as the foremost advocate of racial unity and black nationalism. The Black Power movement, initiated in 1966 by SNCC members, was strongly influenced by Malcolm X.

Library of Congress (Photoduplication).

a tough voting rights bill in late 1964, partly with an eye toward countering Republican gains among Deep South whites with newly registered black Democratic voters. (See Map 28.2.)

Once again, Movement leaders decided to create a crisis that would arouse national indignation, pressure Congress, and force federal action. Martin Luther King Jr. and his aides chose Selma, Alabama, as their target. Selma, a city of 27,000 some fifty miles west of Montgomery, had a notorious record of preventing black voting. Of the 15,000 eligible black voters in Selma's Dallas County, registered voters numbered only in the hundreds. In 1963, local activists had invited SNCC workers to aid voter registration efforts in the community. But they had met a violent reception from Dallas County Sheriff Jim Clark. Sensing that Clark might be another Bull Connor, King arrived in Selma in January 1965, just after accepting the Nobel Peace Prize in Oslo. "We are not asking, we are demanding the ballot," he declared. King, the SCLC staff, and SNCC workers led daily marches on the Dallas County Courthouse, where hundreds of black citizens tried to get their names added to voter lists. By early February, Clark had imprisoned more than 3,000 protesters.

Despite the brutal beating of Reverend James Bevel, a key SCLC strategist, and the killing of Jimmy Lee Jackson, a young black demonstrator in nearby Marion, the SCLC failed to arouse the level of national indignation it sought. Consequently, in early March, SCLC staffers called on black activists to march from Selma to Montgomery, where they planned to deliver a list of grievances to Governor Wallace. On Sunday, March 7, while King preached to his church in Atlanta, a group of 600 marchers crossed the Pettus Bridge on the Alabama River, on their way to Montgomery. A group of mounted, heavily armed county and state lawmen blocked their path and ordered them to turn back. When the marchers did not move, the lawmen attacked with billy clubs and tear gas, driving the protesters back over the bridge in a bloody rout. More than 50 marchers had to be treated in local hospitals.

The dramatic "Bloody Sunday" attack received extensive coverage on network television, prompting a national

Map 28.2 IMPACT OF THE VOTING RIGHTS ACT OF 1965

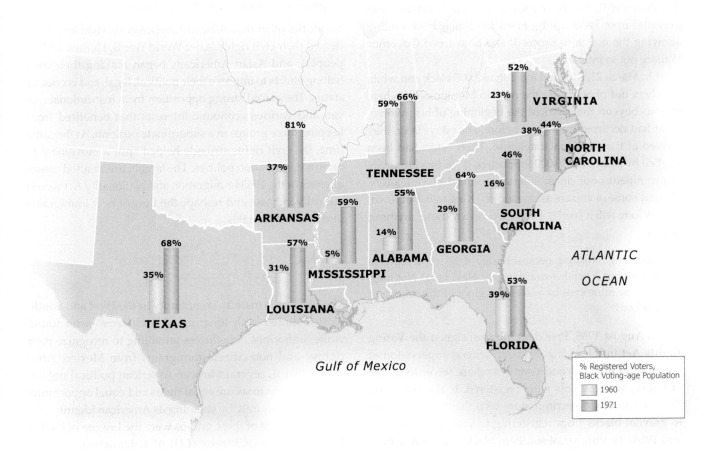

Voter registration among African Americans in the South increased significantly between 1960 and 1971.

uproar. Demands for federal intervention poured into the White House from all over the country. King issued a public call for civil rights supporters to come to Selma for a second march on Montgomery. But a federal court temporarily enjoined the SCLC from proceeding with the march. King found himself trapped. He reluctantly accepted a face-saving compromise: In return for a promise from Alabama authorities not to harm marchers, King would lead his followers across the Pettus Bridge, stop, pray briefly, and then turn back. This plan outraged the more militant SNCC activists and sharpened their distrust of King and the SCLC.

Just when it seemed the Selma movement might die, white racist violence revived it. A gang of white toughs attacked four white Unitarian ministers who had come to Selma to participate in the march. One of them, Reverend James J. Reeb of Boston, died of multiple skull fractures. His death brought new calls for federal action. On March 15, President Johnson delivered a televised address to a joint session of Congress to request passage of a voting rights bill. In a stirring speech, the president fused the political power of his office with the moral power of the Movement. "Their cause must be our cause, too. Because it is not just Negroes, but really all of us who must overcome the crippling legacy of bigotry and injustice. And," he concluded firmly, quoting the Movement's hymn, "we shall overcome." Johnson also prevailed upon federal judge Frank Johnson to issue a ruling allowing the march to proceed, and he warned Governor Wallace not to interfere.

On March 21, King led more than 3,000 black and white marchers out of Selma on the road to Montgomery, where the bus boycott that marked the beginning of his involvement had occurred nine years before. Four days later, they arrived at the Alabama statehouse. Their ranks had been swelled by more than 30,000 supporters, including hundreds of prominent politicians, entertainers, and black leaders. "I know some of you are asking today," King told the crowd, " 'How long will it take?' " He went on in a rousing, rhythmic cadence:

> How long? Not long, because the arc of the moral universe is long but it bends toward justice. How long? Not long, because mine eyes have seen the glory of the coming of the Lord!

In August 1965, President Johnson signed the **Voting Rights Act** into law. It authorized federal supervision of registration in states and counties where fewer than half of voting-age residents were registered. It also outlawed literacy and other discriminatory tests that had been used to prevent blacks from registering to vote. Between 1964 and 1968, the number of southern black voters grew from 1 million to 3.1 million. For the first time in their lives, black Southerners in hundreds of small towns and rural communities could enjoy full participation in American politics. Ten years after the Montgomery bus boycott, the civil

rights movement had reached peaks of national influence and interracial unity.

Yet even amid this triumph, the growing mood of desperation among African Americans in northern ghettoes suggested the limits of the Movement and interracial unity. There had been a violent uprising in New York's Harlem in the summer of 1964 and a far more widespread and destructive rebellion in the Watts section of Los Angeles in August 1965. (See Chapter 29.) These marked the first of the "long, hot summer" uprisings that would alienate many white citizens who had been sympathetic to the nonviolent civil rights struggle. They served notice as well that the growing frustration and alienation of northern blacks, increasingly defined by a militant turn to the rhetoric of "black power," could not be addressed with the same principles, tactics, and solutions that had made the southern civil rights movement successful.

28.4 Civil Rights Beyond Black and White

How did the African American struggle for civil rights inspire other American minority groups?

Minorities other than African Americans also had long been denied their civil rights. After World War II, Latinos, Indian peoples, and Asian Americans began making their own halting efforts to improve their political, legal, and economic status. They faced strong opposition from institutional racism and various economic interests that benefited from keeping these groups in a subordinate position. At the same time, the civil rights struggle helped spur a movement to reform immigration policies. The largely unintended consequences of the 1965 Immigration and Nationality Act would radically increase and reshape the flow of new immigrants into the United States.

28.4.1 Mexican Americans and Mexican Immigrants

The Mexican American community in the West and Southwest included both longtime U.S. citizens—who found white authorities nonetheless unwilling to recognize their rights—and non-citizen immigrants from Mexico. After World War II, several Mexican American political organizations sought to secure equal rights and equal opportunity for their community by stressing its American identity. The most important of these groups were the League of United Latin American Citizens (LULAC), launched in Texas in 1928, and the GI Forum, founded in Texas in 1948 by Mexican American veterans of World War II. Both emphasized learning English, assimilating into American society, improving education, and voting to gain political power.

LULAC successfully pursued two important legal cases that anticipated *Brown v. Board of Education*. In *Mendez v. Westminster*, a 1947 California case, and in the 1948 *Delgado v. Bastrop ISD* case in Texas, the Supreme Court upheld lower-court rulings that declared segregation of Mexican Americans unconstitutional. Like *Brown*, these two decisions did not immediately end segregation, but they offered pathbreaking legal and psychological victories to Mexican American activists. LULAC won another significant legal battle in the 1954 *Hernandez* decision, in which the Supreme Court ended the exclusion of Mexican Americans from Texas jury lists.

Mexican migration to the United States increased dramatically during and after World War II. The *bracero* program, a cooperative effort between the U.S. and Mexican governments, brought some 300,000 Mexicans to the United States during the war as temporary agricultural and railroad workers. American agribusiness came to depend on Mexicans as a key source of cheap farm labor, and the program continued after the war. Most *braceros* endured harsh work, poor food, and substandard housing in migratory labor camps. Some migrated into the newly emerging *barrios*—Hispanic neighborhoods—in cities such as San Antonio, Los Angeles, El Paso, and Denver. Many *braceros* and their children became American citizens, but most returned to Mexico. Another group of postwar Mexican immigrants were the *mojados*, or "wetbacks," so called because many swam the Rio Grande to enter the United States illegally.

This continued flow of immigrant workers into the Southwest heightened tensions within the Mexican American community. LULAC and the GI Forum contended that Mexican American civil rights activists needed to focus their efforts on American citizens of Mexican descent. Thus, they lobbied to end the *bracero* program and enforce stricter limits on immigration from Mexico to help maintain strict boundaries between Mexican American citizens and Mexican immigrants. Yet within Mexican American communities, where citizens and noncitizens shared language and work experience and made families together, this distinction had always been blurry.

In 1954, trying to curb the flow of undocumented immigrants from Mexico, the Eisenhower administration launched the massive "Operation Wetback." Over the course of three years, Immigration and Naturalization Service (INS) agents rounded up some 3.7 million allegedly undocumented migrants and sent them back over the border. INS agents made little effort to distinguish so-called illegals from *braceros* and Mexican American citizens. Many families were broken up, and thousands who had lived in the United States for a decade or more found themselves deported. Many deportees were denied basic civil liberties, such as due process, and suffered physical abuse and intimidation. The breakup of families caused enormous resentment and anger, as did the contradictory policies of the federal government. As Ernesto Galarza, a leader of the National Agricultural Workers Union, put it, "While one agency of the United States government rounded up the illegal aliens and deported them to Mexico . . . another government agency was busily engaged in recruiting workers in Mexico to return them to U.S. farms."

LEAGUE OF UNITED LATIN AMERICAN CITIZENS Lieutenant Governor Gordon Allott of Colorado presents an official proclamation to Fred E. Gonzales, president of the state chapter of the League of United Latin American Citizens (LULAC), designating the week of Feb. 14–20, 1954, as LULAC week in Colorado. After World War II, LULAC grew to about 15,000 members active in 200 local councils.

The government campaign against aliens pushed LULAC, the GI Forum, and other activist groups to change their strategy in a critical way. The campaign to win full civil rights for American citizens of Mexican descent would increasingly be linked to improving the lives—and asserting the rights—of all Mexican immigrants, both documented and undocumented. If the government and the broader American public refused to distinguish among a Mexican national, a resident alien of the United States, a naturalized American citizen, and a native-born Spanish-speaking American, why should Mexican Americans cling to these distinctions? By the 1960s, a new civil rights movement emerged, *la raza* ("the race"), based on the shared ethnicity and historical experiences of the broader Mexican American community.

28.4.2 Puerto Ricans

The United States seized Puerto Rico in 1898, during the final stages of the Spanish-American War. The Jones Act of 1917 made the island an unincorporated territory of the United States and granted U.S. citizenship to all Puerto Ricans. Over the next several decades, Puerto Rico's economic base shifted from a diversified, subsistence-oriented agriculture to a single export crop—sugar. United States absentee owners dominated the sugar industry, claiming most of the island's arable land, previously tilled by small farmers growing crops for local consumption. Puerto Rico's sugar industry grew enormously profitable, but few island residents benefited from this expansion. By the 1930s, unemployment and poverty were widespread and the island was forced to import its foodstuffs.

Small communities of Puerto Rican migrants had begun to form in New York City during the 1920s. The largest was on the Upper East Side of Manhattan—*el barrio* in East Harlem. During World War II, labor shortages led the federal government to sponsor the recruitment of Puerto Rican workers for industrial jobs in New Jersey, Philadelphia, and Chicago. But the "great migration" took place from 1945 to 1964. During these two decades, the number of Puerto Ricans living on the mainland jumped from fewer than 100,000 to roughly 1 million. Economic opportunity was the chief impetus for this migration, because the island suffered from high unemployment and low wages.

The advent of direct airline service between Puerto Rico and New York in 1945 made the city easily accessible. The Puerto Rican community in East (or Spanish) Harlem mushroomed, and new communities in the South Bronx and Brooklyn began to emerge. By 1970, there were about 800,000 Puerto Ricans in New York—more than 10 percent of the city's population. New Puerto Rican communities also took root in Connecticut, Massachusetts, New Jersey, and the Midwest. Puerto Ricans frequently circulated between the island and the mainland, often returning home when economic conditions on the mainland were less favorable.

The experience of Puerto Rican migrants both resembled and differed from those of other immigrant groups in significant ways. Like Mexican immigrants, Puerto Ricans were foreign in language, culture, and experience; unlike Mexicans, they entered the continental United States as citizens. Many Puerto Ricans were also black. Racial and ethnic discrimination came as a double shock, since Puerto Ricans, as citizens, came to America with a sense of entitlement. In New York, Puerto Ricans found themselves barred from most craft unions, excluded from certain neighborhoods, and forced to take jobs largely in the low-paying garment industry and service trades. Puerto Rican children were not well served by a public school system insensitive to language differences and too willing to track Spanish-speaking students into obsolete vocational programs.

By the early 1970s, Puerto Rican families were substantially poorer on average than the total U.S. population, and they had the lowest median income of any Latino group. The steep decline in manufacturing jobs and in the garment industry in New York during the 1960s and 1970s hit the Puerto Rican community especially hard. The structural shift in the U.S. economy away from manufacturing and toward service and high-technology jobs reinforced the Puerto Rican community's goal of improving educational opportunities for its members. The struggle to establish and improve bilingual education in schools became an important part of this effort. Most Puerto Ricans, especially those who had succeeded in school and achieved middle-class status, continued to identify strongly with their Puerto Rican heritage and Spanish language.

28.4.3 Japanese Americans

The harsh relocation program of World War II devastated the Japanese American community on the West Coast. (See Chapter 25.) But the war against Nazism also helped weaken older notions of white superiority and racism. During the war, the state of California had aggressively enforced an alien land law by confiscating property declared illegally held by Japanese. In November 1946, a proposition supporting the law appeared on the state ballot. Thanks in part to a campaign by the Japanese American Citizens League (JACL) reminding voters of the wartime contributions of Nisei (second-generation Japanese American) soldiers, voters overwhelmingly rejected the referendum. One JACL leader hailed the vote as proof that "the people of California will not approve discriminatory and prejudiced treatment of persons of Japanese ancestry." Two years later, the Supreme Court declared the law unconstitutional, calling it "nothing more than outright racial discrimination."

The 1952 Immigration and Nationality Act (see Chapter 26) removed the old ban against Japanese immigration and also made Issei (first-generation Japanese Americans) eligible for naturalized citizenship. Japanese Americans, who lobbied hard for the new law, greeted it with elation. "It gave the Japanese equality with all other immigrants," said JACL leader Harry Takagi, "and that was the principle we had been struggling for from the very beginning." By 1965, some 46,000 immigrant Japanese, most of them elderly Issei, had taken their citizenship oaths under the new act.

28.4.4 Indian Peoples

The postwar years also brought significant changes in the status and lives of Indian peoples. Congress reversed New Deal policies that had stressed Indian sovereignty and cultural independence. Responding to a variety of pressure groups, including mining and other economic interests wishing to exploit natural resources on reservations, Congress adopted a policy known as "termination," designed to cancel Indian treaties and terminate sovereignty rights. In 1953, Congress passed **House Concurrent Resolution 108**, which allowed Congress to terminate a tribe as a political entity by passing legislation specific to that tribe. Supporters of termination had varied motives, but the policy added up to the return of enforced assimilation for solving the "Indian problem."

Between 1954 and 1962, Congress passed 12 termination bills covering more than 60 tribes, nearly all in the West. Even when tribes consented to their own termination, they discovered that dissolution brought unforeseen problems. For example, members of the Klamaths of Oregon and the Paiutes of Utah received large cash payments from the division of tribal assets. But after these one-time payments were spent, members had to take poorly paid, unskilled jobs to survive. Many Indian peoples became dependent on state social services and slipped into poverty and alcoholism.

Along with termination, the federal government gave greater emphasis to a relocation program aimed at speeding up assimilation. The Bureau of Indian Affairs encouraged reservation Indians to relocate to cities, where they were provided with housing and jobs. For some, relocation meant assimilation, intermarriage with whites, and loss of tribal identity. Others, homesick and unable to adjust to an alien culture and place, either returned to reservations or wound up on the margins of city life. Still others regularly traveled back and forth. In some respects, this urban migration paralleled the larger postwar shift of rural peoples to cities and suburbs.

Indians increasingly came to see termination as a policy geared mainly toward exploiting resources on Indian lands. By the early 1960s, a new movement was emerging to defend Indian sovereignty. The National Congress of American Indians (NCAI) condemned termination, calling for a review of federal policies and a return to self-determination. The NCAI led a political and educational campaign that challenged the goal of assimilation and created a new awareness among white people that Indians had the right to remain Indians. When the termination policy ended in the early 1960s, it had affected only about 3 percent of federally recognized Indian peoples.

Taking their cue from the civil rights movement, Indian activists used the court system to reassert sovereign rights. Indian and white liberal lawyers, many with experience in civil rights cases, worked through the Native American Rights Fund, which became a powerful force in western politics. A series of Supreme Court decisions, culminating in *United States v. Wheeler* (1978), reasserted the principle of "unique and limited" sovereignty. The Court recognized tribal independence except where limited by treaty or Congress.

The Indian population had been growing since the early years of the century, but most reservations had trouble making room for a new generation. Indians suffered increased rates of poverty, chronic unemployment, alcoholism, and poor health. The average Indian family in the early 1960s earned only one-third of the average family income in the United States. Those who remained in the cities usually became "ethnic Indians," identifying themselves more as simply "Indians" than as members of specific tribes. By the late 1960s, ethnic Indians had begun emphasizing civil rights over tribal rights, making common cause with African Americans and other minorities. The National Indian Youth Council (NIYC), founded in 1960, tried to unite the two causes of equality for individual Indians and special status for tribes. But the organization faced difficult contradictions between a common Indian identity, emphasizing Indians as a single ethnic group, and tribal identity, stressing the citizenship of Indians in separate nations.

28.4.5 Remaking the Golden Door: The Immigration and Nationality Act of 1965

The egalitarian political climate created by the civil rights movement nurtured efforts to modernize and reform the country's immigration policies. In 1965, Congress passed a new **Immigration and Nationality Act**, abolishing the national origins quotas that had been in place since the 1920s and substituting overall hemispheric limits: 120,000 visas annually for immigrants from the Western Hemisphere and 170,000 for those from the Eastern Hemisphere (with a limit of 20,000 from any single country). The act was intended to redress the grievances of Eastern and Southern European ethnic groups who had been largely shut out since 1924. President Johnson played down its importance. "It does not affect the lives of millions," he said when he signed the bill into law. "It will not reshape the structure of our daily lives, or really add importantly to our wealth or our power."

But the new law proved LBJ's prediction wrong. Exempted from numerical quotas were immigrants seeking family reunification with American citizens or resident aliens. In addition, preferences were extended to people from the nations of the Eastern Hemisphere who had specialized job skills and training in fields like medicine and engineering. The high priority given family reunification created an unprecedented cycle of "chain immigration and sponsorship" of people seeking to join relatives already in the United States. As initial immigrants attained permanent resident or citizenship status, they would sponsor family members and relatives to come over. Once these family members and relatives arrived in the United States and became resident aliens or citizens, they in turn could sponsor their family members, and so on. (See Figure 28.1.)

The consequences for Asian American communities in particular were profound. The number of Asian Americans soared from about 1 million in 1965 to 11 million by the end of the century. Immigrants from India and the Philippines included a high percentage of health care professionals, whereas many Chinese and Korean immigrants found work in professional and managerial occupations or began their own small businesses. At the same time, low-skilled and impoverished Asians poured into the "Chinatowns" and "Koreatowns" of cities like New York and Los Angeles, taking jobs in restaurants, hotels, and garment manufacturing. Four times as many Asians settled in the United States in this period as had in the entire previous history of the nation. This new wave also brought a strikingly different group of Asian immigrants to America. In 1960, the Asian American population was 52 percent Japanese, 27 percent Chinese, and 20 percent Filipino. In 1985, the composition

KOREATOWN Signs in "Koreatown" in Los Angeles reflect the demographic changes that followed the Immigration and Nationality Act of 1965. By 2010 the city's Asian population had reached over 1.5 million, including the largest Korean community (approximately 250,000) outside of Korea.

LHB Photo/Alamy Stock Photo.

Figure 28.1 FOREIGN-BORN POPULATION BY COUNTRY OF BIRTH: 2010

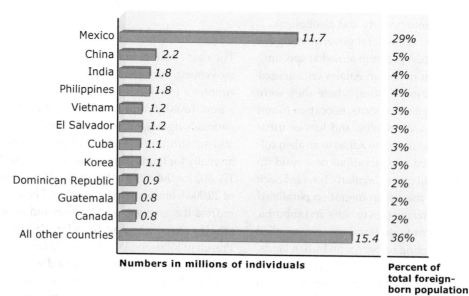

Country	Numbers in millions of individuals	Percent of total foreign-born population
Mexico	11.7	29%
China	2.2	5%
India	1.8	4%
Philippines	1.8	4%
Vietnam	1.2	3%
El Salvador	1.2	3%
Cuba	1.1	3%
Korea	1.1	3%
Dominican Republic	0.9	2%
Guatemala	0.8	2%
Canada	0.8	2%
All other countries	15.4	36%

Following the Immigration and Nationality Act of 1965, the nation experienced a sharp shift in immigrants' countries of origin. By 2010, a large majority of new immigrants arrived from Latin American and Asian countries.

had become 21 percent Chinese, 21 percent Filipino, 15 percent Japanese, 12 percent Vietnamese, 11 percent Korean, 10 percent Asian Indian, 4 percent Laotian, and 3 percent Cambodian.

The 1965 act also created conditions that increased undocumented immigration from Latin America. The new limits on Western Hemisphere migration, along with the simultaneous ending of the *bracero* program, tempted many thousands to enter the United States illegally. The Immigration and Naturalization Service arrested and deported 500,000 undocumented aliens each year in the decade following the act, most of them from Mexico, Central America, and the Caribbean. By the 1980s, more than 80 percent of all legal immigrants to the United States came from either Asia or Latin America; if one included undocumented immigrants, the figure would surpass 90 percent.

Conclusion

The mass movement for civil rights was arguably the most important domestic event in twentieth-century American history. The struggle that began in Montgomery, Alabama, in December 1955 ultimately transformed race relations in thousands of American communities. By the early 1960s, this community-based movement had placed civil rights at the very center of national political life. It achieved its greatest successes by invoking the Constitution—the supreme law of the land—to destroy legal segregation and win individual freedom for African Americans. The Civil Rights Act of 1964 and the Voting Rights Act of 1965 testified to the power of an African American and white liberal coalition. Yet the persistence of racism, poverty, and ghetto slums challenged a central assumption of liberalism: that equal protection of constitutional rights would give all Americans equal opportunities in life. By the mid-1960s, many black people had begun to question the core values of liberalism, the benefits of alliance with whites, and the philosophy of nonviolence. At the same time, a conservative white backlash against the gains made by African Americans further weakened the liberal political consensus.

In challenging the persistence of widespread poverty and institutional racism, the civil rights movement called for deep structural changes in American life. By 1967, Martin Luther King Jr. was articulating a broad and radical vision linking the struggle against racial injustice to other defects in American society. "The black revolution," he argued, "is much more than a struggle for the rights of Negroes. It is forcing America to face all its interrelated flaws—racism, poverty, militarism, and materialism. It is exposing evils that are deeply rooted in the whole structure of our society." Curing these ills would prove far more difficult than ending legal segregation.

Key Terms

Brown v. Board of Education Supreme Court decision in 1954 that declared that "separate but equal" schools for children of different races violated the Constitution. p. 693

Southern Manifesto A document signed by 101 members of Congress from southern states in 1956 that argued that the Supreme Court's decision in *Brown v. Board of Education of Topeka* itself contradicted the Constitution. p. 694

Southern Christian Leadership Conference (SCLC) Black civil rights organization founded in 1957 by Martin Luther King Jr. and other clergy. p. 696

Congress of Racial Equality (CORE) Civil rights group formed in 1942 and committed to nonviolent civil disobedience. p. 691

Albany movement Coalition of activists from SNCC, the NAACP, and other local groups formed in 1961 in Albany, Georgia. p. 701

March on Washington Historic gathering of more than 250,000 people in Washington, D.C., in 1963 marching for jobs and freedom. p. 705

Civil Rights Act of 1964 Federal legislation that outlawed discrimination in public accommodations and employment on the basis of race, skin color, sex, religion, or national origin. p. 706

Freedom Summer Voter registration effort in rural Mississippi organized by black and white civil rights workers in 1964. p. 707

Nation of Islam (NOI) Religious movement among black Americans that emphasizes self-sufficiency, self-help, and separation from white society. p. 707

Voting Rights Act Legislation in 1965 that overturned a variety of practices by which states systematically denied voter registration to minorities. p. 710

House Concurrent Resolution 108 Resolution passed in 1953 that allowed Congress to pass legislation to terminate a specific tribe as a political entity. p. 713

Immigration and Nationality Act Act passed in 1965 that abolished national origin quotas and established overall hemisphere quotas. p. 713

CHRONOLOGY

1948

President Truman issues executive order desegregating the armed forces

1954

In *Brown v. Board of Education,* Supreme Court rules segregated schools inherently unequal and unconstitutional

1956

Montgomery bus boycott ends in victory as Supreme Court affirms district court ruling that segregation on buses is unconstitutional

1957

President Eisenhower deploys federal troops to protect African American students integrating Central High School in Little Rock, Arkansas

1960

Sit-in movement begins in Greensboro, North Carolina, spreads throughout the South, and results in founding of the Student Non-Violent Coordinating Committee (SNCC)

1961

Freedom Rides force confrontation over federal enforcement of integration in the South

1963

SCLC initiates desegregation campaign in Birmingham, Alabama

March on Washington in August

1964

Mississippi Freedom Summer project

President Johnson signs Civil Rights Act of 1964

1965

Voting Rights Act enacted following voter registration campaign in Selma, Alabama

Immigration and Nationality Act passed

Chapter 29
War Abroad, War at Home
1965–1974

AMERICAN SOLDIERS IN VIETNAM Three American soldiers carry a wounded comrade to safety on a stretcher. Vietnam, 1969.

SSG Paul Halverson/US Army Photos.

 Contents and Focus Questions

American Communities

Uptown, Chicago, Illinois

During the Freedom Summer of 1964, while teams of northern college students traveled south to join voter registration campaigns among African Americans, a small group moved to Chicago to help the city's poor people take control of their communities. They targeted Uptown, a neighborhood north of the Loop, the city center. The student organizers hoped to mobilize the community "so as to demand an end to poverty and the construction of a decent social order."

With the assistance of the Packinghouse Workers union, the students formed Jobs or Income Now (JOIN), opened a storefront office, and invited local residents to work with them to demand jobs and better living conditions. They spent hours listening to people, drawing out their ideas, and helping them develop scores of programs. They helped establish new social clubs, a food-buying cooperative, a community theater, and a health clinic.

Chicago JOIN was a project sponsored by the Students for a Democratic Society (SDS). Impatient with the nation's chronic poverty and Cold War politics, a small group of students had met in June 1962 in Port Huron, Michigan, and formed a new kind of campus-based political organization. They issued a declaration of principles, drafted mainly by graduate student Tom Hayden. "We are people . . . bred in at least modest comfort, housed now in universities," *The Port Huron Statement* opened, "looking uncomfortably to the world we inherit." Poverty and social injustice, it continued, were not the only problems. A deeper ailment plagued American society. Everyone, including middle-class students with few material wants, suffered from a sense of "loneliness, estrangement, and alienation." *The Port Huron Statement* defined the SDS as a political movement that would bring people "out of isolation and into community" so that not just the poor but all Americans could overcome their feelings of "powerlessness [and hence] resignation before the enormity of events."

The SDS began with a campaign to reform the university, especially to disentangle the financial ties between campus-based research programs and the military-industrial complex. By its peak in 1968, the SDS had 350 chapters and between 60,000 and 100,000 members. Its principle of participatory democracy—with its promise to give people control over the decisions affecting their lives—appealed to a wider following of more than a million students.

The SDS also sent small groups of students to live and organize in the poor communities of Boston, Louisville, Cleveland, and Newark, as well as Chicago. Ultimately, none of these projects recruited large numbers of people. Nevertheless, organizers did succeed, to some degree, in realizing the goal specified in its slogan: "Let the People Decide." By late 1967, the SDS prepared to leave JOIN in the hands of the people it had organized, which was its intention from the beginning.

Initially, even Lyndon Baines Johnson promoted civic participation. The Great Society, as the president called his domestic program, promised more than the abolition of poverty and racial inequality. In May 1964, at the University of Michigan, the president described his goal as a society "where every child can find knowledge to enrich his mind and to enlarge his talents," where "the city of man serves not only the needs of the body and the demands of commerce but the desire for beauty and the hunger for community."

By 1967, the Vietnam War had pushed aside such ambitions. If SDSers had once believed they could work with liberal Democrats like Johnson, they now interpreted social injustice at home as the inevitable consequence of the president's destructive foreign policies. The SDS threw its energies into building a movement against the war in Vietnam. President Johnson, meanwhile, pursued a foreign policy that would swallow up the funding for his own plans for a war on poverty and would precipitate a very different war at home, Americans against Americans. As hawks and doves lined up on opposite sides, the Vietnam War created a huge and enduring rift.

The dream of community did not vanish, but consensus became increasingly remote by the late 1960s. By that time, parents and children were at odds over values and aspirations, urban uprisings were rocking the nation, and political leaders were struck down by assassins' bullets. New protest groups—Black Power, Women's Liberation, Gay Liberation, as well as Chicano, Native American, and Asian groups—were staking out a highly charged "politics of identity." A powerful backlash brought the election of Richard Nixon, who went on to disgrace the office of president. Meanwhile, the United States continued to fight—and eventually lost—the longest war in its history to that time.

Chicago

29.1 The Vietnam War

Why did President Johnson escalate the war in Vietnam?

The Vietnam War had its roots in the Truman Doctrine and its goal of containing communism. (See Chapter 26.) In 1954, after the Communist forces of Ho Chi Minh defeated the French colonialists and created a new government in the north, Vietnam emerged as a major zone of Cold War contention. President John F. Kennedy called it "the cornerstone of the Free World in Southeast Asia," a barrier to the spread of communism throughout the region and perhaps the world. President Johnson's Secretary of Defense Robert McNamara warned that failure in Vietnam would result in "a complete shift of world power," with the "prestige and integrity" of the United States severely damaged. With the stakes so high, Johnson concluded that Americans had little choice but to fight—and to win. Ultimately, however, more than 58,000 Americans died in an overseas war that proved unwinnable and that deepened divisions at home.

29.1.1 Johnson's War

Although President Kennedy had built up the defense budget and sent military advisers to assist South Vietnam's efforts to fight Communist rebels (see Chapter 27), it was his successor, Lyndon B. Johnson, who made the decision to engage the United States in a major war there. Like Kennedy, he was determined to avoid the fate of President Truman, who had been damaged politically after "losing" China to communism and producing a stalemate in Korea. Johnson decided he would not become the president who lost Southeast Asia to communism.

Throughout the winter and spring of 1964, as conditions worsened in South Vietnam, Johnson's advisers quietly laid the groundwork for a sustained bombing campaign against North Vietnam. In early August, they found a pretext to set this plan in motion. The National Security Agency—which decades later would admit to receiving faulty intelligence— reported two attacks against U.S. destroyers by North Vietnamese patrol boats in the Gulf of Tonkin, off the coast of North Vietnam. Although the second alleged attack never took place, the report prompted Johnson to order retaliatory air strikes against bases in North Vietnam.

Johnson appealed to Congress to give him the authority "to take all necessary measures" to defend U.S. armed forces and "to prevent further aggression." The **Gulf of Tonkin resolution** moved unanimously through the House and passed the Senate on August 7 with only two dissenting votes.

Ironically, Johnson continued his presidential campaign in 1964 with a call for restraint in Vietnam. He assured voters that, "we are not about to send American boys nine or ten thousand miles away from home to do what Asian boys ought to be doing for themselves." This strategy helped him win a landslide victory over conservative Republican Barry Goldwater of Arizona, who had advocated systematic bombing of North Vietnam as a prelude to invasion.

With the election behind him, Johnson faced a hard decision. U.S. forces failed to slow the Communist insurgency into South Vietnam. Meanwhile, the United States-backed government in Saigon, the capital city of South Vietnam, appeared near collapse. His advisors pressed him to chart a new course if he hoped to avoid, as National Security Advisor McGeorge Bundy put it, a "disastrous defeat."

29.1.2 Deeper into the Quagmire

In early February 1965, the Johnson administration found a rationale to escalate the war. The Vietcong had dispatched a suicide bomb squad to the U.S. military base at Pleiku in the central highlands of Vietnam, killing 7 and wounding more than 100 Americans. Johnson ordered immediate reprisal bombing and—one week later, on February 13—authorized Operation Rolling Thunder, a campaign of gradually intensifying air attacks against North Vietnam.

Once Rolling Thunder began, President Johnson hesitated to speak frankly with the American public about his plan to send in more ground troops. Initially, he announced that only two battalions of Marines were being assigned to Danang to defend the airfields where bombing runs began. But six weeks later, 50,000 U.S. combat troops were in Vietnam. By November 1965, the total topped 165,000, and more troops were on the way.

The strategy pursued by the Johnson administration and implemented by General William Westmoreland—a war of attrition—was based on the premise that continuous use of heavy artillery and air power would eventually exhaust North Vietnam's resources. Meanwhile, U.S. ground forces would defeat the Vietcong in South Vietnam and thereby restore political stability to South Vietnam's pro-Western government. As Johnson once boasted, the strongest military power in the world surely could crush a Communist rebellion in a "pissant" country of peasants.

In practice, the United States wreaked havoc in South Vietnam, tearing apart its society and bringing ecological devastation to its land. Intending to eradicate the support network of the Vietcong, U.S. ground troops

CIVILIAN CASAULTIES IN VIETNAM The massive bombing and ground combat created huge numbers of civilian casualties in Vietnam. The majority killed were women and children.

Black Star.

conducted search-and-destroy missions throughout the countryside. They attacked villagers and their homes. Seeking to ferret out Vietcong sympathizers, U.S. troops turned over the course of the war as many as 4 million people—approximately one-quarter of the population of South Vietnam—into refugees. By late 1968, the United States had dropped more than 3 million tons of bombs on Vietnam. Using herbicides such as Agent Orange to defoliate forests, the United States also conducted the most destructive chemical warfare in history.

29.1.3 The Credibility Gap

Johnson's popularity had surged at the time of the Gulf of Tonkin resolution, but it waned rapidly. At the same time, public support for the war also began to decline. To stem the tide, Johnson worked hard to control the news media. Despite his efforts, he found his administration accused of intentional deceit. Moreover, by refusing to announce his decisions and the rationales behind the escalation, Johnson failed to build a public consensus for his actions.

During the early 1960s, network news had either ignored Vietnam or unquestioningly supported U.S. policy. Beginning with a CBS News report by Morley Safer in August 1965, however, the tenor changed. Although government officials described the U.S. operation in the South Vietnamese village Cam Ne as an attack on "fortified Vietcong bunkers," the *CBS Evening News* showed Marines setting fire to the thatched homes of civilians.

Scenes of human suffering and devastation, broadcast daily by 1967, ultimately weakened the administration's moral justification of U.S. involvement as a defense of freedom and democracy in South Vietnam. Reporters described the varieties of American cluster bombs, which released up to 180,000 fiberglass shards, and showed photographs and film clips of the nightmarish effects of the defoliants used on South Vietnam's forests to uncover enemy strongholds. And every night, network television news tallied the soaring American body count, from 26 per week in 1965 to 180 per week in 1967.

Skeptics stepped forward in the U.S. Congress. Democratic Senator J. William Fulbright of Arkansas, who chaired the Senate Foreign Relations Committee and who had personally speeded the passage of the Gulf of Tonkin resolution, became the most vocal critic of Johnson's war policy. A strong supporter of the Cold War, Fulbright had nevertheless concluded that the war in Vietnam was both unwinnable and destructive to domestic reform. Meanwhile, some of the nation's most trusted European allies called for restraint in Vietnam.

The impact of the war, which cost Americans $21 billion per year, was also felt by Americans at home. Johnson convinced Congress to levy a 10 percent surcharge on individual and corporate taxes. Later adjustments tapped the Social Security fund, heretofore safe from interference.

Inflation raced upward, fed by spending on the war. Although Johnson promised that the end of the war was in sight, more and more Americans began to question his credibility and to mistrust his handling of the war.

29.2 A Generation in Conflict

How did campus protests shape national political debate?

As the Vietnam War escalated, Americans from all walks of life began to doubt the wisdom of the administration's leadership. Much of this skepticism initially took on a distinctly generational character. At the forefront were the baby boomers just coming of age, who broadened the meaning of politics to encompass not only U.S. foreign policy but also everyday life.

This so-called Sixties Generation began to combine protest against the war in Vietnam with a broader, penetrating critique of American society, raising controversial issues such as free speech, sexuality, and recreational drugs. Through music, dress, and even hairstyle, "flower children"—or hippies, as they were called—expressed a deep estrangement from the values and aspirations of their parents' generation. Meanwhile, with the help of massive state and federal funding, state universities and community colleges grew rapidly during the 1960s, and the number of college students nationwide nearly doubled. A sizable minority of these students likewise experimented with new lifestyles, to a large extent underwritten by the prosperity that marked the Vietnam War era.

29.2.1 "The Times They Are A-Changin' "

In the fall of 1964, civil rights activists returned from Freedom Summer in Mississippi to the 27,000-student Berkeley campus of the University of California and decided to picket Bay Area stores that practiced discrimination in hiring. When the university administration tried to stop them from setting up information booths on campus, 18 student groups objected, claiming that their right to free speech had been abridged. The administration sent police to break up the protest rally and arrest participants. After university president Clark Kerr threatened to press charges against the free speech movement's leaders, a huge crowd gathered. Joining folk singer Joan Baez in singing "We Shall Overcome," nearly 1,000 people marched toward the university's administration building, where they planned to stage a sit-in until Kerr rescinded his order. The police moved in, detaining nearly 800 protestors in the largest mass arrest in California history.

Mario Savio, a Freedom Summer volunteer and philosophy student, explained that the **free speech movement** aspired to more than just the right to conduct political

JOAN BAEZ AT FREE SPEECH PROTEST, 1964 Thousands of students gathered at a free speech rally on the University of California-Berkeley campus in December 1964. They joined the popular folk singer Joan Baez in singing "We Shall Overcome," the key protest anthem of the Civil Rights movement, and then marched to the university's administration building, where they staged a huge sit-in. The police arrested nearly 800 protesters in the largest mass arrest in California history.

Everett Collection Historical/Alamy Stock Photo.

activity on campus. Its members wanted, in the phrase coined by the SDS, participatory democracy. Across the country—and in many nations around the world—college students began to demand a say in their education. Students also spoke out against campus rules that treated students as children instead of as adults. After a string of campus protests, most large universities relinquished *in loco parentis* (in the place of parents) policies and allowed students to live in off-campus housing and to set their own hours.

Across the bay in San Francisco, other young adults staked out a new form of community—a **counterculture**. In 1967, the "Summer of Love," the population of the Haight-Ashbury district swelled by 75,000 as youthful adventurers from around the world gathered for a huge "be-in." Although the *San Francisco Chronicle* featured a headline reading "Mayor Warns Hippies to Stay Out of Town," masses of long-haired young men and women dressed in bell-bottoms and tie-dyed T-shirts congregated to listen to music, take drugs, and "be" with each other. In the fall, the majority of revelers returned to their homes, bringing with them the new hippie lifestyle.

Although the generational rebellion took many forms, the revolution in sexual behavior triggered countless quarrels between parents and their maturing sons and daughters. During the 1960s, more teenagers experienced premarital sex and far more talked about it openly than in previous eras. With birth control widely available, including the newly developed "pill," many young women were no longer deterred from sex by fear of pregnancy. "Sex doesn't mean the downfall of society, at least not the kind of society that we're going to build," one student explained. Many heterosexual couples chose to live together outside marriage, a

practice few parents condoned. A much smaller but significant number formed communes—approximately 4,000 communes by 1970—where members could share housekeeping and child care as well as sexual partners.

Mood-altering drugs played a large part in this counterculture. Soon-to-be-former Harvard professor Timothy Leary urged young people to "turn on, tune in, drop out" and also advocated the mass production and distribution of LSD (lysergic acid diethylamide), which was not criminalized until 1968. Marijuana, illegal yet readily available, was often paired with rock music in a collective ritual of love and laughter.

Many considered the Woodstock Music Festival the apotheosis of the counterculture. At a farm near Woodstock, New York, more than 400,000 people gathered in August 1969 for three days of "peace and music" featuring Jimi Hendrix, Baez, Santana, the Grateful Dead, and Jefferson Airplane, among other popular artists. Thousands took drugs while security officials and local police stood by; some stripped off their clothes to dance or swim; and a few even made love in the grass.

The Woodstock Nation, as the counterculture was mythologized, did not actually represent the sentiments of most young people. Nor would its good vibes persist. The attitudes and styles of the counterculture, especially the efforts to create a new community, did speak for the large minority seeking a peaceful alternative to the intensifying climate of war. The slogan "Make Love, Not War" linked generational rebellion and opposition to the U.S. war in Vietnam.

29.2.2 From Campus Protest to Mass Mobilization

College students spearheaded a campaign against the Vietnam War. Three weeks after the announcement of Operation Rolling Thunder in 1965, campus activists called for a daylong boycott of classes so that students and faculty might meet to discuss the war. "Teach-ins" soon spread across the United States and to Europe and Japan. Meanwhile, the SDS mobilized 20,000 people in an antiwar march on the nation's capital. (See Communities *in* Conflict.)

Students also protested against war-related research on their campuses. The expansion of higher education in the 1960s had depended largely on federally funded programs, including military research on counterinsurgency tactics and chemical weapons. Student protesters demanded an end to these programs and, receiving no response from university administrators, turned to civil disobedience. Students also disrupted campus interviews of companies such as Dow Chemical, which manufactured the napalm used in chemical warfare. Momentum grew, and demonstrations and disruptions took place on campuses in every region of the country.

The peace movement spread well beyond the campus. In April 1967, a daylong antiwar rally in Manhattan's Central Park drew more than 300,000 people. Meanwhile,

Communities *in* Conflict

The Prospects for Peace in Vietnam, April 1965

"How much more of Mr. Johnson's freedom can we stand?"

During the early months of 1965, President Johnson changed course in Vietnam by launching the "Rolling Thunder" campaign that sent massive bombing missions over North Vietnam and by introducing U.S. ground troops to fight the Vietcong in the South. In response, his opponents became yet more vocal in expressing their dissent. On college campuses, the Students for a Democratic Society (SDS) took the lead in organizing small, local demonstrations against the war and calling on peace activists throughout the United States to join a march in Washington on April 17 to protest the war.

In part to mollify critics of escalation, Johnson decided to present the government of North Vietnam with an opportunity for "unconditional discussions" about a plan for peace. He also offered $1 billion in aid for a development project along the Mekong River, described by some in his administration as an extension of his Great Society policy abroad. He announced all this in a speech at Johns Hopkins University on April 7, 1965, which was televised to 60 million viewers. Johnson's speech, called

"Peace without Conquest," won approval from many Americans and briefly prompted optimism about prospects for peace.

But ten days later, the 20,000–25,000 peace activists who gathered in Washington, D.C., were far from appeased by the president's offer. Paul Potter, the president of the SDS and the final speaker at the rally, offered his own interpretation of the progress of the war and its significance for Americans. In his speech, titled "Naming the System," Potter directly answered Johnson's claims in the "Peace without Conquest" address. In speaking of "the system," the SDS president connected the injustices of war in Southeast Asia with the inequities borne by Americans in their own country. His speech inspired many, who then went home with renewed dedication to the peace movement and radical social change.

- **What are the main points of disagreement between President Johnson and Paul Potter?**

- **In connecting the war to social injustices at home, what political or social challenges stand out in Potter's critique of "the system"?**

President Lyndon Johnson Calls for "Peace without Conquest" (April 7, 1965)

Viet Nam is far away from this quiet campus. We have no territory there, nor do we seek any. The war is dirty and brutal and difficult. And some 400 young men, born into an America that is bursting with opportunity and promise, have ended their lives, on Viet-Nam's steaming soil.

Why must we take this painful road?

Why must this Nation hazard its ease, and its interest, and its power for the sake of a people so far away?

We fight because we must fight if we are to live in a world where every country can shape its own destiny. And only in such a world will our own freedom be finally secure. . . .

The first reality is that North Viet-Nam has attacked the independent nation of South Viet-Nam. Its object is total conquest.

Of course, some of the people of South Viet-Nam are participating in attack on their own government. But trained men and supplies, orders and arms, flow in a constant stream from north to south. . . .

Over this war and all Asia is another reality: the deepening shadow of Communist China. The rulers in Hanoi are urged on by Peking. This is a regime which has destroyed freedom in Tibet, which has attacked India, and has been condemned by the United Nations for aggression in Korea. . . .

Why are these realities our concern? Why are we in South Vietnam?

We are there because we have a promise to keep. Since 1954 every American President has offered support to the people of South Viet-Nam. We have helped to build, and we have helped to defend. Thus, over many years, we have made a national pledge to help South Viet-Nam defend its independence. And I intend to keep that promise. . . .

We are also there to strengthen world order. Around the globe, from Berlin to Thailand, are people whose well-being rests, in part, on the belief that they can count on us if they are attacked. To leave Viet-Nam to its fate would shake the confidence of all these people in the value of an American commitment and in the value of America's word. The result would be increased unrest and instability, and even wider war.

We are also there because there are great stakes in the balance. Let no one think for a moment that retreat from Viet-Nam would bring an end to conflict. The battle would be renewed in one country and then another. The central lesson of our time is that the appetite of aggression is never satisfied. To withdraw from one battlefield means only to prepare for the next. We must say in Southeast Asia as we did in Europe in the words of the Bible: "Hitherto shalt thou come, but no further." . . .

Our objective is the independence of South Viet-Nam, and its freedom from attack. We want nothing for ourselves, only that the people of South Viet-Nam be allowed to guide their own country in their own way. We will do everything necessary to reach that objective. And we will do only what is absolutely necessary.

In recent months attacks on South Viet Nam were stepped up. Thus, it became necessary for us to increase our response and to make attacks by air. This is not a change of purpose. It is a change in which we believe that purpose requires. . . .

These countries of Southeast Asia are homes for millions of impoverished people. Each day these people rise at dawn and struggle through until the night to wrestle existence from the soil. They are often wracked by disease, plagued by hunger, and death comes at the early age of 40.

For our part I will ask the Congress to join in a billion dollar American investment in this effort as soon as it is underway.

The task is nothing less than to enrich the hopes and the existence of more than a hundred million people. And there is much to be done.

The vast Mekong River can provide food and water and power on a scale to dwarf even our own TVA. . . .

Source: Public Papers of the Presidents of the United States: Lyndon B. Johnson, 1965, pp. 394–397, as excerpted in "The Wars for Viet Nam," Vassar College website.

SDS President Paul Potter, "Naming the System" (April 17, 1965)

Not even the President can say that this is a war to defend the freedom of the Vietnamese people. Perhaps what the President means when he speaks of freedom is the freedom of the American people. . . .

How much more of Mr. Johnson's freedom can we stand? How much freedom will be left in this country if there is a major war in Asia? By what weird logic can it be said that the freedom of one people can only be maintained by crushing another? . . .

What kind of system is it that allows good men to make those kinds of decisions? What kind of system is it that justifies the United States or any country seizing the destinies of the Vietnamese people and using them callously for its own purpose? What kind of system is it that disenfranchises people in the South, leaves millions upon millions of people throughout the country impoverished and excluded from the mainstream and promise of American society, that creates faceless and terrible bureaucracies and makes those the place where people spend their lives and do their work, that consistently puts material values before human values—and still persists in calling itself free and still persists in finding itself fit to police the world? What place is there for ordinary men in that system and how are they to control it, make it bend itself to their wills rather than bending them to its?

We must name that system. We must name it, describe it, analyze it, understand it and change it. For it is only when that system is changed and brought under control that there can be any hope for stopping the forces that create a war in Vietnam today or a murder in the South tomorrow or all the incalculable, innumerable more subtle atrocities that are worked on people all over—all the time.

How do you stop a war then?

. . . If the people of this country are to end the war in Vietnam, and to change the institutions which create it, then the people of this country must create a massive social movement—and if that can be built around the issue of Vietnam then that is what we must do.

By a social movement I mean . . . people who are willing to change their lives, who are willing to challenge the system, to take the problem of change seriously. By a social movement I mean an effort that is powerful enough to make the country understand that our problems are not in Vietnam, or China or Brazil or outer space or at the bottom of the ocean, but are here in the United States. . . .

But that means that we build a movement that works not simply in Washington but in communities and with the problems that face people throughout the society. That means that we build a movement that understands Vietnam in all its horror as but a symptom of a deeper malaise, that we build a movement that makes possible the implementation of the values that would have prevented Vietnam, a movement based on the integrity of man and a belief in man's capacity to tolerate all the weird formulations of society that men may choose to strive for; a movement that will build on the new and creative forms of protest that are beginning to emerge, such as the teach-in, and extend their efforts and intensify them; that we will build a movement that will find ways to support the increasing numbers of young men who are unwilling to and will not fight in Vietnam; a movement that will not tolerate the escalation or prolongation of this war but will, if necessary, respond to the administration war effort with massive civil disobedience all over the country. . . .

For in a strange way the people of Vietnam and the people on this demonstration are united in much more than a common concern that the war be ended. In both countries there are people struggling to build a movement that has the power to change their condition. The system that frustrates these movements is the same. All our lives, our destinies, our very hopes to live, depend on our ability to overcome that system.

Source: SDS President Paul Potter, "Naming the System" (April 17, 1965). From the website of Students for a Democratic Society, Document Library. Reprinted by permission.

60,000 protesters turned out in San Francisco. By summer, Vietnam Veterans Against the War had begun to organize returning soldiers and sailors, encouraging them to cast off the medals and ribbons they had won in battle. Government officials took a hard line against protesters. Secretary of State Dean Rusk warned that, "the net effect of these demonstrations will be to prolong the war, not to shorten it."

Some demonstrators concluded that peaceful protest alone had little impact on U.S. policy and decided to change tactics—"from protest to resistance"—and to serve as moral witnesses. Despite a 1965 congressional act providing for a five-year jail term and a $10,000 fine for destroying a draft card, thousands of young men burned their cards. Approximately a half-million more refused induction. Two Jesuit priests, Daniel and Philip Berrigan, raided the draft board office in Catonsville, Maryland, in May 1968 and poured homemade napalm over records. Other activists determined to "bring the war home" went beyond civil disobedience. An estimated 40,000 bombing incidents and bomb threats took place from January 1969 to April 1970; more than $21 million worth of property was damaged, and 43 people were killed.

Parallel wars were now being fought: one between two systems of government in Vietnam, and another between the American government and masses of its citizens. Those Americans sent to Vietnam were caught in between.

29.2.3 Teenage Soldiers

Although nearly 11,000 women served in the armed forces in Vietnam, 90 percent as nurses, men—young men—filled out the combat units. Whereas the average age of World War II soldiers was 26, the average age of those who fought in Vietnam hovered around 19. Until late 1969, the Selective Service System—the draft—gave deferments to college students and to workers in selected occupations and drew disproportionately from the African American communities. Eleven percent of the population, African Americans made up 14.3 percent of the draftees between 1965 and 1970. Meanwhile army recruiters focused on poor communities by advertising the armed forces as a provider of vocational training and social mobility. Working-class young men, disproportionately African American and Latino, signed up in large numbers under these inducements. They also bore the brunt of combat. High school dropouts were the most likely to serve in Vietnam and by far the most likely to die there. The casualty rate for African Americans during the early years of the war was disproportionately higher than the overall death rate for U.S. forces in Southeast Asia. These disparities created a rupture that would last well past the end of the war.

Yet these young soldiers were not entirely isolated from the changes affecting their generation. Many G.I.s smoked marijuana, listened to rock music, and hung psychedelic posters in their barracks, but most condemned antiwar protest as the self-indulgent behavior of their privileged peers who did not have to fight. As the war dragged on, however, some soldiers showed their frustration. By 1971, many G.I.s were putting peace symbols on their combat helmets and joining antiwar demonstrations. Sometimes entire companies refused to carry out duty assignments or even to enter battle. A smaller number took revenge by intentionally wounding or killing—"fragging"—reckless commanding officers with grenades meant for the enemy. Some African American soldiers complained about fighting "a white man's war" and emblazoned their helmets with slogans like "No Gook Ever Called Me Nigger."

The war's course fed these feelings of disaffection. U.S. troops entering South Vietnam expected a warm welcome from the people whose homeland they had been sent to defend. Instead, they encountered anti-American demonstrations. Moreover, despite their superior arms and air power, soldiers found themselves stumbling into booby traps as they chased an elusive guerrilla enemy through deep, leech-infested swamps and dense jungles swarming with fire ants. They could never be sure who was friend and who was foe.

Vietnam veterans returned to civilian life quietly and without fanfare. Tens of thousands suffered debilitating physical injuries. They reentered a society divided over the cause for which they had risked their lives or endured grave physical injuries. As many as 40 percent of the 8.6 million who served came back with drug dependencies or symptoms of posttraumatic stress disorder, haunted and depressed by troubling memories of atrocities. Moreover, finding and keeping a job proved to be particularly hard in the shrinking economy of the 1970s.

29.3 War on Poverty

What were the goals of Johnson's Great Society?

Hoping to build on the New Deal legacy, President Johnson pledged to expand the anti-poverty program that he had inherited from Kennedy. Over the next several years, he used the political momentum of the civil rights movement and the overwhelming Democratic majorities in the House and Senate to push through the most ambitious reform program since the 1930s. Ironically, violence at home as well as abroad ultimately undercut his aspiration to wage "an unconditional **war on poverty**." (See Figure 29.1 and Figure 29.2.)

29.3.1 The Great Society

In his State of the Union message in 1964, President Johnson announced his plans to build a Great Society. Taking advantage of the era's prosperity, he pledged to continue President Kennedy's program while presenting his own

Figure 29.1 COMPARATIVE FIGURES ON LIFE EXPECTANCY AT BIRTH BY RACE AND SEX, 1950–1970

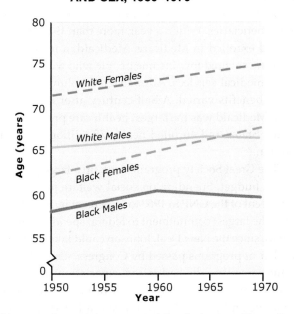

Shifting mortality statistics suggested that the increased longevity of females increasingly cut across race lines, but did not diminish the difference between white people and black people as a whole.

Figure 29.2 COMPARATIVE FIGURES ON INFANT MORTALITY BY RACE, 1940–1970

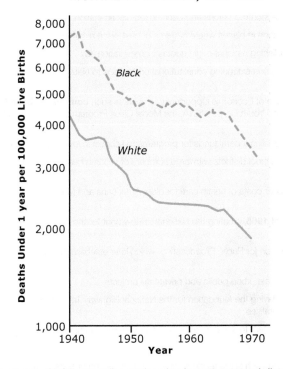

The causes of infant mortality, such as inadequate maternal diets, prenatal care, and medical services, were all rooted in poverty, both rural and urban. Despite generally falling rates of infant mortality, nonwhite people continued to suffer the effects more than white people did.

grand agenda. He sponsored legislation strengthening elementary and secondary education, created the Department of Transportation, and established the National Endowments for the Humanities and the Arts and the Corporation for Public Broadcasting.

One of the most ambitious of these plans was the **Office of Economic Opportunity (OEO)**. The new agency coordinated a network of community-based programs designed to help the poor help themselves by providing opportunities for education and employment. The results of these new federally funded programs were mixed. The Job Corps provided vocational training mostly for urban black youth, but trainees often found themselves learning factory skills that were already obsolete. The Neighborhood Youth Corps provided work for about 2 million young people, but nearly all the jobs were low paying and dead end. Educational programs proved more successful. VISTA (Volunteers in Service to America), a kind of domestic Peace Corps, brought several thousand idealistic volunteers into poor communities for social service work.

The most innovative and controversial element of the OEO was the Community Action Program (CAP), which mandated "maximum feasible participation" of local residents. In theory, community action would empower the poor by giving them a direct say in mobilizing resources. What often resulted was a tug-of-war between local government officials and the poor over who should control funding. Such was the case in Chicago, where Mayor Richard Daley complained that letting the poor head anti-poverty programs was "like telling the fellow who cleans up [at the newspaper] to be the city editor."

More successful and popular were the so-called national-emphasis programs, designed in Washington and administered according to federal guidelines. The Legal Services Program, staffed by attorneys, helped millions of poor people in legal battles with housing authorities, welfare departments, police, and slumlords. Head Start and Follow Through reached more than 2 million poor children and significantly improved the long-range educational achievement of participants. Comprehensive Community Health Centers provided basic medical services to patients who could not afford to see doctors. Upward Bound helped low-income teenagers develop the skills and confidence needed for college. Birth control programs dispensed contraceptive supplies and information to hundreds of thousands of poor women. (See Figure 29.3.) Among Native Americans, the OEO promoted educational reforms, initiated and directed by tribal peoples themselves, that respected traditional culture while providing children with skills for working outside Indian country.

The best-funded and enduring programs grew from an expansion of Social Security, especially the amendments that created Medicare and Medicaid in 1965. **Medicare**

Figure 29.3 PERCENT OF POPULATION BELOW POVERTY LEVEL, BY RACE, 1959–1969

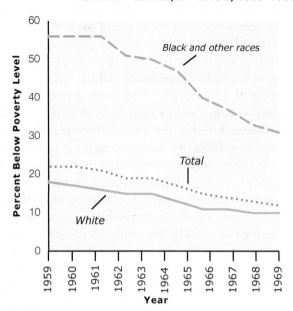

The poverty threshold for a nonfarm family of four was $3,743 in 1969 and $2,973 in 1959.

From *Congressional Quarterly*, Civil Rights: A Progress Report, 1971. Copyright 1971 by CQ-ROLL CALL GROUP.

supplied hospital and medical insurance to people age 65 or older without regard to income or medical history. Former President Harry Truman, a longtime advocate of national health insurance, and his wife, Bess, became the first beneficiaries. Within a year, more than 19 million people had enrolled in Medicare. Medicaid, a means-tested program, covered low-income people who were unable to afford medical services. Administered voluntarily by the states, benefits varied. A half-century after its establishment, Medicaid was the largest health care program in the United States and enrolled nearly 75 million adults and children.

The Great Society programs took up a large part of the federal budget. Spending on social welfare jumped from 7.7 percent of the GNP in 1960 to 16 percent in 1974. Having made the largest commitment to federal spending on social welfare since the New Deal, Johnson could take pride in the number of programs passed by Congress. (See Table 29.1.) At the same time, he had raised expectations higher than could be reached without a more drastic redistribution of economic and political power. Even in the short run, the president could not sustain the welfare programs and simultaneously fight a lengthy and expensive war abroad. Ultimately he admitted that the "bitch of a war in Asia" ruined "the woman I really loved—the Great Society."

Table 29.1 GREAT SOCIETY: MAJOR LEGISLATION

Civil Rights	**Civil Rights Act of 1964**, forbidding segregation in public accommodations and banning job discrimination
	Voting Rights Act of 1965, ensuring minority voter registration in places where patterns of past discrimination existed
	Immigration and Nationality Services Act of 1965, abolishing national-origin quotas in immigration law
	Civil Rights Act of 1968, banning discrimination in housing and extending constitutional protections to Native Americans on reservations
War on Poverty	**Economic Opportunity Act of 1964**, establishing the Office of Economic Opportunity to oversee such **community-based antipoverty programs** as the Job Corps, the Neighborhood Youth Corps, VISTA, the Model Cities Program, Upward Bound, the Community Action Program, and Project Head Start
Education	**Elementary and Secondary Education Act of 1965**, providing federal funds for programs to schools in low-income areas
	Bilingual Education Act of 1968, providing federal aid to school districts with large numbers of children needing to learn English as a second language
Health	**Social Security Act of 1965**, funding Medicare to help cover costs of health care for older Americans and Medicaid to provide funds for medical care of welfare recipients
Culture	**National Foundation on the Arts and Humanities Act of 1965**, creating the National Endowment for the Arts and the National Endowment for the Humanities
	Public Broadcasting Act of 1967, chartering the Corporation for Public Broadcasting, which later established the Public Broadcasting Service (PBS) and National Public Radio (NPR)
Transportation	**Urban Mass Transportation Act of 1964**, funding large-scale urban public and private rail projects
	National Traffic and Motor Vehicle Safety Act of 1966, laying the foundation for the National Highway Traffic Safety Administration to effect policy to reduce traffic injuries and fatalities
	Highway Safety Act of 1966, permitting the federal government to set standards for motor vehicles and highways
	Department of Transportation, established in 1966
Consumer Protection	**Nine major enactments** between 1965 and 1968, covering such areas as cigarette warning labels, motor safety, "fair packaging and labeling," child safety and flammable fabrics, meat and poultry packaging, "truth in lending," and radiation safety
Environment	**Nine major enactments** between 1964 and 1968, covering such areas as wilderness and endangered species protection, land and water conservation, solid waste disposal, air pollution, aircraft noise abatement, and historic preservation
	National Environmental Policy Act of 1969, consolidating many of these gains, passed in the first year of the Nixon administration

29.3.2 Crisis in the Cities

With funds for new construction limited during the Great Depression and World War II, and the postwar building boom taking place in the suburbs, the infrastructure of the nation's cities declined. In 1961, Jane Jacobs identified this trend that, in her estimation, resulted in an "urban crisis." In *The Death and Life of Great American Cities*, she traced the problems to urban planners who invested in business districts at the expense of neighborhoods and local communities. Although city officials did spearhead civic revitalization programs, more often than not developers sliced up poor neighborhoods with new superhighways, demolished them to build new office complexes, or, as in Chicago's Uptown, favored residential developments for the middle class rather than for the poor. In 1968, a federal survey showed that 80 percent of those displaced under these urban renewal programs—dubbed "Negro removal" by former residents—were people of color.

Employment opportunities declined along with the housing stock. Black unemployment was nearly twice that of white unemployment. Moreover, the proportion working in the low-paying service sector continued to rise. In short, in major urban areas African Americans were steadily falling further behind whites.

Despite deteriorating conditions, millions of Americans continued to move to the cities, mainly African Americans from the Deep South, white people from the Appalachian Mountains, and Latinos from Puerto Rico. By the mid-1960s, African Americans had become near majorities in the nation's decaying inner cities. Many had fled rural poverty only to find themselves earning minimum wages at best and living in miserable, racially segregated neighborhoods. These conditions brought urban pressures to the boiling point.

29.3.3 Urban Uprisings

Just as the Vietnam War was heating up, more than 100 urban uprisings rocked the nation during the "long, hot summers" of 1964–1968. (See Map 29.1) The first major uprising erupted in August 1965 in the Watts section of Los Angeles. There, one in three men was unemployed, and the nearest hospital was 12 miles away. It took only a minor arrest to set off the uprising, which quickly spread outward for 50 miles. After six days, 34 people lay dead, 900 were injured, and 4,000 more had been arrested. The Los Angeles police chief blamed civil rights agitators, the mayor accused Communists, and both feigned ignorance when the media reported that white police assigned to "charcoal alley," their name for the Watts district, had customarily called their nightsticks "nigger knockers." "We are on a powder keg in a dozen places," President Johnson observed.

The following summer, large-scale uprisings occurred in San Francisco, Milwaukee, Dayton, and Cleveland.

On July 12, 1967, in Newark, New Jersey—a city with severe housing shortages and the nation's highest black unemployment rate—the beating and arrest of a black taxi driver by a white police officer sparked five days of looting and burning of buildings that ended with 25 people dead. One week later, Detroit police raided a bar and arrested the after-hours patrons. Army tanks and paratroopers were brought in to quell the disturbance, which lasted a week and left 34 people dead and 7,000 under arrest.

In July 1967, President Johnson created the National Advisory Commission on Civil Disorders to investigate the riots. Headed by Illinois Governor Otto Kerner, the commission indicted "white racism" for creating an "explosive mixture" of poverty and police brutality. But the Johnson administration and Congress disregarded the commission's advice to direct funds into housing and jobs and to reduce segregation. By this time, the escalating costs of the Vietnam War left little federal money for antipoverty programs. Senator William Fulbright noted, "Each war feeds on the other, and, although the President assures us that we have the resources to win both wars, in fact we are not winning either of them."

29.4 1968: Year of Turmoil

Why did divisions within American society deepen in 1968?

The urban uprisings of the summer of 1967 marked the most drawn-out violence in the United States since the Civil War. Rather than offering a respite, however, 1968 proved to be even more turbulent. The bloodiest and most destructive fighting of the Vietnam War resulted in a hopeless stalemate that soured most Americans on the conflict and undermined their faith in U.S. invincibility in world affairs. Disillusionment deepened in the spring when two of the most revered political leaders were struck down by assassins' bullets. Once again, protesters and police clashed on the nation's campuses and city streets, and millions of Americans asked what was wrong with their country.

29.4.1 The Tet Offensive

On January 30, 1968, the North Vietnamese and their Vietcong allies launched the Tet Offensive (named for the Vietnamese lunar New Year holiday), stunning the U.S. military command in South Vietnam. The Vietcong pushed into the major cities and provincial capitals of the South, as far as the courtyard of the U.S. embassy in Saigon. U.S. troops ultimately halted the offensive, with comparatively modest casualties of 1,100 dead and 8,000 wounded. The North Vietnamese and Vietcong suffered more than 40,000 deaths, about one-fifth of their total forces. Civilian casualties ran to the tens of

Map 29.1 URBAN UPRISINGS, 1965–1968

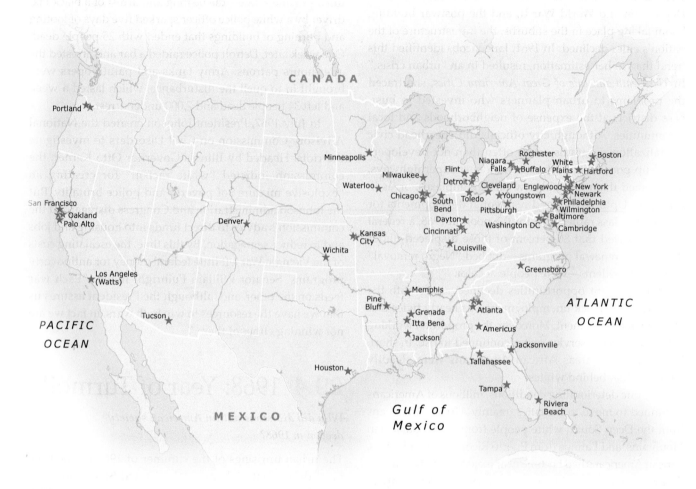

After World War II, urban uprisings precipitated by racial conflict increased in African American communities. In Watts in 1965 and in Detroit and Newark in 1967, rioters struck out at symbols of white control of their communities, such as white-owned businesses and residential properties.

thousands. As many as 1 million South Vietnamese became refugees, their villages totally ruined. (See Map 29.2.)

The Tet Offensive, despite the U.S. success in stopping it, marked a turning point, not least because it weakened the resolve of many Americans. Television news coverage provoked dismay and horror. Viewers saw the beautiful, ancient city of Hue devastated almost beyond recognition. They heard a news reporter quote a U.S. officer who casually remarked about Ben Tre, a village in the Mekong Delta, "It became necessary to destroy the town to save it."

The United States chalked up a major military victory, but lost the war at home. For the first time, polls showed strong opposition to the war, 49 percent concluding that the entire operation in Vietnam was a mistake. Meanwhile, in Rome, Berlin, Paris, and London, huge crowds protested U.S. involvement in Vietnam. President Johnson, facing the 1968 election campaign, watched his popularity plummet to an all-time low.

On March 31, the haggard-looking president appeared on television to declare a pullback in bombing over North Vietnam and his readiness to enter into comprehensive peace talks with Hanoi. He then shocked the nation; "I shall not seek, and I will not accept, the nomination of my party for another term as president." Like Truman almost 30 years earlier, Johnson had lost his presidency in Asia.

29.4.2 King, the War, and the Assassination

On April 4, 1967, in New York City, Martin Luther King Jr. spoke out forcefully against the war in Vietnam. He abandoned his customary caution in criticizing U.S. military policy and described in vivid terms its detrimental impact on the poor in the United States and on the peasantry in Vietnam. The time had come, he said, to "break

Map 29.2 THE SOUTHEAST ASIAN WAR

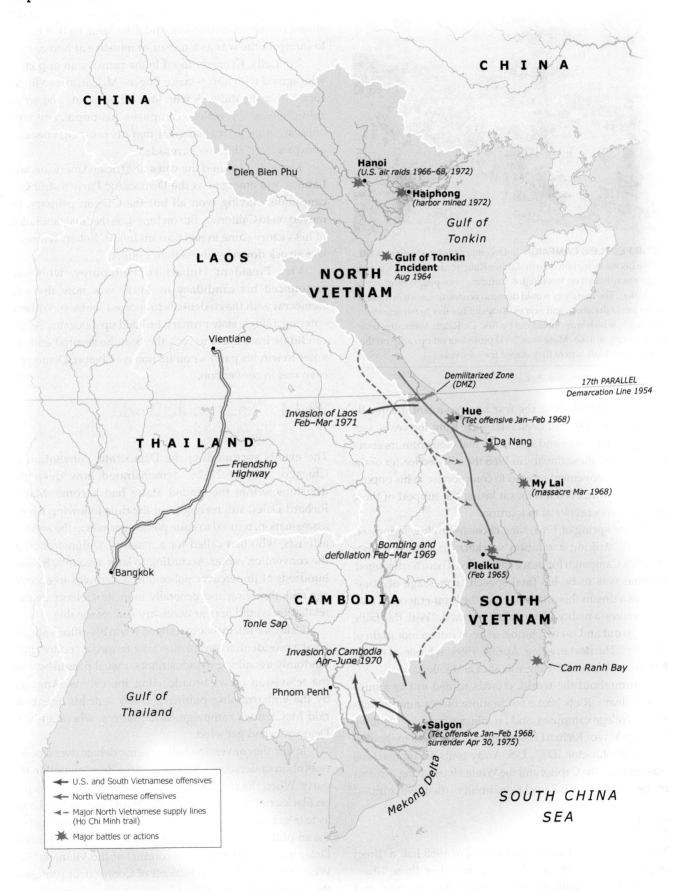

CHINA

CHINA

Dien Bien Phu

Hanoi
(U.S. air raids 1966–68, 1972)

Haiphong
(harbor mined 1972)

LAOS

Gulf of Tonkin

Gulf of Tonkin Incident
Aug 1964

NORTH VIETNAM

Vientiane

Demilitarized Zone (DMZ)

17th PARALLEL
Demarcation Line 1954

Invasion of Laos Feb–Mar 1971

Hue *(Tet offensive Jan–Feb 1968)*

THAILAND

Friendship Highway

Da Nang

My Lai *(massacre Mar 1968)*

Bombing and defoliation Feb–Mar 1969

Bangkok

CAMBODIA

Tonle Sap

SOUTH VIETNAM

Pleiku *(Feb 1965)*

Invasion of Cambodia Apr–June 1970

Cam Ranh Bay

Gulf of Thailand

Phnom Penh

Saigon
(Tet offensive Jan–Feb 1968, surrender Apr 30, 1975)

Mekong Delta

SOUTH CHINA SEA

← U.S. and South Vietnamese offensives

← North Vietnamese offensives

◄– Major North Vietnamese supply lines (Ho Chi Minh trail)

✴ Major battles or actions

The Indochinese subcontinent, home to long-standing regional conflict, became the center of a prolonged war with the United States.

POOR PEOPLE'S CAMPAIGN In December 1967, just a few months before his assassination, Martin Luther King, Jr., announced a plan to stage a new march on Washington featuring poor people from across the nation. The marchers would demand economic justice including better jobs, education, and homes. King did not live to participate in the march, which was carried out by Rev. Dr. Ralph Abernathy later in the spring of 1968. More than 3,000 protesters set up camp on the Washington Mall, where they stayed for six weeks.

Everett Collection Inc/Alamy Stock Photo.

silence" and to oppose the war by nonviolent means. By this time, the FBI had been harassing King for years, tapping his telephones and spreading malicious rumors about him. Despite these threats, in 1968 the beloved leader of the civil rights movement refused to compromise in his opposition to the war, even if it meant losing the support of those liberal Democrats loyal to Johnson.

In the spring of 1968, King chose Memphis, Tennessee, home of striking sanitation workers, to launch a Poor People's Campaign for peace and justice. There he delivered, in what was to be his final speech, a message of hope. "I have a dream this afternoon that the brotherhood of man will become a reality," King told the crowd. "With this faith, I will go out and carve a tunnel of hope from a mountain of despair." The next evening, April 4, 1968, as he stood on the balcony of his motel, King was shot and killed.

Throughout the world, crowds turned out to mourn King's death. Riots broke out in more than a hundred cities, on college campuses, and on military bases in Vietnam. Chicago Mayor Richard Daley ordered his police to shoot to kill. In Washington, D.C., U.S. Army units set up machine guns outside the Capitol and the White House. King's dream of the nation as a "Beloved Community" died with him.

29.4.3 The Democrats in Disarray

The dramatic events of the first part of 1968 had a direct impact on the presidential campaign. For those liberals dissatisfied with Johnson's conduct of the war, and especially for African Americans suffering the loss of their greatest leader, Senator Robert F. Kennedy of New York

emerged as the candidate of choice. Kennedy enjoyed a strong record on civil rights, and, like King, he had begun to interpret the war as a mirror of injustice at home.

Ironically, Kennedy faced in the primary an opponent who agreed with him, Senator Eugene McCarthy of Minnesota. McCarthy did well with liberal Democrats and white suburbanites. On college campuses, his popularity with antiwar students was so great that his campaign became known as the "children's crusade."

Kennedy captured the votes of African Americans and Latinos and emerged as the Democratic Party's strongest candidate. Having won all but the Oregon primary, he moved on to California. But on June 4, as the final tabulation of his victory came in just past midnight, Robert Kennedy was struck down by an assassin's bullet.

Vice President Hubert H. Humphrey, who had announced his candidacy in April, was now the sole Democrat with the credentials to succeed Johnson. Without entering a single state primary, he lined up delegates. As the candidate least likely to rock the boat, he secured enough votes to win his party's nomination well before Democrats even met in convention.

29.4.4 "The Whole World Is Watching!"

The events surrounding the Democratic convention in Chicago, August 21–26, demonstrated how deep the divisions within the United States had become. Mayor Richard Daley, still reeling from the riots following King's assassination, refused to issue parade permits to the antiwar activists, who had called for a massive demonstration at the convention center. According to later accounts, he sent hundreds of undercover police into the crowds to encourage rock throwing and generally to incite violence so that retaliation would appear necessary and reasonable.

Daley's strategy boomeranged when his officers staged what a presidential commission later termed a "police riot," randomly assaulting demonstrators, casual passersby, and the television crews broadcasting the events. Angered by the embarrassing publicity, Daley sent his agents to raid McCarthy's campaign headquarters, where antiwar Democrats had gathered.

Inside the convention hall, a raging debate over a peace resolution underscored the depth of the division within the party. When the resolution failed, McCarthy delegates put on black armbands and sang "We Shall Overcome." Later, as tear gas used against the demonstrators outside turned the amphitheater air acrid, the beaming Humphrey praised Daley and lauded Johnson's conduct of the Vietnam War. When Senator Abraham Ribicoff of Connecticut protested the "Gestapo tactics" of the Chicago police, television cameras focused on Daley saying, "You Jew son of a bitch . . . go home!" Meanwhile, the crowd outside chanted, "The whole

BERNARD PERLIN, *MAYOR DALEY,* **1968** In 1968, Richard J. Daley held the power of a traditional city boss, having been elected mayor of Chicago four times. In December of that year, the National Commission on Violence released a report that concluded that Chicago police, acting under Daley's orders, had been "unrestrained and indiscriminate" in their attacks on demonstrators at the National Democratic Convention held that August. In response, Daley brazenly announced a 22 percent salary increase for members of the city's police and fire personnel.

Library of Congress (Photoduplication).

world is watching! The whole world is watching!" Indeed, through satellite transmission, it was.

In 1968 protest spread worldwide. Across the United States the antiwar movement picked up steam. In Paris, students and workers scrawled on building walls such humorous and half-serious slogans as "Be Realistic, Demand the Impossible!" Meanwhile, demonstrations in Japan, Italy, Ireland, Germany, Czechoslovakia, and England brought young people into the streets to demand democratic reforms in their own countries and an end to the U.S. war in Vietnam.

29.4.5 The Republican Victory

The Republicans stepped into the breach. Presidential contender Richard Nixon deftly built on voter hostility toward youthful protesters and the counterculture. He wooed a growing constituency that he later termed the "silent majority"—those Americans who worked, paid taxes, and did not demonstrate or picket. Recovering from election defeats for president in 1960 and for California governor

in 1962, Nixon claimed to be the one candidate who could restore law and order. He chose as his running mate the governor of Maryland, Spiro T. Agnew, known for treating dissent as near treason. (See Map 29.3.)

After signing the landmark Civil Rights Act of 1964, President Johnson said privately, "I think we just delivered the South to the Republicans for a long time to come." Republican strategists moved quickly to make this prediction come true. They also recognized the growing electoral importance of the Sunbelt, where populations grew with the rise of high-tech industries and of retirement communities. A powerful conservatism dominated this region, home to many military bases, defense plants, and an increasingly influential religious right.

The 1968 campaign exposed the increasing conservatism of white voters even outside the South. The most dramatic example was the relative success of Alabama Governor George Wallace's third-party bid for the presidency. Wallace took state office in 1963 promising white Alabamans, "Segregation now! Segregation tomorrow! Segregation forever!" In 1968, he waged a national campaign

Map 29.3 THE ELECTION OF 1968

Numbers on states represent Electoral Votes.

	Electoral Vote (%)	Popular Vote (%)
RICHARD M. NIXON (N) (Republican)	301 (56)	31,785,480 (43.4)
Hubert H. Humphrey (H) (Democrat)	191 (36)	31,275,165 (42.7)
George C. Wallace (W) (American Independent)	46 (8)	9,906,473 (13.5)
Other candidates (Dick Gregory, Socialist Labor; Fred Halstead and Paul Boutelle, Socialist Workers; Eugene McCarthy, Peace and Freedom; E. Harold Munn and Rolland E. Fisher, Prohibition)	—	221,134 (0.3)

Although the Republican Nixon-Agnew team won the popular vote by only a small margin, the Democrats lost in most of the northern states that had voted Democratic since the days of FDR. Segregationist Governor George Wallace of Alabama polled more than 9 million votes.

and won five southern states and nearly 14 percent of the popular vote nationwide.

The Nixon-Agnew team ushered in the greatest political realignment since Franklin Roosevelt's victory in 1932. They captured the popular vote by the slim margin of 43.4 percent to Humphrey and Maine Senator Edmund Muskie's 42.7 percent, but they took nearly all the West's electoral college votes. Bitterly divided by the campaign, the Democrats would remain out of presidential contention for more than two decades, except when the Republicans suffered scandal and disgrace. The Republicans in 1968 had paved the way for the conservative ascendancy.

29.5 The Politics of Identity

How did race, gender, and sexual orientation gain new political importance in the 1960s?

Richard Nixon campaigned promising to "bring Americans together again." But, if anything, the divisions among Americans—especially among the young—grew sharper during his presidency. The tragic events of 1968 brought whole sectors of the counterculture to political activism. (See Table 29.2.) With great media fanfare, gay liberation and women's liberation movements took shape while young Latinos, Asian Americans, and Indian peoples pressed their own claims. In different ways, these groups drew their own lessons from Black Power, the nationalist movement that formed in the wake of Malcolm X's death. Soon, "Brown Power," "Yellow Power," and "Red Power" became the slogans of movements constituted distinctly as new communities of protest.

The identity politics would continue to thrive into the twenty-first century, broadening the content of literature, film, television, popular music, and even the curricula of the nation's education system. Collectively, the various movements pushed issues of race, ethnicity, gender, and sexual orientation to the forefront of American politics and simultaneously spotlighted the nation's cultural and social diversity as a major resource.

29.5.1 Black Power

Impatient with tactics based on voting rights and integration, many young activists spurned the civil disobedience of

Table 29.2 PROTEST MOVEMENTS OF THE 1960s

Year	Organization/Movement	Description
1962	Students for a Democratic Society (SDS)	Organization of college students that became the largest national organization of left-wing white students. Calling for "participatory democracy," the SDS involved students in community-based campaigns against poverty and for citizens' control of neighborhoods. The SDS played a prominent role in the campaign to end the war in Vietnam.
1964	Free Speech Movement	Formed at the University of California at Berkeley to protest the banning of on-campus political fundraising. Decried the bureaucratic character of the "multiuniversity" and advocated an expansion of student rights.
1965	Anti–Vietnam War Movement	Advocated grassroots opposition to U.S. involvement in Southeast Asia. By 1970, a national mobilization committee was organizing a demonstration of a half-million protesters in Washington, D.C.
1965	*La raza*	A movement of Chicano youth to advance the cultural and political self-determination of Mexican Americans. *La raza* included the Brown Berets, which addressed community issues, and regional civil rights groups such as the Crusade for Social Justice, formed in 1965.
1966	Black Power	Militant movement that emerged from the civil rights campaigns to advocate independent institutions for African Americans and pride in black culture and African heritage. The idea of Black Power, a term coined by Stokely Carmichael, inspired the formation of the paramilitary Black Panthers.
1968	American Indian Movement (AIM)	Organization formed to advance the self-determination of Indian peoples and challenge the authority of the Bureau of Indian Affairs. Its most effective tactic was occupation. In February 1973, AIM insurgents protesting land and treaty violations occupied Wounded Knee, South Dakota, the location of an 1890 massacre, until the FBI and BIA agents drove them out.
1968	Women's Liberation	Movement of mainly young women that took shape following a protest at the Miss America beauty pageant. Impatient with the legislative reforms promoted by the National Organization for Women, founded in 1966, activists developed their own agenda shaped by the slogan "The Personal Is Political." Activities included the formation of "consciousness-raising" groups and the establishment of women's studies programs.
1968	Asian American Political Alliance (AAPA)	Formed at the University of California at Berkeley, the AAPA was one of the first pan-Asian political organizations to struggle against racial oppression. The AAPA encouraged Asian Americans to claim their own cultural identity and to protest the war against Asian peoples in Vietnam.
1969	Gay Liberation	Movement to protest discrimination against homosexuals and lesbians that emerged after the Stonewall Riots in New York City. Unlike earlier organizations such as the Mattachine Society, which focused on civil rights, gay liberationists sought to radically change American society and government, which they believed were corrupt.

King's generation for direct action and militant self-defense. In 1966, Stokely Carmichael, who had helped turn the Student Nonviolent Coordinating Committee (SNCC) into an all-black organization, began to advocate **Black Power** as a means for African Americans to take control of their own communities.

The **Black Panther Party**, founded in Oakland, California, in 1966 by Huey P. Newton and Bobby Seale, demanded "land, bread, housing, education, clothing, and justice." Members—about 5,000 in 30 cities—adopted a paramilitary style that infuriated the authorities. Monitoring police brutality was their major activity. In several communities, volunteers also ran free-breakfast programs for schoolchildren, established medical clinics, and conducted educational classes. Persecuted by police and the FBI, their leaders were arrested, prosecuted, and sentenced to long terms in jail that effectively destroyed the organization.

Black Power nevertheless continued to grow into a multifaceted movement. The Reverend Jesse Jackson, for example, rallied African Americans in Chicago to boycott the A&P supermarket chain until the firm hired 700 black workers. A dynamic speaker and skillful organizer, Jackson encouraged African Americans to support their own businesses and services.

Cultural nationalism became the most enduring component of Black Power. In their popular book *Black Power* (1967), Carmichael and Charles V. Hamilton urged African Americans "to assert their own definitions, to reclaim their history, their culture; to create their own sense of community and togetherness." Thousands of college students responded by calling for more classes on African American history and culture. At San Francisco State University, students—with the help of Black Panthers— demanded a black studies department. After a series of failed negotiations with administrators, activists called for a campus-wide strike in December 1968 and shut down the university. Strikes for "Third World Studies" soon broke out on other campuses, including the University of Wisconsin at Madison, where the National Guard was brought in to quell the protest.

Meanwhile, trendsetters put aside Western dress for African-style dashikis and hairstyles, and black parents gave their children African names. Many well-known activists and artists, such as Imamu Amiri Baraka (formerly LeRoi Jones), Muhammad Ali (formerly Cassius Clay), and Kwame Touré (formerly Stokely Carmichael), rejected their "slave names." The new holiday Kwanzaa, created in 1966, followed Christmas as a weeklong celebration of African heritage and culture. This deepening sense of racial pride was summed up in the popular slogan "Black Is Beautiful."

29.5.2 Sisterhood Is Powerful

In 1966, Betty Friedan's best-selling *Feminine Mystique* (see Chapter 27) sparked the formation of the **National Organization for Women (NOW)**. Members campaigned for the enforcement of laws banning sex discrimination in work and in education, for maternity leaves, and for government funding of daycare centers. NOW also backed the Equal Rights Amendment, first introduced in Congress in 1923, and demanded the repeal of legislation that prohibited abortion or restricted birth control.

By the late 1960s, a different kind of movement had emerged: women's liberation. The women's liberation movement attracted young women who had been active in civil rights, the SDS, and campus antiwar movements. Impatient with the NOW's legislative agenda and angered

HUEY NEWTON This iconic image features Huey P. Newton, co-founder with Bobby Seale of the Black Panther Party in 1966. The photograph, attributed to cinematographer Blair Stapp, conveys determined resistance. The caption on the original poster reads: "The racist dog policemen must withdraw immediately from our communities, cease their wanton murder and brutality and torture of black people, or face the wrath of the armed people.

Library of Congress.

WOMEN STRIKE FOR EQUALITY Originating with Betty Friedan and sponsored by the National Organization for Women, the "Women's Strike for Equality" commemorated the fiftieth anniversary of the passage of the nineteenth amendment to the Constitution, which granted women the right to vote. The "strike" took the form of a huge parade of between 20,000 and 50,000 protesters along Fifth Avenue in New York City. Coordinated "sister" events occurred in dozens of cities across the United States. The event marked the first "Women's Equality Day," which continues to be celebrated on August 26..

Science History Images/Alamy Stock Photo.

by the sexism of male activists, these women organized separately under the slogan "Sisterhood Is Powerful."

The women's liberation movement issued a scathing critique of patriarchy—that is, the power of men to dominate all institutions, from the family to business and government to the protest movements themselves. One New York group created a lot of publicity for the movement by storming the 1968 Miss America beauty pageant in Atlantic City. They crowned a live sheep as queen and threw "implements of female torture" (bras, girdles, curlers, and copies of *Ladies' Home Journal* magazine) into a "freedom trash can."

The media focused on such audacious acts, but the majority of activists were less flamboyant women simply trying to rise above the limitations imposed on them because of their gender. They met more often outside the limelight in consciousness-raising groups, where they examined the relationship between

public events and private lives. Here women established the constituency for the movement's most important principle, expressed in the aphorism "The personal is political." Believing that no aspect of life lacked a political dimension, consciousness-raising groups explored the power dynamics of the family, marriage, the workforce, and government.

Some activists staged sit-ins at *Newsweek* magazine's office to protest demeaning media depictions of women. Others established health clinics, daycare centers, rape crisis centers, and shelters for women fleeing abusive husbands or lovers. Feminist bookstores and publishing companies, such as the Feminist Press, reached out to eager readers. In January 1972, *Ms.* magazine hit the newsstands. Meanwhile, campus activists demanded women's studies programs and women's centers, not least to prepare women for steady participation in the workforce. (See Figure 29.4.) Between 1970 and 1975, as many as 150 women's studies programs were established at colleges throughout the United States.

The women's liberation movement remained, however, a bastion of white middle-class women. The appeal to sisterhood did not unite women across race or class or even sexual orientation. Lesbians, who charged the early NOW leaders with homophobia, found large pockets of "heterosexism" in the women's liberation movement and broke off to form their own organizations. African Americans remained wary of white women's appeals to sisterhood and formed their own "womanist" movement

Figure 29.4 WOMEN IN THE WORKFORCE, 1940–1980

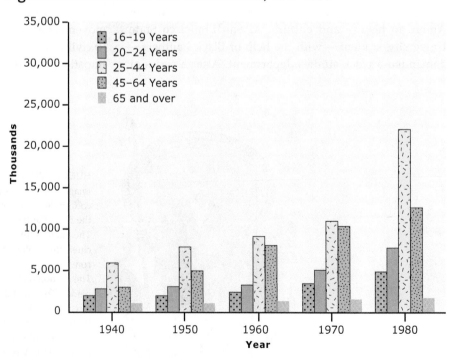

Women showed steady gains in workforce participation since the 1940s, but especially so during their peak child-bearing and child-rearing ages.

U.S. Bureau of the Census.

to address their distinct cultural and political concerns. Similarly, by 1970, a Latina feminist movement addressed issues uniquely relevant to women of color in an Anglo-dominated society.

29.5.3 Gay Liberation

In the mid-1950s, two pioneering homophile organizations, the Mattachine Society and the Daughters of Bilitis, had campaigned against discrimination in employment, the armed forces, and all areas of social and cultural life. But it was during the tumultuous late 1960s that a sizable movement formed to encourage gays and lesbians to "come out" and "Say It Loud: Gay Is Good, Gay Is Proud."

The major event prompting gays to organize followed repeated police raids of gay bars. On Friday, June 27, 1969, New York police raided the Stonewall Inn, a well-known gay bar in Greenwich Village, and provoked an uprising that lasted the entire night. The next day, "Gay Power" graffiti appeared throughout the neighborhood.

In New York City, the Gay Liberation Front (GLF) announced itself as "a revolutionary homosexual group of men and women . . . who reject society's attempt to impose sexual roles and definitions of our nature." Taking a stand against the war in Vietnam, the GLF quickly adopted the forms of public protest, such as street demonstrations and sit-ins, developed by civil rights activists and given new direction by anti-war protesters.

Changes in public opinion and policies followed. Several churches opened their doors to gay activists. In 1973, the American Psychiatric Association, which since World War II had viewed homosexuality as a treatable mental illness, reclassified it as a normal sexual orientation. Meanwhile, a slow process of decriminalization of homosexual acts between consenting adults began. In 1975, the U.S. Civil Service Commission ended its ban on the employment of homosexuals.

The gay liberation movement encouraged more than legal and institutional changes. "Gay Is Good" (like "Black Is Beautiful" and "Sisterhood Is Powerful") called to a large hidden minority to demand public acceptance of their sexual identity. In 1970, to commemorate the first anniversary of the Stonewall raid, Gay Pride parades took place in at least eight American cities.

29.5.4 The Chicano Rebellion

To many Americans, the Chicano movement seemed to burst onto the scene in 1965, when the United Farm Workers (UFW), a union of mainly migrant workers, struck against grape growers of the San Joaquin Valley in California. By 1968, strike leaders César Chávez and Dolores Huerta were heading a nationwide boycott of non-union-picked grapes and lettuce.

While Chávez emerged as a national hero, many young Mexican Americans spearheaded an urban-based movement based on identity politics, which Chávez himself rejected. They adopted the slang term *Chicano*, in preference to Mexican American, to express a militant ethnic nationalism. Chicano militants demanded not only their full civil rights, but also recognition of their distinctive culture and history.

High school students were at the forefront of this new movement. In March 1968, the Brown Berets, a group modeled on the Black Panthers, helped to plan the "blow out" (walkout) that sent nearly 15,000 Chicano teenagers into the streets of East Los Angeles. The high school students demanded educational reform, including courses on the history, literature, art, and language of Mexican Americans. After the police arrested the protesters, students in San Antonio and

CÉSAR CHÁVEZ Labor activist César Chávez spearheaded the organization of Chicano agricultural workers into the United Farm Workers (UFW), the first successful union of migrant workers. In 1965, a strike of grape pickers in the fields around Delano, California, and a nationwide boycott of table grapes brought Chávez and the UFW into the media spotlight. Like Martin Luther King Jr., he advocated nonviolent methods for achieving justice and equality.

Denver expressed their solidarity by conducting their own blow outs. Meanwhile, college students demanded Chicano studies programs.

The larger Chicano movement found vivid expression in the performing and visual arts, and in literature. *El Teatro Campesino*, founded by Luis Valdez, began as a touring company that performed plays on the back of a flatbed truck and in union halls during the Delano grape strike. Teatro branched out to comprise film as well as on-stage drama drama and flourished as an exploration of the political dimensions of Mexican American society. One of the most popular and visible media was the mural, often inspired by the art of Mexican masters such as Diego Rivera. Artistic expression found its way into music and dance. The rock group Los Lobos, for example, dedicated its first recorded album to the UFW. One of the most important writers to capture the excitement of the Chicano movement was Oscar Zeta Acosta, whose *The Revolt of the Cockroach People*, published in 1973, renders into fiction some of the major events of the era.

29.5.5 Red Power

At the forefront of the **Red Power** movement was the **American Indian Movement (AIM)**. Founded in 1968, AIM represented mainly urban Indian communities and expressed a pan-Indian identity. Like the Black Panthers and Brown Berets, its young, militant leaders organized initially to monitor law enforcement practices. They soon built a network of urban centers, churches, and philanthropic organizations as well as the "powwow circuit" that publicized news of protest and educational activities across the country. (See Map 29.4.)

The movement's major catalyst was the occupation of the deserted federal prison on Alcatraz Island in San Francisco Bay. On November 20, 1969, a group of 89 "Indians of All Tribes" claimed the island according to the terms of an 1868 Sioux treaty that gave Indians rights to unused federal property on Indian land. For the next 19 months, nearly 100 Indians occupied the land. Although the protestors ultimately failed

Map 29.4 MAJOR INDIAN RESERVATIONS, 1976

Although sizable areas, designated Indian reservations represented only a small portion of territory occupied in earlier times.

to achieve their specific goals, which included a deed to the land and federal funding for a cultural center, they rallied the larger Indian community.

Another series of dramatic events began in 1972, when AIM sponsored the **Trail of Broken Treaties** caravan. First the participants went to Washington, D.C., where they staged a weeklong occupation of the Bureau of Indian Affairs. AIM insurgents then headed west, to the Pine Ridge Reservation, the site of the 1890 massacre at Wounded Knee, South Dakota. There, in the spring of 1973, they demanded a restoration of treaty rights and began a siege that lasted 10 weeks. Dozens of FBI agents with shoot-to-kill orders poured in, leaving two Indian activists dead and an unknown number of casualties on both sides.

The Red Power movement culminated in the "Longest Walk," a five-month march in 1978 from San Francisco to Washington, D.C. Again activists emphasized the history of the forced removal of Indians from their homelands and the U.S. government's repeated violations of treaty rights. By this time, several tribes had won by court rulings, legislation, or administrative fiat small parts of what had been taken from them. Despite these victories, many tribal lands continued to suffer from industrial and government waste-dumping and environmental degradation. On reservations and in urban areas with heavy Indian concentrations, alcohol abuse and ill health remained serious problems. Identity politics also inspired an "Indian Renaissance" in literature. Vine Deloria Jr.'s *Custer Died for Your Sins: An Indian Manifesto* (1969) argued for the retention of tribal customs within modern society. Inspired by other writers such as N. Scott Momaday and Leslie Silko, Indian activists often turned to their elders to learn tribal ways, including traditional dress, spiritual and healing practices, and language.

29.5.6 The Asian American Movement

In 1968, groups of Chinese, Japanese, and Filipino students began to identify for the first time as Asian Americans. Students at San Francisco State University formed the Asian American Political Alliance (AAPA), while UC-Berkeley students mobilized to "express Asian American solidarity in a predominantly white society."

These groups stood firmly against the Vietnam War, condemning it as a violation of the national sovereignty of the small Asian country. They also protested the racism directed against Southeast Asian peoples and proclaimed their solidarity with their "Asian brothers and sisters" in Vietnam.

Throughout 1968 and 1969, Asian American college students boycotted classes and demanded the establishment of ethnic studies programs. Meanwhile, artists, writers, documentary filmmakers, oral historians, and anthropologists worked to recover the Asian American past. Maxine

Hong Kingston's *Woman Warrior: A Memoir of a Girlhood among Ghosts* (1976) became a major best-seller.

Looking to the example of the Black Panthers, Yellow Power activists also took their struggle into the community. In 1968, a group presented the San Francisco municipal government with a list of grievances about conditions in Chinatown and organized a protest march down the neighborhood's main street. The Redress and Reparations Movement, begun by Sansei (third-generation Japanese Americans), encouraged children to ask their parents about their wartime internment experiences and prompted older civil rights organizations, such as the Japanese American Citizens League, to raise the issue of reparations. Trade unionists organized new Asian American workers, mainly in service industries and garment trades. Other campaigns reflected the growing diversity of the Asian population. Filipinos, the fastest-growing group, demonstrated against the United States–backed Philippine dictator Ferdinand Marcos. Students from South Korea similarly denounced the repressive government in their homeland. Samoans publicized the damage caused by nuclear testing in the Pacific Islands.

29.6 Coming Apart

What were the most important successes and failures of the Nixon administration?

Richard M. Nixon inherited not only an increasingly unpopular war but also a nation riven by internal discord. "We live in a deeply troubled and profoundly unsettled time," he noted. "Drugs, crime, campus revolts, racial discord, draft resistance—on every hand we find old standards violated, old values discarded." Additionally, he saw no resolution to the war in Vietnam. Nevertheless, without specifying his plans, he took office promising a "just and honorable peace" in Southeast Asia and the restoration of law and order at home. Yet, as president, Nixon let pragmatist sensibility guide him and consequently puzzled both friends and foes. He ordered unprecedented illegal government action against private citizens while agreeing with Congress to enhance several welfare programs and improve environmental protection. He widened and intensified the war in Vietnam, yet made stunning moves toward détente with the People's Republic of China. An architect of the Cold War in the 1950s, Nixon became the first president to foresee its end. Nixon worked hard in the White House, centralizing authority and reigning defiantly as an "imperial president"—until he brought himself down.

29.6.1 A White House of Contradictions

Nixon took the oath of office on the Capitol steps and pledged to answer the "crisis of the spirit" that plagued

Americans. However, as the first president in more than a century to face opposition from both houses of Congress, each dominated by a sizable Democratic majority, his prospects were dim. Moreover, his interest in domestic policy paled beside his interest in foreign affairs, and he began with only a vague agenda. Slow getting started, Nixon nevertheless came up with some surprises for the conservatives and liberals alike.

Seven months after his inauguration, on August 8, 1969, Nixon finally presented his domestic program, which he called the "New Federalism." His plan for general revenue sharing—returning a portion of federal income tax dollars to hard-pressed states and cities—became the State and Local Fiscal Assistance Act of 1972 and helped tamp down the financial crisis in many localities. Nixon also surprised conservatives by proposing the Family Assistance Plan, which guaranteed an income to poor children; the senate voted it down. Nixon also embraced a policy of fiscal liberalism. In August 1971, he ordered the dollar's value to float against other currencies on the world market rather than being tied to a fixed value of gold, thereby ending the international monetary policy established at Bretton Woods. His 90-day freeze on wages, rents, and prices, designed to halt the inflation caused by the massive spending on the Vietnam War, also closely resembled Democratic policies. Finally, Nixon's support of adjustments or quotas favoring minority contractors in construction projects created an explosive precedent for "set-aside" programs later blamed on liberals. Determined to win reelection in 1972, Nixon supported new Social Security, Medicare, and Medicaid benefits, and subsidized housing for the poor. He also sponsored more regulatory agencies and rules than any administration since the New Deal. For example, Nixon oversaw the creation of the Environmental Protection Agency, the Occupational Safety and Health Administration, and the National Oceanic and Atmospheric Administration.

Yet, for the most part, Nixon remained committed to the "Southern Strategy" that brought him into office and the principles behind it. He lined up with conservatives on most civil rights issues and thus enlarged his Southern Republican base. He slowed school desegregation and rejected the court-ordered busing programs required to achieve racial balance. His nominees to the Supreme Court were far more conservative than those appointed by Eisenhower.

Nixon's foreign policy, apart from Vietnam, also defied the expectations of liberals and conservatives alike. Nixon pursued a policy of détente that replaced U.S.-Soviet bipolarity with multilateral relations that included the People's Republic of China, a rising world power more rigidly communist than the Soviet Union. "Ping-pong diplomacy" began in April 1971, when the Chinese hosted a table tennis team from the United States. Nixon sent his national security advisor, Henry Kissinger, on a secret mission a few months later. Finally, in February 1972, Nixon flew to Beijing. Heralding a new era in East-West diplomacy, Nixon claimed that he succeeded in bridging "16,000 miles and twenty-two years of hostility."

Next, the president went to Moscow to negotiate with Soviet leader Leonid Brezhnev, who was anxious about U.S. involvement with China and eager for economic assistance. Nixon agreed to cooperate on science and technology, including a joint space mission, and also completed negotiations of the **Strategic Arms Limitation Treaty** (SALT, known later as SALT I). A limited measure, SALT I represented the first success at strategic arms control since the start of the Cold War and a major public relations victory for the leaders of the two superpowers.

Nixon's final major diplomatic foray was far less effective. The president sent Kissinger on a two-year mission of "shuttle diplomacy" to mediate Israeli-Arab disputes, to ensure the continued flow of oil, and to increase lucrative U.S. arms sales to Arab countries. The Egyptians and Israelis agreed to a cease-fire in their October 1973 Yom Kippur War, but little progress toward peace in the area was achieved.

Apart from the highly publicized tour to China, Nixon revealed little publicly about his policy for other parts of the globe. Unknown to most Americans, he accelerated the delivery of arms supplies to foreign dictators, including the shah of Iran, Ferdinand Marcos of the Philippines, and the white supremacist apartheid government in South Africa. In Latin America, Nixon gave financial assistance and military aid to repressive regimes such as that of Anastasio Somoza Debayle of Nicaragua, notorious for its blatant corruption and repeated violations of human rights.

Still more controversial was Nixon's plan to overthrow the democratically elected socialist government of Salvador Allende in Chile. The CIA destabilized the regime by funding right-wing parties, launching demonstrations, and preparing the Chilean army for a coup. In September 1973, a military junta killed President Allende and captured, tortured, or murdered thousands of his supporters. Nixon and Kissinger warmly welcomed the new ruler, General Augusto Pinochet, granting him financial assistance to restabilize the country.

Toward the end of Nixon's term, members of Congress who had been briefed on these policies began to break silence, and reports of clandestine operations flooded the media. Several former CIA agents issued anguished confessions of their activities in other countries. More troubling to Nixon was that, in spite of all his efforts, the United States continued to lose ground as a superpower.

29.6.2 A Widening Divide

Despite Nixon's campaign pledges, the Vietnam War raged for four more years before a peace settlement was reached. (See Figure 29.5.) Much of the responsibility for prolonging the war rested with Kissinger, who insisted that the United States could not retain its global leadership by appearing weak to

Figure 29.5 U.S. MILITARY FORCES IN VIETNAM AND CASUALTIES, 1961–1981

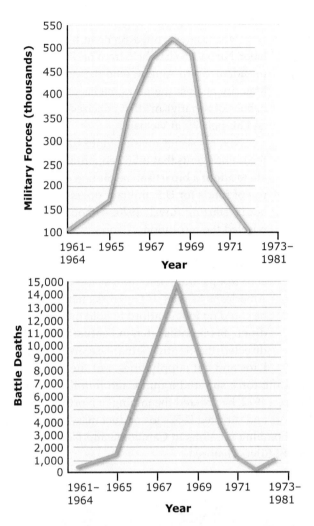

The U.S. government estimated battle deaths between 1969 and 1973 for South Vietnamese troops at 107,504 and North Vietnamese and Vietcong at more than a half-million. Although the United States suffered fewer deaths, the cost was enormous.

U.S. Department of Defense, *Selected Manpower Statistics*, annual and unpublished data; beginning 1981, National Archives and Records Service, "Combat Area Casualty File" (3-330-80-3).

Figure 29.6 PUBLIC OPINION ON THE WAR IN VIETNAM

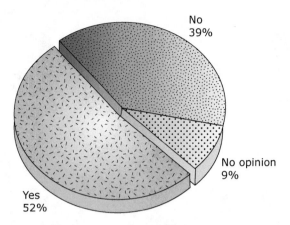

By 1969, Americans were sharply divided in their assessments of the progress of the war and peace negotiations. The American Institute of Public Opinion, founded in 1935 by George Gallup, charted a growing dissatisfaction with the war in Vietnam.

From THE GALLUP POLL 1835–1971 by George Gallup. Copyright © 1972 Gallup Inc.

either allies or enemies. Together, Nixon and Kissinger overpowered those State Department members who understood that the majority of Americans, aware of the mounting casualties, no longer supported the war. (See Figure 29.6.) They also kept their most important actions secret from the public.

In public, Nixon followed a policy of "Vietnamization." On May 14, 1969, he announced that the time was approaching "when the South Vietnamese . . . will be able to take over some of the fighting." During the next several months, he ordered the withdrawal of 60,000 U.S. troops. In private, Nixon mulled over the option of a "knockout blow" to the North Vietnamese.

In March 1969, Nixon had made one of the most controversial decisions of his presidency. Without seeking congressional approval or informing the public, he ordered the bombing of the tiny, neutral nation of Cambodia. Nixon hoped in this way to end North Vietnamese infiltration into the South, but he also decided to live up to what he privately called his "wild man" or "mad bomber" reputation. The enemy would be unable to anticipate the location or severity of the next U.S. strike, Nixon reasoned, and would thus feel compelled to negotiate.

News of Nixon's plan to invade Cambodia broke a year later, on April 30, 1970, and triggered the largest series of demonstrations and police-student confrontations in the nation's history. On May 1, students responded angrily to Nixon's expansion of the war. On several campuses, students attacked or burned down buildings used for military training. To quell the disruption at Kent State University in Ohio, the governor called out the National Guard, a decision that ended in disaster. After several skirmishes with students, the National Guard shot into an unarmed crowd, killing four and wounding nine. Huge demonstrations took place on campuses nation-wide, and 450 colleges closed or saw students and faculty join in strikes. Thirty-seven college and university presidents signed a letter calling on the president to end the war, not escalate the fighting. The following weekend, on May 10, more than 100,000 anti-war protestors headed to Washington, D.C., to demonstrate against both the invasion of Cambodia and the killings at Kent State. Then, on May 14, at Jackson State University, a black school in Mississippi, state troopers entered a campus dormitory and began shooting wildly, killing 2 students and wounding 12 others.

After the Kent State killings, Nixon, without emotion, had addressed the nation, saying, "when dissent turns

KENT STATE On May 4, 1970, members of the Ohio National Guard fired on antiwar protestors, killing four and wounding nine demonstrators at Kent State University. This Pulitzer Prize–winning photograph by John Filo, a 22-year-old photojournalism student, shows Mary Ann Vecchio, a 14-year-old runaway, crying out over the body of student Jeffrey Glenn Miller.

John Filo/Getty Images.

killings at Kent State, a group of 200 construction workers attacked them. The "Hard Hat Riot" was followed a few weeks later by a rally of 20,000 blue-collar workers supporting Nixon's conduct of the war. Nixon later named Brennan his secretary of labor. Nixon also had help from his short-term vice president, Spiro Agnew, who defended the Silent Majority against the news media—the "nattering nabobs of negativism" that criticized the president and his policies in Vietnam.

Nixon's secret missions into Cambodia, and the tragic events that followed, prompted the Senate to adopt a bipartisan resolution outlawing the use of funds for U.S. military operations in Cambodia, starting July 1, 1970. Although the House rejected the resolution, Nixon saw the writing on the wall. He had planned to negotiate a simultaneous withdrawal of North Vietnamese and U.S. troops, but—having lost the trust of many Americans as well as congressional legislators—he could no longer afford to hold out for this condition. Six months later, in February 1971, Nixon directed the South Vietnamese army to invade Laos and cut supply lines, but the demoralized invading force suffered a quick and humiliating defeat. In April 1972, he ordered the mining of North Vietnamese harbors and directed B-52s to conduct massively destructive bombing missions in Cambodia and North Vietnam. (See SEEING History.)

to violence it ends in tragedy." He also used the occasion to cast protesters as "bums." Nixon found an ally in Peter Brennan, head of the construction workers' union in New York. On May 8, 1970, as anti-war protesters—mainly high school and college students—gathered in memory of the

"HARD HAT RIOT" On May 8, 1970, New York City construction workers surged into Wall Street in Lower Manhattan, violently disrupting an antiwar rally and attacking the protesters with lead pipes and crowbars. Known as the "Hard Hat Riot," the well-publicized event was followed later in the month by a march, 100,000 strong, of hard-hat workers unfurling American flags and chanting "All the way U.S.A."

ASSOCIATED PRESS.

SEEING History

Kim Phuc, Fleeing a Napalm Attack near Trang Bang

In 1972, during the phase of the war termed "Vietnamization," South Vietnamese aircraft bombed the village of Trang Bang, about 25 miles from Saigon. They were attacking North Vietnamese and Vietcong fighters, but mistakenly targeted a Buddhist pagoda. The incendiary bombs contained black, oily napalm that burned the villagers gathered there.

News photographer Nick Ut had been assigned to meet up with the South Vietnamese army at Trang Bang. "When we [the reporters] moved closer to the village we saw the first people running," he recalled in 1999. "I thought 'Oh my God' when I suddenly saw a woman with her left leg badly burned by napalm. Then came a woman carrying a baby, who died, then another woman carrying a small child with its skin coming off. When I took a picture of them I heard a child screaming and saw that young girl who had pulled off all her burning clothes. She yelled to her brother on her left. Just before the napalm

was dropped soldiers [of the South Vietnamese Army] had yelled to the children to run but there wasn't enough time."

The Associated Press, which syndicates photographs to the media worldwide, at first refused to transmit the picture because of the nine-year-old girl's nudity but eventually concluded that the news value of the photograph was such that it could run, provided no close-up of the girl be transmitted. Ut, who took the severely burned girl to the hospital before delivering his film, won a Pulitzer Prize for the photograph.

In 1996, Phan Thi Kim Phuc, then 33, came to the United States, visited the Vietnam Veterans Memorial in Washington, D.C., and resolved to form a foundation to help children victimized by war. She still wants the photograph to be seen: "Let the world see how horrible wars can be."

- **What does this photograph suggest about the role of the news media during the Vietnam War?**

- **In focusing on civilians, what does Nick Ut's photograph suggest about the course of the war?**

KIM PHUC, FLEEING A NAPALM ATTACK NEAR TRANG BANG

Nick Ut/ASSOCIATED PRESS.

Unknown to the public, Nixon also sent Kissinger to Paris for negotiations with delegates from North Vietnam. They agreed to a cease-fire specifying the withdrawal of all U.S. troops and the return of all U.S. prisoners of war. Knowing these terms ensured his country's defeat, South Vietnam's president refused to sign the agreement. On Christmas Day 1972, hoping for a better negotiating position, Nixon ordered one final wave of bomb attacks on North Vietnam's cities. To halt the bombing, the North Vietnamese resumed negotiations. But the terms of the Paris Peace Agreement, signed by

North Vietnam and the United States in January 1973, differed little from the settlement Nixon could have procured in 1969.

The last U.S. troops withdrew from Vietnam in March 1973. Two years later, in April 1975, the North Vietnamese took over Saigon, and the communist-led Democratic Republic of Vietnam soon united the small nation.

The war was finally over. It had cost the United States 58,000 lives and $150 billion. The nation had not only failed to achieve its stated war goal, but also had lost an important post in Southeast Asia. Equally important, the United

States proved it could not sustain the policy of containment introduced by President Truman.

Even before the withdrawal of U.S. troops, reports of chilling war crimes had begun to haunt Americans. In 1971, the army court-martialed a lieutenant, William L. Calley Jr., for the murder of "at least" 22 Vietnamese civilians during a 1968 search-and-destroy mission subsequently known as the **My Lai Massacre**. Calley's platoon had destroyed a village and slaughtered more than 350 unarmed South Vietnamese, raping and beating many of the women before killing them. "My Lai was not an isolated incident," one veteran attested, but "only a minor step beyond the standard official United States policy in Indochina."

29.6.3 Dirty Tricks and the 1972 Election

As Nixon approached the 1972 reelection campaign, he tightened his inner circle of White House staff who assisted him in withholding information from the public, discrediting critics, and engaging in assorted "dirty tricks." They also formed a secret squad, "the plumbers," to halt troublesome information leaks. This team, headed by former CIA agent E. Howard Hunt and former FBI agent G. Gordon Liddy, assisted in conspiracy at the highest levels of government.

The first person on the squad's "hit list" was Daniel Ellsberg, a former researcher with the Department of Defense, who in 1971 had turned over to the press secret documents outlining the history of U.S. involvement in Vietnam. The so-called **Pentagon Papers** exposed the role of presidents and military leaders in deceiving the public and Congress about the conduct of the United States in Southeast Asia. Nixon directed the Department of Justice to prosecute Ellsberg on charges of conspiracy, espionage, and theft. Meanwhile, Hunt and Liddy, seeking to discredit Ellsberg, broke into the office of his former psychiatrist, but found nothing. By 1973, the charges against Ellsberg had been dropped after the Nixon administration itself stood guilty of misconduct.

During the 1972 presidential campaign, the Committee to Re-Elect the President (CREEP) enjoyed a huge war chest and spent a good portion on "dirty tricks" designed to divide the Democrats and disgrace them in the eyes of the voting public. They charged George McGovern, Nixon's Democratic opponent, with advocating "abortion, acid [LSD], and amnesty" for draft resisters and deserters. They also informed the news media that McGovern's running mate, Senator Thomas Eagleton, had earlier undergone electric shock therapy for depression, thus forcing his resignation from the Democratic team.

In the short run, the Republicans tallied a monumental success. Nixon presented himself as the candidate of "middle Americans," the Great Silent Majority, and won reelection by a landslide, winning every state but Massachusetts. More important in the long run, the Republicans

captured the once solidly Democratic South and the majority of blue-collar, Catholic, and urban voters.

Nixon had achieved the grandest moment of his long and complex political career. Nevertheless, the most audacious plan of his reelection committee—wiretapping the Democratic National Committee headquarters—ultimately backfired.

29.6.4 Watergate: Nixon's Downfall

On June 17, 1972, a security team had tripped up a group hired by CREEP to install listening devices in the Washington, D.C., Watergate apartment and office complex where the Democrats were headquartered. The police arrested five men, who were later found guilty of conspiracy and burglary. Although Nixon disclaimed any knowledge of the plan, two *Washington Post* reporters, Bob Woodward and Carl Bernstein, followed a trail of evidence back to the nation's highest office.

Televised Senate hearings opened to public view more than a pattern of presidential wrongdoing: They showed an attempt to impede investigations of the **Watergate** case. Testifying before the committee, a former Nixon aide revealed evidence of secret tape recordings of conversations held in the Oval Office. After special prosecutor Archibald Cox refused

NIXON BIDS FARWELL TO WHITE HOUSE STAFF Richard Nixon bid a final farewell to his White House staff as he left Washington, D.C., on August 9, 1974. The first president to resign from office, Nixon had become so entangled in the Watergate scandal that his impeachment appeared certain. He was succeeded by Vice President Gerald Ford. After taking the oath of office later that day, President Ford remarked that the wounds of Watergate were "more painful and more poisonous than those of foreign wars."

Bob Daugherty/ASSOCIATED PRESS.

to allow Nixon to claim executive privilege and withhold the tapes, the president ordered Cox fired. This "Saturday Night Massacre," as it came to be called, further tarnished Nixon's reputation and swelled curiosity about the tapes. On June 24, 1974, the Supreme Court voted unanimously that Nixon had to release the tapes to a new special prosecutor, Leon Jaworski.

The Watergate tapes proved that Nixon not only had known about plans to cover up the Watergate break-in, but had in fact ordered it. In July 1974, the House Judiciary Committee adopted three articles of impeachment, charging Nixon with obstructing justice, abusing the power of his office, and acting in contempt of Congress.

Charges of executive criminality had clouded the Nixon administration since his vice president left in disgrace. In 1972, Spiro Agnew admitted to accepting large kickbacks while serving as governor of Maryland. Pleading no contest, Agnew resigned in October 1973.

A delegation from Congress, led by Senator Barry Goldwater, approached Nixon with the news that impeachment and conviction were certain. On August 8, 1974, in a televised address, Nixon announced his intention to step down, becoming the first U.S. president to resign from office. "By taking this action," he said, "I hope that I will have hastened the start of that process of healing which is so desperately needed in America." Waiting in the wings was Agnew's successor, Vice President Gerald Ford, a moderate Republican U.S. representative from Michigan. After swearing the oath of office, Ford also reassured the public that "our long national nightmare is over." He later backstepped by pardoning Nixon unconditionally for all the federal crimes he might have committed while in office. This controversial action, which may have cost him his own election in 1976, reinforced public cynicism toward government and politicians in general.

Conclusion

The resignations of Richard Nixon and Spiro Agnew did little to relieve the feeling of national exhaustion that followed the Vietnam War. U.S. troops pulled out of Vietnam in 1973 and the war officially ended in 1975, but bitterness lingered over the unprecedented—and, for many, humiliating—defeat. Moreover, confidence in the government's highest office was severely shaken. The passage of the War Powers Act in 1973—written to compel any future president to seek congressional approval for armed intervention abroad, and passed over Nixon's veto—dramatized both the widespread suspicion of an "imperial presidency" and a yearning for peace.

In 1968, seven prominent antiwar protesters had been brought to trial for allegedly conspiring to disrupt the Democratic National Convention in Chicago. Just a few years later, the majority of Americans had concluded that

presidents Johnson and Nixon had conspired to do far worse. They had intentionally deceived the public about the nature and fortunes of the war. This moral failure signaled a collapse at the center of the American political system. Since Dwight Eisenhower left office warning of the potential danger embedded in the "military-industrial complex," no president had survived the presidency with his honor intact. Watergate, then, appeared to cap the politics of the Cold War, its revelations only reinforcing futility and cynicism.

But the upheaval that marked these years left the nation deeply divided. The opposing sides had lined up not merely in relation to the conflict in Southeast Asia, but also on sharp moral and cultural differences that would shape politics for decades to come. The United States was left psychologically at war with itself.

Key Terms

Gulf of Tonkin resolution Joint resolution after a request to Congress from President Lyndon Johnson, in response to North Vietnamese torpedo boat attacks, in which he sought authorization for "all necessary measures" to protect American forces and stop further aggression. p. 719

free speech movement Student movement at the University of California at Berkeley, formed in 1964 to protest limitations on political activities on campus. p. 720

counterculture Various alternatives to mainstream values and behaviors that became popular in the 1960s, including experimentation with psychedelic drugs, communal living, a return to the land, Asian religions, and experimental art. p. 721

war on poverty Set of programs introduced by Lyndon Johnson between 1963 and 1966 designed to break the cycle of poverty by providing funds for job training, community development, nutrition, and supplementary education. p. 724

Office of Economic Opportunity (OEO) Federal agency that coordinated many programs of the war on poverty between 1964 and 1975. p. 725

Medicare Basic medical insurance for the elderly, financed through the federal government; program created in 1965. p. 725

Black Power Philosophy emerging after 1965 that real economic and political gains for African Americans could come only through self-help, self-determination, and organizing for direct political influence. p. 733

Black Panther Party Political and social movement among black Americans, founded in Oakland, California, in 1966 and emphasizing black economic and political power. p. 733

National Organization for Women (NOW) Organization founded to campaign for the enforcement of laws related to women's issues. p. 733

Red Power Term for pan-Indian identity. p. 736

American Indian Movement (AIM) Group of Native American political activists who used confrontations with the federal government to publicize their case for Indian rights. p. 736

Trail of Broken Treaties Event staged in 1972 by the American Indian Movement that culminated in a

weeklong occupation of the Bureau of Indian Affairs in Washington, D.C. p. 737

Strategic Arms Limitation Treaty Treaty signed in 1972 by the United States and the Soviet Union to slow the nuclear arms race. p. 738

My Lai Massacre Killing of as many as 500 Vietnamese civilians by U.S. forces during a 1968 search-and-destroy mission. p. 742

Pentagon Papers Classified Defense Department documents on the history of the United States's involvement in Vietnam, prepared in 1968 and leaked to the press in 1971. p. 742

Watergate A complex scandal involving attempts to cover up illegal actions taken by administration officials and leading to the resignation of President Richard Nixon in 1974. p. 742

CHRONOLOGY

1964 — Lyndon Johnson defeats conservative Barry Goldwater for president

1965
President Johnson authorizes Operation Rolling Thunder, the bombing of North Vietnam

First major march on Washington for peace is organized

Watts uprising begins a wave of rebellions in black communities

1968 — Tet Offensive in Vietnam, followed by international protests against U.S. policies

Martin Luther King Jr. and Robert Kennedy assassinated

Richard Nixon elected president

1972
Nixon reelected in a landslide

1973 — Paris Peace Agreement ends war in Vietnam

1974
House Judiciary Committee adopts articles of impeachment against Nixon

Nixon resigns the presidency

Chapter 30
The Conservative Ascendancy 1974–1999

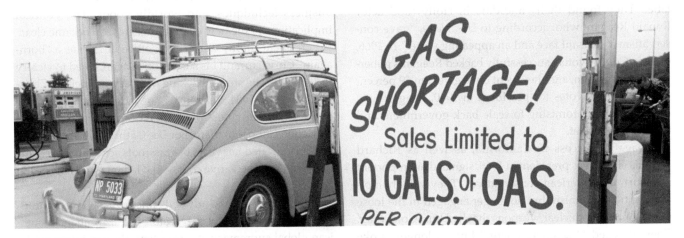

"GAS SHORTAGE!" A gas station rations gas to its customers during the gasoline shortage and energy crisis of the 1970s.

Owen Franken-Corbis/Getty Images.

 ## Contents and Focus Questions

American Communities

Grassroots Conservatism in Orange County, California

In 1962, Bee Gathright, a Brownie leader and mother of three young girls, invited her neighbors to her suburban Garden Grove home to hear a political talk by a man from the nearby Knott's Berry Farm Freedom Center. "This is when I discovered that I was a conservative," she later recalled. She convinced her skeptical husband, Neil, an aerospace engineer, to share her new conviction. They soon joined the California Republican Assembly, a volunteer organization committed to electing conservatives to office. In 1964, the Gathrights' home served as a local headquarters for the presidential campaign of conservative Arizona Senator Barry Goldwater.

In Orange County in the 1960s and 1970s, thousands of "kitchen table" activists like the Gathrights began a transformation of American politics that culminated in the presidential election of Ronald Reagan in 1980. Most of them were white, middle-class men and women, including large numbers of professionals and small business owners.

World War II and Cold War defense-related spending accelerated the county's growth, creating thousands of new manufacturing jobs in towns formerly dominated by large lemon and orange groves. By 1960, more than 700,000 people lived in Orange County, an increase of nearly 400 percent since 1940, and the population doubled again to top 2 million in the 1980s.

Although Goldwater's 1964 campaign ignited great enthusiasm in Orange County, his national defeat forced conservatives to consider ways to shed the "extremism" label. They found their candidate in Hollywood actor Ronald Reagan, who, according to *U.S. News*, "gave conservatism a pleasant face and an appealing voice." In 1966, Orange County voters successfully backed Reagan's gubernatorial campaign, and they went on to give him 69 percent of the county's votes for president in 1980. Reagan won their hearts by promising to scale back government and balance the budget.

Reagan's success in California, as well as Richard Nixon's election as president in 1968, signaled an important new turn for American conservatives. They still championed anti-communism but no longer engaged in the loose talk about using nuclear weapons that had hurt Goldwater. They attacked "big government," but no longer spoke openly about repealing popular New Deal programs like Social Security. Instead, they focused on the "social issues" that increasingly troubled and mobilized Orange County's grassroots activists. Their concerns, largely defined by a "backlash" against the antiwar movement, counterculture, women's liberation, and urban uprisings, emphasized so-called family values, in which opposition to sex education, obscenity, abortion rights, gay liberation, and the Equal Rights Amendment were all linked. On the economic side, conservatives began to tap a deep well of resentment over rising property taxes and high inflation.

Two central themes of this new conservatism resonated with millions of Americans well beyond Orange County. One was the 1978 "revolt" of homeowners that led to a sharp reduction in the property tax rate and soon spread to other states. Orange County also helped form the second

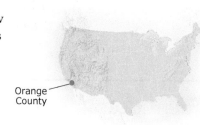

Orange County

new force reshaping conservatism, "born-again" evangelical Christianity. The region's religious revival featured educated professionals and middle-class suburbanites who turned to Christianity for spirituality and as a way to assert order amid rapid cultural and social change. "Born-again" Christians found community not only in Sunday services, but also in a wide range of tightly organized activities: Bible study groups, summer retreats, "singles' fellowships," prayer breakfasts, and "Christian" consumer culture, which allowed people to simultaneously embrace faith, modern business techniques, and worldly goods. The political implications of the new evangelicalism soon became clear.

President Jimmy Carter took office in 1976 as a "born-again" Christian, and his successor, Reagan, raced to victory in 1980 with the strong backing of newly politicized Christian voters. In 1984, Reagan acknowledged the importance of the Christian voters of Orange County by opening his reelection campaign there. For Bee Gathright, Reagan's victories vindicated her years of grassroots activism that set the nation on a conservative course that led into the twenty-first century.

Unlike Carter, who advised Americans to accept limits, Reagan promised to not only restore but also enhance American global supremacy. As president, Reagan introduced a new economic program—"Reaganomics"—that reduced income taxes for wealthy Americans and at the same time increased federal spending for the largest military buildup in American history. Abolishing the Great Society antipoverty programs, he fostered the growth of a two-tiered society characterized by a disproportionate number of women and children filling the ranks of the nation's poor. Meanwhile, the increases in military spending complemented Reagan's foreign policy, which included a revival of Cold War patriotism, interventions in the Caribbean and Central America, and labeling the Soviet Union an "evil empire." However, it was Reagan's successor, George H. W. Bush, who presided during one of the most dramatic events of the era: the dissolution of the Soviet Union. By this time, December 1991, the conservative ascendancy was holding tight, and would do so even through the presidency of the "New Democrat" Bill Clinton.

30.1 Age of Limits

What explains the weakness of the U.S. economy in the 1970s?

In the 1970s, the prosperity that followed World War II ground to a halt, and Americans saw their standard of living decline. In addition, the decade presented Americans with an unfamiliar combination of skyrocketing prices and rising unemployment—"stagflation."

The United States had come to an unhappy turning point in its economic history. Emerging from World War II as the world's richest nation and retaining this status through the 1960s, the country suddenly found itself falling behind Western Europe and Japan. The proportion of families living in poverty, which had shrunk during the 1960s, grew at an alarming rate. To add to a growing sense of crisis, the natural environment seemed to be on the brink of disaster. Nixon's successors, presidents Gerald Ford and Jimmy Carter, hoped to restore integrity to the office that Nixon had tarnished, but when it came to easing the sense of an impending doom, they promised little and, as many voters concluded, delivered even less.

30.1.1 A Troubled Economy

The most vivid sign of the troubled economy, the energy crisis, seemed to appear suddenly in the fall of 1973, although it had been decades in the making. The United States, which used about 70 percent of all oil produced in the world, had a sufficient domestic supply until the mid-1950s. By 1973 the nation was importing one-third of its crude oil, mainly from the Middle Eastern countries around the Persian Gulf. On October 17, the Arab members of the government-controlled **Organization of Petroleum Exporting Countries (OPEC)**, in retaliation for U.S.

support of Israel during the Yom Kippur War, announced an embargo on oil shipments to the United States and its Western European allies. (See Map 30.1.) The government was unprepared for the embargo or for the severe oil shortage and skyrocketing prices that followed. Five months later, OPEC ended the embargo, but limited production to keep prices high.

The effects of the oil embargo rippled throughout the economy. Half of all the inflation since 1940 occurred in just 10 years. Interest rates rose, driving mortgages out of reach for many would-be home buyers. The cost of gasoline, oil, and electricity jumped to new heights, as did apartment rents, telephone bills, and restaurant checks. (See Figure 30.1.) Tuition skyrocketed along with unemployment, and many young men and women who could neither afford to go to college nor find a job moved back home.

One of Nixon's advisors proclaimed "an Energy Pearl Harbor," and Carter likewise referred to the energy crisis as a moral equivalent of war. Both Nixon and Ford initiated a number of energy-saving policies that had only a slight impact. Moreover, their interventionist policies angered their conservative allies, who avoided governmental activism

---

Map 30.1 WORLD'S LEADING OIL PRODUCERS: 1973–1984

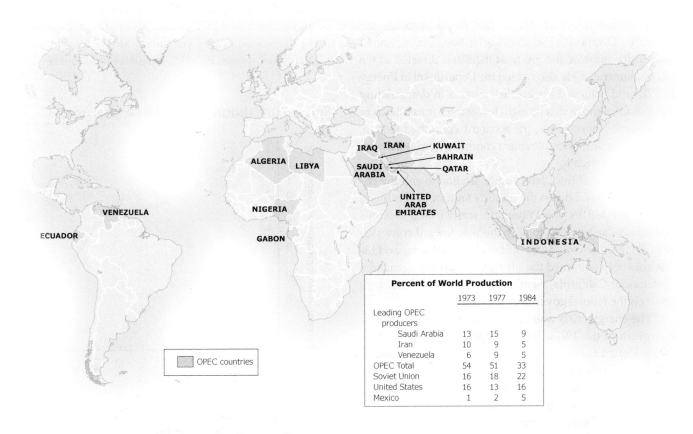

Percent of World Production			
	1973	1977	1984
Leading OPEC producers			
Saudi Arabia	13	15	9
Iran	10	9	5
Venezuela	6	9	5
OPEC Total	54	51	33
Soviet Union	16	18	22
United States	16	13	16
Mexico	1	2	5

In 1973, at the time of the oil embargo against the United States, the OPEC nations controlled half of worldwide oil production.

Figure 30.1 DECLINE OF U.S. OIL CONSUMPTION, 1975–1981

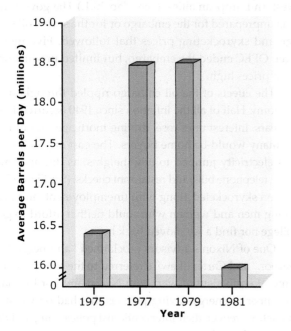

Boycotts causing shortages and high prices spurred the reduction in oil consumption. However, in the 1980s, consumption once again began to rise to reach record highs.

Department of Energy, *Monthly Energy Review*, June 1982.

and preferred instead to let the free market provide the corrective. Democratic President Carter, however, expanded some price controls and antitrust measures directed at the oil conglomerates. He also created the Department of Energy in 1977 and achieved his greatest success in deregulating the airlines, a move that brought lower fares for millions of passengers. Nevertheless, the economy continued to stall, and inflation and unemployment continued to rise through the end of the decade.

The failure of the Carter administration to end the crisis further ground down the public's faith in government, already eroded by the Watergate scandal and Nixon's resignation, and helped to pave the way toward conservatism. By intervening, conservatives charged, Carter and his advisors only worsened the situation. Ronald Reagan, then governor of California, went so far as to blame the energy crisis on the federal government.

The energy crisis was only one factor in the economic downturn of the 1970s. It had deeper roots in the failure of the United States to keep up with the rising industrial efficiency of other nations. Manufacturers from Asia, Latin America, and Europe now produced cheaper and better products, including automobiles, long considered the monopoly of Detroit. Automakers in the United States, determined to reduce costs, turned to "outsourcing"—that is, making cars and trucks from parts cheaply produced abroad and imported into the United States. In high-tech electronics, the United States could scarcely compete with Japanese

companies. For the first time in the twentieth century, the balance of trade had tipped: Americans were importing more goods than they were exporting.

An AFL-CIO leader complained that the United States was becoming "a nation of hamburger stands . . . a country stripped of industrial capacity and meaningful work." Between 1970 and 1982, the AFL-CIO, since the early 1930s a leading source of support to the Democratic Party, lost nearly 30 percent of its membership. (See Figure 30.2.)

The only real union growth took place among public employees, including teachers, civil service workers, and health professionals. With the production of steel, automobiles, and heavy machinery suffering from foreign competition, the so-called "Rust Belt" states suffered severe population losses (see Map 30.2). Of the 19 metropolitan areas that lost population, all were old manufacturing centers where unions were once strong. Bruce Springsteen, the most popular new rock artist of the decade, gave poignant expression to industrial decline in his break-out album "Born to Run," released in 1975.

Typical of hard times, an increasing number of women sought jobs to support their families. By 1980, more than half of all married women with children in their care were working outside the home. Yet despite their numerical gains, women lost ground relative to men. In 1955, women earned 64 percent of the average wages paid to men; in 1980, they earned only 59 percent. The growing service economy accounted for this dip: Women clustered in occupations where the lowest wages prevailed. Single women with children fared worse. By 1992, female-headed households

Figure 30.2 UNION MEMBERSHIP, 1940–1990

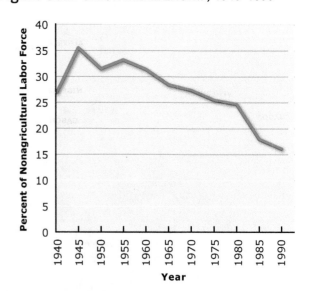

After reaching a peak during World War II, union membership steadily declined. In the 1980s, overseas production took an especially big toll on industrial unions.

Bureau of Labor Statistics, in Mary Kupiec et al., eds., *Encyclopedia of American Social History*, Vol. II. New York: Scribner's, 1993, p. 4188. Copyright © 1993 Scribner's. Reprinted by permission of Cengage Learning.

Map 30.2 POPULATION SHIFTS, 1970–1980

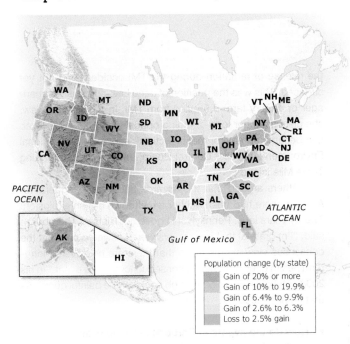

Population change (by state)
- Gain of 20% or more
- Gain of 10% to 19.9%
- Gain of 6.4% to 9.9%
- Gain of 2.6% to 6.3%
- Loss to 2.5% gain

Industrial decline in the Northeast coincided with an economic boom in the Sun Belt, encouraging millions of Americans to head for warmer climates and better jobs. The Southwest and West changed dramatically. Aided by air conditioning, water diversions, public improvements, and large-scale development and subsidies to agribusiness, California became the nation's most populous state; Texas moved to third, behind New York.

accounted for more than one-third of the nation's poor, a trend sociologists described as the "feminization of poverty."

African Americans and Hispanics were hit especially hard by the economic downturn. Through Title VII of the Civil Rights Act, which outlawed workplace discrimination by sex or race, and the establishment of the Equal Employment Opportunity Commission to enforce it, African American women managed to climb the lower levels of the job ladder. By 1980, northern black women's median earnings were about 95 percent of white women's earnings. But despite these gains, as more and more African American women headed their own households, poverty became an increasingly likely experience. Hispanic women, whose labor force participation leaped by 80 percent during the decade, were restricted to only a few occupations, mostly at or only slightly above the minimum wage. Their poverty rate grew to nearly equal that of African American women. Overall, by 1992, 33 percent of African Americans and 29 percent of Hispanics lived in poverty.

30.1.2 The Endangered Environment

The oil crisis of 1973 and the high prices of energy that followed helped to underscore the environmental downside of the post-World War II economic boom. Air and water pollution, climate change, and depletion of the ozone layer became major political issues and inspired a major environmental movement.

The roots of the modern environmental movement trace back to marine biologist Rachel Carson's 1962 best-seller, *Silent Spring*, which detailed the devastating effects of DDT and other pesticides. By the end of the decade, concerned citizens were advocating conservation practices such as recycling glass bottles and newspapers, and providing popular support for the proclamation of Earth Day, first celebrated on April 22, 1970. Long-standing organizations such as the Sierra Club, Audubon Society, and National Wildlife Federation picked up thousands of new members. Newer groups, such as the Environmental Defense Fund and Friends of the Earth, joined to advocate the development of renewable energy sources such as solar and wind power in place of fossil fuels such as oil and coal.

Sometimes environmental campaigns succeeded in blocking massive construction projects, such as nuclear energy plants; more often they halted small-scale destruction of a natural habitat or historic urban district. One of the most dramatic campaigns took place in Love Canal, near Buffalo, New York, following the discovery of high rates of cancer, miscarriages, and birth defects in the community. There, toxic wastes dumped by the Hooker Chemical Laboratory had oozed into basements and backyards, and homemaker Lois Gibbs organized her neighbors to draw national attention to the grim situation. In 1978, after a health emergency was declared, the state of New York bought their properties, fenced off the public school and 500 houses, and moved the residents to new homes.

Congress responded to growing pressure by passing during the 1970s more than 20 new bills and amending earlier legislation to protect endangered species, reduce pollution caused by automobile emissions, limit and ban the use of some pesticides and fluorocarbon gases, and control strip-mining practices. The **Environmental Protection Agency (EPA)**, established in 1970, grew to become the federal government's largest regulatory agency. (See Communities *in* Conflict.)

Business-based groups fought back and sometimes found unexpected allies. City officials, both Democratic and Republican, generally avoided congressional mandates for reduction in air pollution by requesting lengthy extensions of deadlines for compliance. Top union officials, including AFL-CIO president George Meany, denounced environmentalists as enemies of economic growth, and United Auto Workers lobbyists joined auto makers in resisting compulsory gas mileage and tighter emissions controls in new models. Again and again, environmentalists met defeat. Activists lost a key campaign in 1973 when Congress approved the Trans-Alaskan Pipeline—800 miles of pipe, which often leaked—connecting oil fields in Alaska with refining facilities in the Lower 48. Despite the introduction of lead-free gasoline, the air in major metropolitan areas grew worse because automobile traffic increased.

Communities *in* Conflict

Three Mile Island, Harrisburg, Pennsylvania

"[Radiation] is affecting all of us."

On March 28, 1979, mechanical failures and judgment errors at the nuclear generating facility at Three Mile Island (TMI), near Harrisburg, Pennsylvania, caused the breakdown of the plant's cooling system and risked a catastrophic core meltdown. Although the company that ran the facility denied that there was any danger, nearly 150,000 horrified residents fled their homes. What had seemed an isolated event had national repercussions. Elevated radioactivity was found in milk supplies several hundred miles away. Massive demonstrations against nuclear power culminated in a rally of more than 200,000 people in New York City.

The TMI accident climaxed in a debate that had been building throughout the 1970s. The OPEC oil embargo and energy crisis had encouraged communities to explore nuclear energy. But just four years before the TMI accident, more than 2,300 scientists petitioned Congress and the president to warn against rapid expansion.

Events surrounding the accident suggested at least two possible positions. One side insisted that the harm caused by the release of radiation during the TMI accident had not yet surfaced. This was the position of Jane Lee, an assistant manager of a dairy farm 3.5 miles from TMI. In a 1980 interview, she discussed her long-standing opposition to nuclear power. Lee became an environmental activist, served on the regional Environmental Quality Control Board, and opposed restarting Three Mile Island.

Others argued that the hazards had been exaggerated. After all, there had been neither a meltdown nor an explosion. Twenty years later, Pennsylvania governor Richard Thornburgh said, "I'm grateful that our prayers were answered and that the consensus view seems to be that there are no adverse long-term health or environmental consequences of the event." In his 2003 autobiography, Thornburgh spoke of the painful decisions that he had faced.

- **How do the events at Three Mile Island provide a context for examining the energy crisis of the 1970s?**

- **In view of today's fears of global warming, does the near-disaster at Three Mile Island take on new meaning?**

Environmental Activist Jane Lee Opposes Nuclear Power (1980)

I'm on pretty firm ground when I say that I know, over and above the accident, that we have been exposed to more than our share of radiation because of the total incompetency of the people who are operating that plant. There is no question about it. The [government-sponsored] Kemmeny Commission report, if you read it, proves beyond a shadow of a doubt that the people who were operating the plants down there simply do not know what they're doing. And the same people are still operating them. They want to bring Unit 1 on line. During the accident they kept telling us there was nothing to worry about, that everything was under control, and all the time *nothing* was under control. Most people don't know we still have an ongoing accident at TMI. . . .

What I'm about to tell you is only the tip of the iceberg. Back in 1973 I began to log incidences of abortions, stillbirths, birth defects and abnormalities in farm animals and livestock. At first I logged just what was happening here on this farm. Then as I began to get reports, I began to find out that it wasn't just this farm that was having problems—it was most of the farms in approximately a five-mile radius of TMI. . . .

The radiation is striking at the reproductive system, the area most vulnerable to radiation. . . .

For two weeks just after the accident, there wasn't a sign of a bird anywhere . . .

Anywhere. When the farmers go out to plow their fields, the birds usually hover all over the fields. It was the weirdest thing to plow the ground without a sign of a bird.

There wasn't a sign of a bird! York County, where I live, is notorious for its starlings, but this year the starlings never showed up. Now, starlings don't just come like average birds. They come by the hundreds of thousands in wave after wave and cloud after cloud. In fact, we were saying that something was going to have to be done abut the starlings because they were so bad. But they never showed up this year. . . .

We have a housing development near here which sits up real high. When those plants were operating, many times I could see the steam go over the top and settle right on that development. There are pockets of women up there who are having miscarriages. There's been two suits filed already in the area against Met. Ed. The women had stillborns. We don't know yet how far-ranging this is because in the Hershey Medical Center the cancer department is so secret that nobody can go into there and get the statistics. . . .

A lot of people here are developing pneumonia. I'm really surprised at how many. These days, you don't hear of pneumonia like you used to. This is part and parcel of radiation, it destroys the immunity system. . . .

[After the accident] we had a metallic taste in our mouths. It tasted like, you know, like when you're a kid and you put money in your mouth? That's what it tasted like. And we all had it. . . .

[Radiation] is affecting all of us. The radioactive materials are going from the waste into our environment.

They're coming back to us through the food chain. So it doesn't make any difference how close you live or how far away you live from a nuclear plant. We're all going to be affected. And in five years, if we continue with the operation of nuclear power plants, the people in this country are not going to be strong enough to go out and work on a job, much less defend their nation. That is a fact. We are not going to be strong enough because it is going to destroy the immunity system. And it will affect all of us. Every last one of us, I don't care where we live.

It isn't going to go away by pretending it doesn't exist. And the longer it's postponed the greater the danger is. Now that's my feeling. Somebody has to speak out. I went for three years with people making fun of me, telling me I was crazy and I didn't know what I was talking about. Now we all live in fear. All of us. I'm not alone anymore.

Source: Robert Leppzer, *Voices from Three Mile Island: The People Speak Out* (Trumansburg, NY: The Crossing Press, 1980), pp. 21, 23, 37, 44, 45, 48, 50. Copyright © 1980 The Crossing Press. www.turningtide.com/voicesfromtmi.htm.

Pennsylvania Governor Richard Thornburgh Recalls the Three Mile Island Accident (2003)

It later became clear that, while some of the reactor fuel heated to the point of melting, a disastrous "meltdown" was never close to occurring. Detectable amounts of radiation escaped into our air, water and even milk, but these amounts were limited enough that their impact, if any, on public health remains debatable to this day. And a massive evacuation of the up to 200,000 people residing in the area, with its potential for panic, injury and even loss of life, would have been far more dangerous and damaging than was the accident itself. But at 7:50 on that March morning, we knew none of this. The thought of issuing a general evacuation order entered my mind immediately and never left during the days to follow. . . .

Our first task was to find out exactly what was happening. This was to prove far more difficult than any of us could have imagined. The utility (Metropolitan Edison), its parent company (General Public Utilities), state and federal regulators, and other groups and institutions issued increasingly contradictory assessments, telling the public either more or less than they knew of the accident and its consequences. Self-appointed experts exaggerated either the danger or the safety of the situation. The credibility of the utility, in particular, did not fare well. On that first day it sought to minimize the accident, assuring us, inaccurately, that "everything is under control" and that "all safety equipment functioned properly." When company technicians found that radiation levels in the surrounding area had climbed above normal, the company neglected to release that information to the public. It also vented some radioactive steam into the air for two and one-half hours at midday on Wednesday, without informing us or the public.

Thus it fell to Lieutenant Governor William Scranton III . . . to tell the people of central Pennsylvania that "this situation is more complex than the company first led us to believe" and that . . . further discharges were possible . . . but that off-site radioactivity levels had been decreasing during the afternoon and there was no evidence that they had ever reached a danger point. . . .

Shortly after noon on that third day of the crisis . . . I recommended that pregnant women and preschoolers leave the area within five miles of the plant until further notice, and that all schools within that zone be closed as well. I also ordered the opening of evacuation centers at various sites outside of the area to shelter those who had no place to go. "Current readings," I stated, "are no higher than they were yesterday [but] the continued presence of radioactivity in the area and the possibility of further emissions lead me to exercise the utmost of caution. . . ."

In general, reviews of our handling of TMI were favorable. . . . There were, of course, critics as well, mostly focusing upon my unwillingness to order a "precautionary" evacuation in light of all the uncertainty. In time, I was to be labeled both "antinuke" (by the industry) and "pronuke" (by environmentalists) for various positions taken after the accident. . . . In a May 1979 address to the American Society of Newspaper Editors, I called for "a middle ground between those who would abandon [nuclear power] and those who would expand it tomorrow. . . . The question is not yes or no, but how best we can use it and keep it under control. . . . [If] we can't prepare ourselves to control it, then we must prepare ourselves to do without it."

Source: Excerpts from, *Where the Evidence Leads: An Autobiography*, by Dick Thornburgh, 2003. Reprinted by permission of the University of Pittsburgh Press.

30.1.3 The Limits of Global Power

Jimmy Carter was the first Democratic president since the 1930s who declined to call himself a liberal, offering instead personal integrity as his chief qualification for the nation's highest office. He had campaigned as a moderate and capitalized on Ford's unpopular Nixon pardon and—with his running mate, Senator Walter Mondale of Minnesota—won just over 50 percent of the popular vote and a 297-to-240 margin in the electoral college. (See Map 30.3.) If his outsider status helped win the election, Carter's lack of experience in national politics did little to prepare him to govern. He had little understanding of how Washington worked, and despite a Democratic majority in Congress, he accomplished little. Carter gained reforms in civil service, Social Security, and Medicare, and created the

Map 30.3 THE ELECTION OF 1976

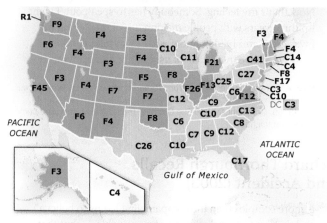

	Electoral Vote (%)	Popular Vote (%)
Numbers on states represent Electoral Votes.		
JIMMY CARTER (C) (Democrat)	297 (55)	40,828,929 (50.1)
Gerald R. Ford (F) (Republican)	240 (45)	39,148,940 (47.9)
Ronald Reagan (R)	1	—
Other candidates (McCarthy, Independent, Libertarian)	—	1,575,459 (2.1)

Incumbent Gerald Ford could not prevail over the disgrace brought to the Republican Party by Richard Nixon. The lingering pall of the Watergate scandal, especially Ford's pardon of Nixon, worked to the advantage of Jimmy Carter, who campaigned as an outsider to national politics. Although Carter and his running mate, Walter Mondale, won by only a narrow margin, the Democrats gained control of both the White House and Congress.

departments of Energy and Education, but inflation proved intractable. An outspoken fiscal conservative, he could not deliver on his promise to turn the economy around or even lower the federal deficit. Carter managed to discredit the liberal tradition of the Democratic Party even while distancing himself from it, making his presidency the symbol of a larger political collapse.

Although President Carter produced at best a mixed record on foreign policy, he managed to instill a modicum of new idealism into his policies. Unlike his predecessors, he placed international human rights at the top of his agenda and condemned policies that allowed the United States to support "right-wing monarchs and military dictators" in the name of anticommunism. His secretary of state, Cyrus R. Vance, worked to punish or at least to censure repressive military regimes in Brazil, Argentina, and Chile. For the first time, leading U.S. diplomats spoke out against the South African apartheid regime. In line with this policy, Carter tried to reform operations at the CIA, particularly to halt covert interventions in the

affairs of foreign governments. He scored his biggest moral victory in foreign affairs—and further raised the ire of conservatives—by pressuring the Senate to ratify new treaties in 1978 that would turn the Panama Canal over to Panama by the year 2000.

Carter also succeeded in achieving full diplomatic relations with the People's Republic of China in January 1979 and in paving the way for cultural and trade exchanges between the two nations. The agreement angered conservatives because it stipulated that the United States sever ties with its ally, the national regime in Taiwan.

Carter came closest to achieving his goals in the Middle East. Early in his administration, he met privately with Israeli Prime Minister Menachem Begin to encourage conciliation with Egypt. When negotiations between the two countries stalled in 1978, Carter brought Begin together with Egyptian President Anwar el-Sadat for a 13-day retreat at Camp David, Maryland. The **Camp David Accords**, signed in September 1978, set the formal terms for peace in the region. Egypt became the first Arab country to recognize Israel's right to exist, as the two nations established mutual diplomatic relations for the first time since the founding of Israel in 1948. In return, Egypt regained control of the Sinai Peninsula, including important oil fields and airfields.

But disappointment lay ahead. Carter staked his hopes for regional peace on the final achievement of statehood, or at least political autonomy, for Palestinians in a portion of their former lands now occupied by the Israelis. The accords specified that Israel would eventually return to its approximate borders of 1967. However, although Begin agreed to dismantle some Israeli settlements in the Sinai, the Israeli government continued to sponsor more and more Jewish settlements, expropriating Palestinian holdings. The final status of the Palestinians remained in limbo.

But mired in problems inherited from his predecessors, Carter often found himself disoriented and, despite his commitment to human rights, putting aside his principles. He chose to stabilize repressive regimes in nations considered vital to U.S. interests, such as South Korea and the Philippines. In Nicaragua, the overthrow in 1979 of the brutal dictator Anastasio Somoza Debayle, longtime U.S. ally, left Carter without a successor to support. When the new Sandinista revolutionary government pleaded for help, Congress turned down Carter's request for $75 million in aid to Nicaragua. Meanwhile, in El Salvador, the Carter administration continued to back a repressive government. At odds with his own commitment to peace and international cooperation, Carter also called for ever-larger increases in the military budget.

Carter's reliance on moral principles failed to bring about **détente** with the Soviet Union, a prospect dimmed

CAMP DAVID PEACE ACCORDS Egyptian President Anwar Sadat and Israeli Prime Minister Menachem Begin shake hands at the signing of the Middle East Peace Treaty in Washington, D.C., March 1979. President Carter had invited both leaders to Camp David, the presidential retreat in Maryland, where for two weeks he mediated between them on territorial rights to the West Bank and Gaza Strip. Considered Carter's greatest achievement in foreign policy, the negotiations, known as the Camp David Peace Accords, resulted in not only the historic peace treaty but also the Nobel Peace Prize for Begin and Sadat.

ANTI-AMERICAN DEMONSTRATORS Iranians demonstrate outside the U.S. Embassy in Tehran, raising a poster with a caricature of President Carter. The Iran hostage crisis, which began November 4, 1979, when a mob of Iranians seized the embassy, contributed to Carter's defeat at the polls the following year. More than 60 embassy employees were held hostage for 444 days.

by his campaign for international human rights. Only after softening his criticism of the Soviet policy toward political dissidents did Carter achieve, in June 1979, the SALT II agreement on arms control. But the thaw proved only temporary. Just six months later, 30,000 Soviet troops invaded neighboring Afghanistan to put down a revolt by Islamic insurgents. Noting that the Soviet occupation of Afghanistan posed "a grave threat to the free movement of Middle East oil," President Carter issued his own corollary to the Monroe Doctrine by affirming the right of the United States to use military force if necessary to protect its interests in the Persian Gulf. He backed up his increasingly hard-line policies by halting exports of grain and high technology to the Soviet Union, by supporting Afghan resistance against the Russians, and by canceling American participation in the 1980 Moscow Olympics. The prospect of détente dried up.

30.1.4 The Iran Hostage Crisis

The limits on the United States as a global power played out at the end of the Carter administration in the Middle East. For decades, the United States had depended on a friendly government in Iran. After the CIA had helped to overthrow the reformist, constitutional government and installed the Pahlavi royal family and the shah of Iran in 1953, millions of U.S. dollars had poured into the Iranian economy and the shah's armed forces. President Carter had toasted the shah for his "great leadership," and overlooked the rampant corruption in government and underestimated a well-organized opposition. By early 1979, however, a revolution

led by the Islamic leader Ayatollah Ruhollah Khomeini overthrew the shah.

After Carter had allowed the deposed shah, Mohammad Reza Pahlavi, to enter the United States for medical treatment, a group of Khomeini's followers retaliated. Led by angry students, they stormed the U.S. Embassy in Tehran on November 4, 1979, taking more than 60 American employees hostage and demanding the return of the shah to Iran for trial and execution.

"The United States will not yield to blackmail," Carter announced in refusing the militants' demands. Months passed without a resolution. Finally, in April 1980, the president ordered U.S. military forces to stage a nighttime helicopter rescue mission. But a sandstorm caused some of the aircrafts to crash and burn, leaving eight Americans dead, their charred corpses displayed by the enraged Iranians. Short of an all-out attack, which surely would have resulted in the hostages' deaths, Carter had used up his options.

The political fallout was heavy. Secretary of State Vance had advised the president to pursue negotiations over military confrontation. To protest Carter's decision, Vance resigned, the first secretary of state in 65 years to leave office over a political difference with a president. The price of oil rose by 60 percent, further highlighting Carter's failure to solve the energy crisis. Gas lines grew longer, inflation once again soared, and it was clear that Carter's program for economic recovery had failed. On moral grounds, the president appeared to have violated his own human rights policy, which he intended to be his distinctive mark on American foreign affairs.

30.1.5 "Crisis of Confidence"

The president's approval rating was already sliding downward before the Iran hostage crisis began. Several months earlier, Carter, along with 130 invited guests, withdrew to Camp David to assess his priorities. In his first public speech after the 10-day retreat, the president announced that the nation was experiencing a "crisis of confidence . . . that strikes at the very heart and soul and spirit of our national will."

Carter appeared to echo several popular pundits who had proclaimed the 1970s, in novelist Tom Wolfe's phrase, the "Me Decade." The years of his administration, the president agreed, were marked by a turning inward of many Americans. Health foods and diet crazes, a mania for physical fitness, and a quest for happiness through therapy drew in many middle-class white Americans. The "human potential movement" and transcendental meditation, with their emphasis on emotional tranquility, found numerous advocates among Wall Street brokers, Pentagon officials, and star athletes. "After the political turmoil of the sixties," historian Christopher Lasch confirmed in a best-selling book, "Americans have returned to purely personal preoccupations."

Carter was so impressed by Lasch's insights into the national *zeitgeist* that he invited him to the White House for advice in writing his speech. Vice President Mondale, after reading a draft, warned that the president would sound "too much like an old scold and a grouch"; his staffers referred to the draft as the "America is going to hell speech." Carter, however, did not yield. On July 15, in a televised address, he gave what came to be known as his "malaise" speech, although he never used that word. Carter addressed, as he had many times before, the energy crisis, and warned Americans that its solution would not be easy. Calling for national unity, he then asked Americans to show more faith in their leaders and to adjust to limits imposed by an austere era.

Carter's plan backfired. Many Americans resented the president for heaping blame on the public and advising them to eschew materialism and accept the limits. They therefore went into the Iran hostage crisis already looking for a national leader who, unlike Carter, would accept responsibility, restore confidence, and promise a limitless future.

30.2 Turning Right

What explains the rise of the New Right in the 1980s?

The failures in U.S. foreign policy, accompanied by the faltering economy, played a large part in mobilizing what several observers termed "the politics of resentment." Sizable numbers of white taxpayers begrudged the tax hikes required to fund the welfare programs that benefited minorities and expanded social services for the poor and, at the same time, slowed economic development. In economically hard-pressed urban areas, conservative white voters who resented the gains made by African Americans, Latinos, and women formed a powerful backlash movement against liberalism.

What distinguished the New Right from the earlier conservatism was an emphasis on "moral values" and its populist character. One element in this coalition comprised conservative ideologues, some of them former Democrats who had become disenchanted with liberalism. By far, the largest component comprised evangelical or born-again Protestants like the Gathrights who organized to become a powerful political force.

30.2.1 The New Conservatism

By the mid-1970s, a new variation of conservatism appeared on the political landscape: neoconservatism. The unsettling social movements of the 1960s had prompted some prominent Democrats to turn against New Deal-style liberalism and move gradually to the Republican Party. In magazines like *Commentary*, *The Public Interest*, and *The New Leader*, leading writers continued to affirm the principle of equal opportunity, but forcefully rejected the goal of equality of outcome. They therefore sought to repeal **affirmative action** programs, especially quotas, and to dismantle the Great Society programs enacted during the Johnson administration and cautiously defended by Carter.

The heart of the neoconservatism was, however, foreign policy. Unlike earlier conservatives and many mainstream Republicans, neoconservatives severed the link between conservatism and isolationism. Angered over the failure to pursue victory in Vietnam, neoconservatives called for a stronger national defense against international communism. They opposed Carter's move toward détente with the Soviet Union and accused the president of allowing communists to advance in Third World countries.

Neoconservatism was not an organized movement, writer Irving Kristol explained, but a "current of thought." Nevertheless, its promoters succeeded in raising sufficient funds to play an important role in the rightward turn in American politics. Richly funded by corporate donors, university-trained scholars and especially social and political scientists established or expanded think tanks to engage other specialists in policy-shaping discussions. The growing intellectual prominence of neoconservatives also smoothed the way for broader public support. Toward the end of the 1970s, the American Enterprise Institute, for example, earmarked more than $1.6 million for public programs. The Heritage Foundation, richly funded by the beer baron Joseph Coors, produced policy papers for members of Congress, while the Cato Institute, supported largely by Kansan Charles G. Koch, promoted a free market economy. The John M. Olin Foundation, funded by the chemical and munitions manufacturer, focused on law as well as economics, and through The Federalist Society for Law and Public Policies moved Second Amendment and campaign finance issues to the forefront of conservative politics. At the state level, the American Legislative Exchange Council, founded in 1973, produced model bills, including specific language, for conservative legislators to sponsor in their assemblies. Through these complementary efforts, conservative policy experts helped to reshape the Republican Party.

30.2.2 The Religious Christian Right

Meanwhile, grassroots New Right activists focused more directly on the "moral" issues defined by evangelical Christians, who numbered more than 50 million by the late 1970s. During the 1970s, mainline Protestant denominations—Lutherans, Episcopalians, Presbyterians, Methodists—lost as many as 20 percent to 30 percent of their members, while evangelical and Pentecostal congregations such as the Southern Baptists and Assemblies of God grew rapidly. These "born-again" Christians, along with many Catholics and Mormons, had typically avoided electoral politics before the 1970s. By the end of the decade, encouraged by their leadership, they began to endorse conservative positions on foreign and domestic policy.

New Right Christians found their first major political issue following a Supreme Court ruling in 1970 stripping tax-exempt status from so-called "segregation academies"—that is, private Christian schools that were founded to resist the racial integration specified in *Brown v. Board of Education*. They widened their political reach to promote a fierce anticommunism as well as a balanced-budget amendment to the Constitution. They sought unsuccessfully to return prayer to the public schools, opposed the teaching of evolution, and endorsed the Supreme Court's reinstatement of the death penalty in 1976. Even more strongly, evangelical Christians promoted what they perceived as "traditional family values" and moved these principles from the margins to the center of the Republican Party.

Evangelical ministers took to the airwaves and frequently mixed conservative politics with appeals for both prayer and money. Ministers such as Oral Roberts, Bill Graham, Jimmy Swaggart, and Jim and Tammy Bakker had pioneered televangelism in the 1950s and usually avoided politics. Pat Robertson formed the Christian Broadcasting Network in 1961, which added conservative messages to its religious programming.

By the late 1970s, more than 1,400 radio stations and 30 TV stations specialized in religious broadcasts that reached perhaps 20 million weekly and became a major source of fund-raising for conservative organizations and campaigns.

In 1979, the Reverend Jerry Falwell, a Bible Baptist, appealed to listeners of his *Old Time Gospel Hour* to join him in the Moral Majority. As a major political lobbying group that claimed 2 million to 3 million members, the Moral Majority advocated tough laws against homosexuality and pornography, and promoted a reduction of government services (especially welfare payments to single mothers) and increased spending for a stronger national defense. The Moral Majority also waged well-publicized campaigns against public school integration and especially the busing of schoolchildren to achieve racial balance. Falwell, who toured the country to get evangelical Christians "saved, baptized, and registered," declared a huge success in claiming 4 million new conservative voters lined up, most notably, for Ronald Reagan in the 1980 presidential election.

30.2.3 The Pro-Family Movement

The Moral Majority—along with other conservative organizations formed in the late 1970s, such as Focus on the Family and Concerned Women of America—were committed to turning back the "moral decline" that had descended on the nation during the 1960s. They reviled the women's liberation movement that advanced political economic equality for women, a demand that threatened the security of women who accepted their homemaker and childrearing responsibilities and depended on men's support and protection. But all around them women were entering the labor force at a fast rate—some taking advantage of greater opportunities, others doing so by necessity. In 1976, only 40 percent of jobs paid enough to support a family. Moreover, the divorce rate doubled during the decade, leaving many women reliant on only their own wages. Against trends, the Moral Majority and its allies aspired to turn back the clock and reestablish "traditional family values."

Defeating the Equal Rights Amendment (ERA) stood at the top of their political agenda. Approved by Congress in March 1972, nearly 50 years after its introduction (see Chapter 22), the ERA stated: "Equality of rights under the law shall not be denied or abridged by the United States or by any State on account of sex." Endorsed by many women's organizations, including the Girl Scouts of America, and by both the Democratic and Republican parties—and most aggressively by First Lady Betty Ford—the amendment appeared likely to be ratified by individual states. Then, in 1972, after 22 states had ratified the ERA, the pace slowed, and an organized opposition rushed forward under the banner "Stop Taking Away Our Privileges."

Phyllis Schlafly, a self-described suburban housewife, had made two unsuccessful runs for Congress before

PHYLLIS SCHLAFLY Phyllis Schlafly rallied her supporters in 1977 in Washington, D.C., to demonstrate against the Equal Rights Amendment. She had also renamed her STOP-ERA group the Eagle Forum, which would continue to serve, as she put it, as "the alternative to women's lib."

Library of Congress (Photoduplication).

organizing the STOP-ERA campaign. Passage of the ERA, she warned, could "mean Government-funded abortions, homosexual schoolteachers, women forced into military combat and men refusing to support their wives." The traditional family was, she explained, "the basic unit of society" that allowed women and their babies the right "to be supported and protected."

Under Schlafly's skilled leadership, STOP-ERA activists mounted large, expensive campaigns in each swing state and overwhelmed pro-ERA resources. An Oklahoma group, Women Who Want to Be Women, for example, campaigned against the ERA and locally against a legislative bill that would fund day care facilities. They produced thousands of copies of their *Pink Sheet* flyer and lobbied their representatives with freshly baked bread. Schlafly's supporters also built a strong religious-based coalition, with southern Protestants, western Mormons, northeastern Catholics, and Orthodox Jews temporarily putting aside differences to join forces to defeat the amendment that they believed was "against God's plan."

Although 35 states had ratified the ERA by 1979, the amendment remained three votes short of passage. Despite a three-year extension, the ERA died in Congress in 1982, with 85 percent of the Democrats and only 30 percent of the Republicans voting in its favor.

Meanwhile, the anti-ERA campaign had grown into a comprehensive "pro-family" movement that opposed abortion as well as family planning through contraception. In 1973, the Supreme Court had ruled in *Roe v. Wade* that state laws decreeing abortion a crime during the first two

trimesters of pregnancy constituted a violation of a woman's right to privacy. Opponents of *Roe*, energized by the National Right-to-Life Committee, organized in 1967, sought to overturn the ruling. They also rallied for a constitutional amendment defining conception as the beginning of life and then argued that the "rights of the unborn" supersede a woman's right to control her own body. These activists also supported amendments limiting abortion that had been introduced in Congress by 1976, including the successful Hyde Amendment that banned the use of federal funds to fund abortions.

Antiabortion groups, such as the Orange County Pro-Life Political Action Committee, founded in 1973, also rallied against sex education programs in public schools. They picketed Planned Parenthood counseling centers, intimidating potential clients. A spate of arson attacks in 1976 and a series of bombings by antiabortion extremists two years later led to the foundation of the National Abortion Federation, which collects statistics on violence against abortion providers.

30.2.4 The 1980 Election

Despite the upsurge of conservatism, Carter went into the 1980 presidential campaign determined to win a second term. In the Democratic primary, he had defeated his popular opponent, Massachusetts Senator Edward Kennedy. But his prospects for winning the general election, he knew, depended to a large extent on an uptick in the economy and a resolution to the hostage crisis in Iran. Shortly before the election, however, his approval rating dropped to the lowest recorded for an incumbent president until that time.

On the Republican side, Ronald Reagan had been building his campaign since his near-nomination in 1976. Most Americans, however, knew him mainly from his Hollywood movies and television appearances. Although never a big star, on-screen he appeared tall, handsome, and affable. In 1966, with the financial backing of some wealthy conservatives, he won the race for California governor, securing 72 percent of the Orange County vote, and in 1970 he won reelection. As governor, Reagan cut the state welfare rolls, reduced the number of state employees, and funneled a large share of state tax revenues back to local governments. He vigorously condemned student protesters and black militants, thereby tapping into the conservative backlash against the 1960s' activism. By 1980, Reagan was well known as a steadfast conservative imbued with unlimited optimism about the future of the nation.

Reagan and vice presidential candidate George H. W. Bush rode the crest of the swelling conservative wave and repeatedly asked voters "Are you better off now than you were four years ago?" Drawing on his acting experience, Reagan emerged "the great communicator." While Carter implored Americans to tighten their belts, Reagan promised to increase their spending power by cutting their taxes and shrinking the government. Reagan and Bush also embraced the conservative heart of the GOP platform and assured voters that "America's best days lie ahead."

The Republicans won in a huge landslide that astounded even their loyal supporters. Carter and Mondale won only 41.2 percent of the popular vote to Reagan's 50.9 percent, and only 49 votes in the electoral college to Reagan's 489. The Republicans won control of the Senate for the first time since 1952 and with the largest majority since 1928. White Southerners and blue-collar ethnic voters, the traditional supporters of the Democratic Party, had defected to the Republicans in large numbers, although women and African Americans voted for Reagan in far smaller numbers.

The Christian Right vote proved crucial. With Democrats battered politically, Reagan moved into the White House on a high note: After 444 days, the Iranian militants released the American hostages on January 20, 1981, the day he took the oath of office. (See SEEING History.)

30.3 The Reagan Revolution

What economic assumptions underlay "Reaganomics"?

No other twentieth-century president except Franklin D. Roosevelt left as deep a personal imprint on American politics as Ronald Reagan. Ironically, Reagan himself began his political life as an ardent New Deal Democrat. But by the time he entered the White House in 1981, shortly before his 70th birthday, Reagan had rejected the activist welfare state legacy of the New Deal era and interpreted his victory as a popular mandate for the conservatism that had been growing since Nixon took office. "In the present crisis," he declared in his first inaugural address, "government is not

---

SEEING History

The Inaugurations of Carter and Reagan

Presidents-elect commonly plan their inauguration ceremonies to reflect symbolically their values and campaign pledges. In 1977, Jimmy Carter staged a "people's inaugural," and hoped to emphasize the unassuming style and frugality that would mark his presidency. He took the oath of office wearing a plain business suit and then broke tradition to walk hand-in-hand with his wife, Rosalynn, along the parade route. There were no flowers on display on the cold January day, and the White House reviewing stand was heated by solar energy.

Ronald Reagan hoped to convey a different message, one not of thrift but of wealth and security. On January 21, 1981, he became the nation's fortieth president wearing a formal black coat, striped pants, and black shoes, and accompanied First Lady Nancy Reagan down the parade route in a limousine.

Everything about Reagan's inauguration, including eight formal balls spread across four days of festivities, reflected what Nancy Reagan described as her aspiration to put the White House "symbolically back up on a hill in people's minds, to have stature and loftiness." The Reagans hired a public relations expert to ensure that every event was telecast. All the inaugural balls, concerts, and receptions, including the opening evening event (an $800,000 light show and concert on the steps of the Lincoln Memorial), were planned to entertain and astound at-home audiences. Festivities at the Washington, D.C., balls were also beamed through a $2 million satellite hookup to

"mini-balls" held simultaneously across the nation. The Reagan inauguration cost nearly five times that of Carter.

Newspapers and magazines published many photographs of Nancy Reagan, noting that she had restored high style to the image of the First Lady. Whereas Rosalynn Carter had worn an old blue chiffon evening dress to the inaugural ball in 1977, Nancy Reagan had chosen a hand-beaded, crystal-studded gown designed by a leader in the fashion industry. Overall, her inaugural wardrobe was estimated to cost around $25,000. Unlike Rosalynn Carter, who appeared at the swearing-in ceremony in a modest cloth coat, Nancy Reagan chose a full-length mink.

Reagan's inauguration, touted by the press as the most expensive in U.S. history, showcased the theme the president-elect had chosen for his administration: "America—A New Beginning." Not the belt-tightening, "homespun ways" of the Carter presidency, noted one reporter, but an unabashed celebration of wealth would prevail.

- **Why did the newly elected President Carter choose to celebrate thrift and humility?**

- **Why did his successor, Ronald Reagan, choose to celebrate wealth?**

- **What had happened in the United States between the mid-1970s and the beginning of the 1980s to make such a display of wealth and power acceptable to the public?**

THE INAUGURATIONS OF CARTER AND REAGAN

Left: White House Photography, right: Bettmann/Getty Images.

RONALD REAGAN Ronald Reagan, the 40th president of the United States, was known for his ability to articulate broad principles of government in a clear fashion. The most popular president since Dwight Eisenhower, he built a strong coalition of supporters from long-term Republicans, disillusioned Democrats, and evangelical Protestants.

Wally McNamee/Getty Images.

the solution to our problem, government is the problem." Pledged to downsize the federal government, the nation's 40th president inaugurated the "Reagan Revolution" and ushered in a new age in American political life. (See Map 30.4.)

30.3.1 Reaganomics

"It is time for us to realize that we are too great a nation to limit ourself to small dreams," Reagan announced in his inaugural address, and he called for "an era of national

Map 30.4 THE ELECTION OF 1980

	Electoral Vote (%)	Popular Vote (%)
RONALD REAGAN (R) (Republican)	489 (91)	43,201,220 (50.9)
Jimmy Carter (C) (Democrat)	49 (9)	34,913,332 (41.2)
John B. Anderson (Independent)	—	5,581,379 (6.6)
Other candidates (Libertarian)	—	921,299 (1.1)

Numbers on states represent Electoral Votes.

Ronald Reagan won a landslide victory over incumbent Jimmy Carter, who managed to carry only six states and the District of Columbia. Reagan attracted millions of traditionally Democratic voters to the Republican camp.

renewal." The building block would be supply-side economics, emblematic of America conservatism and dubbed "Reaganomics" by the media. Supply-side theorists urged a sharp break with the Keynesian policies that had prevailed since the New Deal era. (See Chapter 24.) During recessions, Keynesians traditionally favored moderate tax cuts and increases in government spending to stimulate the economy and reduce unemployment. By putting more money in people's pockets, they argued, greater consumer demand would lead to economic expansion. By contrast, supply-siders called for simultaneous tax cuts, reductions in public spending, and deregulation. This combination, commonly known as "trickle-down economics," would give private entrepreneurs and investors greater incentives to start businesses, take risks, invest capital, and thereby create new wealth and jobs. Whatever revenues were lost in lower tax rates would be offset by revenue from new economic growth. At the same time, spending cuts would keep the federal deficit under control and thereby keep interest rates down.

George Gilder, conservative author of the best-selling *Wealth and Poverty* (1981), summarized the supply-side view; "A successful economy depends on the proliferation of the rich." On the political level, supply-siders looked to reward the most loyal Republican constituencies: the affluent and the business community. At the same time, they hoped to reduce the flow of federal dollars to two core Democratic constituencies: the recipients and professional providers of health and welfare programs.

Reagan quickly won bipartisan approval for two key bills that culminated in the largest tax cut in the nation's history. The **Economic Recovery Tax Act of 1981** brought across-the-board cuts for corporations and individuals. The new legislation also reduced the maximum tax on all income from 70 percent to 50 percent, lowered the maximum capital gains tax—the tax paid on profitable investments—from 28 percent to 20 percent, and eliminated the distinction between earned and unearned income. This last measure proved a boon to the smallest but richest fraction of the population, which derives most of its income from rent, dividends, and interest instead of from wages. With the help of conservative southern and western Democrats in the House, the administration also pushed through a comprehensive program of spending cuts, awkwardly known as the Omnibus Reconciliation Act of 1981. This bill mandated huge cuts affecting more than 200 social and cultural programs. While reducing spending on domestic programs, the Reagan administration greatly increased the defense budget, a trend already under way during Carter's final two years as president.

Meanwhile, the Reagan administration created a chilly atmosphere for organized labor. In the summer of 1981, some 13,000 federal employees, all members of the Professional Air Traffic Controllers Organization (PATCO), went on strike. The president retaliated by firing all the strikers, and a crash course started by the Federal Aviation Administration permanently replaced them. Conservative appointees to the National Labor Relations Board and the federal courts toughened their anti-union positions. By 1990, fewer than 15 percent of American workers belonged to a labor union, the lowest proportion since before World War II.

Deregulation also served as a key element of Reaganomics. Reagan issued executive orders freezing all new federal regulation and appointed Vice President Bush to head a review task force. The president's appointments to head the Environmental Protection Agency, the Occupational Safety and Health Administration, and the Consumer Product Safety Commission abolished or weakened hundreds of rules governing environmental protection, workplace safety, and consumer protection, all to increase the efficiency and productivity of business. Secretary of the Interior James Watt opened up formerly protected wilderness areas and wetlands to private developers. Secretary of Transportation Andrew L. "Drew" Lewis Jr. eliminated regulations passed in the 1970s aimed at reducing air pollution and improving fuel efficiency in cars and trucks.

Following supply-side theory, the Reagan administration weakened the Justice Department's Antitrust Division, the Securities and Exchange Commission, and the Federal Home Loan Bank Board. Large corporations, Wall Street stock brokerages, investment banking houses, and the savings and loan industry were all allowed to operate with a much freer hand than ever before. The appointment of Alan Greenspan to Chair of the Federal Reserve in 1987, to succeed Carter appointee Paul Volcker, greatly encouraged trends toward speculation in market trading. By the late 1980s, the unfortunate consequences of deregulation would become apparent in a series of unprecedented scandals in the nation's financial and banking industries.

Despite these setbacks, Reagan's enormous personal popularity overwhelmed the Democratic ticket in the 1984 election. Walter F. Mondale and running mate Geraldine Ferraro, the first woman to run for vice president, could not steal the thunder of the incumbent's promise of "hope, confidence, and growth." Reagan's campaign ads, with their theme "It's morning again in America," helped to secure one of the biggest presidential landsides in American history. Reagan won 59 percent of the popular vote and carried every state but two. Majorities of women and blue-collar voters cast their ballots for the president. Even a quarter of all registered Democrats voted for Reagan.

30.3.2 Unraveling the Great Society

Midway through his administration, President Reagan specified the key elements in his approach to problems of social welfare. He vowed to create new programs to help poor people "escape the spider's web of dependency." Although no Republican at the time would jeopardize either Social Security or Medicare, which continued to win overwhelming approval from the majority of Americans, conservatives looked to the Reagan administration to eradicate the "welfare culture" that, in the president's words, promoted "the breakdown of the family." His budgets singled out for cuts basic welfare programs such as food stamps, school lunches, subsidized housing, and other so-called poverty programs. The long-standing federal program Aid to Families with Dependent Children introduced new eligibility requirements, a revision that shrank the number of participants by more than half and at the same time reduced average payments. Overall, between 1982 and 1985, federally funded programs targeted to the poor were reduced by $57 billion, and even in the light of social crisis Reagan discouraged the creation of new programs.

Like many conservatives, Reagan preferred to avoid dealing head-on with issues of race and civil rights, although his record shows a distinctive pattern. He had earlier opposed the Civil Rights Act of 1964 and the Voting Rights Act of 1965, and during his presidential campaign made clear his "states' rights" philosophy. As president he opposed the extension of the Voting Rights Act, which he disparaged as "humiliating the South." A sizable, organized lobbying campaign prompted him to sign the bill in 1982. Reagan also opposed affirmative action programs, designating them as "reverse racism." His administration reduced funding to the Equal Employment Opportunity Commission as well as the civil rights division of the Department of Justice. Only a veto-proof vote in Congress kept Reagan from turning back legislation proclaiming Martin Luther King Jr.'s birthday a national holiday 1983.

During Reagan's administration, homelessness emerged as a chronic social problem. Often disoriented, shoeless, and forlorn, growing numbers of street people slept over heating grates, on subways, under bridges, and in parks. Homeless people wandered cities by day panhandling and struggling to find scraps of food. The Department of Housing and Urban Development placed the number of the nation's homeless between 250,000 and 350,000. Advocates for the homeless estimated that the actual number was as high as 3 million.

Who were the homeless? Analysts agreed that at least a third were mental patients who had been discharged from psychiatric hospitals amid the deinstitutionalization trend of the 1970s. Following the development of antipsychotic medication in the 1950s, public mental institutions began to shut down, releasing more than 90 percent of severely ill individuals for outpatient care. Toward the end of his presidency, Carter had signed the Mental Health Systems Act, which provided funding for community-based treatment centers; Reagan's congress repealed most of its provisions. Federal funding for mental health decreased by 30 percent.

The majority of homeless had serious health problems, such as alcohol or other substance abuse, and were unable to hold jobs. Veterans made up between a quarter and a third of the homeless population, with the majority having served in Vietnam. But the ranks of the homeless also included female-headed families, battered women, and elderly people with no place to go. Some critics pointed to the decline in decent housing for poor people and the deterioration of the nation's health care system as the major causes.

Concurrent with the rise of homelessness were upticks in substance abuse and traffic in illegal drugs. In 1982, Reagan renewed the **war on drugs** declared by President Nixon in 1971. In a highly publicized campaign, he rolled out statistics to show that illegal drug addiction and drug trafficking had taken on frightening new dimensions since the days when they were a sign of youth rebellion. By the 1980s, even the urban poor could afford the new arrival, "crack," a cheap, smokable, and highly addictive form of cocaine. The "crack epidemic" spread between 1984 and 1990, ruined hundreds of thousands of lives, and led to a dramatic increase in crime rates. Studies showed that more than half the men arrested in the nation's largest cities tested positive for cocaine. The crack trade also spawned a new generation of drug dealers who were willing to risk jail and death for enormous profit. In city after city, drug wars over turf took the lives of dealers and innocents, both caught in escalating violence. By the end of the 1980s, opinion polls revealed that Americans identified illicit drug use as the nation's number one problem.

The Reagan administration launched a multibillion-dollar paramilitary operation to halt drug trafficking, but directed scant resources to help users. In 1986 Congress passed the Anti-Drug Abuse Act, which established mandatory prison sentences for some violations. In its wake, arrest and incarceration became the common answer, and the prison population grew enormously for non-violent offenses. Critics charged that the war on drugs disproportionately targeted people of color and, moreover, focused on supply from abroad when it needed to look at demand here at home. They urged more federal money for drug education, treatment, and rehabilitation, dismissing as insufficient First Lady Nancy Reagan's "Just Say No" advertising campaign aimed at children.

The Reagan administration also grappled with the outbreak of **acquired immune deficiency syndrome (AIDS)**, identified in 1981 as a new, usually fatal viral disease that destroyed the body's natural defense against illness and made its victims susceptible to a host of opportunistic infections. Because the majority of early victims were homosexual men who acquired AIDS through sexual contact, many Americans perceived AIDS as a disease of homosexuals. But other victims became infected through intravenous drug use, blood transfusions, heterosexual transmission, or birth from AIDS-carrying mothers. In 1983, the Centers for Disease Control and Prevention established an AIDS hotline to respond to questions about the disease but allocated more funds to research into Legionnaire's Disease than into AIDS.

AIDS provoked fear, anguish, and anger. Jerry Falwell told Moral Majority followers that "AIDS is not just God's punishment for homosexuals, it is God's punishment for the society that tolerates homosexuals." Pat Buchanan, Reagan's communications director, called AIDS "nature's revenge on gay men."

The AIDS crisis also brought an upsurge of organization and political involvement. In 1982 in New York City, the Gay Men's Health Crisis formed as the first AIDS service organization to offer counseling and education. In city after city, the gay community responded with energy and determination to advocate "safe sex" to lessen the chances of infection. Hollywood celebrities also stepped forward.

AIDS AND ACTIVISM The People with AIDS Coalition (PWAC), a self-help, non-profit organization founded in New York City in 1985 by individuals who had contracted AIDS, embarked on an educational campaign to dispel negative images, but also to demand assistance from state and federal governments. Their motto became "Fighting for Our Lives." AIDS activists protested against the policies of President Ronald Reagan, who didn't use the word "AIDS" in public until 1987 and refused to speak out about the epidemic.

Act Up AIDS/Alamy Stock Photo.

In 1985 Elizabeth Taylor became the founding chair of the American Foundation for AIDS Research; Madonna sought donations at her concerts. In 1987, *And the Band Played On*, a bestselling book by journalist Randy Shilts, described what had become a burgeoning movement of activists, health workers, and scholars as well as the reticence of the Reagan administration to deal with this highly politicized problem. Although officials in his Health and Human Services agency described the epidemic as "Our Number One Health Priority," Reagan—playing to anti-gay prejudices among conservatives—largely ignored the epidemic, and Congress provided scant funds for research or education. Only in 1988 was Reagan's surgeon general, C. Everett Koop, authorized to inaugurate a major AIDS education campaign.

30.3.3 The Reagan Doctrine

President Reagan matched the zeal of his conservative admirers and made vigorous anticommunism the centerpiece of his foreign policy. In 1982, speaking before the National Association of Evangelicals, he described the Soviet Union as "an evil empire . . . the focus of evil in the modern world." In February 1985, in his State of the Union address, he expanded on this theme and outlined the key elements in what became known as the Reagan Doctrine. Reagan moved beyond President Truman's "containment" policy and confidently promised to "roll back" communism by providing support to anticommunist insurgents and resistance movements anywhere in the world, and immediately in Africa, Asia, and Latin America.

Soon after taking office, Reagan acted to circumvent the 1979 Soviet invasion of Afghanistan. He greatly expanded the U.S. aid initiated by the Carter administration to include supplies of weapons and antiaircraft missiles. The CIA, in one of its most expensive covert operations, provided training and sent billions of U.S. dollars to the Islamic militants opposed to the Soviet occupation. These fundamentalist "holy warriors" managed to drive out the Soviet Union in 1989, but also eventually gave rise to the Taliban and Osama bin Laden's al-Qaeda, which would emerge in the 1990s as major agents of global terrorism.

Reagan's main strategy, however, was based on the idea of peace through strength. Claiming that the nation's military strength had fallen dangerously behind that of the Soviet Union, he shifted budget priorities toward defense programs. Critics disputed this assertion, pointing out that the Soviet advantage in intercontinental ballistic missiles (ICBMs) was offset by U.S. superiority in submarine-based forces and strategic aircraft. Nonetheless, the administration proceeded with plans to secure global military supremacy and created the largest military buildup in peacetime.

In 1983, President Reagan introduced his **Strategic Defense Initiative (SDI)**, a plan for a space-based antimissile defense system that would give the United States the capacity to shoot down incoming missiles with laser beams and homing rockets. As critics pointed out, this plan was unworkable, impossibly expensive, and likely to destabilize existing arms treaties. Despite disagreements within his own administration, Reagan pressed ahead, but without achieving any convincing results. Nevertheless, the Soviets viewed the SDI as an offensive strategy to ensure a first-strike advantage to the United States. U.S.-Soviet relations deteriorated, and the prospect of meaningful arms control dimmed in this atmosphere.

The Reagan administration also adopted a strategy of war by proxy and directed its resources toward Central America, hoping to reestablish the nation's historical control over the Caribbean basin. (See Map 30.5.) Claiming that

Map 30.5 THE UNITED STATES IN CENTRAL AMERICA, 1978–1990

United States intervention in Central America reached a new level of intensity with the so-called Reagan Doctrine. The bulk of U.S. aid came in the form of military support for the government of El Salvador and the Contra rebels in Nicaragua.

all problems throughout the Western Hemisphere stemmed from a "Moscow-Havana" alliance, the administration worked to support anticommunist groups in Cuba and elsewhere in Latin America.

In October 1983, the administration directed U.S. Marines to invade Grenada, claiming that the tiny island governed by Marxists since 1979 had become a Cuban military base and, therefore, would soon serve as "an outpost of communism" and terrorism. Condemned by the United Nations General Assembly as "a flagrant violation of International law," the invasion gave President Reagan his first definitive success in rolling back communist influence.

In promoting the Reagan Doctrine, the president also supplied overt and covert aid to anticommunist resistance movements led by right-wing dictators. His administration directed nearly $5 billion to shore up El Salvador's pro-American yet highly repressive regime. By 1983, right-wing death squads had tortured and assassinated thousands of opposition leaders. In neighboring Nicaragua, the Reagan administration claimed that the revolutionary Sandinista government posed "an unusual and extraordinary threat to the national security" of the United States. His officials accused the Sandinistas of shipping arms to the rebels in El Salvador. In December 1981, Reagan approved a CIA plan to arm and organize Nicaraguan exiles, known as **Contras**, to fight against the Sandinista government. In 1984, the CIA secretly mined Nicaraguan harbors. When Nicaragua won a judgment against the United States in the World Court over this violation of its sovereignty, the Reagan administration refused to recognize the court's jurisdiction in the case and ignored the verdict. Predictably, the U.S. covert war pushed the Sandinistas closer to Cuba and the Soviet bloc.

In 1984, Congress sought to rein in the covert war by passing legislation that forbade government agencies from supporting "directly or indirectly military or paramilitary operations" in Nicaragua. Denied funding by Congress, President Reagan turned to the National Security Council (NSC) to find a way to keep the Contra war going. Between 1984 and 1986, the NSC staff secretly assisted the Contras, raising enough money privately to support the largest mercenary army in hemispheric history. In 1987, the revelation of this unconstitutional scheme exploded before the public as part of the Iran-Contra affair.

30.3.4 The Iran-Contra Scandal

The revelations of what became known as the Iran-Contra scandal laid bare the contradictions in Reagan's foreign policy. The scandal also revealed how overzealous and secretive government officials circumvented Congress,

subverted the Constitution, and compromised presidential authority under the guise of patriotism.

Through his presidency, Reagan was challenged by the terrorism that defined the politics of the Middle East, notably the seizing of Western hostages and the bombing of commercial airplanes and cruise ships. Many of these attacks were desperate acts of retaliation by small pro-Palestinian sects or Islamic extremists opposed to U.S. support of Israel. However, the Reagan administration insisted that behind international terrorism lay the sinister influence of the Soviet bloc, the Ayatollah Khomeini of Iran, and Libyan leader Muammar el-Qaddafi. In the spring of 1986, the president, eager to demonstrate his antiterrorist resolve, ordered the bombing of government and military sites in Libya in a failed effort to kill Qaddafi.

As a fierce war between Iran and Iraq escalated, the administration tilted publicly toward Iraq, treating Iraq's dictator, Saddam Hussein, as an ally and providing much sophisticated weaponry. But in 1986, Reagan's advisers changed course and began secret negotiations with Iran, a nation the United States had declared a sponsor of international terrorism. Violating Reagan's declared policy forbidding negotiations over hostages, they came up with a complicated plan beginning with an offer to supply Iran with weapons ostensibly in exchange for help in securing the release of Americans who were being held hostage by pro-Iranian Islamic groups in Lebanon. (See Map 30.6.)

Subsequent disclosures elevated the arms-for-hostages deal into a major scandal during the summer of 1987. The American public learned that millions of dollars from the weapons sale had been secretly and illegally diverted into covert aid of the Nicaraguan Contras.

A joint House-Senate committee formed to investigate what was now known as the Iran-Contra affair, and implicated Deputy Director of the National Security Council and Marine Lieutenant Colonel Oliver North. In televised congressional hearings, North appeared in full dress uniform to defend his grossly illegal actions in the name of patriotism. Conservatives saw North as a hero; Reagan's opponents were appalled by North and Admiral John Poindexter's blithe admissions that they had lied to Congress, shredded evidence, and refused to keep the president fully informed, in order to guarantee his "plausible deniability." Both North and Poindexter were later convicted of felonies, but higher courts overturned their convictions on technical grounds. Reagan held fast to a plea of ignorance.

Reagan avoided impeachment, but saw his approval rating drop to the lowest of his presidency. His standing was further jeopardized by shortcomings in his supply-side economic programs. Big deficits kept interest rates high. Foreign investors, attracted by high interest rates on government securities, pushed up the value of the dollar in

Map 30.6 THE UNITED STATES IN THE MIDDLE EAST IN THE 1980s

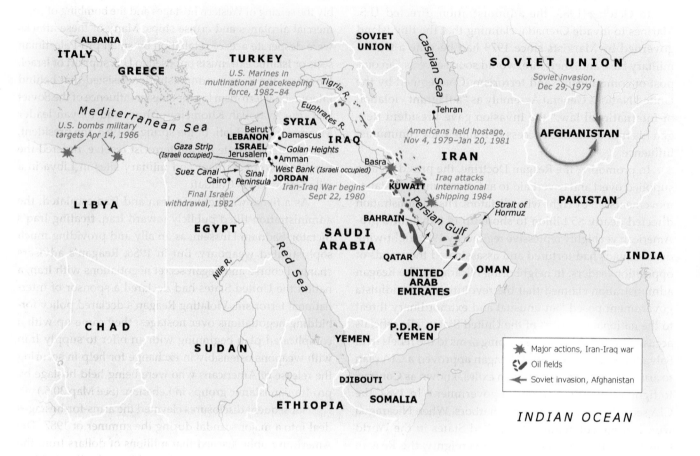

The volatile combination of ancient religious and ethnic rivalries, oil, and emerging Islamic fundamentalism made peace and stability elusive in the Middle East.

relation to foreign currencies. The overvalued dollar made it difficult for foreigners to buy American products, while making overseas goods cheaper to American consumers. Basic American industries—steel, autos, textiles—thus found it difficult to compete abroad and at home. Since World War I, the United States had been the world's leading creditor; in the mid-1980s, it became its biggest debtor. (See Figure 30.3.) The national debt tripled, growing from $914 billion in 1980 to more than $2.7 trillion in 1989. The fiscal crisis developed into a structural problem with profound and long-lasting implications for the American economy.

Nevertheless, in the face of these shortcomings, most Americans experienced an improvement in their standard of living, both in their wages and in consumer options. The very wealthy experienced the greatest gains of all. By the middle of Reagan's term, the economy, spurred on by massive defense spending, headed into one of the longest periods of growth and expansion in American history. The stock market boomed, pushing the Dow Jones Industrial Average to a new high in August 1987. "What I want to see above all," Reagan once remarked, "is that this remains a country where someone can always get rich." That goal remained elusive, but Reagan left office as the most popular president since Franklin D. Roosevelt. Despite the Iran-Contra scandal, he remained untarnished in the firmament of American conservatism.

OLIVER NORTH Lt. Col. Oliver North, who once described the scheme to sell arms to Iran to help the Contras as a "neat idea," is shown testifying in July 1987 before a joint congressional committee formed to investigate the Iran-Contra affair.

Scott J Applewhite/ASSOCIATED PRESS.

30.4 Moving Toward the Center

How did conservativism shape the administrations of both Bush and Clinton in the 1990s?

During the 1988 presidential campaign, moderate Republican George Herbert Walker Bush hoped to ride on Reagan's conservative coattails. He made a clear-cut pledge to voters: "Read my lips: no new taxes." The patrician New Englander and Yale graduate also promised to energize the war against drugs and back initiatives to allow prayer in public schools. Bush won the general election handily over Massachusetts Governor Michael Dukakis in 40 states and with 56 percent of the popular vote. After winning such widespread support, he concluded that he could set his own agenda and distance himself from Reagan. Infuriating conservatives, he promised in his inaugural address to deliver a "kinder and gentler nation."

Four years later, Arkansas Governor Bill Clinton ran for president against Bush as a "new kind of Democrat." Since 1985, he had been active in the Democratic Leadership Council (DLC), a group of Democrats who feared for the fate of their party after the Reagan landslide in the 1984 election. Responding to the conservative challenge, they sought to distance the Democratic Party even further from the liberal tradition established by Franklin D. Roosevelt and revived by Lyndon Johnson in the 1960s, and thereby recapture the blue-collar and white southern defectors "by redefining and reclaiming the political center." Youthful and energetic, Clinton carried this mission to the White House. He moved yet closer to conservatism by presenting a bold agenda that included balancing the federal budget, reforming welfare, reducing crime, promoting economic growth, and ensuring a strong national defense. Trimming the federal government and promoting free markets worldwide became hallmarks of his administration.

30.4.1 New World Order

Toward the end of Reagan's administration, sweeping and unanticipated internal changes within the Soviet Union undermined the entire Cold War framework of international affairs.

Figure 30.3 FEDERAL BUDGET DEFICIT AND NATIONAL DEBT, 1970–1998

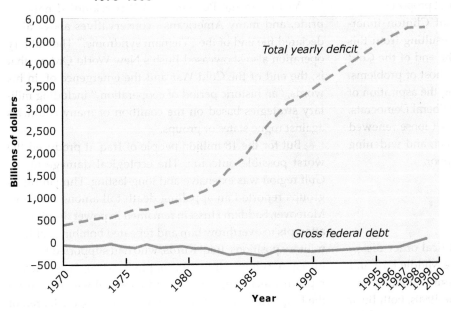

Tax cuts combined with huge increases in defense spending created a sharp increase in the budget deficit during the Republican administrations.

Statistical Abstract of the United States, in Nash et al., *The American People*, 5th ed., p. 988.

In 1985, a reform-minded leader, Mikhail Gorbachev, had taken over as Soviet leader. Under the rubrics of *glasnost* (openness) and *perestroika* (restructuring), Gorbachev encouraged open political discussion, released longtime dissidents from prison, and took the first halting steps toward a profit-based market economy.

In Gorbachev's view, improving the economic performance of the Soviet system depended first on halting the arms race. He had four separate summit meetings with Reagan and agreed to a modest treaty allowing comprehensive, mutual, on-site inspections. But the meetings also provided an important psychological breakthrough. At one of the summits, a Soviet leader humorously announced, "We are going to do something terrible to you Americans—we are going to deprive you of an enemy."

Indeed, the reforms initiated by Gorbachev—and, more immediately, the Soviet withdrawal from Afghanistan—led to the dissolution of the Soviet Union and to the end of communist rule throughout Eastern Europe. In March 1989, the Soviet Union held its first open elections since 1917, and Gorbachev announced that he would not use force to keep the satellite nations in line. In June 1989, after Poland held its first free elections since 1945, pro-democracy demonstrations forced out longtime communist leaders in Hungary, Czechoslovakia, Bulgaria, and Romania. Most dramatic of all were the events in East Germany. The Berlin Wall came down on November 9, 1989, paving the way for German reunification the following year. On Christmas Day 1991, Gorbachev signed a decree officially dissolving the Soviet Union and then resigned as president. President Bush proclaimed the end of the Cold War as an event of "biblical proportions."

Both President Bush and President Clinton inherited a host of enduring uncertainties resulting from this epochal event. They understood that the end of the Cold War complicated rather than resolved a host of problems. The collapse of Soviet communism, long the aspiration of American conservatives as well as most liberal Democrats, did not bring world peace but instead set loose renewed nationalism, ethnic and religious conflict, and widening divisions between the world's rich and poor.

30.4.2 The New Geopolitics of War

Just as dramatically, as the old geopolitical order disappeared, ideological rivalry shifted to the Middle East and to other areas in the world where Islamic militants had forcefully turned against the West. In the 1990s, both Bush and Clinton responded with military force, in alliance with NATO and the UN.

On August 2, 1990, Iraqi troops swept into neighboring Kuwait and quickly seized control of its rich oil fields. The motives of Saddam Hussein, Iraq's military dictator, were mixed. Like most Iraqis, Hussein believed that oil-rich Kuwait was actually an ancient province of Iraq. He also knew that control of Kuwait and its huge oil reserves would give Iraq major Persian Gulf ports for his almost landlocked country and input into the world price of oil. This event prompted President Bush to take action in the first major post-Cold War military operation.

Bush had already demonstrated his willingness to send U.S. troops into battle. After hesitating, in December 1989, he had ordered the largest military operation since the Vietnam War. "Operation Just Cause" succeeded in taking down the Panamanian drug lord and dictator—as well as former CIA ally—General Manuel Antonio Noriega. Bush now responded swiftly to the Middle East crisis.

On August 15, 1990, President Bush ordered U.S. forces to Saudi Arabia and the Persian Gulf in an operation called Desert Shield. The United States led a broad coalition in the United Nations, including the Soviet Union, that condemned the Iraqi invasion of Kuwait and declared strict economic sanctions against Iraq if it did not withdraw. After the UN sanctions failed to budge Hussein from Kuwait, in January 1991 Congress narrowly passed a joint resolution authorizing the president to use military force.

On January 17, 1991, President Bush announced the start of **Operation Desert Storm**. United States-led air strikes began 42 days of massive bombing of Iraqi positions in Kuwait, as well as of Baghdad and other Iraqi cities. The ground war, which began on February 24, took only 100 hours to force Saddam Hussein's troops out of Kuwait. On March 8, before a joint session of Congress, President Bush announced, "Tonight Kuwait is free."

Victory in the **Persian Gulf War** rekindled national pride, and many Americans—conservatives above all—declared the end of the "Vietnam syndrome." The military operation also showcased Bush's New World Order—that is, the end of the Cold War and the emergence of, in his words, "an historic period of cooperation," including military strategies based on the coalition of many countries against rogue states or groups.

But for the 18 million people of Iraq, it produced the worst possible outcome. The ecological damage in the Gulf region was extensive and long-lasting. Human rights groups reported an appalling death toll among civilians. Moreover, Saddam Hussein remained in power despite CIA attempts to overthrow him and repeated bombings of Iraqi military positions. Iraqi Kurds, who had supported the U.S. invasion in hopes it would topple Saddam, faced violent reprisals, including gassing and chemical weapons, from the Iraqi army. Among the region's Muslims, the hatred of Americans intensified and prompted appeals for revenge. Stepping up was Saudi millionaire Osama bin Laden, just a few years earlier a close ally of the United States during the Soviet invasion of Afghanistan. Using his own funds and a vast tribal network, bin Laden built his shadowy al-Qaeda organization, training small groups in terror tactics to be

ARMY NURSE IN IRAQ Female soldiers played a variety of roles during Operation Dessert Storm. This photograph shows an Army nurse moving to a new location during a sand storm and carrying a plant she has nurtured since her deployment.

Harvey O. Stowe/Alamy Stock Photo.

used against Western interests, particularly to force U.S. troops out of the Middle East. The repercussions of the Gulf War were long-lasting.

In 1995, President Clinton followed suit by seeking collective security through multinational military cooperation. He responded—belatedly, his critics charged—to a crisis in the Balkans. Following the collapse of the Soviet Union and the dissolution of Yugoslavia, ethnic and religious rivalry in Bosnia had erupted into a civil war. President Bush, seeing no threat to American interests, had opposed U.S. military intervention. As reports of "ethnic cleansing"—forced removal and murder of Croats and Muslims by Bosnian Serbs—increased, and as the numbers of refugees grew, Clinton joined NATO in bombing Serbian strongholds in Bosnia. After negotiating with Yugoslav president Slobodan Milošević, on November 27 Clinton announced a peace accord that called for a federated, multiethnic state of Bosnia. The following month, the president witnessed the signing of the Dayton Agreement, designed to bring peace and stability to the region.

In Kosovo, Yugoslavia, however, clashes between Serbs and Albanians intensified and spread to neighboring Macedonia and to Albania itself. In March 1999, after negotiations failed, Clinton announced that the United

States had joined "Operation Allied Force," an air campaign conducted by NATO. A settlement was reached in June that depended on the installation of a huge number of UN peacekeeping troops.

The so-called Clinton Doctrine, articulated in 1999 to justify U.S. involvement in the Balkan wars, departed sharply from Cold War policies that sanctioned intervention primarily on the grounds of strategic interest and national security. In October 1993, during Clinton's first year in office, he directed the United States to take part in a UN mission to restore civil order in Somalia, in East Africa. Eighteen ill-equipped American soldiers were killed in battle, their bodies dragged through the streets of Mogadishu, while several thousand Somalian fighters and civilians died in the ill-fated attack. Clinton responded by ordering the withdrawal of U.S. forces by March 1994. Although he insisted that "genocide is in and of itself a national interest where we should act," his administration refused to intervene in 1994 in Rwanda, where an ethnic power struggle led to the mass murder of up to 1 million Tutsis by the Hutu majority.

30.4.3 The Global Economy

If, politically, the Persian Gulf War marked the high point of Bush's popularity, the economy proved his undoing. Just as he was about to take office in 1989, many of the nation's savings and loan institutions, which had been deregulated by Reagan, collapsed. Then, on Friday, October 13, 1989, the stock market took a nosedive, signaling a major recession. American consumers had been spending extravagantly, many falling deep into debt, and now—with the prospect of a recession looming—they pulled back. Real estate prices plummeted, and many businesses filed for bankruptcy. Eventually, Bush reneged on his campaign promise and worked with Democrats in Congress to raise taxes. With the national debt reaching $4 trillion, and with the 1992 presidential campaign heating up, candidate Clinton and his running mate, Tennessee Senator Al Gore Jr., promised to turn the economic tide. In the Democrats' campaign headquarters, a sign humorously reminded the staff "It's the economy, stupid." Economic issues also fueled the independent campaign of Texas billionaire H. Ross Perot, who argued that someone as successful in business as himself was better qualified to solve the nation's economic woes than Washington insiders. The Clinton-Gore ticket won 43 percent of the popular vote and carried 32 states. But Perot's win of 19 percent of the popular vote prompted the newly elected Clinton to focus, as he put it, "like a laser beam on the economy." Once in office, however, the Clinton administration effectively adopted many of the conservative policies that proved so advantageous to Republicans over the previous 12 years.

"Everything from the strength of our economy, to the safety of our cities, to the health of our people," Clinton

declared, "depends on events not only within our border but half the world away." His administration responded forcefully to an economic trend intensifying in the 1990s termed "globalization," which included an international integration of capital, the diminishing importance of national borders, and the flow of knowledge worldwide. The number of transnational corporations grew swiftly, from 7,000 in 1970 to more than 700,000 by the end of Clinton's presidency. In line with the increase in world trade, the global economy grew six times larger in the last half-century. The globalization of finance accompanied the flow of capital across national markets. Clinton stepped forward, promising to enlarge "the world's free community of market democracies" under the leadership of the United States. The editors of *Foreign Affairs* dubbed Clinton the "globalization" president.

During his first term, Clinton pushed through Congress two major trade agreements to expand markets for American products and to encourage "free trade," both building on the conservative economic policies advanced by the Reagan and Bush administrations. Approved in November 1993, the North American Free Trade Agreement (NAFTA) eased the international flow of goods, services, and investments among the United States, Mexico, and Canada by eliminating tariffs and other trade barriers. In 1995, the second trade agreement created the World Trade Organization (WTO), which established international trade rules. Critics and supporters argued over whether these trade agreements would encourage global competition, thereby boosting American export industries and creating new high-wage jobs for American workers, or simply

ANTI-WTO PROTESTS, SEATTLE, 1999 More than 5,000 activists gathered in Seattle in November 1999 to demonstrate against the meeting of the World Trade Organization. The event, which was marked by a violent clash with police and the arrests of dozens of protestors, marked the beginning of a movement for global economic justice.

John G Mabanglo/Getty Images.

erode the U.S. industrial base, shifting manufacturing to low-wage countries such as Mexico, India, and Cambodia and accelerating environmental degradation.

These principles drove Clinton's policy toward the People's Republic of China (PRC). In 1989, Chinese government forces had brutally attacked pro-democracy demonstrators in Beijing's Tiananmen Square. During the 1992 election campaign, Clinton criticized Bush for continuing "to coddle" China in light of such gross human rights violations. Then, after taking office, he modified his position and recommended restoring most-favored-nation (MFN) status to the PRC. Clinton acknowledged that serious human rights abuses continued, but he pointed out that China, the world's most populous nation, had the world's fastest-growing economy—as well as a nuclear arsenal and veto power in the UN Security Council. He promoted free enterprise as a means to advance democracy not only in the PRC but also in other nations, such as Turkey, Saudi Arabia, and Indonesia.

In the United States, Clinton's internationalist, free-trade economic policies appeared to pay off. He presided over the longest economic booms in American history. Between 1992 and 2000, the economy produced more than 20 million new jobs, and by 2000 the unemployment rate had fallen below 4 percent, the lowest in more than 30 years. Many conservatives, however, interpreted Clinton's record as primarily a continuation of the Reagan-era boom.

30.4.4 The Conservative Resurgence

In his first term in office, with Democratic majorities in both the House and Senate, President Clinton presented a policy agenda that angered conservatives. He began by using his executive power to abolish restrictions on some abortion procedures and on medical research using fetal tissue. The first piece of legislation to pass Congress was the Family and Medical Leave Act, earlier vetoed by President Bush, which provided workers with the right to 12 weeks of unpaid leave to care for a newborn or ill family member. On gay rights, however, Clinton was less successful. As a candidate, he had promised to end the ban on gays and bisexuals in the armed forces. After Congress refused, Clinton ultimately compromised and in December 1993 issued an executive order that satisfied virtually no one: "Don't ask, don't tell."

Democrats overcame the resistance of Republicans and the National Rifle Association to pass the Brady Handgun Violence Prevention Act, which required a background check for the purchase of a handgun; a year later, they secured a ban on assault weapons as part of the Violent Crime Control and Law Enforcement Act, signed in September 1994. The bipartisan anticrime act, the largest in U.S. history, targeted violence against women and allocated funds for prosecution of abusers and for shelters for "battered women." It provided specific community guidelines for handling convicted sexual predators, protocols that were amended two years later as

Megan's Law. The act expanded the federal death penalty and provided for 100,000 more police officers and $9.7 billion for prisons. In the long run, the anticrime act included a provision that would prove highly controversial: "three strikes" for habitual federal offenders, which resulted in mandatory sentence laws adopted by states.

On Clinton's campaign promise of guaranteed universal health care, the president could not overcome conservative opposition to a new entitlement program. Among the industrialized nations, the United States and apartheid South Africa alone lacked a national health care system. Moreover, nearly 40 million Americans had no health insurance. Many simply could not afford it; others were denied coverage by private insurers because of preexisting conditions. For millions of others, health insurance was tied to the workplace, and a loss or change of jobs threatened their coverage. Private spending on health care had skyrocketed from $246 billion in 1980 to more than $880 billion during the year Clinton took office.

In a controversial move, President Clinton appointed First Lady Hillary Rodham Clinton, an accomplished attorney, to head a health care task force. The proposed plan, outlined in a 1,342-page legislative bill, mandated employer coverage through regulated health maintenance organizations (HMOs). Opposed by powerful health care interest groups and most Republicans, the plan died in Congress in August 1994, just as the midterm election campaign moved into its final phase.

In the 1994 midterm elections, the defeat of health care reform helped the Republicans gain control of both the House and Senate for the first time in 40 years—a disaster for Clinton and the Democratic Party. With Congress now dominated by conservative Republicans, the new House Speaker and formidable polemicist, Newt Gingrich of Georgia, challenged Clinton's leadership by presenting a set of proposals labeled the Contract with America. The House did indeed pass much of the "Contract," including a large tax cut, an increase in military spending, cutbacks in federal regulatory power in the environment and at the workplace, a tough anticrime bill, and a sharp reduction in federal welfare programs. The Senate passed only a few of these bills.

Meanwhile, Clinton undercut the Republicans by adapting many of their proposals to his own. He pledged to cut taxes and reduce the federal deficit, and declared that "the era of big government is over." He called for "responsibility" on the part of recipients of social programs and spoke of the importance of stable families, promised to be tough on crime, and stressed the need for encouraging private investment to create new jobs. He earlier had also promised to "end welfare as we know it," and he now proposed to terminate the 60-year-old Aid to Families with Dependent Children program (AFDC). Welfare recipients would now have access to aid for only a limited period and only if they were preparing for or seeking work. After Congress passed the Welfare Reform Act in August 1996, Clinton held

"CONTRACT WITH AMERICA" After the 1994 midterm election gave Republicans control of the House of Representatives for the first time in 40 years, the new Speaker, Newt Gingrich of Georgia, presented a list of legislative initiatives to be completed within the first 100 days of the new session. On April 7, 1995, he appeared at a rally on Capitol Hill to celebrate the success of the Republicans' "Contract with America."

John Duricka/ASSOCIATED PRESS.

a public signing ceremony and declared, "Today, we are taking an historic chance to make welfare what it was meant to be, a second chance, not a way of life."

Staking out the political center, Clinton set the tone for his 1996 reelection campaign against U.S. Senator Robert Dole of Kansas, the Republican majority leader of the Senate. He promised to promote policies to strengthen the American family, beginning with the **Americans with Disabilities Act (ADA)**, which he pledged to vigorously enforce. A bipartisan measure introduced during the Reagan administration and enacted in July 1990 with President Bush's encouragement, the act penalized employers who discriminated against qualified workers with disabilities, and required employers and local governments to provide access to public facilities. More controversial was the bipartisan Defense of Marriage Act, which for federal purposes defined marriage as between one man and one woman. In September 1996, Clinton signed the act—reluctantly, he later claimed. In November, Clinton triumphed at the polls, but his was an election victory without coattails: The Republicans retained control of both houses of Congress.

During his final years in office, Clinton had to fend off conservative challenges regarding his moral conduct. A former Arkansas state employee, Paula Jones, charged Clinton with sexual harassment during his gubernatorial term. Around the same time, in 1992, real estate deals involving both Bill and Hillary Rodham Clinton blew up into a scandal known as Whitewater. Complications from these scandals prompted the appointment of an independent counsel, former judge Kenneth Starr, to investigate allegations. In the fall of 1998, Starr instead delivered a report focusing on the president's sexual encounter with a young White House intern, Monica Lewinsky. Starr's report outlined several potentially impeachable offenses, including false testimony under oath, witness tampering, and obstruction of justice, all allegedly committed by the president to keep secret his relationship with Lewinsky. For only the third time in history, in October 1998 the House

IMPEACHMENT On January 7, 1999, Senator Strom Thurmond swore in Chief Justice William Rehnquist to preside over the Senate impeachment trial of President Bill Clinton. At this conclusion of the trial, a month later, Thurmond voted for impeachment and explained his decision to the Chief Justice: "Before today, perjury and obstruction of justice were clearly high crimes and misdemeanors under the Constitution. My vote is consistent with this. The President is not above the law."

ZUMA Press, Inc./Alamy Stock Photo.

of Representatives voted to open an inquiry into possible grounds for impeachment.

Republicans hoping to reap a wholesale victory from the scandal in the midterm elections were bitterly disappointed. Contrary to predictions, the president's party added seats, trimming the Republican majority in the 105th Congress. The election also brought a shakeup in the Republican leadership. Gingrich, who had advanced the unsuccessful campaign strategy focused narrowly on Clinton's impeachment problem, was prompted to resign as Speaker of the House and from his seat in Congress in January 1999 after reports of his own marital infidelity surfaced.

On December 19, 1998, the House voted, strictly along party lines, to impeach the president. In the Senate,

however, Republicans lacked the required two-thirds vote to follow through. On February 12, 1999, the Senate trial concluded with the president's acquittal.

Although Clinton's personal reputation had been badly tarnished, he managed to push through Congress several bills enhancing health and safety regulations. The Republicans joined Clinton to achieve a sweeping deregulation of the banking industry and pass the controversial Financial Services Modernization Act of 1999. The bill, signed by President Clinton in November, repealed major sections of the Glass-Steagall Act of 1933 and allowed banking, securities, and insurance companies to combine and to consolidate services. Bill Clinton left office in 2000 with the highest job approval rating of any president since Dwight Eisenhower.

Conclusion

The success of conservatives in halting and in some cases actually reversing key trends in American politics, from Franklin Roosevelt's New Deal to Lyndon Johnson's Great Society, was made possible by the legacy of the Cold War and the trauma of defeat in Vietnam. But that success also owed a great deal to a deepening anxiety about cultural changes and a growing pessimism about the ability of politicians to offer solutions, especially at the national level. Those community activists struggling to broaden the 1960s' protest movements into an updated, comprehensive reformism encompassing such issues as feminism, ecology, and affirmative action readily recognized that the liberal era had ended.

President Ronald Reagan, a charismatic figure who sometimes invented his own past and seemed to believe in it, offered remedies for a weary and nostalgic nation. By insisting that the rebellious 1960s had been a terrible mistake, lowering national self-confidence along with public

morals and faith in the power of economic individualism, he successfully wedded the conservatism of Christian fundamentalists, many suburbanites, and Sun Belt voters with the more traditional conservatism of corporate leaders. In many respects, the Reagan administration actually continued and added ideological fervor to the downscaling of government services and upscaling of military spending already evident under President Jimmy Carter, while offering supporters the hope of a sweeping conservative revolution.

In the end, critics suggested, supporters of Ronald Reagan and Reaganism could not go back to the 1950s—just as the erstwhile rebels of the 1960s could not go back to their favorite era. Economically, conservatives achieved many of their goals, including widespread acceptance of sharper economic divisions within society and fewer restraints on corporations and investments. But socially and culturally, their grasp was much less secure.

Key Terms

Organization of Petroleum Exporting Countries (OPEC) Cartel of oil-producing nations in Asia, Africa, and Latin America that gained substantial power over the world economy in the mid- to late 1970s by controlling the production and price of oil. p. 747

Environmental Protection Agency (EPA) Federal agency created in 1970 to oversee environmental monitoring and cleanup programs. p. 749

Camp David Accords Agreement signed by Israel and Egypt in 1978 that set the formal terms for peace in the Middle East. p. 752

détente French for "easing of tension," the term is used to describe the new U.S. relations with China and the Soviet Union in 1972. p. 752

Roe v. Wade U.S. Supreme Court decision (1973) that disallowed state laws prohibiting abortion during the first three months (trimester) of pregnancy and established guidelines for abortion in the second and third trimesters. p. 756

Economic Recovery Tax Act of 1981 A major revision of the federal income tax system. p. 759

Deregulation Reduction or removal of government regulations and encouragement of direct competition in many important industries and economic sectors. p. 759

Affirmative Action A set of policies to open opportunities in business and education for members of minority groups and women by allowing race and sex to be factors included in decisions to hire, award contracts, or admit students to higher education programs. p. 754

war on drugs A paramilitary operation to halt drug trafficking in the United States. p. 760

acquired immune deficiency syndrome (AIDS) A complex of deadly pathologies resulting from infection with the human immunodeficiency virus (HIV). p. 761

Strategic Defense Initiative (SDI) President Reagan's program, announced in 1983, to defend the United States against nuclear missile attack with untested weapons systems and sophisticated technologies. p. 762

Contras Nicaraguan exiles armed and organized by the CIA to fight the Sandinista government of Nicaragua. p. 763

Operation Desert Storm U.S. military campaign to force Iraqi forces out of Kuwait. p. 766

Persian Gulf War War initiated by President George H.W. Bush in response to Iraq's invasion of Kuwait. p. 766

Americans with Disabilities Act (ADA) An act that requires employers to provide access to their facilities for qualified employees with disabilities. p. 770

CHRONOLOGY

1973
Roe v. Wade legalizes abortion
Arab embargo sparks oil crisis in the United States

1974
Richard Nixon resigns presidency
Gerald Ford takes office

1976
Democrat Jimmy Carter defeats incumbent Ford in presidential election

1977
President Carter announces human rights as major tenet in foreign policy

1978
Camp David meeting sets terms for Middle East peace

1979
Iranian fundamentalists seize the U.S. Embassy in Tehran and hold U.S. citizens hostage for 444 days
Soviets invade Afghanista

1980
Republican Ronald Reagan defeats incumbent Carter in presidential election

1981
AIDS is recognized and named

1986
Iran-Contra hearings before Congress reveal arms-for-hostages deal and secret, illegal diversion of funds to Nicaraguan rebels

1988
Republican George H. W. Bush defeats Michael Dukakis in presidential election

1990
Iraqi invasion of Kuwait leads to massive U.S. military presence in the Persian Gulf

1991
Operation Desert Storm forces Iraq out of Kuwait

1992
Democrat Bill Clinton defeats incumbent George H. W. Bush and independent candidate Ross Perot in the presidential election

Chapter 31
Inequality in the Global Age 2000–Present

OBAMA INAUGURATION On January 20, 2009, Barack Obama was sworn in as the nation's first African American president.

Ralf-Finn Hestoft/Getty Images.

Contents and Focus Questions

American Communities

Inequality, the Bay Area, California

In late summer 2017, Sheila James described her daily commute to work. Speaking to a *New York Times* journalist, she pinpointed the beginning of her day at 2:15 A.M. No, she was not a baker, the *Times* reporter noted, but an ordinary office worker. At one time she lived just 15 miles from her workplace, but her apartment building was sold

to a developer who evicted its tenants. Ms. James found an affordable apartment, but then had to travel 80 miles, taking two trains, a bus, and a final walk, to reach her destination, the Federal Building in downtown San Francisco.

James was not poor. As a public health adviser, she earned the city's average income. Even so, the cost of rent anywhere in San Francisco was beyond her means.

The median home price was $1.25 million, which put the qualifying income to buy at $254,000 per year. James earned less than a third that amount. Locked out of the housing market, she joined the ranks of the "extreme commuters" of Stockton, California, a city with one of the highest concentrations of long-distance commuters in the nation.

Despite her arduous daily commute, Sheila James held one of the better jobs in the Bay Area's growing service economy. The service sector included highly paid lawyers, financial analysts, and software designers as well as teachers, nurses, and poorly paid fast-food employees and maintenance personnel. In 1965, an estimated 50 percent of all jobs nationwide were in the service sector; the figure grew to nearly 70 percent in 2004 and 80 percent 10 years later.

The Bay Area, home to Facebook, Google, and Microsoft, led the region into a period of unprecedented innovation and corporate and personal wealth. But existing political and geographical bottlenecks caused not only an alarming housing crisis but also an astronomical rise in socioeconomic inequality. By 2016, San Francisco's wealthiest 1 percent of households earned 44 times the average of the bottom 99 percent.

Nationwide, economic and racial inequality had grown over the previous half-century to such an extent that many observers noted the existence of "two Americas." While a corporate official had earned around 20 or 30 times the pay of an employee at the same company a few decades earlier, corporate executive income by 2017 was more than 200 times greater than that of the average employee. In the blue-collar sector, the better-paying industrial jobs continued to disappear as factories closed and companies moved production across borders or overseas. Meanwhile, organized labor continued to decline such that fewer than 15 percent of workers held union memberships, further depressing wages. President Barack Obama called inequality the "defining challenge of our time."

By the 2016 election, accelerating inequality forced itself to the center of American politics. Populist appeals to voters, whether focused on economic inequality or looking to exploit racial and ethnic division, dominated the campaign trail. Candidates gave voice to the increasingly bitter partisan, social, and cultural differences dividing Americans.

31.1 President George W. Bush and the War on Terror

How did the threat of international terrorism transform the American political landscape?

Republican Governor George W. Bush of Texas, son of former president George H. W. Bush, took office after one of the strangest presidential elections in U.S. history. The popular vote went to Democrat Al Gore—Bill Clinton's vice president—and his running mate, Connecticut Senator Joe Lieberman, but by the next morning the number of votes in the electoral college for Bush and running mate Dick Cheney, a former Secretary of Defense, was still in doubt. The cliffhanger ended only after the U.S. Supreme Court, voting five to four along partisan lines, refused a recount of votes in Florida. Finally, on December 12, Gore conceded defeat in the first disputed presidential election since 1876. (See Map 31.1.) With only lukewarm public support, a slim majority in the House of Representatives, and a Senate split evenly, President Bush found himself in a weak position to handle the crisis ahead: terrorism.

31.1.1 Terrorist Attack on America

On September 11, 2001, hijackers crashed two jetliners into New York's World Trade Center towers, while a third

Map 31.1 THE ELECTION OF 2000

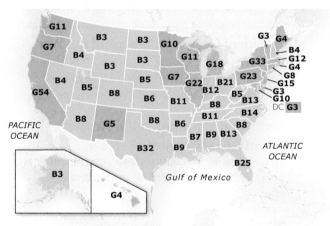

Numbers on states represent Electoral Votes.	Electoral Vote (%)	Popular Vote (%)
GEORGE W. BUSH (B) (Republican)	271 (50.5)	50,456,169 (48.0)
Al Gore (G) (Democrat)	266 (49.5)	50,996,116 (48.0)

The 2000 presidential election was the closest one in U.S. history based on Electoral College vote and the first one to be decided by a decision of the Supreme Court.

jetliner slammed into the Pentagon in Virginia. A fourth plane, diverted from its terrorist mission by courageous passengers, hurtled to the ground near Pittsburgh. At the Pentagon, the death toll reached 184, including 59 people who had been on board the hijacked airliner. In New York City, the collapse of the Twin Towers killed 2,753 people, including hundreds of police and rescue workers who had run into the buildings to help. The damage was devastating. The stark images of the attack, the dramatic collapse of the buildings, and the fear on the faces of thousands fleeing the sites were replayed over and over again on televisions throughout the world. (See SEEING History.)

The 9/11 attacks sparked a massive response. The Federal Aviation Administration halted all air traffic

---

SEEING History

The 9/11 Attacks

The first plane hit at 8:48 A.M., the second at 9:03 A.M. Then, as millions of disbelieving television viewers watched, the 110-story Twin Towers collapsed. Already, many Americans were saying that they would forever remember where they were and what they were doing when they heard the news.

Journalists and ordinary Americans alike repeatedly invoked two twentieth-century catastrophes as parallels to 9/11: the Japanese attack at Pearl Harbor on December 7, 1941, and the assassination of President John F. Kennedy on November 22, 1963. Neither of the earlier disasters played out in real time over modern media, however.

The World Trade Center attack occurred virtually before the eyes of millions. Video cameras caught the image of the second plane hitting the South Tower, panic on the faces of those fleeing, smoke billowing from the towers, and their collapse. Reporters were soon pulling comments from traumatized survivors. The networks immediately preempted regular programming and allowed millions of horrified Americans to watch endless replays. Newscasters drew out the Pearl Harbor analogy as another "Day of Infamy." Within days, programmers edited the videotapes to enhance the drama—adding images of cell phones (to remind viewers of the final calls many of the victims made), overlaying images of the collapsing towers with an unfurling American flag, and piping in patriotic music. To enhance the emotional impact, they borrowed such cinematic techniques as slowing the film's speed and using jump cuts that fast-timed images of the burning towers with close-ups of anguished observers' faces.

Some seventy history-oriented institutions created an Internet site, 911history.net, to collect oral histories and artifacts. Said Diane Kresh of the Library of Congress, "The Internet has become for many the public commons, a place where they can come together and talk." Importance of the Internet aside, the searing pictures of the burning towers will likely remain the preeminent image for 9/11.

THE 9/11 ATTACKS

Spencer Platt/Getty Images.

- **What role did the media play in shaping our understanding of the events of September 11, 2001?**

- **How does the ability of modern media to dramatize the horror and immediacy of such events enhance their "value" to terrorists launching attacks?**

- **In what ways did the 9/11 attacks facilitate the Bush administration's decision to go to war in Iraq?**

nationwide for the first time in U.S. history. President Bush declared the deadly attacks an act of war and vowed to hunt down those responsible for the "evil, despicable acts of terror." Congress, with only one dissenting vote, authorized the president to employ "all necessary and appropriate force" against terrorism. Amid an outpouring of sympathy from European allies, NATO for the first time ever invoked the mutual defense clause in its founding treaty, which in effect supported any U.S. military action.

President Bush identified the Saudi Arabian Osama bin Laden as the prime suspect in the highly coordinated attack and linked the airline hijackers to his al-Qaeda network. An ally of the United States during the Russian invasion of Afghanistan, bin Laden had turned against his former supporter. He went on to build his shadowy al-Qaeda organization, training small groups in terror tactics to be used against Western interests and calling for a *jihad*, or holy war, against the entire non-Muslim world. On February 26, 1993, al-Qaeda terrorists had bombed the World Trade Center, killing 6 people and injuring more than 1,000 others. On August 7, 1998, bin Laden's organization bombed U.S. embassies in Kenya and Tanzania, killing 225 people and injuring more than 5,500 others. Shortly after President George W. Bush took office, the CIA had reported "mounting warning signs" of a "spectacular" attack in the coming weeks or months, and now no one in his administration doubted that bin Laden had directed the deadly 9/11 operation. A few weeks later, bin Laden himself publicly rejoiced in the destruction of the "greatest buildings" in the United States. "Our war on terror begins with Al Qaeda," Bush announced.

31.1.2 The Bush Doctrine: "Preemptive Action"

The 9/11 terrorist attacks prompted dramatic changes in the conduct and goals of American foreign policy. At a memorial service for victims, President Bush warned, "Our responsibility to history is already clear: to answer these attacks and rid the world of evil." He outlined the new principles that would guide his policies; "From this day forward any nation that continues to harbor or support terrorists will be regarded by the United States as a hostile regime."

The first theater of Bush's campaign against terrorism was Afghanistan. With a network spread across the Middle East, bin Laden had based al-Qaeda's operations in Afghanistan, where he enjoyed the protection of a government run by the Taliban, a radical Islamist group. The United States delivered an ultimatum: Hand over Osama bin Laden and other al-Qaeda leaders and close all terrorist training camps. The Taliban refused to comply.

On October 7, 2001, the war in Afghanistan began as a joint U.S.-British military campaign. Although bin Laden

and much of the al-Qaeda leadership managed to escape, the Taliban government toppled.

In his January 2002 State of the Union address, after expressing satisfaction in taking down the Taliban, President Bush pivoted sharply. He now argued that America faced a grave and unprecedented danger not merely from al-Qaeda terrorists, but also from nation-states seeking to develop chemical, biological, or nuclear weapons of mass destruction (WMD). He denounced the regimes of North Korea, Iran, and Iraq as an "axis of evil, arming to threaten the peace of the world."

This new focus on the threat of WMD formed a central element in sweeping reformulation of American foreign policy. Moreover, it signaled a shift toward Iraq and its "evil" leader, Saddam Hussein.

Several months later, Bush outlined what became known as the "Bush Doctrine." Discarding the cornerstones of Cold War policy—containment and deterrence—Bush argued that the war on terrorism "will not be won on the defensive." Instead, the United States must now "be ready for preemptive action"—acting alone, if necessary. Bush pledged to "take the war to the enemy, disrupt his plans, and confront the worst threats before they emerge."

31.1.3 Operation Iraqi Freedom

The first major test of the Bush Doctrine was Iraq. The president had come to believe that "regime change" was necessary to fulfill the larger goals of U.S foreign policy: the promotion of "freedom, democracy, and free enterprise." From the first weeks after the 9/11 attacks, his administration began to plan for a United States-led invasion of Iraq and the overthrow of Saddam Hussein.

Proponents of war reiterated three central arguments. First, Saddam had defied UN resolutions demanding the termination of research on WMDs, and particularly the development of nuclear weapons. Second, he had direct connections to the 9/11 hijackers and to al-Qaeda operatives around the world. Third, toppling him would make possible a democratic Iraq that could then serve as a model for the entire Middle Eastern and Muslim world. The majority of the Iraqi people, the Bush administration also contended, would support a United States-led campaign to oust the brutal dictator, ensuring a swift and fairly painless victory.

Throughout late 2002 and early 2003, while U.S. military planners prepared for the invasion, opponents of war refuted the arguments of the Bush administration. Many political analysts and veteran diplomats doubted that Saddam had the weapon capability credited to him. They charged that Vice President Cheney and Secretary of Defense Donald Rumsfeld had manipulated Pentagon intelligence estimates to make their case. Others doubted Saddam's links to al-Qaeda and argued that war with

Iraq would sideline the hunt for bin Laden. A growing number of Americans questioned the assumption that removing Saddam would make America safer, envisioning an invasion instead as a boost to the recruitment efforts of al-Qaeda and other terrorist organizations. On February 15, 2003, demonstrators staged the largest antiwar protest in history, turning out in more than 300 cities in 60 countries, including 500,000 in New York, 2 million in London, and 3 million in Rome. The international sympathy with the United States that followed the September 11 attacks now dissolved.

Meanwhile, Secretary of State Colin Powell tried but failed to gain support for war from the UN Security Council. Nonetheless, the Bush administration decided to invade Iraq with what it called a "coalition of the willing," with Great Britain as its major partner. On March 19, President Bush announced the beginning of war and ordered the "decapitation strike" against Saddam. (See Map 31.2.) He told the Iraqis "the tyrant will soon be gone, the day of your liberation is near."

The joint U.S.-British "Shock and Awe" of massive aerial bombing overwhelmed the weak Iraqi army fairly easily and secured Baghdad and several other major cities. On May 1, 2003, President Bush announced the end of combat operations. "In the battle of Iraq," the president declared, "the United States and our allies have prevailed."

31.1.4 The Longest Wars

Removing Saddam's regime from power proved far simpler than bringing peace and stability to Iraq. The invasion turned into an occupation, and the plights of ordinary

Map 31.2 THE INVASION OF IRAQ

On March 20, 2003, American and British troops poured into Iraq from bases in Kuwait, crossing the Iraqi border to the east near Safwan. The American Third Infantry Division used armored bulldozers to create wide gaps in the Iraqi defensive line.

"MISSION ACCOMPLISHED" President George W. Bush announces the end of major combat operations in Iraq, May 1, 2003, speaking on the deck of the aircraft carrier USS *Abraham Lincoln*, anchored near San Diego. A banner proclaimed "Mission Accomplished," but American troops would continue to face stiff opposition and endure thousands of casualties battling Iraqi insurgents.

Scott J Applewhite/ASSOCIATED PRESS.

Iraqis and American soldiers worsened quickly. Amid widespread civil disorder, extensive looting, and the disruption of electricity, water, and food supplies, about 4.5 million refugees fled their homes, roughly half of whom left Iraq. Rather than weaken terrorist networks, the U.S. occupation instead strengthened a new generation now drawn to do battle with U.S. forces in Iraq. A year after Bush had confidently declared the fighting over, American troops were still engaged in the toughest battles since the Vietnam War.

Despite the quagmire in Iraq, Bush made the war on terrorism the keynote of his 2004 reelection campaign. He confidently described himself as a "wartime president" and appealed to patriotism and national unity. Defeating the Vietnam War hero Senator John Kerry of Massachusetts, Bush won reelection with a slim margin of 3 million votes. He began his second term with a divided nation and sharply diminishing support for the war in Iraq. Many congressional Democrats, now believing that a military "victory" was impossible, tried to attach deadlines for withdrawal to the president's funding bills.

With only a narrow majority, they could not override the president's vetoes.

Meanwhile, civil disorder in Iraq persisted, despite some major changes in its governance. In January 2005, Iraq conducted its first national elections for an assembly charged with writing a new constitution. In December 2006, after an Iraqi Special Tribunal found Saddam Hussein guilty of crimes against humanity, the ruthless dictator of Iraq since 1979 was executed. A month later, rather than scaling back, Bush unveiled a new and costly plan, a "surge" of some 30,000 additional American troops to Iraq. The goal was to bolster the shaky Iraqi political system. Although the Bush administration touted the success of its new strategy, pointing to a substantial decline in both political violence and attacks on U.S. forces throughout 2007–2008, the larger picture in Iraq remained grim.

The U.S. president continued to defend the war as part of a broader, long-term struggle against global terrorism, but the argument continued to lose credibility. Newly released classified documents showed no direct link between al-Qaeda and Saddam Hussein and, moreover, no WMDs in Iraq, as Bush had charged. While the president blamed "false intelligence," the Senate Intelligence Committee concluded in 2008 that the Bush administration had knowingly "misrepresented the intelligence and the threat from Iraq."

Moreover, the U.S. occupation continued to take a heavy toll on U.S. forces. Tens of thousands of soldiers were commanded to stay in Iraq beyond their regular tour of duty. After returning home, nearly one-third of troops presented signs of post-traumatic stress disorder (PTSD) and other mental health issues. More than 4,500 Americans died in the occupation of Iraq, and nearly 32,000 were wounded, many of them severely. Estimates of Iraqi civilian deaths directly from war-related injuries ranged as high as 193,000 by 2017, and estimates of Iraqi civilian deaths from causes related to the war, such as food shortages, toxic water supplies, and contagious diseases, reached twice that number.

The Iraq occupation as well as continuing combat against the resurgent Taliban in Afghanistan put a heavy strain on the federal budget. To fund these wars—the longest in U.S. history—and concurrently the open-ended war on terror, President Bush pushed the deficit to record levels.

31.1.5 The National Security State

The wars in Iraq and Afghanistan had a major impact on the operation of the federal government and, by extension, on civil liberties. In aftermath of the 9/11 attacks, the Bush administration quickly devised new policies and pushed new legislation through Congress to prevent terrorism. Passed by Congress with little debate just 45 days after terrorist attacks, the **USA PATRIOT Act** gave federal officials greater authority to track and intercept communications for law-enforcement and intelligence-gathering purposes, new powers to curb foreign money laundering, and broader discretion in tightening borders against suspected foreign terrorists. More than 1,000 Muslims, some of them U.S. citizens, were arrested and detained, although only a few of these suspects were actually charged with crimes related to terrorism. The act also allowed government agencies to search telephone and email records and access individual and corporate financial and medical records. Congress passed the USA PATRIOT Act II in 2003, further enlarging the grounds for surveillance and secret arrests.

Several weeks after the 9/11 attacks, the Bush administration established the Office of Homeland Security, which was made into the Cabinet-level **Department of Homeland Security (DHS)** in November 2002. The DHS constituted the largest reorganization of the federal government since the creation of the Department of Defense in 1947. It consolidated 22 different domestic agencies to coordinate the nation's defense against terrorist threats. Its components included the Immigration and Naturalization Service (INS), the U.S. Customs Services, the Secret Services, the Coast Guard, and the **Federal Emergency Management Agency (FEMA)**. The passenger-screening program, previously managed by individual airlines, was upgraded, and the Transportation Security Agency (TSA) was moved into the DHS in 2003.

Troubling questions emerged about security policy involving both American citizens and suspected alien terrorists. Less than a month after the 9/11 attacks, President Bush had issued a secret executive order proclaiming an "extraordinary emergency" that allowed, in Vice President Cheney's words, the military "to work . . . *the dark side*"— that is, to pursue terrorists in the "shadows" of the intelligence world. The military was now able to detain and try by military tribunal anyone, including U.S. citizens, named an "enemy combatant." Imprisoned at U.S. Naval Station Guantanamo Bay in Cuba, more than 770 "terrorist suspects" from more than 40 countries were held without recourse to the customary legal rights of American citizens or international law. Moreover, reports leaked of the "enhanced interrogation" tactics, including sleep deprivation, sensory deprivation, and waterboarding, at Guantanamo and also at CIA "black sites," secret jails overseas. In the spring of 2004, graphic images and descriptions of Iraqi

AIRPORT SECURITY SCREENING The Transportation Security Administration (TSA), founded on November 19, 2001, shortly after the 9/11 attacks, adopted a mission statement: "Protect the nation's transportation systems to ensure freedom of movement for people and commerce." To promote airport security, federal employees screen passengers and luggage for weapons and explosives at more than 450 airports nationwide.

prisoners at Abu Ghraib, the central prison in Baghdad, were broadcast around the world, inciting international outrage and protest. In response, Senator John McCain of Arizona, a former prisoner of war in Vietnam, led Congress to pass the Detainee Treatment Act, which barred "cruel and unusual punishment" already prohibited by the Constitution.

31.2 Social and Cultural Conflict in the Twenty-First Century

How did rising inequality shape government policy and political discourse in the decades after 2000?

At the 1992 Republican National Convention, the conservative Patrick Buchanan gave the opening speech. "There is a religious war going on in our country for the soul of America," he declared. "It is a cultural war, as critical to the kind of nation we will one day be as was the Cold War itself." Many of the issues that fueled the culture wars of the 1980s and 1990s continued to spark conflict in the twenty-first century. Reproductive rights and reproductive technology, gay rights and marriage equality, and gun control all helped to define differences between liberals and conservatives, between Democrats and Republicans. At the same time, the ongoing public debate over America's social and cultural future sharpened by encompassing issues related to growing inequality: immigration, education, poverty, and criminal justice.

31.2.1 Immigration

In October 2006, the U.S. population reached 300 million. With the expanding economy of the Clinton presidency, the nation's population during the 1990s grew by 32.7 million, a number greater than that of any other decade in U.S. history. More than a third of this growth came from the influx of new immigrants. (See Figure 31.1.) By 2011, foreign-born workers made up nearly 15 percent of the workforce, the highest percentage since the 1920s. These developments enlivened discussions about immigrants and immigration

reform, and shaped political campaigns and policy at all levels of government.

The Immigration Act of 1965 had revolutionary, if largely unintended, consequences. The act abolished the discriminatory national origins quotas that had been in place since the 1920s. It also for the first time limited immigration from the Western Hemisphere, while giving preference to people from the nations of the Eastern Hemisphere who had specialized job skills and training. This provision created the conditions for Asian immigrants to become the fastest-growing—as well as the best-educated and highest-earning—ethnic group in the United States.

Still, Asian Americans represented slightly more than 5 percent of the total population. They were an ethnically diverse group, with origins throughout East and Southeast Asia and the Indian subcontinent. Because of this diversity, and despite the common stereotype of the "model minority," wealth inequality was greater among Asian Americans than among white Americans. Emigrants from India and China found the most prestigious jobs in technology and engineering, while Filipinos worked in lower-paying health care positions.

The boom of the U.S. economy in the 1990s had also provided a significant "pull" for Hispanic newcomers, and NAFTA and the greater integration of the U.S. and Mexican economies had further encouraged immigration. By July 2015, the number of Hispanics reached

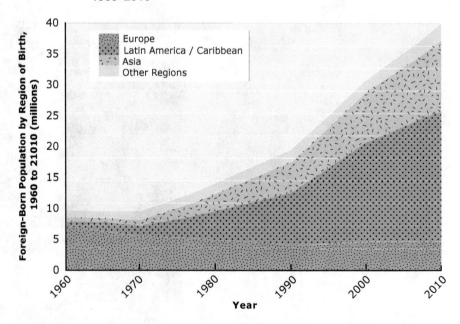

Figure 31.1 FOREIGN-BORN POPULATION BY REGION OF BIRTH: 1960–2010

Latin America and the Caribbean have been the driving force in the increasing number of immigrants to the United States in the twentieth and twenty-first centuries. Mexico and Cuba together have sent the most people, with the Philippines ranking second since 1980.

Note: Other areas include Africa, Northern America, Ocieana, born at sea, and not reported.

Source: U.S. Census Bureau, Census of Population, 1960 to 2000 and the American Community Survey, 2010.

INTERNATIONAL IMMIGRANTS DAY PARADE On June 22, 2013, marchers turned out for the twenty-eighth annual International Immigrants Day Parade along Sixth Avenue in New York City.

56.6 million, or 17.6 percent of the total U.S. population, with two-thirds tracing their origin to Mexico. More than half had settled in Texas, California, and Florida. Los Angeles had the largest Hispanic population of any county in the United States. By 2016, Hispanics made up about half of all unauthorized or "undocumented" immigrants.

Some communities took action against unauthorized immigrants. (See Communities *in* Conflict.) For example, in California in 1994, a successful ballot initiative, **Proposition 187**, denied social services, public schooling, and health care to undocumented immigrants. In 1997, a federal court ruled the California law unconstitutional on the grounds that it breached the federal government's exclusive jurisdiction over immigration. The estimated number of undocumented immigrants peaked in 2007 at nearly 12.2 million and then began to decline.

Refugees presented an even thornier problem. The U.S State Department continued to take pride in the nation's history of welcoming and resettling refugees—more than 3 million since Congress had passed the Refugee Act of 1980, which created standards for screening, admission, and resettlement. However, in the shadow of international terrorism, the influx of refugees from the war-torn Islamic nations of Iraq, Afghanistan, and Syria posed many questions and rekindled fear. Nevertheless, the United States admitted the highest number of Muslim refugees on record in 2016, nearly 39,000. Nearly one-quarter of all refugees settled in California, Texas, and New York.

The social implications of immigration were as far-reaching as political. Children born to new immigrants, despite increasing neighborhood segregation, played together, attended the same schools, and often married outside their racial groups. Between 2000 and 2012, the number of children identifying as multiracial had jumped by 50 percent, making them the fastest-growing youth group in the United States. Moreover, the children of immigrants, especially Hispanics, outperformed their parents in educational achievement. By 2012, Hispanics had become the largest minority group enrolled in college. Still, many observers worried, as did one well-respected historian, that, "The historic idea of a unifying American identity is now in peril."

31.2.2 Education

The growing racial, ethnic, and religious diversity of American society, as well as the expansion of rights for groups such as women, gays, and the disabled, sparked highly controversial educational reforms. During the final decades of the twentieth century, a broad and contentious movement known as **multiculturalism** demanded an overhaul that acknowledged the unique attributes and achievements of formerly marginalized groups and recent immigrants. Reformers advocated major changes in curricular materials,

Communities *in* Conflict

Illegal Immigrants and the Border Fence

*"No fence ever built has stopped history
and this one wouldn't either."*

The plan to build a wall to keep Mexicans from fleeing to the United States did not originate during the presidential campaign of Donald J. Trump. In 2005, the House of Representatives initiated legislation to reform U.S. immigration policy, particularly to stem a flow of illegal immigrants now thought to have brought in 12 million people, more than half from Mexico. Opinions clashed, often along party lines, on proposals for amnesty programs, "guest worker" provisions, and the sanctioning and deportation of illegal migrants. One proposal proved especially divisive: a plan to construct a huge, high-tech, double-layered fence along the 2,000-mile U.S./Mexico border, including powerful lighting, radar, cameras, and even unmanned aircraft. The Border Patrol would also be augmented by 1,500 new troops.

Politicians and experts on immigration reform heatedly debated these issues. The House ultimately passed the Border Protection, Antiterrorism, and Illegal Immigration Act of 2005, but the Senate initially refused to provide funding; only in September 2006 did the upper chamber vote $1.2 billion to construct a 700-mile fence, extending along just one-third of the 2,000-mile border separating the United States from Mexico. Senator Edward Kennedy (D-MA) voiced strong opposition, calling the new legislation "just a bumper sticker solution for a complex problem." Although most Republicans supported the measure, President George W. Bush and some legislators feared that stringent measures would stem the flow of needed workers.

The most extreme opposition came from ultraconservatives, such as the organization Let Freedom Ring, which organized a petition and fund-raising campaign to support construction of the entire fence. Meanwhile, a paramilitary anti-immigration group, the Minutemen, illegally started patrolling the border and constructing a 10-mile-long iron and steel fence. In response, the Mexican government garnered support from 27 other nations to express "deep concern regarding the decision adopted by the United States of America to build and extend a wall on its border with Mexico, considering it to be a unilateral measure that goes against the spirit of understanding."

Bill Richardson, who served in Congress for 17 years and became governor of New Mexico in 2002, spoke for many Democrats, criticizing the proposed border fence and advocating comprehensive immigration reform that would address illegal immigration from Mexico. Richardson is of Mexican American ancestry. Another viewpoint emerges in the statement of Jan C. Ting, a professor of law at Temple University and a former assistant commissioner of the U.S. Immigration and Naturalization Service, who in 2005 called for enhanced border security. Of Chinese American ancestry, Ting ran unsuccessfully for the U.S. Senate in Delaware.

- **How do the writers of these documents employ different perspectives on American history to help make their case?**

- **Do you find contrasting ideals of American patriotism and national interest here as well?**

Governor Bill Richardson Urges Comprehensive Immigration Reform (December 7, 2006)

Today, there are over 11 million illegal immigrants in the United States. Most are law abiding, except for the fact that they have entered this country illegally. And almost all have come here to work—to build a better life for themselves and their families, just as previous generations of immigrants have done.

Eleven million people living in the shadows is a huge problem, and we need to address it intelligently and thoughtfully—and urgently. If Congress fails to do so, it will only get worse, and the demagoguery about it which we have heard so much of recently will only get louder.

As the California-born son of an American father and a Mexican mother, I have known immigrants all my life and I know why they come to America. And as Governor of New Mexico I have known the problem of illegal immigration all too well—we live with this issue every day in my state.

Like it or not, these people have become part of the fabric of our economy and our culture. They have broken the law to enter our country, but they are here—there are

millions of them building and cleaning our homes and offices, picking and cooking our food, caring for our children. These men and women are here illegally, but they work hard, pay taxes, and contribute to the communities they live in.

America needs to SOLVE this problem, not tear itself apart over it. . . .

Governors must promote public safety and ensure that all residents of the state—welcome or unwelcome, legally here or not—are productive, self-supporting, and law-abiding contributors to our community. But treating illegal immigrants like human beings won't make the problem go away. We also need to face up to the problem, and that begins with better border security.

Securing the border must come first—but we must understand that building a fence will not in any way accomplish that objective. No fence ever built has stopped history and this one wouldn't either. The Congress should abandon the fence, lock, stock, and barrel. It flies in the face of America as a symbol of freedom.

This is what we should do: immediately put enough National Guard troops at the border to keep it covered until we can secure it with Border Patrol officers. That should take no longer than three years. If it takes another year, let's do it.

Second, we must hire and train enough Border Guards to actually cover the entire border. I have spent a lot of time at the border and I know we cannot secure it with a fence, but we can secure it with enough trained Border Patrol officers. I propose doubling the number of Border Patrol agents from approximately 12,000 to 24,000. That would secure the border. And you could more than pay for it with the funding for the first segment of that ill-advised fence between Mexico and the United States. Real security, real results, at a fraction of the financial or political cost.

Third, we should give the Border Patrol the benefit of the best surveillance equipment available to our military. And, as suggested by Texas Congresswoman Sheila Jackson Lee, a leader on immigration issues, we should implement a system of "informant visas" and cash rewards for aliens who provide law enforcement with information on human traffickers and document forgers.

We should establish a "fraudulent documents task force" to constantly update law enforcement and border officials on the latest fraudulent documents being marketed for entry into the United States.

Finally, we have to work closely with the Mexican government. Illegal immigration is, at its root, primarily an economic problem: Mexicans need jobs and incomes, and Mexico benefits greatly from illegal immigration to the United States. It is a safety valve for their unemployed, and a major source of revenue in their economy, from the money illegal workers here send home.

Under present conditions, the Mexicans just don't have enough incentive to give us the help we need at the border. Mexico needs to do more to stem the flow. But if we create a reasonable guest worker program and provide a path to legalization for illegal immigrants already here . . . there is every reason to expect Mexico to do its part to create more jobs in Mexico and to help us with border security. . . .

Source: Gov. Bill Richardson, "Speech on Comprehensive Immigration Reform at Georgetown University," Dec. 7, 2006. www.richardsonforpresident.com/issues/immigration.

Law Professor Jan C. Ting Considers "Immigration, National Security, and the Need for a Border Fence" (2005)

[I]t is supremely ironic that four years after 9/11 our national borders remain open and uncontrolled, and our government seems unconcerned. The simple reality is that tonight, four years after 9/11, and every night of the year, thousands of foreigners covertly enter the United States, and we have no idea who they are. Every night. Thousands. Who are they?

It's perhaps an overstatement to say we have no idea, because we do have some idea. We do catch some of them, and that provides us with a kind of sample of who is covertly crossing our borders into the U.S. in violation of our laws. But how big of a sample is it? The official estimate is that the Border Patrol catches 1 out of every 4 illegal border crossers, and this is typically the estimate public officials use in discussing the problem. Three get in for every one caught. But Border Patrol officers speaking off the record, and retired Border Patrol officials speaking for the record, say that the ratio of those getting in to those caught is much higher. . . .

Apprehensions along the southern border make up about 97–98% of the total apprehensions. Most of those apprehended near the southern border are Mexicans. . . .

Even though the number of Border Patrol apprehensions nationally and along the southern border has been fluctuating, the number of OTM's [other than Mexicans] apprehended near the southern border has been clearly and dramatically increasing from 28,598 in 2000 to 65,814 in 2004, despite a lower number of overall apprehensions in 2004. And we already have 100,142 OTM apprehensions for the first eight months of 2005. So the

word is out to the rest of the world what the Mexicans have known for years. The border is wide open, and it's easy for anyone who wants to get into the United States covertly. . . .

Can it possibly be true that, although we can put a man on the moon, although we can put a rover on Mars and hit a comet in outer space with rockets, there's nothing we can do to stop people from walking across our borders into the United States? I think there's plenty that we could do if only we had the political will to do so. And I think it's remarkable that four years after 9/11 we still don't have the political will to do so. Are we not capable of building a fence like the one the Israelis have found effective in preventing terrorists from entering Israel? We can do it. We are in fact fortifying the westernmost 14 miles of our southern border. That leaves only 2,000 miles left on our southern border to go!

The fence is the essential element in any plan to limit illegal immigration across our border. The southern border is the first priority because of the large numbers of illegal entrants compared to our northern border. But we have already had at least one terrorist enter from Canada, so we must also address northern border security once the southern border fence is complete. The fence is essential. . . . Without the fence to control illegal immigration, no reform of immigration is possible. Any reform will fail under the rising tide of illegal immigration and the dangers that accompany it.

Source: Jan C. Ting "Immigration, National Security, and the Need for a Border Fence," Sept. 9, 2005. Reprinted by permission of the author.

teaching strategies, and even staffing. They also aimed to make instruction more relevant by examining such topics as racism and economic inequality. Critics panned multiculturalism as a dangerously divisive, "politically correct" effort that sacrificed objectivity for political ends and thereby gravely compromised academic integrity. Opponents debated: Should the nation's schools provide instruction about sex and birth control, evolution versus creationism, global warming, and a host of other "hot button" issues?

These ongoing debates also addressed the impact of social divisions based on race and wealth. The U.S. Department of Education tracked an increasing gap in proficiency levels between students of color and white students over the decade ending in 2013. This discrepancy, investigators concluded, resulted principally from differences in family wealth. In 2013, 39 percent of black students and 30 percent of Hispanic students lived in poverty, compared with only 10 percent of white and Asian students. Moreover, the majority of poor black and Hispanic students attended a public school where the overwhelming majority—up to 75 percent—of their classmates came from low-income families.

Educators aimed to reverse a second and equally alarming trend: a growing achievement gap between the United States other developed nations. Addressing this issue, President George W. Bush won his earliest congressional victory with the **No Child Left Behind Act (NCLB)**. Passed by Congress with bipartisan support in 2001, the act provided for the implementation of standards for math and reading skills, and required states to test elementary students annually. NCLB depended on standardized tests and thereby changed the practice of teaching and the assessment of teacher success.

NCLB allowed parents to transfer their children out of schools that failed to meet the goals, a policy that complemented a trend toward charter and private schools. Promoted in 1988 by Alfred Shanker, president of the American Federation of Teachers, "schools of choice" operated independently of the public school system, run chiefly by local school districts or not-for-profit institutions. By 2017 the number of charter schools had grown to nearly 7,000, with enrollment topping 3 million students. While the number of charter schools grew, more than 4,000 traditional public schools closed, resulting in a significant transfer of resources from the public education system to privately managed schools. The spread of school voucher programs speeded this development by providing more parents with public tax dollars for tuition at private schools, 85 percent of which were religious.

Despite these policy changes, data did not show a significant improvement in educational achievement. By 2010, for example, the United States ranked twelfth among 37 nations in the number of young people with college degrees; by 2015, the United States ranked 38th out of 71 countries in math proficiency and 24th in science. Moreover, the number of African American and Hispanic students enrolled in impoverished public schools increased between 2001 and 2014. As a consequence, the educational gains from the civil rights arena began to contract or, in some communities, disappeared altogether. Despite increasing racial and ethnic diversity, segregation in the nation's schools had become more pronounced. Critics of this trend viewed it as a consolidation of a two-tier educational system and a major factor in magnifying inequality in the United States.

31.2.3 Poverty

In his 1964 State of the Union address, President Lyndon B. Johnson introduced the war on poverty by stating, "Our aim is not only to relieve the symptoms of poverty, but to cure it and, above all, to prevent it." Fifty years later, amid growing social inequality, poverty resurfaced as a major, controversial national problem.

The twenty-first century ushered in a period of slow economic growth capped by the recession following a major financial collapse in 2007. The unemployment

DETROIT PUBLIC SCHOOL TEACHERS In 2015, Michigan's Republican governor, Rick Snyder, called for a major overhaul of the Detroit school system while students, parents, and teachers protested the deteriorating conditions. Growing class sizes, pay and benefit cuts, and unsafe classrooms topped the list of grievances. Teachers mobilized in various ways, including bringing lawsuits against school districts, staging "sick outs," and ultimately calling for a strike, which is illegal in Michigan law.

Jim West/Alamy Stock Photo.

rate rose from 5 percent at the end of that year to over 10 percent two years later. In turn, the poverty rate rose until finally, in 2016, the U.S. Census Bureau recorded a slight improvement. The poverty rate—defined for a family of two adults and two children as an annual income of $24,339 or less—had dropped to 12.7 percent, approximately its pre-recession level in 2007. Nevertheless, one in eight Americans, or more than 40.6 million people, lived in poverty.

Estimates for childhood poverty ran high, and compared with other developed countries, the United States ranked among the worst. By 2016, as many as 15 million—21 percent of all children—lived below the poverty line. Black and Hispanic children were more likely than white children to live in "deep poverty," defined as less than 50 percent of the federal poverty level. Poverty and lack of affordable health care pushed up the maternal mortality rate to the highest in the developed world.

Economic recession and high unemployment, the shift from high-paying manufacturing jobs to service work, and increasing racial segregation were factors in the rise of urban poverty.

The South Bronx reigned as the poorest congressional district among the 50 states, with at least 40 percent of its quarter-million residents and more than half its children living in high or deep poverty. Once described as a thriving "Jewish borough," this district slid into poverty after World War II, reaching a crisis point in the 1970s when arson or abandonment destroyed 40 percent of the buildings. Nearly 300,000 mainly white residents fled. Following a program of urban renewal and the influx of federal funds for rebuilding, the South Bronx rebounded as an ethnically diverse community. The 2010 U.S. census recorded a growing population 63 percent Hispanic and 36 percent African American. The arts, especially graffiti and hip-hop, began to boom—along with gentrification, high rents, and homelessness.

Even poorer was Puerto Rico, with more than 46 percent of its population living in poverty in 2015. The financial crisis of 2007 had nearly destroyed the local economy, the country's debt hit $70 billion, and the unemployed rate reached more than twice the national average. In addition to the struggle to pay for basic necessities, Puerto Ricans suffered from an epidemic of the mosquito-born Zika virus, which can be passed from a pregnant woman to her fetus and cause serious birth defects. In 2017, a powerful hurricane swept the island and destroyed much of the infrastructure, including power and water supplies. Many residents left for the mainland, causing a population decline projected into the indefinite future.

The nation's rural communities bore the brunt of deep poverty. In Appalachia, historically one of the poorest regions, more than a quarter of the population was too poor to afford homes with adequate plumbing or even kitchens or telephones. Kentucky claimed the three poorest counties in the United States. The collapse of the major extractive industries—coal, timber, and oil—left few replacements in their wake. In Beattyville, classified by the U.S. census as the poorest white town in the nation, residents faced a small downtown of shuttered shops and equally bleak prospects for themselves and their children. One-third of the adult residents had failed to complete high school, and town's median household income was less than one-quarter of the national average in 2012. With half of all families living below the poverty line, Beattyville residents were poorer than they were in 1980. Adding to these disadvantages was a drug crisis not atypical of rural America: opioids, or what residents called "hillbilly heroin."

31.2.4 Criminal Justice

One consequence of growing social inequality showed in the U.S. prison population, which grew fivefold from the 1960s to become the largest in the world, with the second-highest adult incarceration rate anywhere. By 2017, a heavily decentralized prison system ranging from local jails, juvenile correction facilities, and state and federal prisons to military, Indian, and various detention centers held an estimated 2.3 million people. Another 3.7 million people remained on probation, many of them destined to return to the system.

The prison population grew in step with changes in federal policy. As early as the 1960s, funds began

THE SOUTH BRONX, 1977 This image captures the consequences of unemployment, crime, and poverty in the South Bronx in the late 1970s.

to shift from antipoverty programs to crime prevention, to larger police forces and many new prisons, including privately run for-profit prisons. In 1984, Hamilton County, Tennessee, set a precedent by contracting a private firm to run its prisons. Since then, Corrections Corporation of America, renamed CoreCivic, had taken over more than 65 state or federal detention centers.

These law-and-order policies extended to cover a range of nonviolent offenses. The Reagan administration's war on drugs had widened the net for arrests and established lengthier sentences for offenses involving illegal drugs, including marijuana. A majority of incarcerated juveniles had likewise committed nonviolent crimes, mainly probation breaches or truancy. Violations of immigration laws sent thousands to federal prisons or to detention centers operated by the U.S. Immigration and Customs Enforcement (ICE). Women prisoners—nearly three-quarters of them mentally ill, and a majority with past incidences of physical or sexual abuse—went to jail at soaring rates, up 81 percent since 1980. Mainly, they had committed nonviolent drug and property crimes. However, men continued to represent the overwhelming majority: 90 percent of the imprisoned population in 2017. At the time, nearly half of all inmates were serving sentences for drug offenses.

African Americans and Hispanics, together a third of the U.S. population, constituted more than half of the prison population. Despite a use of illegal drugs at rates similar to that of whites, they experienced five to six times the rates of whites' arrest and imprisonment rates. One in three black men faced imprisonment during his lifetime, according to Bureau of Justice estimates. Among black children, one in nine had a parent in jail at some point.

Long sentences; deteriorating conditions including severe crowding, especially in privately run facilities; and abusive guard practices propelled protests by minorities in particular, both within and outside the nation's prisons. Hunger and labor strikes broke out in nearly 30 prisons in at least 12 states in 2016, involving more than 24,000 inmates. The largest round of prison protests in U.S. history also marked the 45th anniversary of the Attica, New York, prison uprising, a painful anniversary that drew further attention to bad conditions and prisoners' rights. (See Figure 31.2.)

The upsurge in mass incarceration inspired scholars and activists to look critically at the criminal justice system. The popular performer and longtime civil rights activist Harry Belafonte, at age 90, dubbed mass incarceration "the new slavery." Best-selling author and scholar Michelle Alexander labeled this trend "the new Jim Crow"—that is, a system of social control and discrimination that systematically denied African Americans their basic civil rights. A sizable network of several thousand black churches sought to inspire a "moral conscience" to end mass incarceration, while other activists advocated a major policy shift from incarceration to drug treatment.

In 2013, **Black Lives Matter (BLM)** organized to protest inequities in the criminal justice system. They focused on

Figure 31.2 INTERNATIONAL RATES OF INCARCERATION PER 100,000

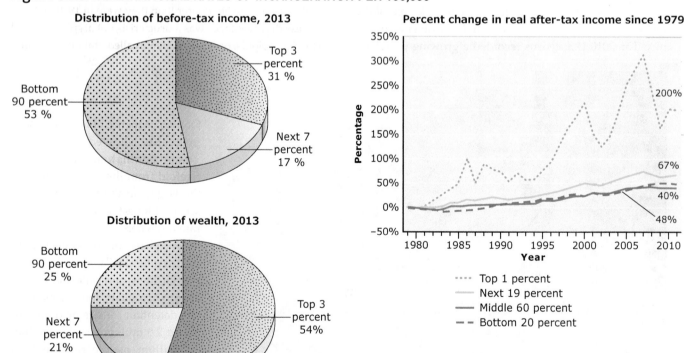

In 2017 the American criminal justice system held in confinement more than 2.3 million people, giving the United States the highest rate of incarceration worldwide. One in five people held was locked up for a drug-related offense.

Source: Walmsley, R. (2016), *World Prison Brief*. London: Institute for Criminal Policy Research. Available online: http://www.prisonstudies.org/world-prison-brief.

BLACK LIVES MATTER, LONDON, 2016 By 2016 the Black Lives Matter movement had a global reach and had extended its activities beyond street protests to intervention in political campaigns.

Mark Kerrison/Alamy Stock Photo.

police brutality directed disproportionately against black men. They pointed out that of the 1,307 people who were killed by police in that year, African Americans outnumbered white Americans by nearly three times. Concurrently, police officers were indicted in fewer than 1 percent of these incidences.

Community organizers Alicia Garza, Patrisse Cullas, and Opal Tometi built an internet-driven movement, *#Black Lives Matter*. They were motivated by the acquittal of George Zimmerman, a white Floridian who had shot to death an unarmed black teen, Trayvon Martin. Over the next year, a decentralized movement grew quickly, especially after a Ferguson, Missouri, police officer shot and killed Michael Brown, like Martin an unarmed black man. In response, BLM activists encouraged thousands of protesters to join them. They were met by well-armed police who used tear gas and pepper spray to disperse the crowds. After several more high-profile police shootings in quick succession, BLM grew to claim more than 40 chapters worldwide.

31.3 Challenges to the Environment

How did responses to environmental disasters reflect racial and social inequality?

"For so many years, talking about the weather was talking about nothing. Now it really is survival," wrote poet and naturalist Terry Tempest Williams in September 2017, as news of monstrous hurricanes in Texas, Puerto Rico, and Florida captured the headlines. Secretary of Defense James Mattis had agreed, acknowledging climate change as a major security issue for U.S. interests at home and abroad that contributed to natural disasters, regional conflicts over resources such as food and water, and the flow of refugees. The quality of the natural environment propelled heated discussions among scientists and politicians who sought to identify major problems and potential solutions.

31.3.1 Climate Change

In 1997, nearly 200 nations signed the Kyoto Protocol to address climate change. After years of negotiations, delegates agreed on a set of goals and timetables for reducing greenhouse emissions from carbon-based fuels, the main cause of global warming according to the scientific consensus at the time. Set to go into effect in 2005, the Kyoto Protocol exempted developing countries, including China and India, because their contribution to the volume of gases at the time had been relatively small. The United States, the largest producer of greenhouse gas in the world, signed the protocol in 1998, but then failed to ratify it. The U.S. Senate held back, fearing harm to the American economy if developing nations received a temporary waiver. Most Republicans additionally charged that environmental regulations were "job killers" that threatened the competitive status of the United States in the world economy.

Some nations, notably in Europe, raced to meet the targets and promised far more drastic reductions in the use of fossil fuels in the decades ahead. Technological advances in "green technology"—solar, wind, thermal, and bio-energy—speeded the installation of equipment in retrofitted and new residential and commercial buildings. Meanwhile, despite conservative voting patterns, Texas and other Sun Belt states achieved some of the highest levels of solar adaptation and use. Nevertheless, by 2012 the results still were falling far short of the goals. Emissions in China and the United States had grown so rapidly as to undo any global progress. "In cumulative terms, we certainly own this problem more than anybody else does," warned David G. Victor, an American expert in climate politics.

Others disagreed. Called "climate deniers" or "climate change skeptics" by their critics, they enlivened the controversy that roiled American politics. President George W. Bush encouraged Republicans to halt or delay governmental action on climate-related issues. His administration relied upon its own experts, who doubted the causal relationship between human activity and climate change. Meanwhile, his opponent in the 2000 presidential campaign, Al Gore, published *An Inconvenient Truth: The Planetary Emergency of Global Warming and What We Can Do About It*, which became a best-selling book and popular documentary film. This opposition played out in the national media, with the nation's four leading newspapers giving equal coverage to both sides of the debate.

Within the scientific community, however, doubts wilted in light of record temperatures, retreating glaciers, rising sea levels, and extreme weather events. Studies of peer-reviewed journals showed that 97 percent of actively publishing scholars agreed that climate change was a real phenomenon resulting from human activities. The majority of scientists additionally concluded that the rate of change was faster than assumed when the Kyoto Protocol was signed.

31.3.2 "Storm of the Century"

Meteorologists used the descriptive "Storm of the Century" to describe a powerful, deadly storm in 1993 that brought tremendous snowfall, high winds, and freezing temperatures from Alabama to Maine. As extreme weather events became increasingly commonplace, however, the phrase proved inadequate to label huge storms that came just years apart. The media substituted "superstorm." Extreme weather events resulted, NASA scientists speculated, from rising temperatures over land and sea that sent more and more moisture into the atmosphere, making superstorms, if not more common, more intense. (See Figure 31.3.)

Hurricane Katrina, making landfall on August 25, 2005, pushed climate change to the center of media reporting and political controversy. The third-strongest storm to that point in U.S. history, Katrina hit sections of Florida, destroying

Figure 31.3 BILLION-DOLLAR DISASTER EVENT TYPES BY YEAR (CPI-ADJUSTED)

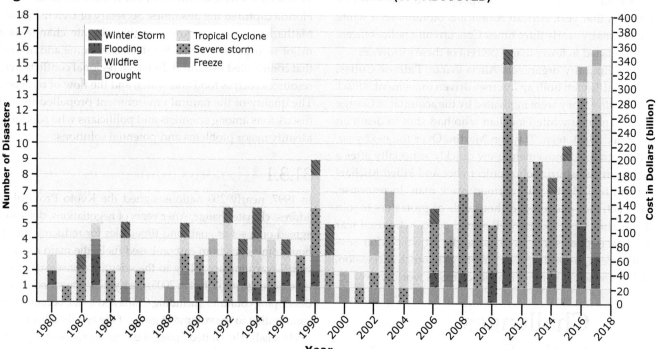

The National Centers for Environmental Information (NCEI) keeps track of severe weather and climate events over time. Since 1980, 219 such disasters—including Hurricanes Harvey, Irma, and Maria in 2017—have cost the nation more than $1.5 trillion in recovery. Notable is the increasing frequency of such events since 2011.

Source: National Centers for Environmental Information (https://www.ncdc.noaa.gov/billions/time-series).

thousands of homes and businesses. The storm then moved ominously toward the Gulf of Mexico and rapidly became a catastrophe for hundreds of thousands of residents in and around New Orleans. It also proved a political catastrophe for the Bush administration, which appeared ill-prepared to deal with the devastation.

A former reporter for the *Boston Globe*, Ross Gelbspan, wrote an op-ed asserting the Hurricane Katrina's "real name is global warming." He claimed that what began as a small storm became "supercharged" while passing over the "relatively blistering" surface temperatures of the Gulf of Mexico. Gelbspan linked Hurricane Katrina to other extreme weather events, including an unexpected blizzard in Los Angeles in the preceding year.

On October 29, 2012, "Superstorm Sandy" came ashore in the United States after a particularly damaging assault on the Caribbean island of Jamaica. Hundreds of people died in its path, and Sandy ranked as the second-most costly hurricane in U.S. history to that point. In New York State alone, more than 2 million customers lost power, the New York Stock Exchange closed for several days, and the East River overflowed, flooding Lower Manhattan, including hundreds of miles of the subways. Regarded as the most destructive storm in New York history, Sandy swept away oceanside sections of neighborhoods in Queens, Brooklyn, and Staten Island, as well as in New Jersey. Scientists attributed much of its power to unusually warm sea-surface temperatures along the East Coast of the United States, which were about 5 degrees above average.

Five years later, in late August 2017, when Hurricane Harvey struck Texas, the relationship between climate change and superstorms resurfaced to drive discussions among scientists and politicians alike. The National Weather Service warned, "This event is unprecedented & all impacts are unknown & beyond anything experienced . . . " Harvey produced the highest rainfall total of any tropical storm to hit the United States.

In the wake of Harvey, vast pools of water covered cities and suburbs that had grown up in recent decades, especially in and around Houston, where wetlands had been replaced by housing and business developments and miles of paving. Many residents feared for their lives and then worried about their homes. Flood insurance had grown too expensive, and federal disaster relief proved far too small for the scale of the destruction. Large chemical- and oil-processing facilities flooded, their contents gushing out into the flood water and from there to the Gulf, with unknowable future effects.

Worse storms lay just ahead. On September 10, 2017, Hurricane Irma struck the American Virgin Islands, Puerto Rico, and Florida, moving inland with flooding that exceeded any previous regional storm. The temporary displacement of millions of residents, magnified by billions of dollars of damage to residences, raised a question mark over the future of

vulnerable areas, including some of the most highly valued real estate in the nation. One week later Hurricane Maria tore through the Caribbean, inflicting yet more catastrophic damage on the U.S. Virgin Islands and Puerto Rico.

31.3.3 Environmental Justice

The circumstances surrounding climate change also reflected the growing inequality in the United States. Rich and poor did not suffer alike. A senior citizen on a fixed income in Dade County, Florida, one of the approximately half-million living there in poverty in 2017, told reporters that he could not afford to evacuate in advance of Hurricane Irma, or to stock up on supplies.

In 2005, this scenario had played out dramatically in the aftermath of Hurricane Katrina. The canal levees had failed, submerging much of New Orleans. The news media seemed to recognize more quickly than federal officials that the city, with a poverty rate approaching 80 percent and two-thirds of its citizens nonwhite, could not withstand the blows. Although local authorities called for evacuation and opened the huge Superdome football arena as a "refuge of last resort," many residents could not escape, simply because they lacked cars. Photographers captured wrenching images of white residents fleeing on the highways while many African Americans were left stranded on rooftops and waiting for rescue. Six days after the hurricane struck, news cameras captured video of dozens of African

HURRICANE KATRINA Hurricane Katrina forced more than a million residents from their homes in the Gulf area. The news media projected images of the many African American victims and enlivened debates about public policy decisions. "We have an amazing tolerance for black pain," the Reverend Jesse Jackson remarked, and charged that race was "at least a factor" in the slow response to the emergency in black neighborhoods. A national poll taken a week after the storm showed that among African Americans, two-thirds reported they believed that "the government's response to the situation would have been faster if most of the victims had been white."

PJF Military Collection/Alamy Stock Photo.

Americans seeking to escape rising flood waters by crossing the Danziger Bridge while city police wielding assault rifles tried to keep them from entering the mainly white neighborhood on the other side. Six of those attempting to flee were shot, two fatally.

The racial dimension of the responses to Hurricane Katrina provided fuel to a burgeoning environmental justice movement. Activists traced their origins back to 1982, when the North Carolina state government chose Warren County, a poor and primarily African American region, as a dump site for 6,000 truckloads of toxic soil. Residents, fearing for the safety of their drinking water, sought to halt the plan. When petitioning failed, they placed their bodies in the path of the trucks headed toward the new hazardous landfill. After weeks of protest and hundreds of arrests, the residents lost their battle. Nevertheless, media coverage helped them launch a national movement. Finally, in 1994, President Bill Clinton directed federal agencies to examine the environmental impact of policies specifically on poor and minority communities, including the location of hazardous sites such as waste disposal, factories, and power plants as well as infrastructure projects such as highways and airports.

Two decades later, in 2014, environmental justice activists rallied again to address the lead poisoning of the mostly African American residents of Flint, Michigan. To save money, government officials had changed the source of the city's water supply from the Detroit River and Lake Huron to the polluted Flint River and then failed to provide sufficient treatment. Eventually, the governor and then the president declared states of emergency. The National Guard began to distribute clean water, and criminal charges were filed against several government employees. By January 2017, lead levels had dropped to comply with federal standards, but so much damage had been done to the pipes that the water remained unsafe to drink.

In early 2016, a grassroots effort aimed to halt the construction of the 1,772-mile-long Dakota Access Pipeline, designed to transport oil from the Bakken fields in western North Dakota to southern Illinois. In light of previous pipeline spills, environmentalists opposed the plan. Members of the Standing Rock tribe, further, considered the pipeline a threat to not only the region's water supply, but also to their ancestral burial grounds. The tribe's preservation officer complained, "The U.S. government is wiping out our most important cultural and spiritual areas. And as it erases our footprint from the world, it erases us as a people." Hundreds of other tribes and tens of thousands of pipelines resisters joined the protest, with up to 4,000 camping out at the site. The highly publicized protest and lawsuits levied by the tribe against the federal government delayed the project. Shortly after taking office, President Trump signed a memorandum allowing construction to proceed. In February 2017 police cleared the camp.

31.4 Barack Obama and the Audacity of Hope

What challenges did Barack Obama face during his presidency?

On January 20, 2009, Barack Hussein Obama became the first African American to take the presidential oath of office. Running on a platform promising change, Obama had inspired many Americans—especially the young, people of color, and first-time voters—to get involved in his quest for the White House. The election took place against the backdrop of the Great Recession, the nation's worst economic downturn since the Great Depression of the 1930s, raising fundamental questions about the strength and the future of the nation's economy.

31.4.1 The Election of 2008

Born in 1961 to a Kenyan father and a white Kansan mother, Obama had grown up in Hawai'i. After graduating from Columbia University in 1983, he moved to Chicago, where he worked for five years as a community organizer. He moved on to Harvard Law School, graduating in 1991, and then returned to Chicago to work as a civil rights attorney and lecturer at the University of Chicago Law School.

Obama made the leap into electoral politics in 1996 and won election to the Illinois State Senate. In 2002, while still a state senator, he began to attract national attention for his vocal opposition to the American invasion of Iraq. In 2004 Obama became only the third African American elected to the U.S. Senate since Reconstruction. He launched his campaign for the presidency barely two years later.

Obama had a carefully thought-out electoral strategy that relied heavily on his experiences as a community organizer. He focused on registering new voters, especially among the young and people of color. Although his policy positions largely resembled those of mainstream liberal Democrats—reform of health care, more funding for education, and new public investment in infrastructure, for example—he carefully framed his appeals to attract independent voters and even Republicans disgruntled with the Bush presidency. His primary opponent, Hillary Clinton (D-NY), was also an accomplished attorney and liberal Democrat. A former first lady, a savvy campaigner and fundraiser, and an influential U.S. Senator, Clinton appealed to many Democrats as a pioneer for women in politics.

Obama clinched the Democratic nomination in June, and then he and his running mate, Senator Joseph R. Biden Jr. (D-DE), took to the campaign trail. Obama's network of organizers turned out huge crowds wherever Obama appeared and raised record-breaking sums, mainly from individual donors. They also used internet social media to reach prospective voters under age 30. The campaign slogans "Change We Can Believe In" and "Yes We Can" reaffirmed Obama's basic message—"the audacity of hope"—and created what many observers believed was a genuine political movement that would persist past Election Day.

The Republican campaign generated no less excitement. Senator John McCain (R-AZ), who had lost his 2000 bid for the nomination to George W. Bush, compared his military credentials and long experience with Obama's thin résumé. Yet McCain's judgment appeared suspect when he announced his surprise pick for vice president, Alaska Governor Sarah Palin. Palin, a mother of five and a social conservative with working-class roots, excited the Republican base and instantly became a national celebrity. A series of televised interviews exposed her uninformed, at times embarrassing grasp of foreign policy and raised serious doubts among many, including some high-level Republicans.

In November, Obama won the election with the biggest margin in 20 years. He took the electoral college, 365 to 173, and the popular vote by nearly 10 million. Observers noted that Obama's victory reversed several long-standing trends. He secured young voters, Latinos, unmarried women, and suburbanites. He also attracted a higher percentage of white voters than either John Kerry in 2004 or Al Gore in 2000, helping him to carry several states, such as Virginia and North Carolina, that had not gone Democratic in decades. But the nation's broken economy also contributed greatly to Obama's victory.

31.4.2 The Great Recession

By late 2007, the global economy was declining sharply to sink, one year later, into deep recession. In the United States, the immediate cause was the burst of the "real estate bubble" that had artificially inflated the values of houses. Approximately 80 percent recent mortgages had been contracted by risky borrowers who had been nevertheless encouraged by the banks to buy with little or no money down and to take subprime or adjustable-rate mortgages. When housing prices slid downward and interest rates moved up, many of these new homeowners could not make their payments, or they realized that the money they still owed on their mortgages far exceeded the market value of their homes, putting them "under water." Hundreds of thousands defaulted on their loans, and the lending agencies took over their properties.

After the real estate market collapsed, the largest financial institutions were left with mortgage-backed stocks and bonds that were nearly worthless. As a result, leading banks, investment houses, and insurance companies faced insolvency. In the fall of 2008, the bankruptcy of Bear Stearns and Lehman Brothers, two of Wall Street's wealthiest investment

banks, shocked the international financial markets. So did the near-collapse of American International Group (AIG), one of the world's biggest insurers.

In its final months, the Bush administration worked frantically to stabilize the financial system, eventually pushing through Congress an unprecedented bailout package. A recalcitrant Congress agreed to pass this legislation only after the biggest one-day decline in the stock market since the crash of 1987. Despite the infusion of funds, banks continued to collapse. Businesses quickly responded by cutting payrolls.

Much of the final phase of the election campaign focused on the economic crisis and helped to give Obama an edge over his Republican opponent. While McCain remained aloof from the tense, high-stakes negotiations going on in Washington, Obama dived into the public debates over how to rescue the economy. By the time he took office in January 2009, however, there was no time for basking in his victory. Wall Street's woes had spread to Main Street, and the recession was deepening. The unemployment rate neared 10 percent, a 16-year high, with more than 11 million Americans unemployed.

31.4.3 Obama Takes Office

President Obama pushed through Congress in February 2009 the largest stimulus package in U.S. history. While Bush's legislative bill had made capital available to big financial institutions, the $787 billion American Recovery and Reinvestment Act targeted ordinary Americans. It combined tax breaks with spending on infrastructure projects, extensions of welfare and unemployment benefits, and education. The Obama administration hoped to jump-start recovery, although many economists warned that the funds allocated were insufficient.

Recovery proved hard to measure. By early 2010, nearly one in four American homeowners found themselves underwater. Millions could not make payments and faced foreclosure on their houses. The stock market crash had wiped out large portions of retirement savings, and many older Americans put off retirement. Many colleges and universities, their endowments cut by one-third or more, raised tuition, putting higher education out of reach for many Americans. Whole industries, such as auto making, continued to teeter on the brink of bankruptcy, and the unemployment rate topped 10 percent. Moreover, Obama faced a fierce Republican opposition. His stimulus bill had passed without a single Republican vote in the House and only three in the Senate. Obama's plan to close the notorious Guantanamo Bay detention camp and relocate its 250 terror suspects also ran into enormous congressional opposition, and the prison remained open.

In foreign policy, Obama acted more successfully to achieve his campaign promises, including ending the unilateral actions that had made President Bush unpopular with many other heads of state. To help reach this goal, he named his primary rival, Hillary Clinton, as secretary of state. While agreeing with Obama that there was "a lot of damage to repair," Clinton also supported his boldest moves in foreign policy, which departed less from Bush-era policies than anticipated.

Obama himself took on the difficult job of restoring America's standing on the global stage. In June 2009, he traveled to Cairo, Egypt, where he called for "a new beginning between the United States and Muslims around the world; one based upon mutual interest and mutual respect; and one based upon the truth that America and Islam are not exclusive, and need not be in competition." The speech, and the largely positive reaction to it, placed the United States in a brighter diplomatic light—if only temporarily.

Renewing his campaign promise, President Obama announced a process for a gradual troop drawdown from Iraq. By summer 2010, Obama had removed all combat troops, leaving roughly 50,000 military personnel as training forces. Then, in December 2011, the last convoy of U.S. soldiers pulled out, signaling an end to the nine-year war with Iraq.

During his campaign, Obama had also pledged to expand the war in Afghanistan. President Bush's failure to capture Osama bin Laden and the revival of the Taliban had once again made that country a haven for al-Qaeda and other terrorist groups. In December 2009, the president announced a new plan, a "surge" of 30,000 additional troops to Afghanistan. This announcement came as he prepared to accept the Nobel Peace Prize, which was awarded to him for his extraordinary role in international diplomacy. While the Afghanistan war intensified, President Obama ordered a covert operation that culminated in the killing of bin Laden in Pakistan on May 2, 2011.

By early 2012, polls indicated that support of the Afghanistan war was collapsing. A majority of Americans reported that the war did not make them feel safer from terrorist threats. Obama himself scaled down his objectives and announced that he no longer considered the conflict there "a war of necessity." In May 2012 he outlined a plan to withdraw U.S. troops by 2014, and in, September he announced the end of the Afghan surge.

On several domestic issues, Obama signaled new directions. The first bill he signed into law, the Lilly Ledbetter Fair Pay Act, allowed workers more time to sue employers over unequal pay. He issued an executive order lifting Bush-era restrictions on funding for international aid groups that facilitated abortions. He overturned a ban on federal funding for stem cell research and ramped up public spending for research on Parkinson's and other diseases. He supported some $30 billion in bridge loans to help automakers General Motors and Chrysler emerge from bankruptcy. For his first Supreme Court nomination, Obama chose Sonia Sotomayor, who became the first ever Latino Supreme Court justice in 2009. His second appointment, former Harvard Law School Dean Elena Kagan, was sworn in the next year.

Obama's biggest legislative challenge was health care reform. Health care represented more than 17 percent of the nation's GDP, yet roughly one in seven Americans lacked health insurance and access to regular medical care. Deep partisan divisions in Congress halted efforts to create a system of universal health insurance similar to Medicare. The **Patient Protection and Affordable Care Act**, the compromise bill that Obama signed in March 2010, would cover 32 million uninsured Americans—many with the help of government subsidies—and would bar insurers from denying coverage to people with preexisting medical conditions and from placing lifetime dollar limits on policies. But with no government-run "public option" to compete with private insurers, the legislation itself reformed some insurance industry practices but did not overhaul the delivery of patient care. Still, not a single Republican in either the House or Senate supported the bill: They considered it an unwarranted expansion of federal power.

BARACK OBAMA GREETS TROOPS IN AFGHANISTAN In 2012, as the next presidential election approached, approximately 68,000 troops still remained in violence-stricken Afghanistan, and more than 2,000 Americans had died there.

Everett Collection Historical/Alamy Stock Photo.

The political fallout was immense. The extremely contentious debate over health care reform epitomized how sharply the two parties, and Americans, were divided. The fundamental split centered on the role of the federal government in American life. Should it be seen as an active agent for improving the lives of ordinary people, or had it become a bloated and wasteful barrier to progress and prosperity?

31.4.4 Republican Resurgence

While Democrats retained a slim majority in the Senate after the 2010 midterm elections, Republicans seized control of the House of Representatives, with disastrous consequences for the Obama administration. During the campaign, Senate Minority Leader Mitch McConnell (R-KY) summed up the goal of his party; "The single most important thing we want to achieve is for President Obama to be a one-term president." Republicans, interpreting their midterm gains as a repudiation of Obama's policies, regrouped to defeat his legislative initiatives. Over the next term, Congress voted 33 times to repeal Obama's signature legislation, the Affordable Care Act.

The 2010 midterm elections presented the Tea Party a major victory. A loose affiliation of local and national groups, the Tea Party had dedicated itself since 2009 to supporting candidates who advocated a strongly conservative agenda. Well-funded by groups such as FreedomWorks and Americans for Prosperity, the latter richly endowed by the billionaire brothers David H. Koch and Charles Koch, the Tea Party pushed Republicans to embrace—without compromise—limited government and lower taxes. Moreover, all but 13 Republican members of Congress signed Grover Norquist's "Taxpayer Protection Pledge," vowing to oppose all proposed tax increases. Obama's hopes for bipartisan cooperation foundered on the shoals of the 112th U.S. Congress, one of the least productive in modern history.

Republicans and Democrats squared off on the problem of the large, unsustainable federal deficit. The report of Obama's bipartisan Presidential Commission, released in December 2010, recommended both spending cuts and increases in revenue, but failed to secure enough support for a successful measure. Congress instead passed the compromise Tax Relief Act of 2010, which basically renewed—but only for two years—the across-the-board tax cuts that had been enacted during President Bush's administration. Democrats and Republicans continued to spar relentlessly over possible mediations, and Congress

"OBAMACARE" President Obama signing the Patient Protection and Affordable Care Act in March 2010. Nicknamed "Obamacare," it represented the most ambitious overhaul of America's health care system since the enactment of Medicare in 1965.

Jewel Samad/Getty Images.

ultimately stalled, earning for itself the lowest approval rate ever.

The impact of the Republican resurgence was even greater at the state level. The 2010 midterm elections awarded 17 states to Republican governors and gave Republicans the largest number of state legislative seats since the Great Depression. Having run on promises to eradicate the budget deficits in their states, Republican governors sponsored severe austerity measures, cutting funds for education and numerous social programs. They also advanced a broad conservative agenda, turning back federal funds for high-speed rail, amending state constitutions to forestall same-sex marriage, restricting the collective bargaining rights of public employees, strengthening anti-immigration policies, weakening child labor laws, tightening voting rights, expanding the right to carry concealed weapons, reducing consumer and environmental protections, and allowing schools to teach creationism or intelligent design as an alternative to evolution. So many new laws restricting women's reproductive rights were passed that by spring 2012, critics charged Republican state legislators with waging a "war on women."

The Republican agenda ignited the largest round of mass demonstrations since the antiwar movement of the late 1960s. In several states, protesters turned out by the hundreds of thousands to express their opposition to the proposed legislation. Some mobilized to attempt to recall state legislators and, in the case of Wisconsin, the new Republican governor, Scott Walker.

The most widespread anti-austerity outpouring was **Occupy Wall Street (OWS)**, which began on September 17, 2011, in Zuccotti Park, in the financial district of New York

City. Thousands of people gathered daily and hundreds camped in tents to focus attention on the steadily growing income gap and the concentration of wealth among a tiny minority of Americans. Popularizing the slogan "We Are the 99%," OWS spread to more than 600 communities in the United States and across more than 80 countries worldwide. By the end of the year, police had shut down most encampments, and Republican legislators had refused to yield, but the reality of economic inequality had forcefully struck home for many Americans.

31.4.5 The 2012 Election

Democrats and Republicans prepared for the 2012 election season by staking out positions on two major issues: the economy and the federal deficit. The U.S. economy had barely inched toward recovery, and stagnation took its toll on the prospects of many Americans. Median family income had fallen since 2000, making the "American dream" of upward mobility unattainable and increasingly unimaginable for much of the middle-class majority. The unemployment rate stubbornly hovered around 9 percent. The poverty rate rose to 16 percent, including 22 percent of all children. In former manufacturing centers, such as Detroit, Cleveland, Cincinnati, and Buffalo, the poverty rate reached upward of 30 percent. Even in regions that showed some recovery, such as New York City, the number of union jobs continued to plummet, indicating that the new jobs created since the recession began in 2008 were in the low-wage service sector. While, in general, Democrats responded by proposing spending programs to "simulate" economic growth, Republicans outlined plans to improve the business climate by lowering taxes and cutting back on government regulations.

The Democratic Party, at its national convention, again endorsed President Obama and Vice President Joe Biden. The Republican Party ultimately winnowed a large field of 10 potential candidates and nominated former Massachusetts Governor Willard "Mitt" Romney for president and a congressional representative from Wisconsin, Paul Ryan, as his running mate. Romney, the first member of the Church of Jesus Christ of Latter-day Saints to be nominated for president, touted his business experience as a major credential. He headed a platform that proclaimed the 2012 election "a referendum on the future of liberty in America."

The two presidential candidates polled neck-and-neck until the final days before the election. Romney, however, lost ground following the release of a secretly recorded video featuring him speaking candidly at a private fundraiser and dismissing Americans too poor to pay income taxes. That 47 percent of the population would vote for Obama, he said disdainfully, and "believe that they are victims . . . And so my job is not to worry about those people. I'll never convince them that they should take personal responsibility and care for their lives." Although both candidates told voters that the economy was their major concern, the social issues central to the "culture wars" of the 1990s—gay rights, reproductive rights, and the role of women in society—came back into play. Other major issues, such as the war in Afghanistan and climate change, surfaced infrequently during the hotly contested campaign. Combined, the two parties established new records in campaign financing, which totaled approximately $2 billion.

After the votes were tallied, the Obama/Biden ticket won the day. Exit polls indicated that the economy was foremost on the minds of voters. In the Senate, Democrats expanded their majority, 55 to 45, while Republicans retained control of the House of Representatives. Seven of eleven gubernatorial races went to the Democrats.

With partisan differences as sharp as they were before the election, and both parties interpreting the results as a validation of their own policies, Obama began his second term on January 20, 2013, with only a slight prospect of getting beyond the legislative impasse. Nevertheless, in his inaugural address, he presented a liberal agenda. He pledged to hold fast to the commitment to Medicare, Medicaid, and Social Security; to address the problem of gun violence; to overhaul immigration policy; and to address climate change. The Republican majority in the House of Representatives, however, blocked most of Obama's initiatives.

The 2014 midterm elections further consolidated Republican power, enlarging their majority in the House of Representatives and turning over the Senate to their majority rule. The GOP also scored decisive victories in the nation's state houses. Not since the 1920s had the Republicans enjoyed as much political power as they did at the opening of the 114th Congress in 2015.

Obama left office with many of his most avid supporters gravely disappointed by his failure to achieve more. Despite his pledge to nurture hope and bring change, economic inequality had continued to entrench itself and now stood at the center of American politics.

31.5 Populism and the Politics of Inequality

How did growing economic and social inequality reshape American politics in 2016?

The 2016 presidential election featured the interplay of two very different versions of "populism," both challenging the established leadership of the two major parties. Senator Bernie Sanders (I-VT) challenged his centrist Democratic primary opponent, Hillary Clinton, from the left before being defeated for the nomination. Republican presidential candidate Donald J. Trump also promised to upset political norms in the name of the working poor, but appealed to the white Americans who felt pushed aside by African Americans and immigrants. The disconnect between Trump's victory in the Electoral College and the popular vote, which he lost by more than 3 million, signaled a political division as deep as at any time since the Civil War.

31.5.1 Widening Economic Inequality

The long-range trend toward widening economic inequality was clear. In 1980, the share of national income going to the bottom 50 percent of earners was 20 percent; by 2014 their share had collapsed to 12.5 percent. During the same period, the share of income going to the top 1 percent grew from 10.7 percent to 20.2 percent. In 1980 adults in the top 1 percent earned on average 27 times more than the bottom 50 percent of adults; by 2014 they earned 81 times more. (See Figure 31.4.) The recovery following the recession of 2008–2009 widened these gaps. Studies revealed that between 2009 and 2013, 85 percent of all income growth went to the top 1 percent, defined as families making at least $389,000 annually. The stagnation of the bottom 50 percent of incomes and the contrasting rise in the top 1 percent coincided with several developments since the early 1980s,

including tax breaks tilted toward the top income earners, widespread deregulation of industries and services (especially in the financial sector), loss of manufacturing jobs to both automation and foreign competitors, dwindling union membership, and an eroding minimum wage.

By 2016 the decades-long trend toward greater economic inequality had become impossible to ignore. Business and employment opportunities were concentrated as never before in a shrinking number of metropolises. The economy in large parts of America, particularly in rural areas and small towns, had been hollowed out, with little prospect for new jobs or future growth.

In 2017 the Economic Innovation Group, an advocacy group dedicated to investors, documented the growing economic inequality in an attempt to map the dimensions of basic community well-being. The group published a Distressed Communities Index (DCI) that reported that one-fifth of U.S. ZIP Codes, which included more than 50 million people, met the criteria for the designation. The South, with 37 percent of the country's population, represented 53 percent of U.S. residents living in distressed ZIP Codes. Equally important, the DCI report indicated that the country's most prosperous and most distressed communities were pulling apart, especially since the Great Recession. The Southeast

---

Figure 31.4 GROWING INCOME INEQUALITY IN THE UNITED STATES

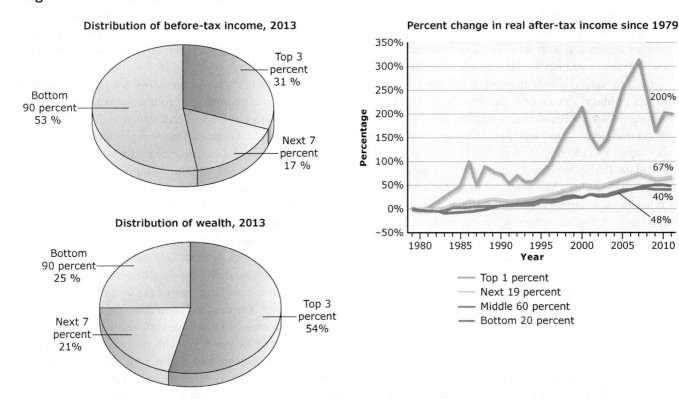

Since the 1970s, income inequality among Americans has grown to such an extent that the United States now has the greatest degree of inequality of all developed countries. The biggest gains were made by those in the top 1 percent of earners, who in 2013 held 40 percent of all the nation's wealth. Most Americans say they wish wealth were more fairly distributed, and further, they believe it is more equally distributed than it actually is.

showed the starkest gap between rural distress and metropolitan prosperity. Lack of a high school degree, unemployment, low median income, vacant properties, and poverty fed this deepening inequality.

31.5.2 A Tale of Two Populisms

While scattered protests, such as the Occupy Wall Street campaign, had highlighted the inequality crisis, by the 2016 election cycle the issue had moved to the heart of national politics. Both the Republican and Democratic presidential contests featured insurgent candidates who made direct populist appeals to alienated and angry voters. The two versions of populism were quite different, and both shook up the establishment of the major parties.

Donald Trump, a wealthy and audacious New York real estate developer, emerged as the dominant figure from a crowded field of Republican candidates. Trump got his start by inheriting his father's housing business in Queens, New York, and then expanded into the world of luxury hotels, high-end apartment houses, and gambling casinos. Although Trump had never run for office before, he was already well known to millions of Americans. His 1987 book *The Art of the Deal* was a best-seller, and as the host of the long-running TV show *The Apprentice*, Trump had become a celebrity. In 2011 Trump made his first foray into politics as a leading voice in the so-called "birther" movement, which claimed—falsely—that President Barack Obama was born in Kenya and therefore was not an American citizen, making him ineligible to serve as president. The attack on Obama's legitimacy, with its clear racial undertones, previewed Trump's strategy for his own presidential run.

Lacking conventional credentials for the presidency, such as military service or experience in office, Trump campaigned for the Republican nomination by largely displacing traditional issues with a *political* populism that was more style or marketing strategy than a set of principles. Candidate Trump repeatedly declared that government and privileged elites had betrayed the American people, leaving them to struggle economically and allowing the nation to be taken advantage of by foreign powers, especially China. Trump rhetorically championed the interests of ordinary people while simultaneously appealing to racial hatred, economic nationalism, and xenophobia. He promised to advance the interests of native-born Americans over immigrants; he celebrated an American national identity often defined in racial, ethnic, and religious terms; and he proposed shielding the country's domestic industry from "unfair" foreign competition by taxing imports and pressuring employers to keep jobs in America for Americans.

Trump shocked most fellow Republicans and millions of others with claims and statements that seemed outside the boundaries of normal political discourse. He disparaged Sen. John McCain, held as a prisoner of war in North Vietnam for five years; "He's not a war hero. He was a war hero because he was captured. I like people who weren't captured." He called for a "complete shutdown of Muslims entering the United States until our country's representatives can figure out what is going on." He attacked Mexican immigrants ("They're bringing drugs. They're bringing crime. They're rapists. And some, I assume, are good people."), and he promised to build a wall along the Mexican border that Mexico would pay for. During the first Republican debate he mocked moderator Megan Kelly with language at best sexist and at worst misogynistic.

In previous elections Trump's rhetorical flourishes might have been seen as the gaffes of a political novice. Yet, rather than dooming his candidacy, they only strengthened his standing with the Republican base. His successful background in sales and the marketing of his name—along with his shrewd use of Twitter, which allowed him to bypass the mainstream media and connect directly to voters—built the Trump "brand" into a potent political movement. His campaign slogans, "Make America Great Again" and "America First," neatly summarized his successful appeals for the GOP nomination. With Governor Mike Pence (R-IN) as his vice-presidential running mate, Trump prepared to test his political populism with the nation as a whole.

Unlike Republicans, Democrats had a presumptive nominee for president: Hillary Rodham Clinton. She had raised an enormous war chest to fund her campaign since her unsuccessful primary challenge to Barack Obama, and she enjoyed the support of the vast majority of Democratic office holders. Indeed, Obama would describe her as the most qualified presidential candidate in our history. And there was enormous symbolic power attached to her campaign to be the first woman president. She inspired women around the country with her promise to break the ultimate glass ceiling, just as Obama had scored his historic breakthrough as the first African American president. On the primary campaign trail Clinton embraced a moderately liberal set of proposals: a $12-an-hour minimum wage; increased infrastructure spending; student debt relief; and an expansion of the "Obamacare" health plan. However, Clinton was also vulnerable to charges that she was too close to Wall Street, the banking industry, and big-money donors to be a true agent of change. For example, between 2001 and 2015, she and her husband, Bill Clinton, had received more than $153 million in speaking fees from Goldman Sachs, Citigroup, Bank of America, and other financial industry giants.

What seemed like a long-shot challenge to Clinton for the nomination emerged with the candidacy of Bernie Sanders. A self-described democratic socialist, Sanders attracted supporters with an *economic* populism that took direct aim at the nation's growing inequality. He depicted a country in profound crisis, emphasizing that the futures of democracy and the middle class were both endangered by the growth of plutocracy. He hammered away at contrasting the interests of working people and those of elites, arguing that the both the economic and political system were "rigged" to favor the wealthy, corporations, and CEOs. Sanders stressed the long-time threat of climate change, one that would require unprecedented federal planning and spending. He called for universal health care and free college tuition at public institutions as a societal right. He supported a $15-an-hour federal minimum wage and called for $1 trillion in infrastructure spending that would create jobs and repair America's roads, bridges, and water systems. Sanders argued for breaking up big banks and restoring campaign finance limits. His program offered a much more ambitious, social democratic, European-style vision than either Clinton or any previous Democrat. Sanders's campaign attracted millions of younger voters, and it successfully raised funds from small donors, accepting no money from corporations or political action committees.

Clinton and Sanders fought for the Democratic nomination over months of primary campaigns. While some Clinton supporters thought Sanders's insurgent candidacy would hurt her in the general election, others welcomed Sanders's challenge as an opportunity to open up debate in the party

and move Clinton to the left. The primaries made clear that Clinton enjoyed a huge advantage in southern states and big cities. There, large African American and Latino populations gave her a broader coalition that Sanders could not overcome. He did carry Michigan in a surprise victory that, in retrospect, might have served as warning to the Clinton campaign that her support was soft in the industrial heartland. Nonetheless, Clinton clinched the nomination and became the first woman ever nominated for president by a major party. She chose Senator Tim Kaine (D-VA) as her running mate. Sanders's economic populism, though it failed to win him the nomination, had nonetheless injected a powerful economic populist vision into national politics.

31.5.3 The Election of 2016

The general election was unlike any in American history. Donald Trump brought a temperamental brashness and insistence on saying (or tweeting) whatever was on his mind, a style like no presidential candidate before him. Many Republicans resisted Trump's appeal, but the realities of partisan politics, and the prospect of controlling all

DONALD TRUMP RALLY, FLORIDA, 2016 During the 2016 campaign, polls showed Florida voters giving an edge to Democrat Hillary Clinton. In response, Donald Trump staged several huge rallies in Florida. On Election Day, he swept the state except in the big cities, such as Miami-Dade County, where Clinton won.

CrowdSpark/Alamy Stock Photo.

three branches of government for the first time in decades, eventually brought nearly all of them into the fold. On the campaign trail and in televised debates with Clinton, Trump kept up his drumbeat of attacks on Mexicans, undocumented immigrants, and Muslims, and he continued to question President Obama's citizenship. He promised to cut taxes, revive manufacturing, and keep American jobs at home—but his racialized appeals to white Americans were even more effective in attracting votes.

Clinton's campaign stressed her experience and the achievements of Obama's presidency, particularly the Affordable Care Act. Millions of women worked tirelessly to elect the country's first woman president. Yet Trump's appeal proved that sexism remained powerful. A month before the election an embarrassing 2005 videotape surfaced, with Trump heard off-camera discussing women in vulgar terms and bragging about his ability to grope them. Trump denied all allegations of sexual assault and laughed off calls to withdraw from the race. On the eve of the election, nearly every poll predicted Clinton's victory.

Election Day revealed a nation deeply and closely divided politically. Although Clinton won the popular vote, Trump carried the Electoral College by 306 to 232. Trump owed his victory to breaking through the so-called "blue wall" of solid Democratic support in the industrial Midwest. His margins of victory in these states were very slim, but large enough for him to clinch his Electoral College victory. Thus out of a total popular vote of nearly 130 million, some 80,000 voters in three states proved the difference. (See Map 31.3)

In an election so close, no one factor explained Trump's victory: not solely Clinton's "unlikability," low turnout among African Americans, Trump's success in courting white working-class voters with racial appeals, or, simply, a hunger for change. Bernie Sanders read Trump's victory as a protest vote, suggesting that Trump won because "his campaign rhetoric successfully tapped into a very real and justified anger, an anger that many traditional Democrats feel." Federal law enforcement and intelligence officials concluded that the Russian government interfered with the election and tipped it toward the Republicans, a charge that led to the appointment of a special counsel to investigate not only the Russians' role but also possible collusion by members of the Trump campaign. Although the Russian investigation cast a dark shadow over Trump's first year in office, he and his followers understood that his brash version of populism had carried him into the White House and secured majorities in both the House and Senate. Republicans looked forward to controlling all three branches of government for the first time since 2000.

31.5.4 Trump in Office

In Trump's first year as president he largely attempted to stick to his campaign promises, particularly in his

Map 31.3 THE ELECTION OF 2016

	Electoral Vote (%)	Popular Vote (%)
Numbers on states represent Electoral Votes.		
DONALD J. TRUMP (T) (Republican)	304 (57.2)	62,985,106 (45.9)
Hillary Clinton (C) (Democrat)	227 (42.7)	65,853,625 (48.0)

Donald J. Trump and running mate Mike Pence won the presidential election, winning over Hillary Clinton and Tim Kaine in the electoral college 304 to 227. However, the Democratic ticket won almost 3 million more votes than their Republican opponents. Just over 52 percent of eligible voters turned out at the polls.

nationalist, **America First** approach to foreign policy. Yet he also discovered the limits of his power, despite Republican control of Congress. By executive order, he tried to ban immigrants and refugees from seven majority Muslim nations, but federal courts soon blocked the directive as unconstitutional religious discrimination. He defiantly announced the country's withdrawal from the multilateral Paris Agreement on climate change, isolating the United States from most of the world on this issue. Arguing that he could negotiate better trade deals for the American worker, he withdrew the nation from the Trans-Pacific Partnership negotiated under President Obama to open up free trade among 12 nations. Trump reaffirmed his intention to renegotiate the North American Free Trade Agreement (NAFTA).

Trump's foreign policy also put "America First." He repeatedly criticized NATO allies for not paying their dues and wondered aloud about upending America's oldest military alliance. He also sought to dismantle the deal, four years in the making, that President Obama had struck to prevent the development of Iran's ballistic missile program. Addressing the war in Afghanistan, then in its sixteenth year, Trump pledged to defeat the Taliban and all terrorists, but renounced nation-building. Trump underscored his deep skepticism of global engagement by proposing to cut the State Department's budget by 32 percent. He nevertheless acted on his campaign promise to bolster the nation's defense, and secured $700 billion for the military budget.

Throughout his first year in office, Trump engaged in provocative, undiplomatic exchanges with many foreign leaders, including Kim Jong-un, the North Korean leader determined to make his nation a nuclear power. The prospect of a new war on the Korean peninsula, possibly begun by accident or even by first strike, worried foreign policy experts across the partisan divide.

On the domestic front, Trump looked less populist and more like a traditional Republican conservative. His cabinet was dominated by Wall Street and corporate executives, including Rex Tillerson, former CEO of ExxonMobil, as secretary of state and Steve Mnuchin, former Goldman Sachs executive, as secretary of Treasury. Most cabinet members worked to roll back Obama's policies, especially in the areas of environmental protection, reproductive health services, and immigration.

Trump championed the repeal of the Affordable Care Act. Republican leadership proposed replacing Obamacare with their American Health Care Act (AHCA), which would have rolled back key provisions and, according to the nonpartisan Congressional Budget Office, initially deprived 14 million Americans of access to health insurance, a figure that would have ballooned to 26 million by 2026. Pushed by the ultra-conservative Freedom Caucus, the House passed the AHCA, but several moderate Republicans joined Democrats to sink the bill in the Senate. Only later in 2017, embedded in their comprehensive tax bill, did they manage to repeal a key requirement, the individual mandate to buy coverage or face a fine.

The Tax Cuts and Job Act, passed in December 2017, represented a major achievement for the Trump administration. It drastically cut the corporate tax rate from 35 percent to 20 percent; collapsed 7 tax brackets into 5, making for less-progressive taxation; and eliminated estate taxes and the alternative minimum tax, a boon for the wealthiest taxpayers. Trump revitalized the supply-side economics of the Reagan era, assuring voters that big tax cuts for corporations and the wealthy would spur economic growth and "trickle down" to bring higher wages and salaries to all. The plan's sponsors acknowledged that the tax overhaul would add $1.5 trillion over 10 years to the national debt. Savings would have to be found in the near term partly by removing deductions for home mortgage interest, state and local taxes, and college tuition loan payments. For the longer term, savings would come by gutting the nation's largest and most popular entitlement programs, including Social Security, Medicare, Medicaid, and the Veterans Administration.

Trump's actions as president pumped new life into various political movements, several dating to his campaign. On January 21, 2017, the worldwide **Women's March** greeted his inauguration by pledging to resist policies infringing on the civil rights of women, immigrants and refugees, LBGQT Americans, and peoples of color. The rallies, attended by 7 million globally, targeted Trump and the policies outlined in his campaign. The Women's March was the largest single-day protest in U.S. history, and was commemorated a year later with a second huge event. Toward the end of Trump's first year in office, social media propelled the "#MeToo" movement, a campaign of thousands of women who had endured sexual harassment, rape, and other abuses by powerful men. The resignations and public shaming of prominent Hollywood executives, television anchors, comedians, actors, newspaper editors, media executives, and sitting legislators empowered more women to break their silence. Inspired in part by Trump's "American First" rhetoric, other activists staged comparatively small rallies to support nationalist and racially exclusivist policies. In August, 2017, a "Unite the Right" group rallied under Confederate and Nazi flags in Charlottesville, Virginia, to protest the removal of a public statue commemorating Confederate figure Robert E. Lee. The event ended in tragedy, as a vehicular attack that killed Heather D. Heyer, a counter-protester. Disconcerting to many was President Trump's qualified condemnation, "We condemn in the strongest possible terms this egregious display of hatred, bigotry, and violence on many sides, many sides."

A tumultuous year for many Americans, Trump's first year in office ended for him on an upbeat note, despite historically low approval ratings. In his State of the Union address, on January 30, 2018, Trump celebrated the booming economy, especially a significant rise in the stock market. Taking into account his accomplishments, he proclaimed a "new American moment" and predicted the advent of bipartisan government. In short, he hailed the "extraordinary success" of his first year as president. "There has never been a better time," he said, "to start living the American dream."

Conclusion

Donald Trump's unlikely election as president both reflected and intensified deep economic, racial, and cultural divisions across a nation of 320 million people. For those who saw Barack Obama's election in 2008 as a momentous breakthrough, Trump's inauguration was a reminder that history rarely travels in a straight line. Fundamental differences over the proper role for federal government in American life grew sharply in late twentieth century politics. By the twenty-first century, that division had widened into a chasm driven by racial, gender, cultural, and partisan tensions that seemed only to get more intense and more fractious.

Key Terms

USA PATRIOT Act Federal legislation adopted in 2001, in response to the terrorist attacks on September 11, to facilitate anti-terror actions by federal law-enforcement and intelligence agencies. p. 778

Department of Homeland Security (DHS) Cabinet-level department created by President George W. Bush to manage U.S. security. p. 779

Proposition 187 California legislation passed in 1994 that cut off state benefits to undocumented immigrants. p. 781

multiculturalism Movement that emphasized the achievements of formerly marginal groups and immigrants. p. 781

No Child Left Behind Act (NCLB) Legislation passed in 2001 that established standards for math and reading skills and implemented testing of proficiency in the nation's elementary schools. p. 784

Black Lives Matter (BLM) Movement formed in 2013 to protest inequities in the criminal justice system and the disproportionate numbers of police shootings of African American men. p. 786

Federal Emergency Management Agency (FEMA) Agency charged with providing assistance to communities hit by natural disasters. p. 779

Affordable Care Act Legislation, also known as "Obamacare," that mandated the federal government to work with insurance companies to cover uninsured Americans, passed in March 2010. p. 792

Occupy Wall Street (OWS) A protest movement begun in 2011 and directed against the growing inequality in income and wages. p. 793

America First The principle behind President Trump's foreign policy, including international trade, that placed the interests of the United States before those of all other nations. p. 798

Women's March A global protest, stated in January 2017, against the policies, behavior, and rhetoric of Donald Trump, which involved nearly 7 million worldwide. p. 799

CHRONOLOGY

2001	George W. Bush becomes president after contested election
	Terrorists attack World Trade Center and Pentagon
	U.S. begins military campaign in Afghanistan
	USA PATRIOT Act passed
	No Child Left Behind Act passed
2003	Invasion and occupation of Iraq
2004	Reelection of George W. Bush
2005	Hurricane Katrina devastates New Orleans and the Gulf Coast
2008	Barack Obama elected president
2010	President Obama signs the Affordable Care Act
2012	Barack Obama is reelected president
2016	Donald J. Trump is elected president
2017	Women's March stages huge worldwide protest

Appendix

THE DECLARATION OF INDEPENDENCE

When in the course of human events it becomes necessary for one people to dissolve the political bands which have connected them with another and to assume, among the powers of the earth, the separate and equal station to which the laws of nature and of nature's God entitle them, a decent respect to the opinions of mankind requires that they should declare the causes which impel them to the separation.

We hold these truths to be self-evident, that all men are created equal; that they are endowed by their Creator with certain unalienable rights; that among these are life, liberty, and the pursuit of happiness. That, to secure these rights, governments are instituted among men, deriving their just powers from the consent of the governed; that, whenever any form of government becomes destructive of these ends, it is the right of the people to alter or to abolish it, and to institute a new government, laying its foundation on such principles, and organizing its powers in such form, as to them shall seem most likely to effect their safety and happiness. Prudence, indeed, will dictate that governments long established should not be changed for light and transient causes; and, accordingly, all experience hath shown that mankind are more disposed to suffer, while evils are sufferable, than to right themselves by abolishing the forms to which they are accustomed. But when a long train of abuses and usurpations, pursuing invariably the same object, evinces a design to reduce them under absolute despotism, it is their right, it is their duty, to throw off such government and to provide new guards for their future security. Such has been the patient sufferance of these colonies, and such is now the necessity which constrains them to alter their former systems of government. The history of the present King of Great Britain is a history of repeated injuries and usurpations, all having, in direct object, the establishment of an absolute tyranny over these States. To prove this, let facts be submitted to a candid world:

He has refused his assent to laws the most wholesome and necessary for the public good.

He has forbidden his governors to pass laws of immediate and pressing importance, unless suspended in their operation till his assent should be obtained; and, when so suspended, he has utterly neglected to attend to them.

He has refused to pass other laws for the accommodation of large districts of people, unless those people would relinquish the right of representation in the legislature, a right inestimable to them and formidable to tyrants only.

He has called together legislative bodies at places unusual, uncomfortable, and distant from the depository of their public records, for the sole purpose of fatiguing them into compliance with his measures.

He has dissolved representative houses, repeatedly for opposing, with manly firmness, his invasions on the rights of the people.

He has refused, for a long time after such dissolutions, to cause others to be elected; whereby the legislative powers, incapable of annihilation, have returned to the people at large for their exercise; the state remaining, in the meantime, exposed to all the danger of invasion from without and convulsions within.

He has endeavored to prevent the population of these States; for that purpose, obstructing the laws for naturalization of foreigners, refusing to pass others to encourage their migration hither, and raising the conditions of new appropriations of lands.

He has obstructed the administration of justice by refusing his assent to laws for establishing judiciary powers.

He has made judges dependent on his will alone for the tenure of their offices and the amount and payment of their salaries.

He has erected a multitude of new offices and sent hither swarms of officers to harass our people and eat out their substance.

He has kept among us, in time of peace, standing armies, without the consent of our legislatures.

He has affected to render the military independent of, and superior to, the civil power.

He has combined with others to subject us to a jurisdiction foreign to our Constitution and unacknowledged by our laws, giving his assent to their acts of pretended legislation—

For quartering large bodies of armed troops among us;

For protecting them by mock trial, from punishment for any murders which they should commit on the inhabitants of these States;

For cutting off our trade with all parts of the world;

For imposing taxes on us without our consent;

For depriving us, in many cases, of the benefit of trial by jury;

For transporting us beyond seas to be tried for pretended offences;

For abolishing the free system of English laws in a neighboring province, establishing therein an arbitrary government, and enlarging its boundaries, so as to render it at once an example and fit instrument for introducing the same absolute rule into these colonies;

For taking away our charters, abolishing our most valuable laws, and altering, fundamentally, the powers of our governments.

For suspending our own legislatures and declaring themselves invested with power to legislate for us in all cases whatsoever.

He has abdicated government here by declaring us out of his protection and waging war against us.

He has plundered our seas, ravaged our coasts, burnt our towns, and destroyed the lives of our people.

He is, at this time, transporting large armies of foreign mercenaries to complete the works of death, desolation, and tyranny already begun with circumstances of cruelty and perfidy scarcely paralleled in the most barbarous ages, and totally unworthy the head of a civilized nation.

He has constrained our fellow citizens, taken captive on the high seas, to bear arms against their country, to become the executioners of their friends and brethren, or to fall themselves by their hands.

He has excited domestic insurrections amongst us and has endeavored to bring on the inhabitants of our frontiers, the merciless Indian savages, whose known rule of warfare is an undistinguished destruction of all ages, sexes, and conditions.

In every stage of these oppressions, we have petitioned for redress in the most humble terms; our repeated petitions have been answered only by repeated injury. A prince whose character is thus marked by every act which may define a tyrant is unfit to be the ruler of a free people.

Nor have we been wanting in attention to our British brethren. We have warned them, from time to time, of attempts made by their legislature to extend an unwarrantable jurisdiction over us. We have reminded them of the circumstances of our emigration and settlement here. We have appealed to their native justice and magnanimity, and we have conjured them, by the ties of our common kindred, to disavow these usurpations, which would inevitably interrupt our connections and correspondence. They, too, have been deaf to the voice of justice and consanguinity. We must, therefore, acquiesce in the necessity which denounces our separation, and hold them, as we hold the rest of mankind, enemies in war, in peace, friends.

We, therefore, the representatives of the United States of America, in general Congress assembled, appealing to the Supreme Judge of the world for the rectitude of our intentions, do, in the name and by the authority of the good people of these colonies, solemnly publish and declare, that these united colonies are, and of right ought to be, free and independent states: that they are absolved from all allegiance to the British Crown, and that all political connection between them and the state of Great Britain is, and ought to be, totally dissolved; and that, as free and independent states, they have full power to levy war, conclude peace, contract alliances, establish commerce, and to do all other acts and things which independent states may of right do. And, for the support of this declaration, with a firm reliance on the protection of Divine Providence, we mutually pledge to each other our lives, our fortunes, and our sacred honor.

THE ARTICLES OF CONFEDERATION AND PERPETUAL UNION*

Between the states of New Hampshire, Massachusetts-bay Rhode Island and Providence Plantations, Connecticut, New York, New Jersey, Pennsylvania, Delaware, Maryland, Virginia, North Carolina, South Carolina, and Georgia.

Article 1

The Stile of this Confederacy shall be "The United States of America."

Article 2

Each state retains its sovereignty, freedom, and independence, and every power, jurisdiction, and right, which is not by this Confederation expressly delegated to the United States, in Congress assembled.

Article 3

The said States hereby severally enter into a firm league of friendship with each other, for their common

defense, the security of their liberties, and their mutual and general welfare, binding themselves to assist each other, against all force offered to, or attacks made upon them, or any of them, on account of religion, sovereignty, trade, or any other pretense whatever.

Article 4

The better to secure and perpetuate mutual friendship and intercourse among the people of the different States in this Union, the free inhabitants of each of these States, paupers, vagabonds, and fugitives from justice excepted, shall be entitled to all privileges and immunities of free citizens in the several States; and the people of each State shall have free ingress and regress to and from any other State, and shall enjoy therein all the privileges of trade and commerce, subject to the same duties, impositions, and restrictions as the inhabitants thereof respectively, provided that such restrictions shall not extend so far as to prevent the removal of property imported into any State, to any other State of which the owner is an inhabitant; provided also that no imposition, duties or restriction shall be laid by any State, on the property of the United States, or either of them.

---

*Agreed to in Congress November 15, 1777; ratified March 1781.

If any person guilty of, or charged with, treason, felony, or other high misdemeanor in any State, shall flee from justice, and be found in any of the United States, he shall, upon demand of the Governor or executive power of the State from which he fled, be delivered up and removed to the State having jurisdiction of his offense.

Full faith and credit shall be given in each of these States to the records, acts, and judicial proceedings of the courts and magistrates of every other State.

Article 5

For the most convenient management of the general interests of the United States, delegates shall be annually appointed in such manner as the legislatures of each State shall direct, to meet in Congress on the first Monday in November, in every year, with a power reserved to each State to recall its delegates, or any of them, at any time within the year, and to send others in their stead for the remainder of the year.

No State shall be represented in Congress by less than two, nor by more than seven members; and no person shall be capable of being a delegate for more than three years in any term of six years; nor shall any person, being a delegate, be capable of holding any office under the United States, for which he, or another for his benefit, receives any salary, fees or emolument of any kind.

Each State shall maintain its own delegates in a meeting of the States, and while they act as members of the committee of the States.

In determining questions in the United States in Congress assembled, each State shall have one vote.

Freedom of speech and debate in Congress shall not be impeached or questioned in any court or place out of Congress, and the members of Congress shall be protected in their persons from arrests or imprisonments, during the time of their going to and from, and attendence on Congress, except for treason, felony, or breach of the peace.

Article 6

No State, without the consent of the United States in Congress assembled, shall send any embassy to, or receive any embassy from, or enter into any conference, agreement, alliance or treaty with any King, Prince or State; nor shall any person holding any office of profit or trust under the United States, or any of them, accept any present, emolument, office or title of any kind whatever from any King, Prince or foreign State; nor shall the United States in Congress assembled, or any of them, grant any title of nobility.

No two or more States shall enter into any treaty, confederation or alliance whatever between them, without the consent of the United States in Congress assembled, specifying accurately the purposes for which the same is to be entered into, and how long it shall continue.

No State shall lay any imposts or duties, which may interfere with any stipulations in treaties, entered into by the United States in Congress assembled, with any King, Prince or State, in pursuance of any treaties already proposed by Congress, to the courts of France and Spain.

No vessel of war shall be kept up in time of peace by any State, except such number only, as shall be deemed necessary by the United States in Congress assembled, for the defense of such State, or its trade; nor shall any body of forces be kept up by any State in time of peace, except such number only, as in the judgement of the United States in Congress assembled, shall be deemed requisite to garrison the forts necessary for the defense of such State; but every State shall always keep up a well-regulated and disciplined militia, sufficiently armed and accoutered, and shall provide and constantly have ready for use, in public stores, a due number of filed pieces and tents, and a proper quantity of arms, ammunition and camp equipage.

No State shall engage in any war without the consent of the United States in Congress assembled, unless such State be actually invaded by enemies, or shall have received certain advice of a resolution being formed by some nation of Indians to invade such State, and the danger is so imminent as not to admit of a delay, till the United States in Congress assembled can be consulted; nor shall any State grant commissions to any ships or vessels of war, nor letters of marque or reprisal, except it be after a declaration of war by the United States in Congress assembled, and then only against the Kingdom or State and the subjects thereof, against which war has been so declared, and under such regulations as shall be established by the United States in Congress assembled, unless such State be infested by pirates, in which case vessels of war may be fitted out for that occasion, and kept so long as the danger shall continue, or until the United States in Congress assembled shall determine otherwise.

Article 7

When land forces are raised by any State for the common defense, all officers of or under the rank of colonel, shall be appointed by the legislature of each State respectively, by whom such forces shall be raised, or in such manner as such State shall direct, and all vacancies shall be filled up by the State which first made the appointment.

Article 8

All charges of war, and all other expenses that shall be incurred for the common defense or general welfare, and allowed by the United States in Congress assembled, shall be defrayed out of a common treasury, which shall be supplied by the several States in proportion to the value of all land within each State, granted to or surveyed for any person, as such land and the buildings and improvements thereon shall be estimated according to such mode as the United States in Congress assembled, shall from time to time direct and appoint.

The taxes for paying that proportion shall be laid and levied by the authority and direction of the legislatures of the several States within the time agreed upon by the United States in Congress assembled.

Article 9

The United States in Congress assembled, shall have the sole and exclusive right and power of determining on peace and war, except in the cases mentioned in the sixth article; of sending and receiving ambassadors; entering into treaties and alliances, provided that no treaty of commerce shall be made whereby the legislative power of the respective States shall be restrained from imposing such imposts and duties on foreigners, as their own people are subjected to, or from prohibiting the exportation or importation of any species of goods or commodities whatsoever; of establishing rules for deciding in all cases, what captures on land or water shall be legal, and in what manner prizes taken by land or naval forces in the service of the United States shall be divided or appropriated; of granting letters of marque and reprisal in times of peace; appointing courts for the trial of piracies and felonies committed on the high seas and establishing courts for receiving and determining finally appeals in all cases of captures, provided that no member of Congress shall be appointed a judge of any of the said courts.

The United States in Congress assembled shall also be the last resort on appeal in all disputes and differences now subsisting or that hereafter may arise between two or more States concerning boundary, jurisdiction or any other causes whatever; which authority shall always be exercised in the manner following. Whenever the legislative or executive authority or lawful agent of any State in controversy with another shall present a petition to Congress stating the matter in question and praying for a hearing, notice thereof shall be given by order of Congress to the legislative or executive authority of the other State in controversy, and a day assigned for the appearance of the parties by their lawful agents, who shall then be directed to appoint by joint consent, commissioners or judges to constitute a court for hearing and determining the matter in question: but if they cannot agree, Congress shall name three persons out of each of the United States, and from the list of such persons each party shall alternately strike out one, the petitioners beginning, until the number shall be reduced to thirteen; and from that number not less than seven, nor more than nine names as Congress shall direct, shall in the presence of Congress be drawn out by lot, and the persons whose names shall be so drawn or any five of them, shall be commissioners or judges, to hear and finally determine the controversy, so always as a major part of the judges who shall hear the cause shall agree in the determination: and if either party shall neglect to attend at the day appointed, without showing reasons, which Congress shall judge sufficient, or being present shall refuse to strike, the Congress shall proceed to nominate three persons out of each State, and the secretary of Congress shall strike in behalf of such party absent or refusing; and the judgement and sentence of the court to be appointed, in the manner before prescribed, shall be final and conclusive; and if any of the parties shall refuse to submit to the authority of such court, or to appear or defend their claim or cause, the court shall nevertheless proceed to pronounce sentence, or judgement, which shall in like manner be final and decisive, the judgement or sentence and other proceedings being in either case transmitted to Congress, and lodged among the acts of Congress for the security of the parties concerned: provided that every commissioner, before he sits in judgement, shall take an oath to be administered by one of the judges of the supreme or superior court of the State, where the cause shall be tried, "well and truly to hear and determine the matter in question, according to the best of his judgement, without favor, affection or hope of reward": provided also, that no State shall be deprived of territory for the benefit of the United States.

All controversies concerning the private right of soil claimed under different grants of two or more States, whose jurisdictions as they may respect such lands, and the States which passed such grants are adjusted, the said grants or either of them being at the same time claimed to have originated antecedent to such settlement of jurisdiction, shall on the petition of either party to the Congress of the United States, be finally determined as near as may be in the same manner as is before prescribed for deciding disputes respecting territorial jurisdiction between different States.

The United States in Congress assembled shall also have the sole and exclusive right and power of regulating the alloy and value of coin struck by their own authority, or by that of the respective States; fixing the standards of weights and measures throughout the United States; regulating the trade and managing all affairs with the Indians not members of any of the States; provided that the legislative right of any State within its own limits be not infringed or violated; establishing or regulating post offices from one State to another, throughout all the United States, and exacting such postage on the papers passing through the same as may be requisite to defray the expenses of the said office; appointing all officers of the land forces in the service of the United States, excepting regimental officers; appointing all the officers of the naval forces, and commissioning all officers whatever in the service of the United States; making rules for the government and regulation of the said land and naval forces, and directing their operations.

The United States in Congress assembled shall have authority to appoint a committee, to sit in the recess of Congress, to be denominated "A Committee of the States," and to consist of one delegate from each State; and to appoint such other committees and civil officers as may be necessary for managing the general affairs of the United States under their direction; to appoint one of their members to preside, provided that no person be allowed to serve in the office of president more than one year in any term of three years; to ascertain the necessary sums of money to be raised for the service of the United States, and to appropriate and apply the same for defraying the public expenses; to borrow money, or emit bills on the credit of the United States, transmitting every half year to the respective States an account of the sums of money so borrowed or emitted; to build and equip a navy; to agree upon the number of land forces, and to make requisitions from each State for its quota, in proportion to the number of white inhabitants in such State; which requisition shall be binding, and thereupon the legislature of each State shall appoint the regimental officers, raise the men and cloath, arm and equip them in a soldierlike manner, at the expense of the United States; and the officers and men so cloathed, armed and equipped shall march to the place appointed, and within the time agreed on by the United States in Congress assembled; but if the United States in Congress assembled shall, on consideration of circumstances judge proper that any State should not raise men, or should raise a smaller number of men than the quota thereof, such extra number shall be raised, officered, cloathed, armed and equipped in the same manner as the quota of each State, unless the legislature of such State shall judge that such extra number cannot be safely spared out in the same, in which case they shall raise, officer, cloath, arm and equip as many of such extra number as they judge can be safely spared. And the officers and men so cloathed, armed, and equipped, shall march to the place appointed, and within the time agreed on by the United States in Congress assembled.

The United States in Congress assembled shall never engage in a war, nor grant letters of marque or reprisal in time of peace, nor enter into any treaties or alliances, nor coin money, nor regulate the value thereof, nor ascertain the sums and expenses necessary for the defense and welfare of the United States, or any of them, nor emit bills, nor borrow money on the credit of the United States, nor appropriate money, nor agree upon the number of vessels of war, to be built or purchased, or the number of land or sea forces to be raised, nor appoint a commander in chief of the army or navy, unless nine States assent to the same: nor shall a question on any other point, except for adjourning from day to day be determined, unless by the votes of the majority of the United States in Congress assembled.

The Congress of the United States shall have power to adjourn to any time within the year, and to any place within the United States, so that no period of adjournment be for a longer duration than the space of six months, and shall publish the journal of their proceedings monthly, except such parts thereof relating to treaties, alliances or military operations, as in their judgement require secrecy; and the yeas and nays of the delegates of each State on any question shall be entered on the journal, when it is desired by any delegates of a State, or any of them, at his or their request shall be furnished with a transcript of the said journal, except such parts as are above excepted, to lay before the legislatures of the several States.

Article 10

The Committee of the States, or any nine of them, shall be authorized to execute, in the recess of Congress, such of the powers of Congress as the United States in Congress assembled, by the consent of the nine States, shall from time to time think expedient to vest them with; provided that no power be delegated to the said Committee, for the exercise of which, by the Articles of Confederation, the voice of nine States in the Congress of the United States assembled is requisite.

Article 11

Canada acceding to this confederation, and adjoining in the measures of the United States, shall be admitted into, and entitled to all the advantages of this Union; but no other colony shall be admitted into the same, unless such admission be agreed to by nine States.

Article 12

All bills of credit emitted, monies borrowed, and debts contracted by, or under the authority of Congress, before the assembling of the United States, in pursuance of the present confederation, shall be deemed and considered as a charge against the United States, for payment and satisfaction whereof the said United States, and the public faith are hereby solemnly pledged.

Article 13

Every State shall abide by the determination of the United States in Congress assembled, on all questions which by this confederation are submitted to them. And the Articles of this Confederation shall be inviolably observed by every State, and the Union shall be perpetual; nor shall any alteration at any time hereafter be made in any of them; unless such alteration be agreed to in a Congress of the United States, and be afterwards confirmed by the legislatures of every State.

These articles shall be proposed to the legislatures of all the United States, to be considered, and if approved of by them, they are advised to authorize their delegates to ratify the same in the Congress of the United States; which being done, the same shall become conclusive.

THE CONSTITUTION OF THE UNITED STATES OF AMERICA

We the people of the United States, in order to form a more perfect union, establish justice, insure domestic tranquillity, provide for the common defense, promote the general welfare, and secure the blessings of liberty to ourselves and our posterity, do ordain and establish this Constitution for the United States of America.

Article I

Section 1. All legislative powers herein granted shall be vested in a Congress of the United States, which shall consist of a Senate and House of Representatives.

Section 2. 1. The House of Representatives shall be composed of members chosen every second year by the people of the several States, and the electors in each State shall have the qualifications requisite for electors of the most numerous branch of the State legislature.

2. No person shall be a representative who shall not have attained to the age of twenty-five years, and been seven years a citizen of the United States, and who shall not, when elected, be an inhabitant of that State in which he shall be chosen.

3. Representatives and direct taxes[1] shall be apportioned among the several States which may be included within this Union, according to their respective numbers, which shall be determined by adding to the whole number of free persons, including those bound to service for a term of years, and excluding Indians not taxed, three fifths of all other persons.[2] The actual enumeration shall be made within three years after the first meeting of the Congress of the United States, and within every subsequent term of ten years, in such manner as they shall by law direct. The number of representatives shall not exceed one for every thirty thousand, but each State shall have at least one representative; and until such enumeration shall be made, the State of New Hampshire shall be entitled to choose three, Massachusetts eight, Rhode Island and Providence Plantations one, Connecticut five, New York six, New Jersey four, Pennsylvania eight, Delaware one, Maryland six, Virginia ten, North Carolina five, South Carolina five, and Georgia three.

4. When vacancies happen in the representation from any State, the executive authority thereof shall issue writs of election to fill such vacancies.

5. The House of Representatives shall choose their speaker and other officers; and shall have the sole power of impeachment.

Section 3. 1. The Senate of the United States shall be composed of two senators from each State, chosen by the legislature thereof,[3] for six years; and each senator shall have one vote.

2. Immediately after they shall be assembled in consequence of the first election, they shall be divided as equally as may be into three classes. The seats of the senators of the first class shall be vacated at the expiration of the second year, of the second class at the expiration of the fourth year, and of the third class at the expiration of the sixth year, so that one third may be chosen every second year; and if vacancies happen by resignation, or otherwise, during the recess of the legislature of any State, the executive thereof may make temporary appointments until the next meeting of the legislature, which shall then fill such vacancies.[4]

3. No person shall be a senator who shall not have attained to the age of thirty years, and been nine years a citizen of the United States, and who shall not, when elected, be an inhabitant of that State for which he shall be chosen.

4. The Vice President of the United States shall be President of the Senate, but shall have no vote, unless they be equally divided.

5. The Senate shall choose their other officers, and also a president pro tempore, in the absence of the Vice President, or when he shall exercise the office of the President of the United States.

6. The Senate shall have the sole power to try all impeachments. When sitting for that purpose, they shall be on oath or affirmation. When the President of the United States is tried, the chief justice shall preside: and no person shall be convicted without the concurrence of two thirds of the members present.

7. Judgment in cases of impeachment shall not extend further than to removal from office, and disqualification to hold and enjoy any office of honor, trust or profit under the United States: but the party convicted shall nevertheless be liable and subject to indictment, trial, judgment and punishment, according to law.

Section 4. 1. The times, places, and manner of holding elections for senators and representatives, shall be prescribed in each State by the legislature thereof; but the Congress may at any time by law make or alter such regulations, except as to the places of choosing senators.

2. The Congress shall assemble at least once in every year, and such meeting shall be on the first Monday in December, unless they shall by law appoint a different day.

Section 5. 1. Each House shall be the judge of the elections, returns and qualifications of its own members, and a majority of each shall constitute a quorum to do business; but a smaller number may adjourn from day to day, and may be authorized to compel the attendance of absent members, in such manner, and under such penalties as each House may provide.

2. Each House may determine the rules of its proceedings, punish its members for disorderly behavior, and, with the concurrence of two thirds, expel a member.

3. Each House shall keep a journal of its proceedings, and from time to time publish the same, excepting such parts as may in their judgment require secrecy; and the yeas and nays of the members of either House on any question shall, at the desire of one fifth of those present, be entered on the journal.

4. Neither House, during the session of Congress, shall, without the consent of the other, adjourn for more than three days, nor to any other place than that in which the two Houses shall be sitting.

Section 6. 1. The senators and representatives shall receive a compensation for their services, to be ascertained by law, and paid out of the Treasury of the United States. They shall in all cases, except treason, felony, and breach of the peace, be privileged from arrest during their attendance at the session of their respective Houses, and in going to and returning from the same; and for any speech or debate in either House, they shall not be questioned in any other place.

2. No senator or representative shall, during the time for which he was elected, be appointed to any civil office

---

[1]See the Sixteenth Amendment.
[2]See the Fourteenth Amendment.
[3]See the Seventeenth Amendment.
[4]See the Seventeenth Amendment.

under the authority of the United States, which shall have been created, or the emoluments whereof shall have been increased, during such time; and no person holding any office under the United States shall be a member of either House during his continuance in office.

Section 7. 1. All bills for raising revenue shall originate in the House of Representatives; but the Senate may propose or concur with amendments as on other bills.

2. Every bill which shall have passed the House of Representatives and the Senate, shall, before it become a law, be presented to the President of the United States; If he approves he shall sign it, but if not he shall return it, with his objections, to that House in which it shall have originated, who shall enter the objections at large on their journal, and proceed to reconsider it. If after such reconsideration two thirds of that House shall agree to pass the bill, it shall be sent, together with the objections, to the other House, by which it shall likewise be reconsidered, and if approved by two thirds of that House, it shall become a law. But in all such cases the votes of both Houses shall be determined by yeas and nays, and the names of the persons voting for and against the bill shall be entered on the journal of each House respectively. If any bill shall not be returned by the President within ten days (Sundays excepted) after it shall have been presented to him, the same shall be a law, in like manner as if he had signed it, unless the Congress by their adjournment prevent its return, in which case it shall not be a law.

3. Every order, resolution, or vote to which the concurrence of the Senate and the House of Representatives may be necessary (except on a question of adjournment) shall be presented to the President of the United States; and before the same shall take effect, shall be approved by him, or being disapproved by him, shall be repassed by two thirds of the Senate and House of Representatives, according to the rules and limitations prescribed in the case of a bill.

Section 8. The Congress shall have the power

1. To lay and collect taxes, duties, imposts, and excises, to pay the debts and provide for the common defense and general welfare of the United States; but all duties, imposts, and excises shall be uniform throughout the United States.

2. To borrow money on the credit of the United States;

3. To regulate commerce with foreign nations, and among the several States, and with the Indian tribes;

4. To establish a uniform rule of naturalization, and uniform laws on the subject of bankruptcies throughout the United States;

5. To coin money, regulate the value thereof, and of foreign coin, and fix the standard of weights and measures;

6. To provide for the punishment of counterfeiting the securities and current coin of the United States;

7. To establish post offices and post roads;

8. To promote the progress of science and useful arts, by securing for limited times to authors and inventors the exclusive right to their respective writings and discoveries;

9. To constitute tribunals inferior to the Supreme Court;

10. To define and punish piracies and felonies committed on the high seas, and offenses against the law of nations;

11. To declare war, grant letters of marque and reprisal, and make rules concerning captures on land and water;

12. To raise and support armies, but no appropriation of money to that use shall be for a longer term than two years;

13. To provide and maintain a navy;

14. To make rules for the government and regulation of the land and naval forces;

15. To provide for calling forth the militia to execute the laws of the Union, suppress insurrections and repel invasions;

16. To provide for organizing, arming, and disciplining the militia, and for governing such part of them as may be employed in the service of the United States, reserving to the States respectively, the appointment of the officers, and the authority of training the militia according to the discipline prescribed by Congress;

17. To exercise exclusive legislation in all cases whatsoever, over such district (not exceeding ten miles square) as may, by cession of particular States, and the acceptance of Congress, become the seat of the government of the United States, and to exercise like authority over all places purchased by the consent of the legislature of the State in which the same shall be, for the erection of forts, magazines, arsenals, dockyards, and other needful buildings; and

18. To make all laws which shall be necessary and proper for carrying into execution the foregoing powers, and all other powers vested by this Constitution in the government of the United States, or any department or officer thereof.

Section 9. 1. The migration or importation of such persons as any of the States now existing shall think proper to admit, shall not be prohibited by the Congress prior to the year one thousand eight hundred and eight, but a tax or duty may be imposed on such importation, not exceeding ten dollars for each person.

2. The privilege of the writ of habeas corpus shall not be suspended, unless when in cases of rebellion or invasion the public safety may require it.

3. No bill of attainder or ex post facto law shall be passed.

4. No capitation, or other direct, tax shall be laid, unless in proportion to the census or enumeration herein-before directed to be taken.[5]

5. No tax or duty shall be laid on articles exported from any State.

6. No preference shall be given by any regulation of commerce or revenue to the ports of one State over those of another: nor shall vessels bound to, or from, one State be obliged to enter, clear, or pay duties in another.

---

[5]See the Sixteenth Amendment.

7. No money shall be drawn from the treasury, but in consequence of appropriations made by law; and a regular statement and account of the receipts and expenditures of all public money shall be published from time to time.

8. No title of nobility shall be granted by the United States: and no person holding any office of profit or trust under them, shall, without the consent of the Congress, accept of any present, emolument, office, or title, of any kind whatever, from any king, prince, or foreign State.

Section 10. 1. No State shall enter into any treaty, alliance, or confederation; grant letters of marque and reprisal; coin money; emit bills of credit; make any thing but gold and silver coin a tender in payment of debts; pass any bill of attainder, ex post facto law, or law impairing the obligation of contracts, or grant, any title of nobility.

2. No State shall, without the consent of the Congress, lay any imposts or duties on imports or exports, except what may be absolutely necessary for executing its inspection laws: and the net produce of all duties and imposts laid by any State on imports or exports, shall be for the use of the treasury of the United States; and all such laws shall be subject to the revision and control of the Congress.

3. No State shall, without the consent of the Congress, lay any duty of tonnage, keep troops, or ships of war in time of peace, enter into any agreement or compact with another State, or with a foreign power, or engage in war, unless actually invaded, or in such imminent danger as will not admit of delay.

Article II

Section 1. 1. The executive power shall be vested in a President of the United States of America. He shall hold his office during the term of four years, and, together with the Vice President, chosen for the same term, be elected, as follows:

2. Each State shall appoint, in such manner as the legislature thereof may direct, a number of electors, equal to the whole number of senators and representatives to which the State may be entitled in the Congress: but no senator or representative, or person holding any office of trust or profit under the United States, shall be appointed an elector.

The electors shall meet in their respective States, and vote by ballot for two persons, of whom one at least shall not be an inhabitant of the same State with themselves. And they shall make a list of all the persons voted for, and of the number of votes for each; which list they shall sign and certify, and transmit sealed to the seat of the government of the United States, directed to the president of the Senate. The president of the Senate shall, in the presence of the Senate and House of Representatives, open all the certificates, and the votes shall then be counted. The person having the greatest number of votes shall be the President, if such number be a majority of the whole number of electors appointed; and if there be more than one who have such majority, and have an equal number of votes, then the House of Representatives shall immediately choose by ballot one of them for President; and if no person have

a majority, then from the five highest on the list the said House shall in like manner choose the President. But in choosing the President, the votes shall be taken by States, the representation from each State having one vote; a quorum for this purpose shall consist of a member or members from two thirds of the States, and a majority of all the States shall be necessary to a choice. In every case after the choice of the President, the person having the greatest number of votes of the electors shall be the Vice President. But if there should remain two or more who have equal votes, the Senate shall choose from them by ballot the Vice President.[6]

3. The Congress may determine the time of choosing the electors, and the day on which they shall give their votes; which day shall be the same throughout the United States.

4. No person except a natural born citizen, or a citizen of the United States, at the time of the adoption of this Constitution, shall be eligible to the office of President; neither shall any person be eligible to the office who shall not have attained to the age of thirty-five years, and been fourteen years a resident within the United States.

5. In case of the removal of the President from office, or of his death, resignation, or inability to discharge the powers and duties of the said office, the same shall devolve on the Vice President, and the congress may by law provide for the case of removal, death, resignation or inability, both of the President and Vice President, declaring what officer shall then act as President, and such officer shall act accordingly until the disability be removed, or a President shall be elected.

6. The President shall, at stated times, receive for his services a compensation which shall neither be increased nor diminished during the period for which he shall have been elected, and he shall not receive within that period any other emolument from the United States, or any of them.

7. Before he enter on the execution of his office, he shall take the following oath or affirmation:—"I do solemnly swear (or affirm) that I will faithfully execute the office of President of the United States, and will to the best of my ability, preserve, protect and defend the Constitution of the United States."

Section 2. 1. The President shall be commander in chief of the army and navy of the United States, and of the militia of the several States, when called into the actual service of the United States; he may require the opinion in writing, of the principal officer in each of the executive departments, upon any subject relating to the duties of their respective offices, and he shall have power to grant reprieves and pardons for offenses against the United States, except in cases of impeachment.

2. He shall have power, by and with the advice and consent of the Senate, to make treaties, provided two thirds of the senators present concur; and he shall nominate, and by and with the advice and consent of the Senate, shall appoint ambassadors, other public ministers and consuls,

---

[6]Superseded by the Twelfth Amendment.

judges of the Supreme Court, and all other officers of the United States, whose appointments are not herein otherwise provided for, and which shall be established by law; but the Congress may by law vest the appointment of such inferior officers, as they think proper, in the President alone, in the courts of laws, or in the heads of departments.

3. The President shall have power to fill up all vacancies that may happen during the recess of the Senate, by granting commissions which shall expire at the end of their next session.

Section 3. He shall from time to time give to the Congress information of the state of the Union, and recommend to their consideration such measures as he shall judge necessary and expedient; he may, on extraordinary occasions, convene both Houses, or either of them, and in case of disagreement between them with respect to the time of adjournment, he may adjourn them to such time as he shall think proper; he shall receive ambassadors and other public ministers; he shall take care that the laws be faithfully executed, and shall commission all the officers of the United States.

Section 4. The President, Vice President, and all civil officers of the United States, shall be removed from office on impeachment for, and conviction of, treason, bribery, or other high crimes and misdemeanors.

Article III

Section 1. The judicial power of the United States shall be vested in one Supreme Court, and in such inferior courts as the Congress may from time to time ordain and establish. The judges, both of the Supreme and inferior courts, shall hold their offices during good behavior, and shall, at stated times, receive for their services, a compensation, which shall not be diminished during their continuance in office.

Section 2. 1. The judicial power shall extend to all cases, in law and equity, arising under this Constitution, the laws of the United States, and treaties made, or which shall be made, under their authority;—to all cases of admiralty and maritime jurisdiction;—to controversies to which the United States shall be a party;[7]—to controversies between two or more States;—between a State and citizens of another State;—between citizens of different States;—between citizens of the same State claiming lands under grants of different States, and between a State, or the citizens thereof, and foreign States, citizens or subjects.

2. In all cases affecting ambassadors, other public ministers and consuls, and those in which a State shall be party, the Supreme Court shall have original jurisdiction. In all the other cases before mentioned, the Supreme Court shall have appellate jurisdiction, both as to law and fact, with such exceptions, and under such regulations as the Congress shall make.

3. The trial of all crimes, except in cases of impeachment, shall be by jury; and such trial shall be held in the State where the said crimes shall have been committed; but when not committed within any State, the trial shall be such place or places as the congress may by law have directed.

Section 3. 1. Treason against the United States shall consist only in levying war against them, or in adhering to their enemies, giving them aid and comfort. No person shall be convicted of treason unless on the testimony of two witnesses to the same overt act, or on confession in open court.

2. The Congress shall have power to declare the punishment of treason, but no attainder of treason shall work corruption of blood, or forfeiture except during the life of the person attained.

Article IV

Section 1. Full faith and credit shall be given in each State to the public acts, records, and judicial proceedings of every other State. And the Congress may by general laws prescribe the manner in which such acts, records and proceedings shall be proved, and the effect thereof.

Section 2. 1. The citizens of each State shall be entitled to all privileges and immunities of citizens in the several States.[8]

2. A person charged in any State with treason, felony, or other crime, who shall flee from justice, and be found in another State, shall on demand of the executive authority of the State from which he fled, be delivered up to be removed to the State having jurisdiction of the crime.

3. No person held to service or labor in one State under the laws thereof, escaping into another, shall, in consequence of any law or regulation therein, be discharged from such service or labor, but shall be delivered up on claim of the party to whom such service or labor may be due.[9]

Section 3. 1. New States may be admitted by the Congress into this Union; but no new State shall be formed or erected within the jurisdiction of any other State, nor any State be formed by the junction of two or more States, or parts of States, without the consent of the legislatures of the States concerned as well as of the Congress.

2. The Congress shall have power to dispose of and make all needful rules and regulations respecting the territory or other property belonging to the United States; and nothing in this Constitution shall be so construed as to prejudice any claims of the United States, or of any particular State.

Section 4. The United States shall guarantee to every State in this Union a republican form of government, and shall protect each of them against invasion; and on application of the legislature, or of the executive (when the legislature cannot be convened) against domestic violence.

Article V

The Congress, whenever two thirds of both Houses shall deem it necessary, shall propose amendments to this Constitution, or, on the application of the legislatures of

---

[7]See the Eleventh Amendment.

[8]See the Fourteenth Amendment, Sec. 1.
[9]See the Thirteenth Amendment.

two thirds of the several States, shall call a convention for proposing amendments, which in either case shall be valid to all intents and purposes, as part of this Constitution, when ratified by the legislatures of three fourths of the several States, or by conventions in three fourths thereof, as the one or the other mode of ratification may be proposed by the Congress; Provided that no amendment which may be made prior to the year one thousand eight hundred and eight shall in any manner affect the first and fourth clauses in the ninth section of the first article; and that no State, without its consent, shall be deprived of its equal suffrage in the Senate.

Article VI

1. All debts contracted and engagements entered into, before the adoption of this Constitution, shall be as valid against the United States under this Constitution, as under the Confederation.[10]

2. This Constitution, and the laws of the United States which shall be made in pursuance thereof; and all treaties made, or which shall be made, under the authority of the United States, shall be the supreme law of the land; and the judges in every State shall be bound thereby, any thing in the Constitution or laws of any State to the contrary notwithstanding.

3. The senators and representatives before mentioned, and the members of the several State legislatures, and all executive and judicial officers, both of the United States and of the several States, shall be bound by oath or affirmation to support this Constitution; but no religious test shall ever be required as a qualification to any office or public trust under the United States.

Article VII

1. The ratification of the conventions of nine States shall be sufficient for the establishment of this Constitution between the States so ratifying the same.

2. Done in Convention by the unanimous consent of the States present the seventeenth day of September in the year of our Lord one thousand seven hundred and eighty-seven, and of the independence of the United States of America the twelfth. In witness whereof we have hereunto subscribed our names.

[Signatories' names omitted]

* * *

Articles in addition to, and amendment of, the Constitution of the United States of America, proposed by Congress, and ratified by the legislatures of the several States, pursuant to the fifth article of the original Constitution.

Amendment I [First ten amendments ratified December 15, 1791]

Congress shall make no law respecting an establishment of religion, or prohibiting the free exercise thereof; or abridging the freedom of speech, or of the press; or the right of the people peaceably to assemble, and to petition the government for a redress of grievances.

Amendment II

A well regulated militia, being necessary to the security of a free State, the right of the people to keep and bear arms, shall not be infringed.

Amendment III

No soldier shall, in time of peace be quartered in any house, without the consent of the owner, nor in time of war, but in a manner to be prescribed by law.

Amendment IV

The right of the people to be secure in their persons, houses, papers, and effects, against unreasonable searches and seizures, shall not be violated, and no warrants shall issue, but upon probable cause, supported by oath or affirmation, and particularly describing the place to be searched, and the persons or things to be seized.

Amendment V

No person shall be held to answer for a capital or otherwise infamous crime, unless on a presentment or indictment of a grand jury, except in cases arising in the land or naval forces, or in the militia, when in actual service in time of war or public danger; nor shall any person be subject for the same offense to be twice put in jeopardy of life or limb; nor shall be compelled in any criminal case to be a witness against himself, nor be deprived of life, liberty, or property, without due process of law; nor shall private property be taken for public use, without just compensation.

Amendment VI

In all criminal prosecutions, the accused shall enjoy the right to a speedy and public trial, by an impartial jury of the State and district wherein the crime shall have been committed, which district shall have been previously ascertained by law, and to be informed of the nature and cause of the accusation; to be confronted with the witnesses against him; to have compulsory process for obtaining witnesses in his favor, and to have the assistance of counsel for his defense.

Amendment VII

In suits at common law, where the value in controversy shall exceed twenty dollars, the right of trial by jury shall be preserved, and no fact tried by a jury shall be otherwise reexamined in any court of the United States, than according to the rules of the common law.

Amendment VIII

Excessive bail shall not be required, nor excessive fines imposed, nor cruel and unusual punishments inflicted.

---

[10]See the Fourteenth Amendment, Sec. 4.

Amendment IX

The enumeration in the Constitution of certain rights shall not be construed to deny or disparage others retained by the people.

Amendment X

The powers not delegated to the United States by the Constitution, nor prohibited by it to the States, are reserved to the States respectively, or to the people.

Amendment XI [January 8, 1798]

The judicial power of the United States shall not be construed to extend to any suit in law or equity, commended or prosecuted against one of the United States by citizens of another State, or by citizens or subjects of any foreign State.

Amendment XII [September 25, 1804]

The electors shall meet in their respective States, and vote by ballot for President and Vice President, one of whom, at least, shall not be an inhabitant of the same State with themselves; they shall name in their ballots the person voted for as President, and in distinct ballots, the person voted for as Vice President, and they shall make distinct lists of all persons voted for as President and of all persons voted for as Vice President, and of the number of votes for each, which lists they shall sign and certify, and transmit sealed to the seat of the government of the United States, directed to the President of the Senate;—The President of the Senate shall, in the presence of the Senate and House of Representatives, open all the certificates and the votes shall then be counted;—The person having the greatest number of votes for President, shall be the President, if such number be a majority of the whole number of electors appointed; and if no person have such majority, then from the persons having the highest numbers not exceeding three on the list of those voted for as President, the House of Representatives shall choose immediately, by ballot, the President. But in choosing the President, the votes shall be taken by States, the representation from each State having one vote; a quorum for this purpose shall consist of a member or members from two thirds of the States, and a majority of all the States shall be necessary to a choice. And if the House of Representatives shall not choose a President whenever the right of choice shall devolve upon them, before the fourth day of March next following, then the Vice President shall act as President, as in the case of the death or other constitutional disability of the President. The person having the greatest number of votes as Vice President shall be the Vice President, if such number be a majority of the whole number of electors appointed, and if no person have a majority, then from the two highest numbers on the list, the Senate shall choose the Vice President; a quorum for the purpose shall consist of two thirds of the whole number of Senators, and a majority of the whole number shall be necessary to a choice. But no person constitutionally ineligible to the office of President shall be eligible to that of Vice President of the United States.

Amendment XIII [December 18, 1865]

Section 1. Neither slavery nor involuntary servitude, except as a punishment for crime whereof the party shall have been duly convicted, shall exist within the United States, or any place subject to their jurisdiction.

Section 2. Congress shall have power to enforce this article by appropriate legislation.

Amendment XIV [July 28, 1868]

Section 1. All persons born or naturalized in the United States, and subject to the jurisdiction thereof, are citizens of the United States and of the State wherein they reside. No State shall make or enforce any law which shall abridge the privileges or immunities of citizens of the United States; nor shall any State deprive any person of life, liberty, or property, without due process of law; nor deny to any person within its jurisdiction the equal protection of the laws.

Section 2. Representatives shall be apportioned among the several States according to their respective numbers, counting the whole number of persons in each State, excluding Indians not taxed. But when the right to vote at any election for the choice of electors for President and Vice President of the United States, representatives in Congress, the executive and judicial officers of a State, or the members of the legislature thereof, is denied to any of the male inhabitants of such State, being twenty-one years of age, and citizens of the United States, or in any way abridged, except for participating in rebellion, or other crime, the basis of representation there shall be reduced in the proportion which the number of such male citizens shall bear to the whole number of male citizens twenty-one years of age in such State.

Section 3. No person shall be a senator or representative in Congress, or elector of President and Vice President, or hold any office, civil or military, under the United States, or under any State, who having previously taken an oath, as a member of Congress, or as an officer of the United States, or as a member of any State legislature, or as an executive or judicial officer of any State, to support the Constitution of the United States, shall have engaged in insurrection or rebellion against the same, or given aid or comfort to the enemies thereof. But Congress may by a vote of two thirds of each House, remove such disability.

Section 4. The validity of the public debt of the United States, authorized by law, including debts incurred for payment of pensions and bounties for services in suppressing insurrection or rebellion; shall not be questioned. But neither the United States nor any State shall assume or pay any debt or obligation incurred in aid of insurrection or rebellion against the United States, or any claim for the loss or emancipation of any slave; but all such debts, obligations, and claims shall be held illegal and void.

Section 5. The Congress shall have the power to enforce, by appropriate legislation, the provisions of this article.

Amendment XV [March 30, 1870]

Section 1. The right of citizens of the United States to vote shall not be denied or abridged by the United States or by any State on account of race, color, or previous condition of servitude.

Section 2. The Congress shall have power to enforce this article by appropriate legislation.

Amendment XVI [February 25, 1913]

The Congress shall have power to lay and collect taxes on incomes, from whatever source derived, without apportionment among the several States, and without regard to any census or enumeration.

Amendment XVII [May 31, 1913]

The Senate of the United States shall be composed of two senators from each State, elected by the people thereof, for six years; and each senator shall have one vote. The electors in each State shall have the qualifications requisite for electors of the most numerous branch of the State legislature.

When vacancies happen in the representation of any State in the Senate, the executive authority of such State shall issue writs of election to fill such vacancies: Provided, That the legislature of any State may empower the executive thereof to make temporary appointments until the people fill the vacancies by election as the legislature may direct.

This amendment shall not be so construed as to affect the election or term of any senator chosen before it becomes valid as part of the Constitution.

Amendment XVIII[11] [January 29, 1919]

After one year from the ratification of this article, the manufacture, sale, or transportation of intoxicating liquors within, the importation thereof into, or the exportation thereof from the United States and all territory subject to the jurisdiction thereof for beverage purposes is thereby prohibited.

The Congress and the several States shall have concurrent power to enforce this article by appropriate legislation.

This article shall be inoperative unless it shall have been ratified as an amendment to the Constitution by the legislatures of the several States, as provided in the constitution, within seven years from the date of the submission hereof to the States by Congress.

Amendment XIX [August 26, 1920]

The right of citizens of the United States to vote shall not be denied or abridged by the United States or by any State on account of sex.

Congress shall have the power to enforce this article by appropriate legislation.

Amendment XX [January 23, 1933]

Section 1. The terms of the President and Vice President shall end at noon on the 20th day of January and the terms of Senators and Representatives at noon on the 3d day of January, of the years in which such terms would have ended if this article had not been ratified; and the terms of their successors shall then begin.

Section 2. The Congress shall assemble at least once in every year, and such meeting shall begin at noon on the 3d day of January, unless they shall by law appoint a different day.

Section 3. If, at the time fixed for the beginning of the term of President, the President-elect shall have died, the Vice President-elect shall become President. If a President shall not have been chosen before the time fixed for the beginning of his term, or if the President-elect shall have failed to qualify, then the Vice President-elect shall act as President until a President shall have qualified; and the Congress may by law provide for the case wherein neither a President-elect nor a Vice President-elect shall have qualified, declaring who shall then act as President, or the manner in which one who is to act shall be selected, and such person shall act accordingly until a President or Vice President shall have qualified.

Section 4. The Congress may by law provide for the case of the death of any of the persons from whom, the House of Representatives may choose a President whenever the right of choice shall have devolved upon them, and for the case of the death of any of the persons from whom the Senate may choose a Vice President whenever the right of choice shall have devolved upon them.

Section 5. Sections 1 and 2 shall take effect on the 15th day of October following the ratification of this article.

Section 6. This article shall be inoperative unless it shall have been ratified as an amendment to the Constitution by the legislatures of three-fourths of the several States within seven years from the date of its submission.

Amendment XXI [December 5, 1933]

Section 1. The Eighteenth Article of amendment to the Constitution of the United States is hereby repealed.

Section 2. The transportation or importation into any State, Territory, or possession of the United States for delivery or use therein of intoxicating liquors in violation of the laws thereof, is hereby prohibited.

Section 3. This article shall be inoperative unless it shall have been ratified as an amendment to the Constitution by conventions in the several States, as provided in the Constitution, within seven years from the date of the submission thereof to the States by the Congress.

Amendment XXII [March 1, 1951]

No person shall be elected to the office of the President more than twice, and no person who has held the office of President, or acted as President, for more than two years of a term to which some other person was elected President shall be elected to the office of the President more than once.

---

[11]Repeated by the Twenty-first Amendment.

But this article shall not apply to any person holding the office of President when this article was proposed by the Congress, and shall not prevent any person who may be holding the office of President, or acting as President, during the term within which this article becomes operative from holding the office of President or acting as President during the remainder of such term.

This article shall be inoperative unless it shall have been ratified as an amendment to the Constitution by the legislatures of three-fourths of the several States within seven years from the date of its submission to the States by the Congress.

Amendment XXIII [March 29, 1961]

Section 1. The District constituting the seat of Government of the United States shall appoint in such manner as the Congress may direct.

A number of electors of President and Vice President equal to the whole number of Senators and Representatives in Congress to which the District would be entitled if it were a State, but in no event more than the least populous State; they shall be in addition to those appointed by the States, but they shall be considered, for the purposes of the election of President and Vice President, to be electors appointed by a State; and they shall meet in the District and perform such duties as provided by the twelfth article of amendment.

Section 2. The Congress shall have power to enforce this article by appropriate legislation.

Amendment XXIV [January 23, 1964]

Section 1. The right of citizens of the United States to vote in any primary or other election for President or Vice President, for electors for President or Vice President, or for Senator or Representative in Congress, shall not be denied or abridged by the United States or any State by reason of failure to pay any poll tax or other tax.

Section 2. The Congress shall have power to enforce this article by appropriate legislation.

Amendment XXV [February 10, 1967]

Section 1. In case of the removal of the President from office or of his death or resignation, the Vice President shall become President.

Section 2. Whenever there is a vacancy in the office of the Vice President, the President shall nominate a Vice President who shall take office upon confirmation by a majority of both Houses of Congress.

Section 3. Whenever the President transmits to the President pro tempore of the Senate and the Speaker of the House of Representatives his written declaration that he is unable to discharge the powers and duties of his office, and until he transmits to them a written declaration to the

contrary, such powers and duties shall be discharged by the Vice President as Acting President.

Section 4. Whenever the Vice President and a majority of either the principal officers of the executive departments or of such other body as Congress may by law provide, transmit to the President pro tempore of the Senate and the Speaker of the House of Representatives their written declaration that the President is unable to discharge the powers and duties of his office, the Vice President shall immediately assume the powers and duties of the office as Acting President.

Thereafter, when the President transmits to the President pro tempore of the Senate and the Speaker of the House of Representatives his written declaration that no inability exists, he shall resume the powers and duties of his office unless the Vice President and a majority of either the principal officers of the executive departments or of such other body as Congress may by law provide, transmit within four days to the President pro tempore of the Senate and the Speaker of the House of Representatives their written declaration that the President is unable to discharge the powers and duties of his office. Thereupon Congress shall decide the issue, assembling within forty-eight hours for that purpose if not in session. If the Congress, within twenty-one days after receipt of the latter written declaration, or, if Congress is not in session, within twenty-one days after Congress is required to assemble, determines by two-thirds vote of both Houses that the President is unable to discharge the powers and duties of his office, the Vice President shall continue to discharge the same as Acting President; otherwise, the President shall resume the powers and duties of his office.

Amendment XXVI [June 30, 1971]

Section 1. The right of citizens of the United States who are eighteen years of age or older to vote shall not be denied or abridged by the United States or by any State on account of age.

Section 2. The Congress shall have power to enforce this article by appropriate legislation.

Amendment XXVII[12] [May 7, 1992]

No law, varying the compensation for services of the Senators and Representatives, shall take effect until an election of Representatives shall have intervened.

---

[12]James Madison proposed this amendment in 1789 together with the ten amendments that were adopted as the Bill of Rights, but it failed to win ratification at the time. Congress, however, had set no deadline for its ratification, and over the years—particularly in the 1980s and 1990s—many states voted to add it to the Constitution. With the ratification of Michigan in 1992 it passed the threshold of 3/4ths of the states required for adoption, but because the process took more than 200 years, its validity remains in doubt.

PRESIDENTS AND VICE PRESIDENTS

1. George Washington (1789)
   John Adams (1789)

2. John Adams (1797)
   Thomas Jefferson (1797)

3. Thomas Jefferson (1801)
   Aaron Burr (1801)
   George Clinton (1805)

4. James Madison (1809)
   George Clinton (1809)
   Elbridge Gerry (1813)

5. James Monroe (1817)
   Daniel D. Thompkins (1817)

6. John Quincy Adams (1825)
   John C. Calhoun (1825)

7. Andrew Jackson (1829)
   John C. Calhoun (1829)
   Martin Van Buren (1833)

8. Martin Van Buren (1837)
   Richard M. Johnson (1837)

9. William H. Harrison (1841)
   John Tyler (1841)

10. John Tyler (1841)

11. James K. Polk (1845)
    George M. Dallas (1845)

12. Zachary Taylor (1849)
    Millard Fillmore (1849)

13. Millard Fillmore (1850)

14. Franklin Pierce (1853)
    William R. King (1853)

15. James Buchanan (1857)
    John C. Breckinridge (1857)

16. Abraham Lincoln (1861)
    Hannibal Hamlin (1861)
    Andrew Johnson (1865)

17. Andrew Johnson (1865)

18. Ulysses S. Grant (1869)
    Schuyler Colfax (1869)
    Henry Wilson (1873)

19. Rutherford B. Hayes (1877)
    William A. Wheeler (1877)

20. James A. Garfield (1881)
    Chester A. Arthur (1881)

21. Chester A. Arthur (1881)

22. Grover Cleveland (1885)
    T. A. Hendricks (1885)

23. Benjamin Harrison (1889)
    Levi P. Morgan (1889)

24. Grover Cleveland (1893)
    Adlai E. Stevenson (1893)

25. William McKinley (1897)
    Garret A. Hobart (1897)
    Theodore Roosevelt (1901)

26. Theodore Roosevelt (1901)
    Charles Fairbanks (1905)

27. William H. Taft (1909)
    James S. Sherman (1909)

28. Woodrow Wilson (1913)
    Thomas R. Marshall (1913)

29. Warren G. Harding (1921)
    Calvin Coolidge (1921)

30. Calvin Coolidge (1923)
    Charles G. Dawes (1925)

31. Herbert C. Hoover (1929)
    Charles Curtis (1929)

32. Franklin D. Roosevelt (1933)
    John Nance Garner (1933)
    Henry A. Wallace (1941)
    Harry S. Truman (1945)

33. Harry S. Truman (1945)
    Alben W. Barkley (1949)

34. Dwight D. Eisenhower (1953)
    Richard M. Nixon (1953)

35. John F. Kennedy (1961)
    Lyndon B. Johnson (1961)

36. Lyndon B. Johnson (1963)
    Hubert H. Humphrey (1965)

37. Richard M. Nixon (1969)
    Spiro T. Agnew (1969)
    Gerald R. Ford (1973)

38. Gerald R. Ford (1974)
    Nelson A. Rockefeller (1974)

39. James E. Carter Jr. (1977)
    Walter F. Mondale (1977)

40. Ronald W. Reagan (1981)
    George H. Bush (1981)

41. George H. Bush (1989)
    James D. Quayle III (1989)

42. William J. Clinton (1993)
    Albert Gore (1993)

43. George W. Bush (2001)
    Richard Cheney (2001)

44. Barack H. Obama (2009)
    Joseph Biden (2009)

45. Donald J. Trump (2017)
    Michael Richard Pence (2017)

PRESIDENTIAL ELECTIONS

Year	Number of States	Candidates	Party	Popular Vote*	Electoral Vote[†]	Percentage of Popular Vote*
1789	11	GEORGE WASHINGTON	No party designations		69	
		John Adams			34	
		Other Candidates			35	
1792	15	GEORGE WASHINGTON	No party designations		132	
		John Adams			77	
		George Clinton			50	
		Other Candidates			5	
1796	16	JOHN ADAMS	Federalist		71	
		Thomas Jefferson	Democratic-Republican		68	
		Thomas Pinckney	Federalist		59	
		Aaron Burr	Democratic-Republican		30	
		Other Candidates			48	
1800	16	THOMAS JEFFERSON	Democratic-Republican		73	
		Aaron Burr	Democratic-Republican		73	
		John Adams	Federalist		65	
		Charles C. Pinckney	Federalist		64	
		John Jay	Federalist		1	
1804	17	THOMAS JEFFERSON	Democratic-Republican		162	
		Charles C. Pinckney	Federalist		14	
1808	17	JAMES MADISON	Democratic-Republican		122	
		Charles C. Pinckney	Federalist		47	
		George Clinton	Democratic-Republican		6	
1812	18	JAMES MADISON	Democratic-Republican		128	
		DeWitt Clinton	Federalist		89	
1816	19	JAMES MONROE	Democratic-Republican		183	
		Rufus King	Federalist		34	
1820	24	JAMES MONROE	Democratic-Republican		231	
		John Quincy Adams	Independent-Republican		1	
1824	24	JOHN QUINCY ADAMS	Democratic-Republican	108,740	84	30.5
		Andrew Jackson	Democratic-Republican	153,544	99	43.1
		William H. Crawford	Democratic-Republican	46,618	41	13.1
		Henry Clay	Democratic-Republican	47,136	37	13.2
1828	24	ANDREW JACKSON	Democrat	647,286	178	56.0
		John Quincy Adams	National-Republican	508,064	83	44.0
1832	24	ANDREW JACKSON	Democrat	687,502	219	55.0
		Henry Clay	National-Republican	530,189	49	42.4
		William Wirt	Anti-Masonic	33,108	7	
		John Floyd	National-Republican		11	2.6

*Percentage of popular vote given for any election year may not total 100 percent because candidates receiving less than 1 percent of the popular vote have been omitted.

[†]Prior to the passage of the Twelfth Amendment in 1904, the electoral college voted for two presidential candidates; the runner-up became Vice-President. Data from *Historical Statistics of the United States, Colonial Times to 1957* (1961), pp. 682–683, and *The World Almanac*.

PRESIDENTIAL ELECTIONS (continued)

Year	Number of States	Candidates	Party	Popular Vote	Electoral Vote	Percentage of Popular Vote
1836	26	MARTIN VAN BUREN	Democrat	765,483	170	50.9
		William H. Harrison	Whig		73	
		Hugh L. White	Whig	739,795	26	49.1
		Daniel Webster	Whig		14	
		W. P. Mangum	Whig		11	
1840	26	WILLIAM H. HARRISON	Whig	1,274,624	234	53.1
		Martin Van Buren	Democrat	1,127,781	60	46.9
1844	26	JAMES K. POLK	Democrat	1,338,464	170	49.6
		Henry Clay	Whig	1,300,097	105	48.1
		James G. Birney	Liberty	62,300		2.3
1848	30	ZACHARY TAYLOR	Whig	1,360,967	163	47.4
		Lewis Cass	Democrat	1,222,342	127	42.5
		Martin Van Buren	Free-Soil	291,263		10.1
1852	31	FRANKLIN PIERCE	Democrat	1,601,117	254	50.9
		Winfield Scott	Whig	1,385,453	42	44.1
		John P. Hale	Free-Soil	155,825		5.0
1856	31	JAMES BUCHANAN	Democrat	1,832,955	174	45.3
		John C. Frémont	Republican	1,339,932	114	33.1
		Millard Fillmore	American			
			("Know Nothing")	871,731	8	21.6
1860	33	ABRAHAM LINCOLN	Republican	1,865,593	180	39.8
		Stephen A. Douglas	Democrat	1,382,713	12	29.5
		John C. Breckinridge	Democrat	848,356	72	18.1
		John Bell	Constitutional Union	592,906	39	12.6
1864	36	ABRAHAM LINCOLN	Republican	2,206,938	212	55.0
		George B. McClellan	Democrat	1,803,787	21	45.0
1868	37	ULYSSES S. GRANT	Republican	3,013,421	214	52.7
		Horatio Seymour	Democrat	2,706,829	80	47.3
1872	37	ULYSSES S. GRANT	Republican	3,596,745	286	55.6
		Horace Greeley	Democrat	2,843,446		*43.9
1876	38	RUTHERFORD B. HAYES	Republican	4,036,572	185	48.0
		Samuel J. Tilden	Democrat	4,284,020	184	51.0
1880	38	JAMES A. GARFIELD	Republican	4,453,295	214	48.5
		Winfield S. Hancock	Democrat	4,414,082	155	48.1
		James B. Weaver	Greenback-Labor	308,578		3.4
1884	38	GROVER CLEVELAND	Democrat	4,879,507	219	48.5
		James G. Blaine	Republican	4,850,293	182	48.2
		Benjamin F. Butler	Greenback-Labor	175,370		1.8
		John P. St. John	Prohibition	150,369		1.5

*Because of the death of Greeley, Democratic electors scattered their votes.

PRESIDENTIAL ELECTIONS (continued)

Year	Number of States	Candidates	Party	Popular Vote	Electoral Vote	Percentage of Popular Vote
1888	38	BENJAMIN HARRISON	Republican	5,447,129	233	47.9
		Grover Cleveland	Democrat	5,537,857	168	48.6
		Clinton B. Fisk	Prohibition	249,506		2.2
		Anson J. Streeter	Union Labor	146,935		1.3
1892	44	GROVER CLEVELAND	Democrat	5,555,426	277	46.1
		Benjamin Harrison	Republican	5,182,690	145	43.0
		James B. Weaver	People's	1,029,846	22	8.5
		John Bidwell	Prohibition	264,133		2.2
1896	45	WILLIAM MCKINLEY	Republican	7,102,246	271	51.1
		William J. Bryan	Democrat	6,492,559	176	47.7
1900	45	WILLIAM MCKINLEY	Republican	7,218,491	292	51.7
		William J. Bryan	Democrat; Populist	6,356,734	155	45.5
		John C. Woolley	Prohibition	208,914		1.5
1904	45	THEODORE ROOSEVELT	Republican	7,628,461	336	57.4
		Alton B. Parker	Democrat	5,084,223	140	37.6
		Eugene V. Debs	Socialist	402,283		3.0
		Silas C. Swallow	Prohibition	258,536		1.9
1908	46	WILLIAM H. TAFT	Republican	7,675,320	321	51.6
		William J. Bryan	Democrat	6,412,294	162	43.1
		Eugene V. Debs	Socialist	420,793		2.8
		Eugene W. Chafin	Prohibition	253,840		1.7
1912	48	WOODROW WILSON	Democrat	6,296,547	435	41.9
		Theodore Roosevelt	Progressive	4,118,571	88	27.4
		William H. Taft	Republican	3,486,720	8	23.2
		Eugene V. Debs	Socialist	900,672		6.0
		Eugene W. Chafin	Prohibition	206,275		1.4
1916	48	WOODROW WILSON	Democrat	9,127,695	277	49.4
		Charles E. Hughes	Republican	8,533,507	254	46.2
		A. L. Benson	Socialist	585,113		3.2
		J. Frank Hanly	Prohibition	220,506		1.2
1920	48	WARREN G. HARDING	Republican	16,143,407	404	60.4
		James M. Cox	Democrat	9,130,328	127	34.2
		Eugene V. Debs	Socialist	919,799		3.4
		P. P. Christensen	Farmer-Labor	265,411		1.0
1924	48	CALVIN COOLIDGE	Republican	15,718,211	382	54.0
		John W. Davis	Democrat	8,385,283	136	28.8
		Robert M. La Follette	Progressive	4,831,289	13	16.6
1928	48	HERBERT C. HOOVER	Republican	21,391,993	444	58.2
		Alfred E. Smith	Democrat	15,016,169	87	40.9

PRESIDENTIAL ELECTIONS (continued)

Year	Number of States	Candidates	Party	Popular Vote	Electoral Vote	Percentage of Popular Vote
1932	48	FRANKLIN D. ROOSEVELT	Democrat	22,809,638	472	57.4
		Herbert C. Hoover	Republican	15,758,901	59	39.7
		Norman Thomas	Socialist	881,951		2.2
1936	48	FRANKLIN D. ROOSEVELT	Democrat	27,752,869	523	60.8
		Alfred M. Landon	Republican	16,674,665	8	36.5
		William Lemke	Union	882,479		1.9
1940	48	FRANKLIN D. ROOSEVELT	Democrat	27,307,819	449	54.8
		Wendell L. Willkie	Republican	22,321,018	82	44.8
1944	48	FRANKLIN D. ROOSEVELT	Democrat	25,606,585	432	53.5
		Thomas E. Dewey	Republican	22,014,745	99	46.0
1948	48	HARRY S TRUMAN	Democrat	24,105,812	303	49.5
		Thomas E. Dewey	Republican	21,970,065	189	45.1
		J. Strom Thurmond	States' Rights	1,169,063	39	2.4
		Henry A. Wallace	Progressive	1,157,172		2.4
1952	48	DWIGHT D. EISENHOWER	Republican	33,936,234	442	55.1
		Adlai E. Stevenson	Democrat	27,314,992	89	44.4
1956	48	DWIGHT D. EISENHOWER	Republican	35,590,472	457*	57.6
		Adlai E. Stevenson	Democrat	26,022,752	73	42.1
1960	50	JOHN F. KENNEDY	Democrat	34,227,096	303†	49.9
		Richard M. Nixon	Republican	34,108,546	219	49.6
1964	50	LYNDON B. JOHNSON	Democrat	42,676,220	486	61.3
		Barry M. Goldwater	Republican	26,860,314	52	38.5
1968	50	RICHARD M. NIXON	Republican	31,785,480	301	43.4
		Hubert H. Humphrey	Democrat	31,275,165	191	42.7
		George C. Wallace	American Independent	9,906,473	46	13.5
1972	50	RICHARD M. NIXON‡	Republican	47,165,234	520	60.6
		George S. McGovern	Democrat	29,168,110	17	37.5
1976	50	JAMES E. CARTER JR.	Democrat	40,828,929	297	50.1
		Gerald R. Ford	Republican	39,148,940	240	47.9
		Eugene McCarthy	Independent	739,256		
1980	50	RONALD W. REAGAN	Republican	43,201,220	489	50.9
		James E. Carter Jr.	Democrat	34,913,332	49	41.2
		John B. Anderson	Independent	5,581,379		
1984	50	RONALD W. REAGAN	Republican	53,428,357	525	59.0
		Walter F. Mondale	Democrat	36,930,923	13	41.0

*Walter B. Jones received 1 electoral vote.
†Harry F. Byrd received 15 electoral votes.
‡Resigned August 9, 1974: Vice President Gerald R. Ford became President.

PRESIDENTIAL ELECTIONS (continued)

Year	Number of States	Candidates	Party	Popular Vote	Electoral Vote	Percentage of Popular Vote
1988	50	GEORGE H. W. BUSH	Republican	48,901,046	426	53.4
		Michael Dukakis	Democrat	41,809,030	111	45.6
1992	50	WILLIAM J. CLINTON	Democrat	43,728,275	370	43.2
		George H. W. Bush	Republican	38,167,416	168	37.7
		H. Ross Perot	United We Stand, America	19,237,247		19.0
1996	50	WILLIAM J. CLINTON	Democrat	45,590,703	379	49.0
		Robert Dole	Republican	37,816,307	159	41.0
		H. Ross Perot	Reform	7,874,283		8.0
2000	50	GEORGE W. BUSH	Republican	50,459,624	271	47.9
		Albert Gore	Democrat	51,003,328	266	49.4
		Ralph Nader	Green	2,882,985	0	2.7
2004	50	GEORGE W. BUSH	Republican	59,117,523	286	51.1
		John Kerry	Democrat	55,557,584	252	48.0
		Ralph Nader	Green	405,623	0	0.3
2008	50	BARACK H. OBAMA	Democrat	69,456,897	365	52.9
		John McCain	Republican	59,934,814	173	45.7
2012	50	BARACK H. OBAMA	Democrat	65,915,796	332	51.1
		Mitt Romney	Republican	60,933,500	206	47.2
2016	50	DONALD J. TRUMP	Republican	62,985,106	304	45.9
		Hillary Clinton	Democrat	65,853,625	227	48.0

Text Credits

Chapter 17 **Page 370:** Henry Watson wrote to a partner, 1865. In Michael W. Fitzgerald, The Union League Movement in the Deep South (LSU Press, 1989); Michael W. Fitzgerald (1989) """To Give Our Votes to the Party""": Black Political Agitation and Agricultural Change in Alabama, 1865–1870. In The Journal of American HistoryVol. 76, No. 2 (Sep., 1989), pp. 489–505. DOI: 10.2307/1907987; Two Hale County former slaves, Brister Reese and James K. Green, won election to the Alabama state legislature. In Michael W. Fitzgerald, The Union League Movement in the Deep South (LSU Press, 1989). **Page 373:** Act to Establish a Bureau for the Relief of Freedmen and Refugees", March 3, 1865. In Paul Skeels Peirce (1904) The Freedmen's Bureau: A Chapter in the History of Reconstruction, Volume 1. Ardent Media. **Page 374:** Representative Thaddeus Stevens told Pennsylvania Republicans in September 1865. In Michael Andrew Grisson (1989) Southern by the Grace of God. Pelican Publishing Company. **Page 375:** Civil Rights Act of 1866. In United States. Circuit Court (9th Circuit), Lorenzo Smith Boswell Sawyer. (1882) Reports of Cases Decided in the Circuit and District Courts of the United States for the Ninth Circuit, Volume 6. A.L. Bancroft. **Page 378:** The Fifth Amendment. The Constitution of the United States of America. U.S. Government Printing Office. **Page 380:** Charles Rodenbough (2009) Pine House - The Day Emancipation Dawned. Lulu.com</url>; Whitelaw Reid (1866) After the War: a Southern Tour: May 1, 1865, to May 1, 1866. Moore, Wilstach & Baldwin; Patience Johnson remarks from William Watts Ball (1932) The State That Forgot: South Carolina's Surrender to Democracy. Bobbs-Merrill Company. **Page 381:** Allen Freeman Davis, Harold D. Woodman (1992) Conflict and consensus in early American history. D.C. Heath and Co. **Page 383:** General Oliver O. Howard, Freedmen's Bureau commissioner (1908) Autobiography of Oliver Otis Howard, Major General, United States Army: pt. 1. Preparation for life. pt. 2. The Civil War. Baker & Taylor Company; Mobile Daily Register (May 30 1869) correspondent. Published by William d'Alton Mann. **Page 385:** The Harper's Weekly, November 16, 1867. A Journal of Civilization, Volume 11. **Page 386:** Caption: A drawing by Harper's Weekly illustrator William L. Sheppard titled "Electioneering in the South," July 25, 1868. Published by Harper & Brothers. **Page 387:** Thomas Settle, "The Spring Garden Speech," June 22, 1867. In Charles Rodenbough (2009) Pine House - The Day Emancipation Dawned. Lulu Press, Inc. **Page 389:** Alabama Department of Archives and History, Montgomery, Alabama. **Page 390:** "Affairs in Insurrectionary States: Report and Minority Reviews, Alabama, vol. 2," Senate Reports, 42nd Congress, 2nd Session, vol. 2, pt. 9, no. 41. **Page 392:** Abraham Lincoln, "Speech on Slavery", July 1, 1854, (1894) Early Speeches, Springfield Speech, Cooper Union Speech, Inaugural Addresses, Gettysburg Address, Selected Letters, Lincoln's Lost Speech. Doubleday & McClure Company. **Page 394:** Frederick F. Low Gave Evidence before the Congressional Committee. In George Frederick Seward (1881) Chinese Immigration in Its Social and Economical Aspects. C. Scribner's Sons. **Page 398:** J.M. Dalzell, in a Letter about the shift of Federal attention to John Sherman, July 29, 1877. In Eric Foner (1988) Reconstruction: America's unfinished revolution, 1863–1877. Harper & Row.

Chapter 18 **Page 401:** Evan G. Barnard (1936) A Rider of the Cherokee Strip. Houghton Mifflin Company. pp. 391–94. **Page 404:** Luther Standing Bear (1933) Land of the spotted eagle. Houghton Mifflin Company; Sitting Bull reportedly quoted. In Dan Georgakas (1973) The broken hoop: the history of Native Americans from 1600 to 1890, from the Atlantic coast to the Plains. Zenith Books. **Page 406:** Chief Joseph Speaks in Washington, D.C. In Jarold Ramsey (1980) Coyote Was Going There: Indian Literature of the Oregon Country. University of Washington Press. **Page 408:** Harper's Weekly, Volume 37. (1893) Harper's

Magazine Company. **Page 413:** Amanda Mae Ellis (1959) The Strange, Uncertain Years. Shoe String Press. **Page 414:** New York Tribune editor Horace Greeley quoted. In (1975) Will the Family Farm Survive in America?: Joint Hearings Before the Select Committee on Small Business and the Committee on Interior and Insular Affairs, United States Senate, Ninety-fourth Congress, First Session . . . United States. Congress. Senate. Select Committee on Small Business. U.S. Government Printing Office. **Page 415:** (1980) To All Inquiring Friends: Letters, Diaries, and Essays in North Dakota, 1880–1910. Department of English, University of North Dakota. **Page 420:** Frederick Jackson Turner (1893) "The Significance of the Frontier in American History": Annual Report of the American Historical Association. University Microfilms. **Page 421:** Alice Cunningham Fletcher (1893) A Study of Omaha Indian Music. University of Nebraska Press. **Page 422:** Indian Commissioner Thomas Jefferson Morgan wrote in 1889. In Fifty-Eighth Annual Report of the Commissioner of Indian Affairs to the Secretary of Interior. Washington, D.C. Government Printing Office. http://digicoll.library.wisc.edu/cgi-bin/History/History-idx?type=turn&entity=History.AnnRep89.p0010&id=History.AnnRep89&isize=M; "Maka' sito'maniyaS" Translation. In James Mooney (1896) The Ghost-dance Religion and the Sioux Outbreak of 1890, Volume 14, Issue 2. U.S. Government Printing Office. **Page 423:** "The Legal Status of the Indian" by Philip Garrett. In Proceedings of the Ninth Annual Meeting of the Lake Mohonk Conference of Friends of the Indian 1891 Pamphlet. First Session, October 7, 1891. Edited by Isabel C. Barrows. Government Printing Office.

Chapter 19 **Page 430:** Samuel Fielden's Remarks. In Stewart Rapalje, Robert Linn Lawrence, Gustav Adolf Endlich, James Shrewsbury Erwin (1887) The Criminal Law Magazine and Reporter, Volume 9. Frederick D. Linn & Company; The Chicago Tribune Report (Haymarket Square, Chicago, May 4, 1886). In Dyer Daniel Lum, August Vincent Theodore Spies (1969) The Great Trial of the Chicago Anarchists. Arno Press; I.G. Blanchard & Reverend Jesse H. Jones's The "Eight-Hour Song", December 2, 1889. First appeared as a poem by Blanchard in Boston Daily Evening Voice (August 7, 1866) and Workingman's Advocate (August 18, 1866). Later Jesse Jones added the music. In Philip S. Foner (1975) American Labor Songs of the Nineteenth Century. Urbana: University of Illinois Press; Arbeiter-Zeitung (Workers' Newspaper), the local German-language newspaper, editor August Spies greeted May 1, 1886 hailed as "Emancipation Day ". In Norman L. Freeman (November 6, 1887) Anarchist Case: Advance Sheets of the Illinois Reports comprising Ages 1 to 267, inclusive of Volume 122. Supreme Court of Illinois. **Page 433:** George Eastmann quoted. In (1890) The Photographic Times, Volume 20. Scoville Manufacturing Company. **Page 434:** Jay Gould described, Striker at the copper mine at Coeur d'Alene, Idaho. 1892, The New York World (1892); Andrew Carnegie (1902) The Empire of Business (New York: Doubleday, Page & Co.), pp. 3–18. **Pages 438, 442:** United States. Bureau of Labor, Charles Patrick Neill (1910) Report on Condition of Woman and Child Wage-earners in the United States: In 19 Vols. . . . U.S. Government Printing Office. **Page 439:** Charles Bagot Labatt (1913) Employers' liability, statutes and contracts, compensation acts, blacklisting, rights in products of service. Lawyers Co-operative Publishing Company. **Page 445:** Jacob A. Riis (1890) How the Other Half Lives: Studies Among the Tenements of New York. Charles Scribner's Sons.

Chapter 20 **Page 456:** Senator Albert J. Beveridge, April 21, 1898. In John Braeman, Albert J. Beveridge: American Nationalist (Chicago: University of Chicago Press, 1971). **Page 458:** (1959) The Iowa Journal of History and Politics. State Historical Society of Iowa; Tammany Hall politician George Plunkit quoted. In (1951) The Iowa Journal of History and Politics. State Historical Society of Iowa; (1835) The Political Mirror: Or, Review of Jacksonism. J.P. Peaslee. **Page 462:** William Allen White, Emporia Gazette editor remarking on Mary Elizabeth Lease, Alexandra Kindell, Elizabeth S. Demers Ph.D. (2014) Encyclopedia of Populism in America: A Historical Encyclopedia [2 volumes]. ABC-CLIO. **Page 463:** Jeffersonian motto, People's Party, better known as the Populist party. In Edward McPherson (1882) A Handbook of Politics for 1868 [to 1894] Philp & Solomons. **Page 465:** Eugene V. Debs quoted. In Nick Salvatore (1982) Eugene V. Debs: Citizen and Socialist. University of Illinois Press. **Page 467:** Official Proceedings of the Democratic National Convention Held in Chicago, Illinois, July 7, 8, 9, 10, and 11, 1896, (Logansport, Indiana, 1896), 226–234. Reprinted in The Annals of America, Vol. 12, 1895–1904: Populism, Imperialism, and Reform (Chicago: Encyclopedia Britannica, Inc., 1968), 100–105. **Page 470:** Alice Fletcher, World's Columbian Exposition. In David Ware Stowe (2004) How Sweet the Sound: Music in the Spiritual Lives of Americans. Harvard University Press; Josiah Strong, prescient commentary in 1885. In Abraham Seldin Eisenstadt (1962) American History: Recent Interpretations, Volume 2. Crowell; (1900) Missionary Review of the World; 1878–1939, Volume 23, Part 2. Funk & Wagnalls Company. **Page 471:** Rudyard Kipling (1899) "The White Man's Burden" Doubleday and McClure Company. **Page 472:** James G. Blaine, 1886 quoted. In Edward P. Crapol (1973) America for Americans: economic nationalism and Anglophobia, 1876–1896. University of Wisconsin—Madison. **Page 474:** President William McKinley Speech at the Dinner of the Commercial Club of Cincinnati, October 30, 1897. In (January 1,1897) The Bulletin of the American Iron and Steel Association, Volumes 31–32. American Iron and Steel Association. **Page 475:** (1898) New York World. Joseph Pulitzer; (1938) The Chinese Social and Political Science Review, Volume 22. Chinese Social and Political Science Association. **Page 476:** (1897) The Bulletin of the American Iron and Steel Association, Volumes 31–32. American Iron and Steel Association. **Page 478:** Jim Cullen (1996) The art of democracy: a concise history of popular culture in the United States. Monthly Review Press; Theodore Roosevelt (1903) The Works of Theodore Roosevelt: American ideals and other essays, social and political. Scribner.

Chapter 21   Page 482: Jane Addams, "The Subjective Necessity for Social Settlement," Essay., 1892. In (1912) Twenty Years at Hull-House, with Autobiographical Notes, New York: The MacMillan Company. **Page 483:** Lillian Wald (1989) Lillian D. Wald, Progressive Activist. Feminist Press at CUNY. **Page 485:** Jacob August Riis (1907) The Making of an American. Library of Alexandria. **Page 487:** Jane Addams, "The Subjective Necessity for Social Settlement," Essay., 1892. In (1912) Twenty Years at Hull-House, with Autobiographical Notes, New York: The MacMillan Company; Muller v. Oregon. No. 107. Argued January 15, 1908. Decided February 24, 1908. 208 U.S. 412. [https://supreme.justia.com/cases/federal/us/208/412/case.html]. **Page 488:** Rheta Childe Dorr (1910) "What Eight Million Women Want". Boston, Small, Maynard & Company; George Washington Plunkitt, Interview with William Riordon (1905) "Plunkitt of Tammany Hall". New York: A.A. Knopf. pp. 3–8. **Page 489:** Frederic C. Howe, 1906. In Bernard Bailyn (1977) The Great Republic: A History of the American People. D.C. Heath and Company. **Page 492:** Poster Advertisement, 1918 Referendum on statewide Prohibition in Ohio. From "The Ohio Dry Campaign of 1918," Ohio State University History Department. Available online at http://ehistory.osu.edu/exhibitions/ohiodry/brdsds. In Thomas Streissguth (2009) The Roaring Twenties. Infobase Publishing. **Page 493:** Maimie Pinzer,"The Maimie Papers: Letters from an Ex-prostitute", (New York: Feminist Press at the City University of New York in cooperation with the Schlesinger Library of Radcliffe College, 1997). **Page 494:** Richard Watson Gilder (November 1903) "The Kindergarten: An Uplifting Social Influence in the Home and the District," Kindergarten Magazine. Chicago, Ill.: Kindergarten Magazine Co. p. 132; Elwood Cubberley (1909) "Changing Conceptions of Education". Boston: Houghton Mifflin Co. pp. 15–16. **Page 496:** Interview with Joe R., a Polish immigrant, July 21, 1974, POHP. In John E. Bodnar, Roger Simon, Michael P. Weber (1983) Lives of Their Own: Blacks, Italians, and Poles in Pittsburgh,

1900–1960. University of Illinois Press. **Page 497:** "In the Factory" by Morris Rosenfeld, the Survey, June 6, 1914, from The Survey Vol. XXXII: April,1914– September, 1914 (New York: Survey Associates, Inc.). **Page 499:** United States. Commission on Industrial Relations (1916) Industrial Relations: Final Report and Testimony. U.S. Government Printing Office; Industrial Workers of the World (IWW) Philosophy. In United States. Bureau of Labor Statistics, Estelle May Stewart (1936) Handbook of American Trade-unions: 1936 edition. U.S. Government Printing office. **Page 500:** United States. Dept. of Labor (1976) The U.S. Department of Labor Bicentennial History of the American Worker. U.S. Government Printing Office; John Reed, "Statement of Purpose for The Masses," Opening manifesto, 1912. The Masses Publishing Co. In John Reed Papers, 1903–1967 (MS Am 1091). Houghton Library, Harvard University. **Page 502:** Margaret Sanger, Woman Rebel, 1914. The Margaret Sanger Papers. The U.S. National Archives and Records Administration. **Page 503:** Booker T. Washington, Address at the Opening of the negro Exhibit in the Atlanta Exposition. In Henry Addison Nelson, Albert B. Robinson (1896) The Church at Home and Abroad, Volume 19. Presbyterian Board of Publication and Sabbath School Work; W.E.B. Du Bois, The Souls of Black Folk (1903) Chicago, A. C. McClurg & Co. **Page 504:** W.E.B. Du Bois, The Niagara Movement Declaration of Principles, 1905. Originally published in the Cleveland Gazette (July 22, 1905) Gazette Pub. Co. **Page 506:** John Muir (1901) Our National Parks. Boston, Massachusetts: Houghton Mifflin Company. **Page 507:** (1921) The Illustrated London News, Volume 158. Illustrated London News & Sketch Limited. **Page 508:** Woodrow Wilson (1913) The New Freedom: A Call for the Emancipation of the Generous Energies of a People. New York: Doubleday, Page & Company. **Page 510:** Lillian Wald (1934) Windows on Henry Street. Boston, Little, Brown, and Company.

Chapter 22   Page 514: Edward M Coffman, "The War to End All Wars: The American Military Experience in World War I", (Lexington, KY: University Press of Kentucky, ©1998.); Theodore Roosevelt quoted. In Alan Wolfe (1984) The Rise and Fall of the Soviet Threat: Domestic Sources of the Cold War Consensus. South End Press. **Page 515:** Alvin Cullum York (1928) Sergeant York, His Own Life Story and War Diary. Doubleday, Doran, Incorporated; American Legion, 1919 Preamble. In Fred L. Holmes (1925) State of Wisconsin Blue Book; Theodore Roosevelt to Henry L. Sprague, January 26, 1900. In (1906) A square deal. Allendale Press. **Page 516:** Secretary of State Elihu Root Letter, 1905. In George Black (1988) The Good Neighbor: How the United States Wrote History of Central America and the Caribbean. Pantheon Books. p. 74; Theodore Roosevelt to Henry L. Sprague, January 26, 1900. In (1906) A square deal. Allendale Press. **Page 517:** President Woodrow Wilson quoted. In Ray Stannard Baker (1927) Woodrow Wilson: Life and Letters, Volume 1. Doubleday, Page & Company; Woodrow Wilson: "Address to the Salesmanship Congress in Detroit, Michigan," July 10, 1916. Online by Gerhard Peters and John T. Woolley, The American Presidency Project. http://www.presidency.ucsb.edu/ws/?pid=117701. **Page 520:** (1815) The Law Times: The Journal and Record of the Law & the Lawyers, November 1914 to April 1915, Volume 138. Published at the office of The Law times. **Page 521:** Wilson's Slogan in the 1916 presidential campaign. In Randolph Chandler Downes (1970) The Rise of Warren Gamaliel Harding 1865–1920. Ohio State University Press. p. 597; Woodrow Wilson's War Message to Congress, February 3, 1917. **Page 523:** Randolph Bourne, unfinished essay "The State" 1918. (1919) Untimely Papers. New York, B. W. Huebsch. **Page 524:** Alexander T. Hussey, Raymond M. Flynn (1919) The History of Company E, 308th Infantry (1917–1919). Knickerbocker Press; Editorial (June 1917) The Crisis. Vol. 14, No. 2. p. 59. The Crisis Publishing Company; W.E.B. Dubois editorial (May 16, 1918) The Crisis. The Crisis Publishing Company. **Page 527:** Food Administration (Food and Fuel Act) Campaign. U.S. Food Administration. Library of Congress. **Page 528:** Cairns Collection of American Women Writers (1918) The Saturday Evening Post, Volume 191. Saturday Evening Post Company. **Page 531:** Carrie Chapman Catt, National American Woman Suffrage Association (NAWSA) quoted. In Woodrow Wilson, Arthur Stanley Link (1985) The papers of Woodrow Wilson, Volume 51.

Princeton University Press. **Page 533:** Eugene V. Debs quoted. In (1930) Constitutional Amendment Making War Legally Impossible: Hearing Before a Subcommittee . . . on S.J. Res. 45, April 12, 1930. **Page 539:** The Covenant of the League of Nations, Article X. Frederick Pollock (1920) The League of Nations. The Lawbook Exchange, Ltd. **Page 540:** Democrat James Reed of Missouri quoted. In Stephan Thernstrom (1989) A History of the American People: Since 1865. Harcourt Brace Jovanovich; Selig Adler (1957) The Isolationist Impulse: Its Twentieth-Century Reaction. London: Abelardschuman, Inc. **Page 541:** Senator Warren G. Harding, May 14, 1920. "Return to Normalcy Speech". In TeachingAmericanHistory.org. Ashland University.

Chapter 23 Page 546: Marcus Loew quoted. In (1980) Time, Volume 115, Issues 18–26. Time Incorporated; Julius Klein (January 22, 1923) "Trade Follows the Motion Pictures," idem Commerce Reports; "What are Motion Pictures Doing for Industry?" (1926) Annals of the American Academy of Political and Social Science, November 1926. pp. 79–83. **Page 550:** Robert and Helen Lynd (1929) Middletown: A Study in American Culture. Harcourt, Brace & World; Henry Ford, 1922 quoted. In Melvin Kranzberg, Joseph Gies (1975) By the sweat of thy brow: work in the Western world. Putnam. **Page 552:** Warren Harding quoted. In Carl Brent Swisher (1951) The theory and practice of American National Government. Houghton Mifflin; Steven F. Hayward (2012) The Politically Incorrect Guide to the Presidents: From Wilson to Obama. Regnery Publishing. **Page 553:** Herbert Hoover (1922) American Individualism. Doubleday, Page; "Statement of Hon. R. James Woolsey, Former Director of Central Intelligence, 1993–1995. In Floyd D. Spence (1997) Threats to U. S. National Security: Hearing Before the Committee National Security, U. S. House of Representatives. DIANE Publishing. **Page 559:** Roland Marchand (1985) Advertising the American Dream: Making Way for Modernity, 1920–1940. University of California Press. **Page 561:** Zelda Fitzgerald, 1924 quoted. In Nancy Milford (1970) Zelda: A Biography. Harper & Row. **Page 563:** Al "Scarface" Capone quoted. In Mary Bennett Peterson (1971) The Regulated Consumer. Green Hill Publishers. **Page 564:** Senator Henry Cabot Lodge, Immigration Restriction League quoted. In (1891) Congressional Record: Proceedings and Debates of the . . . Congress. U.S. Government Printing Office. **Page 566:** Jonathan Wright (2005) Shapers of the Great Debate on the Freedom of Religion: A Biographical Dictionary. Greenwood Publishing Group. **Page 568:** Alice Paul, National Woman's Party (NWP), a brief Equal Rights Amendment (ERA) to the Constitution, introduced in Congress in 1923. In (1929) Equal Rights Amendment: Hearings Before the United States Senate Committee on the Judiciary, Seventieth Congress, Second Session, on Feb. 1, 1929. U.S. Government Printing Office; Mary Anderson, director of the Women's Bureau in the Department of Labor. In (1929) Social Work Year Book, Volume 1. Russell Sage Foundation; M. Carey Thomas, ERA defense. In Allison L. Hepler (1996) Women in labor: mothers, medicine, and occupational health, 1890–1980. Temple University. **Page 569:** Abraham Hoffman (1974) Unwanted Mexican Americans in the Great Depression: Repatriation Pressures, 1929–1939. Tucson: The University of Arizona Press. **Page 571:** Harlem's largest newspaper, the Amsterdam News, explained Garvey's continuing appeal to African Americans. In Edmund David Cronon (1949) Marcus Garvey and the Universal Negro Improvement Association: A Study in Negro Nationalism. University of Wisconsin—Madison; Langston Hughes quoted. In Gilbert Osofsky (1966) Harlem; the making of a ghetto: Negro New York, 1890–1930. Harper & Row; Langston Hughes (June 23, 1926) "The Negro Artist and the Racial Mountain," The Nation 122. **Page 572:** James Weldon Johnson, 1927. In Raymond Jackson Wilson (1970) Reform, Crisis, and Confusion, 1900–1929. Random House; Gertrude Stein, 1925, remarked to Ernest Hemingway. In (1964) A Moveable Feast. New York: Scribner; Jake Barnes, war hero character in Ernest Hemingway (1926) The Sun Also Rises; F. Scott Fitzgerald (1920) This Side of Paradise, New York: Charles Scribner's Sons.

Chapter 24 Page 578: Fisher No. 2 strikers told New York Times. In (1957) The Communist, Volume 16, Issue 3; Maurice Sugar (1937) "Sit Down!" The Maurice Sugar Collection, Papers 1907–1973, 58 1/2 Linear Feet, Accession Number 232, Box 14, Folder 21–22. Walter P.

Reuther Library. Wayne State University. **Page 581:** Dorothea Lange: A Photographer's Life, by Milton Meltzer (Syracuse University Press, 1978) p. 71; Lorena A. Hickok, Richard Lowitt, Maurine Hoffman Beasley (1981) One Third of a Nation: Lorena Hickok Reports on the Great Depression. University of Illinois Press; Joseph S. Hall, Latrobe, Pa. to Bruce McClure, Secretary, Civil Works Administration, April 4, 1934, CWA Administrative Correspondence, Box 54, National Archives; Dr. Nathan Ackerman, Psychiatrist, Family Institute for Living. In Studs Terkel (1970) Hard Times: An Oral History of the Great Depression. Pantheon Books; Anna Novak, Chicago stockyard worker, interview, May 1939. In Robert A. Slayton (1988) Back of the Yards: The Making of a Local Democracy. University of Chicago Press; Lizabeth Cohen (2008) Making a New Deal: Industrial Workers in Chicago, 1919–1939. Cambridge University Press. pp. 248–249. **Page 582:** President Herbert Hoover, December 8, 1931 Annual Message to the Congress on the State of the Union. Online by Gerhard Peters and John T. Woolley, The American Presidency Project. http://www.presidency.ucsb.edu/ws/?pid=22933. **Page 583:** Franklin D. Roosevelt, Nomination Acceptance Speech, Democratic National Convention, July 2, 1932. "I Pledge You—I Pledge Myself to a New Deal for the American People." Online by Gerhard Peters and John T. Woolley, The American Presidency Project. http://www.presidency.ucsb.edu/ws/?pid=75174. **Page 584:** Franklin D. Roosevelt, Inaugural Address on March 4, 1933. Online by Gerhard Peters and John T. Woolley, The American Presidency Project. http://www.presidency.ucsb.edu/ws/?pid=14473. **Page 587:** Huey Long, Share Our Wealth Society. In John M. Murrin, Paul E. Johnson, James M. McPherson, Alice Fahs, Gary Gerstle (2013) Liberty, Equality, Power: A History of the American People, Volume II: Since 1863, Concise Edition. Cengage Learning. **Page 588:** Rexford G. Tugwell, Resettlement Administration 1935 quoted. In Carol Corden (1977) Planned cities: new towns in Britain and America. Sage Publications. **Page 589:** Frederick Douglass, "Should the negro Enlist in the Union Army", August 1863. In James S. Price (2011) The Battle of New Market Heights: Freedom Will Be Theirs by the Sword. Arcadia Publishing. **Page 590:** Franklin D. Roosevelt, Joliet, Illinois, October 14, 1936. In (1938) Public Papers of the Presidents of the United States: F.D. Roosevelt, 1936, Volume 5. Washington, D.C.: United States Government Printing Office; Lizabeth Cohen (2008) Making a New Deal: Industrial Workers in Chicago, 1919–1939. Cambridge University Press. **Page 592:** A woman's experience recounted in Kansas City Times, 1935. In Giles Slade (2013) American Exodus: Climate Change and the Coming Flight for Survival. New Society Publishers. **Page 593:** From Decade of Betrayal: Mexican Repatriation in the 1930s by Francisco Balderrama and Raymond Rodriguez. Copyright © 1995 University of New Mexico Press, 1995. **Page 596:** John Collier, Commissioner of Indian Affairs quoted. In Edward Jewitt Wheeler, Isaac Kaufman Funk, William Seaver Woods (1934) The Literary Digest, Volume 117, Part 2. Funk & Wagnalls; John Collier, Minutes of the plains Congress, Rapid City Indian School Rapid City, South Dakota, March 2–5, 1934. In Vine Deloria (2002) The Indian Reorganization Act: Congresses and Bills. University of Oklahoma Press. **Page 597:** Howard Gorman, a Navajo political leader responding to Collier. In Ruth Roessel, Broderick H. Johnson (1974) Navajo livestock reduction: a national disgrace. Navajo Community College Press; Franklin D. Roosevelt, Second Inaugural Address, January 20, 1937. Washington, U.S. Govt. Printing Office. **Page 598:** Clifford Burke Interview with radio host and author Studs Terkel, Hard Times 1969. In Bill Mullen, Sherry Lee Linkon (1996) Radical Revisions: Rereading 1930s Culture. University of Illinois; (1935) Friends' Intelligencer, Volume 92. **Page 599:** Eleanor Roosevelt (1933) It's Up to the Women. Frederick A. Stokes Company. **Page 601:** Anzia Yezierska quoted. In Ethan Goffman, Daniel Morris (2009) The New York Public Intellectuals and Beyond: Exploring Liberal Humanism, Jewish Identity, and the American Protest Tradition. Purdue University Press. **Page 602:** Roy Stryker, chief of the Historical Section of the Resettlement Administration. In Roy Emerson Stryker, Nancy Wood (1973) In this Proud Land: America 1935–1943 as Seen in the FSA [Farm Security Administration] Photographs; John Steinbeck (1939) Grapes of Wrath. Penguin Books; Elizabeth Noble quoted. In Richard H. Pells (1973) Radical Visions and American Dreams: Culture and

Social Thought in the Depression Years. University of Illinois Press; Granville Hicks, an editor of the radical magazine the New Masses, flatly declared. In Richard H. Pells (1973) Radical Visions and American Dreams: Culture and Social Thought in the Depression Years. University of Illinois Press. **Page 604:** Cary Grant character's lines in She Done Him Wrong film, 1933. Paramount Pictures.

Chapter 25   Page 610: Benito Mussolini, 1934. In (1932) The New Age Magazine, Volume 40. Supreme Council, 33,° Ancient and Accepted Scottish Rite of Freemasonry of the Southern Jurisdiction, U.S.A.; (1941) Congressional Record: Proceedings and Debates of the . . . Congress, Volume 86, Part 17. U.S. Government Printing Office. **Page 613:** Geoffrey Perret (1985) Days of Sadness, Years of Triumph: The American People, 1939–1945. University of Wisconsin Press. **Page 615:** Quipped Andrew G. Truxall and Francis E. Merrill. In William M. Tuttle Jr. (1993) "Daddy's Gone to War": The Second World War in the Lives of America's Children. Oxford University Press. **Page 617:** Dewitt, John L. Final Report: Japanese Evacuation from the West Coast, 1942. Washington D.C.: U.S. Govt. Print. Off., 1943. http://www .archive.org/details/japaneseevacuati00dewi; (1942) The Proceedings of the Louisiana Academy of Sciences, Volumes 6–10. Louisiana Academy of Sciences. **Page 618:** Placards, NAACP demonstrations, 1944. In Laura Elizabeth Hein, Mark Selden (1997) Living with the Bomb: American and Japanese Cultural Conflicts in the Nuclear Age. M.E. Sharpe. **Page 621:** (1941) Congressional series of United States public documents. U.S. Government Printing Office. **Page 629:** Leo Szilard and other 58 scientists signed a petition to the President of the United States, July 3, 1945. In Szilard Petition, First Version (1945) U.S. National Archives, Record Group 77, Records of the Chief of Engineers, Manhattan Engineer District, Harrison-Bundy File, folder #76; Report of the Committee on Political and Social Problems Manhattan Project "Metallurgical Laboratory" University of Chicago, June 11, 1945. U.S. National Archives, Record Group 77, Records of the Chief of Engineers, Manhattan Engineer District, Harrison-Bundy File, folder #76. **Page 631:** General Dwight D. Eisenhower quoted. In John Toland (1966) The Last 100 Days. Random House. **Page 632:** Sec. of War Henry Stimson, informed Churchill by writing him a note at the Potsdam Conference. In Winston S. Churchill (1953) Triumph and Tragedy. (Boston: Houghton Mifflin. pp. 638–639. **Page 633:** Editorial, Nippon Times, August 10, 1945. In Ralph Edward Weber (1972) As Others See Us: American History in Foreign Press. Holt, Rinehart and Winston; A Declassified intelligence document of April 30, 1946. In Gar Alperovitz, Sanho Tree (1996) The Decision to Use the Atomic Bomb. Vintage Books.

Chapter 26   Page 636: Henry Luce, the publisher of Time, Life, and Fortune magazines. In Life magazine (February 17, 1941). **Page 637:** President Truman quoted. In (1944) Carry on, Volumes 23–24. Women's Overseas Service League; Assistant Secretary of State for Economic Affairs Will Clayton quoted. In Charles L. Mee (1985) The Marshall Plan. Simon & Schuster. **Page 639:** Winston Churchill, Iron Curtain speech, in Westminster College, Fulton, Missouri, March 5, 1946. "Sinews of Peace," In (2006) The Origins of the Cold War: U.S. Choices After World War II. Watson Institute for International Studies; Harry Truman (1955) Memoirs. Doubleday & Company, Inc. **Page 641:** North Atlantic Treaty Organization (NATO), April 1949 alliance provisions. In United States. Congress (1949) Congressional Record: Proceedings and Debates of the . . . Congress, Volume 95, Part 6. U.S. Government Printing Office. **Page 642:** Robert H. Ferrell, entitled a chapter of one of his books with the anti-proverb. In (1994) Harry S. Truman: A Life. University of Missouri Press. **Page 643:** Democratic Assemblyman William W. Ward quoted. In (1961) The Railroad Telegrapher: 1961, Volume 78. Order of Railroad Telegraphers. **Page 644:** (1949) Public Papers of the Presidents of the United States, Harry S. Truman, 1949: Containing the Public Messages, Speeches, and Statements of the President, January 1 to December 31, 1949. United States Government Printing Office. **Page 645:** Truman quoted. In (1999) Public Papers of the Presidents of the United States, William J. Clinton, 1997, Book 1, January 1 to June 30, 1997, Book 1. Government Printing Office; FBI director J. Edgar Hoover warned. In Isidor F. Stone (1959) I.F. Stone's Weekly, Volumes 7–8. Kraus Reprint Co. **Page 646:**

Mrs. Lela Rogers, mother of actress Ginger Rogers testimony. In Alvah Cecil Bessie (1967) Inquisition in Eden. Seven Seas. **Page 647:** Republican Senator Joseph R. McCarthy quoted. In Edwin R. Bayley (1981) Joe McCarthy and the Press. University of Wisconsin Press. **Page 648:** Joseph R. McCarthy, "The Red Scare" speech, February 9, 1950. In (1950) State Department Employee Loyalty Investigation: Hearings Before a Subcommittee of the Committee on Foreign Relations, United States Senate 81st Congress, 2d Session, March 8–Apr. 28, May 1–28, 1950, June 28, 1950. **Page 650:** "Invasion USA" Pressbook, 1952. American Pictures Corp. [http://www.conelrad.com/pressbooks/index. php]. **Page 653:** "Zeal for Democracy" program, April 1947, the federal Office of Education. In (March 1948) Education Digest; Mar1947, Vol. 13 Issue 7, p56. **Page 657:** Cliff Roberts quoted. In Blanche W. Cook (1981) The declassified Eisenhower: a divided legacy. Doubleday Publishing; Richard M. Nixon," Checker's Sppech" September 23, 1952 on TV broadcast. In Garry Wills (1970) Nixon Agonistes: The Crisis of the Self-made Man. Houghton Mifflin Harcourt; Dwight D. Eisenhower, "I Shall go to Korea Speech", November 29, 1952. In Kenneth W. Thompson (1994) Institutions and Issues. University Press of America. **Page 658:** Harry S. Truman Farewell Address, January 15, 1953. In (1952) Public Papers of the Presidents of the United States. Federal Register Division, National Archives and Records Service, General Services Administration; Dwight Eisenhower, October 8, 1952. In (1952) United States Army Combat Forces Journal, Volume 3.

Chapter 27   Pages 660–661: Elvis Presley quoted. In Robert Brandt (2001) Tennessee. Fodor's Travel Publications. **Page 661:** Elvis Presley, quoted in The Charlotte Observer, 1956; Nat D. Williams, black Memphis disc jockey and music promoter, quoted. In (1981) The Journal of Country Music, Volume 9. Country Music Foundation. **Page 662:** Dwight D. Eisenhower quoted. In Robert J. Donovan (1956) Eisenhower: The Inside Story. Harper & Brothers; Former GM chief Charles Wilson quoted. In Raymond Simon (1976) Public relations: concepts and practice. Grid Publishing. **Page 664:** Senator Stuart Symington quoted. In (1956) The Michigan Technic, Volumes 75–76. The University of Michigan Library; Col. George C. Reinhardt, Lt. Col. William R. Kintner (Feb 1955) "The Tactical Side of Atomic Warfare" in Bulletin of the Atomic Scientists. Taylor and Francis; Nikita Khrushchev, addressing Western ambassadors at a reception at the Polish embassy in Moscow on November 18, 1956; phrase was originally translated into English by Khrushchev's personal interpreter Viktor Sukhodrev (November 26, 1956) Time Magazine. Meredith Corporation. **Page 667:** Eisenhower quoted. In Joyce Oldham Appleby, Alan Brinkley, James M. McPherson (2003) The American Journey. Glencoe/McGraw-Hill; Eisenhower Press Conference, April 7, 1954. In David F. Schmitz (2005) The Tet Offensive: Politics, War, and Public Opinion. Rowman & Littlefield; Federal Housing Administration, Underwriting Manual: Underwriting and Valuation Procedure Under Title II of the National Housing Act With Revisions to April 1, 1936 (Washington, D.C.), Part II, Section 2, Rating of Location; United States. Congress. Senate. Committee on Banking and Currency. Subcommittee on Housing and Urban Affairs (1969) Housing and urban development legislation of 1969: Hearings, Ninety-first Congress, first session, on bills relating to housing and urban development. U.S. Govt. Printing Office. **Page 669:** Builder William J. Levitt quoted. In Lee Eisenberg (1984) Fifty who made the difference. Villard Books; (1957) U.S. News and World Report, Volume 43, Issues 1–9. U.S. News Publishing Corporation. **Page 671:** Betty Friedan (February 19, 1963)"The Feminine Mystique". W. W. Norton and Co; Mrs. Ada Mae Hardeman quoted. In United States. Congress. Senate. Committee on Government Operations (1972) Establish a Department of Community Development: Hearings, Ninety-second Congress, First Session, on S. 1430. November 16, 17, and 18, 1971, Volume 74, Part 2 - Volume 76, Part 2. U.S. Government Printing Office. **Page 673:** William H. Whyte (1956) Organization Man. Simon & Schuster; C. Wright Mills (1951) White collar: the American middle classes. Oxford University Press. **Page 674:** Harold Wentworth (1960) Dictionary of American Slang. Compiled and Edited by H. Wentworth and S.B. Flexner. Thomas Crowell Company; Life magazine (August 31, 1959); An irate mother's letter to the editors Modern Teen magazine.

In Lisa MacKinney (2008) "Mmmm, he's good-bad, but he's not evil": The Shangri-Las, "Leader of the Pack," and the Cultural Context of the Motorcycle Rider". International Journal of Motorcycle Studies. Volume 4, Issue 1: Spring 2008 [http://ijms.nova.edu/March2008/IJMS_Artcl.MacKinney.html]. **Page 675:** Billboard magazine 1954. In Galen Gart (1954) First Pressings: 1954. Big Nickel Publications. **Page 676:** Marlon Brando character's lines. In The Wild One (1954) Columbia Pictures. **Page 680:** John F. Kennedy: "Inaugural Address," January 20, 1961. The John F. Kennedy Presidential Library and Museum; Dwight D. Eisenhower, Farewell Address, 1961. **Page 681:** (1961) Freedom of Communications: The joint appearances of Senator John F. Kennedy and Vice President Richard M. Nixon and other 1960 campaign presentations. U.S. Government Printing Office. **Page 682:** General Maxwell Taylor and Walt Rostow, "The Taylor Mission Report". In (1971) United States-Vietnam Relations, 1945–1967: Study, Volume 2. U.S. Government Printing Office. **Page 684:** John F. Kennedy Speech, American University Commencement, June 1963. In (1964) Public Papers of the Presidents of the United States: John F. Kennedy, 1963. U.S. Government Printing Office. **Page 685:** Remark on Kennedy's Funeral. Marya Mannes (1964) But Will it Sell? Lippincott Williams & Wilkins.

Chapter 28   Page 689: Excerpt from a speech delivered at Holt Street Baptist Church, Montgomery, Alabama, December 5, 1955. Martin Luther King, Jr. (1991) The Eyes on the Prize: Civil Rights Reader: Documents, Speeches, and Firsthand Accounts from the Black Freedom Struggle, 1954–1990, Penguin Books, New York; Sister Pollard quoted. In Martin Luther King, Jr. (1986) "Our God is Marching On". A Testament of Hope: The Essential Writings and Speeches of Martin Luther King, Jr. HarperCollins. **Page 692:** Horace C. Wilkinson, a former president of the Alabama Bar Association. In (October 1946) "Argument for Adoption of the Boswell Amendment," The Alabama Lawyer: Official Organ State Bar of Alabama. Volume VII; Dick Gregory's dichotomy. In Elijah Wald (2006) Riding with Strangers: A Hitchhiker's Journey. Chicago Review Press; Mamie Till-Bradley (2003) Death of Innocence: The Story of the Hate Crime that Changed America. Random House Publishing Group. **Page 694:** Howard Zinn (December 1, 1962) Kennedy: The Reluctant Emancipator". Nation. pp. 373–76; Ed Cray (1997) Chief Justice: A Biography of Earl Warren. Simon and Schuster. **Page 695:** Albert P. Blaustein, Robert L. Zangrando (1968) Civil Rights and African Americans: A Documentary History. Northwestern University Press; Andrew Young remarked on Selma. In Gary T. Marx (1971) Racial Conflict: Tension and Change in American Society. Little, Brown and Company; Selma's Mayor Joseph Smitherman Interview quoted. In Juan Williams (2013) Eyes on the Prize: America's Civil Rights Years, 1954–1965. Penguin. **Page 696:** James Haskins (1970) Resistance: Profiles in Nonviolence. Doubleday. **Page 697:** Franklin McCain, one of the original four Greensboro students quoted. In Thomas Andrew Bailey, David M. Kennedy (1994) The American spirit: United States history as seen by contemporaries, Volume 2. D.C. Heath and Company. **Page 698:** The Nashville group demonstration rules of conduct In. Carolyn Ruth Calloway (1968) An Analysis of the Non-verbal Means of Persuasion in the Civil Rights Movement, 1960–63: Sit-ins, Marches, and Kneel-ins. University of Wisconsin—Madison; Student Nonviolent Coordinating Committee, April 15, 1960, meeting at Shaw University in Raleigh, North Carolina, Statement of Purpose, drafted by James Lawson. In Christopher Kruegler (1997) Protest, Power, and Change: An Encyclopedia of Nonviolent Action from ACT-UP to Women's Suffrage. Taylor & Francis. **Page 699:** James Farmer, national director of CORE, intention to test a recent Supreme Court decision, Boynton v. Virginia. In Craig Rosebraugh (2004) The Logic of Political Violence: Lessons in Reform and Revolution. PM Press. **Page 700:** Montgomery's police commissioner L.B. Sullivan quoted. In Diane McWhorter (2001) Carry Me Home: Birmingham, Alabama: The Climactic Battle of the Civil Rights Revolution. Simon and Schuster. **Page 705:** John F. Kennedy, June 11, 1963 "The Report to the American People on Civil Rights". [https://www.jfklibrary.org/Asset-Viewer/LH8F_0Mzv0e6Ro1yEm74Ng.aspx]; A. Randolph to John Lewis quoted. In Clayborne Carson (1975)

Toward freedom and community: the evolution of ideas in the Student Nonviolent Coordinating Committee, 1960–1966. University of California at Los Angeles. **Page 706:** Coretta Scott King (September 12, 1969) "He Had a Dream". Life pp. 54–62. **Page 707:** Dave Dennis, CORE quoted. In Howell Raines (1977) My soul is rested: movement days in the Deep South remembered. Putnam; Fannie Lou Hamer, August 22, 1964 Democratic Convention's Credentials Committee. In Steven M. Gillon (2012) The American Paradox: A History of the United States Since 1945. Cengage Learning. **Page 708:** Malcolm X( ) The Autobiography of Malcolm X. Grove Press; Ralph Metcalfe, Jr. (May 20, 1971) "How Blacks Remember Malcolm X". Jet. Volume 40, Issues 6–13; John Lewis on Malcolm X. In Clayborne Carson (1975) Toward freedom and community: the evolution of ideas in the Student Nonviolent Coordinating Committee, 1960–1966. University of California at Los Angeles. **Page 709:** Martin Luther King Jr. quoted. In Peter D. Bishop (1981) A technique for loving: non-violence in Indian and Christian traditions. SCM Press. **Page 710:** President Lyndon B. Johnson televised Speech, May 15, 1965, "Special Message to the Congress: The American Promise"; Martin Luther King Jr., March 25, 1965, State Capitol steps, Birmingham, Alabama. In (1986) A Testament of Hope: The Essential Writings of Martin Luther King, Jr. James Washington ed. San Francisco: Harper & Row. **Page 711:** Ernesto Galarza quoted. In Mexican Farm Labor Program: Hearings Before the Subcommittee on Equipment, Supplies, and Manpower of . . ., 84–1 on H.R. 3822, March 16, 17, 21, and 22,1955. House. Agriculture Committee. United States Congress. **Pages 712–713:** Japanese American Citizens League (JACL) leader Harry Takagi quoted. In Frank F. Chuman (1976) The Bamboo People: the law and Japanese-Americans. Del Mar, Calif.: Publisher's Inc. **Page 713:** President Lyndon B. Johnson, Remarks at the Signing of the Immigration Bill, Liberty Island, New York. October 3, 1965. In (1966) Public Papers of the Presidents of the United States, Lyndon B. Johnson. United States Government Printing Office. **Page 715:** Martin Luther King Jr. Interview. In David J. Garrow (1981) The FBI and Martin Luther King, Jr. From Solo to Memphis. New York: W.W. Norton & Company.

Chapter 29   Page 718: "Agenda for a Generation", The Port Huron Statement by the Students Democratic Society with Tom Hayden as main author. In Rodney P. Carlisle (2007) America in revolt during the 1960s and 1970s. ABC-CLIO; Speech on The Great Society, Lyndon Baines Johnson, University of Michigan Commencement, May 22, 1964. In Lyndon B. Johnson: "Remarks at the University of Michigan," Online by Gerhard Peters and John T. Woolley, The American Presidency Project. http://www.presidency.ucsb.edu/ws/?pid=26262; Senator John F. Kennedy, "America's Stake in Vietnam, the Cornerstone of the Free World in Southeast Asia," address delivered before the American Friends of Vietnam, Washington, D.C. June 1, 1956. In Vital Speeches of the Day, August 1, 1956. Pro Rhetoric, LLC. pp. 617. **Page 719:** Lyndon Johnson, Presidential campaign, October 21, 1964, Akron University, Akron, Ohio. In (September 26, 1964) New York Times. **Page 721:** Ohio State senior explained (April 22, 1964) The Sidelines: Voice of MTSC, The College of Individual Opportunity. Volume 37. No. 13. Middle Tennessee State College. [http://jewlscholar.mtsu.edu/bitstream/handle/mtsu/1402/24248.pdf?sequence=1&isAllowed=y]. **Page 722:** War Psychology. In Paul Potter (April 7, 1965) "The Incredible War" Essay. In Jim Willis (2015) 1960s Counterculture: Documents Decoded. ABC-CLIO. **Page 724:** Sec. of State Dean Rusk quoted. In (1967) The Department of State Bulletin, Volume 56, Part 2. Office of Public Communication, Bureau of Public Affairs. **Page 726:** Lyndon B. Johnson explained to Doris Kearns Goodwin in 1970. In Doris Kearns Goodwin (1976) "Lyndon Johnson and the American Dream." Harper & Row. **Page 727:** Pres. Johnson told CIA Director John McCone. In Nick Kotz (2006) Judgment Days: Lyndon Baines Johnson, Martin Luther King, Jr., and the Laws that Changed America. Houghton Mifflin Harcourt; Senator William Fulbright, referring to the Great Society's war on poverty and the war in Vietnam. In Gary Donaldson (1996) America at War Since 1945: Politics and Diplomacy in Korea, Vietnam, and the Gulf War. Greenwood Publishing Group. **Page 728:** Interview with Associated Press reporter Peter Arnett. Tet Offensive.

In Edwin E. Moïse (2005) The A to Z of the Vietnam War. Scarecrow Press; Lyndon Johnson, March 31 quoted. In Robert Dallek (2004) Lyndon B. Johnson: Portrait of a President. Oxford University Press. **Page 730:** Thai Jones (2007) A Radical Line: From the Labor Movement to the Weather Underground, One Family's Century of Conscience. SUNY Press; Mike Royko (1971) Boss: Richard J. Daley of Chicago. Dutton; MLK, April 3, 1968, Poor People's Campaign for peace and justice. In Mary Craig (1984) Six modern martyrs. Crossroad Publishing Company. **Page 731:** George Wallace, Inaugural Address, January 14, 1963. Alabama Department of Archives and History. [http://archives-alabama-primo.hosted.exlibrisgroup.com/01ALABAMA:default_scope:01ALABAMA_ALMA215244160002743]; Lyndon Johnson signed the 1964 Voting Rights Act. In Theodore Roszak (2006) World, Beware!: American Triumphalism in an Age of Terror. Between The Lines. **Page 733:** Stokely Carmichael and Charles V. Hamilton (1967) Black Power: The Politics of Liberation in America. Vintage Books; Original poster caption, Huey P. Newton, co-founder with Bobby Seale of the Black Panther Party in 1966. In Sol Stern (September 1967) "America's Black Guerillas". Ramparts Magazine. **Page 734:** SLOGAN, National Organization for Women (NOW). Coined by Kathie Sarachild (a.k.a. Amatniek) as part of a leaflet distributed at an anti-Vietnam War event by the Jeanette Rankin Brigade for New York Radical Women, January 15, 1968, Washington, D.C. [http://www.thisdayinquotes.com/2010/01/origin-of-slogan-sisterhood-is-powerful.html]; SLOGAN. In Carol Hanisch (February 1969) "The Personal Is Political," Notes from the Second Year: Women's Liberation. edited by Shulamith Firestone and Anne Koedt. [http://www.carolhanisch.org/CHwritings/PIP.html]. **Page 735:** Gay Liberation Front (GLF) Statement of Purpose, July 31, 1969. In John D'Emilio, Estelle B. Freedman (1988) Intimate Matters: A History of Sexuality in America. University of Chicago Press; Slogan, Gay Pride Opening Day, June 28, 1970. Fred Sargeant (June 22, 2010) "1970: A First-Person Account of the First Gay Pride March. Village Voice, LLC. **Page 737:** Richard M. Nixon, Address at the Dedication of the Karl E. Mundt Library at General Beadle State College, Madison, South Dakota. (June 3, 1969) Online by Gerhard Peters and John T. Woolley, The American Presidency Project. http://www.presidency.ucsb.edu/ws/?pid=2080. **Page 738:** Richard M. Nixon's eight-day visit in China, February 1972. In Richard Milhous Nixon (1978) RN: the memoirs of Richard Nixon. Grosset & Dunlap. **Pages 739–740:** Nixon, after the Kent State killings statement read to the press by Ron Ziegler. In Howard Means (2016) 67 Shots: Kent State and the End of American Innocence. Hachette UK. **Page 740:** Spiro Agnew, California State Republican Party Convention, September 11, 1970. Congressional Record, 92nd Congress, 1970, 116, 32017. U.S. Government Publishing Office. **Page 741:** Horst Faas and Marianne Fulton. "The Bigger Picture". The Survivor: Phan Thi Kim Phuc and the photographer Nick Ut. The Digital Journalist. Dirck Halstead Ed. [http://digitaljournalist.org/issue0008/ng2.htm]; Thi Kim Phuc quoted. In Mark McDonald (June 3, 2012) How Horrible Wars Can Be. The New York Times. **Page 742:** "The Winter Soldier Investigation: An Inquiry into American War Crimes,". In Howard Jones (2017) My Lai: Vietnam, 1968, and the Descent Into Darkness. Oxford University Press; Pres. Gerald Ford, remarked on the wounds of Watergate, August 9, 1974. In [https://geraldrfordfoundation.org/40th/documents/]. **Page 743:** Richard M. Nixon (January 1, 1975) Public Papers of the Presidents of the United States: Richard M. Nixon, 1974.

Chapter 30   Page 745: Bee Gathright quoted. In Lisa McGirr (2015) Suburban Warriors: The Origins of the New American Right. Princeton University Press. **Page 746:** Ronald Reagan, who, according to U.S. News. Kenneth T. Walsh (September 25, 2008) "The Most Consequential Elections in History: Ronald Reagan and the election of 1980. [https://www.usnews.com/news/articles/2008/09/25/the-most-consequential-elections-in-history-ronald-reagan-and-the-election-of-1980]. **Page 748:** AFL-CIO leader complained that the United States. In (1973) U.S. multinationals; the dimming of America: a report. **Page 750:** Gov. Richard Thornburgh. (March 29, 1999) Live Discussion: Governing in a Nuclear Crisis. The Washington Post Company [https://www.washingtonpost.com/wp-srv/national/talk/archive/thornburgh0329.htm]. **Page 753:** (1978) Public Papers

of the Presidents of the United States: Jimmy Carter. Federal Register Division, National Archives and Records Service, General Services Administration. **Page 754:** Christopher Lasch quoted. In (1947) American Perspective, Volume 1. Foundation for Foreign Affairs; President Carter, 1979 quoted. In Iwan W. Morgan (1994) Beyond the Liberal Consensus: A Political History of the United States Since 1965. C. Hurst & Co. Publishers. **Page 755:** David C. Huckabee, "Equal Rights Amendment: Ratification Issues," Memorandum, March 18, 1996 (Congressional Research Service, Library of Congress, Washington, DC). **Page 757:** Nancy Reagan quoted. In Leslie Bennetts (January 21, 1981) New York Times; Ronald Reagan, Republican National Convention, July 17, 1980. In Lou Cannon (1991) President Reagan: The Role Of A Lifetime. Simon & Schuster; Reagan Election Rhetoric, Presidential Debate: Reagan vs. Carter, October 28, 1980. In Rodney P. Carlisle (2005) Encyclopedia of Politics: The Left and the Right. SAGE Publications. **Pages 757–758:** Ronald Reagan, First Inaugural Address. In Ronald Reagan: "Inaugural Address," January 20, 1981. Online by Gerhard Peters and John T. Woolley, The American Presidency Project. http://www.presidency.ucsb.edu/ws/?pid=43130. **Pages 758–759:** Ronald Reagan: "Inaugural Address," January 20, 1981. Online by Gerhard Peters and John T. Woolley, The American Presidency Project. http://www.presidency.ucsb.edu/ws/?pid=43130. **Page 759:** George Gilder (1981) Wealth and Poverty. ICS Press. **Page 760:** Ronald Reagan, 1984 Campaign ad "Prouder, Stronger, Better," Bernie Vangrin of Hal Riney & Partners was the Art Director of the ad, which was directed and filmed by John Pytka of Levine/Pytka Productions. **Page 761:** President Reagan addressing the National Association of Evangelicals, March 8, 1983. In Jeffery T. Richelson (1997) A Century of Spies: Intelligence in the Twentieth Century. Oxford University Press; Pat Buchanan, Reagan's communications director quoted. In Camille Paglia (February 1999) "Ask Camille: Three-way sex with death" Salon Magazine; Rev. Jerry Falwell quoted. In Hans Johnson and William Eskridge (May 19, 2007) The Legacy of Falwell's Bully Pulpit. The Washington Post Company [http://www.washingtonpost.com/wp-dyn/content/article/2007/05/18/AR2007051801392.html}; People with AIDS Coalition (PWAC) motto. In John D. Stinson (August 1998) People With AIDS Coalition: Records, 1987–93. The New York Public Library, Humanities and Social Sciences Library, 58 lin. ft. (112 archival containers; 2 flat boxes; 1 folder) [https://www.nypl.org/sites/default/files/archivalcollections/pdf/pwac.pdf]. **Page 763:** Joseph Gold (1962) The Fund Agreement in the Courts, Volume 2. International Monetary Fund. **Page 764:** Ronald Regan, 1983 quoted. In Ian Shapiro (2009) The State of Democratic Theory. Princeton University Press. **Page 765:** Republican George Herbert Walker Bush Acceptance Speech, Republican National Convention, August 18, 1988. In Robert North Roberts, Scott J. Hammond, Valerie A. Sulfaro (2012) Presidential Campaigns, Slogans, Issues, and Platforms: The Complete Encyclopedia, Volume 1. ABC-CLIO. **Page 766:** Georgi Arbatov, the director of the Soviet Institute for the Study of the U.S.A. and Canada quoted, Time (May 23, 1988). In Chengxin Pan (2012) Knowledge, Desire and Power in Global Politics: Western Representations of China's Rise. Edward Elgar Publishing; Pres. George Bush (March 6, 1991) Address Before a Joint Session of the Congress on the Cessation of the Persian Gulf Conflict. Public Papers of the Presidents of the United States: George Bush, 1991. Online by Gerhard Peters and John T. Woolley, The American Presidency Project. http://www.presidency.ucsb.edu/ws/?pid=19364. **Page 767:** James Carville, de facto slogan for the Clinton 1992 Presidential Campaign. In Michael Kelly (October 31, 1992) THE 1992 CAMPAIGN: The Democrats—Clinton and Bush Compete to Be Champion of Change; Democrat Fights Perceptions of Bush Gain. New York Times; Bill Clinton, The Washington Post. In (2000) US policy and NATO military operations in Kosovo. U.S. Government Publishing Office. **Pages 767–768:** Bill Clinton Remarks on Foreign Policy, Grand Hyatt Hotel, San Francisco, February 26, 1999. The White House. Office of the Press Secretary [https://www.mtholyoke.edu/acad/intrel/clintfps.htm}. **Page 769:** Bill Clinton, "DADT", Official U.S. Policy on military service by gays, bisexuals, and lesbians. Department of Defense Directive 1304.26 issued on December 21, 1993. Mandated by United States federal law Pub.L. 103–160 (10 U.S.C. § 654), which was signed

November 30, 1993. Government Printing Office. **Page 770:** Bill Clinton, Welfare Reform Act in August 1996. In William J. Clinton (January 1, 1999) Public Papers of the Presidents of the United States: William J. Clinton, 1998; Senator Strom Thurmond, Bill Clinton Impeachment Trial. In THE IMPEACHMENT TRIAL: Statement of Sen. Thurmond (R-S.C.). The Washington Post. [https://www.washingtonpost.com/wp-srv/politics/special/clinton/stories/thurmondtext021399.htm].

Chapter 31   Page 775: Diane Kresh of the Library of Congress quoted. In Matthew Mirapaul (October 15, 2001) ARTS ONLINE: How the Net Is Documenting a Watershed Moment. New York Times. **Page 776:** George W. Bush, Address to the Joint Session of the 107th Congress (September 20, 2001) Selected Speeches of President George W. Bush 2001–2008; George W. Bush (September 14, 2001) National Day of Prayer and Remembrance Service. Selected Speeches of President George W. Bush 2001–2008; George W. Bush (January 29, 2002) State of the Union Address to the 107th Congress. Selected Speeches of President George W. Bush 2001–2008; George W. Bush (June 1, 2002) "Bush Doctrine." West Point Commencement. Selected Speeches of President George W. Bush 2001–2008. **Page 777:** George W. Bush's war ultimatum speech from Cross Hall in the White House (February 26, 2003) In The Guardian. Guardian News and Media Limited, [https://www.theguardian.com/world/2003/mar/18/usa.iraq]; George W. Bush's speech aboard the USS Abraham Lincoln, declaring the end to major combat in Iraq (May 2, 2003) CNN.com. Cable News Network LP, LLLP[http://edition.cnn.com/2003/US/05/01/bush.transcript/]. **Page 779:** Transportation Security Administration (TSA) Mission Statement. Department of Homeland Security. [https://www.tsa.gov/about/tsa-mission]. **Page 780:** Patrick Buchanan, Address to the 1992 Republican National Convention (August 17, 1992) Houston, TX. Text obtained from Buchanan.org, http://buchanan.org/blog/1992-republican-national-convention-speech-148 [=A]. **Page 781:** Arthur Schlesinger. Jr., in his essay. The Disuniting of America, WW Norton & Company, New York, 1992. **Page 782:** Gov. Bill Richardson, "Speech on Comprehensive Immigration Reform at Georgetown University," Dec. 7, 2006. www.richardsonforpresident.com/issues/immigration; Senator Edward Kennedy quoted. In (October 25, 2010) Congressional Record, V. 152, Pt. 16, September 29 2006. US Government Printing Office; (October 26, 2006) "Mexico Gathers Support From 27 Nations for Declaration Opposing U.S. Border Fence Plan". FOX News Network, LLC. [http:// www.foxnews.com/story/2006/10/26/mexico-gathers-support-from-27-nations-for-declaration-opposing-us-border-fence.html]. **Page 784:** President Lyndon B. Johnson, 1964 State of the Union address, introduced the War on Poverty. In (January 1, 1967) Public Papers of the Presidents of the United States: Lyndon B. Johnson, 1966. US Government Printing Office. **Page 787:** Terry Tempest Williams in September 2017 quoted. In Henry Fountain (September 8, 2017) Apocalyptic Thoughts Amid Nature's Chaos? You Could Be Forgiven. New York Times. **Page 788:** David G. Victor, longtime scholar of climate politics at the University of California, San Diego quoted. In Justin Gillis & Nadja Popovich (June 1, 2017) "The U.S. Is the Biggest Carbon Polluter in History. It Just Walked Away From the Paris Climate Deal". New York Times. [https://www.nytimes.com/interactive/2017/06/01/climate/us-biggest-carbon-polluter-in-history-will-it-walk-away-from-the-paris-climate-deal.html]. **Page 789:**

The National Weather Service tweet (August 27, 2017); Reverend Jesse Jackson on Hurricane Katrina. In "Anderson Cooper 360 Degrees" Transcript. (September 2, 2005) CNN.com. Cable News Network LP, LLLP. [http://edition.cnn.com/TRANSCRIPTS/0509/02/acd.01.html]. **Page 790:** (September 8, 2016) Center for Biological Diversity Stands With Standing Rock Sioux Tribe in Opposing Dakota Oil Pipeline. [https://www.biologicaldiversity.org/news/press_releases/2016/dakota-access-pipeline-09-08-2016.html]. **Page 791:** Obama Campaign Slogans, 2008 Presidential Campaign. **Page 792:** Barack Obama Speech in Cairo, Egypt,(June 4, 2009) Remarks by the President on A New Beginning. The White House. Office of the press Secretary. [https://obamawhitehouse.archives.gov/the-press-office/remarks-president-cairo-university-6-04-09] **Page 793:** Mitch McConnell, Senate minority leader quoted. In Michael A. Memoli (October 27, 2010) Mitch McConnell's remarks on 2012 draw White House ire. Los Angeles Times. **Page 794:** Mitt Romney, May 2012 quoted, In Mojo News Team (September 19, 2012) Full Transcript of the Mitt Romney Secret Video. Transcription by Sydney Brownstone, Maya Dusenbery, Ryan Jacobs, Deanna Pan, and Sarah Zhang. Mother Jones and the Foundation for National Progress; Occupy Wall Street (OWS) Slogan (August 2011) Blog "wearethe99percent.tumblr.com" [http://wearethe99percent.tumblr.com/] occupywallst.org; Gov. Willard "Mitt" Romney remarked on 2012 election. In (August 27, 2012) "We Believe in America: 2012 REPUBLICAN PLATFORM". 2012 Republican Party Platform. Online by Gerhard Peters and John T. Woolley, The American Presidency Project. http://www.presidency.ucsb.edu/ws/?pid=101961. **Page 796:** Trump disparaged Sen. John McCain, Family Leadership Summit, Ames, Iowa, July 2015. In Chris Cilliza (October 24, 2017) "John McCain keeps serving his revenge to Donald Trump ice cold". CNN Cable News Network; Woodrow Wilson: "Address to the Daughters of the American Revolution," October 11, 1915. Online by Gerhard Peters and John T. Woolley, The American Presidency Project. http://www.presidency.ucsb.edu/ws/?pid=117704; Jenna Johnson (December 7, 2015) "Trump calls for 'total and complete shutdown of Muslims entering the United States'". The Washington Post. [https://www.washingtonpost.com/news/post-politics/wp/2015/12/07/donald-trump-calls-for-total-and-complete-shutdown-of-muslims-entering-the-united-states/?utm_term=.deb121e257fe]; (June 16, 2015) "Donald Trump announces a presidential bid". The Washington Post. [https://www.washingtonpost.com/news/post-politics/wp/2015/06/16/full-text-donald-trump-announces-a-presidential-bid/?utm_term=.77c96f353e7a]; Donald Trump's Campaign Slogan, 2016 Presidential Election. Donald J. Trump for President, Inc. **Page 798:** Bernie Sanders (November 11, 2016) Bernie Sanders: Where the Democrats Go From Here. New York Times. [https://www.nytimes.com/2016/11/12/opinion/bernie-sanders-where-the-democrats-go-from-here.html]. **Page 799:** Tarana Burke (2006) "#MeToo"Movement [https://metoomvmt.org/]; Lilli Petersen(Aug 13 2017) "Many Sides" Memes & Tweets From Trump's Charlottesville Speech Are Taking Over Twitter. Elite Daily, Inc. Bustle Digital Group. [https://www.elitedaily.com/news/twitter-many-sides-meme-donald-trump-speech-charlottesville/2043241]; (January 30, 2018) President Donald J. Trump's State of the Union Address. [https://www.whitehouse.gov/briefings-statements/president-donald-j-trumps-state-union-address/].

Index